Given In The Memory Of

Katherine Ramzer
Grace Jackson

BY Idessa & Gray

THE CHURCH AND THE FINE ARTS

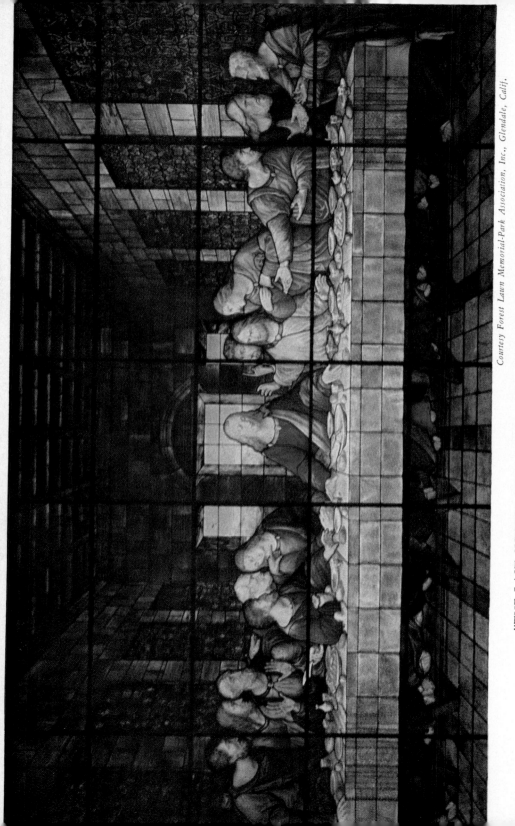

"THE LAST SUPPER" WINDOW—CASELLI-MORETTI (after Da Vinci)

THE CHURCH
AND THE FINE ARTS

AN ANTHOLOGY OF
PICTURES, POETRY, MUSIC, AND STORIES
PORTRAYING
THE GROWTH AND DEVELOPMENT OF THE CHURCH
THROUGH THE CENTURIES

by

CYNTHIA PEARL MAUS

in collaboration with

JOHN P. CAVARNOS
JEAN LOUISE SMITH
RONALD E. OSBORN
ALFRED T. DEGROOT

Fully Illustrated

HARPER & BROTHERS PUBLISHERS
New York

DEDICATED TO
THE CHURCH ECUMENICAL IN ITS WORLD-WIDE TASK
OF PREACHING AND TEACHING
THE CHRISTIAN WAY OF LIFE

✛

Library of Congress catalog card number: 60-7956

CONTENTS

A detailed contents page will be found preceding each of the several sections listed below

	PAGE
"The Last Supper" Window—*Rosa Caselli-Moretti*	Frontispiece
Poem: I am the Church!—*Beulah Hughes*	viii

INTRODUCTION   1

    Poem: God Builds No Churches—*Edgar A. Guest*   4

PART I. THE APOSTOLIC CHURCH OF THE PALESTINIAN AREA   5
(*Cynthia Pearl Maus*)

    § 1. "The Word Became Flesh," 7. § 2. The Ministry of Jesus of Nazareth, 37. § 3. "Go Preach and Teach," 66. § 4. The Church of Christ Is Builded, 94 § 5. The Missionary Outreach of the Apostolic Church, 120.

PART II. THE EASTERN ORTHODOX CHURCH   143
(*John P. Cavarnos*)

    § 1. The Church Spreads Out from Jerusalem, 144. § 2. Alliance of Church and State, 163. § 3. The Fabric of the Faith Is Woven, 183. § 4. Missionary Zeal and Expansion, 202. § 5. Eastern Orthodoxy Around the World, 224.

PART III. THE ROMAN CATHOLIC CHURCH   247
(*Jean Louise Smith*)

    § 1. The Church of Rome Is Established, 248. § 2. The Church Reaches Out, 269. § 3. The Age of Monasticism, 288. § 4. Crusades and Cathedrals, 310. § 5. The Flowering of Christian Art: The Renaissance, 334. § 6. The Age of Romanticism, 356. § 7. The Roman Catholic Church Around the World, 380.

PART IV. THE PROTESTANT REFORMATION IN EUROPE   405
(*Ronald E. Osborn*)

    § 1. The Reformation Begins, 406. § 2. The Reformation Spreads, 434. § 3. The Reformation Reaches Great Britain, 461. § 4. The Reformation Continues, 490. § 5. The Unfinished Reformation, 517.

PAGE

PART V. THE PROTESTANT CHURCH IN NORTH AMERICA   543
(*Alfred T. DeGroot*)

§ 1. The Church in the Colonial Era, 544. § 2. The Church on
the Frontier: The Early West, 564. § 3. The Church on the
Plains and in the Southwest, 587. § 4. Church Development
on the Pacific Coast, 612. § 5. The Church Crosses Canada
and Alaska, 633. § 6. The Church in the Modern Era, 661.
§ 7. Christianity and Education, 686.

PART VI. CHRISTIANITY, A WORLD-WIDE RELIGION   709
(*Cynthia Pearl Maus*)

§ 1. The Church of Christ in Japan, 710. § 2. The Christian
Witness in China, Free China, and Formosa, 733. § 3. The
Christian Witness in Korea, 758. § 4. Christianity in the
Philippines, 782. § 5. The Church of Christ in India, 803.
§ 6. The Church of Christ in Africa, 828. § 7. The Chris-
tian Witness in Latin America, 857.

Acknowledgments   883

Index of Art and Art Interpretations by Artists and Titles   895

Index of Poetry by Authors and Titles   897

Index of Stories by Titles and Authors   899

Index of Music and Music Interpretations by Titles and Authors   901

THE CHURCH AND THE FINE ARTS

I AM THE CHURCH!

I AM THE CHURCH!

The Great Creator drew the plans for me within His heart of love;
The Great Architect gave His dearest Possession that I might be erected;
My one and only Foundation is His Son—whose body was nailed to a tree;
My chief Cornerstone—the Stone which the builders rejected;
My walls—placed without hammer's sound—are built by the martyrs of the centuries;
My steeple points ever toward that Great Architect—Builder throughout eternity;
From my belfry rings out the call for worship to countless multitudes of all ages;
My door swings open to all of every race and every age—bidding them welcome;
        In my sanctuary there is—
          Peace for tired minds,
            Rest for weary bodies,
              Compassion for suffering humanity,
                Forgiveness for repentant sinners,
              Communion for saints,
                Christ—for all who seek Him!

I AM THE CHURCH!

All the *love* of God, the Great Architect,
All the *sacrifice* of Christ, the Great Builder,
All the *dreams* of dauntless prophets,
All the *faith* of hopeful pioneers,
All the *hope* of countless millions,
All the *joy* of conquering Christians, are enclosed within my walls!

I AM THE CHURCH!

Without me, civilization must crumble!
With me is eternity!*

—*Beulah Hughes*

* Reprinted from *Christ and the Fine Arts* (first edition) by special permission of Beulah Hughes.

INTRODUCTION

✛

THIS volume, *The Church and the Fine Arts,* like its predecessors, *Christ and the Fine Arts* (1938; revised and enlarged, 1959), *The World's Great Madonnas* (1947), and *The Old Testament and the Fine Arts* (1954), is a giant resource anthology. It covers the growth and development of the Church through nearly twenty centuries of Christian history, from the viewpoint of the four major fine arts: pictures, with their interpretations; poetry; stories; and music, in the form of hymns, canticles, and chants.

This book—the author's ninth—grew out of numerous requests from professors of church history in church colleges within the author's own communion, the Disciples of Christ, and in other denominations, for a fourth volume in this series, which would represent the wide subject of *The Church and the Fine Arts.*

The suggestion was an intriguing one, and the author worked out a brief outline, indicating to Harper & Brothers, Publishers, that she would undertake the compilation of such an anthology if she might have the assistance of specialists in the fields of church history and the fine arts. Harper & Brothers agreed, and assignments were made on the basis of the following outline:

Part I   THE APOSTOLIC CHURCH OF THE PALESTINIAN ERA
        Dr. Cynthia Pearl Maus. B.A., Northwestern University (1905); Lit.D., Chapman College (1958). Research residence in Europe, the Orient, South America, and Africa. Teacher, author, editor.

Part II   THE EASTERN ORTHODOX CHURCH
        Dr. John P. Cavarnos. B.A., Boston University (1941); M.A., Ph.D., Harvard University (1942, 1957); D.Phil., Athens University (1948). Representative of the Greek Orthodox Church in the National Council of Churches (1954-56). Research specialist, author; Chairman, Department of Classics, Austin College, Texas.

Part III THE ROMAN CATHOLIC CHURCH
        Miss Jean Louise Smith. B.A., Occidental College; M.A., University of Chicago Divinity School; graduate study in the field of the fine arts in Europe and the United States. Research specialist, author, editor.

Part IV THE PROTESTANT REFORMATION IN EUROPE
        Dr. Ronald E. Osborn. B.A., M.A., and B.D., Phillips University; Ph.D., University of Oregon. Lecturer, Ecumenical Institute, University of Geneva (1954-55). Author, editor, Dean and professor of Church History at Christian Theological Seminary (Butler University).

Part V   THE PROTESTANT CHURCH IN NORTH AMERICA
         Dr. A. T. DeGroot. B.A., M.A., and B.D., Butler College (1926, 1928,
         1929); Certificate, University of Grenoble (1938); Ph.D., University of
         Chicago (1939). Chairman, Department of Church History, Brite Col-
         lege of the Bible, Texas Christian University.

Part VI CHRISTIANITY, A WORLD-WIDE RELIGION
         Dr. Cynthia Pearl Maus. B.A., Northwestern University (1905); Lit.D.,
         Chapman College (1958). Research residence in Europe, the Orient,
         South America, and Africa. Teacher, author, editor.

This anthology is not intended to discuss theology, church doctrine, or
dogma. Its purpose is to show the contribution which the Church has made
to the fine arts through the centuries since Christ was born and, in turn, the
contribution which the fine arts have made to the Church in its programs of
study, worship, and service. For more poems have been written, more stories
told, more pictures painted, and more songs sung about *Christ* than any other
person in human history.

Dr. P. T. Forsyth says: "The principle of art is the incarnation of God's
eternal beauty; the principle of religion is the incarnation of God's eternal
human heart. Neither can do the work of the other, yet their work is com-
plementary." This universal love of beauty is one of the resources in human
life that Christianity ought to pervade with its spirit and claim as its own;
for it is to this instinctive love of the beautiful that the artist, the poet, the
storyteller, and the musician make their appeal, obtaining, as a result, a wider
hearing for the truth they present through these universally loved forms of
expression.

All of the fine arts deal with the presentation of truth in a form of beauty.
Christianity deals with the interpretation of truth through God's greatest gift
to humanity—*incarnate love.* Christ Himself said, "A new commandment I
give unto you, that ye love one another" (John 13:34). And Paul says, "Love
never faileth" (I Cor. 13:8, ASV).

The author-compiler of *The Church and the Fine Arts* profoundly believes
that if young people, as well as adults, will strive to make the great masterpieces of art, poetry, stories, and music *live,* through their artistic presentation
of the artist's message, they may become co-workers with Christ in making
truth, beauty, and love so attractive that the unseeing will be led to follow
Him.

Whenever possible, link with the art interpretations in *The Church and
the Fine Arts* visible, eye-gate reproductions of the pictures shown in this
volume. Kodachrome slides may be obtained from the Visual Education
Department, Schauffler Division of Christian Education, Oberlin Graduate
School of Theology, Oberlin, Ohio.

Along with these interpretations of great masterpieces of religious art,
poetry, and stories, use, whenever possible, either vocal or instrumental music
of some of the great hymns, chants, and canticles reproduced in this anthology.

Dr. Paul Hutchinson says: "Among the great religions of the world by
which men seek to worship, Christianity is the most widely spread, has the

most adherents, and makes the most stupendous claims for the divinity of its Founder and the finality of its teachings. Of the two and a half billion human beings on earth, about eight hundred fifty million—one out of every three—are listed as Christians.

"The churches in which Christians worship have developed, during their nearly two thousand years since Christ lived and died, such an astonishing diversity of belief and ritual that it is sometimes difficult to recognize that they all acknowledge the same Lord. Yet there is justification for the habit of including all such diversities in the reckoning. For all, under whatever form, acknowledge *one God;* all declare their loyalty to *one Lord;* all find in *one cross* the symbol of their faith.

"Christianity is a religion which springs historically from Jesus of Nazareth. The first followers of Jesus believed that He traveled about Palestine as a preacher and teacher; that He healed and worked wonders; that He ran afoul of the conservative religious and political forces of that land, was crucified, and rose from the dead. They declared that, in a resurrected and glorified form, He appeared to many of them. They *must* have believed it, for within forty days after Jesus had been executed, what had been a despairing and disintegrating band of disillusioned dreamers was transformed into a company of zealots ready to dare any fate to proclaim that this resurrected Jesus was in fact God's promised Messiah, the *Christ*. The Christian religion is founded on the fact that their Master rose from the dead."*

The early followers of Jesus took in all sincerity His command, "Go ye therefore, and teach all nations, baptizing them in the name of the Father, and of the Son, and of the Holy Ghost: teaching them to observe all things whatsoever I have commanded you; and lo, I am with you alway, even unto the end of the world" (Matt. 28:19-20).

Christ left with His followers a *fellowship of love* known as the Church, of which He was and is the Founder and the chief Cornerstone. On Peter's affirmation, "Thou art the Christ, the Son of the living God," Jesus founded His Church; and He said, "Upon this rock I will build my church; and the gates of hell shall not prevail against it" (Matt. 16:16, 18).

The Church is often spoken of as the "Bride of Christ." Like its Founder, it is universal in scope, ageless, raceless, and classless. It did not belong to the apostles; it does not belong to the Roman Catholic Church, or to the Eastern Orthodox Church, or to any one or all of the infinite variety of Protestant faiths and cults. It belongs to *Christ*. He is its Head, its Founder, its Preserver, and the only Mediator through which men in their quest for eternal life find God. Jesus Himself said: "And whatsoever ye shall ask in my name, that will I do, that the Father may be glorified in the Son. If ye shall ask any thing in my name, I will do it" (John 14:13-14).

The form of organization of the Church was left to man to initiate and direct, and there is *no one form* of organization and administration that has been given divine favor or approval. The primary purpose of the Church is

* Abridged from *The World's Great Religions*, pp. 194-95. Copyright 1957 by Time, Inc. Published by the editors of *Life*. Used by permission of Mrs. Paul Hutchinson and the publishers.

to witness to all men that Jesus Christ is the *living Son* of the *living God,* and their personal Saviour. Jesus said: "I am the way, the truth, and the life: no man cometh unto the Father, but by me" (John 14:6).

The late Edgar A. Guest, in his poem "God Builds No Churches," writes:

> God builds no churches. By His plan
> That labor has been left to man.
>   No spires miraculous arise
>   No little mission from the skies
> Falls on a bleak and barren place
> To be a source of strength and grace.
> The humblest church demands its price
>   In human toil and sacrifice.
>
> Men call the Church the House of God,
> Toward which the toil-stained Pilgrims trod
>   In search of strength and rest and hope
>   As blindly through life's mists they grope.
> And there God dwells, but it is man
> Who builds that house and draws its plan,
> Pays for the mortar and the stone
>   That none need seek for God alone.
>
> The humblest spirit in mortal ken
> Where God abides was built by men.
>   And if the Church is still to grow,
>   Is still the light of hope to throw
> Across the valley of despair,
> Man still must build God's house of prayer.
> God sends no churches from the skies,
>   Out of our hearts they must arise.*

The purpose of this anthology is to help make Christ's message of universal love so beautiful and meaningful that everyone may come to know Him, whom to know aright is life abundant here and hereafter.

All who deal with the use of the fine arts in religious education need to remember that it takes both art and an artist to make truth *live.* No substitute or makeshift can be used without destroying the message which the artist, the poet, the storyteller, or the musician intended to convey.

The author-compiler and her collaborators send out this book in the hope that it will make a lasting contribution toward building in this world Christ's "kingdom of love" by enriching the program of His Church as it ministers to men and women of all races, nations, classes, and cultures the world around.

Springtime, 1960   *Cynthia Pearl Maus*
Los Angeles, California

* From *The Book of Collected Verse.* Copyright 1934 by Reilly & Lee. Used by permission of the publisher.

PART I

THE APOSTOLIC CHURCH OF THE PALESTINIAN AREA

by

CYNTHIA PEARL MAUS

1. "THE WORD BECAME FLESH" .... *page* 7

2. THE MINISTRY OF JESUS OF NAZARETH ... *page* 37

3. "GO PREACH AND TEACH" .... *page* 66

4. THE CHURCH OF CHRIST IS BUILDED ...... *page* 94

5. THE MISSIONARY OUTREACH OF THE
   APOSTOLIC CHURCH .... *page* 120

CONTENTS

PART I SECTION 1

"THE WORD BECAME FLESH"

For the law was given by Moses, but grace and truth came by Jesus Christ.—JOHN 1:17

PICTURES: PAGE
Picture: The Mount of Olives and Gethsemane 8
Interpretation: Picture (The Mount of Olives and Gethsemane) and
   Map (World of the Old Testament): The Background and Founding
   of Christianity — art. by *Maus* 9
Map: World of the Old Testament 10
Interpretation: Christmas Night—*von Uhde* 13
Picture: Christmas Night—*von Uhde* 14
Interpretation: The Holy Family—*Seligmann* 15
Picture: The Holy Family—*Seligmann* 16
Interpretation: Head of Christ—*Sallman* 17
Picture: Head of Christ—*Sallman* 18

POETRY:
Trust the Great Artist—*Clark* 19
His Love Is Always Shining—*Oxenham* 20
Man's Heritage—*Clark* 20
My Father's House—*Clark* 20
Mary, Mother of Jesus—*Spear* 21
Mary and Martha—*Spear* 21
Master Builder—*Clark* 21
John the Baptist—*Marlatt* 22

STORIES:
The Pilgrimage to Bethlehem—*Wallace* 22
The Light of the World Is Come—*Phelps* 26
Wise Men from the East—*Wallace* 29

MUSIC:
Interpretation: O Come, O Come, Emmanuel—*Old Latin* 32
Music: O Come, O Come, Emmanuel—*Ancient Plain Song* 33
Interpretation: Watchman, Tell Us of the Night—*Bowring* 34
Music: Watchman, Tell Us of the Night—*Mason* 35

THE MOUNT OF OLIVES AND GETHSEMANE
Seen from Dome of the Rock, Jerusalem

THE BACKGROUND AND FOUNDING OF CHRISTIANITY

Cynthia Pearl Maus

THE magnificent civilizations of Egypt and Babylon had been in existence many years before Hebrew history began, now about four thousand years ago. The eleventh and twelfth chapters of Genesis tell the story of Abraham's leaving his home in Ur of the Chaldees, with his wife Sarah and his nephew Lot, for that long trek north and west to Haran, a small town far to the northeast of the Holy Land. The exact dates of this journey are unknown, but it fits naturally into the movements of many peoples of the Middle East in those early centuries. Because of the need of water for their herds and flocks, nomadic people moved along the coastal plain east of the Mediterranean and along the valleys of the Tigris and Euphrates rivers.

Abraham and his family remained in Haran for some time before pushing on to the land that came later to be known as Canaan or the Holy Land. They stopped for a while at Shechem, then went to Bethel, and later still to Beersheba. (See map on p. 10.)

Famine in the land drove Abraham and his family into Egypt, but only for a while. On his return he established his camp near Hebron, about twenty miles south of Jerusalem. To this day "Abram's Oak" may be seen in the garden of the old Russian Monastery southwest of the ancient city of Hebron, now called El-Khalil ("the friend") in memory of Abraham, who came to be known as "the friend" although he was a stranger in the land.

The boundaries usually given for the Holy Land are from Dan to Beersheba, about one hundred fifty miles long, and from Gaza to the Dead Sea, a little more than fifty miles wide. This little country contains approximately six thousand square miles. Even if one includes the land east of the Jordan River, the Holy Land is smaller than the State of Maryland. It is bordered on the south and east by wilderness and desert, while steep mountains rise to the north. On the west the Mediterranean Sea breaks against a rugged coastline that offers few natural harbors for the ships that ply its waters.

This small country, which never acquired the political importance or culture of its neighbors, Egypt and Babylon, has nevertheless been a focal point in history for nearly four thousand years. The great highways of travel in the ancient world passed along its borders, and neighboring nations controlled much of its history and destiny. Through these contacts the world came to know of the Holy Land's unique contribution to history: the Judeo-Christian heritage which has shaped in a powerful way the destiny of mankind. For here, in the time of Herod, Jesus was born. Here He lived and here His ministry was fulfilled. On the outskirts of the Holy City, on the Mount of Olives, He spent the night of His betrayal. From Gethsemane (p. 8) He was led to trial and then crucifixion, after a hurried trial by the Jewish Sanhedrin.

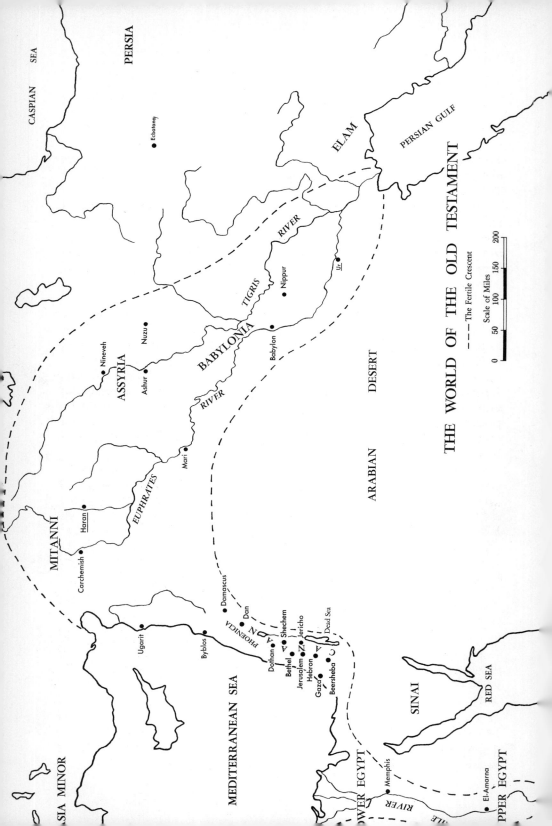

THE WORLD OF THE OLD TESTAMENT

- - - - The Fertile Crescent

Scale of Miles

0   50   100   150   200

CASPIAN SEA

PERSIA

Ecbatana

ELAM

PERSIAN GULF

TIGRIS RIVER

Nippur

Ur

ASSYRIA

Nineveh

Ashur

Nuzu

BABYLONIA

Babylon

RIVER

Mari

EUPHRATES

DESERT

ARABIAN

MITANNI

Carchemish

Haran

ASIA MINOR

Ugarit

Byblos

Damascus

PHOENICIA

Dan

Shechem

Dothan

Bethel

Jericho

Jerusalem

Hebron

Gaza

Beersheba

Dead Sea

MEDITERRANEAN SEA

SINAI

RED SEA

LOWER EGYPT

Memphis

NILE RIVER

UPPER EGYPT

El-Amarna

The background of Christianity, therefore, is Jewish. Jesus was born into a Jewish world under captivity to the Roman Empire. The founder of Christianity was a great Teacher, a great Preacher, and a great Leader tremendously concerned about the individual. He said, "The Kingdom of God is within you.' To Jesus, God the Father was no arbitrary despot; but a heavenly Father, who loved all His earth children, and would not that any of them should perish, but that all might have abundant life here and hereafter.

Jesus never argued about the existence of God. He accepted Him as His heavenly Father, and as the supreme Ruler of the universe. Jesus saw the Law and the Prophets as pointing forward to the Messiah and culminating in Him. He said: "I came not to destroy, but to fulfill." He quoted frequently from the Old Testament; and He welcomed the spiritual insight which caused Peter to declare: "Thou art the Christ (Messiah), the Son of the Living God."

The public ministry of Jesus of Nazareth began with His baptism by immersion at the hands of John the Baptist in the river Jordan (Matt. 3:13-17; Mark 1:9-11; Luke 3:21-22; John 1:29-34). It was followed almost immediately by Christ's temptation in the wilderness (Matt. 4:1-11; Mark 1:12-15; Luke 4:1-13). On His return to Galilee following His temptation, during which period He fasted for forty days and nights, Jesus called at least the first four of His disciples (Matt. 4:18-22; Mark 1:16-20; John 1:35-49), and later all of the Twelve (Matt. 10:1-4). These disciples were with the Master of Men almost constantly during His earthly ministry of teaching, preaching, and healing.

Two sacraments only were observed by the Apostolic Church: baptism by immersion and the Lord's Supper. Both were visible symbols instituted by Jesus in order to confer grace and divine life on all those worthy and desiring to receive it. Much later, in 1439, the Roman Catholic Church fixed the limit of the sacraments at seven, by adding confirmation, penance, matrimony, holy orders, and extreme unction. The sacraments observed by most of the Protestant churches are baptism and the Lord's Supper.

Baptism, in New Testament times, followed an outward or public declaration of one's faith in Christ and intention to follow Him in witnessing to the children of men by changed life. The disciples of Jesus were often spoken of as "followers of the Way." Isaiah 35:8, in prophetic utterance, describes that Way: "And an highway shall be there, and a way, and it shall be called The way of holiness; the unclean shall not pass over it; but it shall be for those: the wayfaring men, though fools, shall not err therein." Later Jesus said to Thomas, the doubting disciple, in answer to his request, "Show us the way": "I am the way, the truth, and the life; no man cometh unto the Father, but by me" (John 14:6).

Jesus Himself, when He came to John the Baptist requesting baptism of him in the Jordan River, said, when John demurred: " 'Suffer it to be so now;

for thus it becometh us to fulfill all righteousness.' Then he suffered him" (Matt. 3:15). Baptism is the entrance door to the Christian fellowship known as the Church (Acts 2:41). Paul describes baptism as a symbol of the death, the burial, and the resurrection of Christ's life on this earth: dead in that we die to sin; burial in that our sins are buried (purged) by the grace of God; and resurrection in that we rise from the baptismal waters to walk a new life with Jesus, the Christ, as our Guide, our Inspiration, and our Mediator at the throne of God (Rom. 6:3-5; Col. 2:12-14).

The Lord's Supper, the second sacrament of the Church, sometimes referred to as the Eucharist, was instituted by Jesus on the night of His betrayal and arrest, as He sat at meat with the Twelve (Matt. 26:20-30; Mark 14:22-30; Luke 22:15-22; John 13:18-38). It was observed by the early Church usually in connection with an evening meal. The apostle Paul quotes Jesus as having said: "For as often as ye eat this bread, and drink this cup, ye do shew the Lord's death till he come" (I Cor. 11:26).

In the Catholic Church the liturgy of the Mass underwent no drastic change from A.D. 500 until 1350. The Roman form of this sacrament had spread throughout Western Europe, but was adapted to local and regional conditions. The major development of the Eucharist during the centuries that followed was in the affirmation of the dogma of transubstantiation, the withdrawal of the cup from the laity in the communion service, the feast of Corpus Christi, and the adoration of the reserved sacrament. The denial of the cup to the laity came slowly and was a natural outgrowth of the acceptance of the dogma of transubstantiation. This dogma holds that by the words of the priest, the bread and wine of the Eucharist actually become the body and blood of Christ; as a result, great care must be taken to prevent any profaning of these elements. Increasingly the clergy attempted to enforce the observance of this feast by requiring fasts and the payment of tithes. Theoretically this was intended to bring the sinner to repentance; actually it sometimes became a means of constraining the unwilling to comply with the wishes of those who had power to exclude them from participation in the Lord's Supper.

When the twelve apostles began to pass away, something was needed to take the place of their personal witness. The Four Gospels—Matthew, Mark, Luke, and John—are the answer to that need. That Mark is the earliest Gospel is agreed upon by most scholars. If we are asked why there are four Gospels, and no more, the answer is that they represented the traditions of important church centers (Mark, Rome; Matthew, perhaps Antioch; Luke, uncertain; and John, Ephesus).

Scholars indicate that the Gospel of Mark was so little read in the early Church that the influence of a large communion like the church in Rome was needed to explain its survival. It is supposed to have been written by John Mark from data supplied by the apostle Peter. It is, therefore, sometimes referred to as Peter's Gospel. The approximate date of writing of the Gospel of Mark is A.D. 65, the years from A.D. 80 to 90 are designated for the Gospels of Matthew and Luke, and about A.D. 100 is the date of John's

Gospel. The remainder of the New Testament consists of the Acts of the Apostles (twenty-eight chapters), the Pauline Epistles (fourteen in number), the general Epistle of James, the First and Second Epistles of Peter, the First, Second, and Third Epistles of John, the general Epistle of Jude, and the Book of Revelation, credited to St. John the Divine.*

✝

CHRISTMAS NIGHT
Fritz von Uhde

THE art of Fritz von Uhde (1848-1911) reveals one deep and abiding element: he loved children. He had three of his own and was himself both mother and father to them, for his wife died when the children were small.

"Christmas Night" (p. 14), painted in 1893, reduces Christmas to its lowest terms—three people. The scene is a barn, fairly roomy and cluttered. A lantern on a peg close at hand throws a frosty glimmer on the actors in this homely drama. It touches the white cloth that transforms Joseph's pack into a pillow; it glances on Mary's head; it flickers on the tiny infant lying on its bed of straw; it lights the forehead and hands of Joseph.

Strangely enough, von Uhde brings Joseph forward and makes him the chief figure. Mary is next in importance, while the Child is the person we notice last. The leading lines of this composition, to be sure, focus upon the Babe, for He is the person who gives significance to all the rest. Yet presently we come back to Joseph as the most interesting and beautiful part of the whole.

All the details are eloquent. Joseph has found himself in a strange town, barred from the inn, friendless, in a stable; and the Child is born.

What to do?—the best possible under the circumstances. Find an old wheelbarrow and turn it upside down for a workbench; find a cracked plate; fetch from his knapsack the little clay stove and dish; whittle a stirring spoon out of a sliver of board; pour out half a cup of meal for gruel. That is just what Mary needs, and Joseph can at least give her that. Look at his face: the face not of a great man but of a good man; and look at his hands—hands that have always worked for others. If Jesus in His mature ministry called God Father, it must have been because He had long since recognized in Joseph the very traits of loving fatherhood that He now felt in the Infinite.

Mary is a peasant girl. Her face is countrified and not beautiful; but in the half-light we see in it something better than beauty. It is the age-old ecstasy of mothers. No matter where the little one is born, the spiritual experience is always the same. God has brought hope and love to fruition, has entered into creative partnership with man and has crowned the mother's suffering with joy.

In this picture, therefore, are some of the chief elements of human character and human happiness. Von Uhde has pushed into the background for the

* Based on data from *A History of Christianity* by Kenneth Scott Latourette. Published 1953 by Harper & Brothers.

CHRISTMAS NIGHT—*VON UHDE*

time being the supernatural and the incomprehensible, and has shown us that wherever there is human ministry—love, faith, hope, devotion, sacrifice —there is Immanuel, God with us.*

✠

THE HOLY FAMILY
Adelbert Franz Seligmann

THERE is little information about Adelbert Franz Seligmann in reference books. He was born in Austria in 1862. His critical writings on the art exhibitions in Vienna appeared in the Parisian *Gazette des Beaux Arts*. This picture, "The Holy Family" (p. 16), was painted in 1888.

Though there are many paintings of the twelve-year-old boy in the Temple and some representing the adult Jesus as carpenter, few other pictures present this phase of the youth of Jesus in the later adolescent years, thinking through His life problems.

The scene is the carpenter shop. As in all Oriental shops, the light comes from one source, the front door. The door in the background in this painting must therefore lead to the back room where the family lives.

In this painting Jesus is the master workman. His father is too old to take the lead any longer but not too old to take an interest. Today he has discovered Jesus standing idle, lost in thought. It is not the first time this has happened; in fact, within the past few months it has occurred with increasing frequency. Joseph is puzzled by it. He steps back into the home and motions the mother to come too. They slip in together and Mary sits on a stool in the corner while both study their son and whisper about this growing habit.

What can it mean? Jesus has always been such a straightforward, open-hearted boy, such a steady workman, so little given to moods and reticences; but now He is often abstracted, silent, almost morose. Always in the shop is a scroll of the Prophets. Frequently when He has been found standing vacantly by His unfinished task the scroll has been in His hand. "And there shall come forth a shoot out of the stock of Jesse, and a branch out of his roots shall bear fruit. And the spirit of Jehovah shall rest upon him, the spirit of wisdom and understanding, the spirit of counsel and might, the spirit of knowledge and of the fear of Jehovah. With righteousness shall he judge the poor, and decide with equity for the meek of the earth.

"Behold I lay in Zion for a foundation a stone, a tried stone, a precious corner-stone of sure foundation: and I will make justice the line and righteousness the plummet.

"The spirit of the Lord Jehovah is upon me, because Jehovah hath anointed me to preach good tidings unto the meek, to bind up the broken-hearted, to proclaim liberty to the captives, and the opening of the prison to them that are bound" (ASV).

* Arranged from *Christ and His Gospel in Recent Art* by Albert Edward Bailey. Copyright 1935 by Charles Scribner's Sons. Used by permission of the publisher.

THE HOLY FAMILY—*SELIGMANN*

Of whom did the prophet speak? Surely not in his day were these things accomplished, and never since has a prophet arisen to fulfill these words. Is the line of the prophets extinct? Could He possibly speak to me—a village carpenter? How does a boy fit himself to be called? Surely "With my soul have I desired Thee in the night; yea, with my spirit within me will I seek Thee earnestly." If I should hear the voice of the Lord saying, "Whom shall I send and who shall go for us?", surely I would answer as Isaiah did, "Here am I; send me!"

But will He call? And shall I know the voice is His?*

Note that the timbers on which Jesus has been working have assumed by chance the shape of a cross, and on the ground are a hammer and three nails. But Jesus does not see them. As yet there is in Him no insight by which such things become significant.

✛

HEAD OF CHRIST
Warner E. Sallman

WARNER E. SALLMAN was born in Chicago, Illinois, in 1892, of Swedish and Finnish parents. Early in his life the Bible illustrations of Gustave Doré set his soul aflame with a burning desire to become a Christian artist. He took an apprenticeship in an art studio at the age of fourteen, studying evenings in the Chicago Art Institute. It was during these years that he was challenged by Dean Sellers: "We need Christian artists. And I hope sometime you will give us your conception of Christ. I hope you'll picture a virile, manly Christ!"

The young artist shared the feeling of divine discontent with the sad, weary, effeminate picturizations of the Christ so often seen. In all humility he felt that the face of Christ should be one of beautiful but rugged simplicity. He hoped some day to create such a picture.

Mr. Sallman was thirty-one when the occasion confronted him. By this time, he was serving as art editor of a religious youth magazine, *The Covenant Companion*. No one had a satisfactory suggestion for the "Christian Life" number which was to appear in February, 1924. The picture had to be finished and in the hands of the engraver early in January.

On the day before the deadline, he worked late at his drawing board, to no avail. "Finally, in the early morning hours," says the artist, "there emerged in one luminous moment a visual picturization of the head of Christ, so clear and definite that I could almost see it on the paper. I hastily made a small thumbnail sketch of the picture before the image got away from me. The next day I made an enlarged charcoal drawing which was completed just in time for the deadline." It was not until sixteen years later, however, that an oil canvas was made following the pattern of the original charcoal sketch.

* Arranged from *Christ and His Gospel in Recent Art* by Albert Edward Bailey. Copyright 1935 by Charles Scribner's Sons. Used by permission of the publisher.

HEAD OF CHRIST—*SALLMAN*

Critics, artists, and churchmen have been unanimous in their praise and acceptance of this picture. No pale, anemic Christ is this. Instead we see a strong young man with clear eyes and thoughtful brow. This Christ needs no halo. His credentials are to be found, not in some external artifice, but in the integrity of His inner life.

Sallman portrays a Christ who is mature, yet ever youthful; courageous, yet humble; manly, yet compassionate; practical, yet mystical; friendly, yet lonely; incisive, yet warm and winsome. One can see Jesus tramping ahead, alone, head erect, determined. In that strong countenance is the look of one who sees His way and will not be denied. Here is one whose personality, met face to face, is too vast to encompass. Here is humanity in its purity, its power, and its perfection. "I wanted to show the reality of the human side of Jesus," says the artist.

The artist has portrayed not only the Son of man, but the divine Redeemer as well. We find in Him far more than a good man who lived a long time ago. He is not only the Man of Galilee—He is the Lord of glory. He confronts us as the perfect Son of God with an offer of redemptive love. He is with us as an elder brother, yet He is above us and beyond us as our Saviour.

In this strong face is a challenge and a promise. Christ came to earth not merely to tell us what we ought to do. He came to do something for us we could not do for ourselves. He came not merely to give good advice; what He offers is something infinitely better. It is the "power of God unto salvation" (Rom. 1:16).*

✦

TRUST THE GREAT ARTIST

Trust the Great Artist, He
Who paints the sky and sea
With shadowed blue, who clothes the land
In garb of green, and in the spring
Sets all the earth a-blossoming—
He guides your destiny.

The magic hand
That colors dawn with flaming rose,
That ere the falling night,
For every soul's delight,
Pours out the streaming gold—
That hand, too, holds your life.

His grasp, amid the strife
Would shape you to His will:
Let Him His wish fulfill;
What though the testings irk,
Fret not; mar not His work.

* Arranged from a booklet, *The Story of Sallman's "Head of Christ,"* by Howard W. Ellis. Copyright 1944 by Kriebel & Bates. Used by permission of the publisher.

Trust the Great Artist, He
Who made the earth and sea.*

—Thomas Curtis Clark

HIS LOVE IS ALWAYS SHINING

Never—once—since the world began
Has the sun ever once stopped shining.
His face very often we could not see,
And we grumbled at his inconstancy;
But the clouds were really to blame, not he
For, behind them, he was shining.

And so—behind life's darkest clouds,
God's love is always shining.
We veil it at times with our faithless fears,
And darken our sight with our foolish tears,
But in time the atmosphere always clears,
For His love is always shining.**

—John Oxenham

MAN'S HERITAGE

These man shares with ox or foal:
The gnaw of hunger, thirst,
And lash of rain are common lot
To flesh and blood accursed
With pain. But this is man's alone:
The search, the deep unrest
Of soul that needs must seek for God—
Inexorable quest!***

—Leslie Savage Clark

MY FATHER'S HOUSE

Who sees a spire against the sky
Shall find, at last, the sign
Of all he sought—nor ever found—
In lands of husks and swine.
Who enters there and kneels, shall know
That place no hands can build
Where man, the prodigal, is Home,
His soul's long hunger filled.***

—Leslie Savage Clark

* From *Meditations under the Sky* by Dorothy Wells Pease, pp. 124-25. Copyright 1957 by Abingdon Press. Used by permission of Mrs. Thomas Curtis Clark and the publisher.
** *Ibid.*, p. 97. Used by permission of Miss Erica Oxenham and the publisher.
*** From *With All Thy Heart* by Leslie Savage Clark. Copyright 1957 by Broadman Press. Used by permission of the author and the publisher.

MARY, MOTHER OF JESUS

"Mary" means "bitter" and "myrrh," two extremes
Portrayed in events of Mary's career;
Favored by God, yet a sword in her dreams,
Blest among women, but widowhood near.
Of low estate, yet mother of our Lord,
To every scene a song of praise she brought,
And from her heart transcendent peace she poured.
She whispered unto Luke each inmost thought.
With Joseph, refugees in foreign land,
In temple seeking Jesus in despair.
Urging others to do each Christ's command,
In upper room with His followers in prayer,
Mary, dispenser of life's sacred leav'n,
Uniting profoundly this earth with heaven.*

—Henry C. Spear

MARY AND MARTHA

Two sisters of the noted Lazarus,
Whose home in Bethany brought Jesus peace.
Martha, who o'er her meals made a great fuss,
While Mary from her worries sought release.
There always will be bodies to be fed,
The "Marthas" will make specialty of that;
The soul is subtle, but also needs "bread,"
The sensitive will sit where Mary sat.
There's not much chance that folk will starve to death,
But many will neglect the better part;
Wise are the souls that list to what Christ saith,
And journey forth to practice Christian art.
"Marthas" who are troubled by many things
Can learn from "Marys" what the Spirit brings.*

—Henry C. Spear

MASTER BUILDER

Only the Hands of Nazareth
Could have used such knotted wood
As the lives of Peter, Thomas, the Twelve,
For building a base that stood
When palaces of Caesar fell,
For laying foundations broad
As love itself, that outlast time
For the carpentry of God.**

—Leslie Savage Clark

* Written especially for this anthology.
** From *With All Thy Heart* by Leslie Savage Clark, p. 59. Copyright 1947 by Broadman Press. Used by permission of the author and the publisher.

JOHN THE BAPTIST

A voice crying in the wilderness:
"Make His paths straight";
Eyes that searched souls
And found their Saviour;
A high heart undismayed
By Pharisees or despots;
A speechless head upon a salver—
This is the stuff that marytrs are made of;
This was the pioneer
Who hewed a way through the wilderness
For One
The latchet of Whose shoes
He thought himself unworthy to unloose.*

—*Earl Marlatt*

✠

THE PILGRIMAGE TO BETHLEHEM
Lew Wallace

IT was the third hour of the day, and many of the people had gone away; yet the press continued without apparent abatement. Of the newcomers, there was a group over by the south wall, consisting of a man, a woman, and a donkey.

The man stood by the animal's head, holding a leading-strap, and leaning upon a stick which seemed to have been chosen for the double purpose of goad and staff. His dress was like that of the ordinary Jews around him, except that it had the appearance of newness.

The donkey ate leisurely from an armful of green grass, unmindful of the woman sitting upon its back in a cushioned pillion. An outer robe of dull woolen stuff completely covered her person, while a white wimple veiled her head and neck. Once in a while, impelled by curiosity to see or hear something passing, she drew the wimple aside, but so slightly that the face remained invisible.

At length the man was accosted: "Are you not Joseph of Nazareth?"

"I am so called," answered Joseph, turning gravely around. "And you— ah, peace be unto you! my friend, Rabbi Samuel!"

"The same give I back to you." The Rabbi paused, looking at the woman, then added, "You were born in Bethlehem, and wend thither now, with your daughter, to be counted for taxation, as ordered by Caesar."

Joseph answered, without change of posture or countenance, "The woman is not my daughter. She is the child of Joachim and Anna of Bethlehem, of whom you have at least heard. She is now my wife."

* From *Cathedral: A Volume of Poems* by Earl Marlatt, p. 88. Copyright 1956 by Earl Marlatt. Published by Parthenon Press. Used by permission of the author and the publisher.

Turning to the left, Joseph's party took the road toward Bethlehem. The descent into the valley of Hinnom was quite broken, garnished here and there with straggling wild olive trees. Carefully, tenderly, the Nazarene walked by the woman's side, leading-strap in his hand.

Slowly they passed the Lower Pool of Gihon, slowly they proceeded, keeping parallel with the aqueduct from the Pools of Solomon. The sun streamed garishly over the stony face of the famous locality, and under its influence Mary dropped the wimple entirely, and bared her head.

She was not more than fifteen. Her form, voice, and manner belonged to the period of transition from girlhood. Her face was perfectly oval, her complexion more pale than fair. The nose was faultless; the lips, slightly parted, were full and ripe, giving to the lines of the mouth warmth, tenderness, and trust; the eyes were blue and large, and shaded by drooping lids and long lashes; and, in harmony with all, a flood of golden hair, in the style permitted to Jewish brides, fell unconfined down her back to the pillion on which she sat. To these charms were added an air of purity which only the soul can impart. Often, with trembling lips, she raised her eyes to heaven, often she crossed her hands upon her breast, as in adoration and prayer; often she raised her head like one listening eagerly for a calling voice. Now and then, midst his slow utterances, Joseph turned to look at her, and, catching the expression kindling her face as with light, forgot his theme, and with bowed head, wondering, plodded on.

So they skirted the great plain, and at length, reached the elevation from which, across a valley, they beheld Bethlehem, its white walls crowning a ridge, and shining above the leafless orchards. The narrow space was crowded. A fear came upon Joseph—a fear lest, if the town were so thronged, there might not be house-room for the gentle Mary. Without delay, he hurried on, past the pillar of stone marking the tomb of Rachel, up the gardened slope until he stopped before the portal of the khan.

The khan at Bethlehem, before which Joseph and his wife stopped, was a good specimen of its class, being neither very primitive nor very princely. The building was purely Oriental; that is to say, a quadrangular block of rough stones, one story high, flat-roofed, externally unbroken by a window, and with but one principal entrance—a doorway, which was also a gateway making what was in the highest degree essential to a respectable khan—a safe enclosure for animals.

In a village like Bethlehem, as there was but one sheik, there could not well be more than one khan; and, though born in the place, the Nazarene, from long residence elsewhere, had no claim to hospitality in the town. When he was come close by, his alarm was not allayed by the discovery of a crowd investing the door of the establishment, while the enclosure adjoining, broad as it was, seemed already full.

"We cannot reach the door," Joseph said, "Let us stop here, and learn, if we can, what has happened."

The wife, without answering, quietly drew the wimple aside. The look of fatigue at first upon her face changed to one of interest. While she was thus looking, a man pushed his way out of the press. The Nazarene spoke to him.

"As I am what I take you to be, good friend—a son of Judah—may I ask the cause of this multitude?"

The stranger replied, "Peace be to you, Rabbi! I am also a son of Judah. When the proclamation went abroad requiring all Hebrews to be numbered at the cities of their birth—That is my business here, Rabbi."

Joseph's face remained stolid as a mask, while he remarked: "I have come for that also—I and my wife."

The man paused again, looking abruptly at Mary, who was now looking at him and listening. Then he said, "Rabbi, will not your wife go to mine? You may see her yonder with the children, under the leaning olive tree at the bend of the road."

Joseph hesitated, but at length replied, "The offer is kind. Let me speak to the gate-keeper myself. I will return quickly."

The keeper sat on a great cedar block outside the gate. A dog squatted on the block by his side. "The peace of Jehovah be with you," said Joseph, at last confronting the keeper. "I am a Bethlehemite. Is there not room for—"

"There is not."

"You may have heard of me—Joseph of Nazareth. This is the house of my fathers. I am of the line of David." These words held the Nazarene's hope. If they failed him, further appeal was idle.

The appeal was not without effect. The keeper of the gate slid down from the cedar block, and said, "Rabbi, I cannot tell you when this door first opened in welcome to the traveler, but it was more than a thousand years ago; and in all that time there is no known instance of a good man turned away, save when there was no room to rest him in. If you care to go with me, I will show you that there is not a lodging-place left in the house."

"The court is large," Joseph said.

"Yes, but it is heaped with cargoes—with bales of silk, and packets of spices, and goods of every kind."

Then for a moment the face of the applicant lost its stolidity. With some warmth he next said, "I do not care for myself, but I have with me my wife, and the night is cold—colder on these heights than in Nazareth. She cannot live in the open air. She is so young! if I make her bed on the hill, the frosts will kill her."

This time the keeper's eyes sought the ground in thought. Suddenly he raised his head; "If I cannot make room for you," he said, "I cannot turn you away. How many are of your party?"

Joseph reflected, then replied, "My wife and a friend with his family, from Beth-Dagon."

"Very well. Bring your people, and hasten; for, when the sun goes down behind the mountain night comes quickly, and it is nearly there now."

The Nazarene went back joyfully to Mary and the Beth-Dagonite; the latter brought up his family, the women mounted on donkeys.

"This is she of whom I spoke," said the Nazarene; "and these are our friends."

Then [the keeper] took the leading-strap from Joseph and said to Mary, "Peace to you, O daughter of David!" Then to Joseph, "Rabbi, follow me."

The party were conducted into a wide passage paved with stone, from which they entered the court of the khan. They went down the slope of the crowded yard slowly. At length they turned into a path running towards the gray limestone bluff overlooking the khan on the west.

"We are going to the cave," said Joseph, laconically.

The guide lingered till Mary came to his side. He said to her, "Better a bed upon the floor where [your ancestor David] has slept than one in the courtyard or by the roadside. Ah, here is the house before the cave."

The guests entered, and stared about them. The house was but a mask for the mouth of a natural cave forty feet long, nine or ten feet high, and twelve or fifteen in width. There was no stalls or partitions of any kind. Dust and chaff yellowed the floor; otherwise the place was cleanly and comfortable.

"Come in!" said the guide. "These piles upon the floor are for travelers like yourselves. Take what of them you need." Then he spoke to Mary. "Can you rest here?"

"The place is sanctified," she answered.

When he was gone, they busied themselves making the cave habitable.

About midnight someone on the roof cried out, "What light is that in the sky? Awake, brethren, awake and see!"

The people, half asleep, sat up and looked; then they became wide-awake, though wonder-struck. Soon the entire tenantry of the house and court and enclosure, were cut gazing at the sky. And this is what they saw. A ray of light, beginning at a height immeasurably beyond the nearest stars, and dropping obliquely to the earth. The apparition seemed to rest on the nearest mountain southeast of the town, making a pale corona along the line of the summit. The khan was touched luminously, so that those upon the roof saw each other's faces, all filled with wonder.

The boldest spoke in whispers. "Saw you ever the like?" asked one.

"It seems just over the mountain there. I cannot tell what it is, nor did I ever see anything like it," was the answer.

"I have it!" cried one, confidently. "The shepherds have seen a lion, and made fires to keep him from the flocks."

A bystander dispelled the comfort. "No, no! Though all the wood in all the valleys of Judah was brought together in one pile and fired, the blaze would not throw a light so strong and high."

After that there was silence on the house-top, broken but once again while the mystery continued.

"Brethren!" exclaimed a Jew of venerable mien, "what we see is the ladder our father Jacob saw in his dream. Blessed be the Lord God of our fathers."*

* Abridged from *Ben Hur, A Tale of the Christ* by Lew Wallace.

THE LIGHT OF THE WORLD IS COME

Elizabeth Stuart Phelps

THE political situation among the Jewish race to which Joseph and Mary belonged was, at this time, extremely interesting. The Hebrews were above all things a hero-loving nation; and their heroes were dead. The Jews revered their prophets. Now there were no prophets. The Jews had experimented with a theocracy and failed in it. Their dejection was proportional to their defeated aspiration.

More humiliating than the enslavement to Babylonia, Greece or Egypt, was enslavement to Rome. By the irony of fortune these proud people were now subjects in their own land, were but the disdained provincials of a vast empire. That is to say, that Caesar Augustus occupied the Roman throne, and Herod, his vassal king, the palace at Jerusalem.

In the year 747, three years before the Christian era, a census preparatory to extra taxation was ordered. The consequence was a tumult. The people were bitterly angry; but to escape from the great hand of Rome was impossible. Caesar Augustus was ruler of the world. Herod, his creature, controlled more territory than any dead Jewish king had ever done. Raging and impotent, the subjects prepared to obey.

To Nazareth, as to other villages in Palestine, the Roman fiat came. Long and severe were the journeys required of the country people who must answer to this enrollment. Every citizen was obliged to register himself at the town whence his family had sprung.

Two plain people of Nazareth started at dawn one winter day to take one of these annoying journeys. Joseph and Mary, husband and wife, traveled as poor people must; on foot, or with one beast of burden between them.

There was a little town, about six miles southeast of Jerusalem, between seventy and eighty miles from Nazareth. Bethlehem was its name. It was the birthplace of David the king; and Joseph, the builder, descendant of David, must register there.

Mary, his wife, went with him. Why did Mary—who had the gravest reasons at that time for wishing rest and shelter—take that cruel journey over one of the roughest of Palestinian pathways to Bethlehem?

Because her heart craved that she should at that time of all others be near her husband, who understood her. Joseph must go to Bethlehem, and go just then. Mary would not allow him to leave her behind. The circumstances were too unusual. Her need of him was absolute.

Her child would have been born in Nazareth, but for this accident of the census. But *was* it only an accident that the census must come just then? Or was it one of those divine incidents in which the great Will rides over little human wills, and brings everything out as no one could possibly have planned? A thousand years before, ancient dreamers had associated strange things with the town of Bethlehem. Did Mary remember them? There, it had been written, the Governor of her people should be sought. There the Wonderful should enter the world.

The two travelers arrived in Bethlehem at nightfall, footworn, chilled and faint. The wife, perishing of fatigue, had passed the stage of physical suffering when one takes care or thought for what is to happen next. Because of her condition, they lagged behind the other travelers, and the town was already brimming over with strangers like themselves, when they arrived. Every house was crowded.

Alarmed by the condition of his wife, Joseph persisted manfully in his determination to find her shelter. Mary asked no questions, expressed no concern. The poor, homesick, young creature was dumb with suffering.

Dully, at length, she heard her husband say that there was a stable behind the inn, and that for the common humanity of the deed, the people of the khan would let her in. He carried her to the stable: she crept among the straw, like the animals around her; and there—hastened probably by her cruel journey—the anguish of motherhood overtook the exhausted wife.

Presently Mary looked about the stable. Women are merciful to each other in this one respect at least, and we are not forbidden to think that some matron of the inn had ministered to this homeless young traveler. The child was not dressed, but tightly wrapped in a long band—the baby clothes of the East. The woman had left the young mother, now, with her husband and the cattle.

The khan to which Joseph and Mary had applied was not a comfortable place; and the stable in which the baby was born was a rude affair. Mary saw that it was a cave in the heart of a rock; a species of grotto. She and Joseph were alone—no, not alone: there lay the child, breathing beside her.

Towards morning, she stirred uneasily, and, out of fitful slumber, broken by conscious suffering, looked about her. It was no dream. She was not at home in happy Nazareth. Joseph had not slept, but stood straight and strong between her eyes and the entrance to the grotto. Voices were audible. Joseph was speaking. Visitors were in the stable.

Day was breaking. The gray light crept in with a kind of reverence, as if the morning were on its knees. In the cold Mary saw the visitors. Their calling was stamped on their dark, weather-tinted faces, and on their rough, warm clothing. They wore mantles of woolen stuff, and heavy sheepskin cloaks.

She heard one say to another: "That was the sign!"

And another answer: "In a manger! There he is!"

Then the shepherds spoke all together, their sentences falling over each other. But Mary—for her ear was delicate and quick—made out as much as this: in their pastures, a mile or more out of Bethlehem, these strong men of iron fist to wolves and robbers, silken to the touch of sheep and lambs, men wakeful of eye and ear by profession, suddenly, in the deep of the night, had seen the sky blossom with celestial forms and faces, and heard the ether ring with celestial tongues and songs.

Half in terror, half in delight, they had hurried to the town to test their wonderful experience. "Ye shall find the babe wrapped in swaddling clothes, lying in a manger." Only one newborn infant in Bethlehem lay in the manger of a public stable.

They went straight out from the stable, and told their experience to anybody and everybody in the crowded town. The village, overflowing with guests from all parts of Palestine, listened to this strange tale; and travelers, returning to their homes, carried the rumor of it everywhere.

The shepherds went back to their sheep. They had seen their only angels. The next night, the next year, brought no more. They talked, all their lives, about this one great experience.

But the young mother did not speak when she heard about the angels, and the sign. She was glad when the shepherds were gone out of the stable. She looked at the baby mutely. Her heart was like a white flower, closing over a drop of dew. She kept these things, and pondered them.

Joseph, too, was quiet. He was one of the plain men who make no fuss about duty. He thought about the shepherds, the angels, their startling message, and the dream of his in Nazareth. It was impossible to think how it would have been, if he had not trusted it, and her. The eyes of the girl wife questioned her husband gently. The mysterious child slept beside them. The hand of Joseph silently clasped that of Mary.

Astrologers from the earliest times have always associated heavenly disturbances with the birth of great men. The expectation of the advent of an extraordinary being among the Jewish people was not, at that time, entirely confined to the Jews. For Persia, the Far East, the civilized world to a certain extent shared it.

Students of the sky followed the march of the stars. Eastern travelers, coming by an unknown route, reached Jerusalem. Here, these idealists asked strange questions, and received significant replies. The Magi, with the persistence of men who have sacrificed too much for an idea to abandon it easily, betook themselves to the palace. Here they had an interview with Herod, one of the most abhorrent and abhorred of monarchs.

He appealed to the priests and teachers of his remarkable and dreaded captives. Their governing body, the Sanhedrin, was called together. The question was officially put to them: Where was this King of theirs to be expected, or to be sought? With ecclesiastical precision the anxious monarch was referred to the Scriptures of the Jewish people, which indicated Bethlehem as the birthplace of their national hero.

The Magi trod the streets of Bethlehem with arrested breath. The mysterious child was now some weeks of age; and the family were no longer boarders in the stable of the khan. They may have been house guests or lodgers at the inn.

At all events, the Eastern travelers found the family readily. All Bethlehem was talking of them and their affairs. The temporary star looked down on the village gossip coldly. Its light and its life were beginning to waste.

Were the travelers Persians, Arabians? Princes or astrologers, or both? How many were there? What tongue did they speak? Greek, perhaps—then the court language of the East. Or did the interpreters connect them with the Aramaic as spoken in Bethlehem?

We only know that they found the object of their wearisome and romantic journey. At last the star and the child had met.

The Magi bent their mitred heads, and knelt before the child. Deeper than the impulsive curiosity or even the deference of the shepherds was the profound, intelligent reverence of these learned foreigners.

Mary, looking on, perplexed and gentle, saw suddenly that the visitors, still upon their rug before the baby, were opening and offering to the child strange things—products of the far East.

Joseph, coming in, perceived at once the meaning of what he saw. For the gifts in the hands, on the laps of the Magi were the typical offerings of subjects to a King. These sages were worshiping a monarch. The glitter of gold shone out of dusky bags. Spicy, Oriental odors filled the air. Frankincense sent up its pungent perfume, strong as the heart of love. And there was myrrh, bitter of life, and as old to the fancy of the East as the ceremonials of death.

Only the wise recognize power in the weak. These Eastern scholars knelt humbly and happily before the babe of Bethlehem. Mary clasped the child and wondered.

The visitors went away quickly. Their faces wore a rapt and reverent look. They vanished quickly from the village, and lost themselves in the first convenient caravan to Arabia. A royal murderer, scowling from his windows, watched in vain for his Eastern guests. He had miscalculated their shrewd simplicity.*

✣

WISE MEN FROM THE EAST
Lew Wallace

Now when Jesus was born in Bethlehem of Judea . . . there came wise men from the east to Jerusalem.—MATTHEW 2:1

THE Arab has impressed his language upon everything south and east of Judea; so, in his tongue, the old Jebel is the parent of numberless wadies which, intersecting the Roman Road, pass into the Jordan. Out of one of these wadies a traveler passed, going to the table-lands of the desert. Judged by his appearance, he was quite forty-five years old. He was clad in the flowing garments so universal in the East; but their style may not be described more particularly, for he sat under a miniature tent, and rode a great white dromedary.

* Abridged from *The Story of Jesus Christ* by Elizabeth Stuart Phelps, pp. 16-26. Published by Houghton Mifflin Company. Used by permission of the author and the publisher.

It may be doubted if the people of the West ever overcome the impression made upon them by their first view of a camel equipped and loaded for the desert. The furniture perched on the [camel's] back was an invention which with any other people than of the East would have made the inventor renowned. It consisted of two wooden boxes, scarce four feet in length, balanced so that one hung at each side; the inner space, softly lined and carpeted, was arranged to allow the master to sit or lie half reclined; over it all was stretched a green awning. In such manner the ingenious sons of Cush had contrived to make comfortable the sunburnt ways of the wilderness, along which lay their duty as well as their pleasure.

For two hours the dromedary swung forward, keeping the trot steadily and the line due east. In that time the traveler never changed his position, nor looked to the right or left. On the desert, distance is not measured by miles or leagues, but by the hour, or halt. A carrier of the genuine Syrian stock can make three leagues easily. Two hours more passed without rest or deviation from the course. Vegetation entirely ceased.

No one, be it remembered, seeks the desert for a pleasure ground. Life and business traverse it by paths along which the bones of things dead are strewn. Such are the roads from well to well, from pasture to pasture. So the man with whom we are dealing could not have been in search of pleasure; neither was his manner that of a fugitive; not once did he look behind him. In such situations fear and curiosity are the most common sensations; he was not moved by them.

Exactly at noon the dromedary, of its own will, stopped, and uttered the cry or moan, peculiarly piteous, by which its kind always protest against an overload, and sometimes crave attention and rest. The master thereupon bestirred himself, waking, as it were, from sleep. He looked at the sun, surveyed the country on every side long and carefully, as if to identify an appointed place. Satisfied, he drew a deep breath, crossed his hands upon his breast, bowed his head, and prayed silently. The pious duty done, he prepared to dismount.

The man as now revealed was of admirable proportions, not so tall as powerful. A strong face, almost negro in color; yet the low, broad forehead, aquiline nose, the hair profuse, straight, and falling to the shoulder were signs of origin impossible to disguise. So looked the Pharaohs and the later Ptolemies; so looked Mizraim, father of the Egyptian race.

The traveler's limbs were numb, for his ride had been long and wearisome; so he rubbed his hands and stamped his feet, and walked round the faithful servant, whose lustrous eyes were closing in calm content with the cud he had already found.

There could be little doubt of the stranger's confidence in the coming of the expected company. In token thereof, he went first to the litter, and, from the cot or box opposite the one he had occupied in coming, produced a sponge and a small gurglet of water, with which he washed the eyes, face, and nostrils of the camel; that done, from the same depository he drew a circular cloth, red-and-white-striped, a bundle of rods, and a stout cane. The latter, after some manipulation, proved to be a cunning device which, when united together, formed a center pole higher than his head. When the pole was planted, and the rods set around it, he spread the cloth over them, and was literally at home. From the litter again he brought a carpet or square rug, and covered the floor of the tent on the side from the sun. That done, he went out, and once more, and with greater care and more eager eyes, swept the encircling country.

"They will come," he said, calmly. "He that led me is leading them. I will make ready."

From the pouches which lined the interior of the cot, and from a willow basket which was part of its furniture, he brought forth materials for a meal: wine, mutton dried and smoked, pomegranates; dates of Central Arabia; cheese and leavened bread, all which he carried and set upon the carpet under the tent.

All was now ready. He stepped out: lo! in the east a dark speck on the face of the desert. He stood as if rooted to the ground; his eyes dilated as if touched by something supernatural. The speck grew and at length assumed defined proportions. A little later, full into view swung a duplication of his own dromedary, tall and white, and bearing the traveling litter of Hindostan. Then the Egyptian crossed his hands upon his breast, and looked up to heaven.

"God only is great!" he exclaimed, his eyes full of tears, his soul in awe.

The stranger drew nigh—at last stopped. He beheld the kneeling camel, the tent, and the man standing prayerfully at the door. He crossed his hands, bent his head, and prayed silently; after which he stepped from his camel and advanced towards the Egyptian. A moment they looked at each other; then they embraced.

"Peace be with thee, O servant of the true God!" the stranger said.

"And to thee, O brother of the true faith!—to thee peace and welcome," the Egyptian replied, with fervor.

The newcomer was tall and gaunt, with lean face, sunken eyes, white hair and beard, and a complexion between the hue of cinnamon and bronze. Save for slippers his costume from head to foot was of white linen. The air of the man was high, stately, severe. He might have been called a Life drenched with the wisdom of Brahma. Only in his eyes was there proof of humanity. They were glistening with tears.

"God only is great!" he exclaimed.

"And blessed are they that serve him!" the Egyptian answered. "But let us wait," he added, "let us wait; for see, the other comes yonder!"

They looked to the north, where, already plain to view, a third camel came careening like a ship. They waited, standing together—waited until the newcomer arrived, dismounted, and advanced towards them.

"Peace to you, O my brother!" he said, while embracing the Hindoo.

And the Hindoo answered, "God's will be done!"

The last comer was all unlike his friends: his frame was slighter; his complexion white; a mass of waving light hair was a perfect crown for his small but beautiful head; the warmth of his dark-blue eyes certified a delicate mind, and a cordial, brave nature. He was bareheaded and unarmed. Under the folds of the Tyrian blanket which he wore with unconscious grace appeared a tunic gathered to the waist by a band, and reaching nearly to the knee; leaving the neck, arms, and legs bare. Sandals guarded his feet. Fifty years, probably more, had spent themselves upon him.

When his arms fell from the Egyptian, the latter said, with a tremulous voice, "The Spirit brought me first; wherefore I know myself chosen to be the servant of my brethren. The tent is set, and the bread is ready for the breaking. Let me perform my office."

Taking each by the hand, he led them within, and removed their sandals and washed their feet, and he poured water upon their hands, and dried them with napkins.

Then, when he had laved his own hands, he said, "Let us take care of ourselves, brethren, as our service requires, and eat, that we may be strong for what remains of the day's duty. While we eat, we will each learn who the others are, and whence they come, and how they are called."

He took them to the repast, and seated them so that they faced each other. Simultaneously their heads bent forward, their hands crossed upon their breasts, and, speaking together, they said aloud this simple grace: "Father of all—God!—what we have here is of thee; take our thanks and bless us, that we may continue to do thy will."

With the last word they raised their eyes, and looked at each other in wonder. Each had spoken in a language never before heard by the others; yet each understood perfectly what was said. Their souls thrilled with divine emotion; for by the miracle they recognized the Divine Presence.*

✢

O COME, O COME, EMMANUEL

LIKE many other early hymns, "O Come, O Come, Emmanuel" expresses the longing of "captive Israel" for the promised Son of God, who was to release the nation from bondage to ancient world empires and unite "all peoples in one heart and mind."

In the twelfth century, when the Latin words of this hymn were written, all church music throughout Europe was sung in Latin. Later the words were translated into various languages. John M. Neale (1818-1866), who translated many ancient hymns (see Interpretation of "All Glory, Laud, and Honor," p. 306), put the first stanza of this hymn into English, and the second and third stanzas were translated by Henry Sloane Coffin.

The music of "O Come, O Come, Emmanuel" is an ancient plain song or

* Abridged from *Ben Hur, A Tale of the Christ* by Lew Wallace.

O Come, O Come, Emmanuel

VENI EMMANUEL. 8. 8. 8. 8. 8. 8.

From Latin, 12th century
Stanza 1 Tr. by JOHN M. NEALE, 1818–1866
Stanzas 2, 3 Tr. by HENRY S. COFFIN, 1877–

Ancient plain song, 13th century

Unison; with spirit

1. O come, O come, Em - man - u - el, And ran - som cap - tive
2. O come, Thou Wis - dom from on high, And or - der all things,
3. O come, De - sire of na - tions, bind All peo - ples in one

Is - ra - el, That mourns in lone - ly ex - ile here
far and nigh: To us the path of know - ledge show,
heart and mind: Bid en - vy, strife, and quar - rels cease;

Un - til the Son of God ap - pear. Re - joice! Re - joice! Em -
And cause us in her ways to go. Re - joice! Re - joice! Em -
Fill the whole world with heav - en's peace. Re - joice! Re - joice! Em -

man - u - el Shall come to thee, O Is - ra - el!
man - u - el Shall come to thee, O Is - ra - el!
man - u - el Shall come to thee, O Is - ra - el! A - MEN.

chant melody that was sung in unison. Later someone, we do not know who, added the harmony that appears in our score (p. 33).

This ancient hymn calls upon "Israel"—a figure of speech referring to God's chosen people or, in other words, the Christian Church—to rejoice in the coming of Emmanuel, the Son of God.

In the second stanza we find a plea for "Wisdom from on high" that will lead us in the path of knowledge.

The third stanza voices the hope that "envy, strife, and quarrels cease," bringing all nations together in heart and mind, and filling the world with peace.

As we sing this magnificent old Latin hymn, we are reminded that the Old Testament prophecies are fulfilled in the life and teachings of Christ of Galilee, and that His Spirit has been guiding the children of men for nearly twenty centuries.

✤

WATCHMAN, TELL US OF THE NIGHT

SIR John Bowring (1792-1872), who gave us the words to this challenging and prophetic hymn, "Watchman, Tell Us of the Night," ranks high among the geniuses of the English-speaking world. He was one of the greatest linguists who ever lived, and over a period of forty years published translations of poetry from the Russian, Batavian, Spanish, Serbian, Bohemian, Magyar, Czech, and Hungarian languages. He is said to have mastered the Chinese language in record time. At various times he represented his government in France, Switzerland, Italy, Syria, Germany, and Siam.

Twice he was a member of the English Parliment. He was governor of Hong Kong in 1854, invested with supreme naval and military power. Although Sir John was technically retired in 1860, his public services continued long afterward, as commissioner to Italy and "minister plenipotentiary and envoy extraordinary" at posts ranging from Hawaii to the various courts of Europe. Many honors were conferred upon him, including membership in most of the learned societies of Europe. In his eightieth year he addressed three thousand people in Plymouth with all the energy of youth. He was buried in Exeter within a stone's throw of the house where he was born.

It is a bit difficult to reconcile this tough, hardened warrior and diplomat, which Sir John was, with the Christian gentleman and sweet singer whose hymns still inspire the Church of Christ the world around.

This great Christian Nativity hymn, "Watchman, Tell Us of the Night," is prophetic in all of its verses. The first verse challenges all men to see, above the mountain heights of history, the brightly beaming star of Bethlehem, foretelling the fulfillment of the hope and joy of Israel.

The second stanza tells us of the Prince of Peace and Truth which the Christ of prophecy brought to earth. The third stanza tells us of the world's

Watchman, Tell Us Of The Night

WATCHMAN 7s. 8 l.

L . Mason, 1830

1. Watchman, tell us of the night, What its signs of prom - ise are,

Trav - 'ler, o'er yon mountain's height, See that glo - ry - beam - ing star.

Watchman, does its beauteous ray Aught of joy or hope fore - tell?

Trav-'ler, yes, it brings the day, Prom-ised day of Is - ra - el. A - men.

2 Watchman, tell us of the night;
   Higher yet that star ascends.
Traveler, blessedness and light,
   Peace and truth, its course portends.
Watchman, will its beams alone
   Gild the spot that gave them birth?
Traveler, ages are its own ;
   See, it bursts o'er all the earth.

3 Watchman, tell us of the night,
   For the morning seems to dawn.
Traveler, darkness takes it flight;
   Doubt and terror are withdrawn.
Watchman, let thy wanderings cease;
   Hie thee to thy quiet home.
Traveler, lo, the Prince of Peace,
   Lo, the Son of God is come !

J. Bowring, 1825

greatest Teacher, the Saviour, and His reign among the children of men.

Bowring's hymn is a moving dramatization of the prophecy of the Messiah. It interprets, in terms of the Messiah, the "morning" of a new day that is coming in Christ Jesus, whose advent is to bless mankind with peace and truth, and it links the Old Testament prophecy with the New Testament imagery of the Star which the Wise Men saw in the East.*

The melody to which this hymn is regularly sung was composed by Lowell Mason (1792-1872). This hymn should be sung with spirit and in moderate time.

* Based on information from *The Gospel in Hymns* by Albert Edward Bailey. Copyright 1950 by Charles Scribner's Sons.

CONTENTS

PART I   SECTION 2

THE MINISTRY OF JESUS OF NAZARETH

✣

For the works which the Father hath given me to finish, the same works that I do, bear witness of me, that the Father hath sent me.—JOHN 5:36

✣

PAGE

PICTURES:
Interpretation: "The Last Supper" Window—*Caselli–Moretti* 38
Picture: "The Last Supper" Window—*Caselli–Moretti* .... Frontispiece
Interpretation: Judas Iscariot—*del Sarto* 41
Picture: Judas Iscariot—*del Sarto* 43
Interpretation: "The Lord Turned and Looked at Peter"—*Beecroft* 42
Picture: "The Lord Turned and Looked at Peter"—*Beecroft* 45
Interpretation: The Ascension—*von Uhde* 44
Picture: The Ascension—*von Uhde* 47

POETRY:
Credo—*Oxenham* 46
Apostle Peter—*Spear* 48
Jerusalem—*Jones* 48
Apostle John—*Spear* 49
And It Was Night—*Anderson* 49
Apostle Matthew—*Spear* 50
In the Garden—*Jones* 50
Nameless, Not Unknown—*Marlatt* 51
Mary Magdalene—*Spear* 51
The Star—The Cross—The Empty Tomb—*Luck* 51
The Road to Emmaus—*Jones* 52

STORIES:
"This Is My Beloved Son"—*Phelps* 52
Peter, the Man of Impulse—*Brown* 55
One of the Twelve Fell Away (A Poetic Story)—*Devanesen* 59

MUSIC:
Interpretation: The King of Love My Shepherd Is—*Baker* 62
Music: The King of Love My Shepherd Is—*Dykes* 63
Interpretation: Here at Thy Table, Lord—*Hoyt* 65
Music: Here at Thy Table, Lord—*Sherwin* 64

"THE LAST SUPPER" WINDOW

(Frontispiece)

Rosa Caselli-Moretti

THE story begins in Italy—when Dr. Hubert Eaton [founder of Forest Lawn Memorial-Park] stood before Leonardo da Vinci's masterpiece, "The Last Supper," in the convent of Santa Maria delle Grazie, in Milan. With him was his friend, Professor Armando Vene, Royal Superintendent of Fine Arts of Italy. On that day in 1924, Dr. Eaton shared with Professor Vene a sense of personal tragedy—for this great picture would soon be lost to the world.

Although now a total wreck, this monumental masterpiece was still perhaps the most impressive picture in the world, and conveyed an idea of Leonardo's powers of invention. The design and the preparations for the execution had been carefully calculated by the master, and the picture itself was completed within three years.

Fifty years after it was finished, the picture began to deteriorate; the seeds for its rapid decay were sown by Leonardo himself, who, in order to be able to work with deliberation, was tempted to paint "a tempera" upon the dry wall, instead of "fresco" (a method of painting on freshly spread plaster before it dries). Thus, the pigments were not absorbed, and by the middle of the sixteenth century they were already crumbling away. In 1652, the great painting was deliberately mutilated when the legs of the figures were cut away to make a door. Twice in that century the work was repainted. The vandalism of Napoleon's troops (1796), who used the refectory as a stable, hastened the ruin of this stupendous masterpiece of the Renaissance. But even in its decay it testified to the superhuman depth and creative power of the master.

Yes, the painting was doomed—and although it was no longer the same painting which Leonardo had given to the world, its loss would be a tragedy. Then inspiration came. A few days before, Dr. Eaton had seen the magnificent stained-glass rose window in the ancient cathedral at Assisi.

The rose window itself had only recently been repaired by a young girl at Perugia—the last of a family which had made stained glass for many centuries. And so—when Dr. Eaton gazed upon the great painting, "The Last Supper"—he remembered the stained-glass window at Assisi.

On the next day, Dr. Eaton drove through the hills under the blue Italian sky to visit the studio in Perugia, and with the aid of an interpreter learned that Rosa Caselli-Moretti would be happy to be given the task of reproducing Leonardo's painting in stained glass. And it was her artist's mind which conceived the daring plan of re-creating the painting directly from Leonardo's original sketches. Because of the many changes made by artists who attempted to restore it, the painting at Milan was no longer Leonardo's. But fortunately in the museum were Leonardo's priceless original sketches, which Rosa Caselli-

Moretti knew she could borrow. Using these sketches, she planned to reproduce the original painting.

"And how long will it take?" Dr. Eaton asked. "Five years, possibly six," was the answer.

Dr. Eaton came home. The years passed. With infinite care, Memorial Court of Honor was designed and built. Five years stretched into six—and then word came from Europe that the figure of Judas had broken five times in the firing. It seemed as if it was not meant that the figure of the traitor who had portrayed our Lord should ever be completed.

Weeks of suspense followed. Then at last reassuring news came from across the ocean. "The Last Supper" Window was finished; and on April 28, 1931, it was enshrined in its appointed place in Memorial Court of Honor.

The genius of Leonardo is nowhere else so evident as in this masterpiece, for the picture does not lose its beauty as you draw closer to it. The detail grows ever clearer as one stands directly beneath it. The scales on the fish are as distinct as the hills of Judea in the background.

The face of Jesus is not quite completed. Leonardo tried vainly for years to depict the divinity of that face. At last he gave up in despair, saying, "I do not finish the face of Christ; no one can finish it."

The lighting behind "The Last Supper" Window is natural—it is God's own daylight. The figures, which are twice life-size, are never quite the same. In the morning they are brilliant; in the afternoon they become softer—and as twilight falls, the colors slowly fade. Finally, there is nothing but darkness until the morning sun, like an invisible artist, paints the picture once more for the new day.

But meanwhile, as the evening light fades, there comes an unforgettable moment. The face of Jesus, the gentle Saviour, remains when everything else has disappeared. It is as if the disciples slip quietly from the room, leaving Him in tranquil meditation.

This well-loved scene is precious to us not merely because its original was painted by a great master, but because it illumines a poignant and dramatic hour of the last night on earth of our Lord, Jesus Christ.

"Now it came to pass, when Jesus had finished all these sayings, He said unto His disciples, 'Ye know that after two days is the feast of the passover,' and He sent Peter and John, saying, 'Go and prepare us the passover, that we may eat.' And they went and made ready. And when the hour was come, Jesus sat down, and the twelve apostles with Him.

"And as they sat and did eat, Jesus said, 'Verily I say unto you, one of you shall betray me.' And they began to be sorrowful, and to say unto Him, one by one, 'Is it I?' And he answered, 'It is one of the twelve.' "

At the end of the table, on the far left, Bartholomew, also called Nathaniel, rises and asks fearfully, "Is it I, Lord?"

And James—sometimes called the Lesser—next to Bartholomew, reaches out to restrain the impetuous fisherman, Peter, who had drawn his knife in sudden rage, seeking to find guilt in the eyes of a traitor.

Andrew, brother of Peter, sits on his left, stunned by the accusation—and he too wonders sorrowfully, "Is it I?"

Judas, frozen with guilty terror, clutches his bag of coins, heedless of the salt knocked over by his hand, spilling across the table. The salt—spilled by a traitor—to be a symbol forever after of warning, an omen of bad luck, to be handed down in legend from generation to generation even until this day!

While John the Beloved Disciple droops in anguish at the thought of his Master betrayed, Jesus said, "Woe unto that man by whom the Son of Man is betrayed! It had been good for that man if he had not been born."

Judas then said, "Master, is it I?" Jesus said unto him, "Thou hast said."

And His disciples heard, but did not understand. For "no man at the table knew for what intent Jesus spake thus unto Judas." How could they know that the bag held so tightly in the greedy hand of Judas Iscariot contained thirty pieces of silver—the price of a life—the earthly life of Jesus?

None of them understood—none of them believed there could be one among them who would betray Jesus unto His enemies. Judas trembled.

"And Jesus took bread, and gave thanks, and brake it and gave unto them, saying, 'This is my body which is given for you, do this in remembrance of me.' And he took the cup and gave thanks, and gave it to them, saying, 'Drink ye all of it. For this is my blood of the new testament which is shed for many for the remission of sins.'

"And Jesus said unto Judas, 'That thou doest, do quickly.' And Judas went immediately out; and it was night.

"When he was gone out, Jesus said, 'Let not your heart be troubled, ye believe in God, believe also in me. In my Father's house are many mansions; I go to prepare a place for you.' And Jesus saith, 'I am the way, the truth and the life: no man cometh unto the Father, but by me.'

"And Jesus said, 'Arise, let us go hence.' And Jesus went forth with his disciples unto the Mount of Olives."

Jesus went forth—to be betrayed and crucified.

We call this "The Last Supper," and yet, was it not really the first? For when Jesus said, as He offered bread and wine to His disciples, "Do this in remembrance of me," He gave the world a communion service which through all the ages since has remained our grateful remembrance of Jesus Christ, and the divine symbol of our belief and hope of immortality.

As one studies "The Last Supper" (frontispiece) from left to right one finds:

Bartholomew (Nathaniel), sincere and honest, springs to his feet in amazement.

James the Lesser, youthful and slightly bearded.

Andrew the fisherman, calms his brother, Peter.

Judas, isolated in the foreground, has just spilled the salt.

Peter, old and rugged, with drawn knife, seems to ask, "Which one, Master?"

John, the beloved, always at the Lord's right hand, bows his head in anguish at the thought of betrayal.

Thomas, rugged and forever the doubting Thomas.

James the Greater, brother of John, is horrified at the accusation.

The youthful Philip rises fearfully.

Matthew turns to the others in utter disbelief.

Thaddeus (Jude), who wrote the shortest book in the Bible, frowns angrily.

Simon, the eldest of the group, shows his surprise.*

✠

JUDAS ISCARIOT
Andrea del Sarto

ANDREA DEL SARTO (1487-1531) was born at Florence, where the famous Mariotto Albertinelli had his shop. Like many other gifted children of his day, he was apprenticed at an early age to a goldsmith, an occupation he disliked. In 1498 he began to study art seriously, under Piero di Cosimo. Rosini says, "He was not allowed to make a line which was not perfect." Piero retained him for several years, allowing him to spend much time studying the famous cartoons of da Vinci and Michelangelo.

Del Sarto's art masterpieces show the influence of both Albertinelli and Fra Bartolommeo more than that of his teacher Piero. His field was clearly that of the devotional type, but was marked more by his sense of beauty than by the deep religious feelings which so clearly inspired other great artists of the Renaissance.

In 1527 he completed his fresco of the Last Supper at St. Salvi, the last work of importance which he was to execute. He died on January 22, 1531, at the age of forty-three, apparently from the plague that was then sweeping through Florence. Some of his biographers seem to feel that his unpretentious funeral was a great slight to his merits as a painter, but the lack of ceremony may have been due to the natural precaution against spreading contagion.

The picture of Judas Iscariot found on p. 43 is enlarged from the head of Judas in del Sarto's "The Last Supper." In this portrayal, Judas is not placed away alone. He is next to the Master, the contrast in the expressions on the two faces thus emphasized by their proximity. Judas is painted with auburn hair, high color, and sharpened features, as an ardent Jewish patriot interested in rebellion against Roman domination and in the re-establishment of the new Kingdom of God which his Master talked about. To his mind, however, the kingdom was merely temporal.

* Abridged from a booklet, "*The Last Supper*" *Window*. Copyright 1955 by Forest Lawn Memorial-Park Association, Inc. Used by permission.

Andrea del Sarto has caught the character of Judas by picturing him as a person, who, for this moment at least, is stabbed by the realization that he is to be the one to betray his Lord. Jesus has just said, "One of you shall betray me." The others draw away in consternation and surprise that such a thing could be, but their expressions do not indicate guilt. Judas, in contrast, has guilt written on every line of his face and in every gesture. He puts his hand to his heart, as though he could not bear to expose it, and his eyes look away, not daring to gaze directly at the Master or any of his friends. His is an isolation of the soul rather than of the body, and this is the most cruel isolation of all.

Contrary to the theory that Judas might have been weak as a person, Andrea del Sarto pictures him as a man of character. But his potentialities for good have been misplaced and misdirected. This not unsympathetic portrayal causes one to speculate, "What if Judas had acted otherwise and had followed his moment of self-realization to a constructive end?" It did not happen, of course, but this artist's portrait makes us think more about this strange and terrible Judas.

✛

"THE LORD TURNED AND LOOKED AT PETER"
Herbert Beecroft

HERBERT BEECROFT has given us an unusual blond Christ, looking out at us as He looked upon Peter in the courtyard of the high priest's house on the night of His betrayal and arrest.

The artist was born in Reading, England, in 1865, and for fourteen years worked in London as a lithographic artist. With the coming of a new process in printing he became a lecturer, sketching before his audiences as he talked.

In 1905 he accepted an offer to tour Australia, and not long after his arrival there gave up entertaining and started painting portraits. Most of his more important works were on religious subjects and were painted during the last thirteen years of his life, while he was living in Australia. He died shortly after the beginning of World War II. His pictures are well known in England, but it is in Australia that the majority of his best works will be found, as will the original of this painting, "The Lord Turned and Looked at Peter" (p. 45).*

All the Gospels tell the story of Peter's denial of his Lord, but it is in the twenty-second chapter of Luke that we find the fullest account. Peter followed Jesus "afar off" when he was taken to the high priest. And when the servants kindled a fire in the outer court, he sat down among the enemies of Jesus to warm himself. A servant who noticed him said, "This man was

* Color prints may be obtained from Frost & Reed, Ltd., 10 Clare St., Bristol 1, England, or Rudolf Lesch Fine Arts, Inc., 225 Fifth Ave., New York, 16, N. Y.

JUDAS ISCARIOT—*DEL SARTO*

also with Him," but Peter denied it, saying, "I knew Him not." Later another accused Peter of being one of Christ's disciples, and again Peter denied it, saying, "Man, I am not." An hour later, when one of the group said, "Of a truth this fellow was with Him: for he is a Galilean," Peter again denied it with an oath, saying, "I never knew the man." Immediately the cock crew. Jesus, passing by, heard the words and turned and looked at Peter. Then Peter remembered the words of the Lord: "Before the cock crow, thou shalt deny me thrice," and he went out and wept bitterly.

In this painting the artist has caught the exact moment of Christ's look at Peter in the midst of his third denial. There is in His eyes both sorrow and understanding. In spite of Peter's weakness, his impetuous assertions and denials, he would yet become the rock upon which Jesus would build His church. Peter's later boldness on the day of Pentecost, when three thousand were added to the Church, and his heroic life of service for his Master have proved that Christ's confidence in the basic goodness of men, despite their many weaknesses, is never in vain.

There is a legend that when the Christians were being persecuted to death in Rome, Peter was there. And when he saw men being burned to death or thrown to the lions for their faith, it was too much for him, and he ran away to deny his Lord for a fourth time. Just outside the walls of that ancient city, Peter met a man carrying a cross. At first he did not recognize Him, and said to Him, "Quo vadis?" which translated means, "Where are you going?"

The man replied sadly, "I am going to Rome to be crucified again." Then Peter recognized his Master, and once more that finer impulse of Christian devotion laid hold of him. He turned and went back into Rome to bear testimony to the living Christ even though it cost him his life. He finally overcame his greatest weakness—impulsive self-preservation—and when he had beat out the music of his life to the end, it was a *Te Deum* of praise and thanksgiving.

✛

THE ASCENSION
Fritz von Uhde

There are very few satisfactory "Ascensions." This is perhaps due to the artist's endeavor to make a spectacular picture, to show a superradiant Christ rising amid clouds and angels to reassume the glory that was His before the world was. Such attempts place the emphasis wrongly. A true Ascension should picture not so much what the event meant to Christ—for we have no means of determining that—but what it meant to His disciples. And assuredly the glimpse of heavenly glories into which their Master and friend was received could assuage for only a moment the sense of loneliness and personal grief which must have been theirs. The Ascension was in reality less a revelation of bliss than a realization of infinite loss.

Von Uhde has conceived of the incident in this human fashion. The cloud

"THE LORD TURNED AND LOOKED AT PETER"—*BEECROFT*

that is to receive Christ out of their sight has no miraculous brilliancy; it is just vapor, blowing up from below in patches that fitfully conceal the treetops. We feel the upward and outward drift of the cloud that like a Fate is bearing Christ forward to some untried form of life of which He knows only that the Father is there. And we cannot surely say whether Christ is treading the air or merely ascending Olivet a few steps in advance of His friends. On one thing we are certain: Christ is leaving them. He is passing on to a larger work in which His spiritual rather than His bodily presence shall be the operating force.

They are staying behind to cherish a great memory and to work out the problems involved in the Great Commission. They show by look and gesture that life is henceforth to be desolate. Not yet has Pentecost come with its revelation of hope, with its Comforter who shall bring to their remembrance the true meaning of their Master's life.

This parting is for them a second tragedy, the outcome of which they cannot see. Their anxious question, "Wilt thou at this time restore the kingdom of Israel?" shows us how difficult it was for them to shake themselves free from the idea of an earthly Messianic kingdom: not only will He not restore it, but He will withdraw from their sight altogether, for in no other way can He teach them that the Kingdom of God is within the soul. So Von Uhde has pictured here on their faces not so much wonder and ecstasy—though perhaps the young woman on the right and the one near Jesus express that—but longing, yearning, entreaty, and almost despair. And Christ turns His face toward them in affectionate farewell and encouragement; He stretches one hand forth to them in blessing, while with the other He reaches up to clasp the Father's hand.

The Ascension is a parable of the infinite progression of man toward the divine, an illustration of Browning's truth that "man's reach should exceed his grasp"; and of Tennyson's noble figure that the Gleam of Merlin may not be overtaken short of eternity. Yet to that infinite quest Christ calls us by the very fact of His Ascension, though the pursuit take us from earth to the heavens and from the shore to the fathomless reaches of the great deep, as we, too, "follow the gleam."*

✝

CREDO

Not what, but *Whom,* I do believe,
    That, in my darkest hour of need,
    Hath comfort that no mortal creed
    To mortal man may give;—

Not what, but *Whom!*
    For Christ is more than all the creeds,
    And His full life of gentle deeds
    Shall all the creeds outlive.

* Abridged from *The Gospel in Art* by Albert Edward Bailey, published by Pilgrim Press. Used by permission of the publisher.

THE ASCENSION—*VON UHDE*

Not what do I believe, but *Whom!*
  Who walks beside me in the gloom?
  Who shares the burden wearisome?
  Who all the dim way doth illume,
  And bids me look beyond the tomb
  The larger life to live?—

Not what do I believe,
  But *Whom!*
  Not what,
  But *Whom!**

—*John Oxenham*

APOSTLE PETER

A fisherman on the seat of Galilee,
A "Simon" changed by Jesus to a "rock."
Of John the Baptist first a devotee,
And then he joined with Jesus' holy flock.
With love and force protected he his Lord,
Stayed by upon the "mount" and "garden," true.
"Thou art the Christ, to leave I can't afford,
Lord, wash my feet and hands and body, too."
Then Peter showed his love, fed Jesus' sheep,
And with the gospel net he fished for men.
After denial he went out to weep,
But never broke his Master's heart again.
Within the gospel story Peter's part
Is written in the book ascribed to Mark.**

—*Henry C. Spear*

JERUSALEM

The way of palms He passed in simple state
  And they that hailed Him knew a breathless awe,
  The lame leapt at His side, the blind eyes saw
That Heaven descended to the desolate;
But where the temple rises chief priests wait—
  And He in whom the Roman found no flaw,
  Whose Love was greater than the ancient Law,
Rides to His death beyond the city gate.

Jerusalem, what can efface the stain!
  Not full six days since He has entered in,
  And now the nails of Calvary pierce Him through;

* From *Bees in Amber* by John Oxenham, preface. Used by permission of Miss Erica Oxenham and Methuen Co., Ltd.
** Written especially for this anthology.

Yet wronged, forsaken, bearing mortal pain,
Immortally He pardons your dark sin;
Forgive them for they know not what they do.*
—*Thomas S. Jones, Jr.*

APOSTLE JOHN

A fisherman whom Jesus called to serve,
A cousin of the Master whom he served,
A favored place that he so much deserved,
Revealed relationship to God above.
He explained each Jerusalem event,
A witness of what Jesus said and did,
He helped to cultivate what Spirit meant,
Apostle of the love he lived amid.
The last disciple at the cruel cross,
He took Christ's mother Mary to his home.
The first one at the tomb to count his loss,
He found that Jesus left no one alone.
A seer and prophet of the gospel road,
His words of God give all a living code.**
—*Henry C. Spear*

AND IT WAS NIGHT

So, after receiving the morsel, he immediately went out; and it was night.—
JOHN 13:30, RSV.

Judas went out and closed the door—
        And it was night.
In his mouth was the taste of the hallowed bread,
Through his mind rang words which his Lord had said;
But for pieces of silver, he turned away,
His Friend and Saviour to betray.
Not for him the farewell words of love,
Telling of mansions prepared above—
He turned aside from the message sweet,
From the gentle hands that had bathed his feet,
And rushed with greed to the silent street—
        And it was night.

        He walked by his Teacher's side no more.
            Ah, what delight
        He might have known had he returned!
        At last, at last he might have learned

* From *Sonnets of the Cross* by Thomas S. Jones, Jr., No. XXIII. Published by the Society of SS. Peter and Paul, London. Used by permission of the publisher.
** Written especially for this anthology.

A branch of the holy vine to be;
He might have watched at Gethsemane;
For his Master's life, when the rest had fled;
He might have seen his Saviour rise,
Heard holy winds rush from the skies—
But he turned his back on paradise—
　　　How dark the night!*
　　　　　　　　　　　—*Margaret Chaplin Anderson*

APOSTLE MATTHEW

Collecting Roman taxes was his job;
As publican with sinners he was classed;
He was aware of hatred from the mob,
From Jewish patriots he was outcast.
But Jesus said to Matthew: "Follow Me!"
And Levi rose and went the Jesus way.
He lived to learn the truth that set him free,
And found that joy of service was rich pay.
He wrote a life of Jesus for the Jews,
To prove He was Messiah unto them;
To all the ages it has been good news,
And unto Matthew was a diadem.
He chose to follow Jesus and obey,
And found a joy that came with every day.**
　　　　　　　　　　　—*Henry C. Spear*

IN THE GARDEN

At dusk of dawn the fragant garden slept
　　Full of a mystery the night had known,
　　When Mary entered, trembling and alone,
And as she trod the grassy way she wept;
But from the place of deepest shadow crept
　　A light most radiant—there was no stone!
　　And the cold rock in which He rested shone
Where two archangels holy vigil kept.

Wondering, she saw the flame-white seraphim
　　At the dark entrance bidding her rejoice,
　　Yet on the flowers her tears fell one by one;
Then turning comfortless in search of Him
She heard the quiet music of a Voice,
　　And Christ stood there against the rising sun.***
　　　　　　　　　　　—*Thomas S. Jones, Jr.*

* From *The Christian Herald* (April 1958). Used by permission of the author and the publisher.
** Written especially for this anthology.
*** From *Sonnets of the Cross* by Thomas S. Jones, Jr., No. XXIV. Published by the Society of SS.
Peter and Paul, London. Used by permission of the publisher.

NAMELESS, NOT UNKNOWN

(The thief on the cross)

A twisted soul
Upon a gallows-tree,
Who saw in the forgiving eyes of One
Aglow with fortitude
The vision of enduring good
And life that flashes on
Unquenchably,
And heard, above the anguish of a man,
His voice:
"Today . . . with me"—
How meaningless are names
Upon a stone
Or in a mouldering necrology!
This lad is nameless, but not unknown.*

—*Earl Marlatt*

MARY MAGDALENE

First among the women who helped their Christ
Mary of Magdala with thankful heart;
Demons from her mind her Lord had enticed,
She tried to repay by doing her part.
She followed Jesus to the cross—His goal,
And guided Jesus' mother to John's home.
She seemed to discern 'twixt the flesh and soul,
Anointed Jesus' body for the tomb.
She saw two angels on guard at the cave,
And saw her Master rise up from the soil.
Christ asked her not to touch Him in the grave,
For He had not ascended to His God.
There is no more than self that one can give,
Mary Magdalene will always live.**

—*Henry C. Spear*

THE STAR—THE CROSS—THE EMPTY TOMB

A still, deep night—Judean hills—
The Angels' song from afar;
God's love immortal sent to earth
Watched o'er by one white Star.

* From *Cathedral: A Volume of Poems* by Earl Marlatt, pp. 119-20. Copyright 1956 by Earl Marlatt.
Published by Parthenon Press. Used by permission of the author and the publisher.
** Written especially for this anthology.

"My Father's business"—hear Him say—
One purpose—gain, or loss—
From Nazareth to Calvary,
And thus to the bitter Cross!

A dawn, gold-veiled—a Garden fair,
Where fragrant roses bloom'd,
The ones who came their grief to share
Rejoiced! The empty tomb!

Redeemer, Christ, our Lord and King,
In love, we Thee Adore!
The Star, the Cross, the empty tomb,
Our hope forevermore!*

—*Clarice White Luck*

THE ROAD TO EMMAUS

As they were hastening from Jerusalem
    There came a Man whose footfall gave no sound
    Nor left a trace upon the dusty ground,
And He made plain all mysteries to them:
The prophet line that led to Bethlehem
    Aflame with vision, and the Love unbound
    In that still dawn when life immortal crowned
The lonely death upon the dark Tree-stem.

The little room was reached at eventide,
    And as He sat and blessed the food there seemed
    A light upon them, though the day was dead;
They saw then Who had journeyed by their side
    Only to lose Him—and each thought he dreamed:
    But on the table lay the broken bread.**

—*Thomas S. Jones, Jr.*

✠

"THIS IS MY BELOVED SON"

Elizabeth Stuart Phelps

IT was a mild day in the late autumn of the year. The Jordan, a picturesque, and for its entire course a lonely river—scarcely sixty miles from Gennesaret to the Dead Sea in a straight line, but two hundred by its windings—had been for months the scene of unusual activity. Everybody was talking of a recluse who had suddenly left his retirement, and was teaching upon the banks of the stream.

* Written especially for this anthology.
** From *Sonnets of the Cross* by Thomas S. Jones, Jr., No. XXV. Published by the Society of SS. Peter and Paul, London. Used by permission of the publisher.

The forerunners of revolutions are among the most interesting men in history, but they are among the least understood. He who was called John the Baptist was a person of extraordinary beauty of spirit. Few men who have been important to human affairs have sunk themselves so utterly in the depths of the cause to which they have offered dedication.

He did not so much as stop to think what men would think of him, or whether they would think of him at all. He was the servant of a great idea, and he did not offer it the discourtesy of any visible interest in himself.

This religious enthusiast wore a single garment of the roughest weave of camel's-hair cloth; and his headdress was the simplest possible arrangement of stuff, sufficient to protect from the sun. He was tall and grave. He discoursed of serious things. The dark-skinned faces lifted to his grew sober. Fear sat upon many; hope on others; attention on all.

The Messianic expectation was in the air of Palestine. The Temple and the market-place buzzed with it, the caravans whispered of it, Roman rulers feared it, and Jewish scribes consulted it; the waves of the Galilean Sea repeated it, and the Jordan reflected it.

The horizon of Nazareth was past its warmth and color, for winter was at hand. The traveler thought of this as he turned his face towards a ford in the Jordan, which lay perhaps twenty miles away. Jesus had grown to manhood in a world of flowers, but when he went out to the *first act* of his public life, he walked in the dying of the year. Did he think of this, as he made his solitary way toward Jordan? For he went alone, moved by the voices which speak only to separateness.

Behind him lay the assured past—his youth, sheltered, peaceful; all the calm and cheerful years that precede responsibility; monotonous labor, respected and respectable, but safe; his gentle home; his mother a widow now, for Joseph of the strong arm and great fatherly heart was dead; his mother, needing him.

Whither did his steps tend as he trod the banks of the Jordan? Whither did his purpose move? Beyond the investigation of a local religious revival, of which Nazareth talked like the rest of the world, what did that journey mean?

Had he been asked, he would have made no answer it may be said that he did not distinctly know himself. Be it what it would—for joy or for anguish, for success or for failure—let the answer come!

Through the thick growth of the river banks he came out suddenly upon the glancing stream. He of Nazareth, being unobserved, gathered himself against the shadow of the reeds, and, standing silently, looked and listened.

John the Baptizer had no velvet tongue. The banks of the river rang with tremendous exhortations. "Repent! repent! Look to your sins! The time is short. The kingdom is at hand. The Kingdom of Heaven cometh!

"Your deliverer is within reach! He whom ye have trusted in and waited for is close at hand. Behold, He cometh! Prepare the way for Him!"

The people, hearing these stirring words, and wrought upon with the eloquence of the young speaker, took upon themselves a natural conclusion. His listeners pressed upon him. "Thou," they cried, "art He! Thou art He whom we have sought so long!"

"Nay—nay, I am not He. I am not worthy to unloose the fastening of His sandal. He cometh after, but He is preferred before. He is before me and above me. I baptize you with this water.

"There cometh One," he murmured, "He shall bathe you with fire, and with the Spirit which is Holy. Repent! for He is mightier than I!" As he spoke these words he perceived suddenly that he was observed by a stranger apart on the banks of the stream. The color fled quickly from the dark face of the young prophet. He ceased abruptly, and strode towards the figure.

Neither could have put into language what that moment meant to each. The face of John grew rapt, that of the Nazarene troubled. On John fell the double responsibility of recognition and of interpretation; he must identify Christ to himself, as well as to the people. One gesture did it—one swift Oriental gesture of reverence, of worship. John's eyes suffused, head bowed, hands outstretched; he cried: "Thou art He!"

The waters of the ford, deepening where they now stood, ran calmer and darker. The slender leaves of a willow on the banks dropped into the stream and floated down. Doves shimmered overhead. The sky was warm and deep. The Nazarene stepped down into the water.

Startled, incredulous, shocked, John perceived that Jesus was seeking the submission of baptism. The young prophet's whole nature rose in noble revolt against the situation in which he so unexpectedly found himself. "Nay, nay! Comest Thou to me? Rather I to Thee!"

But Jesus, smiling, had His will: "Suffer it to be so now; for thus it becometh us to fulfill all righteousness." Saying this He waded into the water and received from the awed and trembling hands of His kinsman the rite of dedication to a religious life. When He came up out of the shining river, a cream-white dove that had been flying to and fro across the Jordan rose high in the heavens, circled into sight again, and with a few encircling movements settled gently upon the head of Jesus of Nazareth.

A little murmur ran through the crowd at the beautiful sight; the people, who must always talk of whatever happens, turned to say something each to his neighbor. But Jesus and John, who did not speak, listened with abated breath. "Didst thou hear aught?"

"Didst *thou?*"

It was said that the stranger, standing in the Jordan with the light of a fresh religious vow upon His lifted face, with prayer in His eyes and the dove circling to His brow, had been identified by Heaven in mystical language: "This is my beloved Son, in whom I am well pleased!"

The newly-baptized man was quickly made aware that He had become the center of observation. Certain of the bolder in the throng pressed curiously forward toward the stranger. But the Nazarene, stunned with the awful credentials which John had given over to Him, and thrilling with the mystical experience of the past hour, turned abruptly away. With bowed head He passed through the shivering river reeds in the direction of the desert.*

✛

PETER, THE MAN OF IMPULSE
Charles R. Brown

"THERE is one glory of the sun and another glory of the moon and another glory of the stars, and one star differeth from another in glory." All glorious, yet all different.

So also is the Kingdom of God! Men differ in temperament, in training, in fitness for the various tasks which are laid upon them. Divine grace is not a steamroller which irons all the wrinkles and individuality out of people. It brings out in a finer way the personal traits in every life.

Here was a man whose name stands first in every list of the apostles! "Now the names of the twelve apostles are these, Peter, James and John, Andrew, Philip, Thomas" and all the rest. His name stood always at the head of the column. He was no modest, shrinking petunia, blossoming in the backyard or wasting his fragrance on the desert air. He was out on the front porch talking, acting, taking the lead. He was heard as well as seen.

He was a man of impulse, a rushing, impetuous type of man, like a mountain stream hurrying over the rocks on its way to the valley below. He was quick on the trigger. His reactions came in spurts. The moment he felt an impulse, he was on his feet suiting his action to that mood. He moved fast, and thought it over later.

Let us notice the strength of such a nature, and then its weakness, and then what the Lord can make of that sort of man! First the strength of it! The man who can make up his mind and act promptly in business, in politics, in the presence of danger, while other men are still thinking it over and talking about it, has a certain advantage. He always strikes while the iron is hot.

Jesus saw this man with a net in his hands, fishing. He said to him, "Follow me and I will make you a fisher of men." Peter had been taking fish for the market; now he was summoned to "take men" for the service of God.

The man of impulse decided then and there that he would do it. He forsook his net, leaving it there in the water, and followed Christ.

Peter was fishing on another occasion, without success. He had fished all night and had caught nothing. Just at daybreak Jesus stood on the shore calling out to the seven men in the boat: "Have you caught anything? Have you any meat?" The others began to talk about how good it was that the Lord had come to them just at the time when they were all discouraged. Peter did

* Abridged from *The Story of Jesus Christ* by Elizabeth Stuart Phelps, pp. 63-76. Published by Houghton Mifflin Company. Used by permission of the author and the publisher.

not wait to make any remarks. He girt his fisher's coat about him and jumped overboard and swam ashore to be the first to greet his Lord.

When Jesus was at Caesarea Philippi, he wondered how men were regarding His ministry. "Whom do men say that I am?"

The disciples answered that there was a wide difference of opinion. Some said that he was John the Baptist risen from the dead; some said Elijah come to life again; others said Jeremiah, or one of the prophets.

"But *ye*, whom say *ye* that I am?"

Peter burst out, "Thou art the Christ, the Son of the living God." He knew what he believed and why he believed it—flesh and blood had not revealed it to him, but an inward experience of divine help. He was ready then and there to stake his all upon the claim that Jesus was the Saviour of the world. His mind was quite made up and he stood ready to act.

There came a day when the Master was speaking about forgiveness. "If thy brother trespass against thee, go and tell him his fault between thee and him alone. If he hear thee, thou hast gained thy brother. Forgive as you would be forgiven! If ye forgive men their trespasses, your heavenly Father will also forgive you your trespasses. The sins you loose on earth will be loosed in heaven."

Then Peter burst out: "Lord, how oft shall my brother sin against me and I forgive him? Until seven times?"

Jesus, however, suggested a still higher standard of forgiveness. "Until seventy times seven!" Peter accepted it, apparently—and I doubt not but that this warm-hearted, impulsive man would have forgiven anyone who had wronged him seventy times seven if the man had asked it. He had that quality of mercy which is twice blessed—it blesseth him that gives and him that takes. He did pray for mercy, and that same prayer taught him the need of showing mercy.

Many of our modern problems are so vast, so intricate, so baffling, that we could sit down and talk about them until the Day of Doom without getting anywhere. The time comes for men to get on their feet and do something about it. "Wisdom," someone said, "is knowing what to do next, skill is knowing how to do it, and virtue is doing it."

Not everyone that talketh endlessly about it, but he that doeth the will of the Father shall enter the Kingdom of Heaven. Thank God for the Peters of the world, who do not stand forever shivering on the brink—they plunge in.

In the second place, notice the weakness of the man. When Jesus celebrated the Last Supper with His disciples, He took a towel and a basin of water and washed their feet. They had been disputing on their way to the supper as to which one should be the greatest in the Kingdom of Heaven. Jesus could not say to a group of men filled to the eyes with pride and selfish ambition: "This is my body which is broken for you. Feed upon me in your hearts by faith and be thankful. Love one another as I have loved you." The words would have stuck in His throat. He must first wash the dust from their feet and wash the conceit out of their minds.

When He came to Peter, the man drew back. "Never," he said. "Thou shalt never wash my feet." Then at a word from Christ, he melted down into a desire for a still closer intimacy. "Lord, not my feet only, but my hands and my head!"

That same night, there was a tragic scene in the life of this impulsive man. When Jesus saw arrest and crucifixion awaiting Him there in the dark, He told His disciples that, in all probability, they would forsake Him. Peter felt very sure of himself. "Though all men should forsake thee, I never will."

But what a sorry showing this man made before the cock crew! He was standing at the fire warning himself after Jesus had been arrested. People were discussing the matter and a servant-girl said, pointing to Peter: "Here is one of them! He is a follower of the Galilean." Peter replied, "I never knew Him."

His accent, however, was Galilean and a man remarked, "His speech betrayeth him—he is one of them." Again Peter denied, "I tell you, I never knew Him."

Then a number of people said all at once, "We have seen this man following Him." Then there came an ugly oath and the third denial of his Lord. Jesus heard the oath "and he turned and looked at Peter." Not a word of reproach, but a look of infinite disappointment! That look was all there was, but it was enough and to spare. This impulsive man broke down and cried like a child—"he went out and wept bitterly."

What a strange combination of courage and cowardice, of rugged strength and instability! It goes with the impulsive temperament. Such men are always striking twelve either in some high noon of glorified action or some midnight of dismal failure. It is never nine o'clock in the morning or three o'clock in the afternoon with them—they are at one extreme or the other. "There is a tide in the affairs of men which taken at the flood leads on to fortune." Take them at high tide, and you may count on something splendid. Omitted, all the voyage of those lives may be bound in shallows and in miseries. The ebb tide brings defeat.

Here is another instance of Peter's fickleness! When he went forth to preach the gospel, he had a vision. He saw a lot of four-footed beasts and fowls and creeping things. He heard a voice saying, "Rise, Peter, kill and eat."

He answered, "No! I never have eaten anything common or unclean."

Then the voice came again, "What God hath cleansed, call not thou common." And when Peter came to think upon his vision, he realized that this wiping out of artificial distinctions between the various animals, whose flesh is good for food, would apply also to men. Jews or Gentiles, Barbarians or Scythians, bond or free, he was not to call any man common or unclean on the ground of race difference. This was a big, long step ahead to be taken by a man who had been brought up in a narrow creed.

Peter took that step. When Cornelius, a Roman centurion, asked him to come to his house, Peter went. He stood there in the home of that Roman official saying: "Ye know that it is an unlawful thing for a man that is a Jew to come unto one of another nation. But God hath shown me that I should not call any man common or unclean. God is no respecter of persons, for in every nation he that feareth Him and worketh righteousness is accepted of Him. Therefore I came as soon as I was sent for."

This was good, broad Christian doctrine, and Peter was ready to act upon it. When the Holy Spirit came upon those who heard his words, he baptized them as Christians. At Antioch also, Peter ate with Gentile Christians and gave them the right hand of fellowship.

In the third place, what use did the Lord make of such a man? He did not refuse to enroll him as an apostle because he was fickle. He set before him an open door into those very qualities which he lacked. He gave him a new name to live up to. His name had been Simon; Jesus said to him, "Thou shalt be called Peter"—*petros,* a rock. When Jesus gave Simon that new name, it was a steady challenge to this fickle soul to do its best. It put stamina and backbone into him. The moral gristle of his uncertain nature was moving up permanently into the vertebrate class. "Thou art Peter," *petros,* a rock, "and on this rock I will build my church."

There is an angel standing in every block of marble, rough hewn though it comes from the quarry. Send for the sculptor that he may bring it out. There is a rock of strength in any fickle, impulsive nature—send for the Saviour that He may bring it out. God deals with them all, not in terms of what they are, but in terms of that which He sees it is possible for them to become.

Read on! Read on—we have not come to the end of the chapter yet! "Now when the day of Pentecost [the church's birthday] was fully come, Peter standing with the eleven said, 'Ye men of Judea, Jesus of Nazareth was approved of God by signs which He did. You took Him with wicked hands and slew Him. God has raised Him up and exalted Him to His own right hand as a Saviour. Now therefore repent and be baptized, every one of you, into the name of this Jesus for the remission of your sins. It is your only hope.'"

"And when the people saw the boldness of Peter and John, they took knowledge of them that they had been with Jesus." Somehow the two men had caught the spirit of that matchless life. There was a certain quality in them which was Christlike. And when the Jewish officials urged them not to speak any further in the name of Christ, Peter flatly refused to be bound by their command. "We ought to obey God rather than men." He was carrying on—he was showing himself indeed "Peter, a rock."

When Jesus called Peter "a rock," it helped the man to move ahead at a rapid pace toward that moral stability which the new name denoted. There is nothing strange about the fact that with all the faults and blunders which can be charged up against Peter, he is perhaps the best loved of all the Twelve.

We are glad that his name stands first on every list. We are glad that his name was given to the greatest church building in Christendom, St. Peter's at Rome. We are glad that on the inside of the massive dome of that church these words are inscribed in stately Latin, "Thou art Peter and on this rock I will build my church and the gates of Hell shall not prevail against it." *

✤

ONE OF THE TWELVE FELL AWAY

(A Poetic Story)

Chandran Devanesen

He was pale and handsome
with a shock of red hair
that glowed on his head
like a danger signal.
His fingers were long and tapering
but they twitched nervously.
He kept wiping his hands on his robe
as if there was a stain on them
that refused to come off.

Now what was there one noticed about his face?
It wasn't effeminate; it wasn't cruel;
no, it wasn't even sensual.
        Then what was it?
It was a weak face.
Yes, that's what it was—
a weakness in the line of his mouth,
in the abutment of his chin.

He looked so young and almost helpless
that you couldn't help pitying him.
He had a hollow, despairing sort of laugh.
He bit his nails, looked furtively at his palms,
and told me he had been a traitor.

        It was funny, he said,
        but the Man he had betrayed
        had often pitied him.

Why did he betray Him?
Oh, for quite ordinary motives,
motives that are likely to suggest themselves
to any ordinary young man.
There was a woman involved.

There usually is—
when one is young and passionate.
That was the trouble with him.

* Abridged from *These Twelve* by Charles R. Brown, pp. 3-22. Copyright 1926 by Charles R. Brown. Published by Harper & Brothers. Used by permission of the publisher.

He was always in a passion
about everything he did.
That's the trouble, he said, with all young men.
They are so passionate about everything.
And passion doesn't last—like love.

He may not have been conscious of it,
but he joined the Master
because he wanted this woman.
So many of us, he said, rather defensively,
so many of us, mix up personal issues
with larger causes.

He was politically conscious, progressive;
he wanted to see his country free.
He hated the foreign oppressors.
And hating is as easy as loving
when you are young.
His Master was to head the rebellion
that would break the foreign yoke forever.

He would be at the Master's side to see that He did.
His Master would be King,
but he would be King-maker.

        That was his youthful dream.
        That was his picture of the future
        framed by the dark tresses
        of the women he loved.
        That was why he was one
        of the twelve.

He was always thinking of her
as he walked along with the twelve.
He would give her costly silks and perfumes.
He would give her chests of sandalwood
filled with precious stones,
and black Nubian slaves to wait upon her
as she stretched her sleek beauty
on a gem-studded couch . . .
All this would he do when the Master was King.

There would be no more of this despicable
stealing from the common purse
to give her cheap little trinkets.
But day followed day, month followed month,
and nothing happened.
In vain did he rave
that it was wrong political strategy,

this knocking about the countryside,
this dallying with hungry mobs
that clustered round them like flies,
when the seat of sovereign power was in Jerusalem.

    And she was growing impatient
    of his spendid dream.
    She wanted him to buy a little field,
    to build a little house,
    to settle down.
    Women do not like wanderers.
    They like their men by the fireside.

And so he ate his heart out
until nothing was left but a black emptiness.
And in that void something moved,
something as black as the pit of hell,
as fascinatingly ugly as a snake.
It was the first thought of treachery.

Treachery, did he say?
But it didn't look like treachery then.
It was a superb bit of logic,
a perfect piece of rationalization.
His master said He was the Son of God.
Then how could earthly power harm Him?
He was not hindering but helping Him,
pushing Him into a dangerous situation
where He would have to assert Himself
and proclaim His kingly power.

    It was such a neat and tidy little scheme.
    His master would get His kingdom,
    and he would get his woman
    her plot of land.

When he saw Him by the light of torches
among the olive trees on Gethsemane
and kissed Him, he did not think
it was the seal of death.

    He thought it was a kiss of acclamation,
    a heralding of kingly triumph.
    He bought the little field for her.
    It cost him all the thirty shekels of silver
    which the High Priest had thrust
    into his trembling hand.

But everything went wrong.
The clever little scheme broke down
pitilessly exposing the selfishness
hidden under the thick folds of rationalization.
Yes, it was plain, ordinary selfishness,
nothing monstrous, nothing villainous;
the ordinary selfishness of a young man
wrapped up in his love affair,
his worldly ambitions,
his pet political theories.
And yet it was the great betrayal of Love
by the selfish passions of youth.

He went to tell her what he'd done.
But she told him what he'd done
with a horror in her eyes
that reflected three crosses on Golgotha.

It was then he really died
though later his body swung from a tree
in the pleasant little field meant for love,
the field of Aceldama, the field of blood.
It was then that I noticed
the halter round his neck.

It was strange, he said
the way he felt it was always there
when he had put it on.
He had woven it with his life,
his rope of destiny.
Before he turned to go
he said with a wan, ghostly smile
that his name was
                Judas Iscariot.*

✢

THE KING OF LOVE MY SHEPHERD IS

OF all the poems ever written, the Twenty-third Psalm is probably the best-loved and known all over the world. Someone has said: "It has been quoted in tent and tabernacle, in lowly cottage and Bedouin tent, in the palaces of kings and in cathedrals and churches the world around."

The Twenty-third Psalm has been translated and paraphrased perhaps more often than any other piece of literature. In highlands and lowlands, in peace and in war, on land and on sea, this hymn, "The King of Love My

* From *The Cross Is Lifted* by Chandran Devanesen, pp. 53-58. Copyright 1954 by The Friendship Press. Used by permission of the author and the publisher.

The King of Love My Shepherd Is

DOMINUS REGIT ME. 8. 7. 8. 7.

HENRY W. BAKER, 1831–1877   JOHN B. DYKES, 1823–1876

Shepherd Is,' continues to express the same joyous faith in the "Good Shepherd" of which John says: "I am the good Shepherd: I came that they may have life, and may have it abundantly. I know mine own, and mine own know me, even as the Father knoweth me, and I know the Father; and I lay down my life for the sheep" (10:11, 10, 14, 15, ASV).

H. Augustine Smith says, in his book, *Lyric Religion*, "The best-known translations, excepting, of course, the matchless un-metrical King James version of the Bible, are the famous Scottish paraphrase, 'The Lord's My Shepherd, I'll Not Want,' and Baker's, 'The King of Love My Shepherd Is.'"

The outstanding work of Henry W. Baker's life was his chairmanship of the committee which edited the Anglican Church's *Hymns Ancient and Modern*. For more than twenty years he remained at the head of this committee, which was formed in 1857. He lived to see the publication of the first edition in 1861 and the revised edition in 1875.

Thirty-three hymns from his own pen are included in the revised edition. It is the hymnal used in fifteen thousand churches and chapels throughout England and Wales. It has been generally adopted by the Episcopal Church of Scotland, and is used throughout British colonies, as well as in the British army and navy. It is estimated that more than fifty million copies have been circulated throughout the world.

This hymn tune gets its name from the Latin title of the Twenty-third Psalm, *Dominus Regit Me;* it was composed by John B. Dykes (1823-1876).*

* Abridged from *Lyric Religion* by H. Augustine Smith. Published by The Century Company.

Here at Thy Table, Lord *

BREAD OF LIFE. 6. 4. 6. 4. D.

MAY P. HOYT   WILLIAM F. SHERWIN, 1826–1888

1. Here at Thy ta - ble, Lord, This sa - cred hour, O let us
2. Sit at the feast, dear Lord, Break Thou the bread; Fill Thou the
3. So shall our life of faith Be full, be sweet; And we shall
4. Come then, O ho - ly Christ, Feed us, we pray; Touch with Thy

feel Thee near, In lov - ing pow'r; Call - ing our thoughts a - way
cup that brings Life to the dead; That we may find in Thee,
find our strength For each day meet; Fed by Thy liv - ing bread,
pierc-ed hand Each com - mon day; Mak - ing this earth - ly life

From self and sin, As to Thy ban-quet hall We en - ter in.
Par - don and peace; And from all bond-age win A full re - lease.
All hun - ger past, We shall be sat - is-fied, And saved at last.
Full of Thy grace, Till in the home of heav'n We find our place. A-MEN.

*From *Christian Worship*, p. 451. Published by Bethany Press.

HERE AT THY TABLE, LORD

THIS hymn (p. 64), whose words were written by May P. Hoyt, a contemporary poetess, is one of the best-loved and most inspiring of all the communion
hymns. It is personal in its appeal and a challenge to each one to "examine
himself," as Paul says: "Wherefore whosoever shall eat this bread, and
drink this cup of the Lord, unworthily, shall be guilty of the body and blood
of the Lord. But let a man examine himself, and so let him eat of that
bread and drink of that cup" (I Cor. 11:27-28).

It contains also an appeal for the mystical presence of Christ to be with
each participant as he sits at the Lord's table, and reminds each one to be
conscious as he partakes of the bread and the wine that it is in memory of
Him who gave His life for mankind, and who would not that any should
perish, but that all might come to life eternal.

William F. Sherwin is the composer of the tune "Bread of Life" to which
this hymn is usually sung. The tune fits the sentiment of the words, and
helps each member of the body of Christ to enter into the deep spiritual
significance of the Eucharist.

CONTENTS

PART I SECTION 3

"GO PREACH AND TEACH"

━━━━━━━━━━━━━━━━━━━━━━━━✠━━━━━━━━━━━━━━━━━━━━━━━━

Go ye therefore, and teach all nations, baptizing them in the name of the Father, and of the Son, and of the Holy Ghost: . . . and lo, I am with you alway, even unto the end of the world. Amen.—MATTHEW 28:19-20

━━━━━━━━━━━━━━━━━━━━━━━━✠━━━━━━━━━━━━━━━━━━━━━━━━

PICTURES: PAGE
Interpretation:"Go Preach"—*Burnand* 67
Picture: "Go Preach"—*Burnand* 68
Interpretation: St. Paul—*Bartolommeo* 69
Picture: St. Paul—*Bartolommeo* 70
Interpretation: St. Paul Before the Altar of the Unknown God—*Ch'en* 71
Picture: St. Paul Before the Altar of the Unknown God—*Ch'en* 72

POETRY:
Paul—*Marlatt* 73
Stephen—*Spear* 73
Worship—*Clark* 74
Memorial—*Clark* 74
Peter—*Marlatt* 74
Apostle Paul—*Spear* 75
John Mark—*Spear* 75
Stephen—Paul!—*Oxenham* 75
O Lord, Forgive!—*Pugh* 76
Quo Vadis?—*Oxenham* 77

STORIES:
Jesus, As Seen by Joseph of Arimathea—*Gibran* 77
The Gospel According to Andrew—*Barton* 80
The Gospel According to Judas—*Barton* 85

MUSIC:
Interpretation: To All the Nations, Lord—*Tiplady* 90
Music: To All the Nations, Lord—*Milligan* 91
Interpretation: O God of Love! O King of Peace!—*Baker* 92
Music: O God of Love! O King of Peace!—*Oliver* 92

"GO PREACH"

Eugene Burnand

THE TWO fundamental things that mattered to Eugene Burnand were his faith and his art. He was born in 1850 at Moudon, a small town in the Canton Vaud, Switzerland. His father, a colonel in the Swiss Army, wanted him to become an architect, but as he grew, the desire to become a painter increased. As soon as he had completed his training as an architect, he began to study painting seriously, first at Geneva and later in Paris, where he worked for several years.

While living in Paris he met and married in 1878 the daughter of the famous engraver, Paul Girardet, and settled in Versailles. Because of his desire to keep closely in touch with the artistic world of his day, he changed his place of residence frequently, living first in Paris, then in Switzerland, and later in Italy. He died suddenly in Paris on February 4, 1921, but not until he had become recognized as one of the really great painters of his day.

This painting, "Go Preach," presents the Great Commission of Jesus to His disciples in simplest terms: it is a personal appeal for loyalty and service, from a great Teacher to His pupil. It is not the historic Jesus of Nazareth calling Peter or John; it is instead the eternal Christ appealing to youth—in every land, and through all the centuries. Christ is here pointing out a way of life, summoning youth to follow an ideal, to accept a companionship, to assume a task.

How does one know this? First, observe the face and eyes of Christ. They bear the stamp of the dreamer, the idealist. The eyes are seeing things in the large rather than in detail; the mind behind them is occupied with principles and grand objectives.

Next look at the young man's face. The disciple is earnestly trying to make out a specific goal, something to work out, accomplish. There is no vagueness in his mind about this call; he is about to tackle a "job."

The difference in the two faces is intentional. Burnand has interpreted correctly the historic and perpetual relationship between Christ and His disciples. Christ has a vision of a world redeemed, of the Kingdom of God, the brotherhood of man, human nature transformed by love from selfishness and individualism to organization and co-operation. That is a grand and compelling ideal that is indeed over the horizon and partly in the clouds; but it grips men powerfully, especially young men and women, and sets them on fire for service.

Down through the ages young enthusiasts have picked out their specific jobs, their own limited and human objectives. Paul sees his task to be the founding of churches, Dorcas makes coats for the poor at Joppa, Athanasius works out a trinitarian formula for the creed. Ambrose trains choirs to enrich the liturgy at Milan. Charlemagne founds a hospital for pilgrims in Jeru-

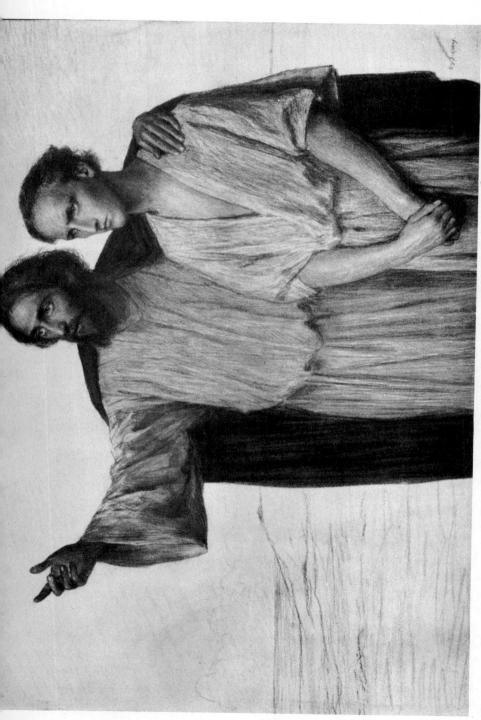

"GO PREACH"—BURNAND

salem. St. Francis of Assisi washes the wounds of lepers. Luther nails his world-shaking challenge on the church at Wittenberg. Howard reforms the prison system of England. Wilberforce frees slaves. Jane Addams brings hope to youth on the city streets. Millions down through the ages have caught the vision of God's kingdom over the horizon and have followed the Gleam each in his own way always under the inspiration of the Great Teacher, the Christ.

What a wonderful partnership it is! The challenge and the response, the infinite and the finite, the far-off ideal and the task near at hand.*

✠

ST. PAUL
Fra Bartolommeo

AMONG several beautiful paintings of the apostle Paul, this one from the brush of Fra Bartolommeo (1475-1517) ranks as one of the greatest. (See p. 70.)

The artists of the fifteenth and sixteenth centuries blended two schools of art. Michelangelo drew more from the vigorous thirteenth-century masters, and Raphael from the more sensuous followers of Masaccio and Lippi. Michelangelo tried to put the Christian soul into his works; Raphael tried to bring realism into religion through painting. Fra Bartolommeo's works show the influence of both of these artists.

It is impossible to appraise properly the paintings of Fra Bartolommeo without considering the influence upon him of Savonarola. The controversy surrounding this great preacher in the years from 1492 to his torture and death at the stake in 1498 entered into the lives of all the people of Florence, either to draw them to devotion or to stir them in the opposite direction. It was natural that Fra Bartolommeo would be greatly affected by such a man. Savonarola had said: "True beauty is neither in form nor color, but in light. God is light, and His creatures are the more lovely as they approach the nearer to Him in beauty. . . . The body is the more beautiful according to the beauty of the soul within it." It is certain that this divine light lived ever after in the paintings of Fra Bartolommeo.

After Savonarola had gone calmly to his death beneath the shadow of the old palace, Fra Bartolommeo, the Della Robbias, Credi, and many other artists showed their grief by abandoning for a time the arts they loved. Fra Bartolommeo gave himself to monasticism, and for some years never touched a pencil or brush. But when Santo Pagnini came to the convent of San Marco as its superior, he commanded Fra Bartolommeo to recommence painting. Bartolommeo soon recovered his former skill, as is evidenced by his painting of the meeting of Christ with His disciples at Emmaus (1506), which combines rich coloring with almost perfect form.

* Abridged from *Christ and His Gospel in Recent Art* by Albert Edward Bailey. Copyright 1935 by Charles Scribner's Sons. Used by permission of the publisher.

ST. PAUL—BARTOLOMMEO

The intercourse between Raphael and Bartolommeo was beneficial to both, and it is claimed that they worked together on some pictures, although there is not sufficient evidence to prove this claim.

When Bartolommeo took his final vows to become a monk, everyone thought his career as an artist was at an end. However, his sun had set only to rise again to greater brilliance as Fra Bartolommeo, a name famous in the annals of Christian art.*

✛

ST. PAUL BEFORE THE ALTAR OF THE UNKNOWN GOD
Luke Ch'en

Then Paul stood in the midst of Mars' hill, and said, "Ye men of Athens, I perceive that in all things ye are too superstitious. For as I passed by, and beheld your devotions, I found an altar with this inscription, *To the Unknown God.* Whom therefore ye ignorantly worship, him declare I unto you."—ACTS 17:22–23.

ARCHBISHOP COSTANTINI, the first apostolic delegate to China (1922-23), was a great lover of art, and encouraged it whenever and wherever he could. He was disappointed to find no Roman Catholic artists in China, and called the attention of his missionaries to the wise rules concerning art issued by the Sacred Congregation for the Propagation of the Faith.

In 1928, while visiting an art exhibition in Peking, His Excellency discovered a non-Christian artist by the name of Ch'en Hsü, whose work followed the finest Chinese traditions. He immediately gave the artist a New Testament, with the suggestion that he read it and give him his impressions of portions of it. He also showed him some of the best works of Western Christian art.

Mr. Ch'en's study of the Gospels to be illustrated led to his conversion to Christianity in 1932. The Archbishop baptized him with the Christian name of Luke, so that in succeeding years the artist has always signed himself as Luke Ch'en.

Speaking of his own art work, Mr. Ch'en said: "If I can represent the teachings of our holy church in pictures according to Chinese art, and by means of such natural impressions draw the Chinese to know God, why should I not render so useful and enjoyable a service?"

Later Luke Ch'en became one of the professors in the Catholic University of Peking. Several of his students began to study the Bible, later trying to portray on canvas what they had read and heard. It is significant that almost all of these young art students became followers of Christ through their love for and work in the field of Christian art.

The picture on p. 72, like that on p. 384, is a fine illustration of Luke Ch'en's work as a Christian artist.

* Based on information in the *Bridgman Art Library of Great Artists,* "Fra Bartolommeo," by Leader Scott.

ST. PAUL BEFORE THE ALTAR OF THE UNKNOWN GOD—*CH'EN*

The Greeks were indeed meticulously religious, and in their efforts not to overlook any of the many gods who claimed their loyalty, they had erected an altar on Mars Hill bearing the inscription: "To the Unknown God." Paul, on his visit to Athens in the early period of the Church's missionary work, used this inscription as a way of bringing to the attention of the Greeks the one and only true God. This caught the attention of the philosophical Greek mind and made it possible for Paul to explain to them the plan and purpose of the living God in sending His only begotten Son as the Saviour of all the children of men.

✢

PAUL

He found life a pattern
Woven by the Law
And men colorless threads in the fabric,
Save one,
Whose face shone
As jagged stones carved the last darkness;
And Another,
Whose light and voice
Illumined a desert road.
Thereafter,
Frail but unafraid,
He journeyed into the dawn—
Tearing the pattern to shreds
To free souls
From the tyranny of the dark.*

—*Earl Marlatt*

STEPHEN

The early Christian leaders sought for aid
To render alms to needy widowed folk;
So Stephen was, with others, deacon made,
And soon through miracles for God he spoke.
Misguided Jews, angered by his success,
Aroused a mob to stone him to his death;
The dying Stephen prayed to God to bless
His executioners with his latest breath.
The followers of the Lord were soon dispersed,
And preached the gospel in the heathen lands,
The death of Stephen did not prove a curse,
But led Paul soon to join the Christian bands.

* From *Cathedral: A Volume of Poems* by Earl Marlatt, p. 90. Copyright 1956 by Earl Marlatt. Published by Parthenon Press. Used by permission of the author and the publisher.

Thus Stephen, like the Christ, by dying gave
The gospel to the world with power to save.*

—*Henry C. Spear*

WORSHIP

We need not fear if rites grow worn,
Nor be dismayed
If vestments which our fathers used
Seem threadbare, frayed.
Perhaps they formed a chrysalis
So man could find
New winged ways to worship Him
"With all thy mind!"**

—*Leslie Savage Clark*

MEMORIAL

Though time has scarred the pyramids,
Though weed and vine
Have overrun the tomb of kings,
Unmarred, this sign
Of Love's remembering endures—
The bread, the wine.**

—*Leslie Savage Clark*

PETER

Lifted by the teaching of a Master
From the pallid shores of a lake
To the azure heights it mirrored,
He fell before a woman's scorn:
Three times he denied his Lord;
And immediately the cock crew.

He was crucified head-downward
Because he thought himself unworthy
To die the death of Jesus.

Denial,
Cock-crow,
Crucifixion—
His was a sacred way
That only the strong dare follow.***

—*Earl Marlatt*

* Written especially for this anthology.
** From *With All Thy Heart* by Leslie Savage Clark. Copyright 1957 by Broadman Press. Used by permission of the author and the publisher.
*** From *Cathedral: A Volume of Poems* by Earl Marlatt, p. 89. Copyright 1956 by Earl Marlatt. Published by Parthenon Press. Used by permission of the author and the publisher.

APOSTLE PAUL

Saul of Tarsus, a Jewish Pharisee,
Sat at the feet of wise Gamaliel;
He worked as the Sanhedrin's devotee
In persecuting Christians with a will.
But Christ met Saul on the Damascus road,
The light of truth dawned on his mind and soul,
From thence he lived by the great Christian code,
And set his aim to reach the highest goal.
A missionary to the world was Paul;
Apostle to the Gentiles far and near;
In Christian service sacrificed his all,
His letters make the gospels doubly clear.
Inspirer of reformers of each age,
Apostle Paul adorns the sacred page.*

—*Henry C. Spear*

JOHN MARK

A Christian mother gave Mark to the Church;
And he, in turn, gave us a gospel bold;
The story of the Christ from Peter's heart
Mark put in print as to him it was told.
A Levite, Mark was helper to the priests,
And then was comfort to Apostle Paul,
He gave us food for our religious feasts,
And rallied Gentiles to the Master's call.
Mark saw in Christ the mighty man of deeds;
His miracles proclaimed Him Son of God;
In actions rather than beliefs in creeds
Mark showed the Shepherd with His staff and rod.
To read the gospel according to John Mark,
Will bring any doubter out of the dark.*

—*Henry C. Spear*

STEPHEN—PAUL!

Stephen, who died while I stood by consenting
    Wrought in his death the making of a life,
Bruised one hard heart to thought of swift repenting,
    Fitted one fighter for a nobler strife.

* Written especially for this anthology.

Stephen, the Saint, triumphant and forgiving,
  Prayed while the hot blows beat him to the earth,
Was that a dying? Rather was it living!—
  Through his soul's travail my soul came to birth.

Stephen, the Martyr, full of faith and fearless,
  Smiled when his bruised lips could no longer pray,—
Smiled with a courage undismayed and peerless,—
  Smiled!—and that smile is with me, night and day.

O, was it I that stood there, all consenting?
  I—at whose feet the young man's clothes were laid?
Was it *my* will that wrought that hot tormenting?
  My heart that boasted over Stephen dead?

Yes, it was I. And sore to me the telling.
  Yes, it was I. The thought of it has been
God's potent spur my whole soul's might compelling
  These outer darknesses for Him to win.*

—John Oxenham

O LORD, FORGIVE!

For the sudden flare of temper, Lord,
That flashes, flames, and throws its spark,
And hurls a hurtful threat or word
To pierce a heart and leave a mark,
Forgive! O Lord, forgive!

For words unspoken, Lord, I pray;
The phrases lost because unsaid—
They healed no hurt, nor paused to say
That word by which the heart is fed.
Forgive! O Lord, forgive!

For times, dear Lord, when we should know
Those words which hurt and those which heal;
Since actions do so quickly show
By things we do, the way we feel—
Stand by! Dear Lord, stand by!**

—Samuel F. Pugh

* From *Bees in Amber* by John Oxenham, p. 30. Used by permission of Miss Erica Oxenham and Methuen Co., Ltd.
** From *Between-Time Meditations* by Samuel F. Pugh, p. 57. Copyright 1954 by Bethany Press. Used by permission of the author and the publisher.

QUO VADIS?

Peter, outworn,
And menaced by the sword,
Shook off the dust of Rome;
And, as he fled,
Met one, with eager face,
Hastening cityward.
And, to his vast amaze,
It was the Lord.

"Lord, whither goest Thou?"
He cried, importunate;
And Christ replied,—
*"Peter, I suffer loss.
I go to take thy place,
To bear thy cross."*

Then Peter bowed his head,
Discomforted;
There at the Master's feet,
Found grace complete,
And courage, and new faith,
And turned—with Him,
To Death.

So we,—
Whene'er we fail
Of our full duty,
Cast on Him our load,—
On Him who suffered sore for us,
On Him who frail flesh wore for us,
On Him who all things bore for us,—
On Christ, the Lord.*

—John Oxenham

✠

JESUS, AS SEEN BY JOSEPH OF ARIMATHEA
Kahlil Gibran

YOU WOULD know the primal aim of Jesus, and I would fain tell you. But none can touch with fingers the life of the blessed vine, nor see the sap that feeds the branches. And though I have eaten of the grapes and have tasted the new vintage at the winepress, I cannot tell you all. I can only relate what I know of Him.

* From *Bees in Amber* by John Oxenham, p. 21. Used by permission of Miss Erica Oxenham and Methuen Co., Ltd.

Our Master and our Beloved lived but three prophet's seasons. They were the spring of His song, the summer of His ecstasy, and the autumn of His passion; and each season was as a thousand years.

The spring of His song was spent in Galilee. It was there that He gathered His lovers about Him, and it was on the shores of the blue lake that He first spoke of the Father, and of our release and our freedom. By the Lake of Galilee we lost ourselves to find our way to the Father; and oh, the little, little loss that turned to such gain.

It was there the angels sang in our ears and bade us leave the arid land for the garden of heart's desire. He spoke of the fields and green pastures; of the slopes of Lebanon where the white lilies are heedless of the caravans passing in the dust of the valley. He spoke of the wild brier that smiles in the sun and yields its incense to the passing breeze. And He would say, "The lilies and the brier live but a day, yet that day is eternity spent in freedom."

And one evening as we sat beside the stream He said, "Behold the brook and listen to its music. Forever shall it seek the sea, and though it is forever seeking, it sings its mystery from noon to noon. Would that you seek the Father as the brook seeks the sea."

Then came the summer of His ecstasy, and the June of His love was upon us. He spoke of naught then but the other man—the neighbor, the road-fellow, the stranger, and our childhood's playmates.

He spoke of the traveler journeying from the east to Egypt, of the plow-man coming home with his oxen at eventide, of the chance guest led by dusk to our door. And He would say: "Your neighbor is your unknown self made visible. His face shall be reflected in your still waters, and if you gaze therein you shall behold your own countenance. Should you listen in the night, you shall hear him speak, and his words shall be the throbbing of your own heart. Be unto him that which you would have him be unto you.

"This is my law, and I shall say it unto you, and unto your children, and they unto their children until time is spent and generations are no more."

And on another day He said, "You shall not be yourself alone. You are in the deeds of other men, and they though unknowing are with you all your days. They shall not commit a crime and your hand not be with their hand. They shall not fall down but that you shall also fall down; and they shall not rise but that you shall rise with them. Their road to the sanctuary is your road, and when they seek the wasteland you too seek with them.

"You and your neighbor are two seeds sown in the field. Together you grow and together you shall sway in the wind. And neither of you shall claim the field. For a seed on its way to growth claims not even its own ecstasy.

"Today I am with you. Tomorrow I go westward; but ere I go, I say unto you that your neighbor is your unknown self made visible. Seek him in love that you may know yourself, for only in that knowledge shall you become my brothers."

Then came the autumn of His passion. And He spoke to us of freedom, even as He had spoken in Galilee in the spring of His song; but now His words sought our deeper understanding.

He spoke of leaves that sing only when blown upon the wind; and of man as a cup filled by the ministering angel of the day to quench the thirst of another angel. Yet whether that cup is full or empty it shall stand crystalline upon the board of the Most High. Then He said: "You are the cup and you are the wine. Drink of yourselves to the dregs; or else remember me, and you shall be quenched."

And on our way to the southward He said, "Jerusalem, which stands in pride upon the height, shall descend to the depth of Jahannum the dark valley, and in the midst of her desolation I shall stand alone.

"The temple shall fall to dust, and around the portico you shall hear the cry of widows and orphans; and men in their haste to escape shall not know the faces of their brothers, for fear shall be upon them all.

"But even there, if two of you shall meet and utter my name and look to the west, you shall see me, and these my words shall again visit your ears."

And when we reached the hill of Bethany, He said, "Let us go to Jerusalem. The city awaits us. I will enter the gate riding upon a colt, and I will speak to the multitude. Many are there who would claim me, and many who would put out my flame, but in my death you shall find life and you shall be free.

"The walls that my Father has built around me shall not fall down, and the acre He has made holy shall not be profaned. When the dawn shall come, the sun will crown my head and I shall be with you to face the day. And that day shall be long, and the world shall not see its eventide.

"The scribes and the Pharisees say the earth is thirsty for my blood. I would quench the thirst of the earth with my blood. But from the drops shall rise oak trees and maple, and the east wind shall carry the acorns to other lands.

"I shall not be her king. The diadems of Zion were fashioned for lesser brows. And the ring of Solomon is small for this finger. Behold my hand. See you not that it is over-strong to hold a scepter, and over-sinewed to wield a common sword?

"Nay, I shall not command Syrian flesh against Roman. But with you my words shall wake that city and my spirit shall speak to her second dawn. My words shall be an invisible army with horses and chariots, and without ax or spear I shall conquer the priests of Jerusalem, and the Caesars.

"I shall not sit upon a throne where slaves have sat and ruled other slaves. Nor will I rebel against the sons of Italy. But I shall be a tempest in their sky, and a song in their soul. And I shall be remembered. They shall call me Jesus the Anointed." These things He said outside the walls of Jerusalem before He entered the city. And His words are graven on us as with chisel.*

* Abridged from *Jesus, the Son of Man* by Kahlil Gibran, pp. 53-58. Copyright 1928 by Kahlil Gibran. Published by Alfred A. Knopf, Inc. Used by permission of the publisher.

THE GOSPEL ACCORDING TO ANDREW

William E. Barton

(Written in prison, on the shores of the Black Sea, near the end of a long life of fruitful but inconspicuous labor.)

I WAS there first. I do not say it boastfully, but in simple truth. I am not disputing the record. I know how it reads:

"Now the names of the twelve apostles are these: The first, Simon, who is called Peter, and Andrew his brother"; and so on through the list to where it ends with the names of Simon the Zealot and Judas Iscariot. I am not disputing Simon's right to be called the first, for in our family the rule is illustrated that the first shall be last and the last first. Simon Peter was a greater man than I, and I have been reminded of it too often and in too many ways to think of disputing it. For many years now Simon's name has stood before mine in the list of the apostles, and I suppose it will always be so. Nevertheless, it was I and not Simon who first found Jesus.

I remember that February afternoon when I first saw Jesus. He had just returned from His forty days in the wilderness, and I and the younger son of Zebedee were standing with our teacher, John the Baptist. We were talking about the day's work and of the number of people who had come down from Jerusalem to hear John and of several notable converts whom he had won. We who were John's disciples had come to feel that no man could be greater than John, and were wondering who it could be that John would hail as the Messiah. To me was given the incomparable honor of having been one of the first two men to whom Jesus was pointed out as the Christ. Months afterward at Caesarea Philippi, Peter acknowledged Him as the Christ and won for himself everlasting honor; but John told me that Jesus was the Christ before Peter had ever seen Jesus. The younger son of Zebedee has told this story truthfully.

"Again on the morrow John was standing, and two of his disciples; and he looked upon Jesus as He walked, and saith, Behold, the Lamb of God! And the two disciples heard him speak and they followed Jesus" (John 1:35-36, ASV). "One of the two that heard John speak, and followed him, was Andrew, Simon Peter's brother" (John 1:40, ASV).

That is what I mean when I say that I was the first. I do not desire to rob Peter of any honor which belongs to him. He deserves much. His force of character, his quick decisions which were sometimes wrong, but much oftener right, his readiness to meet an emergency, his warm, generous and courageous nature entitle him to the high regard which has been accorded him. Let no man accuse me of seeking to rob Peter of anything that belonged to him. He was my brother, well beloved; but I came to Jesus before he did.

Peter has told his story. He gave the facts to John Mark and he has written them out in a short and very interesting narrative. Matthew and Luke have made large use of it. To a great extent Mark's Gospel is Peter's; and so, in a very real sense, are those of Luke and Matthew. Peter's story is a thrice-told tale, and it is well told. Peter deserves all the honor which this three-fold narrative accords him. But Peter did not tell Mark everything. More recently John the son of Zebedee has written down his recollections, and they are not only interesting but important. The most interesting thing about them is that they contain so much which neither Mark nor Matthew nor Luke had recorded and yet which is far too precious to be forgotten.

I know very well that I can never write a book like that of John. I cannot even write a book like that of Mark, which is much shorter, and with the story told forthright, without any such embellishments and discourses as John incorporated into his story. But I can tell what I remember and bring together a few things that are already written, but which are so scattered and incidental that people have very nearly forgotten them and many have quite lost their real significance.

Let me go back to that first day when we saw Jesus. At this time I was living in Capernaum with Peter. We were engaged in the fishing business together. I made inquiry among travelers as to the preaching of John and told it that night to Simon and his wife; and Simon said: "Let us go down to Bethabara and hear John."

So we left Capernaum, and took with us provisions, and went to listen to the preaching of John the Baptist, I and my brother Simon, who was later called Peter. We went out into the wilderness to see John, and we saw him. He was not a man clothed in soft raiment, neither was he a reed shaken with the wind. He wore his shaggy coat of camel's-hair as if it had been ermine, and he fastened his leather girdle around his lean body as if he were girding on a sword.

How he preached, and how men listened! All men believed him to be a prophet. Mitred priests and proud Pharisees trembled when they heard his words. Is it any wonder that we fishermen were profoundly moved? Simon and I made haste to enroll ourselves as his disciples. We stepped into the Jordan side by side, but John baptized Simon first. It was always that way. And yet I think it was I who said to Simon before he did to me, "Surely this man is a prophet and when I hear him preach I feel constrained to confess my sin and enroll myself as one who is waiting for the kingdom of God."

While we were at the Jordan, we met the younger son of Zebedee, John, whose home was in Bethsaida and whom we knew very well. He, his brother and his father were our enterprising competitors in the fishing business. Though competitors we were friends, as good fishermen know how to be. Now and then we were partners for a little time, so that we knew them well. John and I, the two younger brothers, were frequently thrown together.

John, the son of Zebedee, was no favorite among the disciples, as anyone can see who reads the story as it is written by Matthew, Mark or Luke. It is only John himself who tells that he was the disciple whom Jesus loved, but

he tells it truly. I think Jesus discovered in him from the beginning something that was capable of being made not only lovable but loving. I have often
wished that I knew what it was that Jesus saw in me that made Him wish to
have me follow Him. My brother Simon and my associate John both became
distinguished in the apostolic group, and I am hardly more than a name
there. All my life I have been accustomed to being overshadowed by Simon;
but now it has come to pass also that John the son of Zebedee—that rough,
hot-tempered, ambitious, younger son of Thunder, stands as far above me as
my great brother Simon, and what is more strange, he won his distinction as
an apostle of love.

I shall never forget that afternoon in February of which I have already
spoken. After John the Baptist had pointed out Jesus we two young men
stood a moment wondering what to do next. John turned and went toward his
hut in the wilderness. Jesus went the other way, the glory of the descending
sun making a halo around Him as He walked from us. We stood for a
moment irresolute, then I began to follow, and John the son of Zebedee went
with me. Jesus turned and spoke to us: "What are you seeking?" He
asked.

We did not know how to answer Him, for we did not know what we were
seeking. There was something in our hearts that impelled us to follow Him,
but we could not have told in words just what it was. We asked Him in whose
house He had lodging, and He invited us to go with Him. So we stepped up
beside Him, John on the right hand and I on the left, and we came to His
lodging a little way back from the Jordan.

I wish I could tell you what we talked about that wonderful evening. In
very truth I cannot remember. It seemed to me very wonderful and my heart
told me that I had found the Master of my life.

But I could not help thinking as we sat there together, "I must find Simon."
So after awhile I slipped out and left Jesus talking with John while I went
and found my brother and brought him to Jesus.

This also I like to remember, that I was following Jesus before He called
me; even before that blessed moment when He turned around and asked us
what we wanted and whom we were seeking I was a follower of Jesus. From
that hour I have not ceased to be His follower. This thought makes me happy
when I remember it.

We left the Jordan on the next day. Before we left Jesus called another
disciple, a fellow townsman of mine, named Philip. Philip had a friend
named Nathaniel whom he brought to Jesus as I had brought my brother
Peter. Jesus found His first six disciples all within twenty-four hours. There
were three pairs of us, myself and Simon, John and later his brother James,
my friend Philip and his friend Nathaniel.

We started for Galilee. Jesus told us that His reason for going at this
time was that He had been invited to a wedding at Cana. John has told the
story of the wedding at Cana, and it is not necessary for me to repeat it. I have
often thought, however, that people have not adequately recognized the
significance of Jesus' first miracle. It was not a work of healing, nor was it

an effort to undo the effects of sin. Jesus did it just to add to the sum of human joy. I hope I shall not seem irreverent if I say that it has always seemed to me that in some respects that miracle more truly than any other that Jesus ever wrought shows the true character of His mission. He did not come to earth simply to make life bearable. He came to augment every reasonable human joy—to bring life abundant.

There is another miracle of Jesus in which I have a special right to be interested, for I think that I helped to make it possible. That was the one in which Jesus fed five thousand people. All four of the men who have told the story of Jesus have written the account of this, but here again it is the son of Zebedee who relates most fully that part of the story in which I have most reason to be interested. He tells this about me: "One of His disciples, Andrew, Simon Peter's brother, saith unto Him, There is a lad here who hath five barley loaves and two fishes; but what are these among so many?" That is a true statement and I do not feel ashamed of it. I was looking after the food supply and that was all there was in sight and I brought that boy to Jesus.

Concerning this miracle also I feel like saying that I do not think it has had all the weight to which its character entitles it. It was in some respects the largest of Jesus' miracles. It touched more human lives than any other. It was not called out by any stern necessity. Those hungry people could all have gotten to some of the little towns along the lake and there have obtained food. They would have suffered some inconvenience, but none of them would have died. Jesus fed them not because they were starving to death, but just because they were hungry. Hunger is not disease, hunger is not sin; food is not medicine. I am very sure that most people have not sufficiently considered how largely the gospel makes its appeal to that which is normal in human life.

Of course I know about Jesus' miracles of healing, and I do not deny their importance; but in a way it is not so important that one sick man should be healed as that five thousand hungry people should be fed.

I think of these things often and I have this feeling that people had admired and wondered at the striking and unusual elements in the ministry of Jesus and have not adequately considered its normality.

I have never been able to determine just why it was that I was just outside the inner circle. Anyone who will read the list of the twelve apostles will see that it is made up of three groups of four each, and that in each group of four except the first there is some variation in order, but always the same name comes first. The first group consisted of two sets of brothers, Simon and Andrew, James and John. The next group was composed of Philip and Nathaniel, Thomas and Matthew. The third was comprised of James, the son of Alphaeus, Thaddeus or Judas, "not Iscariot," Simon the Zealot and Judas Iscariot. In such a grouping, it would surely have seemed inevitable that I should always have been in the innermost circle, and not at the outermost edge even of that. I should have been second in the innermost group. But it was not so.

The first time Jesus manifested this discrimination was at the raising of the daughter of Jairus. We were all present when Jesus was sent for, and all wanted to go with Him, and expected as a matter of course that it would be so; "but He suffered no man to follow with Him, save Peter, and James and John the brother of James" (Mark 5:37, Luke 8:51, ASV). The rest of us simply stood outside with the crowd and waited to learn secondhand what occurred. The awe of the miracle so impressed us that we forgot to be displeased at the time, but we talked about it afterward, and none of us liked it very well, and I had most reason of all to resent it.

At the Transfiguration, again, He took the same three men with Him, and left the rest of us below confronted by a task too great for us. When He came down from the mountain, He healed the epileptic boy, and we who had been trying to heal him not only had to take the blame of the failure, from which Peter and James and John escaped, but we had no share in the glory of the Transfiguration. I am sure that none of those three could have done any better than we, and we did our best.

Again, on the night of His betrayal, He took Peter and James and John with Him into the middle of the garden, and left the rest of us, eight in number, to watch near the gate. We were all tired to death, and we slept, the first three as well as the rest of us; and were all ashamed of it afterward. But the three especially chosen were no more alert than the rest of us. That was the thing that annoyed me, and I may as well admit it. I was overlooked on all the really important occasions. I no longer think of it with the feeling of resentment which I once cherished, but I have never understood it very well. And this is why I saw the ministry of Jesus from a point just outside the inner group. I was one of the first four, but I was not one of the first three; and yet at the beginning I was one of the first two.

I am glad to remember that on one important occasion near the end of His ministry, I was in the innermost group. As Jesus was leaving the temple on the afternoon of Tuesday just before His Crucifixion, we called His attention to the greatness of the building, and He said that the time was not far distant when the temple was to be destroyed.

We talked about it as we climbed up the slope of the Mount of Olives, and wondered what He meant. So I said to my companions, "If you want to know, why do you not ask Him?"

So we went together, "Peter and James and John and Andrew" (Mark 13:3) and asked Him, "To tell us, when shall these things be, and what shall be the sign when all these things are about to be accomplished."

Then Jesus told us the terrible things which are recorded in those stern chapters toward the end of the gospels. We trembled as He spoke these words. But toward the end, He changed His manner and returned to His old manner of speaking in parables, a thing He had not done for some time. He told us the three parables of the Ten Virgins, the Talents, and the Sheep and the Goats.

I have always been glad that I was one of those who asked Him the question. The parable of the talents has always been very dear to me. I have not as many talents as my brother Simon, and perhaps not as many as either of the sons of Zebedee; but I have used my talents faithfully, and He said that I am not to lose my reward.

All these memories come back to me now when I am an old man and in prison on the shores of the Black Sea. My life has been long and my labors have been arduous and fruitful. If I have not been able to do such things as my brother Simon did, at least I have been a devoted follower of my Lord and I have served Him with fidelity. Even in these regions where I have spent my life and have been faithful to the end, my fame is eclipsed by the zeal and organizing ability of one Saul who is called Paulus. They say I am to be crucified; if so, I shall ask this one favor, that I be not nailed to the cross as Jesus was nailed and that the cross be not like His, for I am not worthy to die as my Lord died.

I have lived my life, I have borne my testimony and now I am writing the story as I sit here in prison. I have no expectation that this will be counted worthy to be received into the collection of books that already are held in high honor. It may even be neglected or forgotten and my name among the twelve may be little more than a name, but I know that I have done my duty even though obscurely.

Names do not always denote the character of those who bear them, but if nothing else is remembered about Andrew, let this be remembered, that from the first call of Jesus to the end of his long ministry and even now as he faces death, he has done his duty like a man.*

✛

THE GOSPEL ACCORDING TO JUDAS
William E. Barton

(Written Saturday, the day following the Crucifixion of Christ.)

I DO not write to excuse myself. I know full well that I have sinned beyond the possibility of pardon here on earth and I know not if it be possible in the mercy of God that I shall have forgiveness in heaven. I am not writing with any thought that I shall be able to set aside or even greatly to modify, the merciless judgment which coming generations must pronounce against me; nor can any condemnation by whomsoever uttered surpass that of my own conscience. I have betrayed innocent blood. I have seen Him hanging on a tree whom I believed to be the noblest and best of men, and I know that largely it was my fault. The thirty pieces of silver, until yesterday in my possession, are a millstone round my neck, which it seems must drag me to the bottom of the abyss. My lips are blistered with the memories of the treasona-

* Abridged from *Four Hitherto Unpublished Gospels* by William E. Barton, pp. 71-92, now out of print. Used by permission of Bruce Barton, Executor of Estate of William E. Barton.

ble kiss I gave Him. Life has become unbearable. If I do not die of remorse I shall surely take my own life. Great would be my joy this minute if I could feel myself nailed, not to His cross, for I am not worthy of that honor, but to the cross of one of the two robbers who were crucified beside Him.

Nevertheless there are some things which ought to be said, not in apology for me, but as giving from a different point of view an account of the ministry of Jesus. I was born in Judah; my very name Judas is the glorious name of Judah, with the Greek ending. It meant in the language of our fathers, "One who deserves to be praised." It is more than an honorable name; it is a glorious name. It is the name of the "Lion Tribe." It is the name of the most noble and illustrious of all the twelve tribes of Israel. Jesus Himself traced His birth through this tribe. Ten of His disciples were Galileans; Simon the Zealot and I shared with Jesus the honor of descent from Judah. Simon and I were born in Judah and I was named for that most stalwart of the sons of our father Jacob.

We two—Simon and I—are mentioned last in the lists of the apostles. We who came from the proudest of the tribes had this perpetually to irritate us, that we were looked upon as having hardly any right even to a place among Galileans. Whenever people asked how many apostles Jesus had and what were their names, the lists always began with Simon Peter and Andrew his brother, and the next names were those of the two sons of Zebedee. Then after all the rest, most of them commonplace and insignificant men, came the two names from the one really great tribe, the names of Simon the Zealot and Judas Iscariot.

I know very well that I had no right to even the lowliest place among the disciples of our blessed Lord. I am not deserving of even the least of the honors that came to me in the months of my association with Him. Nevertheless, it is not a light thing to a proud man, a man who is justly proud of his birth and social position, that in every compilation of a list of names of men with whom he is associated, the names of fishermen and publicans should stand above his own. I know that in intellect, in training and business ability and knowledge of the world I was their superior.

I wonder if anyone would believe me when I say that my motives in becoming a follower of Jesus were not wholly bad. My character had in it traits enough that were and are unlovely, but I was sincere in my love for my country. The traditions of the old days, when Israel had a name and a place among the nations, and Judah was chief among the tribes, were very precious to me. From boyhood I was thrilled when I heard about them. I longed for an opportunity to show my devotion to that which had made my nation great. Does anyone suppose that I joined the society of Jesus for the mere sake of the little money which I might possibly be able to filch from the bag? They underrate my ability as a thief, to say the least. I could have found more profitable places to win confidence and betray it for the reward of money. I believed myself a patriot and had some reason for this opinion.

I had no real associate in the apostolic group excepting Simon, the

Cananaean. He was a patriot, and bitterly resented the domination of Rome and contested with the sword every assumed right of aggression. He risked his life for the glory of Israel when the other disciples of Jesus were quietly fishing in the Sea of Galilee. Jesus Himself said that no man had greater love than he who laid down his life for his friends; Simon the Zealot put his life in peril for the principles of the Kingdom of God and he was the only man among them who had ever risked anything for the sake of the kingdom.

I was not a soldier like Simon, but I was a Judean as he was. I loved my country as he did; I associated myself with Jesus from the same motive that carried him into that uncongenial group. I gave up a better home than most of the apostles and better worldly prospects and business opportunity, but my name always appeared at the end of the list, and Simon came next to the bottom, he who had risked the most.

If ever any of the disciples of Jesus should tell the story of His ministry, they would be compelled to tell how again and again the disciples quarrelled among themselves as to who should be the greatest among them. Jesus rebuked it once by calling a little child and saying that he was greatest in the kingdom. We all understood what that meant, but that was not the end of the matter. Jesus had this in mind when He said to us, "See that ye fall not out by the way." Whenever our minds were free from pressing cares, that was the question that came up. I was ambitious and so was Simon; so were all the rest. James and John were insufferable in their ambition. Only a few days ago, as we were approaching Jerusalem, their mother, Salome, came to Jesus and they with her, begging Jesus that they might sit the one on His right hand and the other on His left in His kingdom. I will not deny that Simon and I coveted those places for ourselves, but we had better sense than to get our mothers to tease Him to give them to us. If I was any more ambitious than the others I think it was because I was more intelligent.

I was ambitious; of course I was ambitious. I believed that Jesus was to establish a kingdom and that He would choose as His foremost officials those who from the beginning of His ministry had left their homes and become His followers. I believed that I had something that I could contribute to the movement and that I deserved both recognition and reward. If this was sinful it was a sin which I shared with all the other disciples.

If the kingdom ever came it must come by the overthrow of Rome. If Rome was overthrown it must be by military force. Inasmuch as a little country like ours could never hope to rally an army great enough to stand against Rome, I knew that there must be favorable circumstance, either political or supernatural. I came to Jesus because I believed He had the power to rally men to Him and to organize them into a successful army of resistance against Rome. If we could begin a revolution in our own country, we might hope that we could rout the local Roman guards and hold our territory successfully against forces that Rome would immediately send for our subjection.

Let me confess that I never really loved Jesus. It was not affection for Him that drew me to Him. On the contrary, there was in Him that which made me ill at ease. I felt that He was able to read my character as no other man. In His presence I felt a sense of self-reproach such as no one else ever gave me; but if I did not love Him, I admired Him and was willing to follow Him; for I loved the kingdom about which He preached.

I have said that Simon and I were consistent revolutionists. Jesus knew this when He accepted us as disciples. He knew that Simon had fought with the sword against the Romans and that I, a Judean, had come into His Galilean company because of my very strong sympathy with our national hope. We ought not to be too severely blamed for not understanding Jesus better in this particular. How could we have been expected to know what Jesus meant when He talked about the Kingdom of Heaven? He knew what meaning we gave to that term. If He chose to give it a new meaning, how could we be expected to know it? Was the Kingdom of God which the prophets promised us entirely a matter of spiritual comfort? Did they not see the Messiah coming from Edom with garments dripping and spattered with the blood of the enemies of Jehovah? How was I to be blamed for an idea of the kingdom which I learned from the holy prophets? Even John the Baptist believed in a kingdom not very different from that in which I believed. And so did the other disciples.

I have been accused of stealing. I confess it, for it seems to me a small sin compared with that which now I have committed and must shamefully confess. From time to time I took money from the common purse. But I was suspected of stealing a long while before I stole, and I think suspicion made it easier for me to be a thief. I am by nature a covetous man, yet for a long time I knew of these suspicions and did not steal.

John, the son of Zebedee, never liked me. I have been told that he has attributed to me the discontent among the disciples last Friday night, when Mary of Bethany broke her bottle of perfume and poured it upon His head. I did complain. So did all the others. It seemed to me the most extravagant thing I had ever witnessed. That perfume represented a working man's wages for a year. We had been living none too abundantly, and here was an opportunity to replenish our own treasury for the stern days ahead of us. There had been no incident in all the ministry of Jesus, which seems to me more incomprehensible than His willingness to have so much money wasted upon Him for the satisfaction of a single hour. I confess that I protested, and so did all the others. Indeed, it was that very incident which threw me into such a passion that I began to consider for myself how I could turn our situation into financial advantage. So I went to the high priest, and I earned those thirty pieces of silver to my everlasting shame.

I betrayed Jesus. But I did not mean to murder Him. I believed that He had grown timid. He had never used His mighty power for His own protection. I believed that I could force Him to do so. On Sunday morning He had ridden into Jerusalem in triumph, and our hearts leaped for joy as we saw Him thus proclaiming Himself the Messiah. But after that He seemed more cautious. The days were slipping by, and He was not asserting Himself. He left the Temple Tuesday evening with no indication that He intended to return.

This seemed to me an appalling situation. We had come to Jerusalem, menaced by a great danger and inspired by high ardor. Sunday and Monday everything went His way. He drove the money-changers from the Temple and no man dared to lay hands on Him, but all day Tuesday He fought a losing battle, and when He left the Temple in the afternoon I realized that the end had come unless we could rouse Him to some new act of self-assertion.

How could I force Him to utilize the power which He possessed? All day Wednesday He hid in Bethany. On Thursday He made His secret arrangements for the eating of the Passover and afterward hid in the orchard. To guide the soldiers to His place of hiding would be to force an issue. I was sure that He would rise to the emergency. I said to myself that in a way my betrayal was the expression of my faith.

I acted in covetousness, but far more in resentment. It was my opportunity to vent my long-cherished hostility toward the whole crowd of the Galileans, but I never thought that Jesus would die.

My shame grows deep when I remember the sign by which I betrayed Him. I kissed Him. I agreed with the priests upon this as the token of betrayal. From that hour until now my lips have burned as though they were hot coals in the memory of that shameful act. I stood aside after the kiss and waited for Jesus to manifest His divine power. I thought He would summon twelve legions of angels. I thought they would smite down the guard and that Jesus would return in triumph to the Temple.

Alas! No legion of angels came. The mob bound Him and led Him away. They jeered Him and mocked Him, and all the mighty power which I expected Him to use remained quiescent. If He had it He did not use it. He saved others; Himself He could not save.

They brought Him before Pilate, and He was condemned to die. They led Him forth beyond the wall of the city and crucified Him and with Him two robbers. Would that one of them had been I!

And now He is dead, and the world has lost Him who might have been its Saviour had I not betrayed Him. I with my covetousness and resentment and pride and selfish patriotism, I delivered Him to be crucified. I betrayed Him with a kiss. I sold Him for thirty pieces of silver.

Thank God I did not keep the money. While yet He was hanging on the cross I hastened to the Temple and offered it back to the priests. They would not take the money. They shrugged their shoulders when I proffered it and said I had earned it and it was no further concern of theirs. When I cried out in agony of soul that I had betrayed innocent blood, they said, "That is your own affair and no concern of ours." I flung it down on the floor and came away. Later they used the money to buy a burial place for the poor.

I cannot live with the memory of my guilt and the consciousness of my shame. Behind me is the mocking memory of lost opportunities. Within me are the tortures of a soul self-condemned and to be condemned by all coming generations of mankind. Before me is the blackness and hopelessness of death.

But might it be that His love, which is unto the uttermost, could forgive even me? I must not presume upon such great mercy. Let me fall into the hands of God and not into the hands of man. I heard His word to the penitent robber upon the cross, for I was hiding near. I longed to run and hide my face at His feet and plead for His forgiveness, but I knew I was not worthy. I know His love can save even unto the uttermost, and I wonder if in the life beyond there may be for me one faintest gleam of hope. I do not know. Alas! I do not know.*

✤

TO ALL THE NATIONS, LORD

OUR present world, having experienced two World Wars since the beginning of the century, is in great need of new hymns that will express the heartfelt longings and spiritual aspirations of our age. We are passing through an epoch in which all the nations, especially the small ones that hitherto have known only the domination of larger ones, are manifesting their desire for the privilege of directing their own destinies. Whether their condition will be better or worse for having won their independence is yet to be seen; but the right to be free and independent, if it is right for the individual, is also right for each nation.

This hymn voices the hope and the prayer that each nation may be led into the fullness of truth by which all men must ultimately live, if the abundant life is to be possible for all. Until every man becomes in spirit and truth "his brother's keeper," there can be no "peace on earth." Might does not make right, although for a time might may prevail.

The Church preaches that all men are children of a common Father. It must practice the doctrine of the "fatherhood of God and the brotherhood of man" in every situation in government, in labor relations, in the home, the Church, the school, and in business practices if there is to be freedom and independence for all of God's family on earth.

The words of this comparatively new hymn were written by Thomas Tiplady (1882-   ), and the music score (p. 91) was composed by Cleo C. Milligan.

* Abridged from *Four Hitherto Unpublished Gospels*, pp. 99-119, now out of print. Used by permission of Bruce Barton, Executor of Estate of William E. Barton.

To All the Nations, Lord *

PAX ORBI. 6. 6. 6. 4. 6. 6. 6. 4.

THOMAS TIPLADY, 1882–

CLEO C. MILLIGAN

In moderate time

1. To all the na - tions, Lord, Thy bless- ing rich - ly give;
2. In right - eous - ness a - lone Can per - fect peace take root;
3. Yea, Lord, this truth we know; Yet strife and tu - mult rage;

And lead them to the truth By which men live;
The ar - mis - tice of might Bears not this fruit;
And might - y ar - mies still In war en - gage;

May knowl-edge of Thy ways Their steps sup - port and guide;
One fam - i - ly God made Of men be- neath the sun;
O give to us the will To live by right - eous deed;

And in Thy per - fect peace May they a - bide.
When love and law are one His will is done.
And melt in fires of love Self - will and greed! A - MEN.

*Words from *Hymns for the Times*. Used by permission of Thomas Tiplady and the Hymn Society of America.
Music score from *Christian Worship*. Used by permission of the Christian Board of Publication, Bethany Press.

O GOD OF LOVE! O KING OF PEACE!

This is another of those great hymns of the Church which expresses an earnest desire for peace. (See words and music score below.) The words were written by Henry W. Baker (1821-1877) and the music composed by Henry K. Oliver (1800-1885).

Although this hymn was written during the nineteenth century, it still speaks to the people of this generation, who know that the world must find a way to peace or risk the destruction of mankind. Our skills in creating instruments of death far outreach our progress in achieving peace. No nation really wants war, and yet governments seem unwilling to spend as much time and

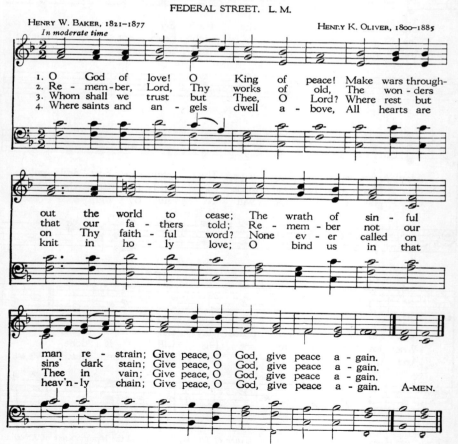

money in exploring the paths to a permanent peace as they do in fashioning weapons of destruction.

We have made so little progress in the art of "loving one another" on an international, world-wide scale, that our fears of the loss of power, of face, of world leadership, and of territory outweigh our willingness to seek peace as the "pearl of great price" and to win it at the cost of personal and national interests and achievements.

We sing, "Give peace, O God, give peace"; yet we know that even God cannot achieve that without man's *will to peace*. When the people refuse any longer to be used as instruments of war, then, and perhaps only then, will the leaders of governments, the world around, seek peace with as much determination as they now seek world domination.

CONTENTS

PART I SECTION 4

THE CHURCH OF CHRIST IS BUILDED

───────────────────────✠───────────────────────

Then they that gladly received His word were baptized; and the same day there were added unto them [the Church] about three thousand souls.—ACTS 2:41

───────────────────────✠───────────────────────

PICTURES: PAGE
   Interpretation: St. Peter—*Bartolommeo* 95
   Picture: St. Peter—*Bartolommeo* 96
   Interpretation: St. Matthew—*Reni* 97
   Picture: St. Matthew—*Reni* 98
   Interpretation: St. John, the Evangelist—*Dolci* 99
   Picture: St. John, the Evangelist—*Dolci* 100
   Interpretation: The Crucifixion of St. Peter—*Michelangelo* 99
   Picture: The Crucifixion of St. Peter—*Michelangelo* 102

POETRY:
   Of Peter—*Clark* 101
   Religion—*Browning* 103
   The Church Within—*Alexander* 103
   The Voice of God—*Neeman* 103
   Architect—*Clark* 103
   The Church—*Asquith* 103
   Intercessors—*Luck* 104
   An Angel Unawares—*Author Unknown* 105
   A Prayer for Our New Church—*Nordlund* 105
   Bless This Church—*Crawford* 106

STORIES:
   Simon, Who Was Called Peter—*Gibran* 106
   Vignettes of the Apostles of the Early Church—arr. by *Maus* 108
   Stephen, the First Christian Martyr—*Foxe* 113

MUSIC:
   Interpretation: The Church's One Foundation—*Stone* 115
   Interpretation: A Christmas Hymn for Peace—*Marlatt* 115
   Music: The Church's One Foundation *or* A Christmas Hymn for Peace—
      Wesley 116
   Interpretation: Here, O My Lord, I See Thee Face to Face—*Bonar* 117
   Music: Here, O My Lord, I See Thee Face to Face—*Mendelssohn* 118

ST. PETER

Fra Bartolommeo

THIS painting is regarded by many as one of the finest of the apostle Peter. It was painted by Fra Bartolommeo during a visit he made to Rome near the end of his life. Because of his illness this picture, with others, was left unfinished, and it is supposed to have been completed by Raphael after Bartolommeo's death in 1517.

Bartolommeo was born in 1475 in a village near Prato. In 1484 the boy was taken away from his home and put to the drudgery of an apprenticeship to art. He had to grind colors, sweep out the studio, run errands, and pick up after his master. From his early youth he showed that innate devotion that marked his entire career.

Bartolommeo's father died, leaving the boy as the head of a family at the age of twelve or thirteen. This was probably responsible for his setting up his own studio, with his young friend Mariotto Albertinelli, while he was still so young. This partnership began about 1490. Bartolommeo learned from Masaccio and Lippi a love for true form and harmonious composition, which he later perfected by a close study of Leonardo da Vinci.

Fra Bartolommeo frequented the cloisters of San Marco to hear Savonarola expound Christianity, feasting his eyes on the speaker's face until it was imprinted on his mind. A year after Savonarola's martyrdom, he painted a faithful portrait of him which remains one of his finest works.

Bartolommeo's early death left to art a valuable legacy—a long list of masterpieces in which religious feeling is expressed in the highest language. He stands forever almost on a level with the great trio: "possessing something of Leonardo da Vinci's grace and color and more than his industry, Michelangelo's force with more softness, and Raphael's sentiment and devotion."*

Fra Bartolommeo's ability to express religious feeling is demonstrated in his portrayal of St. Peter. He pictures a vigorous and thoughtful man—one who has been through the agony of denying his Lord, one who might even yet speak impulsively, but who, at the same time, is "the rock."

This noble figure, delineated with great dignity, is clothed in garments which fall in simple, beautiful folds. Peter's right hand grasps the massive keys to the kingdom, his familiar symbol in art, based on Matthew 16:15-19. He holds a book in his left hand to symbolize the Epistles that bear his name.

But it is the face of the apostle that attracts the eye more than all of these details. The thoughtful expression of the deep-set eyes speaks of one who has known both great sorrow and great spiritual strength. Though other parts of the body are highlighted, the light falls most forcefully on the face, drawing us to it again and again, and making us behold its strength and spirituality.

* Based on information in the *Bridgman Art Library of Great Artists*, "Fra Bartolommeo," by Leader Scott.

ST. PETER—*BARTOLOMMEO*

ST. MATTHEW
Guido Reni

MATTHEW was one of the twelve disciples chosen by Jesus during His earthly ministry. He was also known as Levi (Mark 2:14, Luke 5:29). Eastern Christians hold that Matthew and Zacchaeus were the same (Luke 19:2); Zacchaeus also was a Galilean, a publican, and a tax-collector at Capernaum and later at Jericho. Matthew's Gospel was written primarily to convince the Jews that Jesus was the Messiah, the Christ, whose coming was prophesied in the Old Testament.

George M. Lamsa says, in *Gospel Light*: "Authorship in the East is understood differently than in western lands. A book written about the preaching of Matthew or a compilation of Matthew's writings would be known as the Book of Matthew. This is because the copyist does not consider himself an author of the material he writes or compiles. . . . There is no doubt that one of the apostles wrote the material which is the basis of all the gospels, and that Matthew was the writer."

The picture on p. 98 by Guido Reni shows Matthew sitting near a table as if in the act of writing. His hair is white and his hands are the hands of an old man. By his side is one of the younger "followers of the Christian way," looking intently into Matthew's face as if asking for information about Jesus' earthly life. This may have been John Mark, the scribe who later wrote the Book of Mark, believed by many to have been really the Gospel of Peter. Mark is known to have traveled much with Peter during his missionary journeys.

John Mark was the son of Mary of Jerusalem. She was one of the first converts in that city, and after the Crucifixion the apostles and other early converts met at her house (Acts 12:12). Tradition says that Mark was the young man who fled, leaving his robe behind, when Jesus was arrested (Mark 14:51); some also believe that he was the other disciple who was with Peter when he followed Jesus to the courtyard of the high priest (John 18:15).

We know that Mark spent some time in Cyprus and was later with Peter in the Persian Empire. Peter refers to him as "my son" in his first Epistle, where he says: "The chosen church at Babylon and my son Mark salute you" (I Pet. 5:13). The Gospel of Mark is often referred to as Peter's Gospel. It is quite probable, therefore, that the young man in this painting is John Mark, and that he is inquiring of Matthew about the life and ministry of Jesus.

Guido Reni (1572-1642) is not rated among the greatest Italian artists, but his best works have great beauty, strength, and artistic feeling. His painting of St. Matthew hangs in the Schönborn Gallery in Vienna.

ST. MATTHEW—*RENI*

ST. JOHN, THE EVANGELIST
Carlo Dolci

CARLO DOLCI was born in Florence, Italy, in 1616 and died there in 1686. While not ranking among the greatest painters of his day, many of his paintings of religious subjects, for which he was chiefly known, are regarded as unusually fine.

At least two of his better paintings, "St. Agnes" and a "Madonna and Child," hang in the Palazzo Corsini in Rome. This palace, built in the fifteenth century, was at various times the residence of Cardinal di San Giorgio; of Michelangelo, as a guest of the Cardinal; of Erasmus; and of Queen Christine of Sweden, who died there in 1689. It was purchased by the Italian government in 1884 and has been the *Galleria Nazionale* since 1895.

Another "Madonna and Child" by Dolci hangs in the Borghese Gallery in Rome, and is thought by many to be his finest work on this subject.

His portrayals of the disciples of Jesus are considered to be among his best work. He was noted for the spiritualized quality of his faces, an aspect particularly true of his painting, "St. John, the Evangelist" (p. 100), where John seems to be listening to the voice of inspiration coming to him from the heavens.

With the exception of Paul, John is credited with having given us more of the New Testament than any other follower among the apostolic group, being the author not only of the Gospel which bears his name but of three brief Epistles and the Book of Revelation. John is supposed to have outlived all the other apostles.

This remarkably beautiful painting of St. John the Evangelist hangs in the Pitti Palace in Florence, where many of the greatest masterpieces of art find their permanent home.

For a painting of St. John by the Macedonian artist Manuel Panselenos, done in the Byzantine style, see "St. John and St. Prochorus," p. 206.

✛

THE CRUCIFIXION OF ST. PETER
Michelangelo Buonarroti

MICHELANGELO, said by Delacroix to be "the fountainhead from which all the great painters since have drunk," was born in Caprese, Italy, in 1475 and died in 1564. He was apprenticed at an early age to Ghirlandajo, who was at the time the foremost painter in Florence, and assisted him until he was a better draftsman than his teacher. There in his master's collection of antique sculptures, Michelangelo found his life's calling.

Albert Edward Bailey says: "In the learned society of the Medici court

ST. JOHN, THE EVANGELIST—*DOLCI*

in Florence, and in the fiery preaching of Savonarola he found his inspiration. After Lorenzo de Medici's death and the expulsion of the family from Florence, Michelangelo went to Rome in 1496, where he carved his famous 'Pieta.' Then he returned to Florence, where he carved his world-famous statue of David. Pope Julius called him to Rome in 1505 and ordered him to execute a mausoleum and rebuild St. Peter's Church on a scale grand enough to contain it. These two gigantic tasks, absolutely suited to Michelangelo's genius, were destined, the one never to be completed, and the other to be performed largely by other hands. . . . In 1508 Julius set him to work upon the ceiling of the Sistine Chapel in spite of the artist's protests that he was a sculptor. The result was a stupendous product of his genius, the whole vast design with its 343 major figures conceived and executed by Michelangelo almost single-handed in four years."*

In 1520 he began work on the Medici Chapel of San Lorenzo in Florence, which occupied his time for another fourteen years, but which was never completed. By then he was fifty-nine years of age, and had already outlived Raphael, da Vinci, del Sarto, and Correggio, all artists of his time. Yet he was destined to live thirty years more, long enough to see the extinction of Florence as the art center of the world, the humiliation of his country at the hands of Spain, and the establishment of the Inquisition. With the election of Pope Paul III he was commanded to execute "The Last Judgment" for the Sistine Chapel, which occupied him from 1534 to 1542. His last great work was the erection of the present St. Peter's dome in Rome.

His painting of St. Peter's crucifixion (p. 102) hangs in the Vatican Palace in Rome. Tradition indicates that St. Peter was martyred in A.D. 67. His giant body, in Michelangelo's painting, has already been nailed to a wooden cross, which is being lifted to its upright position in the hole prepared to receive it. Around him are the soldiers and workmen of Nero's brutal Empire. At the right is a group of his frightened and heartbroken friends, helpless to interfere with the decision of the Emperor.

The sagging body of St. Peter on the cross shows the strength of all of Michelangelo's paintings. Peter's alertness, even in his agony, is characteristic of his quick, impulsive nature.

> Only this shall our hearts recall—
> Not that bitter dawn and cock,
> But the love which wrought, in spite of fear,
> Peter, the Rock!**

* From *The Gospel in Art*, p. 458. Used by permission of Pilgrim Press.
** "Of Peter," from *With All Thy Heart* by Leslie Savage Clark, p. 61. Copyright 1957 by Broadman Press. Used by permission of the author and the publisher.

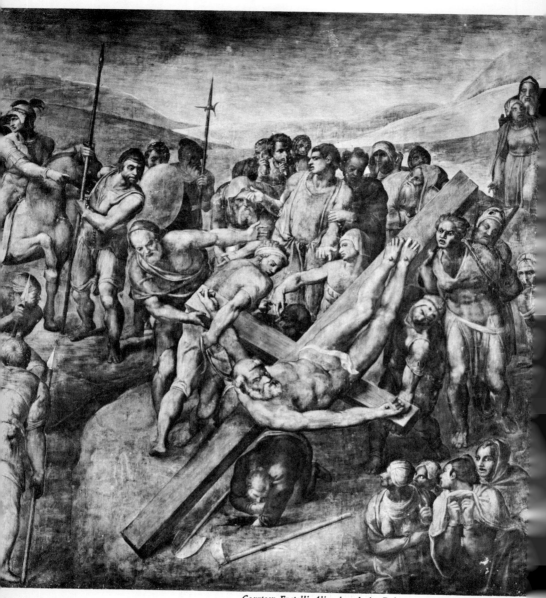

THE CRUCIFIXION OF ST. PETER—*MICHELANGELO*

RELIGION

Religion's all or nothing; it's no mere smile
O' contentment, sigh of aspiration, sir—
No quality o' the finelier-tempered clay
Like its whiteness or its lightness; rather, stuff
O' very stuff, life of life, and self of self.

—*Robert Browning*

THE CHURCH WITHIN

Who builds a church within his heart
And takes it with him everywhere,
Is holier far than he whose Church
Is but a one-day house of prayer.

—*A. L. Alexander*

THE VOICE OF GOD

I sought to hear the voice of God
And climbed the topmost steeple.
But God declared: "Go down again,
I dwell among the people."

—*Louis I. Neeman*

ARCHITECT

He looks too long on yesterday
Who builds a tomb;
No frantic toil on cenotaph
Can stay the doom
Of Time, no pyramid hold back the hour
At man's desire—
Yet he has glimpsed Eternity
Who builds a spire.*

—*Leslie Savage Clark*

THE CHURCH

A DOOR. . . .

I am the church.
I am the door into the fold of God.

* From *With All Thy Heart*, by Leslie Savage Clark, p. 52. Copyright 1957 by Broadman Press. Used by
permission of the author and the publisher.

Through me thirsty wayfarers come into green pastures and beside the
still waters.

By me, seekers from many lands enter into the Presence of the Everlasting Truth.

Youth with high resolve find, through me, the channel of service and
of love.

I am the open portal of the Kingdom.

A SANCTUARY. . . .

I am the church.
I am sanctuary to all who are hard beset.
Peace is granted to those who are fleeing the wrath of their own con-
demnation.
Quietness of soul is my boon to the harassed in a mad and wicked
world.
Protection is my gift to the persecuted and downtrodden in the high-
ways and byways of life.
I am a wall reared against tumult.

A SCHOOL. . . .

I am the church.
I am the school of the soul.
I teach the meek and lowly in heart the ways of life eternal.
My instruction reaches out to the poor and to the rich, to the wise
and to the simple.
Lessons learned of me are as bulwarks of salvation encircling the
obedient.
I am the knowledge of the Lord.

A BULWARK. . . .

I am the church.
I am an impregnable body.
The gates of Hades shall not prevail against me.
The barbed shafts of shallow critics make no marks on my divine
bastions.
Age or custom, the contempt of familiarity, the blatant slurs of evil,
cannot change me.
I am the beloved of God.*

—*Glenn H. Asquith*

INTERCESSORS

My deepest gratitude shall be
To those, O Lord, who pray for me;
In humbleness of heart I bow
And ask Thy blessings on them now:

* From *The Baptist Leader* (December 1941). Used by permission of the author and The American
Baptist Convention.

Bring strength to them in hours of trial;
Grant that there shall be no denial
Of faith in Thee, but greater still
Thy power in them to live Thy will;

God, give these chosen ones of Thine
Thy gracious peace, Thy love divine
Until they live—and yet—not they
But Christ in them; Lord, this I pray.*

—*Clarice White Luck*

AN ANGEL UNAWARES

If after kirk ye bide a wee,
There's some would like to speak to ye;
If after kirk ye rise and flee;
We'll all seem cold and stiff to ye.
There's one that's in the seat wi' ye,
Is stranger here than you, may be;
All here has got their fears and cares—
Add you your soul unto our prayers;
Be you our angel unawares.

—*Author Unknown*

A PRAYER FOR OUR NEW CHURCH

O Master Architect who planned the world,
    Who drew the vaulted arches of the sky,
Help us to plan a temple worthy of Thee,
    Where sacrifice of praise may rise on high.

O Master Builder of the Living Church,
    Help us to build with more than brick or stone,
May faith support, and love cement its walls,
    And welcoming doors swing wide for sad and lone.

Teach us to build a noble edifice
    Unmarred by human faults of life and creed;
Help us to build it broad and large enough
    To satisfy the cries of human need!**

—*Ralph T. Nordlund*

* From *Alabama Christian Advocate* (August 1952). Used by permission of the author and the publisher.
** From *The Christian Herald* (August 1955). Used by permission of the author and the publisher.

BLESS THIS CHURCH

Bless this church, which towers so high,
Reaching through celestial sky.
Bless the door we enter through,
Bringing us so near to You.
Bless the Bible which You gave,
Showing us the higher way,
Bless each page that lies therein
Leading us away from sin.

Bless the altar standing there,
Represented by a prayer.
Help us all on bended knee
To be united, one in Thee.
Bless the windows' colored hues
Bless the sunshine filt'ring through.
Bless the minister, that he
May be ever close to Thee.

Bless this world, and may it be
At peace, O Lord, with Thee.*

—*Mary Ruth Crawford*

✣

SIMON, WHO WAS CALLED PETER

Kahlil Gibran

I WAS on the shore of the Lake of Galilee when I first beheld Jesus my Lord and my Master. My brother Andrew was with me and we were casting our net into the waters. The waves were rough and high and we caught but few fish. And our hearts were heavy.

Suddenly Jesus stood near us, as if He had taken form that very moment, for we had not seen Him approaching. He called us by our names, and He said, "If you will follow me I will lead you to an inlet where the fish are swarming." And as I looked at His face the net fell from my hands, for a flame kindled within me and I recognized Him.

Then my brother Andrew spoke and said, "We know all the inlets upon these shores, and we know also that on a windy day like this the fish seek a depth beyond our nets."

And Jesus answered, "Follow me to the shore of a greater sea. I shall make you fishers of men. And your net shall never be empty." And we abandoned our boat and our net and followed Him.

* These words were written to be sung to the tune "Bless This House," by May H. Blake.

I myself was drawn by a power, viewless, that walked beside His person. I walked near Him, breathless and full of wonder, and my brother Andrew was behind us, bewildered and amazed.

And as we walked on the sand I made bold and said to Him, "Sir, I and my brother will follow your footsteps, and where you go we too will go. But if it please you to come to our house this night, we shall be graced by your visit. Our house is not large and our ceiling not high, and you will sit at but a frugal meal. Yet if you will abide in our hovel it will be to us a palace. And would you break bread with us, we in your presence were to be envied by the princes of the land."

And He said, "Yes, I will be your guest this night."

I rejoiced in my heart, and we walked behind Him in silence until we reached our house. And as we stood at the threshold Jesus said, "Peace be to this house, and to those who dwell in it." Then He entered and we followed Him.

My wife and my wife's mother and my daughter stood before Him and they worshipped Him; then they knelt before Him and kissed the hem of His sleeve. They were astonished that He, the chosen and well beloved, had come to be our guest; for they had already seen Him by the River Jordan when John the Baptist had proclaimed Him before the people. And straightway my wife and my wife's mother began to prepare the supper.

My brother Andrew was a shy man, but his faith in Jesus was deeper than my faith. And my daughter, who was then but twelve years old, stood by Him and held His garment as if she were in fear He would leave us and go out again into the night. She clung to Him like a lost sheep that has found its shepherd.

Then we sat at the board, and He broke the bread and poured the wine; and He turned to us saying, "My friends, grace me now in sharing this food with me, even as the Father has graced us in giving it unto us."

These words He said ere He touched a morsel, for He wished to follow an ancient custom that the honored guest becomes the host. And as we sat with Him around the board we felt as if we were sitting at the feast of the great King.

When He left the board we followed Him and sat about Him in the vine-arbor. And He spoke to us and we listened, and our hearts fluttered within us like birds.

He spoke of the second birth of man, and of the opening of the gates of the heavens; and of angels descending and bringing peace and good cheer to all men, and of angels ascending to the throne bearing the longings of men to the Lord God.

Then He looked into my eyes and gazed into the depths of my heart. And He said, "I have chosen you and your brother, and you must needs come with me. You have labored and you have been heavy-laden. Now I shall give you rest. Take up my yoke and learn of me, for in my heart is peace, and your soul shall find abundance and a homecoming."

I said to Him, "Master, we will follow you to the ends of the earth. And if our burden were as heavy as the mountain we would bear it with you in gladness. And should we fall by the wayside we shall know that we have fallen on the way to heaven, and we shall be satisfied."

And my brother Andrew spoke and said, "Master, we would be threads between your hands and your loom. Weave us into the cloth if you will, for we would be in the raiment of the Most High."

And my wife raised her face, and she spoke with joy, and she said, "Blessed are you who come in the name of the Lord. Blessed is the womb that carried you, and the breast that gave you milk."

And the mother of my wife, who sat at the threshold, said not a word. She only wept in silence and her shawl was wet with her tears. Then Jesus walked over to her and said to her, "You are the mother of all these. You weep for joy, and I will keep your tears in my memory."

And now the old moon rose above the horizon. And Jesus gazed upon it for a moment, and then He turned to us and said, "It is late. Seek your beds, and may God visit your repose. I will be here in this arbor until dawn. I have cast my net this day and I have caught two men; I am satisfied, and now I bid you good-night."

Then my wife's mother said, "But we have laid your bed in the house, I pray you enter and rest."

And He answered her saying, "Suffer me to lie this night under the canopy of the grapes and the stars."

And she made haste and brought out the mattress and the pillows and the coverings. And He smiled on her and He said, "Behold, I shall lie down upon a bed twice made." Then we left Him and entered into the house, and my daughter was the last one to enter. And her eyes were upon Him until I had closed the door.

Thus for the first time I knew my Lord and Master. And though it was many years ago, it still seems but of today.*

✚

VIGNETTES OF THE APOSTLES OF THE EARLY CHURCH
Cynthia Pearl Maus

SCHOLARS generally agree that the Christian religion began in Palestine as a sect or group known as "followers of the way." The early leaders of the infant church were known as "apostles," which literally means "those who are sent." Originally there were twelve of these men, corresponding to the *twelve tribes* of Israel. Many believe that their appointment by Jesus implied that His mission was to the entire Jewish nation at a time when there were more Jews living outside Palestine than within its borders. The ten northern tribes had become the "lost tribes" before the advent of Jesus, and never returned from their Babylonian captivity.

The issue of missionary work among the Gentiles came later, and with its inception created no little tension within the early Church of Christ in Palestine. The conservative Jewish converts insisted that in order to become Christians, Gentiles must first be converted to Judaism, while the more progressive favored the admission of Gentiles directly into the Church (Acts 15:1-33).

The names of the apostles are given in four different lists in the New Testament: in Mark 3:14-19, in Matthew 10:2-4, in Luke 6:13-16, and in Acts 1:13, 26. Their names nearly always appear in this order: Simon (called Peter), James and John, brothers, Andrew (Simon Peter's brother), Philip, Bartholomew (also called Nathaniel), Matthew, Thomas, Jacob (or James "the Less," son of Alphaeus), Thaddaeus, Simon "the Canaanite" (or Zealot), and Judas Iscariot, whose place was later taken by Matthias. We know that Peter had a wife, and it is probable that all or most of the apostles were married.

The work of the apostles is described in the earliest gospel, Mark: they were to become followers of Jesus and to be sent out to proclaim the gospel message; they were to possess "power" (authority) to heal sickness and to cast out demons. Jesus Himself gave them the title of apostles.

The subsequent activities of many of the apostles do not seem to have been recorded, although legends have supplied us with some information. This need not come as a surprise, however, when we remember that much of the New Testament, like the Old Testament, was handed down orally for a generation or more before it found permanency in written form. No contemporary biographies, in a modern sense, were written in Hebrew, Greek, or Latin.

After his miraculous conversion on the road to Damascus Paul was recognized as an apostle, but he was not one of the original twelve.

The following brief sketches of the apostles are based on *Christian Martyrs of the World* by John Foxe.

Peter, whose name always stands first in any list of the apostles, was the first to declare his faith in Jesus as the "Christ, the Son of the Living God." He was the first *man* to see the risen Christ on that first Easter morn (Mary Magdalene had already come to the disciples with the glad news that she had seen Jesus alive in the Garden near His tomb).

It was in answer to Peter's affirmation, "Thou art the Christ, the Son of the Living God," that Jesus Himself said: "Thou art Peter, and upon this rock I will build my church; and the gates of hell shall not prevail against it" (Matt. 16:16, 18).

Peter was born in Bethsaida, in Galilee. He was the son of Jona and was, like him, a fisherman. While he denied his Lord on at least three occasions, he was forgiven, and lived to become one of the great personalities of the early Church. Tradition indicates that after performing many miracles and being greatly persecuted at the hands of Palestinian Jews, Peter went to Rome, where the apostle Paul also was.

In the year 64 Nero, the emperor, caused the city of Rome to be set on fire, and then accused the Christians of having kindled the flames which destroyed most of it. He then ordered hundreds of Christians to be killed. The emperor was particularly angry at the apostles because they had converted to Christianity some of the members of his household, so he cast Peter and Paul into prison. After nine months Peter was brought out, scourged, and crucified with his head downward, a painful posture he himself chose because he did not think he was worthy to suffer in the same manner as his Lord. The basilica of St. Peter's Cathedral in Rome (see photograph on p. 251) is supposed to have been erected on the spot where Peter was crucified.

Philip also was born in Bethsaida in Galilee. He was a persuasive interpreter of the Old Testament, and was sometimes called Philip the Evangelist. He was sent on important missions into heathen countries, being deputed to preach in parts of Asia, where he labored diligently. He then went to Phrygia and at Hierapolis found the inhabitants idolizing a great serpent. Philip converted many of them to Christianity, and destroyed the serpent. This so enraged the rulers and priests, who gained much money by the superstitions of the people, that they put him in prison, where he was cruelly scourged and then crucified. His friend Bartholomew succeeded in taking down the body and burying it, but for this he came very near suffering the same fate. Philip's martyrdom took place eight years after that of James, in the year A.D. 52.

James and *John* were the sons of Zebedee, who lived in Capernaum, a city on the Lake of Galilee, not far from Bethsaida. These two brothers cheerfully obeyed the summons to become disciples of Jesus, and leaving their father, followed the Lord. Jesus called them Boanerges, or the Sons of Thunder, on account of their vigorous minds and impetuous tempers. They wanted to bring down fire upon a Samaritan village that had refused hospitality to the Master. Through their mother's intervention they also tried to secure a promise that they should sit on the right and left hand of Christ in His Messianic glory.

James was the first of the apostles to meet a martyr's death. Herod Agrippa, when he was made governor of Judea by the Roman emperor, began persecuting the Christians, and singled out James as an object of his vengeance. When the apostle was led out to die, a man who had brought false accusations against him walked with him to the place of execution. He had doubtless expected to see James looking pale and frightened, but instead he was bright and joyous, like a conqueror who had won a great battle. The false witness became convinced by this that the Saviour in whom the prisoner believed must be the true God. The man himself was thus converted to Christianity and was condemned to die with James. Both were beheaded on the same day, and with the same sword, in the year of our Lord 44.

Bartholomew was the same person as the Nathaniel mentioned in the

Gospel of John. This apostle and martyr preached in several countries, performed many miracles, and healed various diseases. One account tells of his visit to India. He translated Matthew's Gospel into the languages of several heathen nations. The idolaters finally slew him, some say with the sword; others say that he was beaten to death with clubs.

Thomas, according to the Gospel of John, was often dubbed the "doubting Thomas" because he demanded tangible proof of the Resurrection of our Lord. Jesus invited him to put his hands into the wounds He had received and become a man of faith instead of doubt. As soon as Thomas touched the body of his Lord, he exclaimed, "My Lord and my God." There has always been comfort for those living in later generations in the reply of the Master: "Blessed are those who have not seen and yet believe." Thomas seems to have been a carpenter and builder, like Jesus. He preached in Parthia and India, and in India today there are Christians who call themselves "Christians of St. Thomas." Both their hymns and liturgy are in Syriac. After converting many to Christ, Thomas aroused the anger of the pagan priests, and was thrust through with a spear.

Matthew was born at Nazareth, in Galilee, but lived chiefly at Capernaum, where he was collector of tribute. On being called as a disciple, he at once left everything to follow Christ. A second-century Greek writer by the name of Papias (A.D. 135) gives Matthew credit for collecting and preserving in Hebrew the Old Testament prophecies concerning the coming of the Messiah.

After the Ascension of his Master, Matthew continued preaching the gospel in Judea for nine years. When about to leave Judea, in order to go and preach among the Gentiles, he wrote his Gospel in Hebrew for the use of the Jewish people to whom he had preached. It was afterward translated into Greek by James (the Less). Tradition indicates that he then went to Ethiopia, ordained preachers, established churches, and made many converts. He later went to Parthia, where he is said to have met death by the sword about the year A.D. 60.

Simon the Zealot is called "Simon, the Canaanite" in the King James Bible. Very little is known about him. Some have thought that he came from Cana, the village near Nazareth mentioned in the Gospel of John. His zeal caused him to be distinguished by the name Zelotes. According to some legends, he was a missionary to Babylon and the Black Sea region, while others indicate that he preached in Mauritania and other parts of Africa, and even in Britain, where he made many converts. It is believed he was crucified by pagans in the year A.D. 74.

Thaddaeus, brother of James, is another mysterious figure among the twelve apostles. According to Eusebius in his *Church History,* the King of Edessa (in Mesopotamia) is supposed to have written a letter to Jesus asking him to send a teacher if He Himself could not come. Jesus is supposed to have sent Thaddaeus there to preach and to lay the foundation for the important Christian community which existed there in the time of Eusebius. Legends tell of his activities in Armenia, Persia, and Mesopotamia, where he wrought many miracles and made many converts, stirring up the resentment of the people in power, who crucified him in the year A.D. 72.

Andrew was the brother of Peter. He preached the gospel to many Asiatic nations. At Patrae, in Greece, the governor of the country threatened him with death for preaching against the idols, but Andrew fearlessly continued to tell the people about Christ. He was therefore sentenced to be crucified on a cross made of two pieces of wood of equal length, one end of each piece being fixed in the ground. He was fastened to it, not with nails, but with cords, so that death might come more slowly. An ancient writer tells of the apostle's sublime courage: "When Andrew saw the cross prepared, he neither changed countenance nor color, as the weakness of mortal man is wont to do; neither did his blood shrink; neither did he fail in his speech; . . . He said, 'O cross, most welcome, and oft-looked-for; with a willing mind, joyfully and desirously, I come to thee, being the scholar of Him who did hang on a tree; because I have always been thy lover, and have longed to embrace thee!'"

Andrew hung upon the cross three whole days, suffering dreadful pain, but continuing to tell the people around him of the love of Jesus Christ. The people began to believe his words, and asked the governor to let him be taken down from the cross. At last he ordered the ropes to be cut, but when the last cord was severed, the body of the apostle fell to the ground dead. (For a painting of Andrew, see p. 150.)

James the Less was the son of Alphaeus, and was so called to distinguish him from the apostle James, brother of John, sometimes called "the Great." After the Lord's Ascension he was elected bishop of Jerusalem. He wrote his general epistle to all Christians in order to suppress a dangerous error then being circulated, which was "that a faith in Christ was alone sufficient for salvation, without good works." The Jews of Jerusalem were at this time greatly enraged against the Christians, and incited a mob to attack him and stone him to death.

Judas Iscariot, the disciple who betrayed Jesus, has been portrayed by only a few great artists, and then usually in combination with other disciples, as in da Vinci's "The Last Supper." Many artists shared the viewpoint that Judas Iscariot was an unworthy subject. (For Andrea del Sarto's painting of Judas, see p. 43).

Many students of history believe that Judas expected Jesus to perform a miracle and escape His accusers, and that when he discovered the Master steadfastly refused to use His miraculous powers to save Himself, he went out and hanged himself. Later his place among the twelve apostles was filled by the remaining casting lots. The choice fell on a man named *Matthias,* who ever afterward was numbered among the apostles. Matthias is believed to have been martyred at Jerusalem, being first stoned and then beheaded.

Paul was a Jew of the tribe of Benjamin. Born at Tarsus in Cilicia, he was originally called Saul. From his father he inherited the rights of Roman citizenship, probably earned by some ancestor through services rendered the Roman state. Paul was at first a great enemy of the Christians, being present at the stoning of Stephen. After Stephen's death, while Paul was on his way to Damascus, the glory of the Lord shone suddenly upon him, he was struck to the earth, and was made blind for three days. After his recovery he was converted and became an apostle.

After his conversion Paul went to Jerusalem, where he saw Peter, James, and John. Later he went forth with Barnabas to preach. At Iconium, the two came near being stoned to death by the enraged Jews, whereupon they fled to Lycaonia. At Lystra Paul was stoned, dragged from the city, and left for dead. He recovered, however, and escaped to Derbe. At Philippi, Paul and Silas were imprisoned and whipped, and both were again abused at Thessalonica.

Being later taken to Jerusalem, Paul was sent to Caesarea, but appealed to Caesar in Rome. Here he remained a prisoner at large for two years; after his release, he visited the churches in Greece and Rome, and preached in Gaul and Spain. Returning to Rome, he was again imprisoned for nine months with Peter. By Nero's order he was beheaded with a sword.

In Christian art Paul is always shown with the sword in his right hand (see Bartolommeo's painting, p. 70), symbolic not only of the "sword of the spirit" but also of the sacrificial cost of his discipleship.*

✛

STEPHEN, THE FIRST CHRISTIAN MARTYR
John Foxe

THE first Christian martyrs were those who suffered under the persecution of the Romans in the early ages of the Church. For two hundred and forty years, or from the year 64 after Christ, to the time of the emperor Constantine (A.D. 306) the cruel punishments inflicted upon Christians by their heathen enemies are described by ancient historians as being as various and horrible as the mind of man could invent.

"Some," we are told, "were slain with the sword; some burned with fire; some scourged with whips; some stabbed with forks of hot iron; some fastened to the cross or gibbet; some drowned in the sea; some stoned to death; some killed with cold; some starved with hunger; some, with their hands cut off and otherwise disabled, were left naked to the open shame of the world. Yet, notwithstanding the sharpness of their torments, such was the power of the Lord in His saints—that they generally remained faithful to the end."

In reality, Christ, Himself, was the first Christian martyr. He gave up His home in paradise, endured a life of hardship upon earth, and at last suffered a lingering death upon the cross that mankind might be saved from eternal

* Based on information in *Christian Martyrs of the World* by John Foxe, pp. 26-35. Published by Moody Press. Used by permission of the publisher.

punishment for their sins. After His death and Resurrection, His followers endured martyr's deaths for His sake.

Lonely and sorrowful the disciples must have been when the Lord was no longer with them in human form. But though they could no longer see Him with the eyes of the flesh, or hear His voice, they knew that He looked down from heaven upon them and that He had promised to be with them to the end of the world. Thus the apostles were helped and guided in the work He had told them to do—which was to go out into all parts of the world and tell the people of every land that the Saviour of mankind had come, and had died upon the cross that they might be saved.

After the death of Jesus, there were but eleven apostles, for Judas Iscariot, who had betrayed Christ, was no longer with them. Therefore, the apostles cast lots, and Matthias was chosen, so the number of the apostles was twelve again. Soon they separated to carry on the work of converting all the world to the religion of Christ.

The New Testament does not tell us how long the apostles and evangelists (disciples who wrote the Gospels) lived, nor how many of them died. With the exception of Stephen, who was chosen to be a deacon by the apostles, and who was stoned to death; and James, the apostle who was slain by Herod, we do not know the exact fate of any of the others. But ancient writers and historians, who wrote in the early centuries after Christ the traditions and accounts they heard concerning these holy men, indicate that nearly all of them died martyr's deaths, after living lives of toil and hardship while preaching the gospel of Christ to the heathen world.

St. Stephen is sometimes called the first Christian martyr. From the Acts of the Apostles in the New Testament we know that he was the first Christian man to be put to death for his faith in Christ. Thus he followed next to his Master in the path that leads to glory.

Because of the constantly increasing number of disciples, many of whom were poor people, complaints began to be made that some were neglected in the daily almsgiving. Therefore the apostles said, "It is not right that we should cease preaching to serve tables." So Stephen was chosen from among the Lord's disciples, with six others, to be a deacon. He helped in giving alms to the poor and also preached to the people. He was such a good and holy man that he was permitted to work miracles of healing the sick and converting unbelievers. He preached to the Jews in words so full of power and conviction that they could not answer nor contradict him. The principal persons belonging to the Jewish synagogues entered into debate with him, but the soundness of his doctrine and the strength of his reasoning overcame them all. This so angered them that they paid false witnesses to accuse him of blaspheming God and Moses.

On being taken before the council, he made a noble defense. This so much more enraged his judges that they resolved to condemn him to death. At this instant Stephen saw a vision from heaven, and in rapture he exclaimed: "Behold, I see the heavens opened, and the Son of Man standing on the right hand of God!" Then the Jews cried out against him, and having dragged him out of the city, they stoned him to death.

After the martyrdom of Stephen, there was a general persecution against all the Christians at Jerusalem. More than two thousand Christians are believed to have perished during this persecution.*

✤

THE CHURCH'S ONE FOUNDATION

ALTHOUGH this hymn was not composed until the latter part of the nineteenth century, its inspiration is as old as the Church itself, for its message affirms Peter's conviction: "Thou art the Christ, the Son of the living God."

It was in answer to this affirmation that Jesus said: "Upon this rock I will build my church"; and it is about this rocklike affirmation and its enduring character that the poet, Samuel J. Stone (1839-1900), sings in "The Church's One Foundation," written in 1866. This hymn may be sung to one of two tunes: "Aurelia" (the melody given in the music score on p. 116), composed by Samuel S. Wesley in 1864, or "Descant," composed by William Lester Bates in 1930.

This hymn provides one of the finest of the Church's processional and recessional marches. The tramping feet of millions of followers of Christ, who have found in Him the abundant life, can be heard in this great hymn of challenge and dedication. These words of courage and high resolve strengthen one's faith, provide a vision of the great task to which all Christians have been called as helpers, and promise the glowing joy of comradeship with Jesus Christ in helping to complete on earth the Kingdom of God.

It should be sung in moderate tempo and with great fervor and dignity.

A CHRISTMAS HYMN FOR PEACE

THIS poem, written by Earl Marlatt in 1950, will make a great spiritual contribution to your Christmas music. It is sung to the tune "Aurelia," the same tune to which "The Church's One Foundation" is usually sung. The music score appears on p. 116.

Too long, O Lord, Thy people
Have trusted Baal and Mars,
Have offered sons to idols
Beneath the silent stars;
Forgetful that the angels
Who sang the Saviour's birth
Said with the God Who sent them,
"Let there be light on earth."

It shone above a manger
Where humble folk and wise
Found journey's end a radiance
Within a brother's eyes;
And when the darkness deepened
Above the Holy Hill
That Spirit-Voice still counseled
Forgiveness and good-will.

* Abridged from *Christian Martyrs of the World* by John Foxe. Published by Moody Press. Used by permission of the publisher.

The Church's One Foundation

AURELIA. 7. 6. 7. 6. D.

SAMUEL J. STONE, 1839–1900
In moderate time, with dignity

SAMUEL S. WESLEY, 1810–1876

1. The Church's one foun - da - tion Is Je - sus Christ her Lord;
2. E - lect from ev - ery na - tion, Yet one o'er all the earth,
3. 'Mid toil and trib - u - la - tion, And tu - mult of her war,
4. Yet she on earth hath un - ion With God the Three in One,

She is His new cre - a - tion By wa - ter and the word:
Her char - ter of sal - va - tion, One Lord, one faith, one birth;
She waits the con - sum - ma - tion Of peace for ev - er - more;
And mys - tic sweet com - mun - ion With those whose rest is won:

From heaven He came and sought her To be His ho - ly bride;
One ho - ly Name she bless - es, Par - takes one ho - ly food,
Till, with the vi - sion glo - rious, Her long - ing eyes are blest,
O hap - py ones and ho - ly! Lord, give us grace that we,

With His own blood He bought her, And for her life He died.
And to one hope she press - es, With ev - ery grace en - dued.
And the great Church vic - to - rious Shall be the Church at rest.
Like them, the meek and low - ly, On high may dwell with Thee. A - MEN.

O let us hear the singing
Of angel choirs again,
Thy holy spirit bringing
New life and hope to men,
Till peace with wings of healing,
Thy covenantal dove,
Shall make earth's jangled music
A litany of Love. Amen.*

—*Earl Marlatt*

✣

HERE, O MY LORD, I SEE THEE FACE TO FACE

THE REVEREND Horatius Bonar, who gave us this magnificent communion hymn, "Here, O My Lord, I See Thee Face to Face," was one of the greatest of the Scottish hymn writers of the past century. He was descended from a long line of ministers, studied at the University of Edinburgh, and was ordained in 1858 as pastor at Kelso, near the English border. When the division came in the Established Church in 1843, he entered the Free Church ministry.

After twenty-seven years as vicar at Kelso, he was persuaded to take over the large church known as Chalmers Memorial in Edinburgh, built in honor of the leader of the Free Church Movement. He continued to hold this position until his death in 1889.

Throughout his long life, Horatius Bonar was an enthusiastic Bible student. He loved prophecy, and for twenty-five years edited the *Quarterly Journal of Prophecy,* in every issue of which he published one of his own hymns.

His vivid imagination and his flair for poetic expression gave him unusual power as a writer of hymns. Even he could not really tell the dates when many of his hymns were written. He constantly jotted down on slips of paper fragments of verse as they came to him during his travels. Often they were too spontaneous to be of high literary merit, but their vitality and freshness made them popular throughout the English-speaking world. In all he composed more than six hundred hymns, over a hundred of which are still in regular use.

About once a year Horatius Bonar visited his brother, Dr. J. J. Bonar, minister at Grenock, so that they might celebrate Communion together. His brother used to print a special leaflet for this Communion Service, and in October, 1855, Horatius supplied him with eleven stanzas of a new hymn to include in it. Only four of the stanzas of this hymn, "Here, O My Lord, I See Thee Face to Face," appear in present-day hymnals.

The first stanza of this hymn emphasizes the idea of the "real presence" of the mystical Christ, whose Spirit is always present where "two or three are gathered together in His name."

* From *Journey's End,* a 1950 Christmas folder. Used by permission of the author.

Here, O My Lord, I See Thee Face to Face

CONSOLATION. 11. 10. 11. 10.

HORATIUS BONAR, 1808–1889

FELIX MENDELSSOHN, 1809–1847

Rather slowly, with deep reverence

1. Here, O my Lord, I see thee face to face;
2. Here would I feed up - on the bread of God;
3. Too soon we rise; the sym - bols dis - ap - pear;
4. Feast aft - er feast thus comes and pass - es by;

Here would I touch and han - dle things un - seen;
Here drink with thee the roy - al wine of heav'n;
The feast, tho' not the love, is past and gone;
Yet, pass - ing, points to the glad feast a - bove—

Here grasp with firm - er hand th'e - ter - nal grace,
Here would I lay a - side each earth - ly load;
The bread and wine re - move, but thou art here—
Giv - ing sweet fore - taste of the fes - tal joy,

And all my wear - i - ness up - on thee lean.
Here taste a - fresh the calm of sin for - giv'n.
Near - er than ev - er— still my Shield and Sun.
The Lamb's great bri - dal feast of bliss and love. A - MEN.

The second stanza portrays Christ as the "bread of God" and "the wine of heaven." These are symbols of His body, broken for us, and of His blood, shed for us.

The third stanza emphasizes the continuance of the spiritual blessing after the feast has been completed; and the fourth reminds us that these recurring feasts on earth portray for us that eternal feast in heaven which the Lamb and His Bride, the Church, will celebrate (Rev. 21:1-5).

This great hymn is most often sung to a melody by Felix Mendelssohn, and should be sung slowly and with deep reverence.

CONTENTS

PART I SECTION 5

THE MISSIONARY OUTREACH OF THE APOSTOLIC CHURCH

⊹

And so were the churches established in the faith, and increased in number daily.—ACTS 16:5

⊹

PICTURES: PAGE
  Interpretation: Christ or Diana?—*Long* 121
  Picture: Christ or Diana?—*Long* 122
  Interpretation: St. Paul's Cathedral in Rome—*Poletti* 123
  Picture: St. Paul's Cathedral in Rome—*Poletti* 124
  Interpretation: The Last Prayer—*Gérôme* 125
  Picture: The Last Prayer—*Gérôme* 126

POETRY:
  People—*Marlatt* 127
  Liberty, Equality, Fraternity—*Oxenham* 127
  We Must Needs Love the Highest—*Tennyson* 128
  How the Great Guest Came—*Markham* 128
  World Wide Communion—*Clark* 130
  Your Own Version of the Gospel—*Gilbert* 130
  My Petition—*Cushman* 130
  Prayer—*Clark* 130

STORIES:
  Sealed at the Lord's Table—*Eller* 131
  By Invitation of Jesus—*Marshall* 134
  A House for God—*Asquith* 138

MUSIC:
  Interpretation: One Holy Church of God Appears—*S. Longfellow* 139
  Music: One Holy Church of God Appears—*Courteville* 140
  Interpretation: We Would Be Building—*Deitz* 140
  Music: We Would Be Building—*Sibelius* 141

CHRIST OR DIANA?

Edwin Long

EDWIN LONG was one of England's outstanding historical painters of the nineteenth century (1829-1891). He must have spent a great deal of time studying in libraries or museums, for his pictures are filled with historically accurate details.

The setting in which "Christ or Diana?" (p. 122) took place seems to have been a large hippodrome or amphitheater, crowded with hundreds of people. The presence of Roman soldiers in the foreground suggests that this was a Roman theater, perhaps the one in the city of Ephesus dedicated to Diana of the Ephesians. At the left side of the picture appears an image of Diana, the protectress of Ephesus; her head wears a crown, and her hands are outstretched to receive the offerings of her people. This statue is an exact copy of one in the Naples Museum. Acts 19:24-41 contains an account of the worship of Diana.

The group of young girls also at the left are watching anxiously their friend who must make her decision here and now as to whether or not she will worship Diana or the Christian God. Note the prosecuting attorney who is making the charge of bringing a Christian against this young girl; the high priest of the Diana cult, who is glowering at the obstinate backslider; the Roman praetor before whom the case is being tried. The young priestess is holding a little box from which each worshiper takes a pinch of salt to throw on the flame at the altar as an act of worship. From her pleading expression she seems to be saying, "Reach out your hand and take just one little pinch, I beseech you; you can still be a Christian at heart even if you do make this offering to Diana."

No doubt those who are watching can hear from the dungeons under their feet the smothered growling of hungry lions. This is no imaginary danger. Throughout the first and second centuries after Christ, the Christians in Asia Minor were periodically persecuted. From Acts 19:24-41 you will readily understand the problem which this young Christian faces as she stands with her eyes raised to heaven and her right hand outstretched toward the salt box.

With her the decision must be *now*: is it to be Christ or Diana? On the answer to that question lies her fate—a cruel death or Jesus' words, "Thou shalt have no other gods before me." Somehow as her pleading eyes look steadily upward, we seem to know what her decision will be. She, like thousands of others, will join the long list of Christians on whose martyrdom the Church of the living God is built.*

* Arranged from the Abbott Book Library of Art. Reprinted by special permission.

CHRIST OR DIANA?—LONG

ST. PAUL'S CATHEDRAL IN ROME

L. Poletti

THE basilica of St. Paul's Cathedral outside the walls of Vatican City in Rome is one of the finest buildings in that city, which is said to have contained, at one time, nearly a thousand churches. The original cathedral was founded in A.D. 386 by Emperor Valentinian II, continued by Theodosius, and finished under Honorius on the site of an earlier church built by Constantine over the tomb of St. Paul, the first Christian missionary and theologian to bring the gospel's message to pagan Rome. Until the great fire of 1823, which almost totally destroyed it, it was the finest basilica in Rome.

Immediately after the fire Leo XII began its reconstruction, the entire Christian world joining in the task. The architect was L. Poletti. The present church edifice was completed and consecrated by Pope Pius IX in 1854. The plan and dimensions are the same as those of the original structure.

The interior, which is 394 feet long and 197 feet wide, with a ceiling 75 feet high, is most imposing. The eighty gray granite columns were quarried near Baveno, Italy, on Lake Maggiore, and transported on rafts. The high altar is surrounded by a famous tabernacle which is the work of Arnolfo Di Cambio (1285). Along the friezes of the nave and aisles is a long series of mosaic portrait medallions of all the Roman Catholic popes from St. Peter to Pope Benedict XV (1922), with space remaining for perhaps a half-dozen more distinguished prelates of the Church.

The main facade of St. Paul's, fronting on the Tiber River, is decorated with modern mosaics; the reliefs on its exterior represent scenes from the Old Testament.

The triumphal arch, spared by the fire, is adorned with fifth-century mosaics representing Christ and the twenty-four elders of the Apocalypse. Above are the symbols of the four Evangelists, below the two princes of the apostles Paul and Peter pointing to the Saviour.

The mosaics in the semidome of the apse, and those of the arch above it and opposite to it, are reconstructions of a work of the time of Pope Honorius III (1225). In the center is Christ enthroned, holding in His hands an open book inscribed with the words found in Matthew 25:34: "Then shall the King say unto them on his right hand, Come, ye blessed of my Father, inherit the kingdom prepared for you from the foundation of the world."

To the spectator's right as he faces the high altar stand St. Peter and St. Andrew, to his left St. Paul and St. Luke. At the feet of Christ kneels the diminutive figure of Honorius, by whom the mosaic was dedicated. Beneath are the apostles not included in the semidome; the palm trees which separate them are symbolic of their martyrdoms. In the center is the "prepared throne" with the implements of Christ's Passion. All of the apostles bear scrolls on which the articles of the Creed appear.

The Paschal candlestick near the high altar has carvings of animals and

ST. PAUL'S CATHEDRAL IN ROME—*POLETTI*

foliage on it and scenes from the life of Christ, such as soldiers taking Christ before Caiaphas, Peter washing his hands, the Crucifixion, Resurrection, and Ascension.

At the right of the high altar stands a life-sized statue of St. Paul with a sword (symbolic of the sword of the spirit) in his right hand and a book (symbolic of the Word) in his left. At the left of the altar is a life-sized statue of St. Peter holding in one hand the keys of the kingdom.

The cloisters of St. Paul's date back to the thirteenth century. They cover almost a block of ground, forming within a restful, beautiful garden for repose, study, and meditation.

As a cathedral dedicated to the worship of the living God, St. Paul's has few rivals.

✠

THE LAST PRAYER
Jean Léon Gérôme

THE French artist Jean Léon Gérôme (1824-1904) was both a painter and a sculptor, whose interest in historical subjects led him to execute works with what was called "archaeological precision." "The Last Prayer" shows in a remarkably vivid way the persecutions common in pagan Rome during Nero's reign. It is easy to recognize the building; we know that it is used for horse-racing because of the tall monument to the left which marks the turning-point in the race. The scene which now greets our eyes, however, occurs after the races are over, when human beings are to be sacrificed to the "King of the Forest" in order to satisfy the lust of the public for new thrills.

Around the inner rim of the arena we see a number of persons fastened to wooden posts. They have been covered with pitch to give light during the barbarous climax. Some of these human torches have already been lighted, sending smoke and flames to the open sky above. Others hang suspended, awaiting the moment when the torch will be applied to them.

The small group of people huddled to the right of the arena seem to be of all ages. Most of them are kneeling in prayer, but one white-haired old man stands with his eyes lifted to heaven as he commits the souls of these innocent ones to the mercy of the God of love in whom he believes.

Up from the lion's den stalk these huge beasts of the forest, and come forward with half-starved fierceness to attack their prey. The strong tail of the first one has already begun to switch; he knows that these people are meant for him and that they are helpless to get away. The scene is so vivid that one instinctively turns his face away as the lions make their spring and these Christians meet their horrible fate on their knees.

There were about ten different periods in which the Roman authorities tried, by means of various cruel persecutions, to stamp out the Christian

THE LAST PRAYER—GÉRÔME

religion. This picture* (p. 126) portrays one such attempt, probably in the time of Nero (A.D. 65). These Christians, kneeling for their last prayer, have been collected from different church communities in Rome to make a Roman holiday after the races are over. They have been brought forth now as the crowning feature of this great spectacle.

People in every age are courageous when they give themselves, heart and soul, to some great cause. With Jesus, they, too, can pray: "Father, forgive them, for they know not what they do." Against such a faith and such a loyalty, not even the cruel and unrighteous sentence of a Nero can prevail.

✝

PEOPLE

People are strange.
I cannot understand them.

I had a sweetheart
Who seemed to love me.
I gave her roses, sweets, and gems.
I gave her all I had, my heart,
And she broke it.
I cannot forgive her.

God had a world
That should have loved Him.
He gave it beauty, light, and life.
He gave it all He had, His Son,
And it crucified Him.

People are strange,
I cannot understand them.
But God . . .
He loved them.**

—*Earl Marlatt*

LIBERTY, EQUALITY, FRATERNITY

O God, within whose sight
All men have equal right
    To worship Thee,
Break every bar that holds
Thy flock in diverse folds!
Thy Will from none withholds
    Full liberty.

Lord, set Thy Churches free
From foolish rivalry!
    Lord, set us free!
Let all past bitterness
Now and for ever cease,
And all our souls possess
    Thy charity!

Lord, set the people free!
Let all men draw to Thee
    In unity!
Thy temple courts are wide,
Therein let all abide
In peace, and side by side
Serve only Thee!

God, grant us now Thy peace!
Bid all dissensions cease!
    God, send us peace!
Peace in True Liberty,
Peace in Equality,
Peace and Fraternity,
    God, send us peace!***

—*John Oxenham*

* Reproduced by special permission from the Abbott Book Library of Art.
** From *Cathedral: A Volume of Poems* by Earl Marlatt, p. 111. Copyright 1956 by Earl Marlatt. Published by Parthenon Press. Used by permission of the author and the publisher.
*** From *Bees in Amber* by John Oxenham, p. 46. Used by permission of Miss Erica Oxenham and Methuen Co., Ltd.

WE MUST NEEDS LOVE THE HIGHEST

Ah, my God,
What might I not have made of Thy fair world,
Had I but loved Thy highest creature here?
It was my duty to have loved the highest:
It surely was my profit had I known;
It would have been my pleasure had I seen.
We needs must love the highest when we see it.*

—*Alfred Tennyson*

HOW THE GREAT GUEST CAME

Before the Cathedral in grandeur rose,
At Ingelburg where the Danube goes;
Before its forest of silver spires
Went airily up to the clouds and fires;
Before the oak had ready a beam,
While yet the arch was stone and dream—
There where the altar was later laid,
Conrad the cobbler plied his trade.

. . . .

Tall was the cobbler, and gray and thin,
And a full moon shone where the hair had been.
His eyes peered out, intent and afar,
As looking beyond the things that are.
He walked as one who is done with fear,
Knowing at last that God is near.
Only the half of him cobbled the shoes:
The rest was away for the heavenly news.
Indeed, so thin was the mystic screen
That parted the Unseen from the Seen,
You could not tell, from the cobbler's theme
If his dream were truth or his truth were dream.

It happened one day at the year's white end,
Two neighbors called on their old-time friend;
And they found the shop, so meagre and mean,
Made gay with a hundred boughs of green.
Conrad was stitching with face ashine,
But suddenly stopped as he twitched a twine:
"Old friends, good news! At dawn today,
As the cocks were scaring the night away,
The Lord appeared in a dream to me,
And said, 'I am coming your Guest to be!'
So I've been busy with feet astir,
Strewing the floor with branches of fir.

* From *Guinevere.*

The wall is washed and the shelf is shined,
And over the rafter the holly twined.
He comes today, and the table is spread
With milk and honey and wheaten bread."

His friends went home; and his face grew still
As he watched for the shadow across the sill.
He lived all the moments o'er and o'er,
When the Lord should enter the lowly door—
The knock, the call, the latch pulled up,
The lighted face, the offered cup.
He would wash the feet where the spikes had been;
He would kiss the hands where the nails went in;
And then at the last would sit with Him
And break the bread as the day grew dim.

While the cobbler mused, there passed his pane
A beggar drenched by the driving rain.
He called him in from the stony street
And gave him shoes for his bruiséd feet.
The beggar went and there came a crone,
Her face with wrinkles of sorrow sown.
A bundle of fagots bowed her back,
And she was spent with the wrench and rack.
He gave her his loaf and steadied her load
As she took her way on the weary road.
Then to his door came a little child,
Lost and afraid in the world so wild,
In the big, dark world. Catching it up,
He gave it the milk in the waiting cup,
And led it home to its mother's arms,
Out of the reach of the world's alarms.

The day went down in the crimson west
And with it the hope of the blessed Guest,
And Conrad sighed as the world turned gray:
"Why is it, Lord, that your feet delay?
Did You forget that this was the day?"
Then soft in the silence a Voice he heard:
"Lift up your heart, for I kept my word.
Three times I came to your friendly door;
Three times my shadow was on your floor.
I was the beggar with bruiséd feet;
I was the woman you gave to eat;
I was the child on the homeless street!"*

—*Edwin Markham.*

* From *The Shoes of Happiness and Other Poems,* pp. 56-60. Copyright 1915 by Edwin Markham, 1941 by Virgil Markham. Published by Doubleday & Company, Inc. 1941. Reprinted by permission of Virgil Markham.

WORLD WIDE COMMUNION

Now alien tongues repeat Thy name
Half the world away;
And dark hands lift the cup, the bread
This holy day.

Cleanse Thou our hearts from pride of race
These hours we kneel as one,
Enfold us in Thy boundless love,
O Father—Son!*

—*Leslie Savage Clark*

YOUR OWN VERSION OF THE GOSPEL

You are writing a Gospel,
  A chapter each day,
By deeds that you do
  By words that you say.

Men read what you write,
  Whether faithless or true;
Say, what is the Gospel
  According to you?**

—*Paul Gilbert*

MY PETITION

I do not ask
That men may sound my praises
  Or headlines spread my name abroad
I only pray that as I voice the message
  Hearts may find God!**

—*Ralph Spaulding Cushman*

PRAYER

Beyond the golden minaret
The sunbeams blaze,
The muezzin sounds the ancient call
To prayer and praise.

Beside a church with slender spire
My fathers dwell
And kneel in worship there at sound
Of Sabbath bell.

Moslem and Christian, lift to God
And Allah prayer;
Brothers in need who find, alike
His Presence there!**

—*Leslie Savage Clark*

* From *With All Thy Heart* by Leslie Savage Clark. Copyright 1957 by Broadman Press. Used by permission of the author and the publisher.
** Used by permission of the author.

SEALED AT THE LORD'S TABLE
Vernard M. Eller

THE charter of the Church was originally signed and sealed and is continually reviewed and renewed at the Table of the Lord. This, in a nutshell, is what I want to say in the time that is allotted to me: that in the Eucharist we are given a definite concept of the Church.

Although no one would deny that the Eucharist has *become* central in the life of the Church, many would take exception to the proposition that the Church was chartered in the upper room, for, they would maintain, it is Pentecost that marks the birth of the Church. Now I will be happy to grant this point—if, in turn, I may be granted the privilege of figuring according to the Oriental rather than the Western system. In at least some Asiatic countries a person's age is counted not from his birthday but from the time of his conception; and since the Church is a native of the East, the principle ought to apply. The Church was *born* on Pentecost, but it had a very real existence prior to that time.

Laying aside all the fine questions of ecclesiological chronology, it is certain that the Eucharist very early came to be considered as symbolic of the Church itself, the dramatic epitome of the Church's very ground and being, its charter in a very real sense. Paul, for example, in expounding the Eucharistic formulas, calls the bread "the body of Christ," but uses that phrase in a double sense—first, with obvious reference to the physical body of our Lord which was broken on the cross, but secondly, in reference to the Church itself, which in other connections he often calls "the body of Christ." He says: "The bread which we break, is it not a participation in the body of Christ? Because there is one loaf, we who are many are one body, for we all partake of the same loaf" (I Cor. 10:16-17, RSV). Also, the Didache, one of the oldest Christian documents outside the New Testament, gives us a prayer used by the early Church in blessing the bread of the Eucharist. Here again it is made plain that the symbol refers to the Church itself: "As this broken bread was scattered upon the mountains [that is, when growing as wheat], but was brought together and became one, so let thy Church be gathered together from the ends of the earth into thy kingdom" (Didache 9:4). Thus, it is altogether accurate and appropriate to see the Eucharist as a symbol of the Church, a dramatization of its constitution and commission.

As we examine the sacraments with this symbolism in mind, we find that three different aspects, or dimensions, of the Church's being are commemorated. These three correspond to the three divisions of time itself—the past, the present, and the future. The Church, then, is discovered to be a three-dimensional object—though existing in the three dimensions of time rather than of space.

The first dimension commemorated in the Eucharist is the Church's orientation toward the past. In Luke, the formulas read: "This is my body which is given for you. This cup which is poured out for you is the new covenant in my blood" (22:19-20, RSV). Now the words "given" and "poured out" are in the past tense, and the intent of the symbolism is clear. The emblems have direct reference to the incarnation of Christ and, more particularly, to the great act of redemption that consummated that historical life. The Eucharist, obviously, is a celebration of the Crucifixion, which is itself an historical event.

And the Church today, almost two thousand years later, must still keep this event of the past at the focus of its attention. The core around which the entire Christian faith is organized is a cross that is rooted firmly in the historical past, and the Church *must* keep its "backward orientation" ever clear and distinct and central. This we do: first, by accepting that event as efficacious for our own sin and shortcomings; second, by commemorating the event through the re-enactment of the communion service; and third, by witnessing to the event, not only from the pulpit but by each and every means available to each and every member of the Church—the Church which is mindful of its orientation toward the past.

The second dimension of the Church is its orientation to the present. The Christ who instituted the Eucharist is the Lord who is living and personally present with His Church today. Now of course Christ was there in the flesh that night in the upper room, but the Eucharist symbolizes His *continuing* presence in an even more explicit way. Are you aware of the Biblical correlation between the Lord's Supper and the post-Resurrection appearances of Christ? The resurrected Lord seems to have made it a practice to appear to His disciples at mealtime. Recall His disclosure in the breaking of bread with the men on the road to Emmaus, His visit to the eleven who sat at meat, breakfast by the Sea of Galilee. Now the Gospel writers undoubtedly intended that these meals be interpreted as consciously reminiscent of the Last Supper. In any event, the early Christians caught this significance and made their agape-meal and communion a time for enjoying the Lord's actual, on-the-spot presence with them—a celebration of the Resurrection, as it were. In fact, some scholars have suggested that the service was this emphasis almost exclusively—until Paul came along to remind the Church of the historical act of redemption which the emblems also signify.

But Paul's reminder notwithstanding, the communion service today ought to make us just as aware of the actual presence of our Lord as it ever did those early Christians, for we *do* worship the *risen* Christ, the Church *does* have this strong dimension in the present, and the Lord *is* with us—here—now. And because we belong to the Church that has this orientation, we ought always to conduct our worship in a way that recognizes His actual presence at the service, we ought to feel free to converse with Him in prayer on any occasion, and we ought always to trust, obey, and follow the Lord who stands present to help us.

The third dimension of the Church is its orientation toward the future.

As with the others, this element is given explicit attention in the Eucharist—though we, perhaps, are prone to overlook it. But the eschatological, the forward-looking emphasis in the Last Supper is strong and obvious once we open our minds to it. Luke's account in particular points us to this aspect of the matter; he quotes Christ as saying: "I have earnestly desired to eat this passover with you before I suffer; for I tell you I shall not eat it until it is fulfilled in the kingdom of God . . . for I tell you that from now on I shall not drink of the fruit of the vine until the kingdom of God comes . . . as my Father appointed a kingdom for me, so do I appoint for you that you may eat and drink at my table in my kingdom . . ." (22:15-16, 18, 29-30, RSV). In instituting the Last Supper, then, Jesus was saying, in effect: "This meal is a preview, a figure, an antetype of the great heavenly feast which is to come at the end of the age when my kingdom is established in its completeness and perfection. That time is *not* now; there are things to be accomplished, victories yet to be won; therefore, the meal in which we are now participating will be interrupted; it will not be fully consummated at this time. However, the very fact that I have *begun* this meal with you is my guarantee to you that it will be resumed and completed in my kingdom, the guarantee that that kingdom will come and my will be done—no matter what the events of the interim might seem to indicate."

Now, my brethren, the fact is that we—you and I—are living within that interim, and whenever we come to the Lord's Table we do in truth receive a renewal of the guarantee He gave to His disciples that night in the upper room. The Eucharist does symbolize—among other things—a reality that does not exist as yet but for which we have the Lord's own word that it will come and that we can be a part of it. The Church is the one and only institution that can truly claim to be "of the future," for it is the body of the Christ who guaranteed that the feast which is now symbolical will one day become the feast that is actual. And because the Church has this orientation toward the future, we will live confidently, no matter what our personal fortunes or the state of the world; we will live in anticipation and in preparedness for the day that is coming; we will worship the Lord of history as the grounds and the goal of our living hope.

We have been discussing evidences of the fact that the Eucharist is a symbol of the Church in the three dimensions of its life and charter: the past, the present, and the future. In conclusion, let me present one further evidence —this one catching up and tying together all three of these dimensions. It is one of the earliest liturgical prayers used in the Christian Church, well established even in New Testament times, though unfortunately not current in the modern Church. It is a single Aramaic phrase, *maranatha,* which is translated, "Our Lord, come!" That it had achieved the deep liturgical significance that goes beyond language is indicated by the fact that in the benediction to his first letter to the Corinthians Paul brings the term over into his Greek text without making any attempt to translate it. The Revelator uses the same prayer in the benediction of his book but this time in Greek.

The customary usage of the prayer, however, was in the communion service, just preceding the taking of the sacraments. In that connection the phrase could carry any one of three different meanings—or all three at once. *Maranatha* could mean, "The Lord has come; He has come to men in the incarnation and there, in history, has performed the great act of our redemption." *Maranatha* could, on the other hand, mean, "Our Lord, come! Be present with us in this service of communion and dwell with Thy Church as its living head." And finally, *maranatha* could mean, "Our Lord, come; hasten the day when Thou shalt establish Thy kingdom, when every knee shall bow and every tongue confess that Jesus Christ is Lord to the glory of God the Father." Because *maranatha* is the prayer of the three-dimensional Church, it does in fact mean all of these things.

Let us, then, as members of this Church, recall the rich significance of the symbol—both now and at such time as we actually partake of the Eucharist—and join those first Christians in their prayer: *"Maranatha! Our Lord, come!"* *

✠

BY INVITATION OF JESUS
Peter Marshall

Then said he also to him that bade him, When thou makest a dinner or a supper, call not thy friends, nor thy brethren, neither thy kinsmen, nor thy rich neighbors; lest they also bid thee again, and a recompense be made thee. But when thou makest a feast, call the poor, the maimed, the lame, the blind: And thou shalt be blessed; for they cannot recompense thee: for thou shalt be recompensed at the resurrection of the just.—LUKE 14:12-14.

ONE bitterly cold night, when Washington was covered with a blanket of snow and ice, a man sat in his home on Massachusetts Avenue. The house was very comfortable. A crackling log fire in the fireplace threw dancing shadows on the paneled walls. The wind outside was moaning softly like someone in pain, and the reading lamp cast a soft warm glow on the Book this man was reading.

He was alone, for the children had gone to the Shoreham for supper and dancing, and his wife had retired early after a strenuous afternoon's bridge game.

He read the passage of Luke which is our text, and then could read no more. Somehow he could not get away from those simple words. He had read the Bible often, for he was a good man, but never before did the words seem printed in flame. He closed the Bible, and sat musing, conscious for the first time in his life of the challenge of Christ.

* Delivered in Kneeland Speech Contest, Pacific School of Religion, May, 1957. Used by permission.

He felt as though Someone were standing behind him; he knew he was no longer alone. What strange fancy was this? "I must be sleepy and dreamy," he thought to himself. "It is time I went to bed." But it was long ere he fell asleep, for still he was conscious of a Presence in the room.

He tried to sleep, but somehow he could not close the door of his mind to the procession that shuffled and tapped its way down the corridors of his soul. There were beggars. There were sightless eyes that stared straight in front and faces blue with cold. There were crutches that creaked with the weight of a twisted body. He whispered a prayer that if the Lord would give him courage, he would take Him at His word and do what He wanted him to do. Only then did he find peace and fall asleep.

When the morning came, his determination gave him new strength and zest for the day. His first call was on an engraver who knew him well. At the counter he drafted the card he wished engraved. The card read:

<blockquote>
Jesus of Nazareth
Requests the honor of your presence
at a banquet honoring
The Sons of Want
On Friday evening, in a home on Massachusetts Avenue.
Cars will await you at the Central Union Mission
at six o'clock
"Come unto me, all ye that labor and are heavy laden,
and I will give you rest."
</blockquote>

A few days later, with the cards of invitation in his hands, he walked downtown and gave them out, and within an hour there were several people wondering what could be the meaning of the card that a kindly, happy, well-dressed man had placed in their hands. There was an old man seated on a box trying to sell pencils; and another on the corner with a racking cough and a bundle of papers under his arm. There was a blind man saying over and over to himself, "Jesus of Nazareth requests the honor of your presence . . ." A fellow who was fingering a gun in his pocket and bitterly thinking of suicide wondered whether he should wait until night.

At six o'clock, a strange group of men stood waiting in the vestibule of the Central Union Mission, talking softly together. "What is the catch in this, anyhow?" asked one cynical fellow. "What's the game?"

"Well, what difference does it make?" answered another. "I'd stand almost anything for a feed."

A blind man, with a little boy at his side, ventured to remark: "Maybe it's part of the government relief program."

Then the cynic said: "Aw, somebody's kiddin' us, as if we weren't wretched enough already."

Just then someone came over and announced that the cars were at the door; without a word, they went outside. Perhaps there was something incongruous about it all, seeing these men, clutching their thin coats tightly around their thin bodies, huddling together, climbing into two shiny limousines. It was touching to see the lame get in, dragging one foot, and to see the blind man fumbling for the strap. At last they were all inside, and the cars glided off with the strangest and most puzzled load of passengers they had ever carried.

When they dismounted, they stood gazing at the house, its broad steps and lamps; its thick-piled carpets. They entered slowly, trying to take it all in. They were met by the host, a little nervous, but smiling. He did not say much, only, "I am so glad you came."

By and by, they were seated at the table. The host rose in his place, and in a voice that trembled slightly said: "My friends, let us ask the blessing. If this is pleasing to Thee, O Lord, bless us as we sit around this table, and bless the food that we are about to receive. Bless these men. You know who they are, and what they need. And help us all to do what You want us to do. Accept our thanks, in Jesus' name. Amen."

The blind man was smiling now. He turned to the man seated next to him and asked him about the host. "What does he look like?"

And so the ice was broken; conversation began to stir around the table. It was a strange party, rather fantastic in a way, thought the host, as he surveyed his guests. There they were—men who otherwise might be still loitering on the back streets of Washington, crouched in doorways or huddled over some watchman's fire. What an amazing thing that he didn't even know the name of a single man! His guests had no credentials, no social recommendations, no particular graces—so far as he could see. But my, they were hungry!

It was funny, as he sat there talking, how the stories in the Gospels kept coming back to him, and he could almost imagine that the house was one in Jerusalem. It seemed to him that these men would be the very ones that Jesus would have gathered around Him—the legion of the world's wounded, the fraternity of the friendless, pieces of broken human earthenware.

He watched each plate and directed the servants with a nod or a glance. He encouraged them to eat; and he laughed at their thinly disguised reluctance, until they laughed too. As he sat there, it suddenly occurred to him how different was the conversation! There were no off-color stories, no whispering of scandal, no one saying, "Well, I have it on good authority." Instead they were talking about their friends in misfortune, wishing they were here too, wondering whether Charlie had managed to get a bed in the charity ward, whether Dick had stuck it out when he wanted to end it all, whether the little woman with the baby had got a job.

Wasn't the steak delicious! And they marveled that they still remembered how different foods tasted. They were wondering most of all who this man was, and why he had invited them all here.

When the meal was over, there was music. Someone came in and sat down at the piano. He began to play softly, familiar melodies, old songs; and then in a soft but understanding voice, he began to sing. Someone else joined in—a cracked, wheezing voice, but it started the others. Men who had not sung for months, men who had no reason to sing, there they were, all joining in. Soon they began to request this and that, and before they knew it, they were singing hymns: "What a Friend We Have in Jesus," "The Church in the Wildwood," and "When I Survey the Wondrous Cross."

The pianist stopped, and the guests grouped themselves in soft, comfortable chairs around the log fire; some of them smoked. The host moved among them, smiling, his eyes shining. Then he said: "I know you men are wondering what all this means. I can tell you very simply. It is what Jesus would do, if He were here. Now I haven't done much for you tonight, but it has made me very happy to have you here in my home. I hope you have enjoyed it half as much as I have. If I have given you one evening of happiness, I shall be forever glad to remember it, and you are under no obligation to me. This is not my party. It is *His!* I have merely lent Him this house. He was your *Host.* He is your *Friend.* And He has given me the honor of speaking for Him. He is sad when you are. He hurts when you do. He weeps when you weep. He wants to help you, if you will let Him.

"I am going to give each of you His Book of Instructions. I have marked certain passages in it that you will find helpful when you are sick and in pain, when you are lonely and discouraged, when you are blue and bitter and hopeless, and when you lose a loved one. He will speak a message of hope and courage and faith.

"Then I shall see each one of you tomorrow where I saw you today, and we'll have a talk together to see just how I can help you most. I have made arrangements for each of you to get back to your homes; and those who have nowhere to go, I invite to spend the night here."

They shuffled out into the night, a different group. There was a new light in their eyes, a smile where there had not been even interest before. The blind man turned to where his host stood: "God bless you, my friend, whoever you are."

A little wizened fellow who had not spoken all night paused to say, "I'm going to try again, Mister; there's somethin' worth livin' for."

The cynic turned back, "Mister, you're the first man who ever gave me anything. And you've given me hope."

"That is because I was doing it for Him," said the host as he stood and waved good night. When they had gone, he sat again by the fire and looked at the dying embers, until the feeling became overwhelming again that there was Someone in the room. He would never tell anyone how he knew this, but he knew that He was smiling and that He approved.

And that night, on Massachusetts Avenue, a rich man smiled in his sleep. And the One who stood in the shadows smiled too, because some of the least of these had been treated like brothers for His sake.*

---

* Abridged from *Mr. Jones, Meet the Master* by Peter Marshall, pp. 117-27. Copyright 1949-50 by Fleming H. Revell Company, Inc. Used by permission of the publisher.

A HOUSE FOR GOD

Glenn H. Asquith

"WHERE is God's house?" That question from a small boy was a hard one for his mother to answer. After all, everyone must have a place of residence, but what about God? Where is His house?

King Solomon and his people felt guilty when they thought of their lovely homes while God was worshiped out-of-doors or under a tabernacle, and they proceeded to pour out their treasure and their labor to make God the most beautiful house in all the world. Of course, when the house was built in all its splendor, Solomon confessed that not even in it could God be contained. Nevertheless, there was a house for God.

Today—where is God's house? In many new neighborhoods people look in vain for a church building. In many old neighborhoods, the churches are so old and dilapidated that it is hard for strangers to believe that God means much to men and women who go into the musty, old-fashioned structures once a week, while, as they themselves boast, their homes are equipped with all the latest conveniences and comforts. Happily, both situations are being realized with a sense of stewardship, and a great church-building crusade is on.

Present-day church builders are being moved with a vision of the task which has seldom been equaled since Solomon's time. No longer is there merely cautious giving to a "Building Fund," but a glad response to the call, "Let us build a house for God."

In God's house, miraculous things will happen. It will stand as a symbol of divine justice. So much has happened to civilization during the last fifty years that there is the temptation to yield to man's word that "might makes right." God's house will resound to God's word which will remind men that the "wages of sin is death," and that righteousness leads to life eternal. Like Stevenson's clock ticking regularly while outside a terrific storm was uprooting trees and blowing off shingles, the truth of God never varies. In the house of God we come face to face with the One who is the same yesterday, today and forever.

In God's house will be housed the eternal compass showing the way to the Promised Land. In the worries and sins of life thousands who were once on the road have lost the path. In their souls has been realized the bitter truth discovered by the poet that some experiences can "unweave a rainbow." The high aspirations of youth have been frayed out, one by one, until there is little left but cynicism and disillusionment with people and things. When a house of God appears before such wanderers they will come in and the compass will show them a new way.

But perhaps the most marvelous thing which occurs in the house of God is birth and rebirth. Astronomers say that new stars are born when wandering particles of matter find a point of cohesion. Into the house of God come people whose motives and ambitions and thoughts are journeying hit-or-miss with no real purpose, and in the house of God they are brought up against the fact of the Christ. This startling Person becomes the point of cohesion around which the idle impulses of life begin to revolve until a new personality is born.

Above all, the glory of the matchless Creator fills the house. Ordinary men and women are transformed by this glory and they go out to heroic living and triumphant dying.

Where is God's house?

He fills His universe to overflowing. But it has ever been the way of God, to honor with His presence the habitations which men build for Him by gifts of toil and substance and sacrifice. The crusade moves on. Houses for God are being built in small subdivisions, in city squares, in villages, and in the open country—that no one may need to cry out with Job, "Oh, that I knew where I might find Him!"

Who are the builders? Clerks, teachers, housewives, factory hands, professional people—you and I. We are the builders. None of us is very wealthy, none is able to build alone. But where we join hands, God will not lack for a house.

Where is God's house? It is we who are the answerers of that question.*

✛

ONE HOLY CHURCH OF GOD APPEARS

THE REVEREND Samuel Longfellow, author of "One Holy Church of God Appears," was born in Portland, Maine, in 1819. He was a brother of the New England poet, Henry Wadsworth Longfellow. In 1839 Samuel graduated from Harvard, and seven years later from Cambridge Divinity School.

During his long life (1819-1892), he held only three pastorates—Fall River, Massachusetts; Brooklyn, New York; and Germantown, Pennsylvania. His associates said of him: "He was in all respects a man worth knowing for his own sake: a sympathetic pastor, a sunny-hearted gentleman, and a man of deep, earnest, consecrated will."

At his Brooklyn church he developed a series of Sunday evening "Vesper Services." Not only did his own congregation enjoy singing in the spirit of worship and praise at these services, but through them he made a lasting contribution to Christian worship in America. He himself sometimes referred to them as "songs of praise when the evening shadows fall," and wrote the words to this hymn with his vesper services in mind.

Though brief, the hymn emphasizes the contribution which the Church makes to every age as it continues to worship, through meditation, prayer,

* From *The Christian Herald* (January 1954). Used by permission of the author and the publisher.

and praise, the Unseen Presence who instituted the fellowship of love. For within twenty centuries the Church has circled the globe, bringing its prophetic gift of truth to all nations. The living Church, the Bride of Christ, the bread of life, is the source upon which the hungry of the earth must feed if they are to have life abundant here and life eternal thereafter.

The music to which this hymn is usually sung was composed by Raphael Courteville, who died in 1772. It should be sung in moderate tempo and with reverence and devotion.

One Holy Church of God Appears

ST. JAMES. C. M.

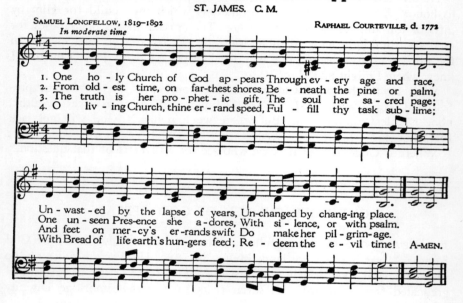

SAMUEL LONGFELLOW, 1819–1892

RAPHAEL COURTEVILLE, d. 1772

In moderate time

1. One   ho - ly Church of   God   ap - pears Through ev - ery   age   and   race,
2. From old - est   time, on   far-thest shores, Be - neath   the   pine   or   palm,
3. The   truth   is   her pro - phet - ic   gift, The   soul   her   sa - cred page;
4. O   liv - ing Church, thine er - rand speed, Ful - fill   thy   task   sub - lime;

Un - wast - ed   by   the lapse   of years, Un-changed by chang-ing place.
One   un - seen Pres-ence   she   a - dores, With   si - lence, or with psalm.
And feet   on   mer - cy's   er - rands swift Do   make her   pil - grim-age.
With Bread of   life earth's hun-gers feed; Re - deem the   e - vil time!   A-MEN.

✠

WE WOULD BE BUILDING

ACCORDING to Purd E. Deitz, the author of the words to this hymn, the story of its inspiration began in Edinburgh, Scotland, where he was doing some graduate work during the winter of 1931-32, and where he first heard "Finlandia" used as a hymn tune.

During the winter of 1934-35, a series of regional conferences on the theme, "Christian Youth Building a New World," was held across the United States, the last of the series being conducted in Philadelphia in March, 1935. As pastor of the Trinity Reformed Church in that city, Mr. Deitz became interested in this movement, and was made chairman of the general committee for the conference. One of the problems that arose was

We Would Be Building *

FINLANDIA. 10. 10. 10. 10. 10. 10.

Purd E. Deitz

In moderate time and flowing rhythm

Jean Sibelius, 1865-1959

1. We would be build - ing; tem-ples still un - done O'er crum-bling walls their
2. Teach us to build; up - on the sol - id rock We set the dream that
3. O keep us build - ing, Mas-ter; may our hands Ne'er fal - ter when the

cross - es scarce-ly lift; Wait-ing till love can raise the bro - ken stone,
hard-ens in - to deed, Ribbed with the steel that time and change doth mock,
dream is in our hearts, When to our ears there come di - vine com - mands

And hearts cre - a - tive bridge the hu - man rift; We would be build - ing,
Th' un-fail-ing pur - pose of our no - blest creed; Teach us to build; O
And all the pride of sin - ful will de - parts; We build with Thee, O

Mas - ter, let Thy plan Re-veal the life that God would give to man.
Mas - ter, lend us sight To see the tow - ers gleam-ing in the light.
grant en - dur - ing worth Un - til the heav'n-ly King-dom comes on earth. A-men.

the difficulty the worship committee encountered in finding a hymn suitable
to the theme of the conference.

One Saturday evening Mr. Deitz tried his hand at writing some words
that would develop this theme and that could be sung to the tune of
"Finlandia." The first stanza tries to express the need for building in terms
of reconstruction: the Church is in need of repair; human relationships are
broken, bridges of understanding down. But the plan must come from Above.

The second stanza uses the figure of modern steel and concrete construction,
with the prayer that we may build wisely and well. While building we must
have the vision of what the completed structure will look like. The final
stanza is a petition for grace to continue building, no matter what may
appear to hinder us, that our work may endure until the kingdom comes.

The thought of "building" is linked with the eternal purpose and power
of God. Building a Christian world is not something that we sally forth to
do in our own strength; that would be building only another tower of Babel.
But there is so much for Christians to do, and only God can give us the
strength to keep on building.

Although this hymn was written especially for that Philadelphia Youth
Conference, it was taken up and used elsewhere, until reports of its use came
from different parts of America and from India, the Philippines, and other
mission fields. During the World Conference of Christian Youth held in
Amsterdam in 1939, it was translated into German and French and used in
the service of worship prepared by the American delegates. Since then it has
found its way into a number of hymnals.*

* Based on information supplied by Purd E. Deitz, and used by his permission.

PART II

THE EASTERN ORTHODOX CHURCH

by

JOHN P. CAVARNOS

1. THE CHURCH SPREADS OUT FROM
   JERUSALEM .... *page* 144

2. ALLIANCE OF CHURCH AND STATE ...... *page* 163

3. THE FABRIC OF THE FAITH IS WOVEN ..... *page* 183

4. MISSIONARY ZEAL AND EXPANSION ...... *page* 202

5. EASTERN ORTHODOXY AROUND THE WORLD *page* 224

NOTE TO THE READER

Readers unfamiliar with the beliefs and practices of the Eastern Orthodox Church will find it helpful to begin their study of Part Two by first reading "America's Fourth Faith" by T. Otto Nall on page 235. Although this article deals specifically with Eastern Orthodoxy in America, it may also serve to orient the reader to the earlier heritage of this major Christian tradition.

CONTENTS

PART II SECTION 1

THE CHURCH SPREADS OUT FROM JERUSALEM

━━━━━━━━━━━━━━━━━━━━━━━━━━━╬━━━━━━━━━━━━━━━━━━━━━━━━━━━

Ye men of Athens, in all things I perceive that ye are very religious. For as I passed along, and observed the objects of your worship, I found also an altar with this inscription, TO AN UNKNOWN GOD. What therefore ye worship in ignorance, this set I forth unto you.—ACTS 17:22-23, ASV.

━━━━━━━━━━━━━━━━━━━━━━━━━━━╬━━━━━━━━━━━━━━━━━━━━━━━━━━━

PICTURES: PAGE
   Interpretation: The Church of the Holy Sepulcher 145
   Picture: The Church of the Holy Sepulcher 147
   Interpretation: Anastasis *or* The Resurrection—*Artist Unknown* 145
   Picture: Anastasis *or* The Resurrection—*Artist Unknown* 148
   Interpretation: St. Andrew—*El Greco* 146
   Picture: St. Andrew—*El Greco* 150

POETRY:
   Ode on the Nativity—*Cosmas of Maiouma* 149
   Transfiguration Canon—*Cosmas of Maiouma* 151
   Thy Kingdom, O Christ God—*Anatolios* 152
   Behold the Bridegroom Cometh—*Author Unknown* 152
   Heavenly King, Comforter—*Author Unknown* 153
   Shepherd of Eager Youth—*Clement of Alexandria* 153

STORIES:
   The Vision of the Leviathan—*Author Unknown* 153
   The Martyrdom of Polycarp—*Author Unknown* 155
   Who the Christians Are—*Author Unknown* 158

MUSIC:
   Interpretation: The Great Doxology—*Traditional Byzantine* 159
   Music: The Great Doxology—*Hartophylax;* transcribed by *Bouzianis* 160
   Interpretation: Nativity Ode—*Romanos the Melodist* 161
   Music: Nativity Ode—Western harmonization by *Bouzianis* 162

THE CHURCH OF THE HOLY SEPULCHER

OUR picture (p. 147) gives a view of the interior of the Greek chapel of the Church of the Holy Sepulcher in Jerusalem. This religious building dates from the fourth century, from the reign of Constantine the Great (324-337).

The Holy Sepulcher, where Christ was buried, had subsequently been covered completely to level the ground for new building requirements. With the progress of Christianity, however, a strong interest was developed for the restoration of this holy place.

In 326 the Holy Sepulcher was uncovered. The emperor Constantine erected the Church of the *Anastasis* (Resurrection) to enclose the Sepulcher rock and site. This edifice gained much renown throughout the Christian world. Its history is long and eventful, and all along identified with the Eastern Orthodox Patriarchate of Jerusalem; and its fortunes often followed the fate of the cradle of Christianity.

In 614 the Persians captured Jerusalem from the Byzantine Empire and destroyed this church. Later it was built and rebuilt. Destroyed in 1009 by the Fatimid Caliph al-Hakim, it was rebuilt in 1048 by the emperor Constantine Monomachos. This was the edifice that the crusaders found when they entered Jerusalem in 1099. Early in the eighteenth century the church constructed by Constantine Monomachos underwent extensive repairs. During the nineteenth century more repairs were made to consolidate the building and take care of the parts that were destroyed or badly damaged by fire.

The Church of the Holy Sepulcher, although originally entirely in the hands of the Greek Orthodox Church, is today the object of interest and concern of various sects, including the Eastern Orthodox. The existing settlement which defines the properties and rights of the diverse groups dates from the beginning of the nineteenth century.

The Greek Orthodox have a prominent part in the Church of the Holy Sepulcher, as is indicated by the picture of the sanctuary of the Greek chapel. Some of the paintings and objects in it are very old, some of more recent date. Small as the sanctuary is, it is filled with icons, lamps, and various other objects and relics. In one way it is rich with precious and valuable articles, and in another the neglect through poverty is apparent. This is true for practically all the properties of the Church of the Holy Sepulcher.

✢

ANASTASIS *or* THE RESURRECTION
Artist Unknown

THE Resurrection scene (p. 148) comes from the Church of St. Luke of Stiris in Phocis, Greece. It is a mosaic and in many ways resembles the

similar compositions of Daphni and of the Nea Moni on the island of
Chios. On the whole, this icon is based on more ancient models.

For the Eastern Orthodox Church the Resurrection, the *Anastasis,* is of
supreme spiritual significance. And this icon, which is rather doctrinal, follows faithfully the Byzantine Orthodox spirit. It embodies humility and
austereness, and at the same time shows the exultation of victory over death
and darkness. At the feet of Christ lie crushed the gates, locks, and chains of
Hades. Christ stands triumphant over the shambles of darkness. He is the
Victor over death.

While holding the cross with His right hand, the Lord takes with His
left hand the right hand of Adam, who is partly kneeling and gazing at the
Saviour with surprise and in a mood of supplication. Near Adam stands Eve.
On the right of Jesus stand two kings of Israel with crowns and haloes.
Other Resurrection compositions, mainly the more recent ones, include more
persons, usually prophets, than does that of St. Luke of Stiris. They represent
Christ holding Adam with His right hand and Eve with His left. In some
works St. John the Baptist is represented, as well as Isaiah, Jeremiah, Abel,
and others.

However, most of the Resurrections seem to be in agreement with regard
to the far-waving folds of Christ's garment; its motion upward signifies
joy and exultation. Christ had descended into the lowest regions of the
earth and there He shattered and trampled over the bars and chains which
held the prisoners down in dark Hades. Now He is risen, and with Him
rise the dead, and the garment itself of the Lord waves, as it were, with
boundless joy. Everything and everybody is in an upward motion. All things
strive to convey the uplifting power of the Resurrection. It is only the
objects of darkness and imprisonment that remain fallen and crushed. All
else stands erect to hear the glad tidings and rejoice at the greatest of victories. Here is a great truth put forth with apocalyptic simplicity.

All the subjects have expressive faces and rather delicate and refined
hands. Christ's expression seems to be the most joyful of all. The garments
are of the traditional sort and color. Although the mosaic has suffered from
the ravages of time, it retains its simple beauty and forcefulness unimpaired.

✛

ST. ANDREW
El Greco

WE have here a masterly execution (p. 150) of a portrait icon by the great
artist Dominico Theotocopuli (1541-1614), who is commonly known as
El Greco, "The Greek." St. Andrew is much esteemed in the Greek Orthodox Church as one of the apostles who spread Christianity in Asia Minor
and Greece and as the founder and first bishop of the church of Byzantium,
later called Constantinople. According to the Apocryphal New Testament

THE CHURCH OF THE HOLY SEPULCHER

Photo by Pericles Papahadjidakis, Athens, Greece

ANASTASIS OR THE RESURRECTION—ARTIST UNKNOWN

and to tradition, he suffered martyrdom at Patras at about A.D. 70, after preaching for over thirty-five years. Here, as in other icons, Andrew is represented with a large X-shaped cross, the instrument used in his martyrdom and death.

This traditional pose was particularly suited to El Greco's technique, and in this icon and that in which Andrew is placed in juxtaposition with St. Francis of Assisi, the artist attains his goal of elongation. Andrew is a towering figure, and his height is matched by an enormous cross. He is old and mature, with an expression of calm resignation. Though his lips are silent and his gaze attentive, his hands are eloquent. It is a pose of painful concentration. The entire life and career of St. Andrew seem to be summarized at this very moment.

According to tradition, Andrew was the first to follow Christ (John 1:40-42), and thus is often known as the "First-called." In John 12:20-23 there is an incident which may indicate why Andrew is so dear to the Hellenic East and the Orthodox Church in general: "And there were certain Greeks among them that came up to worship at the feast: the same came therefore to Philip . . . saying, Sir, we would see Jesus. Philip cometh and telleth Andrew: and again Andrew and Philip tell Jesus. And Jesus answered them saying, The hour is come, that the Son of man should be glorified." This circumstance, coupled with the Hellenic origin of the names of Andrew, Peter, and Philip, shows some tie with the Greeks. It is also true that the Greeks of that era contributed much, in order "that the Son of man should be glorified."

This painting of St. Andrew, like the rest of El Greco's works, had been long neglected. (See also his "St. Jerome," p. 253.) It was the revival of interest in the Hellenic East and Byzantium, and the late revolution in art and taste, that helped bring about the rediscovery of El Greco and his masterpieces. Modern painting itself, which has some affinity to his style, has made him universally popular. However, it should not be overlooked that Dominico Theotocopuli was born and raised in Crete, where the Byzantine iconographic tradition was very strong, and that when he migrated to Italy he fell under the spell of new artistic forces. His skill and ability to combine two apparently opposed modes of art made him unique. To the highly stylized Byzantine technique he added new devices in portraiture and the dramatic style which he had acquired from Titian and Tintoretto.

✢

ODE ON THE NATIVITY

Christ is born, go forth to meet Him,
Christ by all the heaven adored;
Singing songs of welcome, greet Him,
For the earth receives her Lord.

ST. ANDREW—*EL GRECO*

All ye nations shout and sing,
　For He comes, your glorious King.

Once His heavenly image bearing,
　Man has sunk to depths of sin;
Now defiled, debased, despairing,
　Clad in rags and foul within;
But our God, who beauty gave,
　Lifts the soul He comes to save.

From the height of heaven beholding,
　Pity filled the heart of grace,
And our Lord, His love unfolding,
　Made the earth His dwelling-place;
And a virgin mother gave
　God Incarnate, man to save.

Wisdom, Might, and Word Eternal,
　Glory of the Father, Thou!
Hid from man and powers supernal,
　Lo, He wears our nature now!
To the Lord your worship bring,
　Praise Him, your victorious King.*

—Cosmas of Maiouma

TRANSFIGURATION CANON

The choirs of ransom'd Israel,
　The Red Sea's passage o'er,
Uprais'd the hymn of triumph
　Upon the further shore:
And shouted, as the foeman
　Was whelm'd beneath the sea—
Sing we to Judah's Savior,
　For glorified is He.

Amongst His Twelve Apostles
　Christ spake the Words of Life,
And show'd a realm of beauty
　Beyond a world of strife:
When all my Father's glory
　Shall shine express'd in Me,
Then praise Him, then exalt Him,
　For magnified is He!

Upon the Mount of Tabor
　The promise was made good;
When, baring all the Godhead
　In Light itself He stood:
And they, in awe beholding,
　The Apostolic Three,
Sang out to God their Savior,
　For magnified was He!

In days of old, on Sinai,
　The Lord of Sab'oth came,
In majesty of terror,
　In thunder-cloud and flame:
On Tabor, with the glory
　Of sunniest light for vest,
The excellence of beauty
　In Jesus was express'd.

O holy, wondrous Vision!
　But what, when this life past,

* From *Hymns of the Greek Church,* translated by John Brownlie, pp. 28-29.

The beauty of Mount Tabor
  Shall end in heaven at last?
But what, when all the glory
  Of uncreated Light
Shall be the promis'd guerdon
  Of them that win the fight?*

—*Cosmas of Maiouma*

THY KINGDOM, O CHRIST GOD

Firm through the endless years,
  Thy kingdom stands secure,
And Thy dominion evermore,
  Through ages shall endure.

Thou cam'st on us to shine,
  Light from Eternal Light!
And now the Father's brightness rests
  On those who dwelt in night.

O, everything that breathes,
  To Thee gives homage now—
The glory of Almighty God,
  The Father's image, Thou.**

—*Anatolios*

BEHOLD THE BRIDEGROOM COMETH

Behold the Bridegroom cometh
  At the hour of midnight drear,
And blest be he who watcheth
  When his Master shall appear,
But woe betide the careless one
  Asleep when He is near!

O soul of mine, bestir thee
  Lest thou sink in slumber quite,
And the Bridegroom find thee sleeping
  When He cometh in His might.
Awake, awake to praises,
  For He cometh in the night.

That fearful day approacheth,
  Then live, O soul, aright,
And watch the hour, and trim thy lamp
  And keep it burning bright,
Lest the voice be heard, "He cometh!"
  In the middle of the night.

* A cento from J. M. Neale and S. G. Hatherly's *Hymns of the Eastern Church*, 4th ed., p. 80.
** From *Hymns of the Holy Eastern Church*, translated by John Brownlie, pp. 79-80.

Beware when slumber binds thee,
  Lest the Bridegroom pass thee by,
And thou knock without in darkness,
  And for grief and anguish cry;
Take thy lamp, with oil, and trim it,
  For the hour is drawing nigh.*

—*Author Unknown*

HEAVENLY KING, COMFORTER

O King enthroned on high,
  Thou Comforter Divine,
Blest Spirit of all Truth, be nigh
And make us Thine.

Yea, Thou art everywhere,
  All places far or near;
O listen to our humble prayer,
Be with us here!

Thou art the source of life,
  Thou art our treasure-store;
Give us Thy peace, and end our strife
For evermore.

Descend, O Heavenly Dove
  Abide with us alway;
And in the fulness of Thy love
Cleanse us, we pray.**

—*Author Unknown*

SHEPHERD OF EAGER YOUTH

Shepherd of eager youth,
Guiding in love and truth
Through devious ways;
Christ, our triumphant King,
We come Thy name to sing,
And here our children bring,
To sound Thy praise.

Thou art our Holy Lord,
The all-subduing Word,
Healer of strife;
Thou didst Thyself abase,
That from sin's deep disgrace
Thou mightest save our race,
And give us life.

Ever be Thou our Guide,
Our Shepherd and our Pride,
Our Staff and Song;
Jesus, Thou Christ of God,
By Thy enduring word,
Lead us where Thou hast trod,
Make our faith strong.***

—*Clement of Alexandria (150?-?220)*

✞

THE VISION OF THE LEVIATHAN

THE fourth vision which I saw, brethren, twenty days after the former vision, was a type of the persecution which is to come. I was going into the country

* From *Hymns of the Greek Church*, translated by John Brownlie, pp. 54-55.
** *Ibid.*, p. 24.
*** Translated from the Greek by Henry M. Dexter (1821-1890).

by the Via Campana. The place is about ten furlongs from the public road, and is easily reached. As I walked by myself I besought the Lord to complete the revelations and visions which he had shown me by his holy Church, to make me strong and give repentance to his servants who had been offended, "to glorify his" great and glorious "name" because he had thought me worthy to show me his wonders. And while I was glorifying him and giving him thanks an answer came to me as an echo of my voice, "Do not be double-minded, Hermas." I began to reason in myself, and to say, "In what ways can I be double-minded after being given such a foundation by the Lord, and having seen his glorious deeds?" And I approached a little further, brethren, and behold, I saw dust reaching as it were up to heaven, and I began to say to myself, Are cattle coming and raising dust? and it was about a furlong away from me. When the dust grew greater and greater I supposed that it was some portent. The sun shone out a little, and lo! I saw a great beast like some Leviathan, and fiery locusts were going out of his mouth. The beast was in size about a hundred feet and its head was like a piece of pottery. And I began to weep and to pray the Lord to rescue me from it, and I remembered the word which I had heard, "Do not be double-minded, Hermas." Thus, brethren, being clothed in the faith of the Lord and remembering the great things which he had taught me, I took courage and faced the beast. And as the beast came on with a rush it was as though it could destroy a city. I came near to it, and the Leviathan for all its size stretched itself out on the ground, and put forth nothing except its tongue, and did not move at all until I had passed it by. And the beast had on its head four colors, black, then the color of flame and blood, then golden, then white.

After I had passed the beast by and had gone about thirty feet further, lo! a maiden met me, "adorned as if coming forth from the bridal chamber," all in white and with white sandals, veiled to the forehead, and a turban for a headdress, but her hair was white. I recognized from the former visions that it was the Church, and I rejoiced the more. She greeted me saying, "Hail, O man," and I greeted her in return, "Hail, Lady." She answered me and said, "Did nothing meet you?" I said to her, "Yes, Lady, such a beast as could destroy nations, but by the power of the Lord, and by his great mercy I escaped it." "You did well to escape it," she said, "because you cast your care upon God, and opened your heart to the Lord, believing that salvation can be found through nothing save through the great glorious name. Therefore the Lord sent his angel, whose name is Thegri, who is over the beast, 'and shut his mouth that he should not hurt you.' You have escaped great tribulation through your faith, and because you were not double-minded when you saw so great a beast. Go then and tell the Lord's elect ones of his great deeds, and tell them that this beast is a type of the great persecution which is to come. If then you are prepared beforehand, and repent with all your heart towards the Lord, you will be able to escape it, if your heart be made pure and blameless, and you serve the Lord blamelessly for the rest of the days of your life. 'Cast your cares upon the Lord' and he will put them straight. Believe on the Lord, you who are double-minded, that he can do all things, and turns his wrath away from you, and sends scourges on you who are double-minded. Woe to those who hear these words and disobey; it were better for them not to have been born."

I asked her concerning the four colors which the beast had on its head. She answered and said to me, "Are you again curious about such matters?" "Yes," I said, "Lady, let me know what they are." "Listen," she said, "the black is this world, in which you are living; the color of fire and blood means that this world must be destroyed by blood and fire. The golden part is you, who have fled from this world, for even as gold is 'tried in the fire' and becomes valuable, so also you who live among them, are being tried. Those then who remain and pass through the flame shall be purified by them. Even as the gold puts away its dross, so also you will put away all sorrow and tribulation, and will be made pure and become useful for the building of the tower. But the white part is the world to come, in which the elect of God shall dwell, for those who have been chosen by God for eternal life will be without spot and pure. Therefore do not cease to speak to the ears of the saints. You have also the type of the great persecution to come, but if you will it shall be nothing. Remember what was written before." When she had said this she went away, and I did not see to what place she departed, for there was a cloud, and I turned backwards in fear, thinking that the beast was coming.*

✢

THE MARTYRDOM OF POLYCARP

Now when Polycarp entered into the arena there came a voice from heaven: "Be strong, Polycarp, and play the man." And no one saw the speaker, but our friends who were there heard the voice. And next he was brought forward, and there was a great uproar of those who heard that Polycarp had been arrested. Therefore when he was brought forward the proconsul asked him if he were Polycarp, and when he admitted it he tried to persuade him to deny, saying: "Respect your age," and so forth, as they are accustomed to say: "Swear by the genius of Caesar, repent, say: 'Away with the Atheists' "; but Polycarp, with a stern countenance looked on all the crowd of lawless heathen in the arena, and waving his hand at them, he groaned and looked up to heaven and said: "Away with the Atheists." But when the proconsul pressed him and said: "Take the oath and I let you go, revile Christ," Polycarp said: "For eighty and six years have I been his servant, and he has done me no wrong, and how can I blaspheme my King who saved me?"

But when he persisted again, and said: "Swear by the genius of Caesar," he answered him: "If you vainly suppose that I will swear by the genius of

* From *The Shepherd of Hermas* in *The Apostolic Fathers,* Vol. II, translated from the Greek by Kirsopp Lake, pp. 61-67. Used by permission of Harvard University Press and the Loeb Classical Library.

Caesar, as you say, and pretend that you are ignorant who I am, listen plainly: I am a Christian. And if you wish to learn the doctrine of Christianity fix a day and listen." The proconsul said: "Persuade the people." And Polycarp said: "You I should have held worthy of discussion, for we have been taught to render honor, as is meet, if it hurt us not, to princes and authorities appointed by God. But as for those, I do not count them worthy that a defence should be made to them."

And the proconsul said: "I have wild beasts, I will deliver you to them, unless you repent." And he said: "Call for them, for repentance from better to worse is not allowed us; but it is good to change from evil to righteousness." And he said again to him: "I will cause you to be consumed by fire, if you despise the beasts, unless you repent." But Polycarp said: "You threaten with the fire that burns for a time, and is quickly quenched, for you do not know the fire which awaits the wicked in the judgment to come and in everlasting punishment. But why are you waiting? Come, do what you will."

And with these and many other words he was filled with courage and joy, and his face was full of grace so that it not only did not fall with trouble at the things said to him, but that the proconsul, on the other hand, was astounded and sent his herald into the midst of the arena to announce three times: "Polycarp has confessed that he is a Christian." When this had been said by the herald, all the multitude of heathen and Jews living in Smyrna cried out with uncontrollable wrath and a loud shout: "This is the teacher of Asia, the father of the Christians, the destroyer of our Gods, who teaches many neither to offer sacrifice nor to worship." And when they said this, they cried out and asked Philip the Asiarch to let loose a lion on Polycarp. But he said he could not legally do this, since he had closed the Sports. Then they found it good to cry out with one mind that he should burn Polycarp alive, for the vision which had appeared to him on his pillow must be fulfilled, when he saw it burning, while he was praying, and he turned and said prophetically to those of the faithful who were with him, "I must be burnt alive."

These things then happened with so great speed, quicker than it takes to tell, and the crowd came together immediately, and prepared wood and faggots from the workshops and baths, and the Jews were extremely zealous, as is their custom in assisting at this. Now when the fire was ready he put off all his clothes, and loosened his girdle and tried also to take off his shoes, though he did not do this before, because each of the faithful was always zealous, which of them might the more quickly touch his flesh. For he had been treated with all respect because of his noble life, even before his martyrdom. Immediately therefore, he was fastened to the instruments which had been prepared for the fire, but when they were going to nail him as well he said: "Leave me thus, for He who gives me power to endure the fire, will grant me to remain in the flames unmoved even without the security you will give by the nails."

So they did not nail him, but bound him, and he put his hands behind him and was bound, as a noble ram out of a great flock, for an oblation, a whole burnt offering made ready and acceptable to God; and he looked up to heaven and said: "O Lord God Almighty, Father of thy beloved and blessed Child, Jesus Christ, through Whom we have received full knowledge of thee, the God of Angels and powers, and of all creation, and of the whole family of the righteous, who live before thee! I bless thee, that Thou hast granted me this day and hour, that I may share, among the number of the martyrs, in the cup of thy Christ, for the Resurrection of everlasting life, both of soul and body in the immortality of the Holy Spirit. And may I, today, be received among them before Thee, as a rich and acceptable sacrifice, as Thou, the God who lies not and is truth, hast prepared beforehand, and shown forth, and fulfilled. For this reason I also praise Thee for all things, I bless Thee, I glorify Thee through the everlasting and heavenly High Priest, Jesus Christ, through whom be glory to Thee with him and the Holy Spirit, both now and for the ages that are to come, Amen."

Now when he had uttered his Amen and finished his prayer, the men in charge of the fire lit it, and a great flame blazed up and we, to whom it was given to see, saw a marvel. And we have been preserved to report to others what befell. For the fire made the likeness of a room, like the sail of a vessel filled with wind, and surrounded the body of the martyr as with a wall, and he was within it not as burning flesh, but as bread that is being baked, or as gold and silver being refined in a furnace. And we perceived such a fragrant smell as the scent of incense or other costly spices.

At length the lawless men, seeing that his body could not be consumed by the fire, commanded an executioner to go up and stab him with a dagger, and when he did this, there came out a dove, and much blood, so that the fire was quenched and all the crowd marvelled that there was such a difference between the unbelievers and the elect. And of the elect was he indeed one, the wonderful martyr, Polycarp, who in our days was an apostolic and prophetic teacher, bishop of the catholic Church in Smyrna. For every word which he uttered from his mouth both was fulfilled and will be fulfilled.

When the centurion saw the contentiousness caused by the Jews, he put the body in the midst, as was their custom, and burnt it. Thus we, at last, took up his bones, more precious than precious stones, and finer than gold, and put them where it was meet.

Such was the lot of the blessed Polycarp, who though he was, together with those from Philadelphia, the twelfth martyr in Smyrna, is alone especially remembered by all, so that he is spoken of in every place, even by the heathen. He was not only a famous teacher, but also a notable martyr, whose martyrdom all desire to imitate, for it followed the gospel of Christ. By his endurance he overcame the righteous ruler, and thus gained the crown of immortality, and he is glorifying God and the Almighty Father, rejoicing with the apostles and all the righteous, and he is blessing our Lord Jesus Christ, the Saviour of our souls, and Governor of our bodies, and the Shepherd of the catholic Church throughout the world.*

* From *The Martyrdom of Polycarp* in *The Apostolic Fathers*, Vol. II, translated from the Greek by Kirsopp Lake, pp. 323-39. Used by permission of Harvard University Press and the Loeb Classical Library.

WHO THE CHRISTIANS ARE

THE distinction between Christians and other men is neither in country nor language nor customs. For they do not dwell in cities in some place of their own, nor do they use any strange variety of dialect, nor practise an extraordinary kind of life. This teaching of theirs has not been discovered by the intellect or thought of busy men, nor are they the advocates of any human doctrine as some men are. Yet while living in Greek and barbarian cities, according as each obtained his lot, and following the local customs, both in clothing and food and in the rest of life, they show forth the wonderful and confessedly strange character of the constitution of their own citizenship. They dwell in their own fatherlands, but as if sojourners in them; they share all things as citizens, and suffer all things as strangers. Every foreign country is their fatherland, and every fatherland is a foreign country. They marry as all men, they bear children, but they do not expose their offspring. They offer free hospitality, but guard their purity. Their lot is cast "in the flesh," but they do not live "after the flesh." They pass their time upon the earth, but they have their citizenship in heaven. They obey the appointed laws, and they surpass the laws in their own lives. They love all men and are persecuted by all men. They are unknown and they are condemned. They are put to death and they gain life. "They are poor and make many rich"; they lack all things and have all things in abundance. They are dishonored, and are glorified in their dishonor, they are spoken evil of and are justified. "They are abused and give blessing," they are insulted and render honor. When they do good they are buffeted as evildoers, when they are buffeted they rejoice as men who receive life. They are warred upon by the Jews as foreigners and are persecuted by the Greeks, and those who hate them cannot state the cause of their enmity.

To put it shortly, what the soul is in the body, that the Christians are in the world. The soul is spread through all members of the body, and Christians throughout the cities of the world. The soul dwells in the body, but is not of the body, and the Christians dwell in the world, but are not of the world. The soul is invisible, and is guarded in a visible body, and the Christians are recognised when they are in the world, but their religion remains invisible. The flesh hates the soul, and wages war upon it, though it has suffered no evil, because it is prevented from gratifying its pleasures, and the world hates the Christians though it has suffered no evil, because they are opposed to its pleasures. The soul loves the flesh which hates it and the limbs, and Christians love those that hate them. The soul has been shut up in the body, but itself sustains the body; and Christians are confined in the world as in a prison, but themselves sustain the world. The soul dwells immortal in a mortal tabernacle, and Christians sojourn among corruptible things, waiting for the incorruptibility which is in heaven. The soul when evil treated in food and drink becomes better, and Christians when buffeted day by day increase more.

God has appointed them to so great a post and it is not right for them to decline it.

For it is not, as I said, an earthly discovery which was given to them, nor do they take such pains to guard some mortal invention, nor have they been entrusted with the dispensation of human mysteries. But in truth the Almighty and all-creating and invisible God himself founded among men the truth from heaven, and the holy and incomprehensible word, and established it in their hearts, not, as one might suppose, by sending some minister to men, or an angel, or ruler, or one of those who direct earthly things, or one of those who are entrusted with the dispensations in heaven, but the very artificer and Creator of the universe himself. He sent him as God, he sent him as Man to men, he was saving and persuading when he sent him, not compelling, for compulsion is not an attribute of God. When he sent him he was calling, not pursuing; when he sent him he was loving, not judging.*

✛

THE GREAT DOXOLOGY

"THE Great Doxology" is of great antiquity, and is noted for its power and beauty. Both words and music are well combined to deliver in grandiloquent tones a sincere message to the Lord and to praise and magnify Him. God is requested with deep contrition to show His mercy, to guide, teach, heal us, and keep us away from sin. The Latin equivalent to this hymn is the "Gloria in excelsis."

The musical score is in the best Byzantine tradition, which is monophonic. It is set in the third of the eight modes. This type of music preserves the simplicity and power that are so essential in a hymn of this sort.

The Great Doxology is chanted by the choir at the opening of the Divine Liturgy. It is an extended glorification of God, as the very origin of its name suggests. Our score contains only the opening verses:

> Glory to Thee who hast shown us the light.
> Glory to God in the highest,
> And peace on earth, good will among men.
> We praise Thee, we bless Thee,
> We worship Thee, we glorify Thee,
> We thank Thee for Thy great glory.

The second verse comes from Luke, where the birth of Christ is described (2:13-14): "And suddenly there was with the angel a multitude of the

* From *The Epistle to Diognetus* in *The Apostolic Fathers*, Vol. II, translated from the Greek by Kirsopp Lake, pp. 359-65. Used by permission of Harvard University Press and the Loeb Classical Library.

heavenly host praising God, and saying, 'Glory to God in the highest, and on
earth peace, good will toward men.' "

The Great Doxology

Traditional Byzantine

Hourmouzios Hartophylax, 1840
Transcribed from the
Byzantine by
Dean D. Bouzianis

Mode III Plagal *(Barys)*

Dho - xa Si - to dhi - xan - 'ti to fos,

dho - xa   en y - psi - - stis The - o ke e pi ghis i -

ri - ni en an - thro - pis   ev - dho - ki -

a.   Ym - nou - men   Se, evlo - ghou - men   Se prosky - nou - men

Se   dho - xo - lo - ghou - - men   Se,   ef - kha - ri -

stou - men   Si,   dhi - a tin me -

gha - - lin   Sou   dho - - xan.

NATIVITY ODE

IN this "Nativity Ode" of Romanos the Melodist we have the best composition for the occasion in the Orthodox Church. It comes from the Christmas *Kontakion* of this poet, who flourished during the reign of Justinian I (527-565). Romanos had the rare ability to express big ideas in a few well-chosen and well-placed words. To this simplicity and directness can be added his dexterity for combining harmoniously the lyrical with the narrative. The ode enjoyed a unique place of honor in the Byzantine Empire for many centuries. The entire *Kontakion* on the Nativity was chanted every year at Christmas at the imperial palace by a double choir consisting of chanters from the two big churches of Constantinople—Hagia Sophia and the Holy Apostles.

Our Nativity Ode is endowed with excellent dramatic effects. There the Virgin, the birth, Christ the Superessential, the cave, the angels, shepherds, and Magi, the guiding star, and so on are contained in but one stanza with all the force of a dramatic scene. The coming of God is proclaimed with so few words and with the traditional scenes and circumstances. This is a rare feat, and one that can be achieved only by a master. It is therefore with very good reason that Romanos has been surnamed "the Melodist." In fact, some good authorities give him the palm and honor of the great *Akathistos* Hymn, by claiming him as its author.

Romanos was a prolific hymnodist. Some of his other compositions deal with the life and Passion of Christ, Pentecost, the death of St. John the Baptist, and so forth.

The Western harmonization of the melody of the Nativity Ode was successfully done by the composer Dean D. Bouzianis. This was not an easy task, and it was undertaken with the proper reservations. The eminent musician and conductor Dimitri Mitropoulos once expressed the view that he "personally did not agree with European harmonization of Byzantine melodies," and conceded that the problem is "exceedingly difficult." Mr. Bouzianis and the editor of Part II have endeavored to avoid the "de-Byzantinization" of this "classical Christian music," by a strict adherence to the Byzantine prototypes, in so far as this was possible, with the exception of the Nativity Ode and the Cherubic Hymn, which is a Westernized or modern version.

The translation of the text of the "Nativity Ode" from the Greek is as follows:

> The Virgin today bears the Superessential,
> And the earth offers the cave to the Inaccessible.
> Angels with shepherds sing praises,
> And Magi journey with a star.
> For in our behalf was born a new child:
> The God before the ages.

Nativity Ode

From the Christmas Kontakion
of Romanos the Melodist

Western harmonization by
Dean D. Bouzianis*

*Used by permission of Dean D. Bouzianis.

CONTENTS

PART II SECTION 2

ALLIANCE OF CHURCH AND STATE

───────────────────── ✛ ─────────────────────

Render therefore unto Caesar the things that are Caesar's; and unto God the things that are God's.—
MATTHEW 22:21, ASV.

───────────────────── ✛ ─────────────────────

PAGE

PICTURES:
Interpretation: St. Constantine and St. Helen—*Artist Unknown* 164
Picture: St. Constantine and St. Helen—*Artist Unknown* 165
Interpretation: Hagia Sophia at Constantinople—*Anthemios and Isadoros* . 164
Picture: Hagia Sophia at Constantinople—*Anthemios and Isadoros* 167
Interpretation: Basil the Great—*Kontoglous* 168
Picture: Basil the Great—*Kontoglous* 169

POETRY:
From on High, Virgins, Hark the Cry—*Methodios of Olympus* 168
Night Makes Me Sing to Thee—*Synesios of Ptolemais* 170
My Soul Uncrushed by Care—*Synesios of Ptolemais* 171
A Morning Prayer—*Gregory Nazianzen* 171
Infinite Light—*Gregory Nazianzen* 171
What Shall We Bring to Thee—*Anatolios* 172

STORIES:
The Life of St. Anthony—*St. Athanasios* 173
The Conversion of Constantine the Great—*Eusebios* 176
Gorgonia—*Gregory Nazianzen* 178

MUSIC:
Interpretation: Gladsome Light—*Athenogenes* (?) 180
Hymn: Gladsome Light—*Sakellarides;* transcribed by *Bouzianis* 180
Interpretation: We Hymn Thee—*Traditional Byzantine* 182
Hymn: We Hymn Thee—Transcribed from Byzantine by *Bouzianis* 181

ST. CONSTANTINE AND ST. HELEN
Artist Unknown

THESE two saints, mother and son, played important roles in the protection and propagation of Christianity, and many churches in the Orthodox East have been dedicated to them.

Constantine became the first Christian emperor (324-337) of the East Roman or Byzantine Empire. His services to the Church were enormous: persecutions came to an end and the Church itself was granted important privileges and exemptions. During Constantine's reign the First Ecumenical Synod was convoked at Nicaea in 325. This event had far-reaching results, since then and there a close co-operation between Church and State was established and cemented. Furthermore, it was this Constantine, surnamed the Great, who in 330 transferred the capital of the Empire from Rome on the Tiber to Byzantium on the Bosporus. This latter city came to be known as Constantinople. By virtue of his great services to the Church and Christendom in general, Constantine was given the titles of the Thirteenth Apostle and *Isapostolos,* or "Equal-to-the-Apostles."

Helen, mother of Constantine, is said to have done much in the construction of churches and other edifices in the Holy Land in her great effort to preserve the holy cross and other important relics and holy sanctuaries of Christendom. It was during the reign of Constantine that extensive excavations were made to rediscover the historic sites of Jerusalem. (See Interpretation of "Church of the Holy Sepulcher," p. 145.)

The Eastern Church celebrates the memory of Constantine and Helen jointly every year on May 21.

The fresco depicting Constantine and Helen (p. 165) is a very typical one, well fixed in tradition. It belongs to the fourteenth or fifteenth century, and is found in the monastery of St. Stephen in Meteora, Greece. As usual in such icons, Constantine stands on the right of a large cross, his mother on the left. The decoration on their garments also forms the figure of the cross, which symbolizes the constant efforts and struggles of these two saints for the Christian faith and points out the fact of their discovery and protection of the holy cross itself.

The portrait shows more classical naturalism, balance, and symmetry than earlier works. The faces show confidence, mildness, and serenity, and the temporal and spiritual elements seem to blend well in both saints.

✛

HAGIA SOPHIA AT CONSTANTINOPLE

HAGIA SOPHIA is Eastern Christianity's greatest sanctuary and one of the world's major architectural monuments. Without doubt it is the masterpiece

KCΩNSTANTÍNOC   ΗΛΙΆ

ST. CONSTANTINE AND ST. HELEN—*ARTIST UNKNOWN*

of Byzantine art, in the same way that the Parthenon in Athens is the master-piece of classical Greek art.

From the time it was constructed by Emperor Justinian I (527-565), its fame spread far and wide. It was built in the relatively short space of five years (532-537) and dedicated to the Holy Wisdom, which is indeed the meaning of Hagia or St. Sophia. For its erection the best marbles and the rich spoils from the ancient and classical monuments were gathered, and Justinian instructed the builders to employ lavishly gold and silver, precious stones and ivories, and enamels, to lend the temple magnificence and splendor.

The great task was entrusted to two of the foremost architects of the period, Anthemios of Tralles and Isadoros of Miletos, who made Justinian's dream a reality. These architects combined skill with inventiveness and daring, and achieved a most important architectural feat: they successfully placed a huge dome on a square basilica by the use of the architectural device known as the pendentive (triangular arches in the corners). The large dome seems to have been fashioned according to the old idea of a dome-shaped firmament, and when a choir chants one feels that hymns descend from heaven to earth. One feels that of all places this one is most suitable for mystic contemplation, the place to seek the infinite and the undefinable.

The exterior is simple and unpretentious, but the interior is quite the op-posite. Much skill and wealth were expended for the beautiful mosaics and the various ornaments that adorn it. Many of the mosaic panels, however, were made later, in the ninth, tenth, and eleventh centuries.

The sixth-century historian Procopius wrote: "So the church has become a spectacle of marvelous beauty, overwhelming to those who see it, but to those who know it by hearsay altogether incredible. . . . And it exults in an indescribable beauty. For it proudly reveals its mass and the harmony of its proportions, having neither any excess nor deficiency, since it is both more pretentious than the buildings to which we are accustomed, and considerably more noble than those which are merely huge, and it abounds exceedingly in sunlight and in the reflection of the sun's rays from the marble."*

Hagia Sophia has had its share of the glory that is associated with three of the seven Ecumenical Councils, the great triumphs and misfortunes of the Empire, the many coronations of emperors, and the elevation of so many patriarchs. On its holy table was placed the fateful document which brought about the definitive split between the Eastern and Western churches in 1054.

After the fall of Constantinople to the Turks in 1453, Hagia Sophia was converted into a mosque, and its precious mosaics were covered with plaster and whitewash. However, in the early 1930's the American professor Thomas Whittemore started the arduous project of uncovering the mosaics, and slowly some of the original beauty of this Christian shrine has been restored. The Turkish government has allowed Hagia Sophia to be converted into a museum.

* From *Buildings*, translated by Dewing and Downey for the Loeb Classical Library, 1940.

HAGIA SOPHIA AT CONSTANTINOPLE—ANTHEMIOS AND ISADOROS

BASIL THE GREAT
Fotis Kontoglous

THE saint represented on p. 169 is one in whom the Greek Orthodox Church takes great pride. His portrait is a fresco executed by the famous contemporary iconographer Fotis Kontoglous. He is depicted as an ascetic, physically frail, but rich in spiritual resources. To one who has studied the life of this saint, the fresco does credit to his personality.

Basil (329?-379) is the only person in the Eastern Church who bears the title "Great." As monk and Bishop of Caesarea in Cappadocia of Asia Minor, he proved himself a great organizer, administrator, and writer. He was rather frail in health, but in his deeds and words he was a great bulwark for the orthodox and universal church. Well versed in classical Greek literature, he endeavored to bring into the Church as much pagan learning as was possible without in any way injuring the fundamental Christian tenets. He urged the assimilation of what was good and healthy for the life and well-being of the Christians.

Basil can also be called the father of Eastern monasticism. He formulated its standards and rules, which to some extent are still followed in the East. Avoiding on the one hand the oversevere life of the hermits and the stylites and on the other the lax form of monasticism, he struck upon the happy mean, the *cenobitic,* or community living. This is the Basilian order, which still prevails in the Eastern Orthodox Church. For the proper discipline and ordering of monastic life, Basil wrote the so-called *Short Rules* and *Long Rules.*

Basil also wrote many letters, orations, and other works. He was a stanch supporter of orthodoxy against Arianism, and contributed no little in this conflict. Numerous stories and legends are connected with this outstanding saint, whose memory is celebrated on New Year's Day, the day on which he died. On New Year's Eve the so-called *Kalends* or *Kalandae* are sung in his honor. It is also a custom among the Eastern Orthodox to make, in honor of his anniversary, a cake called the *Vasilopita,* "Basil's cake."

The Greek words on the scroll in this fresco are from one of the prayers Basil wrote.

✠

FROM ON HIGH, VIRGINS, HARK THE CRY

Behold the Bridegroom! Hark the cry,
The dead, awaking, rends the sky!
  Go, virgins, He is near,
  Your lamps all burning clear;
He enters where the rising light

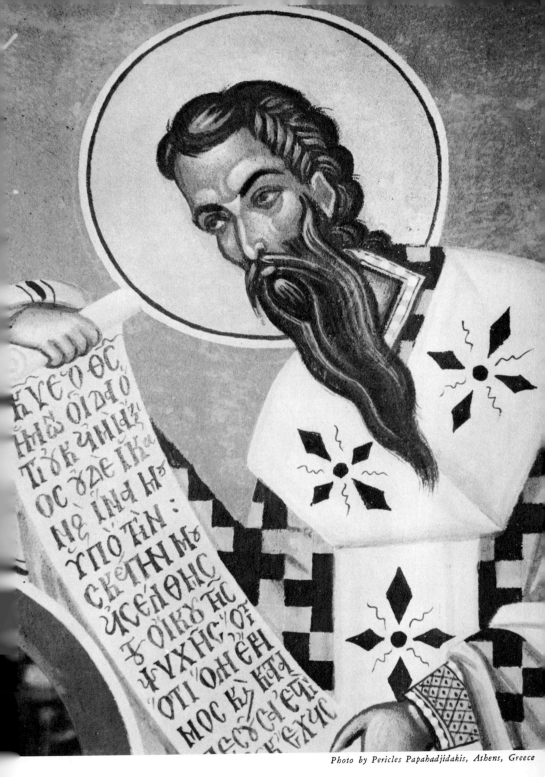

BASIL THE GREAT—*KONTOGLOUS*

Asunder bursts the gates of night.
  In holy garb, with lamp aglow,
  To meet the Bridegroom forth I go.

The smiles of earth that turn to tears,
Its empty joys and foolish fears
  I leave, for Thou dost call—
  Thou art my Life, my All;
I would Thy beauty ever see,
Then let me, Blessed, cling to Thee.
  In holy garb, with lamp aglow,
  To meet the Bridegroom forth I go.

For Thee I leave the world behind—
Thou art my Bliss, O Bridegroom kind;
  My beauty's not mine own—
  'Tis Thine, O Christ, alone;
Thy bridal-chamber I would see,
In perfect happiness to be.
  In holy garb, with lamp aglow,
  To meet the Bridegroom forth I go.

O God, exalted on Thy throne,
Who dwell'st in purity unknown,
  Lo, now we humbly wait,
  Throw wide the Heavenly gate,
And with the Bridegroom, of Thy grace,
Give us at Thy right hand a place.
  In holy garb, with lamp aglow,
  To meet the Bridegroom forth I go.*
                    —*Methodios of Olympus (ca. 825-885)*

NIGHT MAKES ME SING TO THEE

When darkness falls and night is here,
  My hymns of praise in silence rise—
This knows the moon, whose silver sphere
  Shines in the star-bespangled skies.

When morning breaks, and glorious day
  Shines in the dawn and noontide fair—
This knows the sun—a grateful lay
  Springs from my heart in fervent prayer.

When fails the light at sunset gray,
  And twilight listens for my song—
This know the stars—in bright array
  My praises mingle with their throng.**
                    —*Synesios of Ptolemais (ca. 373-ca. 414)*

* From *Hymns of the Greek Church*, translated by John Brownlie, pp. 89-90.
** *Ibid.*, p. 103.

MY SOUL UNCRUSHED BY CARE

O may my soul, uncrushed by care,
  Direct her gaze to where Thou art,
And in Thy splendor find, O Christ,
  The strength of life Thou canst impart.

And freed from sin's depressing load,
  May I pursue the path divine,
And rise above the cares of earth
  Until my life is merged in Thine.

Unsullied life Thy servant grant
  Who tunes his harp to sound Thy praise,
And still my life shall hymn Thy love,
  And glory to the Father raise.

And when I rest in glory bright,
  The burden of my labor past,
In hymns I'll praise Thee more and more
  While the eternal ages last.*
        —*Synesios of Ptolemais (ca. 373-ca. 414)*

A MORNING PRAYER

The morning breaks, I place my hand in Thine,
My God, 'tis Thine to lead, to follow mine;
No word deceitful shall I speak the while,
Nor shall I stain my hand with action vile.

Thine be the day with worthy labor filled,
Strong would I stand to do the duty willed;
Nor swayed by restless passion let me be,
That I may give the offering pure to Thee;

Else were I 'shamed when hoary age I see,
Shamed were this board that bears Thy gifts to me:
Mine is the impulse; O my Christ, I pray,
Be Thou Thyself to me the Blessed Way!**
        —*Gregory Nazianzen (329?-?389)*

INFINITE LIGHT

O Light that knew no dawn,
  That shines to endless day,
All things in earth and heaven
  Are lustred by Thy ray;

* *Ibid.*, p. 104.
** *Ibid.*, p. 98.

No eye can to Thy throne ascend,
Nor mind Thy brightness comprehend.

Thy grace, O Father, give,
    That I may serve in fear;
Above all boons, I pray,
    Grant me Thy voice to hear;
From sin Thy child in mercy free,
And let me dwell in light with Thee.

That, cleansed from filthy stain,
    I may meet homage give,
And, pure in heart, behold
    And serve Thee while I live;
Clean hands in holy worship raise,
And Thee, O Christ my Saviour, praise.

In supplication meek
    To Thee I bend the knee;
O Christ, when Thou shalt come,
    In love remember me,
And in Thy kingdom, by Thy grace,
Grant me a humble servant's place.

Thy grace, O Father, give,
    I humble Thee implore;
And let Thy mercy bless
    Thy servant more and more.
All grace and glory be to Thee
From age to age eternally.*
                        —*Gregory Nazianzen* (329?-?389)

WHAT SHALL WE BRING TO THEE

What shall we bring to Thee?
What shall our offering be
    On this Thy natal morn?
For Thou, O Christ, hast come to earth—
A virgin mother gave Thee birth—
    For our redemption born.

The whole creation broad
Gives praise and thanks to God,
    Who gave His only Son;
And list! the bright angelic throng
Their homage yield in sweetest song
    For peace on earth begun.

* *Ibid.*, pp. 93-94.

The heavens their glory shed,
The star shines o'er His head,
    The promised Christ and King;
And wise men from the lands afar,
Led by the brightness of the star,
    Their treasured offerings bring.

What shall we give Thee now?
Lowly the shepherds bow,
    Have we no gift to bring?
Our worship, lo, we yield to Thee,
All that we are, and hope to be—
    This is our offering.*

—Anatolios

✠

THE LIFE OF ST. ANTHONY

St. Athanasios

ANTHONY was by descent an Egyptian. His parents were of good family and possessed considerable wealth, and as they were Christians he also was reared in the same faith. When he was grown and arrived at boyhood, and was advancing in years, he could not endure to learn letters, not caring to associate with other boys; but all his desire was to live a plain man at home. With his parents he used to attend the Lord's house, and neither as a child was he idle nor when older did he despise them; but was both obedient to his father and mother and attentive to what was read, keeping in his heart what was profitable in what he heard.

After the death of his father and mother he was left alone with one little sister. His age was about eighteen or twenty, and on him the care both of home and sister rested. Now it was not six months after the death of his parents, and going according to custom into the Lord's house, he communed with himself and reflected as he walked how the apostles left all and followed the Saviour; and how they in the *Acts* sold their possessions and brought and laid them at the apostles' feet for distribution to the needy, and what and how great a hope was laid up for them in heaven. Pondering over these things he entered the church, and it happened the gospel was being read, and he heard the Lord saying to the rich man, "If thou wouldest be perfect, go and sell that thou hast and give to the poor; and come follow Me and thou shalt have treasure in heaven." Anthony, as though God had put him in mind of the saints, and the passage had been read on his account, went out immediately from the church, and gave the possessions of his forefathers to the villagers, that they should be no more a clog upon himself and his sister. And all the rest that was movable he sold, and having got together much money he gave it to the poor, reserving a little however for his sister's sake.

* *Ibid.,* pp. 30-31.

And again as he went into the church, hearing the Lord say in the gospel, "be not anxious for the morrow," he could stay no longer, but went out and gave those things also to the poor. Having committed his sister to known and faithful virgins, and put her into a convent to be brought up, he henceforth devoted himself outside his house to discipline, taking heed to himself and training himself with patience. For there were not yet so many monasteries in Egypt, and no monk at all knew of the distant desert; but all who wished to give heed to themselves practiced the discipline in solitude near their own village. Now there was then in the next village an old man who had lived the life of a hermit from his youth up. Anthony, after he had seen this man, imitated him in piety. And at first he began to abide in places outside the village. Then if he heard of a good man anywhere, like the prudent bee, he went forth and sought him; and he returned, having got from the good man as it were supplies for his journey in the way to virtue.

Anthony worked with his hands, having heard, "he who is idle let him not eat," and part he gave to the needy. And he was constant in prayer, knowing that a man ought to pray in secret unceasingly.

Thus conducting himself, Anthony was beloved by all. He subjected himself in sincerity to the good men whom he visited, and learned thoroughly where each surpassed him in zeal and discipline. Thus filled, he returned to his own place of discipline, and henceforth would strive to unite the qualities of each, and was eager to show himself the virtues of all.

But the devil, who hates and envies what is good, could not endure to see such a resolution in a youth, but endeavored to carry out against him what he had been wont to effect against others. First of all he tried to lead him away from the discipline, whispering to him the remembrance of his wealth, care for his sister, claims of kindred, love of money, love of glory, the various pleasures of the table and the other relaxations of life, and at last the difficulty of virtue and the labor of it. In a word, he raised in his mind a great dust of debate, wishing to debar him from his settled purpose. But when the enemy saw himself to be too weak for Anthony's determination, then at length putting his trust in the weapons which are "in the navel of his belly," he attacked the young man, disturbing him by night and harassing him by day, so that even the onlookers saw the struggle which was going on between them. Anthony, however, his mind filled with Christ and the nobility inspired by Him, quenched the coal of the other's deceit. Again the enemy suggested the ease of pleasure and devised other snares, but with no success.

This was Anthony's first victory over the devil. But neither did Anthony henceforth relax his cares and despise him; nor did the enemy as though conquered cease to lay snares for him. Anthony more and more repressed the body and kept it in subjection and accustomed himself to a severer mode of life. He kept vigil to such an extent that he often continued the whole night without sleep. He ate once a day, after sunset, sometimes once in two days, and often even in four. His food was bread and salt, his drink, water only. A rush mat served him to sleep upon, but for the most part he lay upon the bare ground. He gave no thought to the past, but day by day, as if he were at the beginning of his discipline, applied greater pains for advancement.

Thus tightening his hold upon himself, Anthony departed to the tombs, which happened to be at a distance from the village; and having bid one of his acquaintances to bring him bread at intervals of many days, he entered one of the tombs, and the other having shut the door on him, he remained within alone. Therein Anthony was in endless combats with demons. The torture of the blows and stripes he received was very severe, but he endured them all. He was then about thirty-five years old.

Then Anthony set off to the mountain, overcoming temptations on the way. There he took up his abode in a ruined fort across the Nile. Having stored up loaves for six months (this is a custom of the Thebans), and found water within, he lived there, never going forth nor looking at any one who came. Thus he employed a long time training himself, and received loaves, let down from above, twice the year, for nearly twenty years.

After this, when many were eager and wishful to imitate his discipline, and his acquaintances came and began to cast down and wrench off the door by force, Anthony, as from a shrine, came forth initiated in the mysteries and filled with the Spirit of God. He pursuaded many to embrace the solitary life. And thus it happened in the end that cells arose even in the mountains, and the desert was colonized by monks, who came forth from their own people, and enrolled themselves for the citizenship in the heavens. Anthony directed them all as a father. He exhorted them to perseverance and encouraged them against the wiles of Satan. And their cells were in the mountains, like tabernacles, filled with holy bands of men who sang psalms, loved reading, fasted, prayed, rejoiced in the hope of things to come, labored in almsgiving, and preserved love and harmony one with another.

Anthony lived to be one hundred five years old. Up to the end he preserved a uniform zeal for the discipline, and neither through old age was subdued by the desire of costly food, nor through the infirmity of his body changed the fashion of his clothing, nor washed his feet with water, and yet remained entirely free from harm. For his eyes were undimmed and quite sound and he saw clearly; of his teeth he had not lost one, but they had become worn to the gums through the great age of the old man. He remained strong both in hands and feet; and while all men were using various foods, and washings and divers garments, he appeared more cheerful and of greater strength. And the fact that his fame has been blazoned everywhere is clear proof of his virtue and God's love of his soul. For not from writings, nor from worldly wisdom, nor through any art, was Anthony renowned, but solely from his piety towards God. That this was the gift of God no one will deny.*

* Condensed from *A Select Library of Nicene and Post-Nicene Fathers of the Christian Church*, Second Series, Vol. IV, pp. 194-221.

THE CONVERSION OF CONSTANTINE THE GREAT
Eusebios

WHEN Constantine was convinced that he needed some more powerful aid than his military forces could afford him, on account of the wicked and magical enchantments which were so diligently practiced by the tyrant Maxentius in Rome, he sought divine assistance, deeming the possession of arms and a numerous soldiery of secondary importance, but believing the co-operating power of Deity invincible and not to be shaken. He considered, therefore, on what God he might rely for protection and assistance. While engaged in this inquiry, the thought occurred to him, that, of the many emperors who had preceded him, those who had rested their hopes in a multitude of gods, and served them with sacrifices and offerings, had in the first place been deceived by flattering predictions and oracles which promised them all prosperity, and at last had met with an unhappy end, while not one of their gods had stood by to warn them of the impending wrath of heaven; while one alone who had pursued an entirely opposite course, who had condemned their error, and honored the one Supreme God during his whole life, had found him to be the Saviour and Protector of his empire, and the Giver of every good thing. Therefore he felt it incumbent on him to honor his father's God alone.

Accordingly he called on Him with earnest prayer and supplications that He would reveal to him who He was, and stretch forth His right hand to help him in his present difficulties. And while he was praying with fervent entreaty, a most marvelous sign appeared to him from heaven, the account of which it might have been hard to believe had it been related by any other person. But since the victorious emperor himself long afterwards declared it to the writer of this history, when he was honored with his acquaintance and society, and confirmed his statement by an oath, who could hesitate to accredit the relation, especially since the testimony of after-time has established its truth? He said that about noon, when the day was already beginning to decline, he saw with his own eyes the trophy of a cross of light in the heavens, above the sun, and bearing the inscription, CONQUER BY THIS (*In Hoc Signo Vinces*). At this sight he himself was struck with amazement, and his whole army also, which followed him on this expedition, and witnessed the miracle.

He said, moreover, that he doubted within himself what the import of this apparition could be. And while he continued to ponder and reason on its meaning, night suddenly came on; then in his sleep the Christ of God appeared to him with the same sign which he had seen in the heavens, and said to use it as a safeguard in all engagements with his enemies.

Assuming therefore the Supreme God as his patron, and invoking His Christ to be his preserver and aid, and setting the victorious trophy, the salutary symbol, in front of his soldiers and bodyguard, he marched with his whole forces, trying to obtain again for the Romans the freedom they had inherited from their ancestors.

And whereas Maxentius, trusting more in his magic arts than in the affection of his subjects, dared not even advance outside the city gates, but had guarded every place and district and city subject to his tyranny, with large bodies of soldiers, the emperor, confiding in the help of God, advanced against the first and second and third divisions of the tyrant's forces, defeated them all with ease at the first assault, and made his way into the very interior of Italy. Maxentius himself met death on the bridge of the Tiber, and Constantine entered Rome in triumph.

Constantine the Great reigned for about thirty-two years and lived to be over sixty. During his reign he showed much favor to the Christians, and their Church and clergy, and erected many churches. When at length he was convinced that his life was drawing to a close, he felt the time was come at which he should seek purification from sins of his past career, firmly believing that whatever errors he had committed as a mortal man, his soul would be purified from them through the efficacy of the mystical words and the salutary waters of baptism. Impressed with these thoughts, he poured forth his supplications and confessions to God, kneeling on the pavement in the church itself, in which he also now for the first time received the imposition of hands with prayer. After this he proceeded as far as the suburbs of Nicomedia, and there, having summoned the bishops to meet him, addressed them in the following words.

"The time is arrived which I have long hoped for, with an earnest desire and prayer that I might obtain the salvation of God. The hour is come in which I too may have the blessing of that seal which confers immortality; the hour in which I may receive the seal of salvation. I had thought to do this in the waters of the river Jordan, wherein our Saviour, for our example, is recorded to have been baptized; but God, who knows what is expedient for us, is pleased that I should receive this blessing here. Be it so, then, without delay: for should it be His will who is Lord of life and death, that my existence here should be prolonged, and should I be destined henceforth to associate with the people of God, and unite with them in prayer as a member of His Church, I will prescribe to myself from this time such a course of life as befits His service."

After he had thus spoken, the prelates performed the sacred ceremonies in the usual manner, and, having given him the necessary instructions, made him a partaker of the mystic ordinance. Thus was Constantine the first of all sovereigns who was regenerated and perfected in a church dedicated to the martyrs of Christ; thus gifted with the divine seal of baptism, he rejoiced in spirit, was renewed, and filled with heavenly light: his soul was gladdened by reason of the fervency of his faith, and astonished at the manifestation of the power of God. At the conclusion of the ceremony he arrayed himself in shining imperial vestments, brilliant as the light, and reclined on a couch of the purest white, refusing to clothe himself with the purple any more.

He then lifted his voice and poured forth a strain of thanksgiving to God; after which he added these words. "Now I know that I am truly blessed; now I feel assured that I am accounted worthy of immortality, and am made a partaker of divine light." He further expressed his compassion for the unhappy condition of those who were strangers to such blessings as he enjoyed; and when the tribunes and generals of his army appeared in his presence with lamentations and tears at the prospect of their bereavement, and with prayers that his days might yet be prolonged, he assured them in reply that he was now in possession of true life; that none but himself could know the value of the blessings he had received; so that he was anxious rather to hasten than to defer his departure to God. He then proceeded to complete the needful arrangement of his affairs, making every disposition according to his own pleasure.*

✝

GORGONIA**
Gregory Nazianzen

In modesty Gorgonia so greatly excelled, and so far surpassed, those of her own day, to say nothing of those of old time who have been illustrious for modesty, that, in regard to the two divisions of the life of all, that is, the married and the unmarried state, the latter being higher and more divine, though more difficult and dangerous, while the former is more humble and more safe, she was able to avoid the disadvantages of each, and to select and combine all that is best in both, namely, the elevation of the one and the security of the other, thus becoming modest with pride, blending the excellence of the married with that of the unmarried state, and proving that neither of them absolutely binds us to, or separates us from, God or the world (so that the one from its own nature must be utterly avoided, and the other altogether praised): but that it is mind which nobly presides over wedlock and maidenhood, and arranges and works upon them as the raw material of virtue under the master-hand of reason. For though she had entered upon a carnal union, she was not therefore separated from the spirit, nor, because her husband was her head, did she ignore her first Head; but, performing those few ministrations due to the world and nature, according to the will of the law of the flesh, or rather of Him who gave to the flesh these laws, she consecrated herself entirely to God. But what is most excellent and honorable, she also won over her husband to her side, and made of him a good fellow servant, instead of an unreasonable master. And not only so, but she further made the fruit of her body, her children and her children's children, to be the fruit of her spirit, dedicating to God not her single soul, but the whole

* From *The Life of Constantine* by Eusebios of Caesarea, in *A Select Library of Nicene and Post-Nicene Fathers of the Christian Church*, Second Series, Vol. I, pp. 489-90, 492-93, 554-56.
** Sister of Gregory Nazianzen.

family and household. And she made wedlock illustrious through her own acceptability in wedlock, and the fair harvest she had reaped thereby. And she presented herself, as long as she lived, as an example to her offspring of all that was good.

She was sick in body, and dangerously ill of an extraordinary and malignant disease, her whole frame was incessantly fevered, her blood at one time agitated and boiling, then curdling with coma, incredible pallor, and paralysis of mind and limbs: and this not at long intervals, but sometimes very frequently. Its virulence seemed beyond human aid. The skill of physicians, who carefully examined the case, both singly and in consultation, was of no avail; nor were the tears of her parents, which often have great power, nor public supplication and intercessions, in which all the people joined as earnestly as if for their own preservation. Her safety was regarded the safety of all, as, on the contrary, her suffering and sickness was a common misfortune.

What then did this great soul, worthy offspring of the greatest, and what was the medicine for her disorder, for we have now come to the great secret? Despairing of all other aid, she betook herself to the Physician of all, and awaiting the silent hours of night, during a slight intermission of the disease, she approached the altar with faith, and, calling upon Him who is honored thereon, with a mighty cry, and every kind of invocation, calling to mind all His former works of power, and well she knew those both of ancient and later days, at last she ventured on an act of pious and splendid effrontery. She imitated the woman whose fountain of blood was dried up by the hem of Christ's garment [Matt. 9:20]. What did she do? Resting her head with another cry upon the altar, and with a wealth of tears, as she once bedewed the feet of Christ [Luke 7:38], and declaring that she would not loose her hold until she was made whole, she then applied her medicine to her whole body, namely, such a portion of the antitypes of the Precious Body and Blood as she treasured in her hand, mingling therewith her tears. And O the wonder! She went away feeling at once that she was saved, and with the lightness of health in body, soul, and mind, having received, as the reward of her hope, that which she hoped for, and having gained bodily by means of spiritual strength.

Great though these things be, they are not untrue. Believe them all of you, whether sick or sound, that ye may either keep or regain your health. And that my story is no mere boastfulness is plain from the silence in which she kept, while alive, what I have revealed. Nor should I now have published it, be well assured, had I not feared that so great a marvel would have been utterly hidden from the faithful and unbelieving of these and later days.*

* Condensed from *A Select Library of Nicene and Post-Nicene Fathers*, Second Series, Vol. VII, pp. 240, 243.

GLADSOME LIGHT

"GLADSOME Light" or, as it is often also called, "Triune," or "Lamp Hymn,"
is one of the most ancient of Christian hymns. Some attribute it to the apostolic
era, while others cite Athenogenes, who suffered martyrdom late in the third
century. Although its meter is mixed, studded with anapaests, spondees,
dactyls, amphibrachs, and so forth, the message of the words is simple and
direct. The purpose of the hymn is to render thanks to God, at the close of

Gladsome Light

Athenogenes, 3rd Century (?)

John Sakellarides
Transcribed from the
Byzantine by
Dean D. Bouzianis

Mode II

Fos i - la - ron a - ghi as -dho - xis a -thana - -tou Patros oura

ni - ou a - ghi -ou maka - ros I - i -sou Khri - - ste el -

thon - - - tes e -pi tin ili -ou dhy - sin i -dhontes fos e -

spe -ri - non ym -nou - menpa - te - rayi - on ke a - ghi -on

Pnev - ma The -on. A -xi -on Se en pa - si ke -ris ym -

ni - sthe fo - nes e - si - - es Yi - e The - ou zo -

in o dhi - dhous: Dhi -o o

ko - smos Se - dho - xa - zi.

the day, at the time the sun sets and the lamps are lit, whence one of its names.

"Gladsome Light" is usually chanted at the Vespers Entrance, which typifies the gladsome radiance that the person of Christ bestowed upon men. With the singing of this hymn the Holy Doors (of the iconostasis) are opened to represent the coming of the Lord and the opening of God's Paradise to men. The hymn, therefore, fits well in the symbolism of the Eastern Church, and is quite indicative of the joyfulness and humility attending the worship of God. It ends the drama of the daily life with all its cares with a bright and optimistic note. The light of the day is succeeded by the gladsome light that the joyful evening prayer stores within the praying faithful.

In English the Greek text is rendered thus:

> Gladsome Light of the holy glory of the immortal Father,
>   The holy and heavenly, O blessed Jesus Christ,
> We, having come to the sun's setting and seen the evening light,
>   Praise Father, Son, and Holy Spirit.
> Thou God art worthy of praise at all times with joyful voices,
>   Son of God, Giver of life:
> Wherefore the world glorifieth Thee.

WE HYMN THEE

THIS is a brief hymn of unknown authorship. The tendency has been to attribute it to the two prominent authors of Divine Liturgies in the fourth century, St. Basil and St. John Chrysostom, and this all the more since there is no dispute with respect to its date, commonly agreed to be the fourth century. It is interesting to note also that the "We Hymn Thee" goes parallel to the Ambrosian hymn "Te Deum Laudamus."

The chanting of this hymn is done after the priest exclaims, "Thine own of Thine own we offer unto Thee, in behalf of all and for all." During the chanting the priest secretly prays that the Holy Spirit descend upon the Holy Gifts. Four Eastern liturgies—those of SS. Basil, Chrysostom, Mark, and Cyril—fix it in the same place.

An interesting parallel to its text is found in the apostolic treatise called the *Martyrdom of Polycarp* (see p. 155): "I praise Thee, I bless Thee, I glorify Thee through the everlasting and heavenly High Priest, Jesus Christ."

Modern melody versions of this hymn are those of Allemanov, Tchaikovsky, Lomakin, Rozhnov, Smirnov, Vasiliev, and several others.

The words of our hymn are:

> We hymn Thee, we bless Thee,
> We thank Thee, O Lord,
> And worship Thee, our God.

We Hymn Thee

Traditional Byzantine

Mode I

Transcribed from the Byzantine
By Dean D. Bouzianis

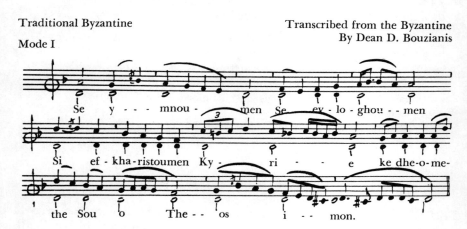

CONTENTS

PART II   SECTION 3

THE FABRIC OF THE FAITH IS WOVEN

Give diligence to present thyself approved unto God, a workman that needeth not to be ashamed, handling aright the word of truth.—II Timothy 2:15, ASV.

PICTURES: PAGE
  Interpretation: Athanasios of Alexandria—*Theophanes of Crete* 184
  Picture: Athanasios of Alexandria—*Theophanes of Crete* 185
  Interpretation: Gregory of Nyssa—*Artist Unknown* 186
  Picture: Gregory of Nyssa—*Artist Unknown* 187
  Interpretation: John Damascene—*Kontoglous* 186
  Picture: John Damascene—*Kontoglous* 189

POETRY:
  The Great Canon—*Andrew of Crete* 188
  Sunday of Orthodoxy Canon—*Theodore of Studium* 190
  Unity of Threefold Light—*Metrophanes of Smyrna* 191
  Thy Paternal Glory—*Joseph of Studium* 191
  Order of Holy Unction—*Arsenios* 192
  The Two Natures of Jesus Christ—*Ephraem the Syrian* 192
  For the Whole Church—*Ephraem the Syrian* 192

STORIES:
  Decree on the Veneration of the Icons—*The Seventh Ecumenical Synod* ... 193
  The Meek Icon—*Kontoglous* 194
  Symeon the Stylite—*Baring-Gould* 196

MUSIC:
  Interpretation: Trisagion—*Traditional Byzantine* 198
  Hymn: Trisagion—*Protopsaltis;* transcribed by *Bouzianis* 199
  Interpretation: Day of Resurrection—*John Damascene* 200
  Hymn: Day of Resurrection—Transcribed from Byzantine by *Bouzianis* ... 200

ATHANASIOS OF ALEXANDRIA

Theophanes of Crete

THE icon of St. Athanasios (293-373) (p. 185) by Theophanes of Crete, the leading artist of the so-called Cretan school, belongs to a great era of Byzantine painting. Theophanes flourished about the middle of the sixteenth century. He worked with his son Simeon on Mount Athos and elsewhere. This icon shows clearly some of the more striking trends of this school of iconographers, which flourished from the fourteenth through the sixteenth century, a period—perhaps the best era of Byzantine painting—which constitutes the third renaissance of Byzantine sacred art.

The Cretan school tended to be conservative. It paid attention to minute details, and was noted for its calligraphic drawing, done with consummate technical skill and refinement. It had both clarity and restraint. In addition, the artists of the Cretan school understood the importance of colors; there is sumptuous coloring in this art.

Artists from the Cretan school have decorated churches from Mistra in the Peloponnesos all the way to Meteora and Mount Athos in Greece and beyond. Incidentally, El Greco, whose paintings of St. Andrew and St. Jerome appear on pp. 150 and 253, springs from this very school.

This icon of Athanasios comes from the monastery of St. Stephen at Meteora. It illustrates well the ability of Theophanes to express in a portrait the traits and qualities of a great physiognomy. The Athanasios in the icon reflects the dynamic and forceful debater at the First Ecumenical Synod at Nicaea in 325, defending Christian orthodoxy against heretical tendencies. Here is the portrait of a man of strong will, resolution, and determination, undaunted in conflict and adversity. In him are united inflexibility and discretion, firmness and charity.

A few months after the Nicene Council ended, the Archbishop of Alexandria died, and Athanasios, the now famous archdeacon, succeeded to the episcopal throne of that leading city. He was consecrated in 326 and distinguished himself in this new capacity. However, his zeal constantly brought him in conflict with the Arians and the pagans who were in league with the heretics. His enemies made many unsuccessful attempts to ruin him with plots, slander, and libel. He was dispossessed of his see several times, after having incurred the disfavor of the emperors Constantine the Great, Constantius, Julian, and Valens. His was a stormy life with all the imprints of the tempestuous fourth century, a golden age for Eastern Orthodoxy.

The words on the open pages of the book Athanasios holds are from the beginning of a prayer similar to the Trisagion in the Divine Liturgy of St. John Chrysostom (see p. 198).

Photo by Pericles Papahadjidakis, Athens, Greece

ATHANASIOS OF ALEXANDRIA—*THEOPHANES OF CRETE*

GREGORY OF NYSSA
Artist Unknown

GREGORY of Nyssa (341?-?395) was a younger brother of Basil the Great. He is one of the glories of Cappadocia and of the whole Greek Orthodox Church. He participated in the Second Ecumenical Synod (381) and his name was honored in the later Councils as befitting a prominent church father.

This mosaic portrait of Gregory of Nyssa gives a faithful glimpse of a man deeply spiritual and contemplative. It comes from the Palatine Chapel at Palermo, Italy, which was founded in 1132 and consecrated eight years later. It belongs to the same period and is wholly Byzantine in design and execution, despite the fact that it was made in Sicily for the chapel of King Roger II, a Norman. The mosaic demonstrates the pre-eminence that Gregory enjoyed abroad. In the icon of Gregory we are convinced that a serious, pious, and contemplative face is looking at us, eager to guide and advise with deep thoughts.

Gregory had a decidedly philosophical bent and aimed at giving to the various doctrines of the Church a rational demonstration. His efforts and success in this endeavor make him the father of pastoral medicine and of Christian anthropology. He also made a serious attempt to create a Christian psychology with the aid of earlier, classical ideas. He was aided in this synthesis of Christian learning by his careful study of the ancient Greek classics, especially the works of Plato and certain scientific and medical works of the past.

He has left many works dealing with problems and issues of Christianity. His treatise *Against Eunomios* is the most complete defense we have of Orthodoxy against the logical and subtle arguments of the Arians. The *Catechetical Discourse* of Gregory is one of the earliest synopses of the Orthodox faith. It has proved to be a popular and very useful work. Another fine treatise is *On the Soul and the Resurrection,* which is modeled on Plato's *Phaedo.*

✤

JOHN DAMASCENE
Fotis Kontoglous

JOHN of Damascus (*ca.* 676-*ca.* 754) in Syria is one of the most highly respected and celebrated Eastern Orthodox Church fathers of the later period. For this reason his portrait is found in many churches the world over. Our selection is a fine panel icon executed by Fotis Kontoglous. It is dedicated to the Archimandrite Damaskinos Lazarides, who is also its present owner. This icon is not a mere picture of the saint, but also a sketch of his life.

Courtesy *Dumbarton Oaks Collection, Washington, D. C.*

GREGORY OF NYSSA—*ARTIST UNKNOWN*

John Damascene was a great fighter in behalf of Orthodoxy and a prolific writer and poet. His life covered the early period of the famous Iconoclastic Controversy which saw the imperial power turned against the veneration of the icons. John fought strenuously against the destruction of the icons by composing three special treatises to defend the use of icons in the Christian faith and present the truly Orthodox point of view on the matter. He explained in clear terms the symbolic nature of the icon, asserting that the icon is not an idol, but that it "stands for something other than itself." The Church later gave him due credit for this extraordinary service.

His major work, *The Fountain of Knowledge,* is a most authoritative synthesis of the doctrines of the fathers. It is the first summary of Christian theology, a *summa theologica,* and has served as the dogmatic handbook of the Middle Ages. John also wrote a large number of hymns, some of which are gems in Eastern Orthodoxy, and easily give him the rank of one of the best melodists of the Orthodox Church. He is credited with having set in order the Greek Orthodox service books.

The pose and attire of John Damascene in our picture make at least three things clear: his character, stormy life, and area of activity. The saint is serene and contemplative, a deep and courageous thinker and writer. The words in the scroll ("We are like sailors on the stormy sea of life. . . .") sum up his stormy career. His attire—the headgear in particular—indicates the area of his activity. For a while John was in the service of the Caliph of Damascus. Then he renounced the world and, giving away his property to the poor, he retired to the monastery of St. Sabas in Palestine. There he was ordained priest and composed his deeply religious hymns. All his works were written in Greek.

The artist Fotis Kontoglous strove to include with much clarity and forcefulness many of the points noted above concerning the life and career of John. In the icon we are face to face with the traditional John Damascene.

✝

THE GREAT CANON

Whence shall my tears begin?
What first-fruits shall I bear?
Of earnest sorrow for my sin?
Or how my woes declare?
Oh Thou! the Merciful and Gracious One!
Forgive the foul transgressions I have done.

With Adam I have vied,
Yea, pass'd him, in my fall;
And I am naked now, by pride
And lust made bare of all;
Of Thee, O God, and that Celestial Band,
And all the glory of the Promis'd Land.

JOHN DAMASCENE—*KONTOGLOUS*

My guilt for vengeance cries;
   But yet Thou pard'nest all,
And whom Thou lov'st Thou dost chastise,
   And mourn'st for them that fall:
Thou, as a Father, mark'st our tears and pain,
And welcomest the prodigal again.

I lie before Thy door,
   O turn me not away!
Nor in mine old age give me o'er
   To Satan for a prey!
But ere the end of life and term of grace,
Thou Merciful! my many sins efface!

The priest beheld, and pass'd
   The way he had to go:
A careless glance the Levite cast,
   And left me to my woe:
But Thou, O Jesu, Mary's Son, console,
Draw nigh, and succour me, and make me whole!

Thou Spotless Lamb divine,
   Who takest sins away,
Remove, remove, the load that mine
   Upon my conscience lay:
And, of Thy tender mercy, grant Thou me
To find remission of iniquity!*

—Andrew of Crete

SUNDAY OF ORTHODOXY CANON

A song, a song of gladness!
   A song of thanks and praise!
The horn of our salvation
   Hath God vouchsaf'd to raise!
A monarch true and faithful,
   And glorious in her might,
To champion Christ's own quarrel,
   And Orthodoxy's right!

Now manifest is glory;
   Now grace and virtue shine:
Now joys the Church, regaining
   Her ornaments divine:
And girds them on in gladness,
   As fits a festal day,
After long months of struggle,
   Long years of disarray.

Awake, O Church, and triumph!
   Exult, each realm and land!
And open let the houses,
   Th' ascetic houses stand!
And let the holy virgins
   With joy and song take in
Their relics and their Icons,
   Who died this day to win!**

—Theodore of Studium

* A cento from J. M. Neale and S. G. Hatherly's *Hymns of the Eastern Church*, 4th ed., p. 18.
** *Ibid.*, p. 102.

UNITY OF THREEFOLD LIGHT

O Unity of Threefold light,
    Send out Thy loveliest ray,
And scatter our transgressions' night,
    And turn it into day;
Make us those temples pure and fair,
    Thy glory loveth well,
The spotless tabernacles, where
    Thou may'st vouchsafe to dwell!

Glorious hosts of peerless might
    That ever see Thy Face,
Thou mak'st the mirrors of Thy Light,
    The vessels of Thy grace:
Thou, when their wond'rous strain they weave,
    Hast pleasure in the lay:
Deign thus our praises to receive,
    Albeit from lips of clay!

And yet Thyself they cannot know,
    Nor pierce the veil of light
That hides Thee from the Thrones below,
    As in profoundest night:
How then can mortal accents frame
    Due tribute to the King?
Thou, only, while we praise Thy Name,
    Forgive us as we sing!*

—*Metrophanes of Smyrna*

THY PATERNAL GLORY

Far from Thy heavenly care,
    Lord, I have gone astray;
And all the wealth Thou gav'st to me,
    Have cast away.

Now from a broken heart,
    In penitence sincere,
I lift my prayer to Thee, O Lord,
    In mercy hear.

And in Thy blest abode
    Give me a servant's place,
That I, a son, may learn to own
    A Father's grace.**

—*Joseph of Studium*

* *Ibid.,* p. 142.
** From *Hymns of the Greek Church,* translated by John Brownlie, p. 23.

ORDER OF HOLY UNCTION

Thou Christ alone art great,
   In Thee we ever find
Infinite love and tenderness,
   And mercy wondrous kind.

Thy sanctifying grace,
   O Christ send from above;
Seal thou our souls and bodies now,
   And heal us all in love.*

                                       —*Arsenios*

THE TWO NATURES OF JESUS CHRIST

Perish not through the names
With which that Living One clothed Himself,
That He might give life to all men!
For that Mighty One put on names
Which fall short of Him through His bodily form,
Because of His mercy towards you.

The name of the Father is true;
The name of the Son is faithful;
That of the Pardoner is worthy of love;
That of the Judge is terrible.
As the Son of man He is circumscribed,
But being unbounded in His nature,
         He is truly God!**

               —*Ephraem the Syrian (306?-?373)*

FOR THE WHOLE CHURCH

Lord! let Thy right hand raise us,
And extend aid to Thy flock;
That our race may be exalted by Thy favor,
For Thine is the victory!
Thou giver of grace to the upright,
Afford us happiness by Thy power;
Let the day of Thy appearing gladden us,
And may we carry oil in our lamps!

Vouchsafe prosperity to Thy Churches,
And sow Thy peace among us;

---

* From *Hymns of the Holy Eastern Church*, translated by John Brownlie, p. 113.

** A cento from *Select Metrical Hymns and Homilies of Ephraem Syrus*, translated from the Syriac by Henry Burgess.

Let tribes and families give thanks
To the name of the Trinity.
O Lord! confirm our souls
In Thy faith and love;
Forgive our trespasses and sins
Through Thy mercy, oh lover of the penitent!*
                    —*Ephraem the Syrian* (306?-?373)

✤

DECREE ON THE VENERATION OF THE ICONS
The Seventh Ecumenical Synod

To make our confession short, we keep unchanged all the ecclesiastical traditions handed down to us, whether in writing or verbally, one of which is the making of pictorial representations, agreeable to the history of the preaching of the gospel, a tradition useful in many respects, but especially in this, that so the incarnation of the Word of God is shown forth as real and not merely phantastic, for these have mutual indications and without doubt have also mutual significations.

We, therefore, following the royal pathway and the divinely inspired authority of our holy fathers and the traditions of the catholic Church, define with all certitude and accuracy that just as the figure of the precious and life-giving cross, so also the venerable and holy icons, as well in painting and mosaic as of other fit materials, should be set forth in the holy churches of God, and on the sacred vessels and on the vestments and on hangings and in pictures both in houses and by the wayside, to wit, the figure of our Lord God and Saviour Jesus Christ, of our spotless Lady, the Mother of God, of the honorable angels, of all saints and of all pious people.

For by so much more frequently as they are seen in artistic representation, by so much more readily are men lifted up to the memory of their prototypes, and to a longing after them; and to these should be given due salutation and honorable reverence, not indeed that true worship of faith which pertains alone to the divine nature; but to these, as to the figure of the precious and life-giving cross and to the Book of the Gospels and to the other holy objects, incense, and lights may be offered according to ancient pious custom. For the honor which is paid to the icon passes on to that which the icon represents, and he who reveres the icon reveres in it the subject represented. For thus the teaching of our holy fathers, that is the tradition of the universal Church, which from one end of the earth to the other hath received the gospel, is strengthened. Thus we follow Paul, who spake in Christ, and the whole divine and apostolic company and the holy fathers, holding fast the traditions which we have received. So we sing prophetically the triumphal hymns of the Church: "Rejoice greatly, O daughter of Sion; Shout, O daughter of Jeru-

* *Ibid.*

salem. Rejoice and be glad with all thy heart. The Lord hath taken away from thee the oppression of thy adversaries; thou art redeemed from the hand of thine enemies. The Lord is a King in the midst of thee; thou shalt not see evil any more, and peace be unto thee forever."*

✝

THE MEEK ICON
Fotis Kontoglous

On the Holy Mountain** there is a monastery which is called Stavronikita, a small and poor monastery, dedicated to the name of St. Nicholas. At first it was built in the memory of St. John the Baptist, but during the period of the enemies of the icons the monks threw many icons into the sea, so that the impious enemies of the icons would not pollute them. Among these icons there was that of St. Nicholas from the monastery of Stavronikita, which was also one of the wonder-making icons of the Holy Mountain. And when this monastery was burned by the corsairs, Patriarch Jeremiah the Elder wanted to rebuild it, again in the name of St. John the Baptist. But as the master workmen were building, the monks cast the nets to catch some fish, and raising them, they found in them this icon of St. Nicholas.

On its forehead an oyster was stuck, and when they pulled to remove it, blood flowed from the wound that the oyster opened. On account of this miracle it was named St. Nicholas the Oyster Fisher, and it is so called to this day. This icon is very old mosaic. Such mosaic icons made on walls abound, but small ones made on wood are very scarce.

When the Patriarch saw this miracle, he dedicated the new monastery to St. Nicholas. And one shell of the oyster the Patriarch made into a tray for the raising of the Virgin at the Holy Table, and the other he made into an amulet which is to be found today in the sacristy of the Moscow Patriarchate. These things took place in 1553.

All the saints are saintly, but St. Nicholas is especially loved by the sailors, whose protector he is. That is why more boats bear his name. Moreover, in his physiognomy he is also the sweetest and the most compassionate, "an icon of meekness." He lived about A.D. 300 during the reigns of two cruel tyrants, Diocletian and Maximian. At first he became monk and then was ordained bishop at Myra of Lycia, because of his fine life which was pleasing to God. Before Constantine the Great became emperor, he suffered much for the faith, was beaten, tortured, and imprisoned. In 325 Constantine convoked the First Ecumenical Synod which enacted the "Creed." Among the 318 assembled fathers was also St. Nicholas.

Though he was severe with the heretics, he was all the more soft and like

---

* Abridged from *A Select Library of Nicene and Post-Nicene Fathers of the Christian Church*, Vol. XIV, p. 550.
** Mount Athos in northern Greece.

a tender father to his flock. He supported the wronged, helped the poor, and consoled the grieved. At one time three men were condemned to death and locked up in the prison to be beheaded the following day. These unfortunate men were innocent and when they heard that the next day their heads would be cut off, they took to prayer and with tears begged St. Nicholas to help them. And the same night the king saw in his dream the saint who told him that the three prisoners were innocent and that the governor Ablavius had falsely accused them. At once there appeared in front of the king the three condemned men and the executioner made them kneel and tied their eyes in order to behead them. But the moment he was raising his sword to strike, St. Nicholas seized it by the blade without cutting himself and held it. Upon seeing these things, the king woke up disturbed before daybreak, ordered the immediate release from the prison of the men that were about to die, and in their place had Ablavius imprisoned.

However, he became the protector of the sailors after his passing away, as a result of a great miracle that he performed. In Constantinople there lived a very pious Christian who loved and honored St. Nicholas exceedingly much. At one time, therefore, he decided to travel on business, and before embarking he went to the church of St. Nicholas to pray with much fervor. When the ship went out on the high sea, it was caught in a heavy storm. About midnight the sailors got up to turn the sails, and from the shouts this man awoke and went to drink water. While he was walking on the deck, he got tangled up in the ropes and the sail struck him and hurled him into the sea. The captain and the sailors tried to save him, but due to the roughness of the sea and the darkness of the night they failed, and the man disappeared from their eyes. But when he sank, dressed as he was, and was going down to the bottom, he said within himself: "St. Nicholas, help me." And as he was dizzy and half-drowned and believed that he was in the other world, he found himself suddenly in the chamber of his home shouting all the while with a loud voice: "St. Nicholas, help me!" And since it was night and quiet, his family heard his shouts, jumped out of bed, and rushed to his room. There they saw their father standing and shouting: "St. Nicholas, help me!" Water was streaming down his clothes. The neighbors also arrived and the house was filled with people. No one could believe his own eyes. Each was asking another what had happened, until the victim of drowning related the miracle. They thanked God and exclaimed: "Lord, have mercy on us."

When the resurrected man dressed himself with dry clothes, he went to the church of St. Nicholas, kneeled before the icon, and wept till dawn. Soon this great miracle was heralded to all Christendom, and from that time the mariners and travelers cry out to St. Nicholas for help, and the priests always mention him with the great saints, "Nicholas the wonder-maker, archbishop of Myra in Lycia."*

* From *Kivotos* (December 1952), pp. 451-54, condensed and translated from the Greek by John P. Cavarnos. Used by permission of the author and the editor.

SYMEON THE STYLITE

Sabine Baring-Gould

SYMEON was born in the village of Gesa, between Antioch and Cilicia, and as a boy kept his father's sheep. One day, forced by heavy snow to leave them in the fold, he went with his parents to the church, and there heard the gospel read, which blesses those who mourn and weep; which calls those enviable who have a pure heart. And when he asked a bystander what he would gain who kept the Beatitudes, the man propounded to him the life of self-sacrifice.

Forthwith, Symeon going out of the church, went to a neighboring monastery, governed by one Timothy; and falling down before the gate, he lay five days, neither eating nor drinking. And on the fifth day the abbot, coming out, asked him, "Whence art thou, my son? What parents hast thou, that thou art so afflicted? Or, what is thy name, lest perchance thou hast done wrong?" Then the lad answered with tears, "No, master! I long to be a servant of God, and to save my soul. Suffer me to enter the monastery, and send me not away."

The abbot accepted him. Symeon was in the convent about four months, serving all without complaint, and in that time he learned the whole Psalter by heart. But the food which he took with his brethren, he gave away secretly to the poor, reserving for himself only food for one day in the seven. But one day, having gone to the well to draw water, he took the rope from the bucket and wound it round his body, from the loins to the neck, and wore it till his flesh was cut into by the rope. One day, some of the brethren found him giving his food to the poor; and when they returned, they complained to the abbot, saying, "We cannot abstain like him; he fasts from Lord's day to Lord's day, and gives away his food." Then the abbot rebuked him, and Symeon answered not. And the angry abbot bade them strip him, and found the rope round him, sunk into the flesh, and with great trouble it was uncoiled, and the skin came off with it; then the monks took care of him and healed him. When he was healed, he went out of the monastery and entered a deserted tank. After a few days he was found, and the abbot descended into the tank. Then the blessed Symeon, seeing him, began to entreat, saying, "I beg you, servants of God, let me alone one hour, that I may render up my spirit. My soul is very weary, because I have angered the Lord."

The lad was returned to the monastery by force, and stayed in the community about one year. After this he came to the Telanassus, under the peak of the mountain, on which he lived till his death, and having found a little house, he remained in it shut up for three years. But eager to advance in virtue, he tried to persuade Blasus, who was the archpriest of the villages around, to leave nothing within by him, for forty days and nights, but to close up the door with clay. The priest warned him that to die by one's own act is no virtue, but a great crime. "Put by me then, father," he said, "ten loaves, and a cruse of water, and if I find my body needs sustenance, I will partake of them." Blasus did so, and at the end of the days Blasus removed the clay, and going in, found the bread and water untouched, and Symeon lying, unable to speak or move. Getting a sponge, he moistened and opened his lips, and then gave him the Holy Eucharist; and strengthened by this immortal food, he chewed, little by little, lettuces and succory, and such like.

When he had passed three years in that little house, he took possession of the peak, which has since been so famous. The fame of the wondrous austerities of this man wrought upon the wild Arab tribes, and effected what no missionaries had been able as yet to perform. No doubt the fearful severities exercised by Symeon on himself are startling and even shocking. But the Spirit of God breathes where He wills. So was it now; on the wild sons of the desert no missionaries had made an impression; their rough hearts had given no echo to the sound of the gospel. Something of startling novelty was needed to catch their attention, and strike their imagination, and drag them violently to the cross. These wild men came from their deserts to see the weird, haggard man in his den. He fled from them as they crowded upon him, not into the wastes of sand, but up a pillar; first up one six cubits, then one twelve cubits, and finally, one of thirty-six. The sons of Ishmael poured to the foot of the pillar, "like a river along the roads, and formed an ocean of men about it." And myriads of Ishmaelites were illuminated by that station on the column. For this most shining light, set, as it were, on a candlestick, sent forth all around its beams, like the sun, and one might see Iberi, Persians, and Armenians coming and receiving divine baptism. But the Arabs coming by tribes, two hundred and three hundred at a time, and sometimes even a thousand, denied with shouts the error of their ancestors; and breaking in pieces the images they had worshiped, and renouncing the orgies of Venus, they received the divine sacraments, and accepted laws from the holy tongue.

On festivals, from the setting of the sun till its appearance again, he stood all night with his hands uplifted to heaven, neither soothed with sleep, nor conquered by fatigue. But in toils so great, and so great magnitude of deeds, and multitude of miracles, his self-esteem is as moderate as if he were in dignity the least of men. Besides his modesty, he is easy of access of speech, and gracious, and answers every man who speaks to him. And from the bounteous God he has received the gift of teaching, and he makes exhortations to the people twice every day. He may be seen also acting as a judge, giving just decisions. This, and the like, is done after the ninth hour. For all night, and through the day to the ninth hour, he prays perpetually. After that he sets forth divine teaching to those who are present, and then, having heard each man's petition, having performed some cures, he settles disputes. About sunset he begins the rest of his converse with God. But though he is employed in this way, he does not give up the care of the churches, sometimes fighting against the impiety of the Greeks, sometimes putting to flight the heretics, and sometimes sending messages to the emperor; sometimes stirring up rulers to zeal for God, and sometimes exhorting the pastors of the churches to bestow more care on their flocks.

Antony, his disciple, thus relates the death of the old hermit. "After a few years it befell one day that he bowed himself in prayer, and remained so three days, Friday, the Sabbath, and the Lord's day. Then I was terrified, and went up to him on the pillar, and stood before his face, and said, 'Master, arise! bless us, for the people have been waiting three days and nights for a blessing from thee.' But he answered not, so I said to him again, 'Wherefore dost thou grieve me, my lord! I beseech thee, put out thy hand to me.' And seeing that he did not answer, I thought to tell no one; for I feared to touch him, and standing about half an hour, I bent down, and put my ear to listen; and there was no breathing. And so I understood that he rested in the Lord; and turning faint, I wept most bitterly; and bending down, I kissed his eyes; and I cried, 'Master, remember me in thy holy rest.' And lifting up his garments, I fell at his feet, and kissed them, and holding his hands, I laid them on my eyes, saying, 'Bless me, I beseech thee, my lord!' "

The body was taken to Antioch, and there buried with great pomp.*

✣

TRISAGION

THIS is a brief hymn in accentual meter, called a *troparion*. The name itself, *Trisagion,* means " 'holy' said three times." The words of the hymn are based on Isaiah 6:3: "Holy, holy, holy, is the Lord of hosts: the whole earth is full of his glory." To this subsequent additions were made. The hymn received its final form sometime before the end of the fourth century.

Tradition is rather vague concerning the authorship. The melody selected for the *Trisagion* comes from the better surviving Byzantine tradition. Ours is in Mode II. As for the matter of age, it seems that the *Trisagion* found a permanent place in the Divine Service during the reign of Emperor Theodosios II (408-451), but it also appears certain that the hymn was known before this time.

Sometimes this hymn is by mistake considered the parallel to the Latin "Ter Sanctus." Actually the "Ter Sanctus" corresponds to another Greek Orthodox hymn, the *Epinikios* or "Triumphal" hymn. The term *Trisagion* is also used to designate the familiar Memorial or Burial Service. The *Trisagion* proper is chanted during the Divine Liturgy by the choir or cantor a little after the Little Entrance, and precedes the reading from the Acts or the Epistles.

Westernized versions of the *Trisagion* are those of Arkhangelsky, Tchaikovsky, Bortniansky, and Arkhiereskoye, and others.

* Abridged from *The Lives of the Saints* by the Reverend Sabine Baring-Gould, Vol. I, pp. 72-80.

The words of the *Trisagion* are quite familiar to the Christian faithful:

Holy God, Holy Mighty, Holy Immortal,
Have mercy upon us.
Glory to the Father, and to the Son, and to the Holy Spirit:
Both now, and always, and unto the ages of ages. Amen.

Trisagion

Traditional Byzantine

Iakovos Protopsaltis, 1800
Transcribed from the
Byzantine by
Dean D. Bouzianis

Mode I

DAY OF RESURRECTION

JOHN Damascene was a highly talented hymnographer and many of his compositions have come down to us, but of all his hymns the Easter Day Canon, which is also called the Golden Canon and the Queen of Canons, stands out. His two other major canons are those of the Ascension and St. Thomas Sunday. Our "Day of Resurrection" hymn comes from the first stanza of the first ode of the Easter Day Canon. In a few words and exultant tones it trumpets far and wide the meaning of Christ's Resurrection. It proclaims that Easter is a change from gloom to gladness, and from death to life eternal. It keynotes victory and immortality.

Day of Resurrection

From the Easter Day Canon
of John Damascene, 8th Century

Transcribed from the
Byzantine by
Dean D. Bouzianis

Mode I

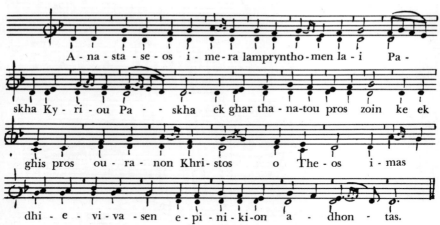

The Easter Day Canon is sung at the midnight Easter service soon after the priest or bishop exclaims, "Christ is risen!" The other eight odes of this canon are variations of the same general theme. The fifth, for example, invites the faithful to drink of the fount of eternal life, for "this is the festival of all Creation." Then the sixth deals with Christ's descent into Hades, to open the gates of heaven to the sons of the earth. The two final odes have perhaps the most triumphant words and phrases. The whole hymn can easily rank among the best compositions of the Eastern Church. Translations like that of Neale do much honor to it, but the full splendor of the hymn can be found and fully appreciated in its original Greek setting, diction, and rhythm and melody.

Inasmuch as the word "canon" has been used extensively in this interpretation, it behooves that the term be defined. The canon is a complex poetical composition consisting of nine odes. These nine odes of the canon are modeled on the Nine Canticles from the Scriptures and are in substance hymns of praise.

The text of "Day of Resurrection" is as follows:

> 'Tis the Day of Resurrection,
> Peoples, let us be bright!
> Easter! The Lord's Easter!
> For from death to life,
> And from earth to heaven hath Christ, who is God,
> Brought us over chanting the hymn of triumph.

CONTENTS

PART II SECTION 4

MISSIONARY ZEAL AND EXPANSION

---†---

For I am not ashamed of the gospel: for it is the power of God unto salvation to every one that believeth; to the Jew first, and also to the Greek. For therein is revealed a righteousness of God from faith unto faith: as it is written, but the righteous shall live by faith.—ROMANS 1:16-17, ASV.

---†---

PICTURES: PAGE
   Interpretation: St. Panteleimon Monastery 203
   Picture: St. Panteleimon Monastery 205
   Interpretation: St. John and St. Prochorus—*Panselenos* 204
   Picture: St. John and St. Prochorus—*Panselenos* 206
   Interpretation: The Transfiguration of Christ—*Kontoglous* 207
   Picture: The Transfiguration of Christ—*Kontoglous* 208

POETRY:
   Let Us Adore God in Holy Trinity—*Emperor Leo VI* 209
   Canon for Apokreos (Sexagesima)—*Theodore of Studium* 209
   The Lord My Creator—*Author Unknown* 210
   All Human Things Are Vanity—*John the Monk* 211
   Tossed on the Sea of Life—*Cosmas of Maiouma* 211
   Song of Cherubim—*Bobrov* 211

STORIES:
   Barlaam and Ioasaph—*John Damascene* 212
   Innocent Veniaminov: The Greatest Missionary of American Orthodoxy—
     Bishop Nicholas 216
   Gregory Palamas: Mystical Illumination—*Payne* 218

MUSIC:
   Interpretation: Cherubic Hymn—*John Chrysostom* (?) 219
   Music: Cherubic Hymn—arr. by *Bouzianis* 220
   Interpretation: Megalynarion—*Traditional Byzantine* 222
   Music: Megalynarion—*Phokaeus;* transcribed by *Bouzianis* 223

ST. PANTELEIMON MONASTERY

MOUNT ATHOS is one portion of the Eastern Orthodox world which has played a very important spiritual and cultural role, and yet is little known to the average person. This place, also called the Holy Mountain, is the only fragment of the Byzantine Empire that has remained more or less intact. It occupies the easternmost prong of the Chalcidice peninsula in Greece. This peninsula is about thirty-five miles long, and at the outer end rises to a sheer peak of over six thousand feet. Extraordinary beauty pervades the entire mountain.

The Athonite peninsula is studded with twenty "ruling monasteries" and a number of dependencies—sketes (religious communities) and hermitages. Seventeen of these are Greek, one Serbian (Chilandari Monastery), one Bulgarian (Zographou Monastery), and one Russian, that of Panteleimon, which means "The All-merciful." Besides these, there are two dependencies belonging to Rumanians. In earlier times there were Iberians and Georgians living on the Holy Mountain. With such a varied population, it is quite evident why this community of monasteries has been called the "Medieval University of Orthodoxy" and the "University of the Balkans." Spiritually, Mount Athos is bound to the Patriarchate of Constantinople, but territorially it comes under the sovereignty of Greece, which guarantees the rights and privileges of all the monks living there and the autonomy of the Athonite community in general.

Mount Athos began to be populated by hermits in early Christian times, and, by virtue of its beauty, security, and the relative richness of its soil, it attracted more solitaries until finally a cluster of monasteries studded the peninsula. The first monastery was founded in the ninth century. The tenth century alone saw eight new monasteries founded there. By the end of the sixteenth century the number of ruling monasteries was fixed at twenty, a figure which still prevails.

The presence of the Russians on the Holy Mountain and their control of the Monastery of St. Panteleimon is a matter of long standing. There has been ascribed to them a monastery on the mountain since the twelfth century. At times circumstances interrupted Russian control of the one monastery. However, in 1834 Russian money and influence helped monks of Russian origin to gain control of the monastery of St. Panteleimon. Gradually it was expanded and strengthened. The Treaties of San Stefano and Berlin of 1878 acknowledged and guaranteed the Russian status. By the beginning of the twentieth century there were about thirty-five hundred Russian monks on Mount Athos, or approximately half the total number. For a while it seemed as if the vast endowments and the influence of the Czars and the monastic population would swing the balance of control of the whole Athonite community. But the Russian revolution changed the situation, and the Russian influence is now negligible.

The Monastery of St. Panteleimon is still very imposing, with its vast buildings and numerous chapels. Its very size and scarcity of monks remind one of great empires—Byzantine and Russian—that were once powerful and generous, but not longer exist. Yet it was such monasteries as this that generations ago trained preachers, iconographers, hagiographers, saints, and writers, and sent them abroad to distribute the gifts of Orthodoxy. But though reduced to relative poverty and other difficulties, the Mount Athos monasteries remain important repositories of immense artistic and cultural wealth. The beautiful churches with their fine icons and precious relics and the libraries with their rich manuscripts all render the Athonite community, this republic of a whole millennium, one of the greatest centers of all Christendom.

✠

ST. JOHN AND ST. PROCHORUS
Manuel Panselenos

THIS icon (p. 206) depicts a historical scene, the composition of the Gospel by St. John the Evangelist, also surnamed the "Theologian," assisted by St. Prochorus. The latter is mentioned in Acts 6:5 as one of the seven deacons. Subsequently he became Bishop of Nicomedia and later died a martyr in Antioch.

John is in his ripe old age, while Prochorus is still very young. The aged evangelist is very attentive and deliberative. From above descends the wisdom and information, which he is dictating slowly to Prochorus. The latter is listening carefully to hear the words dictated and write them down accurately. The words already recorded on the tablet are the opening of the Gospel of John: "In the beginning was the Word . . ."

This dramatic scene is the work of a great artist, Manuel Panselenos of Thessalonike, the outstanding representative of the so-called Macedonian school of art which flourished between the fourteenth and sixteenth centuries. This school combined Eastern Byzantine with Italian influences. To the fundamentally realistic and dramatic style of the East were added the tender and emotional gestures and attitudes. The Macedonian school compares very favorably with the Cretan school in the knowledge and application of color, for both schools flourished side by side for some three centuries.

Churches decorated in the style of the Macedonian school are to be found in Macedonia, Serbia, Peloponnesos, Novgorod, and other places. Mount Athos in Greece boasts of many masterpieces by Panselenos, including this one, which is located in the Church of the Protaton of Karyes. The paintings in the Protaton, which were only recently cleaned by a group of experts, are considered the most remarkable of the works of the Macedonian school on the whole of Mount Athos.

The saints in this painting, John and Prochorus, have a touch of classic

ST. PANTELEIMON MONASTERY

Photo by John P. Cavarnos

ΟΑΙ͡ϹΟΘΕΟ ΛΟΓΟ   ΟΑΠΡΟΧΟΡΟϹ

ST. JOHN AND ST. PROCHORUS—*PANSELENOS*

naturalism. Their bodies are not elongated, and there is little or no attempt to emphasize other-worldly qualities. However, the typical Byzantine abstractness is present, as is evidenced from the background.

For a later painting on the same subject see "St. John, the Evangelist," by the seventeenth-century Italian painter, Carlo Dolci, on p. 100.

✚

THE TRANSFIGURATION OF CHRIST
Fotis Kontoglous

THE Transfiguration, or *Metamorphosis,* as it is called in Greek Orthodoxy, figures prominently in the development of Eastern Orthodoxy, and especially from about the ninth century on.

Matthew 17:1-3 states: "And after six days Jesus taketh Peter, James, and John his brother, and bringeth them up into an high mountain apart, and was transfigured before them: and his face did shine as the sun, and his raiment was white as the light. And, behold, there appeared unto them Moses and Elias talking with him" (cf. also Mark 9:2-4).

That is the scene which this painting (p. 208) depicts. Jesus is the large central figure dressed in white raiment. Moses stands on the left of Jesus holding the Commandments, and Elias on the right. The brightness of the light and a voice from above have frightened the disciples: "Behold, a bright cloud overshadowed them: and behold a voice out of the cloud, which said, This is my beloved Son, in whom I am well pleased; hear ye him. And when the disciples heard it, they fell on their face, and were sore afraid" (Matt. 12:5-7).

Some church writers believed that the Incarnation lay at the heart of the mystery of Christ, while others laid emphasis on the Passion. But for Symeon the New Theologian and Gregory Palamas, the Transfiguration revealed the mystery, for according to them by this event on Mount Tabor Jesus appeared for the first and last time in the true and perfect light of His divinity. Many a mystic in the East has claimed that that light which a person beholds deep within him is the uncreated light of the Transfiguration. For these mystics incessant prayer and contemplation became the important means for achieving the most cherished goal—the seeing of the perfect light of Christ's divinity.

Fotis Kontoglous is the foremost contemporary Greek icon painter. With his paintings and writings he has contributed much to the preservation and perpetuation of the pure Byzantine art tradition. His works are to be found all over Greece, and in Europe, Africa, and the United States.

In this painting, as well as in his icons in general, Kontoglous endeavored to represent faithfully a traditional Byzantine prototype with vigor, clarity, and austere mysticism. As he himself says, "Byzantine art is for me the art of arts. I believe in it as I believe in religion. Not only do I not deny it, but

THE TRANSFIGURATION OF CHRIST—*KONTOGLOUS*

it gives me great satisfaction when someone says this to me, in most cases as an accusation. Only this art nourishes my soul, with its deep and mysterious powers; it alone quenches the thirst that I feel in the arid desert that surrounds us."*

The Greek words at the top of the painting give the title, "The Transfiguration."

✛

LET US ADORE GOD IN HOLY TRINITY

Come ye people, come adore Him,
    God in Holy Trinity;
God the Father, Son, and Spirit,
    Ever Blessed Unity.

Thine the glory, God Almighty,
    To the Son and Spirit given,
Ere upon the world's creation
    Dawned the new-born light of heaven.

Holy, holy, we adore Thee,
    One in power, in nature one;
God the Father, God the Spirit,
    God the Co-Eternal Son.

By the Son the wide creation
    Rose where chaos held its sway;
By the Spirit, God Almighty
    Swept eternal night away.

Son, the Father's love revealing,
    Son, through whom the Spirit came,
Blessed Godhead! endless glory
    Be to Thine exalted name.**

—*Emperor Leo VI*

CANON FOR APOKREOS (SEXAGESIMA)

That fearful Day, that Day of speechless dread,
When Thou shalt come to judge the quick and dead—
    I shudder to foresee,
    O God! what then shall be!

When Thou shalt come, angelic legions round,
With thousand thousands, and with trumpet sound,

* From *Byzantine Sacred Art* by Constantine Cavarnos, p. 24.
** From *Hymns of the Greek Church*, translated by John Brownlie, pp. 60-61.

Christ, grant me in the air
With saints to meet Thee there!

Weep, O my soul, ere that great hour and day,
When God shall shine in manifest array,
Thy sin, that thou may'st be
In that strict judgment free!

The terror!—hell-fire fierce and unsuffic'd:
The bitter worm: the gnashing teeth:—O Christ,
Forgive, remit, protect;
And set me with th' elect!

That I may hear the blessed voice that calls
The righteous to the joy of heav'nly halls:
And, King of Heav'n, may reach
The realm that passeth speech!

Enter Thou not in judgment with each deed,
Nor each intent and thought in strictness read:
Forgive, and save me then,
O Thou that lovest men!

Thee, One in Three blest Persons! Lord o'er all!
Essence of Essence, Power of Power, we call!
Save us, O Father, Son,
And Spirit, ever One!*

—*Theodore of Studium*

THE LORD MY CREATOR

Formed in Thine image bright,
With glory on my head,
I lived within Thy light,
And on Thy bounty fed.

But ah! that evil day!
The tempter's silvery tone
Lured me from God away,
To seek for bliss alone.

Dark came the night of sin,
I mourned my woeful plight,
For all was dark within,
And all around was night.

Shorn of Thy beauty fair,
Gift at my wondrous birth,
Hope fled before despair,
Gone was the joy of earth.

Yea, though the prayer be vain,
Now will I lift mine eyes,
Call me, God, back again,
Back to Thy paradise.

Came there a voice to me
Yea, 'twas Thy voice, my God,
Bidding me come to Thee,
Up to Thy pure abode.

* Ode I, from J. M. Neale and S. G. Hatherly, *Hymns of the Eastern Church,* 4th ed., p. 94.

Trusting Thy mercy great,
Up from my woes I'll rise,
Seeking the golden gate
Opening to paradise.*

—*Author Unknown*

ALL HUMAN THINGS ARE VANITY

All human things decay,
For all is vanity,
  The silver and the gold;
The glory of the great,
The wealth of high estate,
  None can for ever hold.

Death with his icy hand,
Severs each earthly band,
  And bears us all away;
Vain are our earthly dreams,
Shadows our substance seems,
  And nothing lasts for aye.

Immortal Christ, we cry,
O let our prayers come nigh
  Thy throne of heavenly grace;
Rest him whose form we miss,
Grant him in endless bliss
  A lasting dwelling place.**

—*John the Monk*

TOSSED ON THE SEA OF LIFE

Tossed on the sea of life,
  And sick and sore distressed,
I lift my cry to Thee, O Lord,
  Who giv'st the troubled rest.

There, where the waters yawn,
  And cruel monsters grin,
My comrades sink to depths below,
  All in a sea of sin.

My earnest cry I raise,
  Hear Thou the prayer I make,
And from the dark abyss of death
  My soul in mercy take.***

—*Cosmas of Maiouma*

SONG OF CHERUBIM

See the glorious Cherubim
Thronging around the Eternal throne:
Hark! they sing their holy hymn,
To the unknown, Three in One,
All-supporting Deity—
Living Spirit—praise to Thee!

* From *Hymns from the Greek Office Books*, translated by John Brownlie, pp. 57-58.
** *Ibid.*, pp. 17-18.
*** *Ibid.*, p. 42.

Rest, ye worldly tumults, rest!
Here let all be peace and joy;
Griefs no more shall rend our breast,
Tears no more shall dew our eyes.

Heavens directed Spirits rise
To the temple of the skies!
Join the ranks of Angels bright,
Near the Eternal's dazzling light.*

—Bobrov

✝

BARLAAM AND IOASAPH
John Damascene

Now when monasteries began to be formed in Egypt and the fame of the monks reached the Indians, it stirred them up also to the like zeal, insomuch that many of them forsook everything and withdrew to the deserts, and, though but men in mortal bodies, adopted the spiritual life of angels. While matters were thus prospering and many were soaring upward to heaven on wings of gold, as the saying is, there arose in that country a king named Abenner, mighty in riches and power, and in victory over his enemies, brave in warfare, vain of his splendid stature and comeliness of face, and boastful of all worldly honors, that pass so soon away. But his soul was utterly crushed by poverty, and choked with many vices, and sore distraught by the superstitious error of his idol-worship. Besides, he was cursed with childlessness. Such was the king, and such his mind.

Meanwhile the glorious bands of Christians grew and prospered in spite of the threats of Abenner, who became angry thereby and persecuted the faithful. Now while the king was under this terrible delusion and error, there was born unto him a son, a right goodly child, whose beauty from his very birth was prophetic of his future fortunes. Full of the keenest joy at the birth of the child, the king called him Ioasaph (i.e., The Lord gathers), and arranged a great feast for the occasion. At this feast, however, an astrologer made the prophecy that Ioasaph would embrace the Christian religion. King Abenner was grieved at this prophecy and set his son in a palace apart, where none of the annoys of life might come near him. He continued to persecute the Christians and was minded to conceal from his son the astrologer's warning.

As Ioasaph grew to manhood, he desired to know the cause of his imprisonment. One of his tutors, whom he questioned, disclosed confidentially the secret. Soon the son convinced his father to release him. The young man, free now, eagerly sought to inquire into the mystery of life. The description

* Translated from the Russian by Sir John Bowring (1792-1872).

of the nature of death distressed him sorely, as did certain other facts of life. Thenceforth Ioasaph lived in perpetual conflict and distress of mind, and all the pleasures and delights of this world were in his eyes an abomination and a curse. But the eye of God looked upon him, willed that he be saved and know the truth, and made known to him the path whereon he needs must go.

There was at that time a certain monk, learned in heavenly things, graced in word and deed, a model follower of every monastic rule. Whence he sprang, and what his race, I cannot say, but he dwelt in a waste howling wilderness in the land of Senaar, and had been perfected through the grace of the priesthood. Barlaam was this elder's name. He, learning by divine revelation the state of the son of the king, left the desert and returned to the world and the seat of the empire of the Indians. Disguised as a merchant, he entered the city, where was the palace of the king's son. There he tarried many days, and enquired diligently concerning the prince's affairs, and those that had access to him. Learning that the tutor was the prince's most familiar friend, he privily approached him saying:

"I would have thee understand, my lord, that I am a merchant, come from a far country; and I possess a precious gem, the like of which was never yet found, and hitherto I have shewed it to no man. But now I reveal the secret to thee, seeing thee to be wise and prudent, that thou mayest bring me before the king's son, and I will present it to him. Beyond compare, it surpasseth all beautiful things; for on the blind in heart it hath virtue to bestow the light of wisdom, to open the ears of the deaf, to give speech to the dumb and strength to the ailing. It maketh the foolish wise and driveth away devils, and without stint furnisheth its possessor with everything that is lovely and desirable."

The tutor said, "Though, to all seeming, thou art a man of staid and steadfast judgment, yet thy words prove thee to be boastful beyond measure. Time would fail me to tell thee the full tale of the costly and precious gems and pearls that I have seen. But gems, with such power as thou tellest of, I have never seen nor heard of yet. Nevertheless shew me the stone; and if it be as thou affirmest, I then shall bear it to the king's son, from whom thou shalt receive most high honors and rewards. But, before I be assured by the certain witness of mine own eyes, I may not carry to my lord and master so swollen a tale about so doubtful a thing."

Quoth Barlaam, "Well hast thou said that thou hast never seen or heard of such powers and virtues; for my speech to thee is on no ordinary matter, but on a wondrous and a great. But, as thou desiredst to behold it, listen to my words. This exceeding precious gem, amongst these its powers and virtues, possesseth this property besides. It cannot be seen out of hand, save by one whose eyesight is strong and sound, and his body pure and thoroughly undefiled. If any man, lacking in these two good qualities, do rashly gaze upon this precious stone, he shall, I suppose, lose even the eyesight that he hath, and his wits as well. Now I, that am initiated in the physician's art, observe that thine eyes are not healthy, and I fear lest I may cause thee to lose even the eyesight that thou hast. But of the king's son, I have heard that he leadeth a sober life, and that his eyes are young and fair, and healthy. Wherefore to him I make bold to display this treasure. Be not thou then negligent herein, nor rob thy master of so wondrous a boon."

The other answered, "If this be so, in no wise show me the gem; for my life hath been polluted by many sins, and also, as thou sayest, I am not possest of good eyesight. But I am won by thy words, and will not hesitate to make known these things unto my lord the prince." So saying, he went in, and, word by word, reported everything to the king's son. He, hearing his tutor's words, felt a strange joy and spiritual gladness breathing into his heart, and, like one inspired, bade bring in the man forthwith.

So when Barlaam was come in, and had in due order wished him Peace, the prince bade him be seated. Then his tutor withdrew, and Ioasaph said unto the elder, "Shew me the precious gem, concerning which, as my tutor hath narrated, thou tellest such great and marvellous tales." Then began Barlaam to discourse with him thus: "It is not fitting, O prince, that I should say anything falsely or unadvisedly to thine excellent majesty. All that hath been signified to thee from me is true and may not be gainsaid. But, except I first make trial of thy mind, it is not lawful to declare to thee this mystery. Now, if I find in thine heart fruit-bearing ground, and good, I shall not be slow to plant therein the heavenly seed, and manifest to thee the mighty mystery. But I am 'persuaded better things of thee, and things that accompany salvation,' —how that thou shalt see the priceless stone, and it shall be given thee in the light of that stone to become light, and bring forth fruit an hundredfold. Aye, for thy sake I gave diligence and accomplished a long journey, to shew thee things which thou hast never seen, and teach thee things which thou hast never heard."

Ioasaph said unto him, "For myself, reverend elder, I have a longing, an irresistible passion to hear some new and goodly word, and in mine heart there is kindled fire, cruelly burning and urging me to learn the answer to some questions that will not rest. But until now I never happened on one that could satisfy me as touching them. But if I meet with some wise and understanding man, and hear the word of salvation, I shall receive it kindly, and guard it wisely. So if thou knowest any such like thing, conceal it not from me, but declare it." Barlaam answered, "Fair are thy deeds, and worthy of thy royal majesty; seeing that thou hast paid no heed to my mean show, but hast devoted thyself to the hope that lieth within."

Then Barlaam went on to tell two tales much to the point, namely, that spiritual matters are to be valued far above the physical and the external. When he perceived that Ioasaph had understood his message, Barlaam proceeded to preach the word of his divine master, Jesus Christ the Lord, explaining the malice of the devil and the shameful fall of man, the mystery of the Incarnation, the life and ministry of Jesus, the Crucifixion, the Resurrection and the Ascension, and the spread of the Christian faith among all nations.

Barlaam then promised the prince that he shall know the Saviour more perfectly, if he will receive his grace into his soul, and gain the blessing to become his servant.

When the king's son had heard these words, there flashed a light upon his soul. Rising from his seat in the fulness of his joy, he embraced Barlaam, saying: "Most honored sir, methinks this might be that priceless stone which thou dost rightly keep secret, not displaying it to all that would see it, but only to those whose spiritual sense is strong. For lo, as these words dropped upon mine ear, sweetest light entered into my heart, and the heavy veil of sorrow, that hath now this long time enveloped my heart, was in an instant removed. Tell me if my guess be true: or if thou knowest aught better than that which thou hast spoken, delay not to declare it to me."

Again, therefore, Barlaam answered, "Yea, my lord and prince, this is the mighty mystery which hath been hid from ages and generations, but in these last days hath been made known to mankind; and manifestations whereof, by the grace of the Holy Spirit, was foretold by many prophets and righteous men, instructed at sundry times and in divers manners. In trumpet tones they proclaim it, and all looked forward to the salvation that should be: this they desired to see, but saw it not. But this latest generation was counted worthy to receive salvation. Wherefore he that believed and is baptized shall be saved; but he that believeth not shall be damned."

Said Ioasaph, "All that thou hast told me I believe without question, and him whom thou declarest I glorify as God. Only make all plain to me, and teach me clearly what I must do."

After preparing Ioasaph with the proper instruction in the orthodox Christian faith, Barlaam baptized him in the pool of water which was in his garden. Then Barlaam took leave of Ioasaph without accepting a gift at parting, but gave the latter his hair shirt and mantle.

When king Abenner was informed about what had happened, he became exceedingly furious, tortured to death suspected monks, and pleaded with Ioasaph to renounce the new faith and return to the worship of his gods. Since all entreaties and schemes failed to move the son, king Abenner divided his kingdom in two, and allowed Ioasaph to rule his half in his own way.

Ioasaph built a Christian temple in his chief city and led his people to the Christian faith. His fame soon outshone that of Abenner, who finally admitted his error, renounced idolatry, and became a Christian. When years later Abenner died, Ioasaph had his friend Barachias proclaimed king, and he himself went forth into the desert, smitten by the same love of Christ that fired the apostles and the martyrs. In time Ioasaph met Barlaam again and they lived together for many years in the desert. When these two holy men died, king Barachias had their bodies brought to his kingdom for burial.*

* Condensed from the Loeb Classical Library translation of G. R. Woodward and H. Mattingly. Published by William Heinemann Ltd. and Harvard University Press, 1937. Used by permission of Harvard University Press and the Loeb Classical Library.

INNOCENT VENIAMINOV:
THE GREATEST MISSIONARY OF AMERICAN ORTHODOXY

Bishop Nicholas

INNOCENT, Archbishop of Kamchatka, the Kuriles, and the Aleutian Islands, originally named John Popov, was born in the town of Anginskoe in Irkoutsk, Siberia, in the year 1797. The son of a poor sacristan, he studied at the seminary of Irkoutsk, and in 1819 was married and ordained deacon. While a student, the rector of his seminary surnamed him Veniaminov, in order to do honor to the beloved Bishop of Irkoutsk, Benjamin, who had died then (1814).

When in 1823 the Holy Synod of Russia requested the bishop of Irkoutsk to send a priest to the Island of Unalaska to enlighten the natives, and no one wished to accept this difficult and unpleasant task, Veniaminov came forth and gladly accepted. The following year he arrived at the place of his appointment. Unalaska is about the largest of the Aleutian Islands. But in addition to the Aleutians, there were other islands which made up Veniaminov's parish—the Fox, the Privilov, and others. Upon reaching Unalaska, Father John at first lived in a rather crude earthen hut, and then, like a new Robinson Crusoe, constructed with his own hands a wooden house for his family. He made his own furniture, including the clock, for he possessed the skills of a carpenter, watchmaker, and mechanic.

The Aleuts are by nature good and kindhearted. They love their neighbors and have much respect for their parents and elders. At the time of the arrival of Veniaminov they possessed certain other good qualities, but were otherwise living in a wild state and were practically worshipers of idols. Fortunately Father John proved himself equal to the big task as a true missionary in the full sense. Having decided to build a new church edifice, he taught the natives the arts of carpentry and building. The holy table and the iconostasis were his personal work.

However, Veniaminov's more important and far more difficult task was to bring the word of the gospel close to the natives. To this end he studied the native dialects, and in time undertook to translate for the Aleuts the gospel and the liturgical books. The undertaking was exacting, inasmuch as Veniaminov had to invent the very alphabet in order to make the languages of the aborigines instruments of literary expression. He also opened a school on Unalaska to teach the boys how to read and write. By reason of his constant contact with the Aleuts, he became familiar with their customs and traditions, and was thus able to preach more effectively and convert them.

Another obstacle which Veniaminov managed to overcome was that of great distances. His parish being scattered over several thousands of miles, he had to travel constantly. He sailed over wide and wild ocean expanses from one island to another by means of a small boat; and rode in sleds miles and miles over long stretches of endless snow from one settlement to another. He was always cheerful and glad to help, comfort, and save, despite the untold sufferings and privations during his perilous traveling. His greatest reward was the satisfaction he derived from seeing his work bear fruit. The Aleuts were sincerely devoted to him for his constant care and affection for them, and longed and thirsted for his diligent preaching. During his ten-year sojourn on Unalaska he converted to Christianity all the inhabitants of the island. For these exceptional services of his he was decorated and transferred to New Archangel (or Sitka), so that he might convert another people—the Koloshians.

This people had been less exposed to the Christian faith than the Aleuts, and besides were not well disposed toward the Russians. Thus the Koloshians afforded a new challenge for Father Veniaminov. In New Archangel and the surrounding country he followed more or less the same pattern as at Unalaska. He proceeded to familiarize himself with the language, customs, and life in general of the Koloshians, and then to carry on his pastoral work. Slowly he made sacred literature accessible to the people in their native tongue. During his five-year stay at Sitka he steadily increased his Christian flock and gained the love and respect of all who came in contact with him. In addition to his religious missionary work, Veniaminov did much to instruct the natives in the various practical trades and crafts.

Late in 1838 Father John left New Archangel to go to St. Petersburg to get the necessary support for his ever-increasing missionary needs. He sorely needed more priests and the authorization of the Church to print his Aleutian translations of the sacred literature.

At St. Petersburg Father John was promoted to archpriest. In the meantime his wife died and, at the suggestion of the Metropolitan Philaret of Moscow, he entered the monastic orders under the name of Innocent. Here he was invested as an archimandrite or abbot. Soon afterwards a new diocese was organized in Alaska and Innocent was appointed as its first bishop. As bishop, Innocent carried on his missionary work with as great a zeal as ever. His new reward in 1850 was the dignity of archbishop. His diocese was enlarged to include the country of Yakout in Siberia. Now he supervised the translation of the sacred books into the Yakout language.

When the Metropolitan of Moscow, Philaret, died in 1867, Innocent was appointed to succeed him. In this capacity Innocent died in 1879. From an humble priest to the ranks of archbishop and metropolitan, and from the outer limits of his country to the heart of his land Innocent Veniaminov carried the cross with exemplary humility to the very end in the service of the Lord.*

* Compiled from a booklet on the *Life of Veniaminov* (1897) by Bishop Nicholas (U.S.A.), reprinted in *One Church*, vol. 5, nos. 11-12 (1951).

GREGORY PALAMAS: MYSTICAL ILLUMINATION

Robert Payne

WHEN Gregory Palamas was twenty—or according to some records twenty-two—he abruptly left Constantinople and settled among the communities of monks on Mount Athos, which Andronicus II in a golden bull had described as "the second paradise, starry heaven and refuge of all virtues." With Gregory went his two brothers Macarius and Theodore.

On Mount Athos the monks lived lives of serene contemplation. No women were allowed on the mountain; no female animals. The life of the monks was strenuous and masculine. The three brothers put themselves under the monk Theoleptus, later to become Metropolitan of Philadelphia. There for eight years they remained, training themselves in the practice of unceasing prayer. Then they went to live, like the hermits of old, in a high mountain cave at Berea, on the frontiers of Macedonia and Thrace. Gregory's austerities in the harsh Macedonian winters impaired his health, and he never completely recovered from an intestinal disease acquired during those early years of self-mortification. After ten years of living in mountain caves he returned to Mount Athos, where he was soon recognized as a spiritual leader, devoted to the Virgin and the name of Jesus. During this period he began to write the homilies and sermons on the Light of the Transfiguration.

Alone in his cell on Mount Athos, he wrote angelically. He seems to have written with immense speed, the pen hardly touching the paper. And always there is that awareness of light, that light which the Greeks worshiped from the early beginnings. That adoration of the light of God and of the sun and of definition he shared with Homer and Pindar and Gregory Nazianzen. But for Gregory Palamas the supreme light was that which shone on Mount Tabor, the same light which streams in radiance across the Heaven.

In the works of Gregory Palamas the words *beauty, splendor, glory, light, the light of lights* are continually repeated. Like Athanasius, he sees the universe charged with the energy of the Incarnation, but he also sees it charged with the beauty of the Virgin. The earth is a divine place, the beauty of it is almost too much to be borne. The light of the Transfiguration did not cease; it continues always. "Certain saints," he wrote, "after the coming of Christ in the flesh see this light like an endless sea flowing miraculously from a single sun, which is the adored Body of Christ." For him "the Holy Name contains within itself that divine energy which penetrates and changes a man's heart when it is diffused throughout his body." He believed that men are endowed with a divine breath which moves within their physical bodies, and the body acquires holiness by this divine breath pouring into it. The body is not evil; and even the Fall of Man was not entirely evil, for there would have been no Christ without the sin of Adam. He believed that from the first moment of His existence on earth Christ lived within the beatific vision, and he believed that the Virgin died only because it was necessary that she should share the suffering of her Son. He saw no reason to disbelieve in angels, and in his devotional works dedicated to the Virgin he describes how from the age of three she lived in the Holy of Holies of the Temple in Jerusalem, fed by the angels. For him God was not merely essence; He was also energy; and though the essence remained incommunicable, the energy could be perceived by human eyes, in exactly the same way that no man can stare at the sun, but he is aware of its light.

Gregory Palamas said that man, body and soul, was higher than the angels. From the soul came a divine energy which was continually being poured into the body: and the incorporeal angels, though closer to God, are deprived of that vessel into which the divine energy is poured. "Man," said St. Basil, "is a creature who has received the order to become a god." Gregory Palamas answers that he becomes a god when he practices meditation and sees in the place of the heart the blazing light of the Transfiguration.*

✦

CHERUBIC HYMN

THE "Cherubic Hymn" is one of the most solemn and mystical compositions of Eastern Orthodoxy. It takes its name from the references made to the Cherubim. It is included in the liturgies of both St. Basil and St. John Chrysostom, and is solemnly chanted at the Great Entrance or Introit. The first half of the hymn is chanted by the choir as the Holy Eucharistic Gifts are carried from the sanctuary through the body of the church and up to the Holy Table. When the Entrance is completed, then the rest of the hymn follows.

As to the author and the time of composition, there is no conclusive information. Some attribute it to Basil the Great (329?-379), others to John Chrysostom (347-407), and still others to John Scholastikos, patriarch of Constantinople (565-578), and the Emperor Justinian I (527-565). A later historian, Kedrenos, expressed the general opinion that the Cherubic Hymn was formally accepted by an imperial decree (565) in the ceremony of the Divine Eucharist. Recent scholarship states that our hymn has been chanted at the Great Entrance since 574. Up to that time another work—"Let All Mortal Flesh Keep Silence"—was chanted, which tradition attributes to St. James. Thereafter the other hymn was confined to the divine liturgy of St. Basil, and is performed the Great Saturday Morning.

The history of the original melody of the Cherubic Hymn is perhaps even more vague than that of its authorship. However, it is believed that the melodies of it that we possess today have the basic elements of the original one. Needless to say that it must have been rearranged frequently, sometimes

* Abridged from *The Holy Fire* by Robert Payne, pp. 274-79. Copyright 1957 by Robert Payne. Published by Harper & Brothers. Used by permission of the publisher.

Cherubic Hymn*

From a musical setting of the
Divine Liturgy of John Chrysostom

Dean D. Bouzianis

more successfully than others. The arrangement we have used is that of a young American composer of Greek origin, Dean D. Bouzianis. He claims that his music is "Western by tradition but has maintained an Eastern flavor through the use of the melodic interval of the augmented second, harmonic regressions, and other similar devices. In many instances the music is contrapuntal, the same melody being used several times in different voices, combinations, and attitudes for the sake of unity." His Cherubic Hymn is quite original, yet it retains to a good degree the mystical and solemn qualities of the prototype. This successful arrangement was made possible by the composer's broad experience in composition and transcription, and the fact that he has studied Western and Byzantine music in both American and European universities and conservatories.

The very words of the Cherubic Hymn and the manner in which it is chanted make the listener feel that there is a high point coming in the drama of the divine liturgy. Its first half is slow and mystical. One feels uplifted and transported to a different world, forgetting all worldly cares and fixing one's inner attention to Almighty God. Complete solemnity prevails as the Great Entrance is made. Then upon the completion of the Entrance the hymn ends with a crescendo. It has all the majesty of a royal victory. The feeling of triumph and spiritual rebirth seems to be imparted to the whole congregation. All in all this is a most inspiring and moving hymn, and when one is able to fix in mind and heart the words and melody at one and the same time, the experience is unforgettable. It is as if the invisible Christ has been brought close to the faithful, attended by the angelic hosts of the celestial hierarchy which are chanting with exultation.

Other well-known arrangements of the Cherubic Hymn are those of Sakellarides, Krupitsky, Bortniansky, Glinka, Smirnov, Allemanov, Lomakin, Lvov, and others. By virtue of its key position in the liturgy, it has proved a challenge to the best of composers of Eastern Orthodox liturgical music.

✣

MEGALYNARION

THE *Megalynarion* is a liturgical hymn, a kind of *troparion* whose concluding verse has the Greek words *Se megalynomen*, "we magnify thee," whence its name. It is a hymn of praise, in which the *Theotokos*, Mother of God, is glorified. Hence it is also called the "magnifical hymn." Its author is reputed to have been St. Ephraem of Edessa, who flourished during the fourth century.

This hymn, like many others concerned with the Virgin, is indicative of the prominence of the Virgin in the service and hymnography of the Eastern Church. The veneration of the Virgin increased in the eighth century, and is very prominent at present. The *Megalynarion* of our interpretation has a lyric character. The high virtues of the *Theotokos* are magnified and extolled in the highest terms, and thus the Virgin stands revealed as truly the Mother of God.

The English translation of the Greek original is:

> It is truly meet, *Theotokos,* to call thee blessed,
> Who art ever blessed, and most blameless,
> And the Mother of our God;
> More precious than the Cherubim,
> And more glorious by far than the Seraphim,
> Who without corruption didst bear God the Logos,
> Thou the true *Theotokos* we magnify.

Megalynarion

Traditional Byzantine

Mode III

Th. Phokaeus, 1851
Transcribed from the
Byzantine by
Dean D. Bouzianis

A - xi - on es - tin os a - li - thos makari - zin se tin The - o - to - kon, tin a - i - ma - ka - ri - ston ke pa - na - mo - mi - ton ke mi - te - ra tou the - ou i - mon tin ti - mi - o - te - ran ton Khe - rou - vim ke en - dho - xo - te - ran a - syn - gri - tos ton Se - ra - fim, tin a - dhi - a - ftho - ros Theon Lo - ghon te - kou - san, tin on - tos The - o - to - kon Se me - gha - ly - no - men

CONTENTS

PART II   SECTION 5

EASTERN ORTHODOXY AROUND THE WORLD

―✠―

But ye shall receive power, when the Holy Spirit is come upon you: and ye shall be my witnesses both in Jerusalem, and in all Judea and Samaria, and unto the uttermost part of the earth.—ACTS 1:8, ASV.

―✠―

PICTURES: PAGE
    Interpretation: Iconostasis of the Protaton 225
    Picture: Iconostasis of the Protaton 227
    Interpretation: St. Sophia Cathedral of Los Angeles 226
    Picture: St. Sophia Cathedral of Los Angeles 229
    Interpretation: Pantocrator—*Dukas* 228
    Picture: Pantocrator—*Dukas* 230

POETRY:
    Ektenia *or* Great Collect—*Author Unknown* 231
    On Mary Magdalene—*Cassiani* 232
    Good Friday Eve Encomia—*Author Unknown* 233
    Prayer to the Virgin—*Jadovskaya* 234
    Supplant Canon to Jesus—*Theoctistos of Studium* 234
    The Last Kiss—*John Damascene* 235

STORIES:
    America's Fourth Faith—*Nall* 235
    The Miracle of Kaisariani—*Papadiamantis* 238
    The Way of a Pilgrim—*Anonymous* 242

MUSIC:
    Interpretation: This Day Salvation—*Traditional Byzantine* 244
    Music: This Day Salvation—*Protopsaltis;* transcribed by *Bouzianis* 244
    Interpretation: Christ Is Risen—*Traditional Byzantine* 245
    Music: Christ Is Risen—Transcribed from Byzantine by *Bouzianis* 245

ICONOSTASIS OF THE PROTATON

FROM the very early times of Eastern Christianity the sanctuary of a church was separated from the body of the nave by a sort of partition which is called the *iconostasis* or *iconostasion*. These words mean literally "icon stand," since the partition consists of one or more doors and a series of icon panels. The doors themselves also have icons.

Not all iconostases are the same. To a certain extent the size of the particular church is a determining factor. A small church would have an iconostasis with a limited number of icons, and hence only one entrance, the central door, which is called the Royal, or Holy Gate. A larger iconostasis would have two side doors in addition. On the north side of the central gate is the door that is usually called the Server's door, because through it come out the processions at the Great and Little Entrances of the Divine Liturgy. Then on the south side of the Holy Gate is the Deacon's door, which, as its name implies, is used by the deacon as he passes in and out while performing his various functions during the liturgy. The iconostasis of the church of the Protaton on Mount Athos is relatively small, and so has only a central gate. On each side of this entrance are two icons, the principal icons. When the gate is open, one's eyes fall directly upon the holy table, which is the most important part of the sanctuary.

The iconostasis could be all of wood or have marble in the lower part as does that of the Protaton church. The marble is usually white, and various designs are sculptured upon the outer side. Then again there could be one or more rows of icons along the iconostasis. Of course, the rows of icons higher up the iconostasis are much smaller than those of the lower or main row of icons. There is a certain rule with regard to the order in which certain icons appear on the iconostasis. As one is facing the iconostasis, the icon on the right of the main gate is that of Christ Pantocrator, and the one on the left is that of the Virgin. The icon of the patron saint appears next to that of the Virgin.

Before each of the principal icons is suspended a small lamp which is kept constantly lighted. Then over the main gate there is usually placed a large cross, which is sometimes flanked by two lesser crosses over the side entrances.

The present church of the Protaton was perhaps built about the tenth century, and is decorated with some of the best Byzantine frescoes, many of them being reputed to be the works of the famous Panselenos, who flourished in the fourteenth century. The iconostasis is noted for its simplicity, as is the design of the whole church. Every main church, or *catholicon,* of a Mount Athos monastery prides itself of a fine iconostasis. Much work and art have gone into their making. Behind the iconostases, in the sanctuaries, are housed many precious relics and other valuable articles, such as rare Bibles and sacred vessels.

The elaborate candelabra, made of brass plates and suspended rather low from the ceiling, blocks a little one's view of the iconostasis.

✣

ST. SOPHIA CATHEDRAL OF LOS ANGELES

THIS church is one of the largest and most magnificent edifices of Greek Orthodoxy in America, and serves as the cathedral of the West Coast Diocese. The initiative in its construction belongs to the Skouras brothers, the theater magnates—Spyros, George, and the late Charles in particular. The temple was dedicated with much ceremony in 1952, and since that time it has been rightly considered an imposing landmark in Los Angeles.

On the occasion of the dedication, President Harry S. Truman noted: "So beautiful an edifice will forever praise the glory of God. Its embodiment of the architectural traditions of one of the world's great Christian civilizations will serve generations to come as a reminder of the spiritual ties that unite the peoples of Greece and of the United States."

The exterior of the building, following the more conservative Byzantine architectural tradition, is simple. Decoration is reserved for the sides of the transept and the front portals. The front doors themselves are of hand-carved oak with inlaid panels. The plan of the church incorporates the basic elements of the temple's famous namesake in Constantinople. It has the cruciform modification of the basilica and a large dome held up firmly and securely with triangular arches. However, the resemblance ends here, for, by the use of modern materials and principles and inventions, the new St. Sophia has much novelty. For one, the materials used in its construction are steel and concrete. Then, too, it is sound-proof and earthquake-proof, and has many modern conveniences such as lighting, heating, air-conditioning, and public-address system.

The beautiful landscaping of the area surrounding the cathedral lends to the magnificence of the church itself.

The rich interior of St. Sophia bears a sharp contrast to the simple exterior. Much designing and expenditure have gone into its adornment: unusually fine materials and form, light, and color are so blended as to give the interior an exquisite and sumptuous beauty. The large central dome displays in mosaic style the Pantocrator, the Christ Almighty. This dome stands some ninety feet from the floor, a heavenly church suspended, as it were, in mid-air.

The icons with their rich colors and ornaments, the stained-glass windows, the impressive sanctuary partition or iconostasis, the exquisite decorations

ICONOSTASIS OF THE PROTATON

of the arches and the columns, and the magnificent chandeliers, all combine to give the interior an effect of grandeur and opulent beauty. Some of the innovations, especially in the case of the icons, might disturb the more conservative Orthodox, but the over-all effect of St. Sophia dazzles and moves any beholder.

✠

PANTOCRATOR

Demetrios Dukas

THE "Pantocrator," or Christ Almighty, by Demetrios Dukas (p. 230) is a unique work of art here in America. It is the first mosaic of its kind in the United States decorating a church dome, that of the Greek Orthodox Church of the Archangels at Stamford, Connecticut, which was installed in January, 1959. Without doubt, this Pantocrator mosaic has set a high standard in church decoration, a fact noteworthy for the progress of iconography in America, especially since the artist is the first American-born iconographer of incontestable talent and ability.

Mr. Dukas is a graduate of the Boston Museum of Fine Arts. He also studied with Fotis Kontoglous of Athens and collaborated with him in decorating various churches in Greece. Kontoglous himself is recognized as Greece's foremost Byzantine iconographer today (see pp. 169, 189, and 208 for some of his own works). Demetrios Dukas has had unusual experience as a specialist with the Byzantine Institute of America in the restoration of the mosaics and frescoes of the Church of the Saviour (also known as the Kahrieh Djami) at Constantinople. At present he is also on the faculty of the Museum of Fine Arts in Boston. Icons of his are to be seen in several Greek Orthodox churches in America, such as St. Nicholas at Flushing, New York, St. George at his home town, Lynn, Massachusetts, and St. Mary at Minneapolis.

The Pantocrator design measures thirteen feet in surface diameter and eleven and one-half feet straight across. It was executed in the finest Byzantine Greek tradition, and comes the closest to the types of the eleventh century, for example, the Pantocrator of Daphni in Greece. Christ is meek and also a little stern. His gaze is penetrating but kindly. He looks neither to the right nor left, but everywhere, and sees all. Seriousness is combined with the majesty that is quite becoming for the Heavenly Ruler.

Along the edge of the mosaic there is a beautiful iris with the usual bright colors found in the early Pantocrators. Christ appears to be looking down upon the earth after the storm has subsided. He is blessing with His right hand in the Greek fashion, while He is holding the Bible with His left hand, with the index finger curved and pointing to the message in the

ST. SOPHIA CATHEDRAL OF LOS ANGELES

PANTOCRATOR—*DUKAS*

Bible. Only the upper half of Christ is seen peering from the sky. There is much richness and contrast in colors, set in a fine gold background. The garments are of bright mauve and blue. Deep spirituality pervades both the appearance and gestures of Christ as they are expressed through the brilliance of the mosaics. Here there is a complete absence of the secular and unspiritual atmosphere that is found in many modern compositions. The beholder is convinced that he is face to face with a divine and spiritual Being in heaven, rather than an earthly theatrical figure. This feeling is strengthened and confirmed by the presence of the comparably spiritual Virgin and Child in the apse. Thus the Pantocrator in the heavenly dome and the Virgin in the earthly apse give the fine new Church of the Archangels at Stamford a unique position in the array of American Orthodox churches.

It might be very appropriately added that the exquisite decoration of the church in question by Demetrios Dukas parallels the broad experience and superb architectural skill of W. Stuart Thompson and Phelps Barnum, who designed and built this church.

✛

EKTENIA or GREAT COLLECT

Lord, to our humble prayers attend,
Let Thou Thy peace from heaven descend,
And to our souls salvation send.
> Have mercy, Lord, upon us.

Rule in our hearts, Thou Prince of Peace,
The welfare of Thy Church increase,
And bid all strife and discord cease.
> Have mercy, Lord, upon us.

To all who meet for worship here,
Do Thou in faithfulness draw near;
Inspire with faith and godly fear.
> Have mercy, Lord, upon us.

O let Thy priests be clothed with might,
To rule within Thy Church aright,
That they may serve as in Thy sight.
> Have mercy, Lord, upon us.

The sovereign ruler of our land,
Protect by Thine Almighty hand,
And all around the throne who stand.
> Have mercy, Lord, upon us.

In time of war be near to aid,
Strong be the arm for battle made,

Prostrate be every foeman laid.
　　　　Have mercy, Lord, upon us.

Let clouds and sunshine bless the earth,
Give fruits and flowers a timely birth,
Our harvests crown with peaceful mirth.
　　　　Have mercy, Lord, upon us.

Let voyagers by land and sea
In danger's hour in safety be;
The suffering and the captives free.
　　　　Have mercy, Lord, upon us.

Around us let Thy shield be cast,
Till wrath and danger are o'erpast,
And tribulation's bitter blast.
　　　　Have mercy, Lord, upon us.*
　　　　　　　　　　　　　—*Author Unknown*

ON MARY MAGDALENE

Burdened with sin, more, Lord, than I can tell,
I bear the myrrh with those that loved Thee well;
And to the grave lamenting, lo, I bring,
For this last solemn rite, my offering.

The love of sin, ah, that it should be so,
That held my truant spirit long ago—
That love of sin my foolish heart hath found,
And moonless night now circles me around.

O Thou, Who by the clouds that drape the sky,
Bearest the waters of the sea on high,
Accept the offering of my bitter tears,
From springs that issue in a night of fears.

O Thou, who mad'st the heavens of old to bow,
Incline Thine ear and hear Thy servant now,
And let my sighing and my grievous moan,
Enter Thine ear, O God, my God alone.

Prostrate I fall, and in my worship meet,
Would kiss amid my tears Thy stainless feet,
And wipe them with my hair, that by Thy grace,
I with the penitent may take my place.

To Thy fair Paradise, when eve has come,
Take Thou Thy servant in Thy mercy home;

* From *Hymns of the Greek Church*, translated by John Brownlie, pp. 81-83.

From fear of Judgment, and from evil free,
There let me dwell for evermore with Thee.*

—*Cassiani*

GOOD FRIDAY EVE ENCOMIA

Part I

In a grave they laid Thee,
O my Life and my Christ:
And the Armies of the Angels were sore amazed,
As they sang the praise of Thy submissive Love.

How, O Life, canst Thou die?
In a grave how canst dwell?
For the proud domain of Death Thou destroyest now,
And the dead of Hades makest Thou to rise.

Now we magnify Thee,
O Lord Jesus our King;
And we venerate Thy Passion and Burial:
For therewith hast Thou delivered us from death.

Part II

Right is it indeed,
Life-bestowing Lord, to magnify Thee:
For upon the Cross were Thy Hands outspread,
And the strength of our dread Foe hast Thou destroyed.

Right is it indeed,
Maker of all things, to magnify Thee:
For by Thy dear Passion have we attained
Vict'ry o'er the flesh and rescue from decay.

Part III

Ev'ry generation
To Thy grave comes bringing,
Dear Christ, its dirge of praises.

From Thy Cross he brought Thee,
That Arimathaean,
And in Thy Grave he laid Thee.

Myrrh the Women sprinkled,
Store of spices bringing
To grace Thy Tomb ere dawning.**

—*Author Unknown*

* From *Hymns of the Apostolic Church*, 5th series, translated from the Greek by John Brownlie, pp. 127-29.
** From *Orthodox Hymns in English*, translated from the Greek by Michael G. H. Gelsinger, pp. 107-117. Copyright 1939 by Michael G. H. Gelsinger. Used by his permission.

PRAYER TO THE VIRGIN

Mother of intercession! hear me,
  When I offer thee my prayer;
A grievous sinner, clothed in darkness,
  Let me still thy blessings share.

When sorrow, care, and loss befall me,
  When mine enemies gain way;
In the hour of saddest suffering,
  Come thou to my help, I pray.

A holy joy—thirst for salvation—
  Place thou deep within my heart;
To the heavenly kingdom guiding,
  Let me not from truth depart.*

—*Julia Jadovskaya*

SUPPLIANT CANON TO JESUS

Jesu, Name all names above,
  Jesu, best and dearest,
Jesu, Fount of perfect love,
  Holiest, tend'rest, nearest;
Jesu, Source of grace completest,
Jesu purest, Jesu sweetest,
  Jesu, Well of power Divine,
  Make me, keep me, seal me Thine!

Jesu, open me the gate
  That of old He enter'd,
Who, in that most lost estate,
  Wholly on Thee ventur'd;
Thou, Whose Wounds are ever pleading,
And Thy Passion interceding,
  From my mis'ry let me rise
  To a Home in Paradise!

Thou didst call the Prodigal:
  Thou didst pardon Mary:
Thou Whose words can never fail,
  Love can never vary:
Lord, to heal my lost condition,
Give—for Thou canst give—contrition;
  Thou canst pardon all mine ill
  If Thou wilt: O say, "I will!"**

—*Theoctistos of Studium*

* From *Russian Lyrics in English Verse* by C. T. Wilson, p. 215.
** A cento from J. M. Neale and S. G. Hatherly's *Hymns of the Eastern Church*, 4th ed., p. 140.

THE LAST KISS

Part II

Behold and weep me, friends and brethren!
    Voice, sense, and breath, and motion gone;
But yesterday I dwelt among you;
    Then death's most fearful hour came on.

Embrace me with the last embracement;
    Kiss me with this, the latest kiss;
Never again shall I be with you;
    Never with you share woe or bliss.

I go toward the dread tribunal
    Where no man's person is preferr'd;
Where lord and slave, where chief and soldier,
    Where rich and poor alike are heard.

One is the manner of their judgment:
    Their plea and their condition one:
And they shall reap in woe or glory
    The earthly deeds that they have done.

I pray you, brethren, I adjure you,
    Pour forth to Christ the ceaseless prayer,
He would not doom me to Gehenna,
    But in glory give me share!*

—*John Damascene*

✞

AMERICA'S FOURTH FAITH

T. Otto Nall

AN ancient body of Christendom, which claims to embrace more than one hundred and seventy million believers, is becoming recognized today—with Protestantism, Judaism, and Roman Catholicism—as the fourth great religious faith in the United States. It is Eastern (or Greek) Orthodoxy, until now identified by many Americans only as a shadowy land between Protestantism and Catholicism where many of the clergy wear bushy beards, some marry, and the churches observe Christmas in January.

But this little-understood faith—one fourth of the Christian world—is making a new impact upon American life. It claims one thousand parishes in this country and some six million adherents. It is expanding its activities, adding to its seminaries, and establishing youth centers on college campuses. Not long ago, the U. S. Armed Forces for the first time authorized its symbol,

* *Ibid.,* p. 50.

"EO," inscribed as religious identification on servicemen's dog tags, along with Protestant, Catholic, and Jewish identifications. And Eastern Orthodox chaplains now serve with the armed forces.

Looming behind this picture of progress in this country is the grim shadow of world trouble for Orthodoxy. Misfortunes have befallen its Ecumenical (world-wide) Patriarch in Istanbul (formerly Constantinople) that have shoved this peace-loving church into world politics. Both West and East are struggling for its support, but Orthodoxy is not united on where its allegiance—if a church owes any allegiance to a political body—should go.

The Orthodox claim to going back to the apostle Andrew rests in part upon the Epistles of Ignatius of Antioch early in the second century. Later, in 451 A.D., the Bishop of Constantinople was recognized as possessing equal privileges with the Bishop of Rome, Constantinople being the new capital of the empire.

The importance of the respective patriarchs has risen and fallen with the importance of their cities. When, in 330 A.D., Emperor Constantine removed the capital of the empire to Constantinople, it was inevitable that the patriarch there should increase in influence.

The course of history drove wedges into the organized church, causing trouble among the various patriarchates. Alexandria broke away, forming a strain leading to the Coptic Church headed today by a patriarch with residence in Egypt. (Haile Selassie of Ethiopia is of that faith.) Rome and the Eastern patriarchs drifted gradually apart due to nationalistic, economic, and ecclesiastical causes. In 1054 the breach became complete.

Today, Eastern Orthodoxy is composed of twenty-one churches, each of them independent and self-governing. The Ecumenical Patriarch at Istanbul remains the senior, not because of greater authority but because of the long tradition of his city as the center of Orthodoxy. He is first among the patriarchs of Antioch, Jerusalem, Alexandria, Moscow, Belgrade, and Bucharest, and is also revered by the heads of the churches of Greece, Cyprus, Bulgaria, and Albania.

The present Ecumenical Patriarch at Istanbul is Athenagoras I, a towering figure of a man who served his church for a number of years in the United States and, in fact, was once an American citizen. Still a stanch friend of America, he has been in and out of favor with the Turkish government. Currently, he is out of favor. Riots have wrecked his buildings and jeopardized his safety. Many political elements in Turkey, basically a Mohammedan country, are clamoring for Athenagoras' expulsion. That would be virtually like removing the Roman Catholic Pope from Rome.

And if the seat of Orthodoxy in Istanbul is gone, the tradition of leadership for the Ecumenical Patriarch goes with it. Who then would become the "first" among the patriarchs? Who else, many fear, but Patriarch Alexei of Moscow?

Patriarch Alexei has sent recent delegations to Jerusalem, offering aid to the beleaguered Greek Orthodox church there. He provides regular financial aid to the Patriarchate of Alexandria. He is sending a mission of clergymen to India, where the native church traces descent from Thomas, the apostolic "doubter."

Whether it be in Russia, America, Serbia, or Egypt, Orthodoxy tends to take on the coloration of the peoples among whom it finds itself. But all Orthodox churches have a common faith. They all believe in Christ as the Saviour of mankind and the Church as the storehouse of truth and sanctifying grace. They hold that their Church is infallible, but their prayer book says that infallibility belongs "to the whole assembly of true believers," to the whole Church as represented by its council.

The Orthodox community also has a common church government, which in some respects is more like the democracy of Congregationalism than the authoritarianism of Rome.

Furthermore, Orthodoxy has a common basis of worship. Their elaborate ritual—which links them most closely among Protestants to Episcopalians—goes back to the practices of early Christian churches.

In the Church of the Nativity at Bethlehem, there is more than one site of the manger. The Roman Catholics have one; the Greek Orthodox adherents have another; the Armenian Christians still another, yet all are under the roof of the same old church. It is easy to see that, even in the place where the Christ Child was born, his followers do not get on too well together.

The estrangement between Greek and Roman Christians showed up early in the growth of the Christian Church. But the final break did not come until July 6, 1054, when a robed emissary of Pope Leo IX slapped down on the altar of Hagia Sophia Church a paper excommunicating the whole Eastern Church. The charges: wearing beards; allowing priests to marry (they still do but the clergy from whom the bishops are chosen do not); using leavened bread for the Sacrament, and believing that the Holy Spirit proceeds from the Father alone, rather than from the Father and the Son.

There have been attempts at reunion ever since the Middle Ages and the Roman Church still hopes some day to return the Eastern Church to its fold. Most of the effort, however, appears to be one-sided.

In many ways, Orthodoxy has drawn closer to Protestantism than it has to Romanism. It has fellowship with Protestant churches through the World Council of Churches and the National Council of Churches.

In recent years, Eastern Orthodox parishes have joined with Episcopal churches in co-operative activities. In January of 1958, for example, the "high church" Episcopalians and the Eastern Orthodox churches co-operated in the Week of Prayer for Christians United. It is interesting that John Wesley, founder of Methodism, pondering the matter of ordination, admired the method used by the Church of Alexandria and wrote (in 1784): "The presbyters of that venerable apostolic church, on the death of a bishop, exercised the right of ordaining another from their own body, by the laying on of hands."

Yet the Orthodox Church differs greatly from most Protestant churches with which it co-operates. Orthodoxy, for example, holds that there is no salvation for any person outside the visible Church. Under the influence of the Holy Spirit, the Church cannot err in matters of faith. Orthodoxy maintains that bishops, priests, deacons, and other clergy are set apart from other Christians for service in the Church, a doctrine acceptable to Episcopalians but generally inconsistent with the Protestant "priesthood of all believers." When priests and deacons are ordained, however, the Orthodox bishop holds the vestments up to the congregation and asks "Axios?" (Is he worthy?) and the people reply, "Axios!" There is no such democratic gesture in the Roman Catholic Church.

Orthodoxy believes that a body of doctrine is necessary, supernaturally revealed through the Holy Spirit to those who are delegates to the church councils. If any reunion with Roman Catholics—or Protestants—is to come, the Orthodox insist that there must be an "agreement in faith," set forth in ancient creeds.

Orthodoxy has a mystical and sacramentarian view. Christ is the Logos, the word, the Truth of God. In Him the divine and human natures were joined. Men can be saved only through a similar union, effected through the Church's sacraments.

Holy Scripture is not enough; there must be Holy Tradition. It is full of meaningful symbolism.

Orthodoxy stresses "love" and "grace." It can be put this way: If Roman Catholic Christianity is the religion of "law," and Protestant Christianity is the religion of "faith," then Orthodox Christianity is the religion of "love." That shines through all its life.

May God keep it shining during the stormy days ahead.*

✝

THE MIRACLE OF KAISARIANI
Alexander Papadiamantis

LEUTHERIS and I had been married for one year, and the whole year he was constantly sick. He had attracted me when he was thirty, and I was a foolish young girl. As he was ill—with fever all along—the whole neighborhood and my relatives were saying that he had come to be comsumptive. He was tubercular, they were telling me. What a misfortune for me! Doctors, medicines, and preserves were all of no avail. Poverty was beating us, for he himself could not work. Only God knows how I managed things.

Our maid of honor at the wedding expressed the opinion that if I made a vow to Kaisariani, great be her grace, to take him there, that perhaps the

* Abridged from *Together Magazine* (July 15, 1958). Published by Lovick Pierce. Used by permission of the publisher.

Virgin would have pity and cure him. When I heard this, here is what I said to myself, I must confess: "Fine, if perchance the Virgin does not cure him, he may at least die there, that I may bury him on the mountain, in order to spare myself the expenses which I lack, and the other woes and headaches." What is worse, I feared that if he had died at home, something might stick to the clothes and I myself also contract the disease. Everybody was telling me that tuberculosis is contagious.

I didn't have a cent, nor anything valuable in my chest, except for the engagement ring I was wearing. But I did possess a few copper articles, and so I took a pan of mine, brand-new, quite red, and went to our neighbor Panagina.

"Lady Panagina, take this pan for security and lend me four *svantzika;** I want to take my sick husband to the Virgin in Kaisariani, and have no money," said I.

"Here, take these two scanty *svantzika* that I have," said Panagina. "Leave your pan here, and when you are better off, bring the two *svantzika* to get it."

I took the two *svantzika,* even though they fell short for the trip I wanted to make, and thanked her. My husband and I set out at night on the eve of the Ascension. On the way we met a coachman, sponsor of a neighbor of mine. I begged him and he took Leutheris in his coach for most of the way. I went on foot. It was getting dark when we reached Kaisariani. Before we arrived at the church, we met by the stream a shepherd with a flock of sheep. We sat near there to rest and refresh ourselves, before going to the church. The shepherd's wife saw that we sat down and drew near.

Leutheris, who for weeks before had no appetite and ate nothing, when we sat down, said to me: "I am hungry, dear wife. Cut me a little bread."

I cut bread for him, and he began to eat with so much appetite, that I myself was amazed. I had cut him a small slice, knowing that he could not eat. He ate it at once, and asked me to cut him more.

The shepherdess who approached said to me "Is he your husband, my girl? He seems to be emaciated. Does he drink milk, that I may bring you some?"

"He drinks," said I, "because he is ill."

She brought us a large jug full of milk. Leutheris dipped the bread in it, chewed chunks of it, and sipped the milk. I ate bread and olives. The shepherd and shepherdess also gave us fresh bread and two large pieces of cheese. They told us to pass by the next day to have some good roast from the spit. I offered the shepherd some nickels that I had as change from one *svantziko* and told him to keep whatever he wanted for the cheese. But he pushed them back with his elbow, and told me to light a candle to the Virgin for my sick husband.

We went to the church, prayed, and lit a small candle. Then Leutheris sat near the Holy Icon, in the church, and it seemed that he was drowsy. I went out to drink some water at the famous, immortal fountain. It was about

* Currency of modest value.

three after midnight. After a short while I heard some shouts, and some women were telling one another, "To Euresi! . . . it is time . . . . They are going to Euresi! The Dove . . . at Euresi . . . at the cave."

Many women, and some men and children were leaving the area where I stood, and beginning to run uphill. I myself did not know very well what Euresi was, and had hardly ever heard about the Dove. However, that moment I recalled that our maid of honor had been the first person to put in my mind the idea to make a vow to Kaisariani, and had told me that the Virgin's grace is more efficacious at Euresi, where the cave is, and that the Dove descends there, fluttering its wings. Then a lady who knew me a little, and had seen me earlier with my husband on the road, and understood that he was a sick man, turned around and said to me as she was about to get up and leave: "Why don't you, too, come to Euresi? Take your husband and come."

I got up, ran to the fountain, drank some water again, then entered the church, and found Leutheris fast asleep next to the iconostasis. I approached, shook him, and he opened his eyes.

"Why don't you keep away from me?" he said. "I'm drowsy now. Go out to the fountain to get some fresh air."

"Let's go to Euresi," I told him.

"To Euresi? What Euresi?"

I shook him again, dragged him hurriedly, and made him get up. Then I reflected that I had to hurry, in order to catch up with the crowd that was running up the hill, because I didn't know whether it was very near or far away, and I didn't know the way either. Moreover, I had to arrive in time to see the Dove, that my maid of honor had mentioned to me. So I dragged Leutheris and we left the monastery. "The Virgin," I told him, "will cure you."

We set out on the heels of those we saw running in front of us. It was midnight. We walked no little uphill road, and in a short space of time reached the cave. It was a beautiful cave, at the huge rock of ashen color, which was dripping dew all around. The place smelled with thyme, rushes, and wild mint. There was a multitude of people, a crowd of women, many men, and a swarm of children, some standing, others seated, some sick from diverse diseases, wretched and weak, who made the sign of the cross. A priest with the stole stood in the middle; he had performed the Prayer, and was now at the end. They were singing "My Whole Hope," and prostrating. When the priest had said the dismissal, he started to perform the sanctification in a large basin, resembling a baptismal font, made by nature in the rock, wrought by God, as it seems. As the sanctification commenced, the women whispered to one another.

"The Dove will appear now!"

"Now the Dove will descend!"

"Look, now . . . now the Dove will come out!"

Soon, near the end of the sanctification, the moment the priest was about to baptize the cross in the basin, there was suddenly heard a flutter, and the cave resounded, and there appeared for a brief moment a beautiful bird, a dove with white, gray, and golden feathers. It fluttered *frst!* . . . *frst!* . . . and shook its feathers and struck with its wings the water which was in the basin of the sanctification, and at once disappeared. For a few moments water dripped into the basin from the vault of the cave and then stopped. The people watched voiceless, breathless. . . . Then from the chests of many came a "Great Thou art, O Lord!"

The same moment the priest dipped the cross, and sang, "Save, O Lord, Thy People," and then all the people, children, men, women rushed headlong to the basin, taking blessed water with their flasks and goblets, drinking and exclaiming, "Glory to Thee, Lord, glory to Thee!"

With much toil, I also followed the line, dragging Leutheris by the arm and shoulders with all my strength, and we succeeded after much trouble in approaching the priest who illuminated us with his sprinkling. Then I bent over and drank blessed water, and filled my palms and brought them to my husband's mouth to drink. It was a cool, sweet, sanctified water; it had a certain coolness and sweet odor that cannot be imitated.

Afterwards we returned with the whole swarm of people to the church. The next morning, after the mass, we did not forget to pass by the place where the shepherd of the night before had his temporary sheepfold. He gave us milk, yogurt, fresh cheese; then, when the lambs were roasted, he treated us with a large piece of chops and a portion of the shoulder. A family from Plaka seated nearby recognized us and sent us a flask full of wine, and we drank to their health. We had a fine day all told.

In the evening we returned home. On the road home, when it was still dusk, I noticed a small bundle. I stooped, picked it up, and saw that it contained three *svantzika.* The family from Plaka that had treated us with the wine had started out also on foot a little ahead of us and were about a gunshot away from us. At first I wanted to put the bundle in my pocket, then I said: "They are also poor like us; perhaps they dropped it, and it is a sin for me to keep it." I called them. "Did you drop a bundle? What kind was it and how much money did it contain?"

They searched themselves. "No," they said; "we did not lose anything."

Then I said to myself: "Perhaps some well-to-do lady dropped it; it's good luck, and so I'll keep it."

Leutheris was much better. He returned all the way on foot. His appearance improved much. His appetite was restored; he ate and drank well at the festival. In a short time he became well, strong, and lived. He is now eighty years old.

Next morning I went to my neighbor Panagina.

"Here, Mrs. Panagina, take your two *svantzika* and give me my pawn. I had changed the one *svantziko* of the two that you had lent me. I made all the expenses of the trip, I ate and drank well, and I also brought home two big pieces of cheese as well as half a loaf of bread. I returned the two borrowed *svantzika,* and have two more of them left."*

* Translated from the Greek by John P. Cavarnos.

THE WAY OF A PILGRIM

Anonymous

BY the grace of God I am a Christian, by my actions a great sinner, and by calling a homeless wanderer of the humblest birth. My worldly goods are a knapsack with some dried bread, and in my breast pocket a Bible. That is all.

On the twenty-fourth Sunday after Pentecost I went to church to say my prayers there during the Liturgy. The first Epistle of St. Paul to the Thessalonians was read, and I heard in it these words: "Pray incessantly." It was this text, more than any other, which forced itself upon my mind, and I began to think how it was possible to pray without ceasing, since a man has to concern himself with other things also, in order to make a living. I looked at my Bible, and with my own eyes read the words which I had heard, that is, that we ought always, at all times and in all places, to pray with uplifted hands. I thought and thought, but knew not what to make of it.

I went to the churches known for their famous preachers and heard a number of very fine sermons on prayer—what it is, how much we need it, and what its fruits are. But no one said how one could succeed in prayer. I heard a sermon on spiritual prayer, but how it was to be done was not pointed out.

Therefore, I decided to look for some experienced and skilled person who would give me in conversation that teaching about unceasing prayer which appealed to me so much. For a long time I wandered through many places. I read my Bible always, and everywhere I asked whether there was not in the neighborhood a spiritual teacher, a devout and experienced guide, to be found. One day I was told that in a certain village a gentleman had long been living and seeking the salvation of his soul. He had a chapel in his house. He never left his estate, and he spent his time in prayer and reading devotional books. Hearing this, I ran rather than walked to the village named. I got there and found him.

I asked the gentleman to explain to me the meaning of the apostle's words "pray without ceasing." He was silent for a while, looking at me closely. Then he said: "Ceaseless interior prayer is a continual yearning of the human spirit towards God. To succeed in this consoling exercise we must pray more often to God to teach us to pray without ceasing. Pray more, and pray more fervently. It is prayer itself which reveals to you how it can be achieved unceasingly; but it will take some time." This answer did not satisfy me.

Again I set out. I walked at least a hundred and twenty-five miles, and then I came to a large town, a provincial capital, where I saw a monastery. There I met a kind, devout, and hospitable abbot. I beseeched this abbot to explain to me what incessant prayer means. Unable to do so, he referred me to St. Demetrios' book on *The Spiritual Education of the Inner Man*, in which I read the following passage: "The words of the apostle 'pray without ceasing' should be understood as referring to the creative prayer of the understanding. The mind can always be reaching out towards God, and pray to Him unceasingly."

The following morning I thanked the abbot for his hospitality and went on my way. My failure to understand made me sad, and I read the Bible to comfort myself. In this way I followed the main road for five days, till one evening I was overtaken by an old monk who asked me to visit the monastery to which he belonged.

When we entered his cell he began to speak as follows: "The continuous interior prayer of Jesus is a constant, uninterrupted calling upon the divine Name of Jesus with the lips, the spirit, and the heart, while forming a mental picture of His constant presence, and imploring His grace, during every occupation, at all times, in all places, even during sleep. The appeal is couched in these terms: 'Lord Jesus Christ, have mercy on me.' One who accustoms oneself to this appeal experiences as a result so deep a consolation and so great a need to offer the prayer always, that he can no longer live without it, and it will continue to voice itself within him of its own accord. Now do you understand what prayer without ceasing is?"

"Yes, indeed, Father, and in God's name teach me how to gain the habit of it," I cried, filled with joy.

"Read this book," he said. "It is called the *Philokalia*,* and it contains the full and detailed science of constant interior prayer, set forth by twenty-five holy Fathers. The book is marked by a lofty wisdom and is so profitable to use that it is considered the foremost and best manual of the contemplative spiritual life. As the revered Nicephoros said, 'It leads one to salvation without labor and sweat.'"

"Is it then more sublime and holy than the Bible?" I asked.

"No, it is not. But it contains clear explanations of what the Bible holds in secret, and which cannot be easily grasped by our short-sighted understanding."

The old man explained all this to me and illustrated its meaning. We read passages of St. Gregory of Sinai, St. Callistos, and St. Ignatius, and he explained them in his own words. I listened attentively with great delight, fixed it in my memory, and tried as far as possible to remember every detail. In this way we spent the whole night together and went to Matins without having slept at all.

As the teacher sent me away with his blessing, he told me that while learning the prayer I must always come back to him and tell him everything, making a very frank confession and report; for the inward process could not go on properly and successfully without the guidance of a teacher.

After much wandering and traveling and some pleasant experiences I noted that inner prayer bears fruit in three ways: in the spirit, in the feelings, and in revelations. In the first is the sweetness of the love of God, inward peace, gladness of mind, purity of thought, and the sweet remembrance

* "The Love of Spiritual Beauty." It is the title of the great collection of mystical and ascetic writings by Fathers of the Greek Orthodox Church, covering a period of eleven centuries.

of God. In the second, the pleasant warmth of the heart, fulness of delight in all one's limbs, and joyous "bubbling" in the heart, lightness and courage, the joy of living, power not to feel sickness and sorrow. And in the last, light given to the mind, understanding of Holy Scripture, knowledge of the speech of created things, freedom from fuss and vanity, knowledge of the joy of inner life, and finally certainty of the nearness of God and of His love for us.*

✢

THIS DAY SALVATION

"This Day Salvation" is a *troparion* that is chanted on Sundays if the mode for the day is I, II, III, or IV. It follows the Great Doxology. In essence it is a Resurrection hymn that resembles the Easter Victory Hymn, but unlike the latter, it is chanted throughout the year. Simple and concise, it proclaims the central message of Christianity—salvation and victory have been bestowed on mankind through Christ's Resurrection. It has classical

This Day Salvation

Traditional Byzantine

Manuel Protopsaltis, 1819
Transcribed from the
Byzantine by
Dean D. Bouzianis

Mode IV Plagal

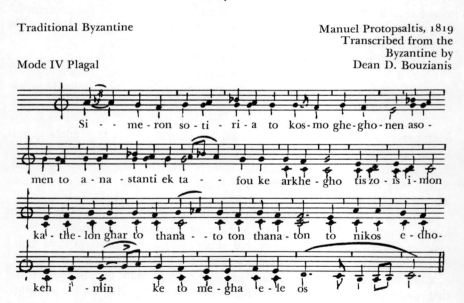

Si - - me - ron so - ti - ri - a to kos - mo ghe - gho - nen aso -

men to a - na - stanti ek ta - - fou ke arkhe - gho tis zo - is i - mon

kal - the - lon ghar to thana - - to ton thana - ton to nikos e - dho-

keh i - min ke to me - gha le - le os

---

* Abridged from *The Way of a Pilgrim*, translated from the Russian by R. M. French.

directness and objectiveness, the characteristics that prevail in the best Byzantine tradition.

The rendition in English of the Greek original is:

> Today salvation hath come unto the world.
> Let us chant to Him that rose from the grave,
>   The Author of our life:
> For having by death destroyed death,
> He hath given us victory and great mercy.

✛

CHRIST IS RISEN

THE title "Christ Is Risen" constitutes the opening words of the famous hymn which comes under various names: "Easter Troparion," "Victory Hymn," "The Glorious Old Hymn of Victory," and so on. The hymn has the form of a *troparion,* which means a short poem in accentual meter. It is chanted at midnight of Good Saturday before Easter Sunday in all Eastern Orthodox Churches, and in the original Greek in most of them. It is the one hymn which contains in so few words the central message of Christianity, which is symbolized in the Eucharistic drama, the greatest of all sacrifices.

Christ Is Risen

Traditional Byzantine

Mode I Plagal

Transcribed from the
Byzantine by
Dean D. Bouzianis

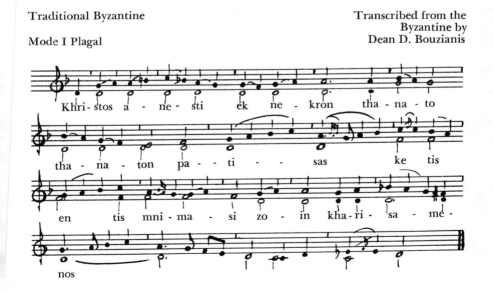

Khri-stos a - ne - sti ek ne - kron tha - na - to

tha - na - ton pa - ti - sas ke tis

en tis mni - ma - si zo - in kha - ri - sa - me -

nos

Easter lies at the heart of Eastern Orthodox Christianity, and its liturgy is an event that needs to be seen in order to be fully appreciated. Its celebration is the most important annual Church event, surpassing even Christmas, and its great message is contained in but three words of our hymn: *Thanato thanaton patisas,* "by (His) death on death He trampled."

At exactly midnight of the celebration of the Easter Liturgy the priest or bishop who is officiating, exclaims "Christos anesti!" or "Christ is risen!" This is the beginning of the Easter *troparion.* The hymn is then chanted over and over again in a tone that becomes more exultant as it is repeated. The faithful are seized by a strong ecstatic joy and all in unison chant with mystical exultation this victory hymn, which in a way resembles the classical Greek *epinikia,* or victory odes. In a precise sense the Easter *troparion* proclaims to man a supreme hope, his victory over death and his release from terror. And this liberation from fear creates boundless joy. Christ's triumph over death makes the faithful rejoice by imparting to them the conviction that they themselves are also sharers of the great victory.

The words of this hymn are few but most meaningful—

> Christ is risen from the dead,
> And by death on death He trampled,
> And to those in the tombs He granted life.

PART III

THE ROMAN CATHOLIC CHURCH

by

JEAN LOUISE SMITH

1. THE CHURCH OF ROME IS ESTABLISHED ... *page* 248

2. THE CHURCH REACHES OUT .... *page* 269

3. THE AGE OF MONASTICISM .... *page* 288

4. CRUSADES AND CATHEDRALS .... *page* 310

5. THE FLOWERING OF CHRISTIAN ART:
   THE RENAISSANCE .... *page* 334

6. THE AGE OF ROMANTICISM .... *page* 356

7. THE ROMAN CATHOLIC CHURCH AROUND
   THE WORLD .... *page* 380

CONTENTS

PART III SECTION 1

THE CHURCH OF ROME IS ESTABLISHED

---✝---

And the Lord added to the church daily such as should be saved.—ACTS 2:47

---✝---

PICTURES: PAGE
  Interpretation: St. Peter's Cathedral, Rome—*Michelangelo and others* 249
  Picture: St. Peter's Cathedral, Rome—*Michelangelo and others* 251
  Interpretation: St. Jerome—*El Greco* 250
  Picture: St. Jerome—*El Greco* 253
  Interpretation: The Emperor Justinian and His Court—*Artist Unknown* ... 254
  Picture: The Emperor Justinian and His Court—*Artist Unknown* 255

POETRY:
  Augustine—*Marlatt* 256
  The Birds—*Dracontius* 256
  Veni Creator Spiritus—*Dryden* 256
  Morning Hymn—*Gregory the Great* 257
  Before Meat—*Prudentius* 258
  Thou Splendid Giver of the Light—*Hilary of Poitiers* 258

STORIES:
  St. Augustine of Canterbury—*Caxton* 259
  Hilary of Poitiers—*Duffield* 260
  Ambrose, the Reluctant Bishop—*Smith* 263

MUSIC:
  Interpretation: The Royal Banners Forward Go—*Fortunatus* (?) 265
  Music: The Royal Banners Forward Go—*Parker* 266
  Interpretation: O Trinity of Blessed Light—*St. Ambrose* (?) 267
  Music: O Trinity of Blessed Light—*Chartres Church Melody* 267

ST. PETER'S CATHEDRAL, ROME

THE basilica of St. Peter is one of the wonders of the world, and perhaps the most stupendous of all. Nothing like it exists anywhere else,
and only those who have seen it can conceive of its stateliness and its magnificence. For nearly two hundred years, the greatest masters of the Renaissance exerted their genius and exhausted all of the resources of their art,
while more than forty popes lavished their treasures on this unparalleled
sanctuary, which stands on the site of the circus of Nero where thousands
of the first Christians suffered martyrdom.

In the year A.D. 67, according to tradition, St. Peter was executed in the
middle of the circus at the foot of the obelisk which now stands in front of
his temple. Close by the circus existed a cemetery where the martyred Christians were buried; and in this cemetery the body of the apostle was deposited.
In the year A.D. 90, the bishop, Anacletus, erected a small oratory over the
grave of St. Peter to mark the spot. Later, at the request of Sylvester I,
Constantine the Great destroyed the old circus and over its northern foundations built the first basilica to the apostle.

The Constantine basilica, which was half as large as the present one, lasted
for eleven hundred years. In the middle of the fifteenth century, ruin
menaced it, and the reigning pope, Nicholas V, determined to reconstruct on
a more extensive scale. Bernardo Rossellino and Leon Battiste Alberti, the
greatest architects of the day, were employed and began the work in 1450.
When Nicholas V died in 1455, the walls of the new construction were only
a few feet high, and for nearly fifty years, under succeeding popes, the
work progressed very slowly until the election in 1503 of the great Julius II,
who had a talent for big undertakings. This pope, keen to detect genius, preferred Bramante to all other architects. The old basilica was gradually demolished, and on April 18, 1506, the foundation stone of the new edifice
was laid.

Leo X, who succeeded Julius II, placed the work in the hands of Giuliano
da Sangello, Fra Giocondo da Verone, and Raphael. The next architects
were Antonio da Sangallo, Baldasare Peruzzi, and Michelangelo, then in his
seventy-second year. Paul III, the reigning pontiff, gave Michelangelo unlimited power to alter, pull down, or remodel the building. When he died in
1564, he had finished the drum of the dome and had left designs and models
for the completion of the work. After the death of Michelangelo various
others were entrusted with the work and finally, in 1626, the new basilica
was dedicated by Urban VIII.

This great achievement of architecture, in which all the artistic forces
of the age contributed, occupied a period of one hundred seventy-six years
in its construction. In addition to the wonders of the basilica, the Vatican
which adjoined it became a repository for great art of the Church. Begun
in 1459 under Nicholas V, the old building of 1150 became the most im-

posing palace in the world. It took more than three hundred years and several popes to bring it to its present state.

The Sistine Chapel with its famed ceiling decorated by Michelangelo shows the Creation story—a task which took the artist eight years to paint. Later in the fifteenth century the foundations were laid for the Vatican Museum. Bramante, Michelangelo, Raphael, Pollaiuolo, Bernini, and other "greats" in Renaissance art were commissioned to do the work which made the museum the largest, most splendid, and most ancient in Europe because of the statuary, frescoes, tapestries, and paintings which fill it. Among the greatest treasures, for example, are Raphael's nine tapestries on Biblical themes, and his frescoes "La Disputa" and "The School of Athens." The Picture Gallery of the Vatican contains paintings by Murillo, Raphael, Perugino, Titian, and others. In the basilica itself, there are impressive marble sculptured tombs, candelabra designed by Pollaiuolo and Cellini, and the poignantly beautiful marble "Pieta" by Michelangelo.*

✠

ST. JEROME
El Greco

ONE of the finest portraits of St. Jerome, who lived in the fourth century, was done by the sixteenth-century artist, El Greco. When we know the facts, this gulf of twelve hundred years between the artist and his subject is not so great after all.

El Greco devoted almost all of his artistic talent to the Church. From his brush came painting after painting on themes of the Church, for the artist was swept into the tide of the Counter Reformation. These reforms of Catholicism gave new life and spirit to the Church. They brought a renewed interest in the Bible and in church history. It was natural, then, that a painter like El Greco should choose for one of his subjects St. Jerome, a Father, Doctor, and great scholar of the Church.

It was logical, too, that El Greco pictured St. Jerome in his study with a Bible, because so much of his life was given to making a Latin version of the Bible. El Greco makes St. Jerome an austere man with a deeply penetrating expression, looking straight out of the canvas at us in a manner which we cannot escape. His finger marks the place in the Bible where he has been reading or possibly translating. The rich, red garment that covers him is the shade of red often used by the Church and sometimes called "ecclesiastical red." Except for the richness of this robe, the general impression is one of an ascetic man—the lean, almost drawn face of the saint tells us this quite plainly.

In this painting as in all of his other religious subjects, El Greco com-

* Adapted from *Wonders of Italy* by G. Fattorusso, pp. 404-406. Used by permission of the author and the publisher.

ST. PETER'S CATHEDRAL, ROME—MICHELANGELO (and others)

bined formality with a storytelling technique. As a youth in Crete—where he was born in 1541—he learned the art of the icon-maker. This disciplined, stylized type of art was intended to inspire the observer to create his own spiritual feelings. In contrast, the storytelling technique that El Greco learned while studying in Titian's studio in Renaissance Italy had as its purpose the recreating of a scene or a personality so that the observer could project himself into it. The combination of the icon approach to art can be observed in the elongation of the figure of St. Jerome, his almost expressionless face, and the rigidity of his posture. The storytelling quality is found in the unmistakable relationship of the saint to the Bible which he holds—there is a warmth of feeling here as well as an almost possessive quality.

El Greco's religious paintings are so numerous as to be in the overwhelming majority of the total of his works. Settling as he did in Toledo, Spain, he found himself in the center of Spanish Catholicism. Because the headquarters of the Inquisition were in that city, priests and monastics constituted a large part of its population. Church commissions for paintings came to El Greco quickly, assuring his future as a popular artist. (For other paintings by El Greco, see pp. 150 and 253.)

As a painter in the service of the Church he became a powerful interpreter of the Counter Reformation. His altarpieces and great canvases depicted the spirit of that movement and, as such, form marvelous commentaries on the great effort that Catholicism was making to purify and strengthen the inner life of the Church. There is no softness, no worldliness to El Greco's work. He is a realist who says what he has to say in a direct and uncompromising manner. The torture which the inquisitors inflicted on heretics prompted him to paint many pictures showing the martyrdom of the saints of old. It required no great imagination for the inquisitors to see themselves in the place of those who were torturing the saints!

The life of El Greco holds a certain mysterious fascination. Born on the island of Crete as Dominico Theotocopuli, he spent his boyhood and young manhood under the influence of Byzantine art. When he was twenty-five he turned his back on all this and went to Venice to work in the studio of the great Titian. There he found the extreme opposite of the formalization of Byzantine art, for all was lush, with rounded forms and glowing colors.

El Greco went from Venice to Rome, where he was warmly received as an artist. After seven years he left Italy to go to Toledo, Spain. It was there that he was given the nickname El Greco, "The Greek," which stayed with him to the end of his days. The genius of El Greco was fired by the environment of religious tension and fervor. For forty years the artist lived in Toledo, amassing a personal fortune and living in splendor, with the Church as his patron. But wealth and fame allowed no compromise for El Greco—he always insisted on interpreting his subjects in his own way. This devotion to his art gives his work an unmistakable integrity.

ST. JEROME—*EL GRECO*

THE EMPEROR JUSTINIAN AND HIS COURT
Artist Unknown

FROM across more than a thousand years of Christian church history—from the sixth century—come the mosaics which so richly adorn the churches of Ravenna, Italy. Still in an excellent state of preservation, they are among the most important legacies of the arts of the early Church.

Standing in the beautiful basilica of St. Vitale, consecrated in 547, one looks high up in the dome of the apse to these softly glowing, jewel-like mosaics. In them the Eastern style of Byzantium came to the Roman world, for the stiff, frontal figures of the Emperor Justinian and the Empress Theodora, and their retinues, look out at us with quiet, expressionless mien. A part of the history of the Christian Church is written in these mosaics.

Justinian and Theodora, rulers of Byzantium with equal rights, had freed Italy from the foreign yoke of the Goths, under whose rule Arianism had been established. This was a humanistic interpretation of Christianity—one which emphasized the human side of Jesus Christ almost to the exclusion of His divine nature.

After Justinian and his queen drove the Goths back into the north country, they made Ravenna the political capital of Italy. As heads of the Church, they declared that henceforth the divinity of Christ should be the acceptable interpretation of Christianity.

The mosaics of St. Vitale are monuments to this decree and to the two rulers who proclaimed it. At the center of the great arch of the apse the figure of Christ is pictured, seated on a blue globe of the world. The walls on either side are covered with mosaics showing the two rulers, coming in procession to offer their gifts to Christ. To the left is the Emperor Justinian carrying for his offering the gold plate or paten, for the bread or wafers of the Mass. This is particularly noteworthy, for in that time the emperor was the only layman allowed to take part in the procession of the Mass. Justinian is crowned and robed in a purple mantle. He is flanked by the archbishop and other dignitaries.

The theme of these mosaics is the redemption of man by Christ and the re-enactment of that redemption by the Eucharist. The sovereigns lay their gifts, the vessels for the elements, at the feet of Christ, and in doing this they represent the desire of all Christians to offer treasure to Christ.

The arts of the early Christian Church are nowhere more magnificent than in these mosaics. To let them speak today, one must know their history and understand also that they were not created for a graceful pastime, but were made by unknown hands to symbolize a truth. Byzantine art was not concerned with naturalistic figures or expressions; it was an effort to create a formalized, symbolic medium which left its interpretation to the viewer. The expressionless features of the people are not accidental and not because of the artist's lack of skill. He who looks is to supply the emotion and feeling.

These bits of colored glass, stone, and jewels, put together with marvelous

THE EMPEROR JUSTINIAN AND HIS COURT—*ARTIST UNKNOWN*

craftsmanship, step out of the past and speak of the Christian Church, not far removed from the days of the Apostolic Church!

✠

AUGUSTINE

A laughing boy,
He loved columns,
Because they towered skyward.
A passionate youth,
He loved beauty
And lost his way in the clouds.
A learned man,
He found his sky again
And, higher than the mists of midnight,
Built the City of God
With Towers that touched the stars.*

—*Earl Marlatt*

THE BIRDS

As they join their various voices
In a melody so bland
To the glory of their Maker—
They seem worthy of His Hand.**
—*Blossius Aemilius Dracontius (5th century)*

VENI CREATOR SPIRITUS

(Fourth Century)

Creator Spirit, by whose aid
The world's foundations first were laid,
Come visit every pious mind,
Come pour Thy joys on human kind;
From sin and sorrow set us free
And make Thy temples worthy Thee.
O Source of uncreated light,
The Father's promised Paraclete!
Thrice holy fount, thrice holy fire,
Our hearts with heavenly love inspire;
Come and Thy sacred unction bring
To sanctify us while we sing.
Plenteous of grace, descend from high,

* From *Cathedral: A Volume of Poems* by Earl Marlatt, p. 93. Copyright 1956 by Earl Marlatt. Published by Parthenon Press. Used by permission of the author and the publisher.
** Translated from the Latin by Thomas Walsh.

Rich in Thy sevenfold energy!
Thou strength of His almighty hand,
Whose power does heaven and earth command.
Proceeding Spirit, our defense,
Who dost the gifts of tongues dispense,
And crown'st Thy gift with eloquence!
Refine and purge our earthly parts;
But, oh, inflame and fire our hearts!
Our frailties help, our vice control,
Submit the senses to the soul;
And when rebellious they are grown
Then lay Thy hand and hold them down.
Chase from our minds the infernal foe,
And peace, the fruit of love bestow;
And lest our feet should step astray,
Protect and guide us on the way.
Make us eternal truths receive,
And practice all that we believe;
Give us Thyself that we may see
The Father and the Son by Thee.
Immortal honor, endless fame
Attend the Almighty Father's name;
The Saviour Son be glorified,
Who for lost man's redemption died;
An equal adoration be,
Eternal Paraclete, to Thee!
          —*Rendered from the Latin by John Dryden (1631-1700)*

MORNING HYMN

Lo, fainter now lie spread the shades of night,
And upward spread the trembling gleams of morn;
Suppliant we bend before the Lord of Light,
    And pray at early dawn,

That His sweet charity may all our sin
Forgive, and make our miseries to cease;
May grant us health, grant us the gift divine
    Of everlasting peace.

Father Supreme, this grace on us confer;
And Thou, O son, by an eternal birth!
With Thee, coequal spirit comforter!
    Whose glory fills the earth.
          —*Gregory the Great (ca. 540-604);*
              translated by Edward Caswall

BEFORE MEAT

Lord, without Thee naught is sweet,
  Naught my life can satisfy,
If Thy favour make not meet
  What I drink and what I eat;
Let faith all things sanctify!

O'er this bread God's grace be poured,
  Christ's sweet fragrance fill the bowl!
Rule my converse, Triune Lord,
  Sober thought and sportive word,
All my acts and all my soul.

—Prudentius (348-ca. 410);
translated by R. Martin Pope

THOU SPLENDID GIVER OF THE LIGHT

Thou splendid giver of the light,
  By whose serene and lovely ray
Beyond the gloomy shades of night
  Is opened wide another day!

But clearer than the sun may shine,
  All light and day in Thee I find,
To fill my night with glory fine
  And purify my inner mind.

Fill with thy spirit every sense,
  That God's divine and gracious love
May drive Satanic temptings hence,
  And blight their falsehoods from above.

That in the acts of common toil
  Which life demands from us each day,
We may, without a stain or soil,
  Live in Thy holy laws alway.

This hope is in my praying heart—
  These are my vows which now I pay;
That this sweet light may not depart,
  But guide me purely through the day.

—Hilary of Poitiers (ca. 300-367); from the Latin

ST. AUGUSTINE OF CANTERBURY
William Caxton

ST. AUGUSTINE was a holy monk and sent in to England, to preach the faith of our Lord Jesu Christ, by St. Gregory, then being pope of Rome. St. Augustine had a great zeal and love for England as is shown all along in his legend. When he saw children of England in the market of Rome to be sold, which were fair of visage, he demanded licence to go into England to convert the people thereof to Christian faith.

When St. Augustine and his fellowship came into England and arrived in the isle of Thanet in East Kent, where King Ethelbert reigned, St. Augustine told the intent of his coming from the court of Rome, and said that he had brought to him right joyful and pleasant tidings, and said that if he would obey and do after his preaching, he should have everlasting joy in the bliss of heaven, and should reign with almighty God in his kingdom. King Ethelbert hearing this, commanded that they should abide and tarry in the same isle, and that all things should be ministered to them that were necessary, unto the time that he were otherwise advised.

Soon after, the king came to them in the same isle, and he being in the field, St. Augustine with his fellowship came and spake with him, having made the sign of the cross, singing by the way the litany, beseeching God devoutly to strengthen them and help. The king received him and his fellowship, and in the same place St. Augustine preached a glorious sermon, and declared to the king the Christian faith openly and the great merit and avail that should come thereof in time coming. When he had ended his sermon the king said to him: "Your promises be full fair that ye bring, but because they be new and have not been heard here before, we may not yet give consent thereto; nevertheless, because ye be come as pilgrims from far countries, we will not be grievous or hard to you, but we will receive you meekly and minister to you such things as be necessary, neither we will forbid you, but as many as ye can convert to your faith and religion by your preaching, ye shall have licence to baptize them, and to accompany them to your law."

Then the king gave to them a mansion in the city of Dorobernence, which now is called Canterbury. And when they drew nigh to the city, they came in with a cross of silver, and with procession singing the litany, praying almighty God of succour and help that he would take away his wrath from the city and to inflame the hearts of the people to receive his doctrine.

Then St. Augustine and his fellowship began to preach there the word of God, and about there in the province, and such people as were well disposed anon were converted, and followed this holy man. And by the holy conversation and miracles that they did, many people were converted and great fame arose in the country. When it came to the king's ear, anon, he came to the presence of St. Augustine and desired him to preach again, and then the word of God so inflamed him, that as soon as the sermon was ended, the king fell down to the feet of St. Augustine and said sorrowfully: "Alas! woe is me, that I have erred so long and know not of him that thou speakest of, thy promises be so delectable that I think it all too long till I be christened, wherefore, holy father, I require thee to minister to me the sacrament of baptism."

St. Augustine, seeing the great meekness and obedience of the king that wanted to be christened, took him up with weeping tears and baptized him with all his household in the Christian faith with great joy and gladness.

When all this was done, St. Augustine, desiring the health of the people of England, went forth on foot to York; and when he came nigh to the city there met him a blind man which said to him: "O thou holy Augustine, help me that am full needy." To whom St. Augustine said: "I have no silver, but such as I have I give thee; in the name of Jesu Christ arise and be all whole," and with that word he received his sight and believed in our Lord and was baptized. And upon Christmas day he baptized, in the river named Swale, ten thousand men without women and children. In the same place they builded a church in the worship of God and St. Augustine.

One time, as St. Augustine was in his prayers, our Lord appeared to him, and comforting him with a gentle and familiar speech, said: "O thou my good servant and true, be thou comforted and do manly, for I thy Lord God am with thee in all thine affection, and mine ears be opened to thy prayers, and for whom thou demandest any petition thou shalt have thy desire, and the gate of everlasting life is open to thee, where thou shalt joy with me without end." And in that same place where our Lord said these words he fixed his staff into the ground, and a well of clear water sprang up in that same place, the which well is called Cerne, and it is in the country of Dorset, whereas now is builded a fair abbey, and is named Cerne after the well. And the church is builded in the same place whereas our Lord appeared to St. Augustine.

Also in the same country was a young man that was lame, dumb, and deaf, and by the prayers of St. Augustine he was made whole.

After this, St. Augustine, full of virtues, departed out of this world unto our Lord God, and lieth buried in Canterbury in the abbey that he founded there in the worship and rule, whereas our Lord God showeth yet daily many miracles. Let us think well of St. Augustine, father and apostle of England, by whom this land was converted unto the Christian faith and by whose ordinance bishops were ordained to minister the sacraments.*

✝

HILARY OF POITIERS
Samuel W. Duffield

ABRA was reading the letter which she had just finished writing. "How does this sound, Mother?" she asked.

* Abridged from *The Golden Legend*, Vol. III, translated by William Caxton in 1483.

Dear Father: How Mother and I miss you! The people of Poitiers miss you too. They stop me in the streets and ask, "How is our bishop, your dear father? Have you heard from him since his exile to the East?" Robert wants to know when you are coming back to open up the singing school again. Oh, Father, why did you speak so strongly against the Arians so that the Emperor Constantius ordered you out of Gaul, out of our lovely city of Poitiers? Please write and tell me why.

Your obedient daughter, Abra

"There, Mother, I've asked him the question that we both wanted to have answered. Now he will have to give us a reply," Abra said as she rolled the parchment and prepared to seal it with wax.

Her mother looked at Abra lovingly. Then she drew her close. "You are twelve years old, my child, and old enough to know that life is not always easy. Your father was born of a fine and noble family, but he was not a Christian until after we were married. He was wonderfully educated—in worldly knowledge—but knew little of Christianity. After our baptism— for I, too, was baptized a Christian with him—he studied the Holy Scriptures like one possessed.

" 'In them we find the only Truth,' he would say to me ofttimes. After he was made Bishop, the faithful Christian people loved him dearly!"

"Yes, Mother. And I love him too! I think it made Father very happy that I was baptized before he left Poitiers, don't you?" Abra asked.

"Yes, dear, I do know it made him happy, for he told me so," her mother said. "But we must not expect too much attention from him when he returns," she added cautiously.

"But Mother, why not?" Abra asked sharply, shocked at the thought that her father might not always seek her company.

"It is only that in our Church bishops do not marry. Before your father was elected to the high position of Bishop of Poitiers, it did not matter so much, for all men understood that he was already a husband and father before he accepted the Christian faith," she explained.

Abra went to the window and looked out over the narrow rugged valley to the rocky hill beyond. She watched the sun set behind the great jagged hill. "He will never stop loving us. That I know," she said thoughtfully.

"You are an unusually discerning girl for your age," her mother replied quietly. "Your father does love us both dearly, and no matter how great he becomes or even if we must live apart from him, his love and kindness will never leave us," she consoled Abra.

Abra waited for her father's reply to her letter for many long weeks. She often stood at the window looking out over the valley, straining her eyes to see if a messenger might be approaching. One day she noticed a cloud of dust in the distance. "Here comes my letter! I know it's coming!" she cried to her mother, who was weaving at her loom.

Down the stairs, out of the door, and along the path Abra flew until she was at the gate just as the messenger arrived. He dismounted and handed her a scroll, sealed with a heavy blob of red wax. Then Abra hurried back to her mother and, with trembling hands, she broke the seal.

Dear Abra: Your sweet letter cheered me and I, too, miss you and your dear mother. I have been busy studying more about our Church and its theology. I am to engage in some discussions with the Oriental bishops here, but I fear that they, like the Arians of the Roman Empire, do not believe that Christ and God, the Father, are alike in substance.

But these are big words and thoughts for you, my daughter, so I shall not trouble you further about them, except, perhaps, to say that should these men care little for my defense of the Orthodox faith, they may send me back to Poitiers before long!

"Oh Mother," Abra said, "I hope he *does* displease them and come home!"

"No doubt he will," her mother smiled. "Your father always speaks his mind. Read on."

Abra took up the scroll.

Keep your soul pure, for it is like the pearl of great value. Pray always to God and forget not the music and the verses of the Church—the music which I taught you. Here are the words and music to a new hymn. I shall think of you standing at your open window, watching the sun come up over the hills, looking to the East and praying for my safe return even as you sing:

> Thou splendid giver of the light,
>   By whose serene and lovely ray
> Beyond the gloomy shades of night
>   Is opened wide another day!

Abra sang hesitantly at first, pondering the unfamiliar music.

"Perhaps your father has learned something of the Greek music," her mother mused. "It sounds just a little different from his Latin hymns. Are there more verses?"

"Oh yes, there are eight. I like them all, but the last one is very beautiful:

> This hope is in my praying heart—
>   These are the vows which now I pay;
> That this sweet light may not depart,
>   But guide me purely through the day."

Three years passed, and one day Abra, now a young lady, was singing the hymn that her father had sent her. Suddenly as she glanced out of the window she saw a column of dust upon the road that wound down the steep hill to the valley below. She strained to see if she could tell who it might be. Suddenly she called out, "It's Father! I know it's Father!" Quickly she spread the word through the household and soon the townspeople took up the cry. A crowd gathered and surged toward the gates of the city. They pressed forward to fling open the gates just as the horse clattered across the drawbridge. The dusty, weary horseman scanned the faces of the crowd. Abra pushed through the throng.

"Let me through! Let me through! I must see who it is!" she pleaded.

"Abra!" the grimy man said joyously as he pressed his daughter close.

Someone overheard and shouted, "It's Hilary, our bishop, home after all these years of exile!"

"Welcome, Hilary!" the people took up the cry.

Abra and her mother soon had reason to be very proud of Hilary, for he became one of the greatest defenders of the Christian faith in all Christendom. Sometimes his bold speaking and fiery writing got him into trouble with the Arians. Sometimes his duties took him on long journeys into Italy to speak and to teach. He became known as the Defender of the Faith, or the Singing Bishop. He wrote many hymns and he opened a school of the chant so that people might learn the beautiful music of the Church.

One day when Abra was a young and lovely woman, she stood sadly at her window looking out over the valley, thinking of how her father had died, worn out from his many labors for the Church. Then, reaching into her desk, she drew out a scroll. Slowly she unfolded it. Then quietly she sang:

> This hope is in my praying heart—
> These are the vows which now I pay;
> That this sweet light may not depart,
> But guide me purely through the day.*

✝

AMBROSE, THE RELUCTANT BISHOP

Jean Louise Smith

It was Palm Sunday in the year 386 and the streets of Milan were teeming with people making their way through the dim light of early morning to the church. It was an orderly, silent crowd which paid little attention to the soldiers who mingled with them. The soldiers, in turn, saw no need to impose themselves upon the people whose sole object was the basilica.

"Think you there will be trouble in the church?" one soldier asked his companion.

"Ah, no. There will be only disappointment. Ambrose, the bishop, will not preach today. After all, his very life is in danger. Only a fool would walk straight into more trouble at a time like this! There is more likely to be an uprising among the Arians whom Ambrose opposes," was the reply.

The soldiers kept a sharp eye on those known to be Arians. They could identify them easily because, like themselves, they were the only part of the throng that was not moving toward the church. The Arians stood silent and glum, watching the Orthodox Christians whose sacred vessels they had requisitioned and into whose churches they were even now demanding entrance for worship.

* Adapted by Jean Louise Smith from *Latin Hymnwriters*, Chap. III, "Hilary of Poitiers and the Earliest Latin Hymns," by Samuel W. Duffield.

"Who is this Ambrose to think he can stand against the tide of our Arian faith?" one of their number was heard to say. "Even the government is on our side and soon the emperor himself will uphold our doctrine. Jesus was not God—any thinking man knows that!"

"Hush! You'll be set upon by the Orthodox for speaking blasphemy!" his companion replied in alarm. " 'Tis no time to shout your ideas to the roof-tops if you value your life."

"Make way! Make way!" came an insistent voice above the silent throng. The crowd parted to allow a commanding, dignified figure carrying a crosier and dressed in priestly robes to go through their midst.

"It's Ambrose, Bishop of Milan, going to preach!" an admiring cheer went up from the churchgoers. It was a cheer that told of their approval of the courage of this man who, in face of violent opposition, was faithful to the performance of his Christian duties as bishop.

As he neared the basilica, Ambrose became the leader of a procession; the people fell in behind him, sweeping along with triumphant steps. When they reached the steps of the church, Ambrose turned for a moment to face his people. Those who stood close saw in his eyes a look of calm confidence and faith. Then he turned and walked unfalteringly into the great church with hundreds of his followers close behind him. The doors were closed and the service began.

The worship proceeded as though it were any other Palm Sunday. When it was time for the sermon, every eye was on the bishop as he mounted to the high pulpit. The silence as he prepared to speak was almost unbearable.

"You know well enough how once I was reluctant to be your bishop. I wanted a quiet life, free from trouble and controversy—with time to study the things of God and His Church. You remember how I fled when you thronged this very basilica and shouted to the Congress of Bishops, met to select a leader to defend your faith against the Arians, that you wanted me to be your bishop!"

Ambrose continued. "Yes, I tried to flee from you and from God that day. But He spoke to me. I had no alternative but to be your leader, for better or for ill in this struggle against the Arian heresy. Whatever happens, we must uphold the faith. We must stand strong in our undying belief that Christ and the Father are one!"

Suddenly there was a movement in the back of the nave as the great double doors were flung open. The sound of the clatter of arms broke the peace of worship. Turning around, the people saw that the church was surrounded by soldiers. Now they were truly frightened, both for their own lives and for the safety of their beloved leader. They drew close to the bishop. Suddenly, as if they were one man, they decided to hold Ambrose captive and keep him within the shelter of the great church until danger was past. "Barricade the doors and protect us!" they pled with the soldiers. "Keep the Arians out of the basilica."

This the soldiers did, and for several days the congregation lived in a kind of encampment within the church and its cloisters. The troops without waited patiently for the people to tire of their self-imposed imprisonment. But no one came out. The week wore on and still the people remained quietly inside, praying and listening to their leader, Ambrose.

One night the soldiers on guard heard strange and wonderful music. From a quiet beginning, the melody rose as wave after wave of voices took it up. All night the beautiful music continued. First one group and then another, answering as from a distance, took up the chant.

"What is this?" those outside the church wondered. "Are these magic incantations that Ambrose has devised to cast a spell of enchantment over his people?" All during the week the singing continued until at last Easter Day arrived. Because there was no change in affairs, the emperor sent word to Ambrose, suggesting a conference that might bring about a measure of peace between Ambrose, the emperor, and the so-called bishop of the Arians. Ambrose had no choice but to submit to the emperor's wishes for compromise and when he returned to the waiting people, still in the church, he said sadly, "The emperor is in the Church, but not over it!" It was his way of comforting them that God was still head of His Church, no matter what earthly rulers might say.

Some would have said that the conference was a failure from the Orthodox Christian point of view. But something else had happened that was to sweep the Christian Church and give it new life. The marvelous music which Ambrose had taught his people during the week within the basilica was caught up with enthusiasm until churches all over Europe were using it. Antiphonal singing—several choirs answering each other in harmonious responses —became the delight of Christian worship. Hymns, canticles, and chants were sung in this manner and even the people learned to take part in musical portions of the worship. Ambrose, father of antiphonal music, in capturing the love of his people had directed it toward the worship of God!

✠

THE ROYAL BANNERS FORWARD GO

FORTUNATUS, one of the great names in early church music, is said to have written this magnificent processional hymn in 569, when a relic of the cross was presented by the Byzantine Empress Sophia to Queen Rhadegunda of Poitiers, France. It was a great occasion and we may imagine the dignitaries of the Church in both France and Italy gathering in Poitiers to solemnize the event. The words tell of the beauty and glory of the Cross of Christ as sanctified by Jesus' death upon it.

Gregory of Tours described the occasion: "Eufronius, Bishop of Tours, came with his clergy with much singing and gleaming of tapers and fragrance of incense, and in the absence of the bishop of the city, brought the holy relics to the monastery."

Fortunatus himself was an Italian-trained church singer, writing verses

The Royal Banners Forward Go*

L. M.

PARKER   HORATIO PARKER, 1894
Majestically

1 The roy - al ban - ners for - ward go, The cross shines forth in
2 Ful - filled is all that Da - vid told In true pro - phet - ic
3 O tree of beau - ty, tree most fair, Or - dained those ho - ly

mys - tic glow Where he, as man, who gave man breath, Now
song of old; How God the na - tions' King should be, For
limbs to bear; Gone is thy shame, each crim-son'd bough Pro -

bows be - neath the yoke of death.
God is reign - ing from the tree.
claims the King of glo - ry now.   A - men.

*From *The Hymnal*, 1940, No. 63 (2nd tune). Published by The Church Hymnal Corporation. Used by permission of The Church Pension Fund.

as well as being able to sing extremely well. Because of an affliction of his eyes, he made a pilgrimage to Tours, in France (Gaul, as it was then called), to visit the birthplace of St. Martin of Tours. He decided to remain there, and entered a monastery. In 599 he was made a bishop. Fortunatus is regarded as the last of the classical church composers and the first of the troubadours. "Welcome, Happy Morning" is another of his hymns that has come down to us and is found in many hymnbooks, Catholic and Protestant.

Horatio Parker (1863-1919) was a well-known American composer who used much of his talent for the service of the Church as both an organist and composer of hymn tunes.

O Trinity of Blessed Light*

ADESTO SANCTA TRINITAS. (L.M.)
In moderate time. Unison.

Chartres Church Melody.

St. Ambrose, 340–97. Tr. J. M. Neale.

O lux beata Trinitas.

O TRINITY of blessèd light,
O Unity of princely might,
The fiery sun now goes his way;
Shed thou within our hearts thy ray.

2 To thee our morning song of praise,
To thee our evening prayer we raise;
Thy glory suppliant we adore
For ever and for evermore.

3. All laud to God the Father be;
All praise, eternal Son, to thee;
All glory, as is ever meet,
To God the holy Paraclete.

*From *Songs of Praise*, No. 51. Published by Oxford University Press, London. Used by permission of the publisher.

O TRINITY OF BLESSED LIGHT

ST. AMBROSE, who is believed to have written the words of this great hymn of praise to the Trinity, was the first important hymn writer of the Church. Living in the latter half of the fifth century, St. Ambrose, as Bishop of Milan, was the originator of the Latin hymn. (See the story in this section, "Ambrose, the Reluctant Bishop.") The natural, beautiful rhythms of Ambrose's hymns caught the imagination of the people in an upsurge of faith so great that the Arians accused him of having bewitched his congregation! Modern hymnbooks contain but few hymns by St. Ambrose—most of the scores he must have written were lost. Among the most frequently seen are "O Trinity of Blessed Light," "Creator of the Earth and Sky," and "O Splendor of God's Glory Bright." The first of these, printed here, is a brief two-stanza hymn of praise to the Trinity, followed by a doxology. As translated by the Catholic hymn writer, J. M. Neale, it follows the original almost exactly, and thus comes to us practically unchanged from nearly sixteen hundred years ago.

The stately "Chartres Church Melody," to which St. Ambrose's words have been set, is from the sixteenth century, during which time several fine hymn tunes were named for the churches where they originated—in this instance, Chartres Cathedral.

Through the words of the hymn, the worshiper directs his praise to the Triune God, praying that the love of God may light his heart, even as his voice is lifted in praise.

CONTENTS

PART III   SECTION 2

THE CHURCH REACHES OUT

—✛—

. . . Faith without works is dead. Seest thou how faith wrought with his works, and by works was faith made perfect.—JAMES 2:20, 22

—✛—

PICTURES: PAGE
    Interpretation: St. Martin's Cross—*Artist Unknown* 270
    Picture: St. Martin's Cross—*Artist Unknown* 271
    Interpretation: The Ardagh Chalice—*Artist Unknown* 272
    Picture: The Ardagh Chalice—*Artist Unknown* 273
    Interpretation: Glastonbury Abbey 274
    Picture: Glastonbury Abbey 275

POETRY:
    Hymn of the World's Creator—*Caedmon* 276
    Alleluia!—*Balbulus* 276
    The Deer's Cry—*St. Patrick of Tara* 277
    The Rune of Hospitality—*Author Unknown* 278
    On His Exile to Iona—*St. Columba* 278
    Communion Hymn-Poem of the Ancient Irish Church—*Anonymous* 279

STORIES:
    St. Hilda: Princess, Abbess—*Baring-Gould* 279
    St. Boniface—*Bell* 280
    Patrick of Ireland—*Leo* 283

MUSIC:
    Interpretation: Hark! A Herald Voice Is Calling—*St. Ambrose* (?) 284
    Music: Hark! A Herald Voice Is Calling—*Monk* 285
    Interpretation: Father, We Praise Thee—*St. Gregory the Great* (?) 286
    Music: Father, We Praise Thee—La Feillée's *Methode du Plain Chant* 286

ST. MARTIN'S CROSS
Artist Unknown

ST. MARTIN'S CROSS stands just in front of the Cathedral of Iona, that "Isle of the Saints" off the western coast of Scotland where St. Columba spent the last years of his life. None of the original monastic buildings of Columba's day remains on the tiny island. St. Martin's Cross and the antiquities there today were a part of the Benedictine monastery which was constructed during the latter part of the Gothic period. In spite of the fact that the Roman missionaries spread over the south of England and up to Scotland, bringing the Roman cross to England, the Celtic Church remained strong in Wales, Cornwall, Ireland, Scotland, and the Western Isles up until the Reformation.

St. Martin's Cross is one of the finest extant examples of Celtic crosses. It is made of red granite and lavishly carved except for its plain base.

The ring or halo around the crossing is the first characteristic of the Celtic cross. Notice how, in St. Martin's Cross, this halo falls just inside the short arms. The circle or halo was the cosmic symbol for eternity, timelessness, and perfection. The circle is one of the oldest symbols of Christianity, and speaks of life eternal and of the resurrection.

The front of St. Martin's Cross (see p. 271) is carved with a design of five panels. (1) At the very center of the crossing the Virgin and Child are surrounded by four angels. (2) Carved on the top arm are three pairs of beasts, biting each other's tails and forming a circle. These, too, are symbolic of eternity. (3 and 4) On the left and right arms, medieval beasts are pictured. (5) The shaft, or long part of the cross, contains a series of carved scenes. Reading from the top (below the Virgin and Child) to the bottom, they are: Daniel in the Lion's Den, a group of three figures (possibly to show the Old Testament story of the sacrifice of Isaac), a group of two figures (one is playing a harp and might be David with King Saul), a group of four figures which are not identified, and finally, at the bottom, six raised bosses interlaced by twelve serpents. The boss or raised circle was a favorite design of Celtic Christian art, as was the interlacing pattern.

The back of St. Martin's Cross is also elaborately carved.

One can imagine Iona, with its three hundred sixty crosses, forming a kind of "Appian Way" of crosses that led down to the sea. Hoary with age, St. Martin's Cross speaks of the Christian Church in Britain centuries ago when the great monasteries were being established. It takes our thoughts back even farther to St. Columba and other saints of the Celtic Church—saints of the dim past whose imprint on the world of Christian art and thought will ever remain.

ST. MARTIN'S CROSS—*ARTIST UNKNOWN*

THE ARDAGH CHALICE
Artist Unknown

IN a carefully guarded case in the National Museum of Ireland is displayed a large chalice or communion cup. For centuries it lay buried in the earth under a thorn bush, protected only by a flagstone. Its discovery near Ardagh, County Limerick, Ireland, aroused great interest, for this chalice is a very early object of Christian art, of which there are all too few.

The Ardagh Chalice was used as a communion vessel for the laity of the Irish Church in the seventh and eighth centuries. It dates back to the time when Irish monks, following the example and pattern set by St. Patrick, wandered up and down and across the breadth of the Green Isle, even going as far afield as Poland, Russia, and Iceland to preach the Word of God and instruct the people in the ways of the Church. The monks traveled in groups, forming a little company. They dressed in long flowing white robes and carried stout walking sticks. Among their number were always those who excelled in music, manuscript illumination, and metal work, so that the arts of the Church could be carried on. Tools and materials for the work were piled into carts and dragged along as part of the equipment for this necessary work.

The Ardagh Chalice was probably made and used by one of these groups of missionaries. It is typical of seventh- and eighth-century Christian art, with broad surfaces relieved by designs of Celtic scrollwork and round bosses. The cup is large, measuring nine and a half inches across and seven inches in height. Made of silver, it has lovely touches of gold, bronze, and enamel. The simple and extremely beautiful outlines of the chalice are accented by decoration that has been placed at carefully chosen points.

The unknown artist, or artists—for more than one person probably worked on it—fashioned the designed bands and medallions of gold, silver, brass, copper, and even lead. The complicated gold filigree work is wild and strong, with patterns of Celtic interlacings, triangles, spirals, zig-zags, circles, and the dots which were common to this early art. It scarcely seems possible that people who must have worked with imperfect and even crude tools could have produced such beautiful work. One feels that the realization that this chalice was to be used in worship inspired the craftsmen to do an almost incredible labor of love—one that amazes modern jewelers. The arts of the Christian Church would be far from complete without this rare example of Irish art. The Chalice of Ardagh speaks of the love and devotion of those far-off missionaries who lavished their time and talents on the Church. It speaks of Christian craftsmen who devoted long years and even a lifetime to make one perfect object which would have an important part in the service of worship.

THE ARDAGH CHALICE—ARTIST UNKNOWN

GLASTONBURY ABBEY

"AT GLASTONBURY one may lay aside the name of England and speak of Britain," the *Catholic Encyclopedia* tells us. The term *Britain* takes us farther back in history than *England,* and Glastonbury claims legends that date to the time just after Christ. Today, as one wanders among the romantic twelfth- to fifteenth-century ruins, one realizes that once they must have been very beautiful and extensive buildings. But it must be remembered that these ruins account for considerably less than half of Glastonbury's history, if we are to hold with the earliest legends.

Joseph of Arimathea is said to have gone to Glastonbury in A.D. 63 when he traveled into Britain after the death of Christ. Traditionally, he established the first Christian Church in England, because, on nearby Wearyall Hill, as a weary pilgrim who stopped to rest, he thrust his staff into the ground and it blossomed into life. This staff, which was said to have been cut from the same tree as Jesus' crown of thorns, became a great thorn tree, and each year at Christmastime it still blooms. St. Joseph is also said to have brought with him the cup that was used by Jesus and His disciples at the Last Supper. This was the Holy Grail around which developed the stories of King Arthur and the Knights of the Round Table. King Arthur and Queen Guinevere were buried at Glastonbury.

None of the earliest buildings is seen today among Glastonbury's ruins. Even the present ruins were preceded by an abbey that was built by St. Dunstan in the tenth century, when previous ancient buildings were despoiled by the Danes. St. Dunstan, who became one of the great abbots of Glastonbury, received his education there as a boy. As founder of the Benedictine order in England, he is one of the great names in that country's church history. It was largely due to him that Glastonbury became a center of learning during the Middle Ages, continuing until a great fire destroyed all of the buildings in 1184.

After the fire, King Henry II decreed that the Benedictine Abbey church of Glastonbury should be rebuilt in a manner befitting a church so rich in history. The magnificent sanctuary, dedicated to the Virgin Mary, St. Peter, and St. Paul, together with the buildings of the abbey necessary to the life of the monks who lived there, was of great importance for five centuries. It is these that we see in their present state of ruin—a state that was brought about by the suppression of monasteries in 1539.

From the accompanying photograph (p. 275) of the sanctuary crossing, looking toward the great west door, something of the magnitude of that church can be seen. The nave had six bays of windows that were decorated with beautiful tracery. Soaring pillars supported a high vaulted roof. The nave was the scene of many an important ceremony, since the Benedictine order had within its rules the stipulation that its churches should be constructed so that the brethren could walk around it in procession. We may well

GLASTONBURY ABBEY

imagine the monks circumambulating the nave, the beautiful chapel of St. Mary which adjoined the chancel, and the Galilee Porch—said to have been one of the loveliest and largest among all of England's churches.

In our imagination we can reconstruct the delicate stone carvings which adorned the pillars, the tracery, and the vaulting. The first wooden ceiling was replaced in the fifteenth century by fine lacy fan vaulting. In the choir, pier upon pier of delicate, slender shafts supported the arches, the uppermost of which became tracery for stained-glass windows. These looked down upon the shrine of St. Dunstan, which was a center of attraction for pilgrims. Smaller chapels accommodated the crypt of St. Joseph of Arimathea and the shrine of St. Patrick, who was said to have spent his last days at Glastonbury.

The abbey buildings adjoined the church. The monks could reach the dormitory by night stairs that led from the south transept of the sanctuary. The abbots' kitchen, a large and interesting ruin, remains today in good condition. From its size one can surmise that a fairly large community was housed at Glastonbury and that it must have been a thriving and busy Benedictine center in its day.

These buildings stood in great splendor, the finest and most impressive Christian Church in the west of England. Their rich Christian tradition and history linked Britain with the first century after Christ, a claim that was made by no other church in all that land.

✣

HYMN OF THE WORLD'S CREATOR

Now must we hymn the Maker of heaven,
The might of the Maker, the deeds of the Father,
The thought of His heart! He, Lord everlasting,
Established of old the source of all wonders;
Creator all-holy, He hung the bright heaven,
A roof high upreared o'er the children of men;
The King of mankind then created for mortals
The world in its beauty, the earth spread beneath them—
He, Lord everlasting, Omnipotent God!
                    —*Caedmon (died 680); from the Anglo-Saxon*

ALLELUIA!

The strains upraise of joy and praise. Alleluia!
To the glory of their King
Shall the ransomed people sing, Alleluia!
And the Choirs that dwell on high
Shall reëcho through the sky, Alleluia!
They on the fields of Paradise that roam,

The Blessed ones, repeat through that bright home, Alleluia!
The planets glittering on their heavenly way,
The shining constellations, join and say, Alleluia!
Ye clouds that onward sweep,
Ye winds on pinions light,
Ye thunders echoing loud and deep,
Ye lightnings wildly bright—
In sweet consent unite your Alleluia!
Ye floods and ocean billows,
Ye storms and winter snow,
Ye days of cloudless beauty,
Hoar frost and summer glow,
Ye groves that wave in spring,
And glorious forests, sing Alleluia!
First let the birds with painted plumage gay
Exhalt their great Creator's praise, and say Alleluia!
Then let the beasts of earth with varying strain
Join in Creation's Hymn and cry again, Alleluia!
Here let the mountains thunder forth sonorous, Alleluia!
There let the valleys sing in gentler chorus, Alleluia!
Thou jubilant abyss of ocean, cry Alleluia!
Ye tracts of earth and continents, reply Alleluia!
To God who all Creation made,
The frequent hymn be duly paid, Alleluia!*

—Blessed Notker Balbulus (840–912)

THE DEER'S CRY

Christ with me, Christ before me, Christ behind me,
Christ in me, Christ beneath me, Christ above me,
Christ on my right, Christ on my left,
Christ when I lie down, Christ when I sit down,
Christ when I arise,
Christ in the heart of every man who thinks of me,
Christ in the mouth of every man who speaks of me,
Christ in the eye that sees me,
Christ in the ear that hears me,
I arise today
Through a mighty strength, the invocation of the Trinity,
Through a belief in the Threeness,
Through a confession of the Oneness
Of the Creator of creation.**

—St. Patrick of Tara (377–460)

* Translated from the Latin by John Mason Neale.
** Anonymous translation from the Gaelic.

THE RUNE OF HOSPITALITY

I saw a stranger yestereen,
I put food in the eating-place,
Drink in the drinking-place,
Music in the listening-place,
And in the blessed name of the Triune
He blessed myself and my house,
My cattle and my dear ones,
And the lark said in her song,
Often, often, often
Goes the Christ in the stranger's guise.
Often, often, often
Goes the Christ in the stranger's guise.

—Author Unknown; from the Gaelic

ON HIS EXILE TO IONA

Too swiftly my coracle flies on her way,
    From Derry I mournfully turned her prow,
I grieve on the errand which drives me today
    To the Land of the Ravens, to Alba, now.

How swiftly we travel! There is a gray eye
    Looks back upon Erin, but it no more
Shall see while the stars shall endure in the sky
    Her women, her men, or her stainless shore.

From the plank of the oak where in sorrow I lie
    I am straining my sight through the water and wind,
And large is the tear of the soft gray eye
    Looking back on the land that it leaves behind.

To Erin alone is my memory given,
    To Meath and to Munster my wild thoughts flow,
To the shores of Moy-linny, the slopes of Loch Leven,
    And the beautiful land the Ultonians know.

O bear me my blessing afar to the west,
    For the heart in my bosom is broken; I fail.
Should death of a sudden now pierce my breast
    I should die of the love that I bear the Gael!*

—St. Columba (521–597)

* Translated from the Irish by Douglas Hyde.

COMMUNION HYMN-POEM OF THE ANCIENT IRISH CHURCH

May the sweet name of Jesus
Be lovingly graven
On my heart's inmost haven.

O Mary, sweet mother,
Be Jesus my brother,
And I Jesus' lover.

A binding of love
That no distance can sever
Be between us for ever;
Yea, O my Saviour, for ever and ever.

—Anonymous translation

✠

ST. HILDA: PRINCESS, ABBESS

Sabine Baring-Gould

THE monastery of Hartlepool was founded about the year 645 by Heiu, a Northumbrian lady, the first woman of her race who embraced conventual life. She received the veil from the hands of Bishop Aidan. After a few years she retired to a solitude, and Aidan replaced her by Hilda, a princess of the blood royal and of the Deirian dynasty. She was grandniece of Edwin, the first Christian king of Northumbria, father of the queen who had shared the throne of Oswy. This illustrious lady seemed to be called by her genius and character, even more than by her rank, to exercise a great influence over religious and political movements in her time.

Born in exile, during the sovereignty of Ethelfrid, among the West Saxons, where her mother died a violent death, she returned with her father, on the restoration of his race in 617. In her early youth she had been baptized, with her uncle King Edwin, by the Roman missionary Paulinus, which did not, however, prevent her from leaning during her whole life to the side of the Celtic missionaries. Before consecrating her virginity to God, she had lived thirty-three years "very nobly," says Bede, among her family and her fellows.

When she understood that God called her, she desired to make to Him a complete sacrifice, and forsook at once the world, her family, and her country. She went immediately into East Anglia, the king of which had married her sister, and whence she designed to cross over to France, in order to take the veil at Chelles, where her widowed sister was one day to devote herself to God, or in one of the monasteries on the banks of the Marne, which sprang from the great Irish colony of Luxeuil, and whither the Saxon virgins already began to resort. She was only a year in all away from her native province. Aidan gave her lands by the Wear, and there she spent a twelvemonth with a few companions, till Heiu retired from governing Hartlepool, when Aidan made Hilda superior of the monastery. Probably Heiu had not ruled very well, for we are told that one of the first things done by Hilda was to introduce order into the monastery.

Nine years later, when the peace and freedom of Northumbria had been secured by the final victory gained by King Oswy over the Mercians, Hilda took advantage of a gift of land granted her by that prince to establish a new monastery at Streaneshalch (the Beacon Headland), now Whitby. There, as at Hartlepool, and during the thirty years that she passed at the head of her two houses, she displayed a rare capacity for the government of souls, and for the consolidation of monastic institutions. This special aptitude, joined to her love of monastic regularity, and her zeal for knowledge and ecclesiastical discipline, gave her an important part to play, and great influence. Her society was sought by St. Aidan, and all the religious who knew her, that they might be guided by her clear judgment and wise experience. Kings even, and princes of her blood, or of the adjacent provinces, often came to consult her, asking enlightenment, which they afterwards joyfully acknowledged themselves to have received. But she did not reserve the treasures of her judgment and charity for the great ones of the earth. She scattered round her everywhere the benefits of justice, piety, peace, and temperance. She was ere long regarded and honored as the mother of her country, and all who addressed her gave her the sweet name of Mother, which she well deserved.

Nor did the royal abbess confine herself to the government of a numerous community of nuns. According to a usage then very general, but principally prevailing in the Celtic countries, a monastery was joined to the nunnery. And Hilda inspired the monks subject to her authority with so great a devotion to the rule, so true a love of sacred literature, so careful a study of the Scriptures, that this monastery, ruled by a woman, became a school of missionaries and bishops.

The poor cowherd Caedmon was reared into an ecclesiastical poet under her care, and became the father of English poetry.

During the last six years of her life Hilda suffered much from fever. But "during all this while she never failed either to return thanks to her Maker, or publicly and privately to instruct the flock committed to her charge." When dying, she called her monks and nuns around her, at early cockcrow, and, after exhorting them to preserve evangelical peace among themselves and toward all men, she passed by death to life eternal.*

✠

ST. BONIFACE
Mrs. Arthur Bell

OF THE MANY noble-hearted men who in the eighth century went forth as missionaries to the heathen, counting all suffering as naught if they could

* Abridged from *The Lives of the Saints* by the Reverend Sabine Baring-Gould.

THE CHURCH REACHES OUT

but win one soul to God, none is more celebrated than St. Boniface, whose baptismal name was Winfred, and whose life story is, fortunately, as well authenticated as it is beautiful and inspiring. The eldest son of wealthy parents, Winfred was born at Crediton in Devonshire about 680, and would have inherited a large fortune had he not from the first resolved to be a monk.

With the reluctant consent of his father he entered a monastery at Nutsall, the modern Nutshalling in Hampshire, where there is still a church dedicated to him. There he remained until he was past thirty, earnestly endeavoring to prepare himself for missionary work. It is related that whether the young monk was performing his allotted tasks in the monastery, pacing to and fro in the convent precincts, or kneeling in prayer before the crucifix in his cell, he constantly heard a voice, inaudible to all but himself, urging him to go and preach the gospel to all nations, and in 716 he obtained the consent of his Superior to obey the divine summons.

With three companions Winfred set sail for Holland, and landed in Friesland, where so many missionaries had already made more or less futile efforts to win the savage inhabitants to the true faith. The country was still distracted by the struggle between Charles Martel and King Radbod, and after trying in vain to obtain a hearing, Winfred was compelled to return home. Soon after this he was elected abbot of the monastery at Nutsall, but he persuaded the Bishop of Winchester to annul the appointment, and to allow him to go to Rome to ask for the aid of the Pope in a fresh missionary journey.

Kindly received by St. Gregory II, who then occupied the Papal See, Winfred, who now took the name of Boniface, received full authorization to preach the gospel in the whole of Germany, and having passed through Thuringia and Bavaria, he came once more to Friesland, where Charles Martel, since the last visit of the missionary, had become the sole ruler. Armed with letters from the Pope to him and to all the minor princes of the Teutonic provinces, St. Boniface was now able to secure their aid in his work of evangelization.

For many years he wandered hither and thither with a little band of enthusiastic helpers, converting thousands to belief in Christ, destroying the heathen idols and other objects of idolatrous veneration, including the celebrated oak at Geismar, with the wood of which he built a chapel, and the image of the god Stuffo, to whom sacrifices used to be offered up on the mountain named after him in the Hartz Mountains.

The remarkable success of St. Boniface led to his being appointed the first Archbishop of Mainz, as well as Primate of All Germany, the latter position giving him the power of founding bishoprics wherever he chose, and from that time until his voluntary resignation of all his ecclesiastical dignities he was perhaps the most powerful man in Northern Europe. The bishoprics of Ratisbon, Paderborn, Erfurt, Wurzburg, Eichstadt, and Salzburg, with the famous Abbey of Fulda, and many other monasteries were founded by him.

He became the trusted friend and adviser of Charles Martel, and, on his death, of his sons and successors, Carloman and Pepin the Short. It was St. Boniface who advised the former, after a reign of three years, to abdicate and retire to the Monastery of Monte Cassino; it was St. Boniface who at Soissons in 751 placed the crown upon the head of Pepin, the founder of the Carlovingian Dynasty and the father of Charlemagne. In spite, however, of the enthralling interest of the political situation, in which he was himself so very important a factor, the heart of St. Boniface remained true to his first love, that of missionary work pure and simple, and at the age of seventy-four he resolved to go forth once more to preach the gospel to the heathen in Friesland, where so many years ago he had made an abortive attempt to obtain a hearing.

Having carefully arranged all his worldly affairs, and appointed as his successor in the See of Mainz an Englishman, named Lullus, who had long worked under him, St. Boniface started with about fifty followers on a new missionary enterprise. Some of the party were armed, but the leader himself had no weapons except a copy of the Holy Scriptures written with his own hand, and the celebrated treatise of St. Ambrose, "De Bono Mortis," which he is said to have been in the habit of carrying with him wherever he went.

At first success attended the efforts of the devoted band, who, after following the course of the Rhine and winning many to the true faith, halted by a little stream in the very heart of Friesland, in order that St. Boniface might confirm a large number of his new converts. Whilst awaiting the arrival of the neophytes, a band of savage warriors suddenly dashed upon the mission party, shouting that they had come to avenge the insults that had been offered to their gods. Some of the younger companions of St. Boniface would fain have fought for their lives, but their leader, standing up in their midst, forbade them to use their weapons, saying: "O my children, let us not return evil for evil. The day that I have long expected has come at last. Fear not those who kill the body, but put your trust in God, who will speedily give you entrance into His kingdom." The brave words had hardly left his lips before the speaker was struck down, all but a few of his followers who escaped by flight, sharing his fate.

Some say that St. Boniface threw himself on the ground with his head resting on the Gospels to await the fatal blow; others that his heart was pierced with a sword, the weapon passing through the Holy Scriptures without injuring one word of the text, or, according to yet another version, through the treatise of St. Ambrose, an incident which is said to have led the tailors of Flanders, who, like the rest of their brethren, pride themselves in careful cutting out, to choose the martyred missionary as their patron. However that may be, a copy of the Bible stained with the blood of St. Boniface is still shown in the Abbey of Fulda, where the remains of the revered archbishop now rest, after being interred for a short time first at Utrecht and later at Mainz.*

* Abridged from *The Saints in Christian Art* by Mrs. Arthur Bell, pp. 110-113. Copyright 1904 by George Bell & Sons, London.

PATRICK OF IRELAND

H. Leo

IN THE village of Bannaven, between Dumbarton and Glasgow, toward the close of the Roman rule in Britain, lived a deacon Calpurnius, with a son Sucath, or Victor, who was afterwards known as Patrick of Cil-Patrick, that is Church-Patrick. This was Patrick, the Apostle of Ireland. He was carefully trained by his father for the church, but at the age of sixteen fell into the hands of pirates, in one of their inroads on the coast. They carried him away to North Ireland and sold him as a slave to an Irish chief, who made him his herdsman. In the solitude of his shepherd life, weighed down by his misfortune, the heart of the young man turned to God, as he himself relates: "I was sixteen years old, and knew not the true God (that is, he had till then only an outward knowledge of Christianity, without experience of its saving truth), but in a strange land the Lord opened the blind eyes of my unbelief, so that I thought, though at a late hour, of my sins, and turned with my whole heart to the Lord my God. And He looked down upon my low estate, my ignorance, and my youth; He cared for me before I knew Him, and ere I could distinguish good from evil, He protected and comforted me, as a father his son."

After six years' captivity, Patrick found means to escape and go home. He recognized God's hand in the attending circumstances. Again, in his thirty-second year, he was so unfortunate as to be made prisoner by the sea-robbers, who were on every side devastating the shores of Britain, now forsaken by the Romans. He was taken to Gaul, but found opportunity, a second time, to return to his people. So quickened was he, as a Christian, by misfortune, that he was roused to an effort to impart his faith to others. His mind turned to the scene of his former captivity. He chose Ireland, familiar as he was with her language and people.

The story of his first visiting Rome and receiving from Bishop Sixtus III, the pope of that period, the Irish mission, is an invention of later times. In that earlier day there was no connection between Rome and the Irish Church. The latter was developed in the same way as was the Church in Britain, previous to the withdrawal of the Romans.

Patrick knew that the Celtic pagan priests or Druids of Ireland would be his foes. If he was to accomplish anything he must endeavor to gain over the chiefs of the country, before the Druids should count him an opponent. This he succeeded in doing. He also gained a Christian from the Irish poets, who by celebrating Christ in song contributed materially to the advancement of Christianity. During his captivity in Gaul, Patrick had observed the cloisters established there already, after the style of those in Egypt, like that of Cassianus in Marseilles. He now devoted the land given him by the Irish chiefs to the founding of monastic establishments in Ireland.

His mission work endured much opposition from pagan chieftains and the Druids. He encountered it successfully, not only making a part of the island Christian, but leaving behind him, in his monasteries, schools that should extend his mission. He attained an advanced old age: some say one hundred and twenty years, reckoning three divisions of forty years, which are hardly to be accepted literally. He may have lived till between ninety and a hundred and ten, a not uncommon age in an active and enthusiastic monastic career. It may have been attained by Patrick, for his activity evinces an extraordinary physical vigor.

As the name of Patrick soon grew very common in Ireland, it is not strange that many things have been ascribed to him that belong to others of his name. The difficulties of his biography are increased by two other facts. The means at his command were insufficient to crush and extirpate the old pagan culture, manners, and literature, to the extent attained by the missionary preachers of Germany. On the contrary, the great political influence of the Irish lords endured, and their old songs exerted undiminished power. But after Christianity had won the day, their praises of pagan heroes were no longer in place. They did not suppress them, however, but introduced the holy Patrick into the song, or into the introductory verses, making him, as far as possible, their mouthpiece. So he grew to be the representative, in poetry, of Christianity.

This is the first circumstance to be mentioned. The second is that when Patrick was made the Christian hero, there were sung in his praise songs that contained far more of myth than of history. The contents of these songs were embodied afterward in his biographies. On their account some have wished to turn Patrick over entirely to the region of fable, banishing him out of history. But the notices of him in Irish poetry and the ascription of days of fasting and like ordinances to him go back to such early times as to place the main features of his life and work beyond doubt.*

✛

HARK! A HERALD VOICE IS CALLING

ONCE attributed to St. Ambrose, "Hark! A Herald Voice Is Calling" is one of the Church's oldest Advent hymns. It was sung at Lauds—the service held at daybreak—during the Advent season in several great monasteries of Britain during ancient times. Of sixth-century origin, this hymn is so well loved that at least eighteen variations have been made by translators during the last few centuries.

The words of the hymn are based on Romans 13:11, the Epistle for Advent, and Luke 21:25, the Gospel for Advent. They tell of the coming of Christ into a world of darkness, that wrongs may be cleared and a better day may dawn. The hymn ends in a stanza which is virtually a doxology.

William Henry Monk, composer of the hymn tune used here, created many hymns and anthems. He was also editor of *Hymns Ancient and Modern*.

* From *Lives of the Leaders of Our Church Universal*, translated and edited by Henry Mitchell Mac-Cracken, pp. 114-16.

Hark! A Herald Voice is Calling*

MERTON. (8 7. 8 7.)

Moderately slow.

W. H. MONK, 1823-89.

[This hymn may also be sung to STUTTGART, 84.]

6th cent. S. P. V.

Vox clara ecce intonat.

HARK! a herald voice is calling:
   'Christ is nigh,' it seems to say;
'Cast away the dreams of darkness,
   O ye children of the day!'

2 Wakened by the solemn warning,
   Let the earth-bound soul arise;
Christ, her Sun, all sloth dispelling,
   Shines upon the morning skies.

3 Lo! the Power, so long expected,
   Comes with pardon down from heaven;
Let us haste, with tears of sorrow,
   One and all to be forgiven;

4 So when love comes forth in judgment,
   Debts and doubts and wrongs to clear,
Faithful may he find his servants,
   Watching till the dawn appear.

5. Honour, glory, might, and blessing
   To the Father and the Son
And the eternal Spirit give we,
   While unending ages run.

*From *Songs of Praise*, No. 61. Published by Oxford University Press, London. Used by permission of the publisher.

Father, We Praise Thee*

GREGORY THE GREAT, 540-604
Tr. PERCY DEARMER

CHRISTE SANCTORUM

11. 11. 11. 5.   La Feillée's *Méthode du Plain Chant*, 1808

Unison; majestically, but not too slowly

1. Fa - ther, we praise Thee, now the night is o - ver; Ac - tive and
2. Mon - arch of all things, fit us for Thy man - sions; Ban - ish our
3. All - ho - ly Fa - ther, Son, and Ho - ly Spir - it, Trin - i - ty

watch - ful, stand we all be - fore Thee; Sing - ing, we of - fer
weak - ness, health and whole-ness send - ing; Bring us to heav - en,
bless - ed, send us Thy sal - va - tion; Thine is the glo - ry

HARMONY

prayer and med - i - ta - tion: Thus we a - dore Thee.
where Thy saints u - nit - ed Joy with-out end - ing.
gleam - ing and re - sound-ing Through all cre - a - tion. A - MEN.

*From *The Hymnal*, No. 44. Words copyright 1941 by Eden Publishing House. Used by permission of Oxford University Press, London.

✢

FATHER, WE PRAISE THEE

THE WORDS to this stately hymn of praise are attributed to St. Gregory the Great (540-604). It was St. Gregory who saw the fair-haired youths in the slave market of Rome and when someone told him that they were Angles, he replied, "Not Angles—they are angels!" He could not rest until Augustine had set out across Gaul to carry the Christian message to England from whence those slaves had come.

Gregory gave up both wealth and title to serve his Church. He established the beautiful, yet severe type of melody known as the Gregorian Chant which became the official music of the Roman Church.

Percy Dearmer, who translated the words of this ancient hymn of the Latin Church, preserved the strength and beauty of the original. God is approached with largeness of spirit, in universal terms that lift man far from his human limitations.

Of the several tunes to which this hymn may be sung, "Christe Sanctorum," given here, has a majesty which matches St. Gregory's words. The tune had its source in the famous *Methode du Plain Chant* published in the eighteenth century by François de la Feillée. It is easily sung in unison; the pace should be slow but not dragging to give the feeling of a great, sweeping processional, moving forward in triumph and dignity.

CONTENTS

PART III SECTION 3

THE AGE OF MONASTICISM

———————————————✠———————————————

. . . Study to be quiet, and to do your own business, and to work with your own hands.—I THESSA-
LONIANS 4:11

———————————————✠———————————————

PICTURES: PAGE
   Interpretation: St. Thomas Aquinas Visiting St. Bonaventura—*Zurbaran* .. 289
   Picture: St. Thomas Aquinas Visiting St. Bonaventura—*Zurbaran* 290
   Interpretation: A Dominican Preaching—*Morone* 291
   Picture: A Dominican Preaching—*Morone* 293
   Interpretation: The Cuxa Cloister 294
   Picture: The Cuxa Cloister 295

POETRY:
   A Hymn Poem—*Bede* 296
   A Charm for Bees—*Anonymous* 297
   To Gabriel of the Annunciation—*Abélard* 297
   Be Thou My Vision—*Anonymous* 298
   Strength, Love, Light—*King Robert of France* 298
   Amergin—*Anonymous* 299

STORIES:
   The Venerable Bede—*Caxton* 299
   St. Joseph of Arimathea—*Windham* 300
   St. Benedict—*Walker* 303

MUSIC:
   Interpretation: All Glory, Laud, and Honor—*Theodulph of Orleans* 306
   Music: All Glory, Laud, and Honor—*Teschner* 307
   Music: Creator Spirit, by Whose Aid—*Attwood* 308
   Interpretation: Creator Spirit, by Whose Aid—*Dryden* 309

ST. THOMAS AQUINAS VISITING ST. BONAVENTURA

Francisco Zurbaran

WHEN an artist or a writer consistently dips into the past for subject matter for his work, one can be fairly sure that an intense sympathy and understanding exists between the artist and that particular portion of history which he chooses to portray. Such was the liking of the seventeenth-century Spanish artist, Francisco Zurbaran (1598-1664), for two thirteenth-century saints, Thomas Aquinas and Bonaventura. Again and again, because of a deep interest in the mystical side of Christianity, Zurbaran's brush turned to these two saints whose lives were devoted to studying mystical and theological subjects.

Zurbaran did a series of paintings portraying the life of St. Bonaventura, the Italian saint who lived between 1221 and 1274 and who was said to have been named by St. Francis of Assisi who cured him miraculously when a child. St. Francis was supposed to have exclaimed, "O buona ventura!" ("O good fortune") when the miracle took place.

St. Bonaventura was a close friend and admirer of St. Thomas Aquinas. In the painting, "St. Thomas Aquinas Visiting St. Bonaventura," Zurbaran shows St. Thomas Aquinas with some of his brother monks, coming to consult with St. Bonaventura. The setting is an austere study where the books are spread out or within easy reach. Evidentally St. Thomas Aquinas has just asked his friend a question—probably on a theological subject which is puzzling him. With dramatic earnestness, St. Bonaventura has arisen to draw aside the curtain of the shrine above his desk, revealing the figure of Christ upon the cross. "There," he seems to be saying, "is the answer and the sum of all theology—behold the Christ, the origin of our faith!" It is as though St. Bonaventura would put a stop to argument, perhaps even disagreement, by this gesture toward the crucified Christ.

Zurbaran chose to put both of these renowned saints into one painting because he realized that the two great doctors of the Church belong together. Their lives covered almost exactly the same span of years. Both were Italian, and both were great scholars who represent the monastic age with its preservation of learning. St. Bonaventura was a Franciscan who at thirty-six was made minister-general of that order. Later on he was created a cardinal bishop. A philosophical and theological writer, St. Bonaventura was known especially for his beautiful life of St. Francis of Assisi.

St. Thomas Aquinas, often referred to as the "Angelic Doctor," spent most of his life in the Dominican order. He was not only a scholar and theologian, but he also had a gift of inspiring others by his teaching. At the University of Paris and at various Italian universities he held chairs of professor of theology. Today, his *Summa Theologica* holds an important place in the theology of the Catholic Church. St. Thomas Aquinas was also a gifted poet and hymn writer.

ST. THOMAS AQUINAS VISITING ST. BONAVENTURA—ZURBARAN

Now that we are acquainted with the two central figures of Zurbaran's painting, "St. Thomas Aquinas Visiting St. Bonaventura," it speaks directly of the character and interest of the two men who are pictured as consulting each other. The fellow monks at St. Thomas Aquinas' side seem to have been talking quietly among themselves. But suddenly a hush falls as St. Bonaventura strikes at the heart of the matter by pointing to Christ on the cross. For a moment, the books of learning take a subordinate place.

Zurbaran has told his story well, and with dramatic and religious intensity. He has indicated something of monastic life through his setting of the monk's study with its simple furnishings and surroundings. The plain, heavy robes of the monks fall to the ground in deep, thick folds.

Francisco Zurbaran, who lived in the first half of the seventeenth century, was an almost legendary figure. As a poor shepherd lad he is said to have drawn upon tree trunks for want of better materials. A priest of his little Spanish village was impressed by the lad's ability and undertook to help him improve his drawing. Zurbaran made great progress and by the time he was twenty, he was making a name for himself in the world of art. Because he was able to portray the mystical side of Christianity so well, the Church piled commission after commission upon him, with the result that nearly everything he painted was for the Church.

Zurbaran stands alone, quite unique in his work. His forcefulness, his wonderful ability to contrast light with shadow, his marvelous techniques with drapery and cloth—these are all important contributions; but more outstanding is the deeply penetrating and spiritual manner in which Zurbaran somehow captured and set down mystical Christianity.

✛

A DOMINICAN PREACHING
Domenico Morone

THIS small painted panel (14½ inches by 13½ inches) of "A Dominican Preaching," by Domenico Morone, gives us an interesting glimpse into the work of the Preaching Friars, as the Dominicans were often called. Painting in 1475, the artist portrayed a Dominican monk preaching from a pulpit in the square of a medieval Italian town. The scene might have been comtemporary with the artist or he could have meant it to show one of the preaching friars who preached up and down the length and breadth of Italy two hundred years before Morone's time.

In the painting, high fortresslike walls of a medieval town surround the square where a group of Dominican nuns and townspeople have gathered to hear a sermon. Morone has pictured a scene from real life—one which could surely have taken place in almost any town in Italy or France during those years when the Dominican friars evangelized through their preaching.

The preacher is clad in the black mantle and white tunic prescribed by his order. From his high pulpit he is addressing the throng with great earnestness. The artist has used the attentiveness of the crowd to the preacher to direct our attention to him. Also part of this focus of attention are the sculptured decorations above the church doorway at the left. In the round medallion is St. Dominic with his special symbols of the lily and the Book. These symbols also appear in the large tympanum above the door where a female saint kneels beside the Madonna and Child.

The symbol of the open Bible, to signify preaching from the Word of God, is also prominent in the cloud, which hovers at the upper portion of the picture. Actually, this cloud was uncovered fairly recently when the panel was cleaned. Looking at it closely, a shadowy figure of a man—God, the Father—can be discerned, holding the open Book. Since the head of the figure is missing, it is clear that there once was more to the upper part of this panel. The presence of the symbols of God, the Bible, and the angel faces was to show that a divine blessing was felt to rest upon the work of the Dominicans, whose preaching centered around the Bible.

This painted panel by Domenico Morone probably belonged to a series of several panels which originally comprised the altarpiece of St. Thomas Aquinas in the Church of San Domenico, Modena, Italy. In this church four altars were dedicated to the four principal Dominican saints. Other panels from this particular altar are by other artists. The panel pictured here was acquired by The National Gallery of Art in Washington, D.C. Another panel from the St. Thomas Aquinas altar is in the Metropolitan Museum, New York, and a third in the Jarves Collection at Yale University. The other four belong to collections abroad.

Domenico Morone, an Italian painter of the latter part of the fifteenth century, is a somewhat obscure figure in a world of art that was overshadowed by better known Renaissance artists. He was chiefly a painter of altarpieces.

Insight into the work of the Dominicans sheds further understanding on the scene Morone has left us here. St. Dominic of Spain, who founded the Dominican order in 1216 shortly before his death, was said to have been religious and self-sacrificing from childhood. After he was ordained a priest, he made a pilgrimage to Rome. On the way he was greatly impressed by the disciples of St. Bernard, with whom he became acquainted when he stopped for a rest at the Abbey of Citeaux in southern France. This visit led him to decide to give himself over to a life of evangelistic preaching. Gradually his own efforts as a preacher became well known, and Rome, recognizing preaching as a means of spreading the teaching of the Church, gave St. Dominic permission to found an order of preaching friars.

It was not long before the work of the Order of Friars Preachers, or Dominicans, spread over Europe. Their rule was strict in many ways, but a unique feature of it was that the monks alternated preaching with study. Also, the order provided a plan of nonpaternalistic government—the monasteries were governed by priors who were elected for a term of office rather than for life, as was the case with most orders.

A DOMINICAN PREACHING—*MORONE*

Through the centuries the Dominican order has become renowned for its contribution to theological thinking. Famous members have included St. Catherine of Sienna, Fra Angelico, Savonarola, and St. Thomas Aquinas. The Dominicans have carried their preaching efforts around the world, establishing missions in India, China, and remote places. Today, Dominicans function as both contemplative and teaching orders.

✤

THE CUXA CLOISTER

IN The Cloisters of the Metropolitan Museum of Art in New York City, one may see several splendid examples of monastic cloisters. The Cuxa Cloister from the Benedictine Abbey of St. Michel de Cuxa, founded in 878, is one of the loveliest of these. This cloister was installed in the present building at Fort Tryon Park, which opened in 1938 as a branch of the Metropolitan Museum. Mr. and Mrs. John D. Rockefeller, Jr. made it possible for the Museum to construct The Cloisters.

The various parts which make up the Cuxa Cloister were brought from southern France, from the area near Spain where the original monastery had once stood. Sacked in 1645, ruthlessly pillaged and plundered one hundred forty years later during the French Revolution, the original Cuxa Cloister was finally divided and sold in parts to interested people in southern France.

Fortunately, most of the Cuxa Cloister was kept together, and what is now seen in New York gives a fairly accurate idea of the original, twelfth-century cloister, except that it is smaller.

Along these covered walks Benedictine monks of seven hundred years ago walked and copied manuscripts. They gathered in informal groups for discussions. In fact, the cloister was the center of the everyday life of a medieval abbey and monastery. The Cuxa Cloister was probably built along one side of the abbey church, like the others of its day, since customarily one of the walks was placed next to the wall of the nave.

The refectory or dining hall generally stood opposite the nave and formed the second wall. Other buildings close to the church and cloister included the Chapter House, in which formal discussions and business transactions were held, the dormitory—usually placed over the Chapter House so that the monks could slip down the little night stairs and into the church for the night offices—and the workshops and storerooms.

Arranged along the warm, south side of the cloister were the little cubicles in which the scribes worked over their parchments, producing the delicate lettering and matchless illuminated paintings of medieval manuscripts. At Cuxa, the scribes could look through the low pillared arches with their lovely carved capitals to a central fountain.

The timbered roof and floor tiles of the present Cuxa Cloister were patterned after some which were commonly used in that particular region of

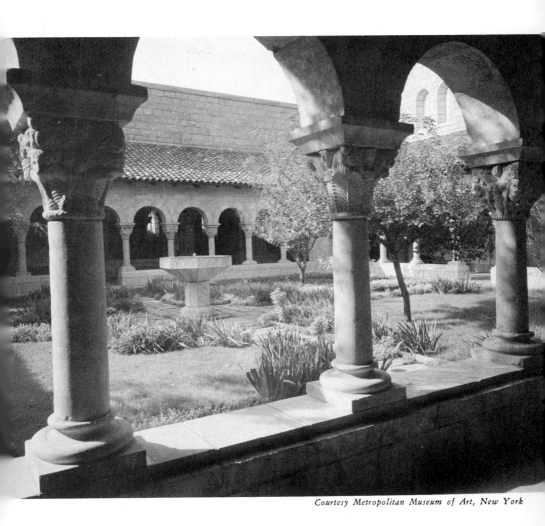

THE CUXA CLOISTER

France during medieval times. The pillars with their carved capitals came from the original Cuxa Cloister. The medieval carvings are of animals, foliage, and floral designs, or episodes from fables or classical stories.

The central fountain in the reconstructed Cuxa Cloister at Fort Tryon Park came from St. Genis des Fountaines in France. There is a little wall fountain along the cloister wall, at the northeast corner, which was originally in the monastery of Notre Dame du Vilar. Both of these fountains came from the same period as the original Cuxa Cloister; they were acquired after careful study as to the best way to complete the setting of the restored cloister in order to make it as much like the twelfth-century original as possible. It requires little imagination to let the present slip away to the past and think of these cloisters as they originally must have been, peopled by devout Benedictine monks.

The Benedictines who made the Cuxa Cloister part of their home had as their founder St. Benedict of Nursia, who was born about 480. (See story, "St. Benedict," later in this section.)

Over each monastery was an abbot, who was elected to his office for life. He was regarded as the father of the house, but his authority was complete. The days and nights of the Benedictine monks were given over to a carefully planned schedule of worship, solitary meditation, reading, manual labor, sleep, and meals. Although each monastery was independent and had its own regulations, it adhered faithfully to the basic Rule of St. Benedict.

The movement spread through France and later into England. As moderation was substituted for austerity, a larger life and work was opened up to the Benedictines, with the result that for centuries they were the preservers of books. They made notable contributions to education and to literature as a result of this.

Some of the famous Benedictine abbeys included St. Gall, Fulda, Glastonbury, and many others. The order exists today and in the United States there are several Benedictine establishments.

✢

A HYMN POEM

A hymn of glory let us sing;
New songs throughout the world shall ring;
By a new way none ever trod
Christ mounteth to the throne of God.

The apostles on the mountain stand,—
The mystic mount, in Holy Land;
They with the virgin mother, see
Jesus ascend in majesty.

The angels say to the eleven:
"Why stand ye gazing into heaven?
This is the Saviour, this is He!
Jesus hath triumphed gloriously!"

Be thou our present joy, Oh Lord!
Who wilt be ever our reward;
And, as the countless ages flee,
May all our glory be in Thee!*

—*The Venerable Bede*

A CHARM FOR BEES

Christ, there is a swarm of bees outside.
Fly hither, my little cattle,
In blest peace, in God's protection,
Come home safe and sound!
Sit down, sit down, Bee.
St. Mary commanded thee.
Thou shalt not have leave,
Thou shalt not fly to the wood!
Thou shalt not escape me,
Nor go away from me.
Sit very still,
And wait God's will!

—*Anonymous; from the High German*

TO GABRIEL OF THE ANNUNCIATION

On with thine embassy;
　Say AVE! say ALL HAIL!
Say THE LORD IS WITH THEE!
　And, that thou mayst avail,
　　Say too the words FEAR NOT!

Virginal Lily, nod
　Gently thy jewelled brow
In the soft breath of God;
　Chastly thou'lt keep thy vow
　　With never stain or spot.

Heareth She, and believes!
　Now the message done;
Credits the word, conceives,
　Brings forth her only Son,
　　Marvellous in emprise;

Jesus the Counsellor
　Unto the sons of men,
Man-God who shall restore
　Unto earth again
　　Peace by His sacrifice!

Who shall blot out our sin
　With His almighty hand,
Bidding us enter in
　Unto the fatherland
　　Over the starry skies!**

—*Pierre Abélard (1079–1142)*

* Translated by Elizabeth Charles in *The World's Great Religious Poetry*, edited by Caroline Hill. Used by permission of the Baptist Home and Hospital.
** Translated from the Latin by H. Y. Henry.

BE THOU MY VISION

Be thou my vision, O Lord of my heart,
Naught is all else to me, save that Thou art.

Thou my best thought by day and by night,
Waking or sleeping, Thy presence my light.

Be Thou my wisdom, Thou my true word;
I ever with Thee, Thou with me, Lord.

Thou my great Father, I Thy dear son;
Thou in me dwelling, I with Thee one.

Be Thou my battle-shield, sword for the fight,
Be Thou my dignity, Thou my delight.

Thou my soul's shelter, Thou my high tower;
Raise Thou me heavenward, power of my power.

Riches I heed not, nor man's empty praise,
Thou mine inheritance now and always.

Thou, and Thou only, first in my heart,
High king of heaven, my treasure Thou art.

King of the seven heavens, grant me for dole,
Thy love in my heart, Thy light in my soul.

Thy light from my soul, Thy love from my heart,
King of the seven heavens, may they never depart.

With the high king of heaven, after victory won,
May I reach heaven's joys, O bright heaven's sun!

Heart of my own heart, whatever befall,
Still be my vision, O Ruler of all.*

—*Anonymous*

STRENGTH, LOVE, LIGHT

O Thou almighty Will
Faint are thy children, till
  Thou come with power;
Strength of our good intents,
In our frail hour, Defense
Calm of Faith's confidence,
  Come, in this hour!

O Thou most tender Love!
Deep in our spirits move:
  Tarry, dear Guest!
Quench thou our passion's fire,
Raise thou each low desire,
Deeds of brave love inspire,
  Quickener and Rest!

* Translated by Eleanor Hull in *1000 Years of Irish Poetry*, edited by Kathleen Hoagland. Copyright 1947, published 1953 by the Devin-Adair Company. Used by permission of the publisher.

O Light serene and still!
Come and our spirits fill,
    Bring in the day;
Guide of our feeble sight,
Star of our darkest night,
Shine on the path of right,
    Show us the way!
                    —*King Robert of France (c. 1000 A.D.)*

AMERGIN

I am the wind which breathes upon the sea,
I am the wave of the ocean,
I am the murmur of the billows,
I am the ox of the seven combats,
I am the vulture upon the rocks,
I am a beam of the sun,
I am the fairest of plants,
I am a wild boar in valour.
I am a salmon in the water,
I am a lake in the plain,
I am a word of science,
I am the point of the lance in battle,
I am the God who creates in the head the fire.
Who is it who throws light into the meeting on the mountain?
Who announces the ages of the moon?
Who teaches the place where couches the sun?
                    —*Anonymous; English (Date Unknown)*

✠

THE VENERABLE BEDE
William Caxton

THE holy and venerable Bede was born in England, and when he was seven years of age he was delivered to Benet Biscop of Jarrow, for to learn, and after his death he was put to Ceolfrith, abbot of the same place, and learned and profited much in the holy life. And the nineteenth year of his age he was made deacon to John, Bishop of York, and in the thirtieth year of his age he was made priest. Then began he to write and to study and to expound holy writ, whereupon he made many noble homilies, and notwithstanding his great business, was daily in the service of religion, as in singing and praying in the church.

He had great sweetness and liking to learn, to teach and to write; he wrote seventy-eight books; he accounted the books and years from the beginning of the world in Historia Anglicana. In the book of Polycronicon is rehearsed that it is a wonder that a man that is without use of school made so many noble volumes in so sober words in so little space of his lifetime. It is said he went to Rome for to show there his books, for to see them according to holy writ and to the lore of the holy church, but hereof some doubt, and say that he never went to Rome. Also it is said that when he was blind he went about for to preach, and his servant that led him brought him whereas were many hopples of stones, to whom he made a noble sermon, and when he had all finished his sermon the stones answered and said, "Amen."

Pope Sergius wrote a letter to the abbot Ceolfrith and prayed to have Bede come to Rome to answer certain questions. Here is to be noted, that how noble and worthy the court of Rome held him, when so noble a court had need to have him to declare and answer the questions that were there moved. Also we ought to hold him noble and holy by the manner of his living and his teaching. He spared not the travail of lecture and of books, and every day among the travail of service and of psalms, he taught his disciples in lessons and in questions. He translated St. John's Gospel into English, and said to his scholars: "Learn ye, my small children, whiles I am alive and with you; I wot not how long I shall abide with you. I have not so lived among you that me shameth to live, neither me dreadeth to die, for we have a good Lord."

On night's time when he had no man to teach then would he devoutly be in prayers and thanking our Lord of all His gifts. The Tuesday before Ascension-day his death approached, and his feet began to swell; he was anointed and kissed his brethren, and prayed them all to remember him, and he gave to divers of his servants things that he had in privity. On the Ascension-day the hair was spread, and he laid him down thereon, and prayed for the grace of the Holy Ghost, and said: "O king of bliss, and Lord of virtues, leave thou us not fatherless, but send thou in to us that behest of the Father, the ghost of soothfastness." And when he had ended that, he gave up the last breath with a sweet odour and savour.*

✠

ST. JOSEPH OF ARIMATHEA
Joan Windham

ONCE upon a time there was a man who was a good and just counselor, and his name was Joseph, and he lived in a place called Arimathea, and he was one of our Lord's disciples. (A disciple is a person who follows and learns from another person. Our Lord had hundreds of disciples, but only twelve apostles.) We don't really know very much about Joseph, except that he was a nobleman and rich, but I'll tell you what we do know.

After our Lord had been crucified and had died the Roman soldiers just

* Abridged from *The Golden Legend*, Vol. VII, translated by William Caxton in 1483.

left him on the cross. The disciples thought what a terrible thing this was, and how dreadful for our lady, too, but they were afraid of the Roman soldiers, and of the Jews who had wanted our Lord to be crucified, and so they didn't do anything about it. So, late in the evening, Joseph, because he was rich and therefore important, went secretly (so that the Romans and the Jews wouldn't know) to Pontius Pilate and asked him please could he take away our Lord's body to bury it?

Now Pilate hadn't really wanted to crucify our Lord at all, and he was feeling very sorry about it, but he did not believe that our Lord could be dead yet. He thought that Joseph was trying to help him to escape. So he sent for the centurion, whose name was Longinus, and he asked him if it was true that our Lord was dead. Longinus said, "Yes, I saw him die." Then Pilate said that Joseph could take away the body and bury it.

So Joseph and another disciple called Nicodemus took our Lord's body down from the cross. Now Joseph's garden was near the place where he was crucified, and in the garden was a new cave in the rock that Joseph had got ready for himself to be buried in when he died. By the time they had got our Lord down it was very late at night, and he did not know of anywhere else near at hand, so he hoped that his own new cave would be nice enough for our Lord, and he thanked God for the honor of being allowed to give it up. So Joseph and Nicodemus put our Lord's body safely there, and they rolled a great rock to the door of the cave so that no one could get in in the night. Then they went sadly home. Now all that is perfectly true, but there are lots of other stories about the things that Joseph did afterwards that are not in the Bible, and I will tell you some of them.

A year after Joseph had given his own new cave to be a burial place for our Lord, St. Philip, who was one of the apostles, sent Joseph and eleven of his friends to England to tell the English people about our Lord. Because, of course, there were no Christians there yet, and no one had even heard of such a thing.

Now there were a lot of tin mines in Cornwall (and there still are) and people used to come from round about Palestine to buy tin. So Joseph and his eleven friends sailed in one of the tin people's boats, and after a time they landed in Cornwall, which is in the bottom left-hand corner of England. They brought with them a very precious thing. It was the silver cup that our Lord had used at the Last Supper when he put wine into it and said, "This is my blood." Do you remember? The cup was called the Holy Grail.

Lots of people collected round to stare at Joseph and his eleven friends, because they had different clothes and they could not speak English. But they went on to a place nearby, to Glastonbury, and they made a camp, and they settled down and got friendly with the people, and soon they could speak English fairly well.

Everyone who used to visit their camp used to look at their chapel and say: "What's that place?"

"It's a chapel."

"What's a chapel?" asked the visitor.

"A place where we worship God," said Joseph.

"Can I see?" asked the visitor.

"Of course you can," said Joseph.

And always, when they went into the chapel and saw the Holy Grail, the people would want to know about it, and Joseph, or one of his eleven friends, would tell them. But they were not allowed to touch the Holy Grail, because of its being so precious. And so, because they couldn't *see* the Christians' God, some of the English people thought that he must be in the cup.

"That's why Joseph won't let us touch it," they said.

"Well," said one of them, "let's steal it just for one day, and then we'll be able to see God."

After that so many of the English people tried to get into the chapel, and so often, that the Christians had to take it in turns to stand guard, and at last Joseph said to them:

"We can't go on like this. One of these days somebody really will steal the Holy Grail, and it is much too precious to be handed round the villages for everyone to stare at and handle. What do you all think that we had better do?"

They thought and they wondered, and at last one of them said: "Couldn't we bury it in a safe place?"

The others all thought that this was a very good idea, and so they buried the Holy Grail by a well at the bottom of a little mountain called Glastonbury Tor. It was a winter's day and Joseph stuck his tall walking stick into the ground to mark the place. And now a wonderful thing happened! You remember that it was a winter's day? Well, the walking stick grew roots and leaves and flowers and turned into a hawthorn tree all in the same afternoon! And what is more, instead of flowering every summer like hawthorns always do, it flowered every winter!

Well, Joseph traveled on and taught the people about being Christians, and they built them chapels, and they never got back to Glastonbury, somehow. Nobody else knew where the Grail was buried, and they thought that the hawthorn tree was Joseph's stick, and that it was very surprising, but they never thought that it was marking anything.

But for hundreds of years people looked and searched for the Holy Grail. It was one of those special things that King Arthur's Knights of the Round Table tried to do, and one of them, called Sir Galahad, is supposed to have seen it once, but we don't know if he really did, because it is all so very long ago. But as far as we know, it never has been found. Or perhaps somebody found it and never knew what a precious thing it was.

Anyway, after years and years some monks came and built a monastery, with a famously beautiful chapel, round Joseph's thorn tree so that it was in their garden and they looked after it for ages until it got very old. At last one of the gardening monks said to the abbot:

"Father Abbot, I am afraid that St. Joseph's thorn tree won't live much longer. It is hundreds of years old. Do you suppose that I might take one or two cuttings so that we'll still have some of it when the old tree dies?"

"I don't see why not," said the abbot, rubbing his chin with his thumb. "It would be a great pity to lose it altogether after all these years."

So the brother gardener made two or three cuttings, and they had just started to grow nicely when Oliver Cromwell's soldiers arrived!

I don't know if you know about Oliver Cromwell, but he was one of the heads of the Puritans who were extraordinary people, and they only thought three things.

One was that they thought that the church was bad, and that all the beautiful churches were bad too.

Two, they thought that kings were bad to have.

Three, they thought people couldn't be happy as well as good, and that Sundays must be solemn and sad, and that churches must be plain and ugly, and that nobody must laugh or sing (because they couldn't be good as well as happy) and worst of all they thought that God was terrible and frightening, and was always watching to see if he could catch you out.

So you can see what extraordinary people they were, can't you? (As a matter of fact there are still some of them about, poor, miserable things.)

Well, Cromwell's soldiers went about smashing the lovely old churches and burning them. Haven't you seen statues and things in old churches with their noses bashed and their fingers broken off? Well, now you know who did it.

When the soldiers got to Glastonbury they pulled down the famously beautiful church, and then they went into the monastery garden and saw the thorn tree.

"What's this?" they shouted. "St. Joseph's thorn? Nonsense, of *course* it can't flower in the winter! What wickedness to tell such lies to the poor people!" And they chopped it down and dug up the roots and made a bonfire of the whole lot! *But* they didn't find the little cuttings that the brother gardener had made!

So we still have St. Joseph's thorn tree. And one or two cuttings have grown at Kew Gardens, so that all will be well if anything happens to the one in Glastonbury. And it really does flower in the winter!

St. Joseph of Arimathea's special day is on March 17, and anyone born on that day can have him for their special saint, specially people who live in Glastonbury.*

✣

ST. BENEDICT

Williston Walker

BENEDICT was born in Nursia, about eighty-five miles northeast of Rome, late in the fifth century. His education in Rome had advanced but little when he adopted the extremest form of asceticism, and dwelt as a hermit in a cave near Subiaco, in the mountains some forty miles eastward of the city. Here he spent three years in the study of the Scriptures and in severe self-mortification, till the monks of a neighboring monastery chose him for their abbot. His strict discipline proved irksome to them, however. He narrowly escaped death by poison at their hands, and gladly betook himself once more to his cave.

He could not now be alone, for his fame attracted disciples. He taught children, he established a group of small monasteries. Subiaco proved at length, however, an uncomfortable place of sojourn by reason of the jealous opposition to Benedict of one of its clergy; and, therefore, he left it, now a man of ripened observation and experience. In 529, he laid, at Monte Cassino, eighty-five miles southeast of Rome, the foundations of what was to be the most famous monastery in Europe, the motherhouse of the Benedictine order. For this monastery he wrote his celebrated "Rule." Here he taught, preached, and lived, a pattern of monastic piety till his death, which occurred after the summer of 542.

Benedict was no scholar, but he had the Roman genius for administration, an earnest belief in monasticism as the ideal Christian life, and a profound knowledge of human nature. In the creation of his "Rule" he built on the work of the regulators of monasticism who had gone before him, but with a moderation and good sense that reveal the keenness of his observation and his capacity to meet existing needs. Monasticism, in his judgment, had its grave perils. Many monks lived unworthily of their profession. Some were no better than vagabonds. These evils were due to lack of discipline. Discipline was a fundamental need; yet it must not be made too heavy a yoke for ordinary men. It is this remarkable combination of strict restraint with some real degree of freedom, of lifelong vows with moderation in requirements, that above all distinguished Benedict's "Rule."

Benedict's conception of the monastic career seems to have been that of a spiritual garrison holding duty for Christ in a hostile world. As such, its discipline was a necessary part of its life. None should enter its service until he had tried the life fully for at least a year's novitiate, during which he should be free to leave. This completed, the would-be monk took the threefold vows which forever cut him off from the world, binding himself to permanent life in the monastery, poverty and chastity, and obedience to its rule and its head.

The government of the monastery was vested in an abbot; and nowhere does Benedict's skill more signally appear than in his provisions for its exercise. While each monk was vowed to absolute obedience to the abbot's commands, even if they seemed to him impossible of fulfilment, the abbot was chosen by the free suffrage of all the monks, he could decide weighty matters only after calling for the judgment of the whole body, and smaller concerns affecting the monastery only on hearing the opinion of the elder brethren. Benedict was wise enough to know that a sensible man, even if given absolute authority in theory, would not long resist the wishes of the majority of those whose advice he was obliged to take in all cases of importance. Under the abbot, and appointed by him "with the advice of the brethren," was to be a provost as an assistant in government, and in large monasteries "deans," also, chosen for the same purpose. That the separation of the monks from the world should be as complete as possible, Benedict prescribed that each monastery, wherever feasible, should be equipped to furnish the necessaries of life, since he deemed wandering outside its walls a chief spiritual danger.

Benedict's regulations concerning food and drink exhibited a similar moderation and wisdom. He would have neither luxury nor undue fasting, and he was especially considerate in the care of those who were ill. Since worship was a large part of monastic life, careful requirements were made for its observance in the "Rule." On the supposed authority of Scripture, Benedict required not merely seven services in the twenty-four hours, but made much of that appointed for two in the morning, the "vigil." In contrast to the prescriptions of some other "Rules," however, the services appointed by Benedict, except the "vigil," were notably brief, demanding only about twenty minutes each. They consisted chiefly in the recitation of the Psalms, the whole book being used each week.

Benedict's most fruitful requirements were regarding labor. "Idleness," said he, in the "Rule," "is hostile to the soul, and therefore the brethren should be occupied at fixed times in manual labor, and at definite hours in religious reading." He saw clearly the moral value of work; and he was broad-minded enough in his conception of labor to include in it that of the mind as well as that of the hands.

A Benedictine monastery that was true to the purposes of the founder of the order was, therefore, a little world in itself, in which the monks lived a strenuous but not overburdened life, involving worship, vigorous labor in the shop and fields, and serious reading. It made every Benedictine monastery the possessor of something of a library; and though Benedict himself says nothing about classical learning, his aim being primarily religious, the Benedictine monasteries soon copied and read the great literary examples of Latin antiquity.

From Italy the Benedictine "Rule" spread rapidly over western Europe. It is almost impossible to exaggerate the services of these monks in the transition period caused by the ruin of the old Roman civilization and the growth in its place of the new life of the Germanic conquerors. That that new life preserved so much of the best the old had to offer in Christianity and civilization alike was largely due to this Benedictine monasticism. Northern Europe was then much like North America at the coming of the first European settlers. It was in large measure a land of forests and untilled soil. The monasteries did what a modern mission station does among barbarous peoples. They instructed in the principles of Christianity, they relieved distress and sickness to a considerable degree, they taught agriculture to the peoples of northern Europe, they preserved such learning as survived the Germanic invasions, they gave the only schools. Above all, they made it possible, in a rude age when men won and held property and place in the world by the sword, for peace-loving, religious-minded people to find a comparatively quiet and sheltered life. They gave the only opportunity that the early Middle Ages had to offer for study, for protection amid constant warfare, and for rest. They were a great missionary force, and a constant reminder to a rude population that there are other interests than those of the body.*

✤

ALL GLORY, LAUD, AND HONOR

IT IS difficult to believe that the words to this joyous hymn of praise were composed while the author was imprisoned. Theodulph of Orleans, who lived during the ninth century and was abbot of a monastery in Florence, Italy, spent part of his life in France, where he was appointed Bishop of Orleans. For some reason, the King of France felt that Theodulph was conspiring against him, and so he ordered that he be imprisoned in a monastery at Angers. While there, he wrote the words to the glorious "All Glory, Laud, and Honor."

John Mason Neale, who lived during the last century, translated the ancient hymn and put it into the familiar language that we know. Neale was deeply interested in translating and reviving great Latin and Greek hymns. "Jerusalem the Golden" and "Art Thou Weary, Art Thou Languid" are two other dearly-loved hymns which he translated with great skill.

Notice how the Triumphal Entry into Jerusalem comes to life through the word-pictures created in this hymn. Not only the "people of the Hebrews, with palms before Thee went" but we, too, are made to feel a part of the procession, led by the children of old, whose "sweet hosannas" ring out clearly in cheerful festivity.

The magnificent tune was composed by Melchior Teschner, a gifted church musician of the seventeenth century.

* Abridged from *Great Men of the Christian Church* by Williston Walker, pp. 107-14. Copyright 1908 by University of Chicago Press. Used by permission of Harper & Brothers.

All Glory, Laud, and Honor*

THEODULPH OF ORLEANS, 820
Tr. JOHN MASON NEALE, 1854

VALET WILL ICH DIR GEBEN (ST THEODULPH)

7.6.7 6 D.

MELCHIOR TESCHNER, 1615

With well defined rhythm

1. All glo - ry, laud, and hon - or To Thee, Re - deem - er, King,
2. Thou art the King of Is - rael, Thou Da - vid's roy - al Son,
3. Thou didst ac - cept their prais - es; Ac - cept the prayers we bring,

To whom the lips of chil - dren Made sweet ho - san - nas ring!
Who in the Lord's name com - est, The King and bless - ed One!
Who in all good de - light - est, Thou good and gra - cious King!

The peo - ple of the He - brews With palms be - fore Thee went;
To Thee, be - fore Thy pas - sion, They sang their hymns of praise;
All glo - ry, laud, and hon - or To Thee, Re - deem - er, King,

Our praise and prayer and an - thems Be - fore Thee we pre - sent.
To Thee, now high ex - alt - ed Our mel - o - dy we raise.
To whom the lips of chil - dren Made sweet ho - san - nas ring! A-MEN.

*From *The Hymnal,* No. 135. Published 1941 by Eden Publishing House. Used by permission of the publisher.

Creator Spirit, By Whose Aid*

VENI, CREATOR (ATTWOOD). (8 8. 8 8. 8 8.)

Moderately slow.

T. ATTWOOD, 1765–1838.

A-men.

*From *Songs of Praise,* No 181. Published by Oxford University Press, London. Used by permission of the publisher.

CREATOR Spirit, by whose aid
The world's foundations first were laid,
Come, visit every pious mind;
Come, pour thy joys on human kind;
From sin and sorrow set us free,
And make thy temples worthy thee.

2 O source of uncreated light,
The Father's promised Paraclete,
Thrice holy fount, thrice holy fire,
Our hearts with heavenly love inspire;
Come, and thy sacred unction bring
To sanctify us while we sing.

3 Plenteous of grace, descend from high
Rich in thy sevenfold energy;
Make us eternal truths receive,
And practise all that we believe;
Give us thyself, that we may see
The Father and the Son by thee.

4. Immortal honour, endless fame,
Attend the almighty Father's name;
The saviour Son be glorified,
Who for lost man's redemption died;
And equal adoration be,
Eternal Paraclete, to thee.

J. Dryden, 1631–1700. *Based on* Veni, creator Spiritus.

CREATOR SPIRIT, BY WHOSE AID

THIS is one of the most important hymns of the Roman Catholic Church, historically speaking, because of its relation to "Veni, Creator Spiritus," a hymn written at the close of the so-called Dark Ages. In one form or another, this hymn has been sung for a thousand years at solemn functions of the Church: at councils, coronations, consecrations, and even during the crusades. Its singing in old times was accompanied on great occasions by the ringing of bells and the use of lights and incense.

This particular version by the well-known seventeenth-century English poet, John Dryden, is a freer one than some of the others which come from the early centuries. It reflects something of the comfortable life and times of the seventeenth century when the rigors of the Dark Ages were well past and forgotten, when life was comfortable and gentlemen in full-bottomed wigs sang with graceful piety Dryden's excellent verses to the accompaniment of excellent music. It lacks the sternness of the older settings when life was a struggle and reality difficult to face.

Thomas Attwood, organist of St. Paul's Cathedral, wrote the music for Dryden's verses at the request of the Bishop of London, who wanted to use them at an ordination service on Trinity Sunday, 1831. It is said that Attwood received the bishop's note only on a Saturday and finished the composition while driving up to London from rural Norwood on Sunday morning. Attwood, who had been a pupil of Mozart, was a competent craftsman and accomplished the feat to his credit. The tune is one of grace and refinement, possessing an elegant charm which suits Dryden's words.*

* Adapted from *Songs of Praise Discussed*, p. 113. Published by Oxford University Press, London. Used by permission of the publisher.

CONTENTS

PART III SECTION 4

CRUSADES AND CATHEDRALS

✠

Put on the whole armour of God, that ye may be able to stand against the wiles of the devil.—
EPHESIANS 6:11

✠

PICTURES: PAGE
  Interpretation: Upper and Lower Church of St. Francis of Assisi 311
  Picture: Upper Church of St. Francis of Assisi 312
  Picture: Lower Church (Interior) of St. Francis of Assisi 313
  Interpretation: Cathedral, Baptistry, and Campanile, Pisa 314
  Picture: Cathedral, Baptistry, and Campanile, Pisa 316
  Interpretation: "Christ Teaching," Cathedral of Notre Dame, Chartres—
    Artist Unknown 315
  Picture: "Christ Teaching," Cathedral of Notre Dame, Chartres—
    Artist Unknown 317

POETRY:
  A Simple Prayer—*St. Francis* 319
  Canticle to IL Poverello—*Marlatt* 319
  Come, Thou Holy Spirit—*Innocent III* 320
  Crusaders' Song—*Author Unknown* 320
  The Basque Song—*Anonymous* 321
  The Love of God—*Rascas* 321
  Thy Kingdom Come—*St. Bernard of Clairvaux* 322
  Francis—*Marlatt* 322

STORIES:
  St. Francis of Assisi—*Brown* 323
  Peter the Hermit—*Haaren* and *Poland* 326
  St. Bernard of Clairvaux—*Bell* 328

MUSIC:
  Interpretation: Brief Life Is Here Our Portion—*Bernard of Cluny* 330
  Music: Brief Life Is Here Our Portion—*Gauntlett* 331
  Interpretation: O What Their Joy and Their Glory Must Be—*Abélard* 331
  Music: O What Their Joy and Their Glory Must Be—Harmonized by
    Dykes 332

UPPER AND LOWER CHURCH OF ST. FRANCIS OF ASSISI

No church in the age of cathedrals rose as fast as the basilica at Assisi. Begun in 1228, two years after the death of St. Francis, it was completed in 1230. The devotion with which the plan for building the church was conceived and the fervor with which it was carried out, can largely be attributed to Brother Elias, who was vicar of the order which St. Francis established. Brother Elias, a close companion of the saint, appealed to Pope Gregory IX immediately on the death of St. Francis, to build a basilica which would be a worthy shrine for the saint.

When the Pope announced that the church was under way, money and gifts poured in from the faithful all over the world. Royalty, church dignitaries, laymen—rich and poor alike—gave in reverence to the saint whose life had captured their imagination and devotion. Umbrian peasants who lived on the sunny slopes and valleys of that part of Italy in which the hill town of Assisi is situated, gave freely of their labor when they were too poor to give money. Thus, the building of the Church of St. Francis was truly a labor of love.

When the church was completed, the body of St. Francis was carried in a triumphal procession from its temporary resting place to the Lower Church, where it was placed in a secret tomb. The townspeople were not allowed inside the church for the ceremony and the few who had prepared the tomb kept its exact location within the church a secret. Eventually the sarcophagus was lost sight of until 1818, when it was located after a long search.

Brother Elias was general overseer, if not the architect of the basilica. He had the assistance of Jacopo Lombardo, and the collaboration of other well-known architects. Situated upon a hill called "The Hill of Paradise," the church of St. Francis was actually two churches: the Upper and the Lower Churches, built one upon the other in the form of a Latin cross. The general style of architecture is Romanesque, with Gothic modifications.

The Lower Church was constructed so as to give the appearance of a crypt. Its massive piers and solid round arches seem to rise from the earth. The builders gave a somberness to the Lower Church which persists in spite of the richness of the decorated walls. Someone has said that the Lower Church symbolizes the suffering of St. Francis on this earth and the Upper Church, so full of light, symbolizes his glory in heaven.

A veritable galaxy of artists adorned the walls of the Lower Church. There Cimabue painted his "Madonna and Child Enthroned Between St. Francis and a Choir of Angels." Simone Martini and Pietro Lorenzetti added frescoes later on. Giotto pictured allegorical aspects of the life of St. Francis over the high altar, and in the right transept he did a magnificent series of frescoes that tell the Christmas story. In later centuries, other artists added their contributions.

The glory of the Upper Church of St. Francis is the splendid series of

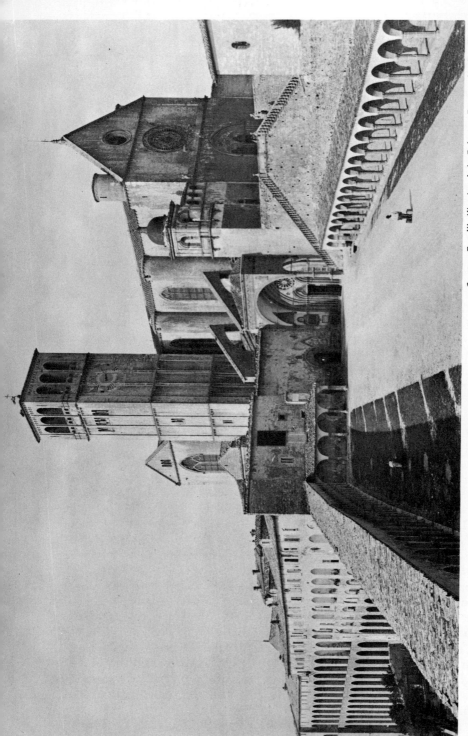

UPPER CHURCH OF ST. FRANCIS OF ASSISI

LOWER CHURCH (INTERIOR) OF ST. FRANCIS OF ASSISI

frescoes by Giotto showing the twenty-eight principal events in the life of St. Francis. Like precious jewels in the sunlight, these paintings cover the lower walls on both sides of the nave with a brilliance that is dazzling. On a sunny day, light from the large windows above them belies their great age. One is struck by the rich shades of rose, beautiful clear blues (as in the greatly loved "St. Francis Preaches to the Birds"), deep, earthy browns, and silvery grays. The colors could have scarcely been brighter when they were damp from Giotto's brush! If ever an artist and his subject belonged together, Giotto and St. Francis did. The artist lived close enough to the time of the saint to catch the feeling of his life and works.

The modern pilgrim to Assisi finds the Upper and Lower Churches of St. Francis so rich in tradition and art masterpieces that he is overwhelmed by their immensity and importance. Yet strangely enough, the simplicity of St. Francis has been kept. Part of this is due to the unswerving focus of attention on St. Francis—every work of art within the church speaks of him with a spirituality that is in keeping with that man of God. Part is due also to the setting of the basilica, high upon a hill overlooking the Umbrian plain. It is easy to imagine, in this unspoiled Italian hill town and countryside, that St. Francis may walk down a dusty path, clad in his rough brown robe, his bare feet thrust into sandals. It is quite wonderful to consider how, for seven hundred years, Assisi, with its beautiful basilica, has kept alive the memory of the saint it cherishes!

✢

CATHEDRAL, BAPISTRY, AND CAMPANILE, PISA

It is unfortunate that the cathedral group at Pisa, Italy, is generally known chiefly for the "leaning tower," as the campanile is popularly called. Both the splendid cathedral and the fine baptistry deserve careful study and appreciation as excellent examples of church architecture of northern Italy.

The style of the cathedral, usually termed "Lombardic" or "Pisan," is similar to that of Roman basilicas, except that it was built in the form of a Latin cross. The rounded arches of the graceful and bold triforium let in far more light than did the Romanesque churches.

The exterior of the cathedral is decorated by the lavish use of colored marble. Three rows of arcades and half-columns mark the side aisles, triforium, and clerestory of the nave. This arcade effect lends both grace and ornament to what would otherwise be a heavy and massive exterior.

The interior of the cathedral at Pisa is remarkable because of the use of colored marble, which is applied in bands, squares, panels, and so forth. There are at least four hundred and fifty columns, all with capitals covered with lavish stone carvings by unnamed artists. Some of this sculpture is so early in its date that it is thought to reflect remnants of a barbaric culture.

A splendid marble pulpit, a masterpiece of sculpturing by the great

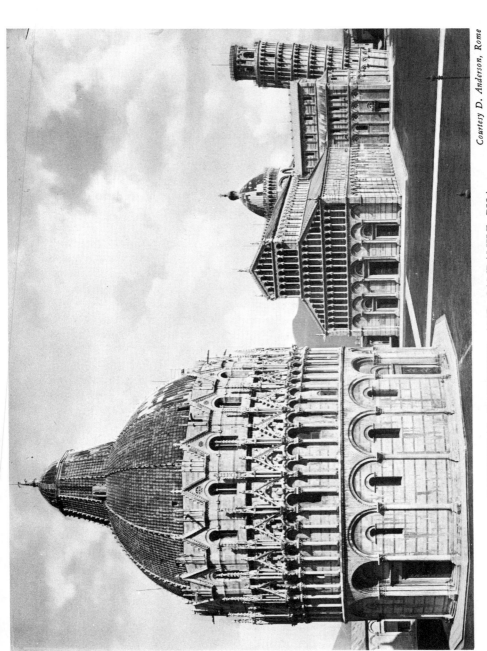

CATHEDRAL, BAPTISTRY, AND CAMPANILE, PISA

Courtesy D. Anderson, Rome

Giovanni Pisano, once occupied a prominent place in the cathedral. This, together with several valued paintings and ornaments, was destroyed by a great fire in 1569. However, the bronze doors by Pisano at the eastern side of the South transept did survive, and may be seen today. Their remarkable panels, done in relief, show the story of Jesus from the appearance of the angel to Zacharias to the Ascension scene.

Much of the cathedral was rebuilt after the fire. Happily, this is one of the few really skillful cathedral restorations which has retained the spirit of the original. At the time of restoration a profusely gilded ceiling of the nave was added, as were the brilliant stained-glass windows in the chapels along the sides of the nave.

The altars of these nave chapels are very beautiful. They were created before the fire, beginning with the year 1500. The master Michelangelo created the designs for these altars. Above each, hangs some masterpiece of painting, framed on either side by a pair of graceful Corinthian columns.

The baptistry was begun in 1153 and took one hundred twenty-five years to complete. Its beautifully decorated, engaged columns harmonize well with the design of the cathedral. The pointed gables and pinnacles, added during the fourteenth century, are slightly discordant.

The interior of the baptistry is most interesting because of the large octagonal bath for adult immersion. A round basin, attached to each oblique side of this bath, is for infant baptism. The baptistry is used by the entire town, the smaller churches having no baptistries of their own. The magnificent pulpit by Niccola Pisano is worthy of attention.

The leaning tower follows the same decorative plan as the cathedral. It is not known for certain whether the lean has been caused by the settling of the foundation or if it was included purposely in the architect's design.

✝

CHRIST TEACHING, CATHEDRAL OF NOTRE DAME, CHARTRES
Artist Unknown

EACH of the three great portals of Chartres Cathedral has its special theme. The Royal or West Portal carvings show the coming of Christ to the world. The sculpture of the North Portal treats of the doctrine of atonement and the Old Testament, while that of the South Portal represents the Church, as it was established in the world. Knowing that the carvings and stained-glass windows of a great cathedral such as Chartres were "the Bible of the people," one can see that these three magnificent entrances to Chartres portray the history of Christianity quite fully.

In studying the statue, "Christ Teaching," it will be interesting to try to put ourselves in the place of a thirteenth-century worshiper and discover how it, and other sculpture of the South Portal, tells the story.

The great South Porch is approached by a flight of seventeen steps. It is

CHRIST TEACHING, CATHEDRAL OF NOTRE DAME,
CHARTRES—*ARTIST UNKNOWN*

comprised of three bays or entrances, each of which is surmounted by a pointed arch, a niche, and a cross. Seven hundred and eighty-three carved figures tell the story of Christ in the midst of His apostles and martyrs.

The figure of Christ, the Teacher, dominates the scene. He stands on a slender shaft which divides the central door. In His left hand, He holds a book, and He lifts His right hand in blessing. Behind His head is a nimbus with the outline of the cross upon it. A lion and a dragon—both of which are mentioned in Psalm 90—rest quietly under His feet.

The unknown sculptor or sculptors have created a calm and beautifully spiritual face for the Christ. It is one of the finest representations in Christendom, and its immortality is attested to by the fact that modern man finds this portrayal of Christ as satisfying as it must have been to Christians living six hundred years ago. There is love and compassion in the face of this Christ. And there is also great strength and peace. Dignity is in every line of the figure.

It is appropriate that the teaching Christ should hold a book—probably the Word of God. Books were rare in those days and they were handmade and beautifully bound. The majority of the manuscripts of the Western World were either parts of the Bible or the Psalter, books of devotions, and other church-related books.

Although the picture on page 317 shows only the figure of Christ, the surrounding carvings are important to any understanding of the total effect of this religious craftsmanship. The carvings immediately below Christ show two scenes which carry out His teachings—acts of charity. The first pictures a man on his knees. He has in his hands loaves of bread to give to the poor, in accordance with Jesus' teachings. He first offers them to Christ for blessing. Below, a man and a woman, said to be the donors of the porch—Pierre Mauclerk, Count of Dreux, and his wife, Ann of Brittany—give a loaf of bread to a beggar.

To the left and to the right of Christ are statues of the twelve apostles. Unlike many representations of this period, most of these figures bear no special symbols, and so it is impossible to identify other than the five who carry their symbols.

Teachings and events in the life of Christ are represented in the other carvings of this porch. Above the door, the Last Judgment is depicted and there are also other sculptures on themes related to the teachings of Jesus about the Last Days and life after death. Twenty-eight statues of kings and queens of the Old Testament are included as part of the "Heavenly Court."

The left bay or entrance of the South Portal concerns many of the martyrs who have died proclaiming the teachings of Jesus. St. Stephen is there, John the Baptist, St. Thomas of Canterbury, and many others. The teaching of the Wise and Foolish Virgins is also included.

The right bay is the bay of the Confessors—those who have gone forth to teach and carry out the instructions that Jesus gave to those who would follow Him. St. Martin, St. Jerome, St. Nicholas—there is not space to name them all—they are a roll call of men and women of the early Church and of medieval times who sought to carry out the teachings of Christ.

Seven hundred and eighty-three carved figures—all bearing on the theme of the teaching of Christ! This magnificent sculpture not only shows many of Christ's teachings, but it also depicts how men and women, in His age and up to the age of the building of Chartres Cathedral, have sought to carry out those teachings.

✛

A SIMPLE PRAYER

Lord, make me an Instrument of your peace.
Where there is hatred, . . . let me sow love.
Where there is injury, . . . pardon.
Where there is doubt, . . . faith.
Where there is despair, . . . hope.
Where there is darkness, . . . light.
Where there is sadness, . . . joy.

O Divine Master, grant that I may not so much seek
To be consoled, . . . as to console,
To be understood, . . . as to understand,
To be loved, . . . as to love,
            for
It is in giving, . . . that we receive,
It is in pardoning, that we are pardoned,
It is in dying, . . . that we are born to eternal life.
               —*St. Francis (1181 or 1182-1226)*

CANTICLE TO IL POVERELLO

"One should always be willing to leave an ecstasy to help a brother."
               —St. Francis of Assisi.

Little Brother Poor Man, we
Beg thee of thy poverty,
Give us riches; vision; grace;
Gold of heaven on kindling face—
Jesus' Little Brother, we
Would be rich like Him and thee.

Jocund Troubadour of God,
Hearing music in the clod,
Cadence of eternity
In wolves and larks and lepers, we
Wait the blessing of thy nod:
Make us troubadours of God.

Little Brother of the Sun,
Shining with the light of One,
Who left supernal ecstasy
To make His brother-poor-men free,
Little Brother of the Sun,
Jesus' will and thine be done.*
                                        Amen.

—*Earl Marlatt*

COME, THOU HOLY SPIRIT

Come, Thou Holy Spirit, come,
And from Thy celestial home
    Shed a ray of light divine;
Come, Thou Father of the poor,
Come, Thou source of all our store,
Come, within our bosoms shine.

Heal our wounds; our strength renew;
On our dryness pour Thy dew;
    Wash the stains of guilt away;
Bend the stubborn heart and will;
Melt the frozen, warm the chill;
    Guide the steps that go astray.**

—*Innocent III (ca. 1160-1216)*

CRUSADERS' SONG

From the Chronicle of the Dukes of Normandy

Take the good and cast the evil,
    Listen, people, to my song,
For 'tis God for whom I'm speaking
    To the valiant and the strong.
Take the Cross, the Cross He died on,
    Oh, repay Him as ye may;
For by dying He redeemed us,
    Can we give Him less today?

Help me, God, in this my pleading!
    Tardy have we been to free
That Thy Cross and that Thy country
    Where the Infidels mock Thee.
'Tis our sins that have delayed us
    Let us cast them and be free,
Leaving everything behind us,
    Finding Paradise with Thee.***

—*Author Unknown*

* From *Cathedral: A Volume of Poems* by Earl Marlatt, p. 103. Copyright 1956 by Earl Marlatt. Published by Parthenon Press. Used by permission of the author and the publisher.
** Anonymous translation from the Latin.
*** Translated from the Old French by Walter Clifford Meller.

THE BASQUE SONG

O little lark, you need not fly
To seek your Master in the sky.
He's near our native sod.
   Why should you sing aloft, apart?
   Sing to the Heaven of my heart,
In me, in me, in me is God.

O travelers, passing in your car,
Ye pity me, who came from far
On dusty feet, rough shod.
   You cannot guess, you cannot know,
   Upon what wings of joy I go
Who travel home with God.

Ships bring from far your curious fare.
Earth's richest morsels are your share,
And prize of gun and rod.
   At richer boards I take my seat
   Have dainties angels may not eat.
In me, in me, is God.

O little lark, sing loud and long
To him who gave you flight and song,
And me a heart of flame.
   He loveth them of low degree,
   And He hath magnifièd me,
And Holy, Holy, Holy is His name.
         —Anonymous translation from the Basque

THE LOVE OF GOD

All things that are on earth shall wholly pass away,
Except the love of God, which shall live and last for aye.
The forms of men shall be as they had never been;
The blasted groves shall lose their fresh and tender green;
The birds of the thicket shall end their pleasant song,
And the nightingale shall cease to chant the evening long.
The kine of the pasture shall feel the dart that kills,
And all the fair white flocks shall perish from the hills.
The goat and antlered stag, the wolf and the fox,
The wild boar of the wood, and the chamois of the rocks,
And the strong and fearless bear, in the trodden dust shall lie;
And the dolphin of the sea, and the mighty whale shall die.
And realms shall be dissolved, and empires be no more,
And they shall bow to death, who ruled from shore to shore;

And the great globe itself, so Holy Writings tell,
With the rolling firmament, where starry armies dwell,
Shall melt with fervent heat—they shall all pass away,
Except the love of God, which shall live and last for aye!*

—Bernard Rascas

THY KINGDOM COME

Thou hope of all the lowly!
   To thirsting souls how kind!
Gracious to all who seek Thee,
   Oh, what to those who find!

My tongue but lisps Thy praises,
   Yet praise be my employ;
Love makes me bold to praise Thee,
   For Thou art all my joy.

In Thee my soul delighting,
   Findeth her only rest;
And so in Thee confiding,
   May all the world be blest!

Dwell with us, and our darkness
   Will flee before Thy light;
Scatter the world's deep midnight,
   And fill it with delight.

O all mankind! behold Him,
   And seek His love to know;
And let your hearts, in seeking,
   Be fired with love and glow!

O come, O come, great Monarch!
   Eternal glory Thine;
The longing world waits for Thee:
   Arise, arise and shine!**

—St. Bernard of Clairvaux (1090-1153)

FRANCIS

Little Brother of the Sun,
The birds of Bevagna,
And the wolf of Gubbio,
He gave up gold and scarlet pomp

---

* Translated from the Limousin (a French Provençal language) by William Cullen Bryant.
** Anonymous translation from the Latin.

To marry Poverty;
And went adventuring,
Singing,
Jesting,
Rebuking lords,
And kissing lepers—
Living a life
As fragrant as lilac-time
And leaving the memory of a soul
Drenched with holy loveliness.*

—*Earl Marlatt*

✠

ST. FRANCIS OF ASSISI

Abbie Farwell Brown

BAREFOOTED in the snow, bareheaded in the rain, St. Francis wandered up and down the world smiling for the great love that was in his heart.

And because it grew from love the smile of St. Francis was a wonderful thing. It opened the hearts of men and coaxed the secrets out of their thoughts. It led human folk whithersoever St. Francis willed. It drew the beasts to his side and the birds to nestle in his bosom. It was like a magic charm.

Great princes knew his smile and they obeyed its command to be generous and good. The sick and sorrowful knew his smile. It meant healing and comfort. Then they rose and blessed God in the name of St. Francis. The wretched beggars in the streets of Assisi knew it. To them the smile of "the Lord's own beggar" meant help and sympathy. Like them he was poor and homeless, often ill and hungry. They wondered that he could smile. But he said, "It does not become a servant of God to have an air of melancholy and a face full of trouble." So they also tried to smile, poor fellows. But how different it was!

The little lambs to whom he gave his special protection and care knew the smile of St. Francis. Once he met two woolly lambkins who were being carried to market. He never had any money, but taking off his cloak, which was all he had to part with, he gave it to buy their lives. And he carried the lambs home in his bosom.

The wilder beasts beyond the mountains, the fierce wolves and shy foxes of Syria and Spain whom he met in his wanderings knew St. Francis. Here was a brother who was not afraid of them and whom they could trust in return, a brother who understood and sympathized. The birds in the trees knew also, and his coming was the signal of peace. Then they sang with Francis, but he was the sweetest singer of them all.

Besides these living things the green fields of Italy, the trees, the meadows,

* From *Cathedral: A Volume of Poems* by Earl Marlatt, p. 93. Copyright 1956 by Earl Marlatt. Published by Parthenon Press. Used by permission of the author and the publisher.

the brooks, the flowers all knew the smile of St. Francis. It meant to them many things which only a poet can tell. But Francis understood, for he was a poet.

Upon all alike his face of love beamed tenderly. For St. Francis of Assisi was a little brother of the whole great world and of all created things. Not only did his heart warm to Brother Sheep and Sister Bees, to his Brother Fish and his little Sisters the Doves, but he called the Sun and Wind his brothers and the Moon and Water his sisters. Of all the saints about whom the legends tell, Francis was the gentlest and most loving. And if

> He prayeth best who loveth best
> All things both great and small,

the prayers of St. Francis must have been very dear to Him who "made and loveth all."

There was none so poor as Francis. Not a penny did he have, not a penny would he touch. Let them be given to those who could not smile, he said. His food he begged from door to door, broken crusts for a single poor meal; more he would not take. His sleeping place was the floor or the haymow, the ruined church, whatever lodging chance gave him. Oftenest he slept upon the bare ground with a stone for his pillow. He wanted to be poor because Christ was poor, and he was trying to live like his Master.

In his coarse brown gown, tied about the waist with a rope, without hat or shoes he wandered singing, smiling. The love which beamed from him like radiance from a star shone back from every pair of eyes which looked into his own. For all the world loved Francis in the time of the crusades. And even today, seven hundred years since that dear beggar passed cheerily up and down the rough Italian roads—even today there are many who love him like a lost elder brother. St. Francis preached to all lessons of charity and peace. His were simple words, for he had not the wisdom of many books. But he knew the book of the human heart from cover to cover. His words were like fire, they warmed and wakened. No one could resist the entreaty and the love that was in them. So thousands joined the Society of Little Brothers of which he was the founder, and became his helpers in works of charity and holiness.

His church was out of doors in the beautiful world that he loved, in mountain, field, or forest, wherever he happened to be wandering. Sometimes he preached by the candlelight of stars. Often the cloistering trees along the roadside made his chapel, and the blue sky was the only roof between him and heaven. Often his choir was of the brother birds in the branches and his congregation a group of brother beasts. For he preached to them also who, though they spoke a different language, were yet children of his Father. And in his little talks to them he always showed the courtesy which one brother owes another.

Once, on returning from a journey beyond the sea, he was traveling through the Venetian country, when he heard a great congregation of birds singing among the bushes. And he said to his companion, "Our sisters, the birds, are praising their Maker. Let us then go into their midst and sing." So they did this, and the birds did not fly away but continued to sing so loudly that the brothers could not hear each other. Then St. Francis turned to the birds and said politely, "Sisters, cease your song until we have rendered our bounden praise to God." So the birds were still until the brothers had finished their psalm. But after that when it was again their turn the birds went on with their song.

Now after a life spent like Christ's in works of poverty, charity, and love, St. Francis came at last to have one spot in the world which he could call his own. It was neither a church nor a convent, a cottage nor even a cell. It was only a bare and lonely mountain top where wild beasts lived and wild birds had a home. This retreat in the wilderness was the gift which Orlando, a rich nobleman, chose to make St. Francis. And it was a precious gift indeed, sorely needed by the Lord's weary beggar. For he was worn with wandering; he was ill and weak, and his gentle eyes were growing dim so that he could not go along the winding ways. But he was happy still.

So one warm September day he went with some of his chosen brethren to take possession of their new home. They left the villages, the farms, and at last even the scattered shepherd's huts far below and behind them, and came into the quiet of the Italian hills. They climbed and climbed over the rocks and along the ravines, till they came in sight of the bald summit where Francis was to dwell. And here in happy weariness he paused to rest under an oak tree and look about upon the beautiful scene.

But suddenly the air was filled with music, a chorus of trills and quavers and carols of the wildest joy. Then the air grew dark with whirring wings. The birds of the mountain were coming from everywhere to welcome home their brother. They flew to him by hundreds, perching on his head and shoulders; and when every other spot was covered they twittered into the hood of his brown mantle. The brothers stood about, wondering greatly, although they had seen St. Francis in some such plight before. But the peasant who led the ass which had brought St. Francis so far stood like one turned to stone, unable to believe his eyes. Here was a miracle the like of which he had never dreamed.

But St. Francis was filled with gladness. "Dearest brethren," he said, "I think it must be pleasant to our Lord that we should dwell in this solitary place, since our brothers and sisters the birds are so glad of our coming."

And indeed, how could they help being glad of his coming, the dear, kind saint? And how they hovered around the shelter of branches which the brethren built for him under a beech tree on the very mountain top! One can picture them at morning, noon, and night joining in his songs of praise, or keeping polite silence while the holy man talked with God.

Many wonderful things happened upon the Monte Alverno while St. Francis dwelt there. But none were more wonderful than the great love of Francis himself; his love which was so big and so wide that it wrapped the

whole round world, binding all creatures more closely in a common brotherhood.

So that every man and every bird and every beast that lives ought to love
the name of that dear saint, their childlike, simple, happy little brother, St.
Francis of Assisi.*

✠

PETER THE HERMIT
John H. Haaren and A. B. Poland

DURING the Middle Ages the Christians of Europe used to go to the Holy
Land for the purpose of visiting the tomb of Christ and other sacred places.
Those who made such a journey were called "pilgrims."

Every year thousands of pilgrims—kings, nobles, and people of humbler
rank—went to the Holy Land.

While Jerusalem was in the hands of the Arabian caliphs who reigned
at Baghdad, the Christian pilgrims were generally well treated. After about
1070, when the Turks took possession of the city, outrages became so
frequent that it seemed as if it would not be safe for Christians to visit the
Saviour's tomb at all.

About the year 1095 there lived at Amiens, France, a monk named Peter
the Hermit.

Peter was presented at a council of clergy and people held at Clermont in
France when his Holiness, Pope Urban II, made a stirring speech. He begged
the people to rescue the Holy Sepulcher and other sacred sites from the
Mohammedans.

The council were so roused by his words that they broke forth into loud
cries, "God wills it! God wills it!"

"It is, indeed, His will," said the Pope, "and let these words be your
war cry when you meet the enemy."

Peter listened with deep attention. Immediately after the council he began
to preach in favor of a war against the Turks. With head and feet bare,
and clothed in a long, coarse robe tied at the waist with a rope, he went
through Italy from city to city, riding on a donkey. He preached in churches,
on the streets—wherever he could secure an audience.

When Peter had gone over Italy he crossed the Alps and preached to the
people of France, Germany, and neighboring countries. Everywhere he kindled the zeal of the people, and multitudes enlisted as champions of the cross.

Thus began the first of seven wars known as the "Crusades" or "Wars of
the Cross," waged to rescue the Holy Land from the Mohammedans.

It is said that more than one hundred thousand men, women, and children
went on the first crusade. Each wore on the right shoulder the emblem
of the cross.

* Abridged from *The Book of Saints and Friendly Beasts* by Abbie Farwell Brown, pp. 211-25.

Peter was in command of one portion of this great multitude. His followers began their journey with shouts of joy and praise.

But they had no proper supply of provisions. So when passing through Hungary they plundered the towns and compelled the inhabitants to support them. This roused the anger of the Hungarians. They attacked the crusaders and killed a great many of them.

After long delays about seven thousand of those who had started on the crusade reached Constantinople. They were still enthusiastic and sounded their war cry, "God wills it!" with as much fervor as when they first joined Peter's standard.

Leaving Constantinople, they went eastward into the land of the Turks. A powerful army led by the sultan met them. The crusaders fought heroically all day long but at length were badly beaten. Only a few escaped and found their way back to Constantinople.

Peter the Hermit had left the crusaders before the battle and returned to Constantinople. He afterwards joined the army of Godfrey of Bouillon.

Godfrey's army was composed of six divisions, each commanded by a soldier of high rank and distinction. It was a well organized and disciplined force and numbered about half a million men.

It started only a few weeks after the irregular multitude which followed Peter the Hermit, and was really the first crusading army, for Peter's undisciplined throng could hardly be called an army.

After a long march Godfrey reached Antioch and laid siege to it.

It was believed that this Moslem stronghold could be taken in a short time; but the city resisted the attacks of the Christians for seven months. Then it surrendered.

And now something happened that none of the crusaders had dreamed of. An army of two hundred thousand Persians arrived to help the Moslems. They laid seige to Antioch and shut up the crusaders within its walls for weeks. However, after a number of engagements in which there was great loss of life, the Turks and Persians were at last driven away.

The way was now opened to Jerusalem. But out of the half million crusaders who had marched from Europe less than fifty thousand were left. They had won their way at a fearful cost.

Still onward they pushed with brave hearts, until on a bright summer morning they caught the first glimpse of the Holy City in the distance. For two whole years they had toiled and suffered in the hope of reaching Jerusalem. Now it lay before them.

But it had yet to be taken. For more than five weeks the crusaders carried on the siege. Finally, on the fifteenth of July, 1099, the Turks surrendered. The Moslem flag was hauled down and the banner of the cross floated over the Holy City.

A few days after the Christians had occupied Jerusalem Godfrey of Bouillon was chosen king of the Holy Land.

"I will accept the office," he said, "but no crown must be put on my head and I must never be called king in the land where once lived the King of Kings."

Peter the Hermit is said to have preached an eloquent sermon on the Mount of Olives. He did not, however, remain long in Jerusalem, but after the capture of the city returned to Europe. He founded a monastery in France and within its walls passed the rest of his life.*

✛

ST. BERNARD OF CLAIRVAUX
Mrs. Arthur Bell

ST. BERNARD is accounted one of the greatest saints of medieval times, and his burning eloquence won for him the name of the Oracle of Christendom in his lifetime, and of one of the Fathers of the Church after his death. The son of a French nobleman, the future saint, who was one of a large family, was born in the Castle of Fontaine, near Dijon, and was, it is said, dedicated to God before he was born, his mother having dreamed that she would give birth to a white dog with russet spots, which would bark furiously as soon as it saw the light; a vision interpreted to mean that the expected little one would be a great preacher.

Whatever truth there may be in this quaint story, St. Bernard appears to have been from the first remarkable for the beauty of his character, and to have won the affection of all with whom he was brought in contact. At school he was worshiped by his companions, and at the University of Paris, to which he was sent to complete his education, he exercised a remarkable influence over his fellow students. On his return home at the age of nineteen, he fell in love with a beautiful young girl who returned his affection, but he had already resolved to crush down all earthly feelings, and is said to have spent several nights standing in a frozen pond with a view to cooling his ardor. This severe discipline nearly cost him his life, but it was thoroughly effectual, and he was never again tempted in a similar manner.

At the age of twenty the young ascetic resolved to withdraw to the Monastery of Citeaux, and, much to the grief of his father, he persuaded three of his brothers to go with him. A pathetic story is told of the parting between the four young men and their little brother Nivard, who was playing in the courtyard of their beautiful home as they were riding forth. St. Bernard turned back to embrace him once more, and said to him as he pointed to the castle, "All this will one day be yours"; to which the child naively replied, "So you take heaven and leave me earth. I don't call that a fair division." Later Nivard, too, joined the Cistercians, and in the end the old father, deserted by all his sons, followed his example.

* From *Famous Men of the Middle Ages* by John H. Haaren and A. B. Poland, pp. 173-79.

On their way to Citeaux, St. Bernard and his brothers were joined by a number of other enthusiasts, all of whom were eagerly welcomed by the abbot St. Stephen, who, however, quickly recognized the exceptional qualities of their leader, and from the first chose him as a counselor, in what were then the difficult circumstances of the little community. St. Bernard had entered the monastery with a view to renouncing the world, and crushing down all the ambition which his great gifts made it impossible for him not to feel, yet which he felt it his duty to relinquish. St. Stephen took an entirely different view of the matter, and, though he encouraged the novice in his secret mortifications of the flesh, he was fortunately successful in convincing him that the gift of eloquence was a sacred charge, to be turned to the glory of God and the spread of religion. The immediate result of this wise advice was that St. Bernard gave full scope to his natural bent, and having been ordained priest, his earnest preaching became the means of winning so many to follow his example, that ere long the monastery, almost empty on his arrival, could no longer hold those who flocked to it, eager to be received into the order.

St. Stephen now resolved to send forth St. Bernard and twelve carefully selected monks to found a new community; and they started with eager enthusiasm, trusting to divine guidance in their selection of a suitable site. Their leader going before bearing the uplifted cross, the chosen twelve walked bravely forth from what had long been their home; and, after many days' journey, halted in a dreary wilderness of Champagne, then known by the forbidding name of the Valley of Wormwood, soon to be changed into that of Clara Vallis, or the Vale of Light, now corrupted into Clairvaux. This, St. Bernard assured his followers, was the spot chosen for them by God, and with unquestioning faith the little band set to work at once to clear a space, cut down trees, and build with their own hands the nucleus of what was eventually to become one of the greatest religious houses of Europe.

In a very few years the fame of St. Bernard of Clairvaux as a preacher had spread throughout the Christian world, and so resistless was the spell of his eloquence, that wives are said to have hid their husbands, and mothers their sons, lest they should be enticed into the cloister by the all-prevailing monk. Crowds flocked daily to Clairvaux to consult the abbot; feudal lords asked him to settle their disputes; vexed questions of theology were submitted to him; the newly-founded Knights Templar appealed to him to draw up their statutes. It was due to his influence that Pope Innocent II was finally triumphant over his rival, the Antipope Anacletus, and the successor of the former, Pope Eugenius III, turned to the famous abbot for advice in every difficulty.

It was St. Bernard who aroused the enthusiasm of France and Germany for the fatal crusade that had such tragic results for Europe; and so great was the enthralling force of his personality, that he was able to convince the shattered remnant of the great army, which had gone forth with such eager hope, that failure was the result, not of the mistaken advice he had given, but of the unworthiness of the soldiers of the cross. It was also, alas! St.

Bernard who, by his bitter animosity, finally broke the spirit and crushed the hopes of the hapless poet and theologian Abélard, whose tragic love story is one of the most pathetic romances of medieval times. Yet, with all his faults, which were the outcome rather of the period at which he lived than of his own character, the Abbot of Clairvaux was truly, as even Luther admitted, "a God-fearing and holy monk," luminously sincere, absolutely unselfish, a typical theologian, a true leader of thought. Under his stern discipline the order founded by St. Robert of Molesme became so modified and transformed that it was looked upon as practically a new institution, and it was often spoken of as the Bernardine instead of the Cistercian. Before his death in 1153, at the comparatively early age of sixty-five, St. Bernard had founded no less than seventy new monasteries, and it was his only sister, St. Humbeline, who, fired by his example, instituted the French sisterhood of the Bernardine nuns.

St. Bernard breathed his last in his monastery at Clairvaux, and was buried in its chapel, but little now remains to recall the memory of the great ascetic, in the valley he loved so well. The simple cells occupied by his monks were replaced in the thirteenth century by a luxurious house, and out of the humble oratory in which the ascetic founder had so often worshiped, grew a stately church, which was, however, destroyed after the Reformation. The abbey buildings were later converted into a prison, so that the beautiful name of the Vale of Light has long ceased to be appropriate.*

✠

BRIEF LIFE IS HERE OUR PORTION

BETWEEN the years 1122 and 1156, a monk named Bernard poured out his heart against the sins and wealth of the Church as contrasted to the wretched poverty of the people. His was the Church of the era of the great crusades and monasteries. Bernard, whose abbot resided in the luxurious monastery of Cluny, was often within those walls and there saw wealth, abundance of food, and lavish worldly appointments. Outside the monastery walls, Bernard walked among the children of the Church, whose lives were characterized by disease and toil without end.

When Bernard could bear the sight of these things no longer, he found himself impelled to write a poem, "De Contemptu Mundi." In it he described the troubles and heartaches of God's common folk, the wickedness and worldliness of the times, and the rewards of the future life. "Brief Life Is Here Our Portion" is based on this long poem.

As you read or sing the verses of the hymn, thinking of the heartbreak and love from which they came, you will discover they are the cry of a righteous soul. In the sixth and the eighth stanzas especially, we catch a glimpse of what life can become for those who strive to build a better world. Bernard of Cluny, a medieval monk, writing in the language of an ancient theology, helps us today to catch the vision and inspiration of the social gospel. He

* Abridged from *The Saints in Christian Art* by Mrs. Arthur Bell, pp. 222-25. Copyright 1904 by George Bell & Sons, London.

Brief Life Is Here Our Portion*

ST. ALPHEGE. (7 6. 7 6.)
In moderate time.   H. J. GAUNTLETT, 1805–76.

Part of Hora novissima.

BRIEF life is here our portion,
  Brief sorrow, short-lived care;
The life that knows no ending,
  The tearless life, is there.

2 For thee, O dear, dear country,
  Mine eyes their vigils keep;
For very love, beholding
  Thy happy name, they weep.

5 Thou hast no shore, fair ocean!
  Thou hast no time, bright day!
Dear fountain of refreshment
  To pilgrims far away!

6 Strive, man, to win that glory;
  Toil, man, to gain that light;
Send hope before to grasp it,
  Till hope be lost in sight.

Bernard of Cluny, 12th cent. Tr. J. M. Neale.

3 There grief is turned to pleasure,
  Such pleasure as below
No human voice can utter,
  No human heart can know.

4 And now we fight the battle,
  But then shall wear the crown
Of full and everlasting
  And passionless renown.

PART II

7 The morning shall awaken,
  The shadows shall decay,
And each true-hearted servant
  Shall shine as doth the day.

8. Then all the halls of Sion
  For ay shall be complete,
And, in the Land of Beauty,
  All things of beauty meet.

*From *Songs of Praise*, No. 459 (2nd tune). Published by Oxford University Press, London. Used by permission of the publisher.

pictured the need for Christians everywhere to set their eyes on things eternal and to labor to make a world that is a "Land of Beauty" where "All things of beauty meet."

Henry John Gauntlett, who composed this musical setting, was an important organist in England during the last century. His greatest contribution was to raise the standard of Gregorian musical arrangements.

✛

O WHAT THEIR JOY AND THEIR GLORY MUST BE

PIERRE ABÉLARD, the author of the words to this hymn, was born in 1079. No more romantically colorful or stormy career exists among hymn writers

O What Their Joy and Their Glory Must Be*

10 10. 10 10

O QUANTA QUALIA

Ad. 1854, from *Méthode du Plain Chant*, 1808;
har. by JOHN B. DYKES, 1868

With dignity

1 O what their joy and their glo - ry must be, Those end - less
2 Tru - ly Je - ru - sa - lem name we that shore, Vi - sion of

Sab - baths the bless - ed ones see; Crown for the val - iant, to
peace that brings joy ev - er - more; Wish and ful - fil - ment can

wea - ry ones rest: God shall be all, and in all ev - er blest.
sev - er'd be ne'er, Nor the thing prayed for come short of the prayer.

3 There, where no troubles distraction can bring,
We the sweet anthems of Sion shall sing;
While for thy grace, Lord, their voices of praise
Thy blessèd people eternally raise.

4 Now, in the meanwhile, with hearts raised on high,
We for that country must yearn and must sigh,
Seeking Jerusalem, dear native land,
Through our long exile on Babylon's strand.

5 Low before him with our praises we fall,
Of whom, and in whom, and through whom are all;
Of whom, the Father; and in whom, the Son;
Through whom, the Spirit, with them ever One. Amen.

A-men.

PETER ABELARD, c. 1129;
Tr. JOHN MASON NEALE, 1854, *alt.*

of Christendom than that of Abélard. Born of a noble French family, he was a brilliant though controversial theological thinker, philosopher, and writer. His enemies were many; he was driven from pillar to post, and sad indeed was his much criticized marriage with Héloïse—a romance that became immortalized in literature.

Abélard's life was set against waving banners and flashing arms of the crusades. More especially, his mind rebelled at the dead uniformity of medieval theology and he was unafraid to speak out against the scholars in debate.

Abélard wrote more than a hundred poems and hymns. "O What Their Joy and Their Glory Must Be" is the most celebrated and the one most certain to have come from his pen. It was written for use at evening prayer in the abbey in which Héloïse spent the last years of her life as abbess. The hymn reflects the sadness of their life and thought—for the two had voluntarily committed themselves to monastic life—and at the same time it expresses a longing for peace in the life to come. The words are a cry that tell the longing of all mankind: rest for the weary, "vision of peace" that shall bring "joy evermore," answered prayer, freedom from troubles. The fourth verse is a paean of praise to God the Father, Son, and Holy Spirit.

This is not a sad hymn in spite of the somberness of its words, for a sweep of exaltation characterizes the plain-chant melody. Its music swells heavenward in ascending chords and each stanza ends on tones of quiet, confident peace.

CONTENTS

PART III SECTION 5

THE FLOWERING OF CHRISTIAN ART: THE RENAISSANCE

--------------------✠--------------------

All things were made by him; and without him was not any thing made that was made.—JOHN 1:3

--------------------✠--------------------

PICTURES: PAGE

Interpretation: The Tribute Money—*Mosaccio* 335
Picture: The Tribute Money—*Masaccio* 336
Interpretation: The Crucifixion—*Grünewald* 337
Picture: The Crucifixion—*Grünewald* 339
Interpretation: Christ Consigning the Keys to St. Peter—*Raphael* 340
Picture: Christ Consigning the Keys to St. Peter—*Raphael* 341

POETRY:

For Inspiration—*Michelangelo* 342
Consider Well—*More* 342
The Life of the Blessed—*Ponce de León* 343
Orazione—*de' Medici* 343
Tomorrow—*de Vega* 344
Whate'er God Will—*Albrecht of Brandenburg* 344
Trust—*Thomas à Kempis* 345

STORIES:

Michelangelo Buonarroti—*Clement* 345
Luca Della Robbia's Singing Gallery—*Smith* 348
The Bell Founder's Window—*Smith* 350

MUSIC:

Interpretation: O Love, How Deep—*Latin Hymn Poem* 352
Music: O Love, How Deep—*"The Agincourt Song"* 353
Interpretation: Therefore We, Before Him Bending—*St. Thomas
     Aquinas* 352
Music: Therefore We, Before Him Bending—*Palestrina* 354

THE TRIBUTE MONEY
Masaccio

HIGH upon scaffolding which covered the walls of the tiny Brancacci Chapel in the Church of the Carmine in Florence, Italy, a young man scarcely twenty years old labored quite unnoticed. Once he had secured permission from his parish priest to paint frescoes on the walls of this dark chapel, Masaccio, whose name means "The Untidy One," was quite content to be ignored, just as long as he was allowed to paint what he wanted in his own way.

During the brief span of his life in the early part of the fifteenth century (1401-1428), Masaccio created a style and manner of painting that revolutionized art and set it in a new and vital direction. Young Masaccio was quite aware of this importance to his painting. He had sought permission to decorate the walls of this little chapel because burning within him was some strange compulsion, a consuming fire that would not be extinguished. He was an artistic genius. Brought up in the traditions of the Church, it was natural that Masaccio should choose Biblical subjects for his frescoes. For the largest and most impressive of these, he decided to portray the story of the tribute money, or the payment of taxes, as told in Matthew 14:24-27, when Jesus instructed Peter to go to a pond and take from the mouth of a fish the gold coin with which to pay the imperial tax. Masaccio was to be one of the very few artists to choose this Bible story as the subject for a painting.

The young artist divided his canvas into three scenes so that he could tell the complete story as it is set down in the Bible. The central group, the most important, shows the disciples and the Roman tax collector (with his back to us) grouped around Jesus in what is a moment of dignified, solemn decision. We know that this is no mere incident because of the extremely serious expressions upon the faces of all present. Nearly every eye is focused upon Jesus, who is giving directions to Peter, indicating the pond at the left. There is no hesitation, no doubt but that these men believe that the One whom they follow knows exactly how to meet the situation, and forthwith, Peter is off to do His bidding.

We see Peter kneeling beside the water over at the extreme left, in the shadows, taking the coin from the fish's mouth. At the right, placed in full light to show the importance of the scene, Peter is pressing the coin into the tax collector's hand with a firm and final gesture.

Thus the New Testament story is told. But to discover what is remarkable about the manner in which it is told, it is necessary to put one's self into fifteenth-century Italy.

In the early part of that century, up to the time of Masaccio, there had been many fine artists who were good colorists. But theirs was a limited technique bound by a two-dimensional way of looking at things, with little, if any,

THE TRIBUTE MONEY—*MASACCIO*

feeling for space. Too, they held to Gothic traditions, relying heavily on symbols, haloes and other devices which seem to us to be stiff and mannered. In contrast, here is something that is alive, that has the feeling of real people who are set in an actual landscape that contains mountains, trees, depth of space. Furthermore, there is a wonderfully rounded composition of the central group. The artist has arranged his people to form a perfect circle, but it is one from which the eye is carried off to the left where Peter is about to go to find the coin.

One more marvelous effect puts this and other works by Masaccio in a class by themselves—the way light and shadow are used. This technique is called *chiaroscuro*. Here, for the first time, an artist sensed how to illuminate his figures, highlighting his landscape and buildings so that the light fell in exactly the right places and darkness or shadow was contrasted with light to gain the best possible effect. Masaccio's use of chiaroscuro has been the marvel of artists for centuries.

Little is known of Masaccio as a person. Incidentally, Thomas, the one to the extreme right of the tax collector, is traditionally considered to be a self-portrait of Masaccio. He lived only twenty-eight years and actually left only a handful of works compared to the wealth of paintings produced by other great-name artists. Those which exist today are in a damaged state, as can be seen in "The Tribute Money."

Young Masaccio was a lonely figure who labored unnoticed and unappreciated in his day. After his death someone, we know not who, found his way down the aisle of the little Church of the Carmine to the small, poorly lit Brancacci Chapel at the right of the altar and saw the amazing frescoes with figures that seemed to live and breathe. The wonder of them spread around Florence and all of Italy so that for a hundred years great artists like Botticelli, Leonardo da Vinci, Raphael, and the great Michelangelo himself, sat long and pondered over them, trying to learn the secret of Masaccio's techniques—a secret they longed to possess!

✠

THE CRUCIFIXION

Matthias Grünewald

"THE Crucifixion" by Grünewald (*ca.* 1465-1528) forms one section of an altarpiece that is universally regarded as one of the most important works in the arts of the Church—indeed in the entire field of painting. Known as the Isenheim Altarpiece, this huge tabernacle, which was originally made for the Antoine Convent at Isenheim, Alsace, now rests in the Schongauer Museum at Colmar, Germany.

When Grünewald was commissioned to execute this altarpiece, he was instructed to design it to fit the needs of the worship of the Church. He worked out the problem by constructing a great tabernacle, eight feet high, consisting of hinged panels which fold in or open out on each other. Each combination of panels may be displayed according to the usage required by the Church. When all the panels are closed, the painting of the Crucifixion is revealed. These two panels, opened once, show a series of paintings depicting the Annunciation, Nativity, and Resurrection. The secondary panels may be opened out still further to reveal carved or sculptured representations from the lives of St. Anthony, St. Augustine, and St. Jerome.

For general use the Crucifixion scene was generally displayed. On special feast days of the Church, the second series of paintings was shown. The inner panels were opened when the Church calendar indicated St. Anthony's feast days. Because the Antoine monastery was also a hospital that "specialized"—as we today would put it—in the treatment of skin diseases, the innermost panels, which show scenes from the life of St. Anthony, portray vividly people in the throes of leprosy and other skin maladies.

The emphasis on suffering shown in the Crucifixion panels is explained in part by this knowledge that the altarpiece was designed for those who, perhaps more than most persons, were able to enter into the physical sufferings of another.

The tragedy of suffering—stark physical agony—is the overwhelming emotion that Grünewald has emphasized in "The Crucifixion." The dead Christ hangs upon a crude wooden cross. His body is fixed in the final writhings of death, His figure contorted, His hands and feet convulsed. The cross is set against an ominous, unrelieved sky, and a stark wasteland of earth. The light that illumines the figure of Christ and those around the cross, seems to come from spiritual other-worldly sources. The somberness of the landscape is broken only by this light and by the harsh, discordant colors of the red, purplish-orange, and crimson garments.

At the left, Mary, the Mother of Jesus, swoons in the arms of John, the Beloved Disciple. She is unable to look upon her Son's death agony any longer. Mary Magdalene, her jar of precious ointments nearby, is kneeling. Her every gesture is agonizing. To the right stands John the Baptist, pointing to Christ. Behind him are the barely discernible words, "He must grow as I increase." They have been painted into a triangular space formed by the position of John's arm. In his other arm, John holds the Word of God open to the place where this statement is found. A lamb, symbolizing the Lamb of God, stands at John's feet. A staff, which ends in a cross and is one of the symbols of John the Baptist, is held in an upright position by the lamb. Nearby is a chalice, a symbol of Christ's Passion.

It is interesting to note how Grünewald has used the hands of the figures in this painting to emphasize the tortured emotions of the people. There is the death convulsion of Christ's hands, the clasped hands of grief of the two Marys, the compassionate, tender hands of John, the Beloved Disciple, and the insistent pointing finger of John the Baptist's hand.

THE CRUCIFIXION—*GRÜNEWALD*

In "The Crucifixion" Grünewald seems to have gathered up all of the suffering of mankind, heaping it upon Christ and the little group around Him.

Little is known of the life of this artist and few are the paintings which he left behind him, but his reputation as a great master of art would have been established by the Isenheim Altarpiece had that been his only work.

✛

CHRIST CONSIGNING THE KEYS TO ST. PETER
Raphael

A VISITOR to the Vatican today will discover, in the long gallery known as the *Galleria degli Arazzi,* a set of ten tapestries illustrating the Acts of the Apostles. These tapestries, designed by Raphael, are among the art treasures of the Vatican. The cartoons or original drawings, even more precious than the tapestries, are in the South Kensington Museum of London.

Raphael was commissioned in 1514 to design cartoons for ten tapestries which were to hang in the Sistine Chapel. The hangings were to serve a practical as well as an artistic purpose, for the great basilica of St. Peter's was still unfinished and without a roof. This meant that the sanctuary could be used only in good weather. When the weather was poor, ceremonies took place in the Sistine Chapel. The tapestries were needed to keep out drafts. Because the marvelous frescoes by Michelangelo covered the ceiling and the upper portions of the walls of the Sistine Chapel, any other work of art placed near them had to be of high standard. Raphael was considered capable of designing the tapestries which were to hang on the lower portions of these walls.

Before the tapestries could be woven, Raphael had to design cartoons or drawings, exactly the size and coloring which the finished tapestries were to be. The cartoons themselves are wonders of art, they are so beautifully drawn and delicately colored. The weavers were unable to dye threads to match these lovely colors, and so the tapestries are far richer and more brilliant in tone. Also, the use of gold and silver threads give the tapestries quite a different effect than the cartoons. Consequently, the cartoons, rather than the tapestries, are considered the greater works of art.

As soon as Raphael completed a cartoon, he sent it to the weavers. The weaving took between three and four years, and in December, 1519, seven of the huge tapestries were hung in the Sistine Chapel. The entire series of ten was up by 1520—an amazing feat, considering the magnitude of the task.

Raphael chose to delineate ten scenes which he called "Acts of the Apostles." More accurately, they depict events in the lives of Peter and Paul.

In "Christ Consigning the Keys to St. Peter," Christ stands to the right, pointing to a flock of sheep with one hand while with the other He emphasizes His words (Matt. 16:13-20). Raphael's introduction of the sheep refers

CHRIST CONSIGNING THE KEYS TO ST. PETER—*RAPHAEL*

Courtesy Fratelli Alinari and Art Reference Bureau, Ancram, N. Y.

to the story in John 21:15 where Jesus instructs Simon Peter, "Feed my lambs." The artist combines two stories of Jesus and Peter in this one tapestry. The chief scene, however, refers to the sixteenth chapter of Matthew, when, in the presence of the other disciples, Jesus honors Peter's confession, "Thou art the Christ, the Son of the Living God," by giving him the keys to the kingdom. The astonishment of the disciples is plain to see. Peter is serious, intent; Andrew and John, just behind him, are beautifully portrayed, and the figure and features of Jesus are of great dignity and spiritual beauty.

The history and adventures of these tapestries and cartoons read like a storybook. For many years some of them were hidden in far-off lands, having been carried away by conquerors. They were cut up, separated, and ravaged. Only comparatively recently have they been assembled and restored.

✠

FOR INSPIRATION

The Prayers I make will then be sweet indeed,
    If Thou the spirit give by which I pray;
    My unassisted heart is barren clay,
Which of its native self can nothing feed;
Of good and pious works Thou art the seed
    Which quickens where Thou say'st it may;
    Unless Thou show us then Thine own true way,
No man can find it! Father, Thou must lead!
Do Thou, then, breathe those thoughts into my mind
    By which such virtue may in me be bred
    That in Thy holy footsteps I may tread;
The fetters of my tongue do Thou unbind,
    That I may have the power to sing of Thee
    And sound Thy praises everlastingly.
        —*Michelangelo Buonarroti (1475-1564);*
        translated by William Wordsworth (1770-1850)

CONSIDER WELL

Consider well that both by night and day
While we busily provide and care
For our disport, our revel and our play,
For pleasant melody and dainty fare,
Death stealeth on full slily; unaware
He lieth at hand and shall us all surprise,
We wot not when nor where nor in what wise.

When fierce temptations threat thy soul with loss
Think on His Passion and the bitter pain,
Think on the mortal anguish of the Cross,
Think on Christ's blood let out at every vein,

Think of His precious heart all rent in twain;
For thy redemption think all this was wrought,
Nor be that lost which He so dearly bought.
                    —*Sir Thomas More* (*1478-1535*)

THE LIFE OF THE BLESSED

Region of life and light!
Land of the good whose earthly toils are o'er!
    Nor frost nor heat may blight
    Thy vernal beauty, fertile shore
Yielding thy blessed fruits for evermore!

    Might but a little part,
A wandering breath, of that high melody
    Descend into my heart,
    And change it till it be
Transformed and swallowed up, O Love! in thee:

    Ah! then my soul should know,
Beloved! where thou liest at noon of day;
    And from this place of woe
    Released, should take its way
To mingle with thy flock, and never stray.
                    —*Luis Ponce de León* (*1460?-1521*)

ORAZIONE

One general song of praise arise
To him whose goodness ceaseless flows;
Who dwells enthroned beyond the skies,
And life and breath on all bestows!
    Great Source of intellect, his ear,
    Benign receives our vows sincere
Rise then, my active powers, your task fulfill,
And give to him your praise, responsive to my will!

    Eternal Spirit, whose command
    Light, life, and being gave to all,
    Oh, hear the creature of thy hand,
    Man, constant on thy goodness call!
    By fire, by water, air, and earth,
    That soul to thee that owes its birth—
By these he supplicates thy blest repose:
Absent from thee, no rest his wandering spirit knows!
            —*Verses selected from "Orazione" by Lorenzo*
                de' Medici (*1449-1492*), *translated by*
                William Roscoe (*1753-1831*)

TOMORROW

Lord, what am I, that, with unceasing care,
Thou didst seek after me, that thou didst wait,
Wet with unhealthy dews, before my gate,
And pass the gloomy nights of winter there?
O strange delusion, that I did not greet
Thy blest approach, and oh, to heaven how lost,
If my ingratitude's unkindly frost
Has chilled the bleeding wounds upon thy feet,
How oft my guardian angel gently cried,
"Soul, from thy casement look and thou shalt see
How he persists to knock and wait for thee!"
And oh! how often to that voice of sorrow,
"Tomorrow we will open," I replied,
And when the morrow came I answered still, "Tomorrow."*
                                       —*Lope de Vega (1562-1635)*

WHATE'ER GOD WILL

(Composed while suffering in exile, 1566)

Whate'er God will, let that be done;
    His will is ever wisest:
His grace will all thy hope outrun,
    Who to that faith arisest.
        The gracious Lord
        Will help afford;
    He chastens with forbearing:
        Who God believes
        And to him cleaves,
    Shall not be left despairing.

My God is my sure confidence,
    My light and my existence;
His counsel is beyond my sense
    But stirs no weak resistance.
        His word declares
        The very hairs
    Upon my head are numbered.
        His mercy large
        Holds me in charge,
    With care that never slumbered.
                       —*Albrecht of Brandenburg; translated
                       by N. L. Frothingham in 1869*

---

* Translated from the Spanish by Henry Wadsworth Longfellow.

TRUST

Always place in God thy trust,
Will and do what's right and true;
Let thy soul be brave and just;
Show thy Lord a humble mind;
Thou shalt thus his favor find;
Love but few and simple things;
Simple life much comfort brings.*

—*Thomas à Kempis*

✠

MICHELANGELO BUONARROTI
Clara Erskine Clement

THIS great artist was born in the castle of Caprese, in 1475. His father, who was of a noble Florentine family, was then governor of Caprese and Chiusu. When the Buonarroti family returned to Florence, the little Michelangelo was left with his nurse at Settignano, where his father had an estate. The home of the nurse was there, and for many years pictures were shown upon the walls of her house which her little charge had drawn as soon as he could use his hands.

When Michelangelo was taken to Florence and placed in school, he became the friend of Francesco Granacci, who was of noble family like himself, and a pupil of the artist Ghirlandajo, one of the best masters in Florence. Already, Michelangelo was unhappy because his father did not wish him to be an artist. At length, however, he became a pupil of Ghirlandajo, and that at a time when the master was engaged on the great work of decorating the choir of the church of Santa Maria Novella, at Florence. Thus Michelangelo came immediately into the midst of wonderful things, and he was soon remarked for his complete devotion to the work about him. One day when the workmen were at dinner, the boy made a drawing of the scaffolding and all belonging to it, with the painters at work on it. When Ghirlandajo saw this he exclaimed: "He understands more than I myself."

It was not long before he corrected the drawing of the plates which his master gave his pupils to copy; then the plates were refused to him. Lorenzo de' Medici soon gave permission to both Michelangelo and Francesco Granacci to study in the gardens of San Marco. Ghirlandajo, we may well suppose, was only glad to be free from a pupil who already knew so much.

Duke Lorenzo had placed many splendid works of art in the gardens of San Marco, and pictures and cartoons were hung in buildings there, so that young men could study them. Many young sculptors worked there, and one

* *In Domino Semper Spera* (15th century), translated by D. Donahoe.

Bertoldo, an old man, was their teacher. Michelangelo now began to model, and his first work was the mask of a faun, which he copied so well as to attract the attention of Lorenzo. He praised Michelangelo, but said: "You have made your faun so old, and yet you have left him all his teeth; you should have known that at such an advanced age there are generally some wanting." When he came again to the gardens, he found a gap in the teeth of the faun so well done that he was delighted with it.

Soon the Duke sent for the father of Michelangelo, and obtained his full consent that the boy should be an artist. The young sculptor was then taken into the palace, where he was treated with great kindness by Lorenzo, and sat at his table, where he met all the remarkable men of the day, and listened to such conversation as is most profitable to a boy. It was the rule that whoever came first to the table should sit next to the Duke, and Michelangelo often had that place.

But all this happy life was sadly ended by the death of Lorenzo de' Medici, and Michelangelo left the palace and used a room in his father's house for his work-shop. After a time, Piero de' Medici induced him to return to the palace; but the young man was ill at ease there, and soon went to Venice. Here he met a sculptor of Bologna, who induced him to visit that city; but the commissions he received so excited the jealousy of other artists in Bologna that he returned again to Florence. He was now twenty years old, and the next work of his which attracted attention was a "Sleeping Cupid," which so resembled an antique statue that it was sold in Rome for a very old work; two hundred ducats were paid for it, though Michelangelo received but thirty ducats. By some means the knowledge of this fraud came to Michelangelo, and he explained that he had known nothing of it, but had also been deceived himself; the result of all this was that he went to Rome, and was received into the house of the nobleman who had bought the "Cupid."

He remained in Rome about three years, during which time he excuted the "Drunken Bacchus," now in the Uffizi Gallery at Florence, and "La Pietà" (or the Virgin Mary seated, holding the dead body of Jesus across her lap), a fine piece of sculpture, now in the Basilica of St. Peter's at Rome.

When Michelangelo returned to Florence he executed some paintings and sculptures, but was soon employed on his "David," one of his greatest works. It was completed and put in its place in 1504, and there it remained more than two centuries—next the gate of the Palazzo Vecchio. A few years ago it was feared that the beautiful statue would crumble in pieces if longer exposed to the weather, and it was removed to a place where it now stands, safe from sun and rain.

When the "David" was completed, Michelangelo was not quite thirty years old, but his fame as a great artist was firmly established. Through all his long life—for he lived eighty-nine years—he was constantly and industriously engaged in the production of important works.

Michelangelo was not merely a great painter, a great sculptor, or a great architect—he was all of these. His most famous painting was that of the "Last Judgment" in the Sistine Chapel of the Vatican. His most famous sculptures were the "David," "La Pietà," the "Tomb of Pope Julius II," "Moses," "The Dying Youth," and the famous statues of "Day" and "Night"; and his greatest architectural work is the cupola of St. Peter's Church. But these are, in truth, a small part of all he did. He served under nine popes, and during his life thirteen men occupied the papal chair. There were great political changes also during this time, and the whole impression of his life is a serious, sad one. He seems to have had very little joy or brightness, and yet he was tender and thoughtful for all whom he loved. He was an old man before he met Vittoria Colonna, who was a very wonderful woman, and much beloved by Michelangelo. He wrote poems to her, which are full of affection and delicate friendship; for to all the other gifts which this great man possessed was added that of poetry, which he used so nobly and purely. The Italians associate the name of Michelangelo Buonarroti with those of Dante Alighieri and the painter Raphael, and speak of these three as the greatest men of their country in what are called modern days.

Michelangelo died at Rome in 1564. He desired to be buried in Florence, but it was feared that his removal there would be opposed. His body was therefore taken through the gate of the city as merchandise; when it reached Florence it was borne to the church of San Piero Maggiore. The funeral was at evening; the coffin, placed on a bier, was borne by the younger artists, while the older ones carried torches; and thus it reached Santa Croce, its final resting-place—the same church in which the poet Dante was buried.

A few months later magnificent services were held in his memory in the church of San Lorenzo, where are his fine statues of "Day" and "Night," made for the Medici chapel of this edifice. A monument was erected to him in Santa Croce, and his statue is in the court of the Uffizi. The house in which he lived, and which is still visited by those who honor his memory, contains many very interesting personal mementos of this great man and of the noble spirit in which all his works were done.

In 1875 a grand festival was made to celebrate the four hundredth anniversary of his birth. The ceremonies on this occasion were very impressive, and at that time some documents relating to his life, which had never before been opened, were given over by command of the king into the hands of suitable persons, to be examined. Mr. Heath Wilson, an English artist residing in Florence, wrote a new *Life of Michelangelo*; and the last time that king Victor Emmanuel wrote his own name before his death, it was on the paper which conferred upon Mr. Wilson the order of the *Corona d' Italia,* in recognition of his services in writing this book.*

* From *Stories of Art and Artists* by Clara Erskine Clement, pp. 58-66.

LUCA DELLA ROBBIA'S SINGING GALLERY

Jean Louise Smith

THE November light was fading fast and it was only by looking a second time that one could see a small boy in the corner of the studio, working close to the window, eager to catch the last rays of daylight.

"Come, my Luca, it is late and supper is ready," called his mother.

"Just another minute, Mother. It will soon be dark, and it is not so easy to work by candlelight."

Although Luca was only twelve years old, he was making a beautiful metal bowl, for as a goldsmith's apprentice he was already fashioning many lovely things in metal. He had not only learned to work in gold, but his skillful chisel could make a block of marble become a beautiful portrayal of a boy. But now, he was eager to finish the bowl so that he might work on the marble bust that he had begun some time earlier.

At the supper table Luca talked with his parents about the cathedral which was the pride of his native city, Florence, in Italy.

"Now that Brunelleschi has found a way to make a dome for the cathedral, we shall soon see many artists at work painting and sculpturing works of art to go inside. This House of God must be the most beautiful in all Italy!" Luca's father said.

"There will be so much to do," said Luca. "How I wish I were old enough to help!"

"Perhaps you can, if you keep up your hard work and study," said his mother.

That night after Luca had helped his mother with the dishes, he lit a candle and carried it over to the corner of the little studio where he had been working earlier in the day. The soft rays of candlelight fell on the block of marble which was soon to become a boy's head—a boy who would portray the laughing, happy mood of the young artist who was its creator. On and on Luca worked, and as it grew cold, he tried to warm himself by putting his feet into a basket of wood shavings. After a time the candle burned too low for further work and finally, sputtering, it went out. With a sigh Luca laid down his chisel and went to his room to go to bed. The moon shone brightly and he went to the window where he stood looking out over the city. Just below him the great dome of the cathedral loomed up.

"Perhaps I *shall* be able to help make our beloved cathedral one of the most magnificent in all Italy," he thought.

As he fell asleep, the words of the psalm that he had learned to sing as a very small boy in the cathedral choir kept going through his mind: "Praise ye the Lord. Praise God in his sanctuary. . . ."

Eighteen years later, Luca della Robbia, a talented young man, was working in the same studio. His chisel had been busy all the years, but now, instead of a small block of marble, he was working with a very large slab, and before him was a huge cartoon, or life-size sketch of a frieze of children, singing, dancing, and playing musical instruments. Luca had been commissioned to make a marble choir gallery or *cantoria* for the great cathedral of Florence, Italy. He had chosen for his theme the psalm which he had learned to sing in the choir as a boy, and on the marble he had decided to inscribe in Latin its words:

> Praise ye the Lord.
> Praise God in his sanctuary:
> Praise him in the firmament of his power.
> Praise him for his mighty acts;
> Praise him according to his excellent greatness.
> Praise him with the sound of the trumpet;
> Praise him with the psaltery and harp.
> Praise him with the timbrel and dance:
> Praise him with stringed instruments and organs.
> Praise him upon the loud cymbals:
> Praise him upon the high sounding cymbals.
> Let everything that hath breath praise the Lord.
> Praise ye the Lord.

For seven long years Luca worked at the marble, and under his chisel the *cantoria* came to life as the happy children on it took form. There were two rows of four panels in front. Each end consisted of a single panel. One of the two end panels pictured a group of seven boys singing from a large music book. The leader was beating time with his hand and another child kept time with his foot. All seven children were singing with enthusiasm, just as Luca had sung when he was a boy. The second end panel was a joyous, happy scene, with the singing boys' arms resting on each other's shoulders as they all looked to read from the same scroll. Luca inscribed the word "Alleluia"—"Praise ye the Lord"—on these two end panels.

Along the length of the gallery or *cantoria*, Luca followed the order of the Psalm which he was illustrating. The panels included: the trumpeters, the players on the psaltery, players on the cithara, and the drummers. In the bottom row, he pictured the choral dancers, players on the organ and harp, the tambourine players, and the cymbal players. They were all happy, lively children, absorbed in singing their praises. Their full cheeks are puffed as they play their musical instruments and their throat muscles are plainly seen.

History does not tell of the day when Luca della Robbia's Singing Gallery was placed high along the wall of the cathedral. By only a slight twist of the imagination, one can fancy the scene—the great nave filled with worshipers who, as the choir sang from the *cantoria*, must have admired the happy singing children carved along the sides of the gallery. Remembering that those were the days when all artists served the Church and all Florentines loved and appreciated art, we may be sure of their enthusiasm for this new work of art in the Church.

Luca della Robbia's Singing Gallery was only one of hundreds of fine sculptured pieces that he, his nephew, and his nephew's son did for the Church. From this family workshop, notable and unique in the Renaissance period, charming glazed terra-cotta bambinos, nativity scenes, and madonnas found their way into the churches of Italy. Andrea and Giovanni della Robbia, inspired by their uncle Luca, carried on his work long after he died. But even their best could not quite measure up to Luca's "frozen music," for Luca della Robbia's dedication of artistic talent to his Church was so devout, so sincere, that it has always said, "Praise ye the Lord. Praise God in his sanctuary!"*

✛

THE BELL FOUNDER'S WINDOW
Jean Louise Smith

PETER watched the thick, gleaming red liquid glass as it boiled vigorously. He poked up the fire under the iron pot so that the flame burned more steadily. The master glazier paused thoughtfully when he came to the pot Peter was watching.

"Keep the fire steady, my boy. This glass is to be for the most beautiful colored window that has yet gone into York Cathedral."

"Who is giving the window this time?" asked Peter.

"Do you not know? It is the Lord Mayor himself, Richard Tunnoc," replied the master glazier.

"Why, he is also head of the Bell Founder's Guild that cast all the beautiful-sounding bells that ring the hour and call us to worship. This is indeed an important window," said Peter. "You can depend on me, sir, to keep the fire at an even temperature."

Peter fell to thinking, as he had often done of late, about how he wished he had gone into the bell foundry as an apprentice instead of the stained-glass studio. Peter was a thoughtful boy and took his church seriously. He was proud of the great cathedral in the city of York, England, where he had always lived. He sang in the boys' choir and was never happier than when he was singing some beautiful chant.

"Music can help people worship," Peter mused, as he watched the rich red molten glass catch the rays of the sun as it streamed through a nearby window. "Music and bells—they truly ring praises to God. I wish I had had a part in casting the bells of York. Every day, every hour, their beautiful music reminds people of God."

Just then the tester interrupted Peter's thoughts by dipping his long lead pipe into the pot to dip out a bit of glass. Then he blew into the pipe and the glass formed a shimmering red bubble.

* Adapted from *Great Art and Children's Worship* by Jean Louise Smith, pp. 50-52. Copyright 1948 by Stone & Pierce. Used by permission of Abingdon Press.

"It's just right. Ah, it will be like the richest of rubies, this glass. I never saw the master blend his dyes more carefully. This will be the finest window we have yet made," said the tester.

When all the various colored glass had been blown and cut into sheets, the master glazier carefully supervised the cutting. The huge pattern, exactly the size that the window was to be, had been cut up, and Peter helped when he was not tending the fires. Peter helped the cutter lay the pattern on the glass.

"I have never seen it more lovely," sighed Peter.

"Look how the sun falls on the tiny bumps and different thicknesses of glass and makes it like precious jewels," said the cutter. "I wonder what story this window will tell."

"They say it will tell us the story of the bells of York," said Peter. "I can hardly wait till it is finished."

Several days later, when all the parts to the window were cut out, every workman and apprentice in the studio gathered to watch the master glazier and his chief assistant put the window together. The huge pattern or plan of the window hung beside the rack where they worked. It was like watching someone put together a picture puzzle, only these glass pieces were held by soft lead. Often the master glazier paused, holding up a bit of glass to the light to admire its rich color and sparkle.

"Look, it does tell the story of the bells," cried Peter eagerly. "See, there in the lower part of the center panel Richard Tunnoc is presenting the archbishop with a model of the window. The side panels show a bell being cast and the turning of a bell in a lathe. And the border of the window has bells of all sizes and shapes." The words tumbled out eagerly as Peter shared his enthusiasm with his friend the cutter.

The Sunday finally came when the "Bell Founder's Window" was in its place in the north aisle of York Cathedral. There was to be a special service of dedication of the window, and Peter was happy that his choir was chosen to sing. He had not seen the window in the cathedral, as yet, for no one was allowed to see it until the service.

The deep throbbing tones of the bells called the people of York to worship, and it seemed as though the whole city answered their call and filled the great cathedral. Peter, from his place in the choir processional, tried to look sideways without turning his head as he passed the new window, but it was not until he was seated in the choir that he had a good look at it. The light that shone through it made the colors glow and sparkle even more beautifully than they had in the pot.

"It is truly a window worthy of the house of God," the archbishop was saying, and Peter believed it, humbly remembering the small part he had had in making it.

"The men who made the bells gladly gave their time and talents, and now all who have made this beautiful window have served God by their labor," continued the archbishop. "Can praise to God be more perfectly expressed than through music of sound and beauty of light and color, as the bells of York and this stained-glass window signify?"

As if to answer the archbishop's question, the people, choir, and clergy repeated together the verse, "And let the beauty of the Lord our God be upon us: and establish thou the work of our hands upon us; yea, the work of our hands, establish thou it."

Peter never forgot those words, and he never again regretted his work in the stained-glass studio.*

✠

O LOVE, HOW DEEP

THE fifteenth-century melody of this hymn has the mark of greatness on it. Its magnificent chords stir the heart and mind to reach toward God in praise. Heard on a fine organ and sung in unison by a congregation that is appreciative of its glory, this hymn possesses unmatched power. No finer tune comes from the Renaissance than "The Agincourt Song," and it deserves more widespread use today. It should be sung in unison, in moderate and steady time, and, except for the third stanza which may be rendered more quietly, a full-voiced majesty should characterize its interpretation.

Historically, the melody is based on a fifteenth-century English melody, probably written to commemorate the success of the British in Normandy. It was very quickly taken over by hymnology when it was discovered that the words of a Latin hymn poem fitted the tune so perfectly. Note how well the words, "O Love, how deep, how broad, how high," fit the tremendous opening chords. Then the melody curves with, "How passing thought and fantasy." The soul soars with words and music as one sings: "That God, the Son of God should take," and then comes a climax in thought and music: "Our mortal form for mortal's sake!" This kind of sequence applies to each verse in the same orderly fashion of thought and music. The hymn is also remarkable for its fine balance of pure praise to God and the personal devotional approach to God. The worshiper is led by reaching out to God to apply God's love and guidance to his own individual daily life.

✠

THEREFORE WE, BEFORE HIM BENDING

NO COLLECTION of hymns from the heritage of the music of the Roman Catholic Church would be complete without the names of St. Thomas Aquinas and Giovanni da Palestrina. "Therefore We, Before Him Bending," combines these two great names of church history in a glorious historical communion hymn that is sung by all Christians, regardless of creed.

* From *Great Art and Children's Worship* by Jean Louise Smith, pp. 56-58. Copyright 1948 by Stone & Pierce. Used by permission of Abingdon Press.

O Love, How Deep*

15th century
Trans. by Benjamin Webb (1820–1885)   L. M.

DEO GRACIAS
"The Agincourt Song," 1415

In unison; majestically

1. O Love, how deep, how broad, how high!
2. For us bap - tized, for us He bore
3. For us to wick - ed men be - trayed,
4. For us He rose from death a - gain,

How pass - ing thought and fan - ta - sy,
His ho - ly fast, and hun - gered sore;
Scourged, mocked, in crown of thorns ar - rayed;
For us He went on high to reign;

That God, the Son of God, should take
For us temp - ta - tions sharp He knew;
For us He bore the cross - 's death;
For us He sent His Spir - it here

Our mor - tal form for mor - tals' sake!
For us the Temp - ter o - ver - threw.
For us at length gave up His breath.
To guide, to strength - en, and to cheer. A - MEN.

Therefore We, Before Him Bending*

TANTUM ERGO (No. 2).　(8 7. 8 7. 8 7.)

Very slow and solemn.

Probably by G. P. DA PALESTRINA, d. 1594.

St. Thomas Aquinas, 1227–74.　*Tr. cento.*

Tantum ergo.

THEREFORE we, before him bending,
　This great sacrament revere;
Types and shadows have their ending,
　For the newer rite is here;
Faith, our outward sense befriending,
　Makes the inward vision clear.

2. Glory let us give, and blessing
　To the Father and the Son;
Honour, might, and praise addressing,
　While eternal ages run;
Ever too his love confessing,
　Who, from both, with both is one.

*From *Songs of Praise*, No. 280. Published by Oxford University Press, London. Used by permission of the publisher.

As the basis for the words, St. Thomas Aquinas drew on an ancient sixth-century Passiontide hymn which was used at Vespers in the Roman rites and at Matins in the Sarum rites. Historians of Latin hymns agree that this hymn is one of the "greats." In simple dignity, the words speak of the timelessness of the Christian faith and its most cherished sacraments which make the "inward vision clear." The doxology of praise, with which the hymn closes, brings us close to the "eternal ages" and binds all Christians together.

St. Thomas Aquinas, that great theologian of the thirteenth century, has been discussed in connection with the painting "Thomas Aquinas Visiting St. Bonaventura," by Francisco Zurbaran (see p. 290). The words to the hymn belong to his period. Though they were sung before the sixteenth century, it was then that Palestrina gave them their grandest musical setting.

The name of Palestrina (1525-1594) stands at the summit of church music. He wrote ninety-three settings for the Mass and over three hundred motets. Palestrina reformed the elaborate and secular music of the Church when it had departed from the high standards set by Gregory the Great. Palestrina's setting for "Therefore We, Before Him Bending," is pure of tone and dignified in spirit. Someone has said that it may be compared to a needlework tapestry with a pattern of soft, rich colors, brightened by a few gold and silver threads.

CONTENTS

PART III SECTION 6

THE AGE OF ROMANTICISM

—✠—

Rejoice with me, for I have found my sheep which was lost.—LUKE 15:6

—✠—

PICTURES: PAGE
Interpretation: Santa Barbara Mission 357
Picture: Santa Barbara Mission 359
Interpretation: Cap-de-la-Madeleine 361
Picture: Cap-de-la-Madeleine 362
Interpretation: The Education of the Virgin—*De la Tour* 363
Picture: The Education of the Virgin—*De la Tour* 364

POETRY:
Praise and Prayer—*Davenant* 365
Christ Crucified—*Crashaw* 365
O Flame of Living Love—*St. John of the Cross* 366
If, Lord, Thy Love for Me Is Strong—*St. Teresa of Avila* 366
Lines Written in Her Breviary—*St. Teresa of Avila* 367
The Soul Wherein God Dwells—*Silesius (Scheffler)* 367

STORIES:
St. Francis Xavier: Apostle of the Indies—*Murray* 368
Junipero Serra: Father of the California Missions—*Hunting* 370
Pére Marquette—*Quill* 373

MUSIC:
Interpretation: My God, I Love Thee—*St. Francis Xavier (?)* 376
Music: My God, I Love Thee—*Gauntlett* 377
Interpretation: Disposer Supreme, and Judge of the Earth—*Santeuil* 376
Music: Disposer Supreme, and Judge of the Earth—*Ravenscroft's Psalter* .. 378

SANTA BARBARA MISSION

SANTA BARBARA, like San Diego and Monterey, was listed on the Spanish maps of California long before the arrival of the Franciscans. It had been so named by Sebastian Vizcíño some sixty years after its discovery by Cabrillo in 1542. From the time of the first march of the Portolá expedition, it had been warmly regarded as a likely spot for mission settlement.

The padres, however, were thirteen years in California before an opportunity for founding a mission at Santa Barbara occurred. By then, Governor Felipe de Neve was their archenemy, who openly preferred civil colonists to mission neophytes. Nevertheless, he had agreed at a meeting in San Gabriel to allow the fathers to place a mission at San Buenaventura and at Santa Barbara although his own interest was in the new presidio [military post] he planned to establish on the later site. It was agreed that all three establishments would be instituted by one expedition. The padres and their military escort started out from San Gabriel in the spring of 1782, but circumstances prevented the governor from participating in the founding of San Buenaventura.

When the governor finally met the expedition at Santa Barbara, the new presidio was quickly established, with Father Serra an eager participant in preparing the military chapel. After this had been completed, the governor replied that Santa Barbara could wait until the Franciscans were willing to follow *reglamento* [regulations] which had been ignored at San Buenavenutra. In their hearts each probably knew that the other would never give in, and since the governor had clearly won the field at Santa Barbara, there was nothing for the defeated padre to do but return to his own mission at Carmel.

It was five years before the father *presidente* received word that a mission would at last be placed at Santa Barbara. By that time, de Neve was gone and his place taken by the former governor, Pedro Fages. Some years before, Father Serra had made the long trip to Mexico in order to secure Fages' removal and it must have been a discouraging experience for the aging padre to learn that his former enemy had returned. The old father did not survive Fages' appointment for long, as he passed away on August 28, 1784, leaving the burden of mission problems to be shouldered by the able and willing Father Lasuén.

The administration of Father Fermin Lasuén has often been called the "Golden Age" of California's mission system. Although this period extended considerably beyond the eighteen years of Father Lasuén's presidency, it was his constructive energy and executive ability that set the pattern for prosperity.

Santa Barbara became an active mission on December 4, 1786, and was the first to be established by Father Lasuén. Launched on the threshold of the prosperous years, the mission enjoyed singular good fortune from the very beginning. Its first permanent church, finished in 1789, was a well-constructed adobe with a red tile roof. Within five years, the church was too small for the increasing mission population and a larger edifice was built. This structure was destroyed by an earthquake in 1812 and the existing stone church was begun shortly thereafter. Completed in 1820, it remained intact for one hundred five years. In 1925 an earthquake shook the building so severely that restoration required more than two years to complete.

The design on the facade of Santa Barbara's church, strongly resembling an ancient Latin temple, was inspired by one of the buildings in Rome of the pre-Christian era. One of the Franciscans had brought from Spain a reprint of a book on architecture originally published twenty-seven years before the birth of Christ by the Roman architect, Vitruvio Polion.

The Indians of the Santa Barbara region found the mission system much to their liking. Shortly after the beginning of the nineteenth century, the mission had more than seventeen hundred neophytes living in some two hundred fifty adobe houses. They were, like those at Ventura, a more adaptable and energetic tribe than any with whom the padres had previously dealt. With the ready assistance of their neophytes, the Franciscans soon made the mission self-sustaining. Part of their industry, a large stone reservoir, is still an active unit in the Santa Barbara city water-supply system.

In 1818, one of the padres at the mission was warned of the approach of the French pirate, Bouchard. He armed and drilled one hundred fifty of his Indian neophytes in preparation for the expected attack. With the aid of these colorful reinforcements, the presidio guard was able to impress the usually reckless Bouchard, and the pirate sailed out of the harbor without venturing to attack the settlement. This was, however, the last instance of co-operation between the Indians and the military.

News of the Mexican revolt arrived in 1822 and from that time onward the Franciscan fathers had increasing difficulties with the presidio. One of the causes of the friction had little to do with the contemporary problems but was deeply rooted in the past. For more than two hundred years those who had been born in the Americas had harbored a smoldering antagonism toward the Spanish-born. This resulted from the fact that the Spanish kings, feeling that Spaniards would be more loyal than colonials, had always sent from Spain the officers who occupied positions of authority. The Spanish-American "creoles," no matter how wealthy or influential, were kept out of the profitable positions of administration.

After the Mexican revolution, creole resentment was reflected in an active campaign against the Spanish-born, and one of the first official pronouncements to reach California was a law ordering all Spaniards under sixty to leave the province. Although the order was never carried out, it added considerably to the problems of the padres, for they were all from Spain. Their authority over the Indians was subjected to attack and soldiers were encouraged to assume the work of policing the natives. Trouble between the Indians and the military was inevitable.

In the spring of 1824, an Indian uprising against the increasing violence of the soldiers occurred at three missions, including Santa Barbara. Here the Indians broke into the almost forgotten armory and succeeded in overcoming

SANTA BARBARA MISSION

the mission guard. In the struggle, two soldiers were wounded and the Spanish reprisals were so severe that all the Indians who were not caught fled from the area. It was not until more than six months later, after a general pardon for all the Indians had been secured by the Franciscan father *presidente,* that any of the neophytes returned to the mission.

The great days enjoyed by Santa Barbara were fast coming to an end. The withering effect of secularization soon overtook the settlement, although there were two men destined to save it from the complete destruction that fell upon most of the other missions. In 1833, the Spanish exclusion policy was followed by the introduction of American-born Franciscans. The new governor, José Figueroa, brought with him ten Zucatecan friars who were placed in charge of all the missions north of San Antonio. Shortly after this, Father Narciso Durán, then *presidente* of the missions, moved his office to Santa Barbara. Here the courageous padre conducted a last struggle to save the mission system. In 1842, Francisco Garcia Diego, first bishop of the Californias, moved his headquarters to the mission at Santa Barbara. The presence of both the bishop and the father *presidente* saved this mission from complete expropriation until 1846, when both good men died within a month of each other.

At that time the ever eager Pio Pico rushed in to make a final sale. He was too late, however, for California became a territory of the United States before the buyer could occupy his newly acquired property. Santa Barbara, the queen of the missions, thus became the only mission to remain in constant occupation by the Franciscan order from the day of its founding down to the present time.

Having been in continuous occupancy, the mission closely resembles its original appearance. This is especially true of the interior, where even the rooms which house the mission's museum have been in uninterrupted use for more than one hundred sixty years. It is logical that the museum's collection, as a result of these long years of accumulation, should be the best organized and documented. Each room in the museum has a central theme. The music room, as an example, contains an extensive collection of instruments and music manuscripts with most of the latter bearing distinctive hand-lettered square notes. The music from which the Indians were taught to sing has each note of the scale lettered in a different color. Other rooms have Indian exhibits of the pre-mission era such as hollowed stone vessels and ancient tools.

At the back of the old church is the choir loft in which the Indian neophytes once sang. The beauty of the interior from this height is most impressive. The unusual decorative effects which give the impression of marble are nowhere more striking than here at Santa Barbara. Beautiful candelabra are suspended from the ceiling by ingenious "S" shaped chains. At the point where the chains are fixed into the ceiling, one sees the startling "flash of lightning" design resembling the Aztec Indian motif. It is hard to believe that its weird, arresting beauty once graced some ancient Roman wall and that its presence on the mission ceiling reflects the debt of some Franciscan padre to Polion's work of two thousand years before.*

    * From *California's Missions,* edited by Ralph B. Wright. Copyright 1950 by California Mission Trails Association, Ltd. Used by permission of the publisher.

CAP-DE-LA-MADELEINE

ONE would never take the modest stone church that stands beside the road leading from Montreal to Quebec for one of Canada's most precious artistic and religious treasures. Built from the stones of the field, the tiny church of Cap-de-la-Madeleine is only sixty feet by thirty feet. The little building dates from 1719, but its history goes to an earlier time, when the Jesuits constructed a small wooden chapel for their mission at Cap-de-la-Madeleine. It is because of this past history that one hundred thousand tourists and pilgrims make their way each year to see the little church that is now a national shrine of French Canada, for it is one of the oldest churches in Canada.

Architecturally, the present building is a variant of the Maillou plan, and as such is similar to many of the old churches of Canada. Maillou, an eighteenth-century architect, built many of Canada's churches, using a round apse and a bell tower or *clocher* surmounting a steeply pitched roof. Cap-de-la-Madeleine has these features, together with small windows and a door cut through very thick walls. Although there have been repairs and restorations since the church was completed in 1719, the building today varies but little from the original. Inside, behind the high altar, is the carved reredos brought from France by the Jesuits in 1690. The ironwork of the entrance door, the sacred altar vessels and other valuable effects are those that were given to the previous church by the court of Louis XIV.

Looking at the present Cap-de-la-Madeleine, one is transported in imagination to the seventeenth century, when the Jesuits brought Christianity to the Indians. Black-robed and wearing their broad-brimmed hats, these missionary-priests tramped through dense forests, traveled in summer by canoe and in winter by snowshoe, so that they might carry out their consuming desire to convert the savages to Christianity. A stranger contrast to the fierce, primitive Indian tribes cannot be imagined than these intelligent, well-educated men who left their books and the quiet of their monasteries for the danger and loneliness of missionary life.

When the Jesuits reached a place where they wished to work, they built a little chapel. The first Cap-de-la-Madeleine, erected in 1659, was one of these. Primitive and tiny, the structure was scarcely more than a shelter with three walls of rough-squared timbers, sharpened at one end so that they could be driven into the ground, side by side. The cracks between the boards were filled with clay. Green branches were bent to form a vaulted roof. The fourth wall was a "door" and consisted of a sheet of bark or heavy cloth which could be rolled up to expose a rude table covered with a white sheet, to serve as an altar. On it stood candles and a crucifix.

Old records indicate that the Indians came in great numbers to this little chapel to learn of the white man's God. Two years later, in 1661, the crude chapel was replaced by a stone church dedicated to St. Mary Magdalene. It too, was small, only thirty feet long by eighteen feet wide. This second church

Courtesy Le Secretariat de la Province de Quebec

CAP-DE-LA-MADELEINE

served both the Indians and the people of the parish until 1719, when it was replaced by the present Cap-de-la-Madeleine.

✛

THE EDUCATION OF THE VIRGIN
Georges De la Tour

THE cultus of the Virgin Mary cannot be overlooked in a study of the Roman Catholic Church and the fine arts, because it gave some of the world's finest artists both interesting and beautiful subject matter. There is something very human, extremely intimate and personal about the young woman who was chosen to be the mother of Jesus.

Many beautiful traditions—apart from the Bible—have grown up about her own birth and childhood. One of these has to do with her education. From the time she was a child, she was supposed to have been prepared in a very special way for the privilege that was to be hers.

Georges De la Tour, a French painter of the seventeenth century, painted one of his loveliest canvases on the theme of the education of the Virgin. He has pictured little Mary and her teacher, perhaps her mother, St. Anne, as French peasants of the highest type, wearing simple homespun garments of dignity and grace. This is an informal home setting, with almost barren furnishings.

The only light comes from the candle which Mary holds, shielding the flame with her right hand. This device of illuminating his subjects with a single candle was a favorite of De la Tour's—so much so that one critic, P. Jamot, says that it expresses the secret of the artist's poetry: "Although it is sometimes held in the hand of a little child, a candle has conquered the enormous night." In this painting, De la Tour probably intended the candle to be a symbol of the light that Mary was to bring to the world through her Son.

The serene faces of Mary and her teacher are beautifully illumined by this light. It spreads over the book, pointing up its importance. Note too, how beautifully and naturally the shielding hand of Mary becomes transparent along the sides and tips of the fingers.

The colors of "The Education of the Virgin" are chiefly cinnabar red highlighted by shades of ivory. The dignity of the figures is notable. The emotion is established as one of quiet serenity and repose. It is as though the teacher has been reading the lesson and some thought in it bears deep reflection, and so the book is lowered into her lap, as wordlessly the teacher and pupil reflect on the truth they have just discovered.

De la Tour's closely knit forms have much to do with his style and design. He uses an economy of line which is at the same time beautifully rhythmic in effect. The simple draperies, the compact, carefully drawn and painted figures, set against extremely simple backgrounds, all combine to create a style that is unique. There is an unmistakable spirituality to this artist's work and it

THE EDUCATION OF THE VIRGIN—DE LA TOUR

springs chiefly from the presence of candlelight and the serene, intelligent, and spiritual facial expressions of his subjects.

Georges De la Tour probably lived all of his life in France. Like other seventeenth-century French artists of his day, he was strongly influenced by Italian art. In his case, Caravaggio, that superb master of light, seems to have been the one from Italy to have made the greatest impression on De la Tour. Unlike most of his contemporaries, he probably never got to Italy to study the masters of art there.

The twentieth century has rediscovered Georges De la Tour and put him where he belongs, among the important artists of his day—an artist whose works have a spiritual quality that sets him apart.

✛

PRAISE AND PRAYER

Praise is devotion fit for mighty minds,
    The diff'ring world's agreeing sacrifice;
Where Heaven divided faiths united finds:
    But Prayer in various discord upward flies.

For Prayer the ocean is where diversely
    Men steer their course, each to a sev'ral coast;
Where all our interest so discordant be
    That half beg winds by which the rest are lost.

By Penitence when we ourselves forsake,
    'Tis but in wise design on piteous Heaven;
In Praise we nobly give what God may take,
    And are, without a beggar's blush, forgiven.
               —*Sir William Davenant* (*1606-1668*)

CHRIST CRUCIFIED

Thy restless feet cannot go
    For us and our eternal good,
As they were ever wont. What though
    They swim, alas! in their own flood?

Thy hands to give Thou canst not lift,
    Yet will Thy hand still giving be;
It gives, but O, itself's the gift!
    It gives though bound, though bound 'tis free!
               —*Richard Crashaw* (*1613?-1649*)

O FLAME OF LIVING LOVE

O flame of living love,
That dost eternally
Pierce through my soul with so consuming heat,
Since there's no help above,
Make thou an end of me,
And break the bond of this encounter sweet.

O burn that burns to heal!
O more than pleasant wound!
And O soft hand, O touch most delicate,
That dost new life reveal,
That dost in grace abound,
And, slaying, dost from death to life translate!

O lamp of fire that shined
With so intense a light
That those deep caverns where the senses live,
Which were obscure and blind,
Now with strange glories bright,
Both heat and light to His beloved give!

With how benign intent
Rememberest thou my breast,
Where thou alone abidest secretly;
And in thy sweet ascent,
With glory and good possessed,
How delicately thou teachest love to me!*

—*St. John of the Cross (1542-1591)*

IF, LORD, THY LOVE FOR ME IS STRONG

If, Lord, Thy love for me is strong
As this which binds me unto Thee,
What holds me from Thee, Lord, so long,
What holds Thee, Lord, so long from me?

O soul, what then desirest thou?
—Lord, I would see Thee, who thus choose Thee.
What fears can yet assail thee now?
—All that I fear is but to lose Thee.

Love's whole possession I entreat,
Lord, make my soul Thine own abode,

* Translated from the Spanish by Arthur Symons.

And I will build a nest so sweet
It may not be too poor for God.

A soul in God hidden from sin
What more desires for thee remain,
Save but to love, and love again,
And, all on flame with love within,
Love on, and turn to love again?*
—*St. Teresa of Avila (1515-1582)*

LINES WRITTEN IN HER BREVIARY

Let nothing disturb thee,
Nothing affright thee;
All things are passing;
God never changeth;
Patient endurance
Attaineth to all things;
Who God possesseth
In nothing is wanting;
Alone God sufficeth.*
—*St. Teresa of Avila (1515-1582)*

THE SOUL WHEREIN GOD DWELLS

The soul wherein God dwells,
What church could holier be?
Becomes a walking-tent
Of heavenly majesty.
How far from here to heaven?
Not very far, my friend.
A single hearty step
Will all the journey end.
Though Christ a thousand times
In Bethlehem be born,
If He's not born in thee,
Thy soul is still forlorn.
The cross on Golgotha
Will never save thy soul:
The cross in thine own heart
Alone can make thee whole.
Hold thou—where runnest thou?
Know heaven is in thee—
Seek'st thou for God elsewhere,
His face thou'lt never see.

* Translated from the Spanish by Henry Wadsworth Longfellow.

Oh, would thy heart but be
A manger for His birth;
God would once more become
A child upon the earth.
Go out, God will go in;
Die thou—and let Him live;
Be not—and He will be;
Wait, and He'll all things give.
O shame, a silk-worm works
And spins till it can fly;
And thou, my soul, wilt still
On thine old earth-clod lie!

—*Angelus Silesius (John Scheffler)*

✜

ST. FRANCIS XAVIER: APOSTLE OF THE INDIES

John O'Kane Murray

ST. FRANCIS XAVIER, one of the glories of the sixteenth century, was born in 1506, at the castle of Xavier, not far from Pampeluna, in the north of Spain. His parents were pious, wealthy, and noble.

From infancy Francis was kind and attractive. He was naturally gifted, and early exhibited an intense love of study. Though all his brothers had embraced the profession of arms, he seemed to care only for books and learning.

His parents wisely seconded his inclination, and at the age of eighteen he was sent to the University of Paris. He was a hard-working, ambitious student. He aimed to conquer the world of knowledge; and, on taking the degree of Master of Arts, he began to teach philosophy.

When St. Ignatius came to continue his studies at the French capital, he made the acquaintance of Xavier.

These rare spirits were attracted to each other. Soon they become bosom friends. "What will it profit a man to gain the whole world and lose his own soul?" said Ignatius one day, with gentle force, to his companion. He pointed out that such a noble soul ought not to confine itself to the vain honors of this world. Celestial glory is the only object worthy of ambition. It is even contrary to reason not to prefer that which is eternal to that which vanishes with the fleetness of a dream.

This pointed reasoning made a deep impression on the ardent soul of Xavier; and, after a short interior struggle, grace completed the conquest. He became a soldier of the cross.

In 1534, on the feast of the Assumption, St. Ignatius and his six companions—one of whom was our saint—made a vow at Montmartre, Paris, to visit the Holy Land, and unite their labors for the conversion of infidels; but if this should not be found practicable, to cast themselves at the feet of the Vicar of Christ, and offer their services wherever he might wish to give them employment. Xavier was ordained priest in 1537.

The great design, however, of converting the Holy Land had to be abandoned, and the new Society of Jesus found a wider sphere for its sublime mission.

At the request of the King of Portugal, two fathers were ordered to plant the faith in the East Indies. One of these was Francis Xavier. He received the benediction of the Pope, and he stepped with a light heart on board the chief vessel of a squadron that sailed from Lisbon on the seventh of April, 1541. It was on that very day that he had completed his thirty-fifth year.

He arrived at Goa in the month of May, 1542, after a long and dangerous voyage, during which he had excited in all the spirit of piety, courage, and cheerfulness. It was during this voyage that he first got the name of "Holy Father," which was ever after given him alike by Mohammedans, pagans, and Christians.

Xavier landed, and spent the greater part of the first night in prayer. He wished to call down the blessing of heaven on his coming labors.

After spending the morning in assisting and comforting the unfortunate in the prisons and hospitals, he walked through the streets of Goa with a bell in his hand, imploring all masters for the love of God to send their children and slaves to catechism. The little ones gathered about him in crowds, and the man of God led them to the church.

The modesty and devotion of the youth by degrees changed the aspect of the whole town. The saint preached in public and visited private houses. His kindness and charity were irresistible, and in six months he accomplished the conversion of Goa. It was more than a miracle.

The pure heart of the great missionary swam in torrents of joy, and from his lips broke songs of gladness. He endured cold, heat, hunger, disease. On the roads his naked feet were torn by thorns and briars, but he never complained. He kept on his way, tireless and resolute. On earth he walked as if already in heaven.

His food was merely rice and water. His labors were incredible. It was a rare thing for him to sleep three hours at night, and a rarer thing to use a bed. His couch was the hard ground.

"The dangers to which I am exposed," he writes to St. Ignatius from the Isle del Moro, "and the pains I take for the interest of God alone, are the inexhaustible springs of my spiritual joy. These islands, bare of all worldly necessaries, are the places in the world for a man to lose his sight with excess of weeping. But they are tears of joy. I never remember to have tasted such interior delights; and these consolations of the soul are so pure, so exquisite, and so constant that they take from me all sense of my bodily suffering." Truly, to be a saint is something beautiful!

His missions grew with marvelous rapidity. He labored, and God blessed his labors. At the end of two years the crop of helpers that he had planted was almost ripe. At Goa, which was his headquarters, he founded a seminary. His first priests were now ready. Today he attempted what seemed impossible yesterday. At one place he baptized ten thousand persons with his own hands in a month.

He established the faith at Malacca. He converted two kings in Ceylon. To him a journey of a thousand miles was nothing.

Nor could his zeal be confined by the boundless regions of India. A mysterious finger pointed to Japan, and he hastened there, accompanied only by three missionaries. It was nine years since he had left Europe, and he had not rested a day.

He learned the language of Japan, and miracles opened the way for the new doctrine. But slow was the progress of truth. The good seed fell on rocks; and even the dauntless Xavier for a moment seemed disconcerted. He regretted having left India. It required all the valor of his resignation to harden himself for a work that seemed impossible.

But where the saints pass, God passes with them. The great apostle redoubled his efforts. Heaven listened to his sighs and tears and prayers, and after two years of suffering that cost him his life, Xavier was master of Japan.

Then he turned his eyes towards that great unknown—China. But before entering on this gigantic enterprise, he returned to Goa, where he found that India numbered half a million Christians. Well might he exclaim: "Glory be to God! this is a fine harvest. Let us sow in the fields." And he embarked for China.

But God was pleased to accept his will in this good work, and took him to Himself. The saint labored hard, but at last he was overcome. After suffering great pain he was put ashore, in a dying condition, in a land that was not China. With the light of heaven shining from his countenance, he passed to everlasting glory on December 2, 1552, saying: "In Thee, O Lord! have I hoped; I shall never be confounded."

The heroic labors of St. Francis Xavier in India and Japan were a repetition of the marvelous preaching of the first apostles of Jesus Christ. His words were powerful. Each of his steps was a victory over the prince of darkness. In the short space of ten years he extended the gospel over an area of nine thousand square miles, penetrated to regions never reached, saved countless souls, and filled the world with the sublimity of his apostleship.*

✠

JUNIPERO SERRA: FATHER OF THE CALIFORNIA MISSIONS
Harold B. Hunting

IN the middle of the seventeen hundreds, about the time that the French and Indian wars were raging on the north Atlantic coast, a Franciscan monk came to Mexico from Spain as a missionary to the Indians. His name was Miguel José Serra. These Franciscans were members of an order of monks founded

* Abridged from *Little Lives of the Great Saints* by John O'Kane Murray, pp. 411-23.

by the great St. Francis of Assisi, who lived in Italy in the twelfth century, and who undertook to imitate literally Jesus' way of love.

The early followers of Francis renounced all possessions and care for money and joyously went everywhere, spreading the gospel of love and helping those who were sick or poor or in any kind of distress. It became a custom that when any man became a Franciscan, he took the name of one of those first followers of the Saint. Miguel Serra chose the name Junipero. The original Junipero had been nicknamed "the jester of the Lord." Once he was caught taking gold lace off the altar of a rich church in order to sell it and give the money to the poor. He was that kind of jester. And Junipero Serra was much that kind of man. He had a passion for helping the poor.

He was born in the Majorca Islands off the coast of Spain, and early became known as a brilliant student and musician. Coming to Mexico, he had wonderful success as a missionary. He was sent to a remote tribe of Indians who seemed to be sunk in the worst kind of savagery. After a few years their lives were completely transformed. The hungry were fed, the naked clothed, and the quarrelsome lived together in peace.

About that time the Spanish governor of Mexico, Don José Galvez, decided that the time was ripe for sending colonists into the mysterious land of California. He selected Father Serra to be the religious head of the expedition. There were to be at first three settlements at points along the coast where harbors had already been discovered. There was to be one at San Diego, another at Monterey, and a third between the two. A mission was to be founded at each place where the gospel would be preached to the Indians. Each mission was to be named after a saint. The Spanish word *San* means saint.

"Don José," said Father Junipero, "you have named a mission after San Diego, and another in honor of San Carlos at Monterey, and a third for San Buenaventura. But is there to be no mission in honor of our Father St. Francis?"

"If St. Francis desires a mission," answered Don José, smiling, "let him show us his harbor."

The expedition set forth partly by land and partly by sea. Father Serra went with the land party. It was a long, hard journey over wild mountain ranges and barren desert plains. Some of the party perished, others deserted. But on July 1, 1769, they came within sight of San Diego harbor where the two ships of the expedition were already riding at anchor. Great was the rejoicing.

After waiting only a few days, Don Gaspar Portola, the military leader, set forth to find Monterey, the other harbor at which they were to establish a settlement. Father Serra remained for the time in San Diego. Never was a port so hard to find as Monterey. The trouble was that the map was wrong. The old sailor who made it had miscalculated and had placed Monterey too far north. So now Don Gaspar and his men went too far north and kept going farther and even farther north. For weeks and months they marched on until, on the morning of November 1, 1769, they camped near the ocean, and sent a few soldiers to scout around in search of game for food. Towards evening the soldiers returned in great excitement.

"Just over the hill to the north," they said, "is an inlet from the ocean, lead-ing into a great harbor. Is this Monterey?" The whole company went with the commander across the hills and soon found themselves looking down upon the dancing, sparkling waters which we call the Golden Gate. White men for the first time were looking upon the world's greatest harbor.

Returning as quickly as possible to San Diego, they told their story. They had failed to find Monterey, but they had found an even better harbor. "God be praised," cried Father Junipero. "Our Father, St. Francis, has indeed made known to us his harbor. We shall name it San Francisco, and build a mission there in his honor."

As the days went by, there came to Father Junipero's mind a great and noble plan. He proposed to build a chain of missions more than seven hundred miles long, from San Diego on the south to San Francisco on the north, each one about a day's journey on horseback from its neighbors on either side. This plan he carried out with tireless energy which overcame every difficulty. Twenty-one missions were built. There they stand today—most of them in ruins, but beautiful. The great highway along which they were strung like pearls on a chain is still one of the chief thoroughfares of California. It is still called by the name the Fathers gave it, *El Camino Real,* that is to say, The King's Highway.

In the happy days when these missions were not in ruins, they were living proofs of what miracles Christlike kindness and patience can work among ignorant and degraded men. Each mission was a community of Indian families and Franciscan monks living and working together. Within a very few years the red men showed the results of their new training, and learned better methods of tilling the soil, herding cattle, building houses, and weaving cloth. They had learned to read and write, and to play certain musical instruments.

The good monks brought into the country new kinds of fruits. In the garden of the mission of San Gabriel one may still see the great gnarled trunk of the oldest grapevine in California, brought from Spain in 1798 by the Franciscan fathers. The original California pepper tree was likewise planted at the mission of San Luis Rey. Within the shelter of these great households there were at one time as many as thirty thousand Christian Indians. Vast areas of land brought forth lush harvests of grain, and there were thousands upon thousands of sheep and cattle on the green hillsides. Loveliest of all were the roses.

In the missions in those days one got up at five o'clock in the morning, and went with the others to prayers where God's blessing was asked upon the new day. Then came breakfast. After breakfast everybody went to work—some to the fields, some to the shops, the women to their spinning wheels and looms, the children to school. At eleven o'clock came dinner, and after dinner there came an hour for games, and then more hours of work. Supper was at six, and after supper until nine there were games again—races and sports of every kind.

Life was sweet in the missions and it was safe. There was justice for all, not only as between white men and white men, but as between Indians and white men. Picture this scene in your imagination—an Indian running for his

life, pursued by Spanish soldiers. The Indian succeeds in reaching the mission
at San Diego and finds refuge in the church. He is accused by the soldiers
of having murdered a Spaniard. The truth is that outside of the missions the
Indians were for the most part being treated as they have usually been treated
by white settlers. This Indian had suffered many wrongs at the hands of the
Spanish soldiers, and had at last struck back in self-defense. Now he stands
among the gentle, brown-robed monks, terror-stricken and breathless. Would
they give him up to the soldiers? They would not.

The soldiers, led by their *commandante,* Captain Riviera, stormed and
blustered. "You will be sorry for this," said he. "I will report this to your
Father Superior."

Away he went to Monterey where Father Junipero Serra was stopping.
Again he insolently demanded that the Indian be surrendered to his soldiers.
But the Father, when he learned the whole story, sternly refused. The soldiers
never succeeded in capturing the Indian. It is not strange that when Father
Junipero died, the Indians fought among each other for shreds of his brown
robe and for locks of his white hair.*

✧

PÉRE MARQUETTE
Father Quill

THE French missionaries are their own best historians. They sent yearly reports
of their missions to their superiors. They wrote curious and edifying letters
to their religious brethren. They left the most luxurious country in Europe to
seek shelter in unwelcome huts of one of the most wretched races of men. To
win these crude beings to the Christian faith it was necessary to know them
intimately in their daily walks.

In their generous enthusiasm the French missionaries forsook the schools,
the camps, the court of their beautiful sunlit land, and from the rock of
Quebec, where generous friends and patrons had built them a college and
supplied them with ample means for their mission, they would evangelize
New France. What a field for their labors! The field stretched from Hudson
Bay to Pennsylvania—and from Nova Scotia to Kentucky! They would visit
the land of the Abnaki in Maine, of the Iroquois in New York, of the Hurons
in Michigan, of the Ottawas in Wisconsin, the Illinois in Illinois—all that
immense expanse of territory within our borders, including New England,
New York, and the states washed by the Great Lakes and the Mississippi. The
French missionaries that labored in this field from 1611 to 1800 number three
hundred and twenty persons.

Far in advance of the oncoming columns of humanity, slowly moving,
marched James Marquette in solitary grandeur. He it was who kindled the
torch whose beams, piercing the forest and flashing over lake and river, en-

* From *Pioneers of Goodwill* by Harold B. Hunting, pp. 24-33. Copyright 1929 by G. Q. LeSourd.
Published by Friendship Press. Used by permission of the publisher.

abled those venturing amid the perilous glooms to pick their way through the gray dawn of our American civilization.

In his rude hut, a thousand miles away from the habitations of civilized man, Marquette wrote:

"I am obliged to render you an account of the mission at La Point de St. Esprit among the Ottawas, according to your orders; on my arrival here, after a month's navigation on snow and through ice which closed my way and kept me in constant peril of life, Divine Providence having destined me to continue this Mission, I went to visit the Indians here who are divided into five towns. The Hurons, to the number of about four or five hundred, still preserve some little Christianity. The nation of the Outouaks is far from the Kingdom of God, being above all other nations addicted to sacrifices and juggleries. They ridicule prayer and will scarcely hear us speak of Christianity. The Kiskakons had resolved in the fall of 1668 to obey God. They were then in the fields, harvesting their Indian corn. They listened with pleasure when I told them I came to La Point for their sake."

The gentle Marquette spent the long and dreary winter alone among these rough creatures on the desolate shore of Chagnamegon. Spring brought Dakotas trooping to the village. From the South, a thirty days' journey, bent on trade, came a band of Illinois. Marquette listened to their stories about the Mississippi—the "Great Water"—flowing no one could tell whence, no one knew whither. Thereupon he formed the settled purpose of exploring this river.

In his next letter he wrote: "If the Indians, who promise to make me a canoe, do not fail to keep their word, we shall go into this; we shall visit the nations which inhabit it, in order to open the way to so many of our Fathers who have long awaited this happiness. The discovery will give us a complete knowledge of the Southern or Western Sea."

In 1670 La Point was abandoned. The Hurons wandered away until they found a good fishing coast just east of Lake Superior. Up went the huts and the chapel. The mission of St. Ignace is born and Marquette is tending his flock and giving account of it: "The Hurons come regularly to prayers and have listened to the instructions I gave them, consenting to what I required of them to prevent their disorders and abominable customs. We must have patience with untutored minds. God alone can fix these fickle minds, and place and keep them in His grace, and touch their hearts, while we stammer at their ears."

It took years to mature and carry out his great plan. Joliet, a Canadian by birth, and a trader and rover by inclination, was sent to join Marquette in 1672. Of his arrival Marquette wrote: "I was delighted because I saw my plans about to be accomplished, and found myself in the happy necessity of exposing my life for the salvation of all these tribes and especially of the Illinois, who had begged me very earnestly to bring the word of God amongst them."

On the seventeenth of May, 1673, the two Frenchmen and five Indian companions started on their journey in two canoes with a small provision of Indian corn and smoked beef.

They skirted the northern shore of Lake Michigan to Green Bay; up the Fox River through Lake Winnebago; through the Upper Fox they found their way to the Wisconsin, reaching the point of previous exploration only after a month. On the seventeeth of June, just below the present city of Prairie du Chien, they shot out upon the virgin waters of the Mississippi. "The Father of Waters" was discovered! Marquette's joy was beyond expression. The dream of his life was realized, the wish of his heart gratified, the toils and dangers of years repaid in that one moment.

For weeks they floated southward seeing no signs of life, but later holding friendly intercourse with the Illinois and other tribes. After delays here and there they reached an Indian village opposite the mouth of the Arkansas. The Indians were in possession of firearms and steel hatchets, evidences of their relations with the English of Virginia or the Spaniards. They were warned that death awaited them by disease or the tomahawk, or capture by the Spaniards. They decided to turn back; the important point was established. The Great River did not flow into the Atlantic or Sea of Virginia, nor into the Gulf of California or Vermilion Sea, but into the Gulf of Mexico.

Returning by toilsome stages they passed up the Illinois River, discovered much of the adjoining country, and reached Green Bay in September. They were gone four months and had paddled twenty-five hundred miles. Joliet returned to Quebec with a report of their success; Father Marquette remained in the country about Chicago and visited the Illinois who received him as "an angel from heaven."

Soon his strength was spent. A prey to hunger, cold, and disease, he tried to reach St. Ignace to die among his brother missionaries. At Mackinaw, on the nineteenth of May, and on the banks of the river that now bears his name, he calmly expired in the loneliness of the forest. They laid his body in a grave by the waters of Lake Michigan. Two years later a party of Kiskakons hunting thereabouts sought out his grave. With a flotilla of thirty canoes they conveyed the rustic casket reverently to St. Ignace. Priests, Indians, and traders all thronged the shore. The relics of Marquette were received with solemn reverence and buried beneath the altar of the little chapel of the mission.

Wisconsin has done herself honor in honoring Marquette for his pure life, his writings, and for his fame as the explorer of the Mississippi, since he was the first white man to traverse her territory and write a description of it. He was the first to map out the confines of that state. He gave a name to the river after which the state is called.

The Congress of the nation has shown wisdom in placing in its capital the statue of "the faithful missionary, whose work among the Indians and explorations within our borders in early days are recognized all over the civilized world."

Marquette's fame is secure. As long as men shall be touched and inspired by what is good and beautiful, saintly and heroic, Marquette must occupy his proud pedestal as the hero whose simplicity of manners, purity of life, serenity of soul, tenacity of purpose, love for man and zeal for religion, make up a personality which the history of our country will find it difficult to match and impossible to surpass.

Marquette, I venture to say, was something more than a man gifted with a thirst for knowledge and a genius for exploration. He must be credited with something more than the mere natural virtues of steadfast courage and noble self-sacrifice. His ambition and enthusiasm were not earth-born. The supernatural had place in his life and character. He was in the world but not of the world. His powers, his activities, his life were dedicated to the cause of Christ. His pure, gentle, patient soul was touched to the finest issue—the greater glory of God.*

✠

MY GOD, I LOVE THEE

PURE devotion to Jesus Christ, not for hope of reward or punishment in a future life, but for the love of God alone, is not often expressed except by saints and mystics. But here, in words attributed to St. Francis Xavier, that great sixteenth-century missionary to India of the Roman Catholic Church, we find noble and pure devotion. No more devoted servant of God ever lived in any age than St. Francis Xavier (see page 368), and so it is quite fitting that he should have written the words to this hymn.

Edward Caswall, who translated the words to the hymn, was a convert to the Roman Catholic Church from the Church of England. He devoted twenty-eight years of his life to serving the poor, the sick, and the impoverished children of his parish in the manufacturing city of Birmingham, England. He found time somehow to translate scores of Latin hymns, many of which are dearly loved by Protestant and Catholic alike.

Henry John Gauntlett, who composed the tune given here, was an exceptional organist and student of Gregorian music. He served as organist in several important London churches, composing psalm and hymn tunes for his choirs. His greatest contribution was taking very old hymns and arranging more singable melodies for them, as was the case with his version of "My God, I Love Thee."

✠

DISPOSER SUPREME, AND JUDGE OF THE EARTH

THIS interesting and rather unusual hymn is one of a great many hymns that were revised for the Cluniac Breviary by Jean-Baptiste Santeuil. Born in Paris

* Abridged from *The Celtic Association of Philadelphia, U.S.A.*, pp. 47 ff., "Pére Marquette and the Early Jesuit Missionaries," a speech by Father Quill.

My God, I Love Thee*

C. M.

ST. FULBERT   HENRY J. GAUNTLETT, 1852

Moderately slow

1 My God, I love thee; not be - cause I hope for heav'n there-by,
2 But for that thou didst all man-kind Up - on the cross em - brace;
3 And griefs and tor-ments num-ber - less, And sweat of ag - o - ny;
4 Then why, most lov - ing Je - sus Christ, Should I not love thee well,

Nor yet for fear that lov - ing not I might for ev - er die;
For us didst bear the nails and spear, And man - i - fold dis-grace,
E'en death it - self; and all for man Who was thine en - e - my.
Not for the sake of win-ning heav'n, Nor a - ny fear of hell;

5 Not with the hope of gaining aught,
  Not seeking a reward;
  But as thyself hast lovèd me,
  O ever-loving Lord!

*6 E'en so I love thee, and will love,
  And in thy praise will sing,
  Solely because thou art my God
  And my eternal King. Amen.

A-men.

Spanish, 17th cent.; Tr. EDWARD CASWALL, 1849, alt.

*From *The Hymnal, 1940*, No. 456, reprinted from *Songs of Praise* (enlarged edition). Used by permission of Oxford University Press, London.

in 1630, Santeuil was a Latin poet who became renowned for his translations of ancient hymns and composition of new ones for the Roman Catholic Church. When the Order of Cluny took steps to revise many of the old Latin hymns of the Roman Breviary so that they might be more singable and more easily understood, Claude Santeuil was asked to take the responsibility for the work. He lived long enough to finish only six hymns.

Disposer Supreme, and Judge of the Earth*

OLD 104TH. (10 10. 11 11.)

Slow and dignified.

Ravenscroft's Psalter, 1621.

A-men.

Based on Supreme quales, Arbiter, *J.-B. de Santeüil (1686).*
Cento. Percy Dearmer.

DISPOSER supreme, and judge of the earth,
Who choosest for thine the meek and the poor;
To frail earthen vessels, and things of no worth,
Entrusting thy riches which ay shall endure;

2 Like clouds are they borne to do thy great will,
And swift as the winds about the world go;
The Word with his wisdom their spirits doth fill,
They thunder like clouds, and the waters o'erflow.

3 They hearten the few, they armour the free,
Thy Reign to advance, thy peace to proclaim;
The wisdom of kindness they lead men to see,
With fire of the Spirit men's hearts they enflame.

4 O loud be their trump, and stirring the sound,
To rouse us, O Lord, from slumber of sin;
The lights thou hast kindled in darkness around,
O may they illumine our spirits within!

5. All honour and praise, dominion and might,
To thee, three in One, eternally be,
Who pouring around us the waves of thy light,
Dost call us from darkness thy glory to see.

*From *Songs of Praise*, No. 211. Published by Oxford University Press, London. Used by permission of the publisher.

After his death, the task fell to Claude's younger brother, Jean, a canon of the monastery of St. Victor. When the new breviary was published it had instant appeal. People liked the revised hymns and the many new ones which Santeuil had written. The excellence of the new hymns led to a popularity which few hymn writers have enjoyed. In all Santeuil wrote 228 hymns. "Disposer Supreme" is one of the best known. Its five verses tell of the responsibility and influence of men who serve the Church as apostles and prophets. The spirit of God rests upon them and within them as they advance the Kingdom of God and witness to the Triune God.

The tune used here was composed as a setting for Psalm 104 for Ravenscroft's *Whole Booke of Psalmes,* published in 1621.

CONTENTS

PART III   SECTION 7

THE ROMAN CATHOLIC CHURCH AROUND THE WORLD

☩

For we are labourers together with God: ye are God's husbandry, ye are God's building.—I CORIN-
THIANS 3:9

☩

PICTURES: PAGE
   Interpretation: The Sacrament of the Last Supper—*Dali* 381
   Picture: The Sacrament of the Last Supper—*Dali* 382
   Interpretation: The Return of the Prodigal—*Ch'en* 383
   Picture: The Return of the Prodigal—*Ch'en* 384
   Interpretation: The Church on the Hill—*Eldershaw* 385
   Picture: The Church on the Hill—*Eldershaw* 386

POETRY:
   The Hound of Heaven—*Thompson* 387
   Give Me Thy Heart—*Proctor* 388
   How Shall I Build?—*Blunt* 389
   A Confession—*Verlaine* 389
   E Tenebris—*Wilde* 390
   The Abbey—*Egurin* 390

STORIES:
   White Martyrdom: The Story of Father Damien—*Henaghan* 391
   The End Is a Beginning—*Nevins* 394
   Father Tabart—*Kittler* 398

MUSIC:
   Interpretation: Crown Him with Many Crowns—*Bridges* 400
   Music: Crown Him with Many Crowns—*Elvey* 401
   Interpretation: O Saviour, Bless Us Ere We Go—*Faber* 402
   Music: O Saviour, Bless Us Ere We Go—*Monk* 403

THE SACRAMENT OF THE LAST SUPPER
Salvador Dali

SALVADOR DALI, the contemporary artist who painted "The Sacrament of the Last Supper," has used religious themes for much of his art during the last few years. Earlier in his career, he was frequently referred to as a "trick" painter. His limp watches and other surrealist works labeled him as an artist who did "paranoic" or illusionary painting.

In the late thirties, Dali's art began to change, and by 1941 he had forsaken surrealism. Dali is a Roman Catholic, and he has indicated that the change in his art was motivated by a religious experience of a very personal nature. He took up the study of theology and after World War II began to devote himself to religious painting.

In 1954, Mr. Chester Dale, president of the Board of Trustees of the National Gallery of Art in Washington, D. C., talked with Salvador Dali at his home in Spain. He urged him to create "The Sacrament of the Last Supper." Dali was fascinated, and decided to do the composition along classical lines and make the painting simple and direct in its message.

He used the structure of the dodecahedron as the basis for the over-all composition. This twelve-sided figure, believed by the Greeks to be a symbol of the universe, Dali divided into several smaller squares and rectangles by drawing diagonal lines to connect the various angles.

The artist has retained some of his old visionary aspects in this representation of the Last Supper. Look, for example, at the figure of Christ. The face is spiritual and at the same time realistic. The illusion lies in placing the figure as though it were standing waist-deep in water. This appears to be the Sea of Galilee—the same body of water that is in Dali's famous "Christ of St. John of the Cross" and in one or two of his other religious paintings. The fishermen's small boats and the same mountains are in all of these paintings.

In Dali's "The Sacrament of the Last Supper" Jesus has just broken the bread. The two halves of the loaves lie at the edge of the table. With His left hand, Jesus points to Himself, and with His right, He points upward. A golden, heavenly light, which is truly wonderful, illumines the scene. The disciples are overcome by the solemnity and meaning of the moment. They bow their heads so low that their faces are completely hidden, making it impossible to distinguish one from the other. Christ is the center; Christ is everything in this representation of the Last Supper. Even the simple, identical robes of the men obliterate their individuality.

Dali has given no clue as to the meaning of the outstretched arms that embrace the scene. In fact, he prefers not to have his paintings analyzed closely, and those who attempt to do so find a difficult task before them.

This we know: on this great canvas, Dali has created for the twentieth century a painting that combines the classical and traditional approach to art

THE SACRAMENT OF THE LAST SUPPER—DALI

with visionary, mystical insight. "The Sacrament of the Last Supper" is one which speaks to modern man. In a mood of timelessness, the painting depicts one of the sacraments of the Church which Christ created for His followers.

✛

THE RETURN OF THE PRODIGAL
Luke Ch'en

So appealing is the theme of Christian forgiveness that it has been the subject of the artist's brush, the poet's meter, and the novelist's plot. Throughout the many centuries since Jesus moved among men, teaching forgiveness, artists have found in the story of the prodigal son a favorite theme for their work.

There is so much of the human side of mankind in that story! The wastrel son and the forgiving father, whose story teaches men to have faith and confidence in each other. Too, the parable portrays God's love for man. Puvis de Chavannes, Pieter Brueghel, Rembrandt—many of the world's greatest artists have pictured the prodigal's return.

Luke Ch'en, a contemporary Chinese Christian artist, has made an especially appealing painting on this theme (see p. 384). He has told it in his native language of art, using a Chinese setting. The father is pictured as an elderly Chinese gentleman, clad in a silk robe. His features bespeak a man of rank; his beard suggests considerable age, greatly venerated in China.

Tenderly the father reaches down to embrace his son, and a world of forgiveness is reflected in his downcast eyes. The son, home from his wanderings and wastefulness, throws himself at his father's feet. Though his head and hands are almost hidden, his posture shows his feelings of sorrow and self-abandonment, and he reaches hopefully toward his father. He has dropped his staff and his basket of meager possessions—he will not need them now. His plain, patched garment will soon be replaced by a fine robe and his bare feet shod with slippers, befitting the son of a man of rank.

The scene is pictured as taking place just outside the home, as though it were happening today. This gives a feeling of timelessness to the story.

Luke Ch'en, who painted "The Return of the Prodigal," is a professor of art at the Catholic University of Peking, as far as is known at the present time. He was converted to Christianity and baptized with the name of Luke in 1932. He was already well established as an artist, and since his conversion he has devoted his talent to painting Christian subjects. (For his painting, "St. Paul Before the Altar of the Unknown God," see p. 72.)

Luke Ch'en says he believes that when he paints the wonders of Christianity according to the ancient rules of Chinese art, the painted objects exert a new and strange effect, so that the Chinese may come to know God through familiar means. His many beautiful, poetic paintings on the life and teachings of Jesus have inspired countless Chinese Christians. They have also inspired many of

敗子回頭

路加陳緣吾畫圖

Courtesy S. V. D. Catholic Universities, Chicago

THE RETURN OF THE PRODIGAL—*CH'EN*

his students to study the Bible and to transfer to canvas their understanding of the Christian way of life.

It has been only for the last fifty years that Chinese artists have used Christian themes. Various societies and guilds of artists have encouraged this indigenous art by helping native artists to continue their training and work. The Church Art Society (Episcopal) is one of these groups. Another source of encouragement came from the Department of Fine Arts of the Catholic University in Peking until it was taken over by the Communists in 1950. Art by Chinese Christians is now being seen more frequently in the Western world, through exhibits in America and elsewhere.

✣

THE CHURCH ON THE HILL

John Roy Eldershaw

"THE Church on the Hill," which John Roy Eldershaw so beautifully painted in water colors, is a picture of the oldest existing Roman Catholic Church in Australia. It dates back more than a hundred years, and in both its setting and history it reflects the fact that it is a pioneer church in the midst of a rugged, vast continent.

The old church is located in the village of Richmond in Tasmania—a section of Australia which is characterized by mountains and rivers. The village, remote from large cities, is situated in a sparsely populated area. It owes its beginnings to an English priest, Dr. Polding, who in 1836 was on his way to Sydney, where he was to be made an archibishop. Against the advice of his friends who knew the area, Dr. Polding insisted that he wanted to go to Richmond to visit a small group of Roman Catholics there. He interested his companion, Father Lawrence Catham, and a few others in going with him on the journey into the interior.

When the governor heard that Dr. Polding had gathered this little party to make the trek, he did his best to dissuade them. He said that the territory which they would need to traverse was inhabited by savage blacks who were known to be dangerous and hostile. Dr. Polding held out, determined to visit his flock, and finally Governor Arthur made a proposition: "I'll match pound for pound any money you can collect toward building a church in Richmond!" Then, offering what protection he could, the governor wished the little party Godspeed.

Dr. Polding and his friends finally approached Richmond. The records tell of no adventures, but the journey through the rugged countryside was undoubtedly difficult. As the men crossed the Richmond Bridge—the oldest bridge in Australia—they found themselves in a little pioneer village, set at the foot of a hill. "There," said Dr. Polding, pointing to the summit, "is a perfect site for Richmond Church!"

Photo by Colin Ballantyne. Courtesy National Gallery of South Australia, Adelaide

THE CHURCH ON THE HILL—ELDERSHAW

As Dr. Polding mingled with the Christians and preached and administered to them, he found that their interest in building a place of worship was keen. A Mr. Cassidy offered a plot of land, and it turned out to be the very hill that Dr. Polding and his party had thought of! Money began to come from various sources. From his flock in Richmond, from others in Sydney, and throughout Tasmania, Dr. Polding collected a thousand pounds. The governor, true to his agreement, gave a similar amount. Work on the stone structure was started in 1836, soon after Dr. Polding's visit to Richmond. On December 31, 1837, the church was ready for worship.

In his water color (p. 386), Mr. Eldershaw admirably portrays the simple, sturdy stone church. Architecturally, the church seems to be part of the hill on which it stands, and it fits into the background of mountains and valleys. In the foreground the artist pictures simple pioneer homes set in fenced-off plots, thus giving an idea of what the village itself is like.

Because Mr. Eldershaw spent a number of years in Tasmania and was fascinated by this rugged pioneer countryside, he succeeded in doing some of his best work there. In "The Church on the Hill" he has captured the feeling of early pioneer days and the rugged simplicity of the homes and churches built for the hardy folk who chose to live in the vast country of Australia. St. John's Church was renovated and restored in 1929, but the same feeling of age and stability which John Roy Eldershaw pictures in his water color was kept by the restorers of the church as they carefully brought it into repair.

John Roy Eldershaw, born in Sydney, Australia, in 1892, is one of that country's finest artists. He studied under Julian Ashton and J. S. Watkins at the Royal Art Society of New South Wales and also at the Central School in London. Soon after he completed his formal schooling, he was recognized as an artist of first rank. Mr. Eldershaw's paintings are found in all of the Australian art galleries and in the Print Room of the British Museum in London. In 1941 "The Church on the Hill" was shown at the Museum of Modern Art in New York City, where it was part of a special exhibition of Australian art. It was cited in many reviews of that show as outstanding among the paintings.

✠

THE HOUND OF HEAVEN

I fled Him, down the nights and down the days;
    I fled Him, down the arches of the years;
I fled Him, down the labyrinthine ways
    Of my own mind; and in the midst of tears
I hid from Him, and under running laughter.
        Up vistaed hopes I sped;
        And shot, precipitated,
Adown Titanic glooms of chasmed fears,

From those strong Feet that followed, followed after.
    But with unhurrying chase,
    And unperturbèd pace,
Deliberate speed, majestic instancy
    They beat—and a Voice beat
    More instant than the Feet—
'All things betray thee, who betrayest Me.'

    I pleaded, outlaw-wise,
By many a hearted casement, curtained red,
  Trellised with intertwining charities;
(For, though I knew His love Who followed,
    Yet was I sore adread
Lest having Him, I must have naught beside.)
But, if one little casement parted wide,
  The gust of His approach would clash it to:
  Fear wist not to evade, as Love wist to pursue.
    Still with unhurrying chase,
    And unperturbèd pace,
Deliberate speed, majestic instancy,
Came on the following Feet,
    And a Voice above their beat—
'Naught shelters thee, who wilt not shelter Me.'*

                  —*Francis Thompson*

GIVE ME THY HEART

With echoing step the worshipers
Departed one by one;
The organ's pealing voice was stilled,
The vesper hymn was done;
The shadows fell from roof and arch,
Dim was the incensed air,
One lamp alone with trembling ray,
Told of the Presence there!

In the dark church she knelt alone;
Her tears were falling fast;
"Help, Lord," she cried, "the shades of death
Upon my soul are cast!
Have I not shunned the path of sin
And chosen the better part?"
A voice came through the sacred air?
"My child, give me thy heart!

"For I have loved thee with a love
No mortal heart can show;

---

* Verses 1 and 2 from *"The Hound of Heaven."*

A love so deep, My Saints in Heaven
Its depths can never know:
When pierced and wounded on the Cross,
Man's sin and doom were Mine,
I loved thee with undying love;
Immortal and divine."

In awe she listened and the shade
Passed from her soul away;
In low and trembling voice she cried,
"Lord, help me to obey!
Break Thou the chains of earth, O Lord,
That bind and hold my heart;
Let it be Thine and Thine alone,
Let none with Thee have part!"

—Adelaide Anne Proctor

HOW SHALL I BUILD?

How shall I build my temple to the Lord,
Unworthy I, who am thus foul of heart?
How shall I worship who no traitor word
Know but of love to play a suppliant's part?
How shall I pray, whose soul is as a mart,
For thoughts unclean, whose tongue is as a sword
Even for those it loves, to wound and smart?
Behold how little I can help Thee, Lord.

The Temple I would build should be all white,
Each stone the record of a blameless day;
The souls that entered there should walk in light,
Clothed in high chastity and wisely gay.
Lord, here is darkness. Yet this heart unwise,
Bruised in Thy service, take in sacrifice.

—Wilfrid Scawen Blunt

A CONFESSION

O my God, Thou hast wounded me with love,
Behold the wound that is still vibrating,
O my God, Thou hast wounded me with love.

Take my hands because they have labored not,
For coals of fire and for rare frankincense,
Take my hands because they have labored not.

Take my heart that has beaten for vain things,
To throb under the thorns of Calvary,
Take my heart that has beaten for vain things.

Take my feet, frivolous travelers,
That they may run to the crying of Thy grace,
Take my feet, frivolous travelers.

Ah, Thou God of terror and God of holiness,
Alas, my sinfulness is a black abyss!
God of terror, God of holiness.

Thou God of peace, of joy and delight,
All my tears, all my ignorances,
Thou God of peace, of joy and delight.

Thou, O God, knowest all this, all this,
How poor I am, poorer than any man,
Thou, O God, knowest all this, all this,
And what I have, My God, I give to Thee.*

—*Paul Verlaine*

E TENEBRIS

Come down, O Christ, and help me! reach Thy hand,
   For I am drowning in a stormier sea
   Than Simon on Thy Lake of Galilee:
The wine of life is spilled upon the sand.
My heart is as some famine-murdered land
   Whence all good things have perished utterly,
   And well I know my soul in Hell must lie
If I this night before God's throne should stand.
"He sleeps, perchance, or rideth to the chase,
   Like Baal, when his prophets howled that name
     From morn till noon on Carmel's smitten height."
     Nay, peace I shall behold before the night,
   The feet of brass, the robe more white than flame,
The wounded hands, the weary human face.

—*Oscar Wilde*

THE ABBEY

Through the deep monastic halls
Ancient chime of Matins calls
Solemnly and mournfully,
Where cloistered knights of prayer
Put away their love-dreams fair,
Thoughts of tourney, and of feast,
In profound obscurity—
Courtiers, poets, who have ceased

* Translated from the French by Arthur Symons.

From their plays and learned to feel
Sorrows sharper than the steel.
In oblivion's shrine, despite
Smothered groanings, they recite,
Sheathing in their anguished breasts
Farewells to glories laid to rest
Deep in abbey crypts of night.
And the bell their story says,
In its bitterness contrite,
To the clouds upon their ways;
Says their boast, desire, and all,
To the sainted nights of prayer
As it sounds the Matins there
O'er the graves conventual.*

—*José M. Eguren*

✤

WHITE MARTYRDOM: THE STORY OF FATHER DAMIEN

John Henaghan

WHAT note shall one strike in approaching the life of Father Damien, the apostle of the lepers, the martyr of far-away Molokai? Will it be a note of tender pathos we shall strike as we recount the incidents that stand out in the life story of one whose daily portion it was to witness and to share in the living death of these pitiable sufferers—the lepers? No, though if one wrote of the horrors of the lepers' life alone it would be a picture too sad to be portrayed in human words.

Will it be a note of triumph and gladness? Yes, it shall be so. For we write not in the tones of pagan despair, but with the glad hopefulness of Christianity, as we tell the story of a man who in the springtime of his life and in the glory of his days went down to a living death—of a man who lit up all the vileness and abominations of Molokai with the torch of Christian hope—of a man who, bravely and unafraid, faced all the horrors of leprosy, toiling and sweating in disease-infested huts, and in the end dying a victim to his zeal.

Father Damien's mission was in Hawaii—the largest of the Sandwich group. The Islands until recently were pagan, full of dark rites, of cruelties, and pitiful strivings after the unknown God. However, in this particular "near-Paradise" where Damien's first years were to be spent, the people had taken kindly to Catholicism and several resident priests had already built a cathedral as well as a number of small chapels.

Damien's life as a young missionary in Hawaii was hard. There were many demands upon his time. His hand was ever ready for a grown man's work. His letters home at this period were frequent, telling of his life, of his activities, of the souls to be comforted, of the churches to be built, and always asking

* Translated from the Spanish by Thomas Walsh.

for a remembrance in prayers. He was delighted with the people, so gentle, so pleasant-mannered, so hospitable.

Leprosy came like a blow on these Hawaiian people and they fell before its rancid breath. There seemed no escape. Men fled; homes were broken up, the government grew alarmed and ordered all those afflicted with the disease to be detained in the island of Molokai. When this edict went forth, a wail of sorrow and of grief was heard throughout the Archipelago.

Damien saw some of his parishioners being hurried off—saw the terrible distress and misery of the poor people—and these scenes so heartrending were indelibly impressed on his mind and treasured there. His thoughts turned often to the unfortunate outcasts in the distant island of Molokai and every day he prayed God to comfort them.

It happened simply like this: The bishop was consecrating a chapel in Maui, and Damien with several of his brother priests was invited to be present at the ceremony. The consecration of the little church in Maui was a truly magnificent ceremony and at its close the zealous bishop took the opportunity at dinner for a close and intimate conference with his devoted priests. In the course of his talk he touched on the spiritual misery of the unfortunate lepers in Molokai. Damien's heart leaped within him. His chance had come. "My lord," he said quietly across the dinner table, "if you will be kind enough to allow it, I will go to Molokai and labor for the poor lepers." The offer was accepted and that day, without any farewells, without any preparation, just as he was, Damien went to Molokai.

And now these outcasts of society were to become Damien's friends, his only familiars. We can picture him waiting for that first dawn which would reveal to him the full extent of the sacrifice before him. On the very first day of his arrival he took inventory of the surroundings. The dwellings of the unfortunate lepers were in a miserable condition; they were nothing but grass huts, unprotected in the rainy season, nothing but plague-stricken hovels. They had no separate abodes; they were all huddled together; the water supply was scanty, thus adding to the infection of the place. They were often in want of the necessaries of life.

It was, in truth, a place forgotten and cut off from the eyes of men. It seemed to be deserted by God till Damien came and raised the standard of the true cross amidst the foul leper huts, and brought hope and joy and the touch of comradeship into their lives. He soon found his way into hearts which long years of suffering and despondency had sealed against all affection. Poor lepers who had no hope of a cure, their bodies doomed, were taught to raise their eyes on high—to believe that the patient bearing of their sad lot would win a reward exceeding great. Murmuring ceased, hope revived, and even the poor disfigured faces reflected the joy and peace that filled their minds. Damien was given the grace and the strength to stand before these outcasts and say, "You suffer, my children. Take heart. Here in your midst is One who can turn your sorrow into joy. Go to Him, then, Who dwells in the Tabernacle. Go to Him. He will console you."

Damien at once set about his work of reform. He harassed the government for better accommodations. He worked in company with the lepers building houses and soon six hundred cotttages stood as the result of his endeavors. He next tackled the water supply. Hitherto water had to be carried from a gulch that was a very great distance from the center of the colony, and the more help-less lepers were able to procure a little only by begging from their healthier companions. He persisted in his demands for an adequate water supply and finally succeeded in getting a quantity of pipe which he lifted into position.

His tenacity of purpose was rewarded when a steady stream of clear, cold water began to pour into the village. He then improved the hospital, secured decent supplies of food and clothing, had a resident doctor appointed to visit the settlement occasionally—there was not a medicine chest in the entire colony before his time. His work soon became known outside and visitors called at the island.

Two meals a day were his limit. A late morning meal, consisting of rice, meat, coffee, and a few "hardtack" biscuits and in the evening, "what was left from dinner with a cup of tea, the water for which I boil over a lamp. You see, I live very well; I do not starve and am not much at home in the daytime."

As he worked and chatted with the lepers, he had always the vision of Christ before him, and the hunger in his heart to do Christ's work among the outcast. That was his comfort as he wended his lonely way to the huts of the plague-stricken, or walked at eventide beside the restless sea. Everywhere in his journeyings up and down the colony he felt this presence of his Lord.

After long years on the island, after much seeking and craving, he secured the assistance of other priests, as well as three nuns, and two lay-brothers. There was an Irish Brother there, tall, auburn-haired, generous-hearted, named Brother James. With the ardor and generosity of the Celt, Brother James devoted himself utterly to the personal service of Damien who was now much in need. Thus, in the evening of his days did God bless Damien with the one thing most completely absent from his life in the colony, human friendship. His work, too, was insured against destruction.

To these devoted friends were added the long-desired community of Sisters. The Sisters initiated a regime of cleanliness as well as the establishment of a modern clinic for the dressing of the lepers' sores. A Girls' Home was placed under their supervision and, in general, things were never so bright. But, one evening when Brother James was getting ready a bath of hot water to bathe Father Damien's feet when he returned footsore and weary after the day's toil, in a moment of abstraction Damien put his foot into the boiling water and felt no pain.

"Are you scalded?" asked Brother James anxiously. Both men looked at each other. Came in that tense moment the realization: Damien was a leper!

Damien a leper! One at last in suffering as he had been one in sympathy. He was in very deed a prisoner now with the others. And in that hour he was not afraid. It was the bargain he had made long ago when he had passed that first night under the spreading pandanus tree; it was the doom he sought. He inquired from the doctor. The verdict was conclusive. The kindly doctor hesitated: "I cannot bear to tell you what you know is the case."

"There is Red martyrdom and White martyrdom," wrote an Irish monk one day on his parchment scroll. "Red martyrdom is achieved when one gives up his life for a sacred cause, white martyrdom is the daily dying to oneself." The slow death of Damien smote him piece by piece.

His visitors marveled at his unalterable patience. He lay there in his wooden shed with the roar of the sea sounding ever more faintly in his dying ear, and the kindly face of the good brother working with sorrow beside him.

"They are all gone," he said, referring to the lepers who had met and welcomed him on that never-to-be-forgotten first day in the colony, "and I shall be seeing them soon."

On April 13, 1889, he died, without a struggle, as if falling asleep. The bell was tolled. A long, low wail rose among the cliffs. The father and friend of the lepers was dead. Death, yes. But not defeat. It was a glorious, magnificient, triumphant victory. The young lad of Tremoloo had walked into history, into a place among the great ones, and is now evermore the exemplar of noble deeds. He was laid to rest under the shade of the friendly pandanus tree which had sheltered him the first night he slept within sound of the seas.

On February 3, 1936, at the request of the Belgian government, the body of Damien was translated to the Chapel of the Fathers of the Sacred Heart at Louvain, Belgium; with unheard-of acclaim, full liturgical pomp and royal salutes it was escorted to the waiting American steamer while the Stars and Stripes dipped in homage to the world hero.

At Antwerp, the King of the Belgians met the solemn cortege in company with the Cardinal Archbishop of Malines. In Belgium he received honors which the poor lepers of Molokai may not bestow . . . but his glory will ever be that he achieved white martyrdom in Molokai.*

✠

THE END IS A BEGINNING
Albert J. Nevins

THE locale is Kaying, Kwangtung, China, two days before Christmas, 1950. Bishop Ford** sits in his cathedral rectory clearing up details because he knows that time is quickly running out. It has been a year since the Reds came to Kaying, and every day the noose draws tighter. Suddenly there are the sounds of cars driving up, the running of feet, and muffled shouts. Red soldiers, acting on a prearranged plan, surround the mission, and officials of the Provincial Police hurry inside. Some officials detain Bishop Ford in a room downstairs, while others direct searches through the rest of the house. That night Bishop

* Abridged from *White Martyrdom* by the Rev. John Henaghan. Copyright 1946 by St. Columban's Foreign Mission Society. Used by permission of the Society of St. Columban's.
** Bishop Francis X. Ford was a missionary belonging to the Catholic Society of Maryknoll, which maintains missionaries in all parts of the world.

Ford sleeps on the dining-room table, as his two soldiers stand guard over him. The next day he is moved to his room, never to leave it until April 14, with but one exception. Around the clock a search goes on. Every inch of space is examined—the cathedral, the bishop's house, the mission, the convent, the combination water-and-bell tower, the student hostel, all the outbuildings. Every book in the mission is subjected to minute scrutiny; every marked passage is noted.

Toward the end of February, the other missioners under arrest in Kaying watch the guards escort Bishop Ford to the front of the new cathedral—a building that he had begun erecting after the war. The cornerstone, ordered months earlier, has arrived, and Bishop Ford is taken down to give directions where it should be placed. The priests watching from the mission window grieve to see their bishop looking pale, gaunt, haggard. The hours of unending questioning are beginning to have effect. The trumped-up charges against Bishop Ford take legal shape and are solemnly printed all over China: Head of the United States spy ring, would-be saboteur of the Communist national-church movement, harborer of agents of the Kuomintang, organizer of an army to overthrow the People's Government.

On the morning of April 14, 1951, Bishop Ford and his secretary, Sister Joan Marie, are taken from the mission by a squad of thirty soldiers. The two Americans are bound like common criminals. The bishop's hands are tied behind his back; another rope is fastened about his neck, extending down his back, and looped around his hands. Every time the weight of his hands and arms pulls downwards, his head is jerked backwards.

The bus carrying Bishop Ford and his secretary is halted on the outskirts of town and the Americans are ordered out to go by foot the rest of the way to the local jail. The Hingning officials have done their work well. The road is lined with slogan-shouting students, armed with sticks, stones, and garbage. When the students spy the American, a great roar goes up. The bishop looks down the threatening line but his step does not falter. He walks slowly and deliberately into the crowd. Behind him comes Sister Joan Marie, followed by soldiers. The roar turns to shouts and screaming. Blows begin to rain down, stones hit the bishop with sickening sounds. Garbage and refuse cover him. Because of the way he has been tied, he is unable to even raise his elbows to defend himself.

Bishop Ford calmly continues his course through the gauntlet, making no protest at the flagellation. Each time he is tripped, he manages somehow to regain his feet. At last, bruised, disheveled, and covered with filth, he stumbles into the comparative safety of the Public Security Office. Sister Joan Marie, who has undergone the same treatment, follows.

The two prisoners are locked up overnight in the Hingning jail. People are brought in to see the "leader of the American spies" and to heap abuse and insults upon both prisoners.

"Where is your God now?" they cry. "What is He doing to help you? Our god is the devil. Our god has power over your God!"

The next day the two Americans are taken to Laulung. The demonstration here has to be cut short because of rain, and Sister Joan Marie is able to persuade a guard to buy some eggs and milk for the bishop—his first food since he was taken from his house in Kaying. The prisoners are led aboard a boat for Ho-yun. Here the guards change the bishop's ropes for heavier ones, adding a little refinement of soaking the ropes in water before trussing the bishop up. As the ropes begin to dry, they tighten up and bite deeply into the flesh.

The federal prison of Canton is a sprawling, red stone, cruciform structure. It is an old building, erected for the purpose of punishing prisoners and not pampering them. It is two stories high, except over one wing where the Reds added a third story to house their interrogation and "persuasion" rooms. The four elongated wings lead into a sort of rotunda, where three guards with machine guns are on constant watch.

After their arrival, Bishop Ford and Sister Joan Marie are taken to separate sections of the prison and locked in reception cells. They are dark, and they give the effect of living at the bottom of an elevator shaft. There is no furniture and the prisoners must sleep on the stone floor. The cells are not private. Sister Joan Marie is placed in a cell with seventeen other women, many of them guilty of the crudest crimes imaginable. Two cups of water are given to each prisoner daily. No clothing is furnished; no blanket, soap, towel, or washbasin.

For the first two months, the new prisoners remain in the reception section undergoing a systematic brainwashing. This psychological treatment lasts for about twelve hours a day, but occasionally extends longer, sometimes until two or three o'clock in the morning. The sessions are bitter, full of hysteria and violence, screams, and denunciations.

When the two Americans are moved to the main section of the prison, conditions are a little better. There are still the crowded cells, the filth, the poor food; but the long brainwashing sessions end, and only brutal interrogation periods remain. Prisoners are given work to do. Sister Joan Marie becomes a water-carrier, a job that lets her move in a limited way around sections of the prison, and that enables her to catch a few glimpses of her bishop. She becomes the only available witness to his final days.

In July, she gets a brief sight of Bishop Ford and rejoices that he looks fairly well. Long months pass, during which she does not see the bishop. The year 1951 slips into 1952, and Sister begins to worry about her superior. Then by an odd accident, she sees him again.

One day early in January, Sister Joan Marie is going about her work. On the damp stone floor of the corridor, her foot slips, and she loses her balance. Prone on the floor, she looks up at a wooden door, the bottom of which has slanted slats to permit ventilation. Through the slats she can see a stairway down which a man is laboriously descending. He is a prisoner, and over his shoulder, like a sack of potatoes, he is carrying another prisoner. From the black cotton gown, she recognizes the carried man as Bishop Ford.

At the bottom of the stairs, the prisoner slips Bishop Ford off his shoulder and stands him on his feet. The bishop's hair has turned white, and his *saam* hangs loosely on his thin frame. He has a stick to use as a cane, but he seems unable to make his feet move. He puts both arms out, standing there wavering.

"Come on. Walk!" says the other prisoner, with a laugh.

"I can't," replies the bishop.

The prisoner carries the bishop down the corridor, out of sight.

"He must be very light," the watching Sister thinks, "because it hardly takes any effort for the other prisoner to carry him."

Two days later, Sister Joan Marie sees the bishop again. This time he is walking slowly, one arm linked in the arm of a fellow prisoner. He is very feeble. His face is emaciated and terribly aged, but peaceful.

Sister sees Bishop Ford once again in February. The bishop is being carried over a prisoner's shoulders, up the stairs, but by this time malnutrition has left her so confused that she notes only the main incident and not the details.

The year moves along. It is now August 16. A guard comes for Sister Joan Marie and leads her to the Red warden's office. There she is told that Bishop Ford is dead. The warden orders her to sign a certificate stating that Bishop Ford died of illness and old age and not from ill treatment. She tries to resist, but in her shocked and weakened condition, she is no match for the Communist. She signs the certificate, noting the day of death: February 21. That was six months earlier, and only a few days after she had last seen the weakened bishop.

The news of the bishop's death proves too much for the Sister, and she falls desperately ill. She is removed to a hospital, her captors fearing that she too, will die and then suspicion will fall upon them for two murders. It now becomes important for them to get her out of the country alive. She was only to be a witness at Bishop Ford's trial; after his death she is longer valuable. The Communists want no martyrs, unless they are their own. That is why the charges hurled against missionaries are always political ones.

On September 2, Sister Joan Marie is brought before Communist officials again. They tell her that in a few days the whole story of Bishop Ford will be released to the public. Because of the bishop's many crimes, reaction will be hard to control. It will be difficult to save her from being torn apart by the people, so to protect her life they are deporting her at once. Two officers immediately escort her to the Hong Kong border, and Sister stumbles across the barrier to freedom.

With Sister Joan Marie's release, the news of Bishop Ford's death speeds around the world. Newspapers and magazines tell of the persecution. Radio broadcasts are beamed behind the Iron Curtain. Orators eulogize the dead prelate. Memorial masses are celebrated on four continents.

The spirit of Bishop Ford is the spirit of Maryknoll. The traditions that formed him are the traditions of the Society to which he gave his life. Bishop Ford's story is the Maryknoll story, and one cannot be understood without the other. The success of any society lies not in statistics but in the men it creates. The meaning of Maryknoll brings one to an understanding of the bishop who died in the prison on Canton's Yellow Flower Road—and not only him, but others, some dead, more alive in many and varied parts of the world, the priests and brothers who compose the Catholic Foreign Mission Society—the men of Maryknoll.*

✠

FATHER TABART
Glenn D. Kittler

AT THE same moment throughout Africa, hundreds of other White Fathers were also starting out to say Mass, in a bush village, a distant hospital, a school perhaps. Knowing this always filled Father Tabart with a sense of fraternity he greatly enjoyed. There, of course, were other societies of missionaries in Africa, but the White Fathers were the largest, and they were the only society dedicated exclusively to Africa. A love for Africa was practically a prerequisite for the society, yet an unnecessary one, for the men who joined the White Fathers had that love from boyhood, a love they couldn't explain but had felt all their lives as vividly as they felt the desire to become priests. It was perhaps a spiritual inheritance from the man who had started the society—Charles Martial Allemand Lavigerie, who had come to Africa as a bishop at the age of forty-one—Tabart's age now—and who had almost single-handedly changed the face of the continent.

Lavigerie had been a tornado of a man, big and powerful, who tackled every problem as if it were a living enemy. He had been one of the first men to maintain that Africa should be for the Africans—a form of political heresy a century ago—and he had organized the White Fathers as a step in that direction. It had seemed an unattainable goal in 1856; even in 1956 it was not much closer, but now the Africans—both the brown man of the Sahara and the black man of the Equator—were better equipped for the job, and the White Fathers were greatly responsible. There had been many obstacles, but Lavigerie was a man who thrived on obstacles, and so were the priests who followed him. The hardships, even deaths, had served to unify the White Fathers, to crystallize their aim: to help the African to help himself.

This unique crusade had created a deep brotherhood among the White Fathers, strengthened them, and gave their efforts greater impact upon the people. True, progress had been slowest in the north, but if Lavigerie had been correct in predicting that by example and acts of charity the priests would inevitably break down the Moslem resistance to Christianity and the social advancement implicit in it, then the only thing to do, Tabart told himself, was to keep hard at the job, just as others that moment were doing all over Africa.

Tabart's road took him high into the mountains, and as he hurried along he saw in distant fields the smoke rising from what he deduced to be insurgent camps. Once or twice he thought he heard sudden movement in the roadside bushes; a lookout probably. Tabart pretended to hear nothing and continued toward the French camp. As a White Father dedicated to Africa, he found his sentiments in the war were with the Arabs. He disapproved of what they were doing, but he could understand why they felt they must. Yet as a priest there was nothing he could do about it, one way or the other; under the circumstances he could only go on with the regular work, as normally as possible. Arabs in Géryville had tried to sound him out, but he had replied merely: "You people should know me well after all these years. Judge me in that light." All he could hope was that they understood.

He rode across the valley to the foot of the big hill, got off his bicycle, and walked up it. At the top, he mounted again for the long downhill ride. He had gone part way when he saw several Arabs rush from the bushes and block his path. He skidded to a stop at their feet. He was about to ask them what was wrong, when they jumped him. Before he could speak, one man struck him brutally across the face. Dazed, he felt himself being pulled from his bicycle and dragged off the road. He spoke, and his voice sounded distant, hollow. He tried to free himself, but the Arabs held him fast. They carried him into the thick bush and threw him to the ground, and when he attempted to get up, they straddled him. One man took out a dagger with one hand and with the other ripped Tabart's rosary off his neck. The morning sun caught the dagger as the man raised it.

Tabart had time to say: "God!"

His body was found five days later. The ground was still black moist from his blood. His throat had been cut almost clean through. He was lying face down, his arm outstretched. There were blood on his fingers and markings in the dust, as if he had put his hand to his wound for blood to write a message. His rosary was missing; so were the bicycle and the Mass kit.

He was brought back to the mission and prepared for burial, and that night the village of Géryville was unusually quiet. Very late, there was a knock on the mission door, and Father Superior went to answer it. Standing in the darkness were several men of the village.

One of them said: "We have come to tell you how sorry we are that this has happened."

"Thank you," Father Superior replied.

"And we want you to know we had nothing to do with it."

"Thank you. I believe you."

"The men who did it were not from around here and they did not know him."

"I'm sure that's understandable," the priest said. "There are many strangers in the hills these days."

"We are going to find out who killed him," the man said, "and we are going to avenge his death."

"Oh, no," Father Superior said quickly. "No vengeance. He would not want that. Vengeance would be against everything he believed in."

Another man asked: "Will you close the mission because of this?"

"I hope not," answered Father Superior. "That depends on the French, but I will do everything to keep it open."

"We want you to stay."

And still another man queried: "Have you chosen those who will lower him into the ground?"

"No," said Father Superior. "I will probably do it myself with the other priest here with me, and perhaps a couple of the French soldiers."

"Would it be possible for us to do it?"

"You mean you want to be his pallbearers?"

"If it is possible. Among our people it is a special honor. It is the greatest tribute of friendship we have."

"Very well," said Father Superior. "You may do it. I'm sure nothing could please Father Tabart more than knowing you considered him your friend."

Next morning, the Arabs were there in the courtyard next to the mission, and when Father Superior gave the signal, they gently lowered Father Tabart into his grave. The illiterate merchant was there, too, and the woman with the sick child, and the young man who wanted to get married, and many others Father Tabart had befriended. The scene proved many things, but above all it proved that no matter what Moslems had been taught to believe about Christians, they could still have no defense against men who loved them. This Lavigerie had predicted a century before when, as Bishop of Algiers, he had founded the White Fathers. And he had predicted much more.*

✠

CROWN HIM WITH MANY CROWNS

MATTHEW BRIDGES (1800-1894) left the Church of England to become a Roman Catholic. On doing so, he published a volume of poems, "The Passion of Jesus," and included in the book were the words to "Crown Him with Many Crowns." From that time on, Matthew Bridges wrote prolifically; his hymns and ritual arrangements appeared and still appear in Roman Catholic books of church music. The majesty and dignity of the words to this great hymn carry the worshiper beyond the bonds of earth to a vision of heaven itself. They express the wonder and power of God and of Jesus Christ as the redeemer of man.

The tune, "Diademata," matches the glory of the words. This music was written by Sir George Elvey, organist of St. George's, Windsor, in England. A devout man as well as a talented musician, Elvey wrote many compositions

* Abridged from *The White Fathers* by Glenn D. Kittler, pp. 5-9. Copyright 1957 by Glenn D. Kittler. Published by Harper & Brothers. Used by permission of the publisher.

Crown Him With Many Crowns*

MATTHEW BRIDGES, 1851 S. M. D. DIADEMATA
George J. Elvey, 1868

Joyously, but with great dignity

1. Crown Him with man - y crowns, The Lamb up - on His throne;
2. Crown Him the Lord of love; Be - hold His hands and side,
3. Crown Him the Lord of peace; Whose power a scep - ter sways
4. Crown Him the Lord of years, The Po - ten - tate of time;

Hark! how the heaven-ly an - them drowns All mu - sic but its own:
Rich wounds, yet vis - i - ble a - bove, In beau - ty glo - ri - fied:
From pole to pole, that wars may cease, Ab-sorbed in prayer and praise:
Cre - a - tor of the roll - ing spheres, In - ef - fa - bly sub - lime:

A - wake, my soul, and sing Of Him who died for thee, And
No an - gel in the sky Can ful - ly bear that sight, But
His reign shall know no end; And round His pierc - ed feet Fair
All hail, Re - deem - er, hail! For Thou hast died for me: Thy

hail Him as thy match-less King Through all e - ter - ni - ty.
down-ward bends His burn-ing eye At mys - ter - ies so bright.
flowers of Par - a - dise ex - tend Their fra-grance ev - er sweet.
praise shall nev - er, nev - er fail Through-out e - ter - ni - ty. A-MEN.

which are models of what church music should be: noble, dignified, profound, and worshipful. "Diademata" is one of his few hymn tunes (most of his music was composed for choir and organ), and a more glorious musical setting for the majestic words could not be found. Words and music combine to lift the worshiper from worldly things and direct his attention and spirit toward God. One gets the feeling of worshiping in a great cathedral with soaring arches and the finest of architectural beauty around him to inspire his mind toward God. "Crown Him with Many Crowns" does through its words and music what a great cathedral does through its architecture: lift the soul toward God in worship.

✠

O SAVIOUR, BLESS US ERE WE GO

FREDERICK WILLIAM FABER, author of the words to this beautiful eventide hymn, was raised in the Church of England, where he took orders and became a clergyman. He changed his views, however, and entered the Roman Catholic Church, forming with eight others a community known as "Brothers of the Will of God." He wrote about one hundred fifty hymns and several books on religious subjects. Many of his hymns are loved and used by Protestants and Catholics alike.

Such is the case with "O Saviour, Bless Us Ere We Go." It is found in hymnbooks of both faiths. The words to the hymns embody Faber's beliefs that men should be "brothers of the will of God." Notice, how, in the first stanza, the Saviour is invited into the heart and mind so that persons may show love for others and trust in God. Faith that God will help all who sin forms the theme of the second stanza, while in the third the worshiper asks Christ to absolve him from evil ways and grant purity and inward peace. The fourth stanza develops the idea that Christian faith and love make one mindful of others. The hymn closes with a beautiful expression of trust and quiet peace that will come when the Saviour is near.

Other hymns by Faber include, "My God, How Wonderful Thou Art," "O Come, and Mourn with Me Awhile," "Faith of Our Fathers," and "Hark! Hark, My Soul!"

William Henry Monk wrote the quiet, gently flowing music which is so well suited to the words of this hymn. He was director of the choir and organist at Kings College, London.

The first three stanzas appear in the music score on p. 403. The fourth and fifth are given below:

> For all we love, the poor, the sad,
>   The sinful, unto thee we call;
> O let thy mercy make us glad;
>   Thou art our Saviour and our all.

O Saviour, Bless Us Ere We Go*

88. 88. 88

ST. MATTHIAS

WILLIAM H. MONK, 1861

With movement

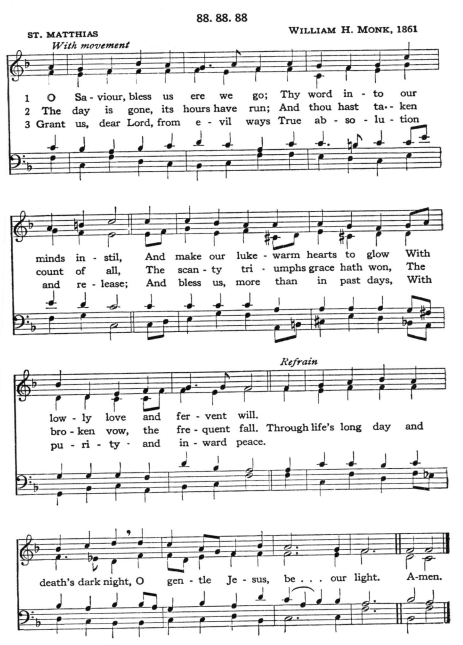

1 O Sa - viour, bless us ere we go; Thy word in - to our
2 The day is gone, its hours have run; And thou hast ta - - ken
3 Grant us, dear Lord, from e - vil ways True ab - so - lu - tion

minds in - stil, And make our luke - warm hearts to glow With
count of all, The scan - ty tri - umphs grace hath won, The
and re - lease; And bless us, more than in past days, With

Refrain

low - ly love and fer - vent will.
bro - ken vow, the fre - quent fall. Through life's long day and
pu - ri - ty - and in - ward peace.

death's dark night, O gen - tle Je - sus, be . . . our light. A - men.

FREDERICK WILLIAM FABER, 1849

*From *The Hymnal, 1940*, No. 182. Published by The Church Hymnal Corporation. Used by permission of The Church Pension Fund.

Refrain

O Saviour, bless us; night is come;
  Through night and darkness near us be;
Good angels watch about our home,
  And we are one day nearer thee.

Refrain

PART IV

THE PROTESTANT REFORMATION IN EUROPE

by

RONALD E. OSBORN

1. THE REFORMATION BEGINS .... *page* 406

2. THE REFORMATION SPREADS .... *page* 434

3. THE REFORMATION REACHES GREAT BRITAIN *page* 461

4. THE REFORMATION CONTINUES .... *page* 490

5. THE UNFINISHED REFORMATION .... *page* 517

CONTENTS

PART IV SECTION 1

THE REFORMATION BEGINS

—✝—

But that no man is justified by the law in the sight of God, it is evident: for the just shall live by faith.—GALATIANS 3:11

—✝—

PICTURES: PAGE
Interpretation: Knight, Death, and the Devil—*Dürer* 407
Picture: Knight, Death, and the Devil—*Dürer* 409
Interpretation: The Bible Goes to Press—Motion Picture 410
Picture: The Bible Goes to Press—Motion Picture 413
Interpretation: "Here I Stand"—Motion Picture 412
Picture: "Here I Stand"—Motion Picture 415

POETRY:
The Word of God—*Huss* (?) 417
Lord, Keep Us Steadfast in Thy Word—*Luther* 417
A Missionary Prayer—*Luther* 418
Morning Prayer for the Day's Work—*Matthesius* 418
An Evening Prayer—*Herbert* 419
The Moravian Emigrants' Hymn—*Isaac* 419
Anabaptist Martyr's Hymn—*Schiemer* 420
Christian Unity (Psalm 133)—*Czerwenka* 420

STORIES:
Through Peril and Fire—*Hall* 421
The Abbot and the Learned Woman—*Erasmus* 424
Martin Luther and the Eisleben Choir—*Baker* 428

MUSIC:
Interpretation: O Lord of All, Our Father—*Bosák* 429
Music: O Lord of All, Our Father—*Hussisches Graduale* 430
Interpretation: Thou Holy Spirit, We Pray to Thee—*Luther* 431
Music: Thou Holy Spirit, We Pray to Thee—*Gesangbuch* 432

KNIGHT, DEATH, AND THE DEVIL

Albrecht Dürer

THE young scholar and monk, Martin Luther, was harassed by the burden of his unrighteousness. Striving with might and main to win acceptance from God, in fact he wore himself out with penances and pilgrimages, buffeting his body in vigils and prostrations and pouring out the torture of his soul in daily confessions, yet only increasing thereby his torment.

This Martin Luther was not only a guilt-ridden individual; he also reflected the age in which he lived, with its hope of heaven and fear of perdition. Popular illustrated books depicted in lurid woodcuts the torments of hell. Manuals intended to help people learn to die well showed in graphic imagery the evil spirits that hovered around the dying, tempting them to abandon God in life's final moment. A very familiar illustration was that of Christ as Judge sitting on the rainbow, in condemnation of the unrighteous, whom we see being dragged by the devils out of their graves and cast writhing into eternal torment.

Death and the Devil, and God standing wrathfully as Judge—these were the presences with whom the medieval world lived.

But here is another picture, which Professor Paul Tillich has called the classic expression of the spirit of the Reformation. It was engraved shortly after Luther's heroic struggle by one of the early converts to the Protestant faith, Albrecht Dürer (1471-1528), who may well be called the artist of the Reformation, despite his early death. The picture is entitled "Knight, Death, and the Devil."

In this picture (p. 409) we see the Knight, symbol of the Christian man, riding his steed through a dark valley, strewn with skulls and beset by skulking beasts. Just to the front of him is Death on his haggard nag, holding before the eyes of the Knight the hourglass of his brief and fleeting day. Behind him is the monstrous, evil figure of the Devil, following to snatch his soul.

But the Knight sees neither, nor thinks on them. His strong face is relaxed and poised. His eyes are straight forward, but resting easily downward, without strain or anxiety. He makes his sure and unperturbed way through the desolate valley toward the lighted hill beyond, on which stands a castle crowned by a church. One could scarcely imagine a greater contrast than the harassed Catholic monk and the triumphant Christian knight.

What has happened to make the difference? Nothing—in outward circumstances. Here in Dürer's picture are the familiar and frightful figures of Death and the Devil—symbols of man's mortality and the evil that constantly besets him. But inwardly the entire world has changed. To understand that change is to hit upon the central secret of Protestant faith.

Why did the men of the late Middle Ages, to whom Luther belonged,

buffet themselves so to win salvation? Luther tells of seeing on the streets
one day Prince William of Anhalt, a young man of position and riches, in the
cowl of a monk who had given all up to become a beggar. There he was, bent
under the weight of his beggar's bag, emaciated, prematurely old, struggling
through the slums of the city, so "worn down by fasting and vigil that he
looked like a death's head." He was striving to lay up treasures in heaven,
yet dogged by the constant fear that he might never attain that blessed
state.

And so the whole of mankind was called upon to bend every nerve and
muscle, submitting to humiliating penances, enduring all kinds of self-mutil-
ations, impoverishing themselves buying indulgences, agonizing to secure the
release of loved ones from the punishments of purgatory. Yet no one could
be quite sure he had become good enough. Some secret sin, some unremem-
bered and unconfessed fault might damn him in that final day.

What was the matter with these men of the sixteenth century? Why did
they drive themselves so mercilessly trying to appease the wrath of God, or to
attain positions of power and success, or to achieve the favors of cosmic
fortune? Well, for precisely the same reasons we do very similar things today
—and in fact, in every day. Why? Perhaps here is the clue: we all feel desperately alone.

No, not entirely alone; for there ride beside us as by the Christian Knight
of old those familiar and inescapable figures of Death and the Devil. Death—
that haunting uncertain certainty of which we rarely speak but of whose presence we can never get rid, by whatever means we try. The sands of the
hourglass flow unceasingly—and we know they will all too soon run out. And
the Devil—that demonic perversity which dogs all our ways—the evil that
lies in wait for us at every turn and drives us to arrogant self-assertion and
pugnacious aggression. We push in where we do not belong, to take what is
not rightfully ours, to rebuff, and hurt, to wound even those whom we love,
to torture those whom we hate, and then to leave ourselves with the thorns
of remorse and bitterness deep in our own hearts.

And because we too ride alone—and yet in company with these two dark
companions and enemies, Death and the Devil—we are beset by the same
anxiety, the same threat of despair as that which drove the monk Martin
Luther so relentlessly. Our strivings and self-lacerations are no less real
simply because they are less lurid. Our Judge too sits upon the rainbow.

And what of the Christian Knight in his armor? What would we not give
to possess that calm strength, that unperturbed peace, that victory over the
world and its evils that are his!

Well, it was the genius of Luther and his colleagues that they woke up to
the fact that they were running a losing race. No one—however swift or
strong—could escape these two enemies. Nor could he ever become good
enough to stand in the presence of the Holy One. Never could all his alms
and penances and righteous works take away the weight of the world's sins
nor lighten the load of his own dread.

KNIGHT, DEATH, AND THE DEVIL—*DÜRER*

So in mid-flight these men stopped and turned to face the depth of their despair. Out of their own emptiness they turned to the fullness of God's love and mercy. Could it possibly be that God knows we are running a losing race? Could it be also that He accepts us not because of what we are but because of what He is? Could it be that He receives us not because of our righteousness, or its lack, but because of His own goodness?

These men of the sixteenth century turned again to what had been virtually a closed book to them, the Bible. And they read it like a new revelation. They found the figure of Jesus, Son of God, who never demanded of any man that he be good, but only that he accept the love of God and give his love in return. Indeed, as Luther pondered the sufferings of Christ the light of God's love broke upon him. He saw that the picture of Christ the relentless Judge sitting remote and wrathful on the rainbow was a perversion. Christ is indeed our Judge, but His judgment is only the darker side of His eternal, seeking, suffering love.

Here in the Word of God made manifest they rediscovered the inexhaustible love of God for His sinful and remorseful children, a love that suffers for and with all those guilt-ridden, fear-driven, anxiety-cursed mortals who exhaust themselves in running away from Him or frantically fight to reach Him. Here they heard Him saying to them all, "Come unto me, all you that labor and are heavy laden . . . and I will give you rest."

But the Reformation leaders did not invent the idea. They discovered it; or rather they received it with eager and rejoicing hearts. This indeed was the world-shaking truth manifest in the flesh by Jesus Christ. This was the secret of Paul's peace—Paul who, like Luther and thousands of others after him, struggled desperately to meet the demands of God's justice and holiness but in vain. Paul's word is that of all who have known the grace of Christ: "Thanks be to God. . . . For the law of the Spirit of life in Christ Jesus has set me free from the law of sin and death (Rom. 7:25-8:2, RSV).*

✤

THE BIBLE GOES TO PRESS
From the Motion Picture, *Our Bible—How It Came to Us*

JUST imagine 908,000 scribes, each carefully copying a Bible in one of a hundred or more languages. That would take a lot of desk space and a tremendous number of man-hours. Allowing sixty-five days out of a year for Sundays and church holidays, each would need to work at least three hundred days in order to complete a whole Bible—272,400,000 man-hours. How could the 1,612,739 Testaments and the 14,918,353 Portions actually distributed in one recent year by the American Bible Society alone have been reproduced under such conditions?

Because of the persistence and inventiveness of a German goldsmith who lived in the fifteenth century, it is not necessary to employ such methods to

* This interpretation was prepared by Walter W. Sikes.

manufacture the Scriptures. In August, 1456, the first printed Bible was issued from the press, printed, illuminated and bound. Perhaps two hundred copies had been produced in the course of five years by only a handful of men using movable metal letters instead of quill pens.

Back of that beginning were long years of experiment. The year 1440 has long been celebrated to honor Gutenberg's achieving a practical method of casting separate metal letters. For ten years he had worked to improve and perfect his methods, experimenting with pamphlets and Latin schoolbooks. Several conditions helped to create the propitious atmosphere for this important invention. The revival of learning was awakening all Europe to an interest in new ideas, and the development of trade by the Hanseatic League and other such organizations provided routes for the spread of written material, thus providing a waiting market and means of filling it. Parchment had been expensive, but by the middle of the fifteenth century, paper, which had been coarse, unsatisfactory, and scarce, was appearing in much better quality and quantity. In experimenting with block printing (carved blocks of wood), with pictures and a few lines of text, the wine press had been improved until it provided a suitable means of securing an even, solid impression. But the need for the right kind of ink and the problem of producing metal letters that would be perfectly aligned were unresolved.

From childhood Johann Gansefleisch, known today by his mother's name of Gutenberg, had been familiar with the technique of working with precious metals and dies. He conceived and developed a process of making a die which might be punched into a brass bar from which, by the use of molds, could be cast any number of a single letter. He developed a mold that would provide at the same time a shank for the letter, by which it could be handled. By this process quantities of similar letters could be made that would line up evenly. This invention would not have been so difficult with the finely calibrated instruments of today, but it was a task demanding tremendous ingenuity five hundred years ago. He also needed to find a suitable metal alloy that would be strong enough to wear well and soft enough not to cut the paper, and a kind of ink that would stick to the surface of the letters evenly, yet would also adhere to the paper smoothly and permanently.

The picture on p. 413 (from a film produced for the American Bible Society) represents Gutenberg's assistant setting type for the first printed Bible about 1450.

Gutenberg borrowed large sums "for the work of the books" and a "a project of considerable importance," as the old records of the lawsuits cryptically expressed it. The lenders wanted results; Gutenberg was a perfectionist; the lenders sued. He lost his materials but he started all over again. It is quite likely that because of these difficulties Gutenberg himself did not print, or at least complete, the Bible that was to be "the great project." This may have been done by Johann Fust, one of the moneylenders, and Gutenberg's former assistant, Peter Schoeffer.

It was planned to have forty lines to a full column, but it soon became clear that this would use too much paper; so the body of the type was filed off to provide forty-one lines and, still further, to provide forty-two lines; and the rest of the book was set with forty-two lines. These first eighty-two leaves were later reprinted, so that of the forty-six copies now known, some have forty-two lines on all pages, but a few have the forty- and forty-one-line pages. Even though Gutenberg may not have printed this Bible himself, and even though the Mainz Psalter may possibly have been published earlier, the Gutenberg Bible is the first Bible printed from movable metal type and the first printed large book—and a magnificent piece of printing.

At a time when manuscript Bibles were selling for around sixty guilders, the paper for this book was the most expensive item, and a copy probably sold for about fifty guilders. But it would have taken at least a year to produce a manuscript Bible, and here was a process whereby in the first instance it took perhaps five years to print two hundred copies. The invention once worked out, the idea spread—but not always with printers as painstaking and exacting as Gutenberg. Out of the small city of Mainz into the great trading centers and over the Alps to Italy, to France, to Spain, to England spread the printing press and this new method of making books. Editions increased from two hundred until in the next century Aldus in Venice was printing 1,000 copies of small books of the Greek and Latin classics. In 1491 Froben in Basle issued the first "Poorman's Bible," so called because of its small size— six inches by four and a half inches.

While more and more Bibles were printed every year—first in Latin, then, in 1466, in German, and later in other languages—the process remained fundamentally the same for over three hundred years. In the eighteenth century various experiments were tried out to avoid resetting type and to speed up the presswork, but it was not until the nineteenth century that the use of stereotyped plates was introduced and the steam press increased the number of copies that could be printed at one time. Then came the linotype and monotype machines, reducing the time for setting type. It was because of these improvements, in addition to Gutenberg's original inventions, that it was possible for printers in various parts of the world to manufacture these 14,918,353 Bibles and Testaments and Portions that the American Bible Society distributed in this five-hundredth year since the completion of that first printed Bible.*

✛

"HERE I STAND"

From the Motion Picture, *Martin Luther*

POPE LEO X was at his hunting lodge. Before many weeks the Most Catholic Emperor, Charles V, was to make a trip from Spain to Germany. Germany?

* Abridged from "500th Anniversary of the Gutenberg Bible" by Margaret T. Hills, in *Bible Society Record*, Vol. 101 (1956), pp. 104-105. Published by the American Bible Society. Used by permission of the author and the publisher.

Courtesy American Bible Society, New York

THE BIBLE GOES TO PRESS

That was where a most obstreperous monk had been making objectionable noises, and interfering with the steady flow of ecclesiastical revenues.

Leo X had appointed a special consistory to handle the situation. The group of about forty were all Italians—except Eck, another German. With well-tempered patience and confidence the consistory had laid before His Holiness a document which condemned only forty-one of the multitude of errors in Luther's ninety-five theses, his books, sermons and growing broadsides and pamphlets.

Sitting in his hunting lodge the pope plucked a figure of speech from the beautiful setting as he inscribed the personal message with which to make the committee's work his own. He wrote: "Exsurge . . ."—"Arise, O Lord, and judge thy cause. A wild boar has invaded thy vineyard. . . ."

A "bull" was an official papal document made impressive with a large seal *(bulla)*. This one condemned Luther because, as Leo wrote to Frederick the Elector, he "gives credence to the opinions of none save himself alone, which no heretic before ever presumed to do." He added that in the consistory which listed the errors of Luther "the Holy Spirit also was present, for in such cases he is never absent from our Holy See."

But the sleep of ages was removing from the minds of men, long drugged by claims of divine rights held by kings and bishops. The invention of printing gave wings to the Bible, long withheld from the common man.

And men everywhere rose to protect Luther! Erasmus, most learned man of his day, spoke not for himself alone but for a new generation reared on Holy Writ when he dismissed the formerly fearsome document by saying, "Papal bulls are weighty, but scholars attach more weight to books with good arguments drawn from the testimony of divine Scripture."

Students at Erfurt threw copies of the bull in the river; at Leipzig, Eck had to run for his life to a cloister.

But popes and emperors long had won over recalcitrant rebels, peasants and their sons—over all common men. For a millennium men without the knowledge of the Word of God for instruction and power were but shadows of reality.

Only an iron will born of the assurance of divine truth caused the peasant-priest to write in letters of fire a pamphlet Against the Execrable Bull of Antichrist: "Where are you now, most excellent Charles the Emperor, kings, and Christian princes? You were baptized into the name of Christ, and can you suffer these Tartar voices of Antichrist? . . . The wrath of God is coming upon the papists, the enemies of the cross of Christ, that all men should resist them. You then, Leo X . . . I call upon you to renounce your diabolical blasphemy."

The pope tried to entice Frederick the Elector, Luther's prince, with an offer of more indulgences, plus a church position for his illegitimate son. Instead, Frederick insisted upon a trial before the Emperor, although the ruler was Spanish and was known to have torn and trampled some of Luther's writings. And so it was arranged, at Worms, in April, 1521.

"HERE I STAND"

A new age trembled to be born. Would empire crush man, privilege repel people, kings and bishops continue to exploit the ignorance and fear of awakening minds and souls? Only a completely convinced and divinely dedicated spirit would be able to bring a new era to birth.

A single individual was pitting his reason and his integrity against established institutions which were the bulwark of society.

Luther's words were not uttered without thought, nor by impulse. A full day was allowed after the first period of the trial before the Saxon monk need answer. At last it came—in words now historic with the prophecy of a new age: "Since then Your Majesty and your lordships desire a simple reply, I will answer without horns and without teeth. Unless I am convinced by Scripture and plain reason—I do not accept the authority of popes and councils, for they have contradicted each other—my conscience is captive to the Word of God. I cannot and I will not recant anything, for to go against conscience is neither right nor safe. God help me. Amen." One version adds, "Here I stand. I cannot do otherwise."

All gains cost. Tragedy accompanied the triumph of the German people who supported Luther, for it divided Christendom into three instead of two factions (the East had rejected Roman claims five hundred years earlier). But now new powers of a mass participation in creative religious life were released.

Sermons sped education, literature freed minds, family life was deemed holy instead of a concession to evil; this Luther dramatized by his marriage.

Princes gave added voluntary devotion to the religious life. An ebb tide cost the loyalty of many impatient peasants, and some learned humanists, but the balance showed vast gains. Roman presumption, rebuked by whole generations of events, retreated.

And down the ages Luther's great principles continue as the signpost of Christian liberty:

The priesthood of believers.
Salvation through faith.
The right and duty of private judgment.*

The photograph, "Here I Stand," shown on p. 415, is from the film, *Martin Luther*, produced by Louis de Rochemont Associates in collaboration with Lutheran Church Productions. Summoned to appear before Charles V, Emperor of the Holy Roman Empire, Martin Luther gives the answer all of Europe is awaiting to the question, "Will you or will you not recant?"

The reply rings down to the present day: "Unless I am so convinced that I am wrong, I am bound by my beliefs by the texts of the Bible. My conscience is captive to the Word of God. To go against conscience is neither right nor safe. Therefore I cannot and will not recant. Here I stand. I can do no other."

* From "Scenes of the Protestant Reformation" by Dr. A. T. DeGroot in *The Christian-Evangelist* (Vol. 92, 1954), pp. 1032-40. Published by Bethany Press. Used by permission of the author and the publisher.

THE WORD OF GOD

The Word of God which ne'er shall cease,
Proclaims free pardon, grace and peace,
Salvation shows in Christ alone,
The perfect will of God makes known.

This holy Word exposes sin,
Convinces us that we're unclean,
Points out the wretched, ruined state
Of all mankind, both small and great.

It then reveals God's boundless grace,
Which justifies our sinful race,
And gives eternal life to all
Who will accept the gospel call.

It gently heals the broken heart,
And heavenly riches doth impart,
Unfolds redemption's wondrous plan,
Through Christ's atoning death for man.

O God, in Whom our trust we place,
We thank Thee for Thy Word of grace;
Help us its precepts to obey,
Till we shall live in endless day.*

—John Huss (?) (ca. 1370-1415)

LORD, KEEP US STEADFAST IN THY WORD

Lord, keep us steadfast in Thy Word;
  Curb those who fain by craft or sword
Would wrest the Kingdom from Thy Son;
  And set at naught all He hath done.

Lord Jesus Christ, Thy power make known,
  For Thou art Lord of lords alone;
Defend Thy Christendom, that we
  May evermore sing praise to Thee.

O Comforter of priceless worth
  Send peace and unity on earth;
Support us in our final strife,
  And lead us out of death to life.**

—Martin Luther (1483-1546)

* Translated by L. F. Kampmann, 1876. This Hussite hymn was sung by the Bohemian Brethren before the sermon. From the *Hymnal and Liturgies of the Moravian Church (Unitas Fratrum)*. Used by permission of the Provincial Elders Conference.
** Translated by Catherine Winkworth, 1863.

A MISSIONARY PRAYER

Thy mercy, Lord, to us dispense,
   Thy blessing on us pour;
Lift up Thy gracious countenance
   Upon us evermore:
Oh, may we fully know Thy mind,
   Thy saving word proclaim,
That many heathen-tribes may find
   Salvation in Thy Name.

Let tongues and kindreds praise the Lord,
   Let every nation praise,
Let all the earth with one accord
   A glad thanksgiving raise,
That sin no more its sway maintains,
   For Christ the Lord is King,
His word defends, His law sustains;
   Shout all ye lands and sing!

Then shall the earth her increase bring,
   Her fruits be multiplied;
Then shall Thy scepter rule, O King,
   Thy word be glorified:
And God, our God, with blessings crown,
   His faithful Church again,
And earth's remotest bounds shall own
   Him, Lord and God!   Amen!*

—*Martin Luther*

MORNING PRAYER FOR THE DAY'S WORK

May Jesus' grace and blessing
Attend me without ceasing;
Thus I stretch out my hand,
And do that work with pleasure,
Which is my call and measure,
My God for me to do ordained.**

—*John Matthesius (1504-1565)*

* Verse 1 translated by W. Delamotte, 1742; verses 2 and 3 by B. Harvey, Jr., 1885. From the *Hymnal and Liturgies of the Moravian Church (Unitas Fratrum)*. Used by permission of the Provincial Elders Conference.

** Translated 1754. John Matthesius was Lutheran pastor and schoolmaster at Joachimsthal in Bohemia. *Ibid.*

AN EVENING PRAYER

Now God be with us, for the night is closing,
The light and darkness are of His disposing;
And 'neath His shadow here to rest we yield us,
    For He will shield us.

Let evil thoughts and spirits flee before us;
Till morning cometh, watch, O Master, o'er us;
In soul and body Thou from harm defend us,
    Thine angels send us.

Let holy thoughts be ours when sleep o'ertakes us;
Our earliest thoughts be Thine when morning wakes us;
All sick and mourners, we to Thee commend them,
    Do Thou befriend them.

We have no refuge, none on earth to aid us,
Save Thee, O Father, Who Thine own hast made us;
But Thy dear presence will not leave them lonely,
    Who seek Thee only.

Father, Thy Name be praised, Thy Kingdom given,
Thy will be done on earth as 'tis in heaven;
Keep us in life, forgive our sins, deliver
    Us now and ever.*

—Petrus Herbert

THE MORAVIAN EMIGRANTS' HYMN

Blest be the day when I must roam
Far from my country, friends and home,
An exile, poor and mean;
My fathers' God will be my Guide,
Will angel guards for me provide,
My soul, my soul in danger screen.

Himself will lead me to a spot
Where all my cares and griefs forgot
I shall enjoy sweet rest.
As pants for cooling streams the hart
I languish for my heavenly part
For God, for God my Refuge blest.**

—Henry Isaac (1450-1517)

* Translated by Catherine Winkworth, 1863. Bishop Petrus Herbert was born in Moravia; in 1562 he became a minister of the Unitas Fratrum and in 1566 he was one of the compilers of the Brethren's Hymn-book. *Ibid.*
** Henry Isaac composed this poem about 1490. The members of the Unitas Fratrum sang these words when bitter persecution compelled them to seek refuge and liberty of conscience in foreign countries. *Ibid.*

ANABAPTIST MARTYR'S HYMN

Thine holy city they destroyed,
Thine altar overthrew they,
Thy servants have they put to death,
Where they could apprehend them:
Of us alone, thy little flock,
But few are still remaining.
Throughout the land, in shameful flight,
Disgraced, they have expelled us.
Scattered are we like flocks of sheep
Without a shepherd near us;
Abandoned stand our home and hearth
And like the owl or birds of night
Seek shelter we in caverns.
In clefts, on crags, in rocky wilds
We make our home—still they pursue;
Like birds or fowl we're hunted.*

—Leonard Schiemer

CHRISTIAN UNITY (Psalm 133)

How good it is, how pleasant to behold
The favored sheep of our good Shepherd's fold,
Obeying Him in love and knowledge grow,
Each sharing in the other's weal and woe.

Fullness of grace in Him the Head abounds;
Hence every blessing to His Church redounds;
He dwells with us, and by His Spirit's light
To love each other teaches us aright.

His precious word like plenteous dew descends,
And fructifying power its fall attends;
Unto the soul refreshment it supplies,
And to salvation makes us truly wise.

When love unfeigned our actions truly show,
The God of peace His blessing will bestow;
O Lord, unite Thy Church for Jesus' sake,
And bless what in Thy Name we undertake.**

—Matthias Czerwenka (1521-1569)

* Quoted by Henry S. Lucas in *The Renaissance and the Reformation.* Published 1934 by Harper & Brothers.

** Translated by Bishop F. W. Foster, 1789. Bishop Czerwenka (Cervenka) of the Unitas Fratrum wrote this paraphrase of Psalm 133 in 1561. From the *Hymnal and Liturgies of the Moravian Church (Unitas Fratrum).* Used by permission of the Provincial Elders Conference.

THROUGH PERIL AND FIRE

Kenneth Hall

THE city of Constance on the Swiss bank of the Rhine River had broken
out in a riot of color. Its normal population of fifty thousand had doubled.
Booths and temporary wooden dormitories had been thrown up just outside
the city's walls. The crowds were laughing and gay, but underneath lurked
a deadly seriousness, for the Council of Constance had been called because of
a crisis in the Roman Catholic Church. That great body was torn by division
and was widely accused of corruption. The dissatisfaction was agitated by the
Bohemian preacher-writer, John Huss.

As Huss wondered what would happen to him at Constance, scenes from
along the trail he had been following for forty-five years must have flashed
through his mind.

John had started on that trail of life, probably in 1369, in the little
Bohemian village of Husinec. From this place he got his surname. Huss first
went to school in a monastery at Husinec, where the monks soon noted the
boy's quick mind. They sent him on to a higher school at nearby Prachatice.

The university of Prague was in those years one of the world's outstanding
centers of learning. Here seven hundred teachers and thirty thousand students
came together in the newly sparked search for knowledge. Huss plunged
earnestly into university life.

At this time Huss's interest in church affairs was being fanned by discussions at the university. Two rival popes, John and Gregory, each claimed to be
the supreme representative of Christ on earth. Shortly John Wycliffe's books
would come in from England to add fuel to the discussion.

Huss, after earning bachelor's and master's degrees at the university, was
called to join the faculty. Even his earliest lectures showed a search for truth
based on the Bible. He was named by the king as preacher at Bethlehem
Chapel. This was a preaching point that had developed out of a desire for
preaching instead of the cathedral rituals. Instead of using Latin, speakers
here spoke in the native tongue.

John proved a fiery preacher, and the crowds flocked to hear him. He
attacked the vices of every class of people. The Bohemian king stood behind
him when criticism came: "Huss is bound by his ordination oath to speak the
truth without respect of persons."

During this ministry Huss also took an interest in church singing. The
Bohemians were a musical people, and they wanted to participate in the
church singing themselves instead of merely listening to a priest's chant. Huss
himself wanted more feeling in the singing and more participation by the
congregation. He translated Latin hymns into Bohemian and also composed
some suitable songs himself.

Such a revolutionary approach did Huss take, however, that he soon found
himself in serious disagreement with high church officials. In a neighboring

province three communion wafers had been found in the ruins of an old church. They had apparently been soaked in blood. The rumor went around that this blood was actually the blood of Christ. Those who paid homage to the wafers, it was said, could expect miraculous results. Pilgrims by the thousands flocked to the spot. Some so-called miracles were reported. Huss was sent by the archbishop to investigate. He found wholesale fraud.

Huss was also getting entangled in theological controversies. The works of Wycliffe came up for study by the university. Huss found himself defending this "morning star of the Reformation," although the faculty decision was that Wycliffe be declared a heretic.

Huss, in company with many others, worked hard to clean up the abuses within the Roman Catholic Church, but by doing so made enemies. Prague's Archbishop Zbynek sent spies to Bethlehem Chapel to accumulate evidence for making heresy charges against John Huss. He heard about this attempt. One day during a sermon he recognized one of these spies. The preacher paused, leaned over the pulpit, and stuck a finger at the man. "Note that down, cowled monk, and carry it to the other side."

The monk did. A lengthy list of charges was prepared. The archbishop sent these charges to Pope Gregory and received from him authority to stamp out heretics. The archbishop set to work with a heavy hand to carry out the papal orders. In the palace courtyard, guarded by soldiers, the archbishop gathered about two hundred books considered heretical—and there set fire to them himself. Bells tolled mournfully while the books went up in flames.

But the burning books set off a storm of protest. Soon the forbidden volumes were recopied. Greater crowds than ever flocked to hear Huss. Bible study multiplied. The pope called Huss to Rome. At the urging of friends, he remained in Prague. The angered pope promptly excommunicated him.

The Bohemian king himself sided with Huss. That man ordered the archbishop's property seized and sold for enough money to make good the loss of the destroyed books. In a rage the archbishop declared an interdict over the whole city. That meant no Christian burials, no marriages, no public services.

The need for a general council to clear up the many pressing questions of church practice and belief had long been felt. Finally such a meeting was agreed to and scheduled for the city of Constance. It was to this city that Huss made his way in 1414 under a "safe conduct guarantee."

Huss's enemies were hard at work. Soon after his arrival he was under arrest. For some time he was in the palace. Later he was moved into a monastery dungeon where he lay in darkness beside a sewage ditch. Here Huss fell ill and drew near death. But Pope John was eager to keep the Council's attention off his own wickedness and on Huss. So he decided that Huss should not be allowed to die just yet and he was moved to more favorable quarters.

Powerful Bohemian nobles worked hard for Huss, but his prospects gradually faded. He was moved to a castle tower where his arms were tied to the wall and his feet chained to a block. The room was cold. The food was scarce and not nourishing. His guards liked to see him suffer. The policy was an attempt to break his spirit.

At last a public hearing before the Council was arranged. While Huss appealed to the rights of the individual and to the Scriptures, the Council considered the power of the church all-important.

Finally the Council's decision was announced. Huss would have to submit himself humbly to the Council, admit publicly that he was in the wrong on all charges brought against him, and promise never to teach his erroneous views again.

Huss quietly refused. He continued to refuse even when man after man came to plead with him. In chains, ill, tormented by his enemies, Huss kept hard at work for a month, writing his supporters not to give up the cause. He poured out his heart in love to the people of Bohemia.

The condemnation ceremonies took place in the cathedral. Huss was ushered in, pale and weak and trembling. Lines of suffering were carved on his face. He was given no opportunity to speak for himself. The articles against him were read. A yard-wide paper cap, picturing devils struggling for his soul, was placed on his head. As this was done the bishops said, "We commit thy soul to the devil!"

Huss responded quietly, "And I commit it to my most gracious Lord Jesus Christ."

Next Huss was taken outside where he saw his writings burned. It made him smile just a bit, for he knew his books were being circulated by the hundreds throughout all of Europe in a flood tide that could never be stopped.

He was led to a spot outside the city gates. There his guards piled wood and straw around him up to his chin. He was given one final chance.

Loudly this time he shouted, "What shall I recant, not being conscious of any errors? In the truth which I have proclaimed . . . I will this day joyfully die."

The torch was touched to his kindling. Huss began to sing a hymn, "Christ, Thou Son of God, have mercy upon us." By the third line smoke and sparks took away his breath, but his lips continued to move in silent prayer until the flames seared out his life.

Huss went peacefully to his reward. But there was to be little peace in the land he left. A storm of indignation swept Bohemia, a storm that was to go on and on and pave the way for Luther and other reformers a century later.*

* Abridged from *They Stand Tall* by Kenneth Hall, pp. 131-39. Copyright 1953 by Gospel Trumpet Company. Used by permission of the author and Warner Press.

THE ABBOT AND THE LEARNED WOMAN
Desiderius Erasmus

NOTE: Erasmus of Rotterdam (1466-1536) was a noted scholar who did much
to popularize classical learning and the reform of abuses within the church. He
greatly influenced Luther and Zwingli, though he himself remained a Roman
Catholic. His *Familiar Colloquies* were widely read and quoted. This particular
dialogue, in which a learned woman, Magdala, gets the best of an ignorant and
unspiritual abbot named Antronius, is typical of Erasmus' program: to ridicule
superstition and unworthiness and to depend on education and moral sincerity to
purify and elevate the common life.

ANTRONIUS. What sort of household stuff do I see?

MAGDALA. Is it not neat?

ANTRONIUS. How neat it is, I cannot tell, but I am sure it is not very becoming either a maid or a matron.

MAGDALA. Why so?

ANTRONIUS. Because here are books lying about everywhere.

MAGDALA. What, have you lived to this age, and are both an abbot and a
courtier, and never saw any books in a lady's apartment?

ANTRONIUS. Yes, I have seen books, but they were French, but here I see
Greek and Latin ones.

MAGDALA. Why, are there no other books but French ones that teach wisdom?

ANTRONIUS. But it becomes ladies to have something that is diverting, to pass
away their leisure hours.

MAGDALA. Must none but ladies be wise and live pleasantly?

ANTRONIUS. You very improperly connect being wise and living pleasantly
together; women have nothing to do with wisdom, pleasure is ladies' business.

MAGDALA. Ought not every one to live well?

ANTRONIUS. I am of opinion they ought so to do.

MAGDALA. Well, can anybody live a pleasant life that does not live a good
life?

ANTRONIUS. Nay, rather how can anybody live a pleasant life that does not
live a good life?

MAGDALA. Why, then, do you approve of living illy, if it be but pleasantly?

ANTRONIUS. I am of the opinion that they live a good life that live a pleasant
life.

MAGDALA. Well, but from whence does that pleasure proceed—from outward
things or from the mind?

ANTRONIUS. From outward things.

MAGDALA. O subtle abbot, but thick-skulled philosopher! Pray, tell me in
what you suppose a pleasant life to consist?

ANTRONIUS. Why, in sleeping and feasting, and liberty of doing what you
please in wealth and in honors.

MAGDALA. But suppose to all of these things God should add wisdom, should you live pleasantly then?

ANTRONIUS. What is that you call by the name of wisdom?

MAGDALA. This is wisdom, to know that a man is only happy by the goods of the mind; that wealth, honor, and descent, neither make a man happier or better.

ANTRONIUS. If that be wisdom, fare it well for me.

MAGDALA. Suppose now that I take more pleasure in reading a good author than you do in hunting, drinking, or gaming, will not you think I live pleasantly?

ANTRONIUS. I would not live that sort of life.

MAGDALA. I do not inquire what you take most delight in, but what is it that ought to be most delighted in?

ANTRONIUS. I would not have my monks mind books much.

MAGDALA. But my husband approves very well of it. But what reason have you why you would not have your monks bookish?

ANTRONIUS. Because I find they are not so obedient, they answer again out of the decrees and decretals of Peter and Paul.

MAGDALA. Why then do you command them the contrary to what Peter and Paul did?

ANTRONIUS. I cannot tell what they teach, but I cannot endure a monk that answers again; nor would I have any of my monks wiser than I am myself.

MAGDALA. You might prevent that well enough, if you did but lay yourself out to get as much wisdom as you can.

ANTRONIUS. I have not leisure.

MAGDALA. Why so?

ANTRONIUS. Because I have not time.

MAGDALA. What, not at leisure to be wise?

ANTRONIUS. No.

MAGDALA. Pray what hinders you?

ANTRONIUS. Long prayers, the affairs of my household, hunting, looking after my horses, attending at court.

MAGDALA. Well, and do you think these things are better than wisdom?

ANTRONIUS. Custom has made it so.

MAGDALA. Well, but now answer me this one thing, suppose God should grant you this power, to be able to turn yourself and your monks into any sort of animal that you had a mind, would you turn them into hogs, and yourself into a horse?

ANTRONIUS. No, by no means.

MAGDALA. By doing so you might prevent any of them from being wiser than yourself.

ANTRONIUS. It is not much matter to me what sort of animals my monks are, if I am but a man myself.

MAGDALA. Well, and do you look upon him to be a man that neither has wisdom nor desires to have it?

ANTRONIUS. I am wise enough for myself.

MAGDALA. And so are hogs wise enough for themselves.

ANTRONIUS. You seem to be a sophistress, you argue so smartly.

MAGDALA. I will not tell you what you seem to me to be. But why does this household stuff displease you?

ANTRONIUS. Because a spinning-wheel is a woman's weapon.

MAGDALA. Is it not a woman's business to mind the affairs of her family, and to instruct her children?

ANTRONIUS. Yes, it is.

MAGDALA. And do you think so weighty an office can be executed without wisdom?

ANTRONIUS. I believe not.

MAGDALA. This wisdom I learn from books.

ANTRONIUS. Books destroy women's brains, who have little enough of themselves.

MAGDALA. What quantity of brains you have left I cannot tell. And as for myself, let me have never so little, I had rather spend them in study than in prayers mumbled over without the heart going along with them, or sitting whole nights in quaffing off bumpers.

ANTRONIUS. Bookishness makes folks mad.

MAGDALA. And does not the rattle of your pot companions, your banterers, and drolls make you mad?

ANTRONIUS. No, they pass the time away.

MAGDALA. How can it be, then, that such pleasant companions should make me mad?

ANTRONIUS. That is the common saying.

MAGDALA. But I by experience find quite the contrary. How many more do we see grow mad by hard drinking, unseasonable feasting, and sitting up all night tippling, which destroys the constitution and senses, and has made people mad?

ANTRONIUS. By my faith, I would not have a learned wife.

MAGDALA. But I bless myself that I have got a husband that is not like yourself. Learning both endears him to me and me to him.

ANTRONIUS. Learning costs a great deal of pains to get, and after all we must die.

MAGDALA. Notable sir, pray tell me, suppose you were to die tomorrow, had you rather die a fool or a wise man?

ANTRONIUS. Why, a wise man, if I could come at it without taking pains.

MAGDALA. But there is nothing to be attained in this life without pains; and yet, let us get what we will, and what pains soever we are at to attain it, we must leave it behind us. Why then should we think much to be at some pains for the most precious thing of all, the fruit of which will bear us company unto another life?

ANTRONIUS. I have often heard it said that a wise woman is twice a fool.

MAGDALA. That indeed has been often said, but it was by fools. A woman that is truly wise does not think herself so. But on the contrary, one that knows nothing, thinks herself to be wise, and that is being twice a fool.

ANTRONIUS. I cannot well tell how it is, that as panniers do not become an ox, so neither does learning become a woman.

MAGDALA. But, I suppose, you cannot deny but panniers will look better upon an ox than a mitre upon an ass or a cow.

What think you of the Virgin Mary?

ANTRONIUS. Very highly.

MAGDALA. Was not she bookish?

ANTRONIUS. Yes; but not as to such books as these.

MAGDALA. What books did she read?

ANTRONIUS. The canonical hours.

MAGDALA. For the use of whom?

ANTRONIUS. Of the order of Benedictines.

MAGDALA. Indeed! What did Paula and Eustochium do? Did not they converse with the Holy Scriptures?

ANTRONIUS. Ay, but this is a rare thing now.

MAGDALA. So was a blockheaded abbot in old times; but now nothing is more common. In old times princes and emperors were as eminent for learning as for their governments. And after all, it is not so great a rarity as you think it. There are both in Spain and Italy not a few women that are able to vie with the men, and in England, and in Germany. Unless you take care of yourselves we shall be divinity professors in the schools, and preach in the churches, and take possession of your mitres.

ANTRONIUS. God forbid.

MAGDALA. Nay, it is your business to forbid it. For if you hold on as you have begun, even geese themselves will preach before they will endure you, a parcel of dumb teachers. You see the world is turned upside down, and you must either lay aside your dress or perform your part.

ANTRONIUS. How came I to fall into this woman's company? If you will come to see me, I will treat you more pleasantly.

MAGDALA. After what manner?

ANTRONIUS. Why, we will dance and drink heartily, and hunt, and play, and laugh.

MAGDALA. I can hardly forbear laughing now.*

* Abridged from *The Whole Familiar Colloquies* of Desiderius Erasmus, translated by Nathan Bailey, pp. 193-96.

MARTIN LUTHER AND THE EISLEBEN CHOIR
Ellen Baker

A DISCOURAGED choirmaster closed his organ at the end of the rehearsal. The choristers were hurriedly putting on hats and coats, eager to go their several ways. Suddenly a boy's clear voice rang out in joyous song in the streets outside the Eisleben church.

"Bring that singer in that I may speak with him," the master said.

The cantor went in search of the singer, who came readily at his bidding and stood attentively before the man still seated on the organ bench.

"What is your name?" the choirmaster asked.

"Martin Luther, sir," was the reply.

"Who taught you to sing?"

"No one taught me, sir. I like to sing, and often earn a few coins by singing in the streets."

"Would you like to sing in my choir?" asked the master.

"I'd be very glad for the chance, sir," Martin answered gratefully.

"Then report for rehearsal Saturday afternoon."

And in this manner Martin Luther was introduced to the Eisleben church choir, and to the world of song.

Luther was born of sturdy peasant stock in the village of Eisleben, Saxony, in the year 1483. His father practiced careful economy during his son's youth in order to give him a college education. Besides singing in the choir at Eisleben, Martin also learned to play on the flute and the lute. He was entered in the University of Erfurt for the purpose of studying law; but in 1505 he left the university and became a monk in the Augustinian monastery at Erfurt. Later he was called from the monastery to become an instructor in the newly established University of Wittenberg. There he was seized with a spirit of unrest, and while studying the Bible he received a new and original conception of the meaning of the Scriptures, which led to his break with the then established Roman Catholic Church.

With the ideals of the Reformation sweeping over the world, Luther was quick to see that congregational singing must become an effective part of all worship. In 1524 Luther's first hymnbook was published. It was printed on three sheets, and contained the words and music of eight new and original congregational hymns. Later there appeared from a Wittenberg press, and published under Luther's direction, a book of sacred songs for three, four, and five voices.

Martin Luther was a great music lover and an ardent composer. Music to him was not only a divine revelation but an aesthetic necessity. He wrote both words and music for his mighty chorale, "A Mighty Fortress Is Our God," which is still found in many hymnals.

Luther died at Eisleben in 1546. His remains were taken to Wittenberg and buried in the Schloss-Kirche. During the burial services three great bands played "A Mighty Fortress Is Our God" in unison.*

✠

O LORD OF ALL, OUR FATHER

ONE of the great gifts of the Reformation was the congregational hymn. For the most part, the liturgical music of the Middle Ages consisted of chants sung by the clergy, with an occasional response of two or three words in Greek or Latin to be sung by the people. Many of them did not know the meaning of the words sung by the priest or even of their own oft-repeated response. The traditional music of the Church has great dignity and spiritual power and is enjoying something of a revival today, but as the centuries before the Reformation passed, more and more it lost touch with the spirit of the people. John Huss and the Protestant leaders who came after him wanted the people to share actively in the worship of God, rather than leave the service so largely in the hands of the clergy. The Reformers emphasized the doctrine of the universal priesthood of believers. Worship should be congregational praise, with all the people taking an active part.

For this reason Huss introduced the congregational hymn into public worship. The hymn tune was more regular than that of the chant and was more easily sung by the people. The words of the hymn followed a rhythmical pattern and were easily remembered because the lines were put into rhyme. Huss himself wrote several hymns (see "The Word of God," the first poem in this section). He liked to think of the congregation preaching a sermon as it sang, just as he did when he stood in the pulpit. The Hussite hymns emphasize their teaching purpose, but are sometimes weak in poetic inspiration.

The disciples of Huss in Bohemia (Czechoslovakia) continued the practice of congregational singing, even after he was put to death in 1415. Through the years various members of their group composed new hymns, and in 1504 the Bohemian Brethren published a collection of these. It has been called the first real hymnbook ever issued for congregational use. One of these Czech poets who lived at the time of Luther was named Kliment Bosák, and he composed the hymn, "O Lord of All, Our Father." It was set to the tune of a Hussite "gradual" or communion hymn, published in 1512. The English translation was made in 1950 by Francis House, who formerly held a high position with the British Broadcasting Corporation and is now one of the associate general secretaries of the World Council of Churches in Geneva, Switzerland.

This hymn is a prayer. It asks God to grant the gift of His Holy Spirit as a guide to His people so that they may be delivered from all corrupt religion. It is a heroic witness of the Reformers' longing to be true to the Word of God.

The music score shows the first stanza in English, French, and German; the English translation of the second and third stanzas appears below.

* From *Uplift Magazine.* Used by permission of the author and the publisher.

O Lord of All, Our Father*

Hussisches Graduale (1512).

*From *Cantate Domino*, No. 47. By Kliment Bosák, translated 1950 by Francis House. Copyright 1951 by World's Student Christian Federation. Used by permission of the publisher.

> O Christ, who to the faithful
>   By God the Father chosen
>   Didst send the Holy Spirit,
>   When Thou from earth hadst risen:
> We pray Thee pour upon us
>   In this our day of testing,
> The Spirit's gift of power,
>   Thy word of truth attesting.

> O Holy Spirit, guide us,
>   The comfortless befriending:
> Approach, Thou bounteous Giver,
>   Thy grace to us extending:
> Thy truth to speak, inspire us,
>   Thy counsels just proclaiming:
> Compel our ears to heed Thee,
>   Our hearts with faith enflaming.

☩

THOU HOLY SPIRIT, WE PRAY TO THEE

MARTIN LUTHER believed in the calling of every Christian. As a matter of conviction he wished to help every believer fulfill his sacred vocation under God. So he translated the Bible into the language of the people. And following the lead of John Huss, he made a large place for congregational song in the services of public worship, as an expression of the priesthood of believers. The radical change from the medieval pattern of worship has been neatly put by Bismarck: "The Roman Catholic service can be held by a priest without a congregation, if need be; the Lutheran service can be held by a congregation without a priest, if need be."

One element of Luther's greatness was his ability to speak to the people in their own language. This was far more than simply preaching the gospel in German rather than Latin. He had a "feel" for the spirit of the people, and they regarded him as truly one of themselves. He loved their folk songs, and one of his favorite pleasures was to gather with family and friends for a session of singing in the evening. When it came to composing hymns to express the new spirit of the Reformation, Luther was particularly well equipped. In the thirty-six hymns which he wrote there is something elemental that speaks to the heart of every man; in them, says Luther D. Reed, the child and the hero are blended.

Like the householder described by Jesus who "bringeth forth out of his treasure things new and old" (Matt. 13:52), Luther retained much that was in the tradition of the Church, even as he sought new ways to bring the gospel to the hearts of men. To him Reformation meant cleansing the Church of corruption and distortion, not the tearing down of everything that had been done

Thou Holy Spirit, We Pray to Thee*

Vorreformatorisch
Johann Walther Gesangbuch (1524).

Nun bit - ten wir den hei - li - gen Geist, Um den
Es - prit de Dieu, crée en nous tous la foi. Tou - te
Thou Ho - ly Spi - rit, We pray to Thee, Strength' our

rech - ten Glau - ben al - ler - meist, Dass er uns be -
puis - san - ce nous vient de toi. Si dans la dé -
faith and in - crease it al - way; Com - fort Thou our

hü - te an un - serm En - de, Wenn wir heim - fahr'n
tres - se Le mal nous pres - se, Af - fer - mis nos
hearts in our ad - vers - i - ty With true be -

aus die - sem E - len - de. Ky - ri - e - leis.
cœurs Et les rends vain - queurs. Ky - ri - e - leis.
lief by night and by day. Ky - ri - e - leis.

*From *Cantate Domino*, No. 39.

since the time of the apostles. He sought wisdom in the great teachers of the Church through the centuries and his heart was strengthened by the devotion of the saints of all ages. A good example of his inclusive spirit is his hymn, "Thou Holy Spirit, We Pray to Thee." The first stanza is a medieval German spiritual folk song which Luther reworked, and to which he added additional stanzas. Thus he made use of a piece already beloved by his people.

The refrain at the end of each stanza is an ancient prayer of the Church. In the Greek language in which the New Testament was first written, *Kyrieleis* means "Lord, have mercy." (The prayer may be found in Matthew 17:15.) Very early in Christian history, in that part of the Mediterranean world where Greek was spoken, *Kyrieleis* became a common response by the congregation in various prayers and litanies. As the Church moved westward into Latin-speaking Europe, the phrase continued to be used without translation—like *Amen,* a Hebrew word from the Old Testament which has gone into all parts of the world among people of many different languages. So even as Luther wrote his hymn in German, he kept the old Greek phrase *Kyrieleis,* which comes directly from the New Testament.

The hymn was translated into English by Miles Coverdale, one of the great translators of the English Bible, in the sixteenth century. And still we sing it today, a prayer for faith, for love, and for courage, in which we join with Christians of every generation.

The first stanza is given in the music score on p. 432. The second and third stanzas appear below:

> Thou sweet Love, grant us all together
> Enchanted to be unfeignedly;
> That we may all have love for one another,
> And of one mind now and always be.
> *Kyrieleis.*

> Be Thou our Comforter in all need,
> Make us to fear neither death nor shame
> But in holy truth to be established,
> That Satan should put us not to blame.
> *Kyrieleis.*

CONTENTS

PART IV   SECTION 2

THE REFORMATION SPREADS

---✠---

For by grace are ye saved through faith; and that not of yourselves: it is the gift of God: Not of works, lest any man should boast.—EPHESIANS 2:8-9

---✠---

PICTURES: PAGE
    Interpretation: St. Peter's Cathedral, Geneva 435
    Picture: St. Peter's Cathedral, Geneva 437
    Interpretation: Reformation Monument, Geneva—*Landowski and*
        Bouchard 438
    Picture: Reformation Monument, Geneva—*Landowski* and *Bouchard* 441
    Interpretation: Waldensian Fresco—*Paschetto* 440
    Picture: Waldensian Fresco—*Paschetto* 443

POETRY:
    In the Midst of the Illness—*Zwingli* 444
    In Convalescence—*Zwingli* 444
    Its Only Joy, Saviour and Lord (Psalm 25)—*Jud* 445
    Sitting Beside the Babylonian Waters (Psalm 137)—*Marot* 445
    We Greet Thee, King of Mercy and of Grace—*Calvin* 446
    Thoughts in a Cathedral—*Clark* 446
    The Vaudois Teacher—*Whittier* 447

STORIES:
    Giving Worship Back to the People—*Farner* 448
    Our Protestant Heritage—*Sikes* 451
    Keeper of the City—*McCrie* 454

MUSIC:
    Interpretation: Lord, Take Thou the Reins to Thee—*Zwingli* 456
    Music: Lord, Take Thou the Reins to Thee—*Zwingli* 457
    Interpretation: We Gather Together—*Anonymous* 458
    Music: We Gather Together—*Old Netherlands Melody;* arr. by *Kremser* .. 459

ST. PETER'S CATHEDRAL, GENEVA

THE Cathedral of St. Peter (shown on p. 437) was built between A.D. 1160 and 1220, the period when the West was becoming covered with churches in proportion to the strength of its faith.

The cathedral, begun in the Romanesque style, was soon to profit by the audacious innovations of the Gothic. It keeps the Romanesque style in the thickness of its walls, and the fortresslike aspect of its towers. From the new style it takes the boldness of its arches, the elegance of its pillars, adorned with sculptured capitals, the impression of space gained on entering the sanctuary, a confidence, a lightness, a boldness of stone leaping heavenwards like a prayer.

Like all cathedrals, St. Peter's is planned in the form of a cross. The visitor entering the nave faces toward the East and the Holy Land where the Son of God became flesh. The impression of space is the result of its carefully calculated proportions, which make it seem vaster than it really is.

The life of the city was concentrated in the cathedral. In war the citizens entrenched themselves there and the church then became a citadel against which dashed a hail of great stones from the catapults.

It was in the cathedral that Bishop Adhemar Fabri in 1387 published the *Franchises* (freedoms), which made Geneva a real little republic.

It was in St. Peter's that syndics and counselors came to Mass on Tuesdays and Fridays "in order that, with God's help, the affairs of the town may be better inspired."

It was there that the bishops had to swear, at their induction, "to respect and endeavor to extend, rather than to diminish, the freedoms of the city."

The ornamentation of the cathedral developed during the centuries. Bonivard, Prior of St. Victor, tells us that "the church was well adorned and embellished with church vestments, chalices, reliquaries, candlesticks, altar ornaments, pictures and paintings"! In the course of centuries we find a slow deformation of Christian worship, a return to ceremonies in which pagan elements mix more with Christian tradition.

Reform was necessary. It burst forth at the beginning of the sixteenth century.

When the Reformation began in Germany, Catholics were found in all Western Europe who sincerely loved their Church and wished to see it return to its true tradition. In Geneva, citizens known under the name of Lovers of the Holy Gospel gathered to study the Word of God and to rediscover in it the vocation of the Church. They welcomed to Geneva French preachers, such as Guillaume Farel. There was in Geneva a genuine popular movement for the Church's return to a more simple religion, more in conformity with that of the apostles. The authorities, however, hesitated, and the bishop, preferring the pleasures of the chase to theological discussions, hurriedly left Geneva.

On August 8, 1535, the Reformers held a service at the convent of Rive.

They flocked there in great numbers that day, like a river about to overflow and burst its banks. Voices rose from the multitude. "St. Peter's! Let us go to St. Peter's!" they roared. Pushed by an irresistible impulse, the crowd surged away to the cathedral. In every street it was as if hot young blood were spurting out of the heart into the arteries. Everyone eventually met again before St. Peter's and crossed the threshold without meeting any resistance. The priests fled, carrying away all the sacred objects they could lay hands on. Farel went up into the pulpit and quite calmly began to preach. The huge but well-controlled crowd was keener to listen to the preacher than to rejoice in its victory. There was no scuffle and no pillaging, although later, in the afternoon, some of the more impetuous Reformers did break a number of statues they considered to be idols.

Some days later, the Council took the step of temporarily forbidding the Mass, pending a propitious moment for a plebiscite, which eventually took place on May 21, 1536, in the cloister of St. Peter's. This meeting was so important that the date of May 21, 1536, is now considered the date of the Reformation in Geneva.

It was Sunday. To the sound of the church bells, the Genevese had gone up to the court of St. Peter's.

Claude Savoye, the head syndic, was in the chair. He prayed to God, and then proposed to the General Council a resolution "concerning men's way of life."

"Is there any wishing to speak against the Word and the doctrine preached in this city? Let him speak!

"Is there any not wishing to live according to the Gospel and the Word of God, as they are preached to us daily since the abolition of the mass? Let him speak!"

A deep silence followed these words. Nobody in Geneva wished to return to the past. Everyone had confidence in the Reformers. And this they affirmed on oath, right hands lifted, "to live under this sacred Gospel law and Word of God, as it is proclaimed unto them." Thenceforth worship was celebrated in St. Peter's according to the Reformed custom. Its form did not much change during the centuries separating us from that time; no new religion was preached in St. Peter's, only the old Christian religion as practiced in the time of the apostles, that is, a religion stripped of all elements foreign to the spirit of the gospel.

When, in July 1536, the Frenchman John Calvin, then twenty-seven years old, and already famous, came to Geneva, he found a Church which had already adopted the Reformation. It lacked, however, a preacher capable of teaching the truths it had recovered to a multitude very ignorant of the Word of God. The Reformation had been too sudden and too revolutionary for order to be in existence yet amid the disturbed conditions of the city. Calvin's work was to organize the city and the Church.

For thirty years Calvin preached in St. Peter's, thirty years during which Geneva was so deeply transformed that Michelet, the historian, has said:

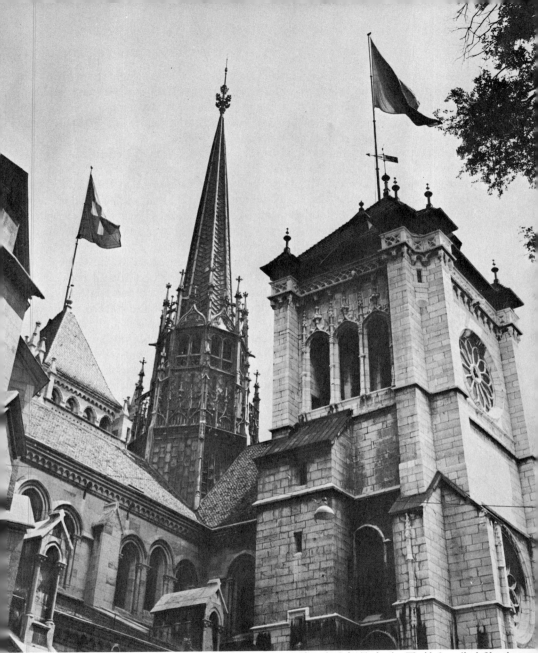

ST. PETER'S CATHEDRAL, GENEVA

438 THE CHURCH AND THE FINE ARTS

"This city, merry and satirical, and changeable as the lake it stands on, in which so many fine minds foundered among medieval superstitions, and so many noble hearts were lost in the defilements of dissipation, became an amazing town where all was fire and prayer, study, labor, and austerity, the great school of faith and of the martyrs."

Geneva was from that time on the city of refuge for all Reformers obliged to leave their own countries. It was the forward rampart of the Reformation, surrounded on all sides by regions still owing allegiance to the Papacy. St. Peter's was once more the citadel where spiritual arms were prepared, and thanks returned to God for His merciful deliverances, and fasts celebrated in humiliation for sorrowful news from France or elsewhere. For many years the whole life of Church and city was concentrated on St. Peter's.

In the nineteenth century numerous foreigners settled there and Geneva, so long an exclusively Protestant city, found itself with an additional population belonging either to the Roman Catholic Church or to other confessions. It thus became cosmopolitan in character. The Church of the Reformation was nevertheless anxious to be faithful to its tradition. Liberal and tolerant toward those not agreeing with its convictions, it affirmed in St. Peter's its desire to continue the work of the Reformers; it humbly but resolutely strove to live according to the Word of God and to spread the gospel in the city and beyond. For the Geneva of the Reformation remained an international center, and it was in this spirit that it was later to extend a most cordial welcome to the headquarters of the World Council of Churches.

St. Peter's remains today the symbol of the city and the faith.

The visitor will take with him from Geneva a memory of a stone church standing on a hill, a living sermon, a call to greater holiness, a light to guide men of all nations, stones which speak aloud.*

✣

REFORMATION MONUMENT, GENEVA
Paul Landowski and Henri Bouchard

THE Swiss city of Geneva has long been a center of world Protestantism. In their struggle for freedom, both political and religious, its citizens drove out their bishop and resisted the armies of the Duke of Savoy, who sought to maintain the authority of the Roman Catholic Church. Independent and Reformed, and set in the heart of Catholic Europe, Geneva became a city of refuge for persecuted Protestants from many lands. Frenchmen, Germans, Italians, Spaniards, Poles, Hungarians, Dutchmen, Englishmen, Scots, and other exiles flocked to the little city.

As political conditions changed in the countries from which they had fled, many returned to their homelands, with a burning zeal and with convictions

* From *St. Peter's Cathedral, Geneva: A Short Outline* by Daniel Buscarlet. Used by permission of the author.

shaped by the mind of Calvin. As a result of their labors, churches in many lands were reformed after the Geneva pattern, those on the continent generally taking the name Reformed while those in Britain (and later America) called themselves Presbyterian. Congregationalists, Baptists, and other major communions also followed Calvin's theology in large measure, even though adopting another plan for church government.

To mark 1909 as the four hundredth anniversary of Calvin's birth and the three hundred and fiftieth anniversary of the founding of the University of Geneva, Professor Lucien Gautier proposed the erection of an International Monument of the Genevan Reformation. Protestants from many lands contributed to the project, and after an open competition, an international jury selected the artists for the task: the architectural firm of Monod, Laverrière, Taillens & Dubois from Lausanne, Switzerland, and two Parisian sculptors, Paul Landowski and Henri Bouchard. The first stone was laid in the anniversary year of 1909.

Situated beneath the ancient fortifications of the city, the monument itself takes the form of a medieval wall, extending for a distance of 328 feet. Its dominant feature is the group of four heroic statues representing the giants of the Reformation—Farel, Calvin, Beza, and Knox. Spaced along the wall are smaller statues of leaders in the spread of Reformed Christianity—Admiral Coligny of France, William the Silent of the Netherlands, Frederick-William of Prussia, Roger Williams of Rhode Island, Oliver Cromwell of England, and Stephen Bocskay of Hungary. Incised in the wall are the words of the Lord's Prayer in French and English and selections from major documents in the progress of Protestantism—the Dutch Declaration of Independence, the Mayflower Compact, the British Bill of Rights, and others. Stirring scenes in the history of the Reformation appear in a series of bas-reliefs. In a commanding position above all the other inscriptions appears the motto of Geneva in letters of monumental size: *Post tenebras lux*—After the darkness, light! At either end rises a massive stone, one bearing the name of Luther, the other that of Zwingli, to manifest the link between the men of Geneva and the prior Reformers.

Straight and sturdy and unyielding, the four central figures (see p. 441) portray the spirit of the Reformation.

At the left stands William Farel, refugee Frenchman who brought Reform to Geneva and in 1535 preached the first Protestant sermon in the ancient cathedral of St. Peter. When he found himself faced with a task too great for his own talents, he persuaded his fellow Frenchman, Calvin, who was passing through the city, to stay and become the leader.

John Calvin dominated the life of Geneva as he does the giants among whom he stands. He was the great system-builder of the Reformation. He composed a system of public morals for Geneva. He devised a system of church government which Presbyterians still follow. He wrote a system of academic regulations for the university which he founded in Geneva. He organized into a system the cardinal doctrines of Protestantism and set them forth in his classic work, the *Institutes of the Christian Religion.*

Theodore Beza was Calvin's right-hand man, first rector of the new university, hymn writer, pastor, and Calvin's successor in the leadership of the church at Geneva.

John Knox completes the group. He stands here as firm and immovable as he often appeared before Mary, Queen of Scots. While in Geneva as a refugee, Knox was pastor of a congregation of English Puritans, delivered daily lectures on the Scriptures, and helped in the translation of the famous Geneva Bible. Then he returned to his homeland to lead the struggle for Reformation there. His prayer was "Give me Scotland, or I die!"

The spirit of the Reformation is embodied in these men: its plainness in the austere Geneva gown which each of them wears instead of priestly vestments; its fearlessness in their stalwart and unflinching stance; its commitment to education in Calvin's book of regulations for the university which Beza holds; its stern conception of righteousness in the expression of their faces. These men may not appear glamorous or winsome, but they put iron in the blood of Protestantism. Wherever the Reformed faith took root, there before long civil liberty also flourished, as Professor James Hastings Nichols demonstrates in *Democracy and the Churches.* Most significant of all, Farel, Calvin, and Knox each clasps a copy of the Bible, the message of salvation.

At the center of the massive slab of stone on which the four Reformers stand is inscribed the ancient trigram, IHΣ, the Greek symbol for the name of Jesus, which appears in the seal of Geneva. "Other foundation can no man lay than that is laid, which is Jesus Christ."

✠

WALDENSIAN FRESCO
Paolo A. Paschetto

AFTER climbing the steep grade into the Italian Alps for miles from the industrial city of Turin, the railroad tracks finally come to an end against the mountain wall. Nestled there in the high valley, surrounded on three sides by towering peaks, lies the little town of Torre Pellice. To go higher, the traveler must take the narrow military road which snakes its way up the sides of the cliffs into the clouds that hover over the Alpine border between Italy and France. Here and there, clinging improbably to the steep slopes or spreading out wherever there is a patch of level ground, are tiny villages which can be reached only by mule trail.

This all but inaccessible region is known as the Waldensian Valleys. Here for generations a sturdy little community of Italian Protestants have borne gallant witness to their Biblical faith. The painting before us celebrates their tenacity under persecution and recalls dramatic incidents in their stirring history. It is a memorial to past heroism and an admonition to fidelity in the present.

Photo by John Taylor for World Council of Churches

REFORMATION MONUMENT, GENEVA— *LANDOWSKI AND BOUCHARD*

Long centuries before the Reformation the rude and earnest mountaineers of this region resisted the claims of priest and pope; against the doctrines and practices of Roman Catholicism they set the simple teachings of the Bible. In the twelfth century Peter Waldo had the New Testament translated into the language of the people and his followers preached the Good News through the High Valleys. Thereafter the Waldenses were known as heretics and, time and again, suffered persecution. Seeking solidarity with like-minded Christians, they identified themselves in the fifteenth century with the Hussites of Bohemia, and after the Reformation in Germany and Switzerland they sought instruction from its leaders, especially those in Basle and Geneva. Oecolampadius was one of their advisers and Farel was another. Finally in a great assembly at Chamforan in 1532 the Waldenses declared themselves a Reformed Church and accepted the teachings of the Swiss preachers as being in accord with the doctrines of the Bible. Thereafter the influence of Geneva was felt in the Waldensian Valleys in many important ways.

The days of suffering were not over. When the Duke of Savoy demanded their submission to the Church of Rome or death, the Waldensians took a solemn oath of faithfulness at Puy in 1561. There they swore "to maintain the Bible whole and without admixture, according to the usages of the true Apostolic Church," even at the peril of their lives, and many made the supreme sacrifice. When, after another century and a quarter of persecution, they had been reduced to a few thousand people, those who were left received permission to take refuge in Geneva; but after three years their longing for the hills of home drew them back to their high valleys, and in 1689 they made their "Glorious Return." At Sibaud they took a new oath, renewing the Covenant of Puy made by their fathers in 1561.

Not till 1848 did the Waldensians receive constitutional guarantees of civil and religious liberty. February 17, the anniversary of that occasion, is celebrated annually with services of worship and gay festivities. On the night before, bonfires are kindled as a public demonstration of joy; one such night at Torre Pellice, the author counted forty-nine bonfires blazing on the mountainsides.

The "Waldensian Fresco" (see p. 443) dominates the plain, unpretentious assembly room in the headquarters building at Torre Pellice, where the annual synod of the church is held. The artist, Paolo A. Paschetto, himself a Waldensian, has set his symbolic painting against a background of Alpine peaks. The picture is dominated by the stubborn oak tree that will not die. Its gnarled roots cling to the inhospitable granite which seems to give no promise of life, but they have sunk themselves so firmly that the rock has splintered while the oak holds fast. The broken stump of many a branch bears mute testimony to repeated efforts to cut off the tree. But it has put forth new sprouts and has leafed out again. The open Bible resting against the trunk is turned to Revelation 2:10—"Be thou faithful unto death." (On the inner and outer walls of all their churches it is Waldensian custom to emblazon verses of Scripture.)

SII FE-
DE LE
FINO
ALLA
MOR-
TE..

89 NOI GIVRIAMO E PROMETTIAMO AL COSPETTO 1939
DELL'IDDIO VIVENTE DI MANTENERE TRA NOI
L'VNIONE E L'ORDINE..GIVRIAMO FEDELTÀ FINO
ALL'VLTIMA GOCCIA   DEL NOSTRO SANGVE

WALDENSIAN FRESCO—*PASCHETTO*

The fresco was painted on the two hundred and fiftieth anniversary of the Glorious Return, and below the picture appear the words of the Oath of Sibaud: "We swear and we promise to maintain among ourselves unity and discipline. We swear fidelity unto the last drop of our blood."

Beneath the words of the oath the artist has painted the crest of the Waldensian Church. It represents a burning lamp surrounded by seven stars (the seven churches of Revelation) surmounted by the motto, *Lux Lucet in Tenebris*—"The light shineth in the darkness."

Among their beloved hills, these mountain men have maintained freedom and faithfulness of worship.

✛

IN THE MIDST OF THE ILLNESS

Comfort, Lord God, comfort!
  The illness grows;
I am in throes
  Of agony and fear.
Therefore draw near
  To me, in grace and mercy.

Thou dost redeem
  Him who can trust,
As all men must,
  And his hopes place
In Thine own grace,
  And for Thee all else set aside.

Relief has come;
  My tongue is dumb,
I cannot speak one word.
  My thoughts are dark and blurred.
Therefore 'tis right
  That Thou the fight
Shouldst carry on
  For me, Thy son.

I am too weak,
  Dangers to seek;
Nor can I fight
  The devil's taunts and evil might;
Yet will my soul
  Be thine for aye, complete and whole.*
    —*Huldreich Zwingli (1484-1531)*

IN CONVALESCENCE

Healed, Lord God, healed!
I do believe
The plague does leave
My body now.
And lettest Thou
The sinners' scourge depart from me,

Then shall my mouth
Through all my days
Show forth Thy praise
And wisdom more
Than e'er before,
Whatever dangers may beset me.

And though I must
Become as dust
And suffer death, I know,
Perhaps with greater woe,
Than did befall
And me appal,
As I did lie
To death so nigh,

Yet will I still
My part fulfill
In this our world
And all things bear, for Heaven's reward,
With help from Thee,
Who art alone to life the key.*
                              —*Huldreich Zwingli* (*1484-1531*)

ITS ONLY JOY, SAVIOUR AND LORD (Psalm 25)

Its only joy, Saviour and Lord,
    To Thee my heart discloses;
Thy hand restores me to the way,
    And every step disposes.
Neither delights nor terrors here
Nor this world's transient story
Can cloud Thy face nor hide from me
    The radiance of Thy glory!

O Holy Spirit, Comforter!
    Possess I now implore Thee
This sinner still by conflicts torn
    And falling down before Thee;
In mercy come to loose my chains,
    The bonds of sin to sever,
That I by faith Thy grace receive,
    Thy name to praise forever.**

                              —*Leo Jud*

SITTING BESIDE THE BABYLONIAN WATERS (Psalm 137)

Sitting beside the Babylonian waters,
By God abandoned, where our captors brought us,
Sadly we thought of Zion, longed for home,
In this far land of exile where we roam.
Those harps which saw us weep upon our pillows
We hung on high upon the leafy willows.

* *Ibid.*, p. 37.
** From *Cantate Domino*, No. 79. Translated by Nansie Anderson, 1949. Used by permission of Mrs. James C. Blackie, Edinburgh.

Our captors then made mock of all our sadness:
"Sing to us now those songs of simple gladness
Which echoed through your city long ago!"
How can we sing with hearts that break with woe?
How can we sing amidst an alien nation
Our sacred hymns of praise and jubilation?

Jerusalem, if ever I forget Thee,
Let my tongue cleave for ever to my palate,
And let my own right hand forget its skill!
O only joy, sole hope that holds me still,
That not a string be by my hand vibrated
Till thou, Jerusalem, art liberated.*

—*Clément Marot (1495?-1544)*

WE GREET THEE, KING OF MERCY AND OF GRACE

We greet Thee, King of Mercy and of grace,
Reigning omnipotent in every place:
So come, O King, and our whole being sway;
Shine on us with the light of Thy pure day.

Thou art the life, by which alone we live,
And all our substance and our strength receive;
Comfort us by Thy faith and by Thy power,
Nor daunt our hearts when comes the trying hour.

Thou hast the true and perfect gentleness,
No harshness hast Thou and no bitterness:
Make us to taste the sweet grace found in Thee
And ever stay in Thy sweet unity.

Our hope is in no other save in Thee;
Our faith is built upon Thy promise free;
Come, give us peace, make us so strong and sure,
That we may conquerors be and ills endure.**

—*John Calvin (1509-1564)*

THOUGHTS IN A CATHEDRAL

Is this a tribute to the Nazarene,
Beloved of children, brother of the poor,
The peasant teacher turned from door to door—
Without a home save on God's friendly green?

* From *Cantate Domino*, No. 91. Translated by Margaret House, 1950. The paraphrase was written by Marot in 1539 and altered by Charles Dombre in 1935. Copyright 1951 by World's Student Christian Federation. Used by permission of the publisher.
** From *Christian Hymns*. Copyright 1945 by The Christian Foundation. Used by permission of The North River Press.

This mitred pomp, these gilded lords of pride,
These surging people awed by prattling priests,
By old tradition, storied fasts and feasts—
Is this for him who on a rude cross died?
How great his gain, who now commands such zeal,
Such loyalty, beyond his fairest thought!
In his high name what wonders have been wrought!
How proud his Kingdom—this we see today!
If he were here—who walked a pilgrim way—
If he were here . . .*

—Thomas Curtis Clark

✝

THE VAUDOIS TEACHER

"The manner in which the Waldenses and heretics disseminated their principles among the Catholic gentry was by carrying with them a box of trinkets, or articles of dress. Having entered the houses of the gentry and disposed of some of their goods, they cautiously intimated that they had commodities far more valuable than these, inestimable jewels, which they would show if they could be protected from the clergy. They would then give their purchasers a Bible or Testament; and thereby many were deluded into heresy."—Rainerus Sacco.

"O lady fair, these silks of mine are beautiful and rare—
The richest web of Indian loom, which beauty's queen might wear;
And my pearls are pure as thy own fair neck, with whose radiant light they vie;
I have brought them with me a weary way—will my gentle lady buy?"

The lady smiled on the worn old man through the dark and clustering curls
Which veiled her brow, as she bent to view his silks and glittering pearls;
And she placed their price in the old man's hand and lightly turned away,
But she paused at the wanderer's earnest call—"My gentle lady, stay!

"O lady fair, I have yet a gem which a purer luster flings,
Than the diamond flash of the jeweled crown on the lofty brow of kings;
A wonderful pearl of exceeding price, whose virtue shall not decay,
Whose light shall be as a spell to thee and a blessing on thy way!"

The lady glanced at the mirroring steel where her form of grace was seen,
Where her eye shone clear, and her dark locks waved their clasping pearls
  between;
"Bring forth thy pearl of exceeding worth, thou traveler gray and old,
And name the price of thy precious gem, and my page shall count thy gold."

* From *The Christian Century* (May 1, 1946). Used by permission of Christian Century Foundation.

The cloud went off from the pilgrim's brow, as a small and meager book,
Unchased with gold or gem of cost, from his folding robe he took!
"Here, lady fair, is the pearl of price, may it prove as such to thee!
Nay, keep thy gold—I ask it not, for the word of God is free!"

The hoary traveler went his way, but the gift he left behind
Hath had its pure and perfect work on that high-born maiden's mind,
And she hath turned from the pride of sin to the lowliness of truth,
And given her human heart to God in its beautiful hour of youth!

And she hath left the gray old halls, where an evil faith had power,
The courtly knights of her father's train, and the maidens of her bower;
And she hath gone to the Vaudois vales by lordly feet untrod,
Where the poor and needy of earth are rich in the perfect love of God!

                                        —*John Greenleaf Whittier*

✛

GIVING WORSHIP BACK TO THE PEOPLE
Oskar Farner

IT WAS an hour of supreme importance in the history of Zurich. The realization now dawned that the time was ripe, that the old order must pass away and a new reality appear! Zwingli proclaimed, in a voice stifled by tears, "Do not be afraid, my friends! God is on our side and He will protect His own. You have indeed undertaken something big and you will encounter much opposition for the sake of the Pure Word of God, which only a few bother to think about. Go forth in the name of God!"

At the end of 1523 began the reorganization of the church service; until then almost everything had remained outwardly the same as under the old order. Zwingli's principle in these reforms was: First of all, be law-abiding! "Do not do anything behind the backs of the authorities and on your own responsibility!" Secondly, be thorough! For "if you do not destroy their nests, the little storks will return." In the municipal churches, men set to work, under the orders of the Council: the three secular priests, Zwingli, Englehart, and Leo Jud, two constables and an honorable master craftsman from every guild, and, finally, the municipal master builder with his locksmiths, stonemasons, carpenters, and handy men. They shut the doors from the inside and removed all the decoration that had now become superfluous; ladders were placed against the painted walls and all the splendid coloring was either scratched away or whitewashed over. Now Zwingli was able to rejoice: "Our temples in Zurich are indeed light; the walls are beautifully white!"

And in other respects, too, the former ceremoniousness was replaced by a sobriety hitherto unknown; the canonical prayers and the sung matins and vespers were no longer heard; no song resounded now through the sacred building; the organs remained for a while unused and then, finally, were removed. The same Zwingli who confesses, "None of the arts is so closely related and bound up with the human spirit as is music," did not lift a finger to give his congregation the evangelical hymn. They should now have an ear for one thing alone: the Word of God.

There were purges in other respects too: the monstrances and other gold and silver equipment used in worship were melted down; the ecclesiastical vestments were sold or removed; the relics were done away with; in the cathedral, the bones of the local saints, Felix and Regula, which previously had been preserved so reverently, were "buried honorably and quietly." No longer did incense rise up to heaven; no longer were banners and crosses carried in procession in the streets. It was already being said, "Let the people keep their images and colorful splendor!" To which Zwingli answered: "God does not want to be honored with outward show but with faith, love and purity, in spirit and in truth. . . . Christ commanded us to teach not by images but by the Word." He went on to say that God's true images were men, especially the poor for whom we should care!

What did it matter if henceforth things looked much less pious, if the monks "let hair grow over their bald heads," if the monasteries emptied and became instead poorhouses and hospitals! When Zwingli came to Zurich there were ninety-two secular priests, thirty monks and ninety-two nuns; when he died there remained only three secular priests, with a number of assistants. But, whereas the former had previously spent their lives as parasites, the latter now shouldered a heavy burden of work. For now there was a sermon every day, generally twice a day, and on Sundays there were also special services for children and for servants.

Every day, except Sundays and Fridays, at seven o'clock in the morning during the summer (eight o'clock in winter), all the pastors, canons, and students would gather together in the cathedral choir and sit down in the pews there. First of all, Master Huldreich steps up to the lectern and prays for the guidance of the Holy Spirit; sometimes Zwingli himself, sometimes one of his colleagues, takes over the preaching in the German language of the passage which has been studied so thoroughly, thus benefiting also other listeners who have meanwhile assembled.

These efforts, spread over many years, culminated in the Zurich Translation of the Bible, to which Zwingli himself contributed a good part. He was an artist in language and could knock the nail on the head when it was a question of making Biblical expressions comprehensible to the simple man. For "Priest and Levite," in the Parable of the Good Samaritan, he suggests "parson and clerk"; for "if the salt has become dull," "if the salt has lost its savor," and so on. And he finds many expressions which sound a homely note in the ears of the Swiss, as, for example, at the beginning of the Twenty-third Psalm, which he translates, "The Lord is my Shepherd, I shall not want. He makes me rest in lovely Alpine pastures."

The keystone of the innovations in worship was introduced on Maundy
Thursday, 1525; then, for the first time, instead of the Mass, Zwingli celebrated the Lord's Supper according to Biblical custom. First of all, from the
pulpit, he summed up what he had long been teaching on this subject: Away
with the bloodless repetition of the bloody sacrifice on Golgotha! The Supper
was instituted by Christ, so that we might remember His act of redemption
with special praise and thanks and be stirred to more complete obedience and
more faithful service to the brotherhood. Finally, away with all the magic
that had been carried on long enough with the holy symbols! Bread remains
bread and wine remains wine. What good would it do us even if we could,
outwardly only, taste with our lips of the body and blood of the Lord! If
there were no faith the most eager eating and drinking would not help one
jot. It is faith alone which can provide meat and drink for the soul. It is the
spirit that quickeneth; the flesh profiteth nothing. Are you serious about it?
Are you worthy of this partaking? To be worthy does not mean to present
oneself without sin; if that were the case, no one would be able to come. He
is worthy of the Lord's Supper, who knows his own unworthiness and calls
to the Saviour: "Lord be merciful to me, a sinner!"

And now the Reformer leaves the pulpit and comes down into the body
of the church. There stands a simple table, over which is spread a linen cloth
and on which are placed the Communion vessels, everything as plain as possible, without any show, no silk or silver or gold, the dishes and cup made only
of wood. With a few assistants, Zwingli now stands at this table and, with
his face turned towards the congregation, begins to pray using only the
German language, so that he can be clearly heard and understood. Then, in
turn with two deacons, he reads out the Liturgy with the Biblical account
of the Institution. And, when they have themselves partaken of the Bread
and the Wine, they go with the vessels to the congregation; from pew to
pew they hand the sacred symbols to the people. First the Bread—it was
unheard-of and had never happened before: they take it themselves and then
pass the rest on to the person sitting next to them. Then the Cup with the
Wine: for the first time since this cathedral was built has the command of
the Master been obeyed within its walls: "Drink ye *all* of this." Having
returned to the table, Zwingli now prays, using the One Hundred Thirteenth
Psalm, and then dismisses the faithful with the impressive injunction that
they must now go out and fulfill the word of reconciliation in their lives.
"Lord, we give Thee praise and thanks for all Thy gifts and blessings, who
livest and reignest, God, world without end." Thereupon the deacons respond:
"Amen!" And finally, Zwingli: "Go in peace!"

Shortly afterwards he wrote to a friend about this first Communion: "The
number who partook of it was greater than I have ever seen before and the
number of those who looked back to the flesh-pots of Egypt was far less
than I expected." And later he wrote that, in Zurich, they had experienced
how the communal celebration of the Lord's Supper had become a power for
peace; members of the congregation who had been living in enmity, now
came and, as if by chance, sat down next to each other, and, having passed the

Bread to each other and drunk of the same Cup, found that they were able to conquer their hate and forget their quarrel.*

✜

OUR PROTESTANT HERITAGE
Walter W. Sikes

TWO monuments of unusual interest for Protestants stand in Geneva. The "Reformation Monument" (see picture on p. 441) faces the campus of the University of Geneva and is surmounted by the high wall of the bastion of the ancient city, along which it runs for some hundreds of feet. At the center rise statues of the four great leaders of the Reformed Church of the sixteenth century in "Protestant Rome."

John Calvin dominates the group in stone as he did in the flesh. It was his spirit, so Roland Bainton reminds us, that "fashioned Geneva, divided Holland, convulsed France, molded Scotland, and guided New England." On his left is Theodore Beza, his associate, successor and biographer.

Flanking these two on one end of the group is William Farel, who had provoked a reluctant Calvin to leave his cloistered life as an intellectual and undertake the role of evangelist, prophet, teacher, and architect of the new religious and civil order in Geneva. The fourth is John Knox, who learned from Calvin how to resist those in authority and returned to Scotland to wrest liberty from a recalcitrant queen.

More than once I have sat, surrounded by the charm and beauty of the public park in front of this spreading monument, contemplating not only these four figures but the several others flanking this central group and pondering the short, massive legend across its face, *Post tenebras lux*—After the darkness, light! Was the world so very dark before Calvin and his associates here lifted the pall?

We now know that the gloom of the "Dark Ages" has been spread on much too heavily by some popular historians with more Protestant bias than sound learning. The later Middle Ages were centuries of high culture and inspiring religion. Besides, the Middle Ages had ended a couple of centuries before Calvin came to Geneva. For whatever else the Renaissance may have been, it certainly was a period of great resurgence of spiritual vitality. Wide learning, the arts and sciences, emphasis upon the worth of man, the power of reason, and the richness of nature had become the focus of attention and had inaugurated a period of great cultural emancipation.

Moreover, these reformers hardly achieved a regime of complete enlightenment themselves. The emancipation of the Renaissance was far from complete. Everyone in this group had suffered more or less violence for the sake of his conscience. Unfortunately they were not willing to allow to others the rights of conscience which they demanded for themselves.

* Abridged from *Zwingli the Reformer* by Oskar Farner, translated by D. G. Sear, pp. 58-66. Copyright 1952 by Lutterworth Press. Used by permission of the publisher.

The other monument in Geneva is a symbol of this unhappy fact. It is to Michael Servetus, whose burning at the stake Calvin energetically promoted and the others approved. Farel, watching the heretic burn and hearing him cry out of the flames, "O Jesus, thou Son of the Eternal God, have pity on me," remarked that Servetus might have been saved if he had placed the adjective "eternal" before the Son rather than before God.

These all regarded the damning crime of Servetus to be his unwillingness to confess the Nicene formula of the Trinity.

Far to the right of the central group in the "Reformation Monument" is the name of Luther. And one must remember that a quarter of a century before the execution of Servetus, Luther had urged "every one who can [to] smite, slay, and stab, secretly and openly" the revolting peasants of Germany; and his followers constituting the first church to bear his name at Wittenberg, having gained the power of a majority, undertook to drive out of the city all Roman Catholics by force.

And at the opposite end of the monument is the name of Zwingli, who at the same time was leading a bloody attempt to crush the Anabaptists, whose rejection of the validity of infant baptism he believed would undermine the principle of the Christian state, since there would be many in the state who were not in the church.

No, the Reformation scarcely broke on the world like a great light.

But if we think now of the second monument, actually erected first, on October 27, 1903, the three hundred fiftieth anniversary of the execution of Servetus, a more significant aspect of the Reformation emerges. It was erected by the Reformed churches of France and Geneva, who declare thereon that they, "respectful and grateful sons of John Calvin . . . firmly devoted to the liberty of conscience according to the true principles of the Reformation and of the Gospel, have erected this expiatory monument." Parenthetically, it is worth remarking that a similar "expiatory monument" was unveiled in 1911 at Vienne, where Servetus practiced medicine for twelve years and wrote many of his works, religious and scientific. This one was the gift of scientists from all over the Western world.

What are these "true principles of the Reformation and of the Gospel," which transcend the intolerance and violence of these early days?

Its central symbol and its informative principle is the open Bible. The Reformation was already breaking on the world when Wycliffe, Tyndale, and their contemporaries were risking their lives to give the Bible to the people. The sixteenth-century Reformers continued to make this effort the focal point of their multifarious efforts. And this effort was fiercely resisted by the guardians of the old order. For a thousand years now the people had been allowed access to the Bible only through creeds and catechisms. More than once Bibles were consigned to the flames, and less frequently those who dared make them available to the people.

The implications of the Protestant restoration of the Bible were revolutionary. Here and not in either the historic confessions or the historical church is to be found the redeeming Word. And the people, not the priests only, are able and responsible to go directly to this prime source of God's revelation, read it, judge it, and act on it for themselves. God and not man—not even those called to be ministers of the Word—is lord of every man's conscience.

The winds of freedom that blew through these open windows were so fresh and so fierce that those who had opened the windows began to slam them shut almost before they were fully open. When Servetus declared that he would "persevere in the confession that Jesus is the Son of God," Oecalampadius of Basel retorted, "I call upon you to confess that He is the Son of God consubstantial and co-eternal. . . . This you must do if we are to hold you for a Christian." This spirit soon crystallized in the Augsburg and Westminster confessions, intended, as were the classic creeds of Nicea and Chalcedon before them, to substitute non-Biblical concepts for Biblical language as tests of orthodoxy. It was not enough that one confess his faith in the words of Scripture.

The principle of the open Bible was destined to overcome this spirit of division and exclusiveness. More and more it has enabled Christians of various levels of understanding and diverse minds to stand together in freedom and in unity. Its profound meaning was impressively stated by John Robinson, beloved pastor of the Pilgrims, as he charged them on their departure for the New World that they be ever as ready to receive whatever revelation God might choose to make "by any other instrument of His" as they had been to listen to him, to Luther, or to Calvin. For he was confident that "the Lord hath yet more light to break forth out of His Holy Word." And the World Council of Churches has made the confession of Christ its only criterion of membership.

Thus if one asks, Which is the *true* Church? the Catholic and the Orthodox can point to a single historical form, his own, and declare, "Here it is, the repository of all truth and the divine expression of it." But no true Protestant can do such a thing. The Reformation principle recognizes that the Word of God stands over every institution, whether religious or secular, always judging its inadequacy, demanding that it see and confess its sins against God and its injustices to men.

Here we find the twin concepts of freedom and responsibility which the Reformation has fostered in the Western world and wherever its sons have gone. These sons have been called upon to resist attacks upon this freedom in the past. They are being so called upon today. The most subtle attack on them has been phrased in the deceptive truism, "Error has no rights." In reply one must say, Neither has truth any rights. Rights belong only to rational creatures. And the right of freedom of inquiry, of expression, of religious conscience belongs to every man.

This means that we must seek truth wherever it is to be found and must correct by criticism the claims of every person or institution.*

* Abridged from *The Christian-Evangelist* (Vol. 92, 1954), pp. 1011 ff. Published by Bethany Press. Used by permission of the author and the publisher.

KEEPER OF THE CITY
C. C. McCrie

IN 1519 there was born at Vezelay Theodore de Besze or Beze, known to all readers of history by the Latin form of the name—Beza.

Pierre De Besze, the father of Theodore, was *bailli* or prefect of the province; Marie De Bourdelot, the mother, was of noble descent. Youthful Theodore was the youngest in a family of seven. His wealthy Parisian uncle visited Vezelay, formed a liking to the seventh child, and offered to be responsible for his education. At the University of Orleans the youth became a good classical scholar, and studied law, as his father designed him for the legal profession.

When a student at Orleans, Theodore Beza came under the influence of a German, who largely influenced his character and convictions, and practically determined his career in life. This was Melchior Wolmar, a noted scholar of his day, who had at one time under his tuition a greater Frenchman than Beza—Jean Calvin from Noyon. What Beza owed to his teacher at Orleans can be gathered from an autobiographical letter to Wolmar. He styles the day upon which he became a member of the Orleans household his "second birthday, the beginning of all the good things which I have received from that time forward, and which I trust to receive hereafter in my future life."

After taking his degree in law, Beza went to Paris. Thanks to his father's other brother, the Abbot of Froidmont, Theodore had for income the revenues of two riches benefices, yielding an annual revenue of seven hundred golden crowns, while there was every prospect that, on the death of the ecclesiastic, his nephew would succeed him, and that meant an increase of five thousand golden crowns every year. With this affluence of means and these brilliant prospects, Beza gave himself to classical studies, literary pursuits, and pleasure seeking. He led the life of a brilliant devotée of *belles lettres,* and of a man of society. But Beza was not happy; he was not at peace. His father insisted that he should enter upon the practice of law. To the son the prospect was abhorrent, the *palais* or parliament house was a veritable house of bondage. His uncle, the Abbé, advised the life of a courtier. That was not less repugnant.

Late in 1584 Beza was visited with a severe illness: so severe that for a time it was regarded as fatal. From the bed of sore suffering and extreme weakness he, who was already converted, rose a consecrated, resolute man. The benefices were surrendered, and, with his wife, to whom he had been secretly married, Beza made his way to Switzerland, and received a kindly welcome at Geneva from John Calvin. Within a year he became professor of Greek in the *Académie* of Lausanne. From 1549 to 1558 Beza exercised a fruitful ministry in the Pays de Vaud, influencing the youth who were preparing for the ministry of the gospel, having helpful intercourse with colleagues, scholars, and theologians residing in Lausanne and neighboring towns, and using his graceful, facile pen in completing the Huguenot Psalter and in producing his classic Latin translation of the New Testament.

After nine years' work Beza resigned his professorship at Lausanne and returned to Geneva. From this point in his career Beza's lifework was done in the city of Calvin, and it readily falls into two periods. In the first of these, he was the coadjutor of Calvin; in the second he was the successor of the great Reformer.

Officially during the first period Beza was rector of the newly-founded university; he aided Calvin in his work as theological lecturer, and he was also pastor of one of the city churches. In addition Beza gave much of his time and strength to the extension and defense of Protestantism in his native country. He was in France when the Massacre of Vassy (Sunday, March 1, 1562), was perpetrated by orders of the Duke of Guise. Beza at once sought and obtained an audience of Charles IX and Catherine de Medici, at which Antoine De Bourbon was also present. The last-named potentate had changed sides, and was no longer an ardent supporter of the Reformation. It was to this shifty weakling that Beza addressed the words which have become historical: "Sire, it belongs in truth to the Church of God, in whose name I speak, to endure blows and not to inflict them. But it will also please Your Majesty to remember that she is an anvil that has worn out many hammers."

Beza returned to Geneva in May, 1563. Calvin was rapidly failing, and so, at the joint request of his colleagues and of Calvin himself, Beza undertook to bear a portion of the load of work which was pressing heavily upon the enfeebled leader. The leader died on May 27, 1564. Beza was appointed his successor as President or Moderator of the "Venerable Company of Pastors," and so entered upon the second period of his lifework at Geneva.

From 1590 to 1592 the little community of Geneva was menaced with danger from an implacable enemy, the Duke of Savoy. The privations of a state of siege were intensified by something approaching famine. But in the hour of darkness and danger the voice of Beza, now threescore and ten, was raised from the old pulpit of St. Pierre on behalf of the rights and liberties of the Republic. In 1594, when seventy-five years of age, he wrote: "With the exception of a trembling of the hand that almost prevents my tracing a line, I am well enough, thank God! to preach every Sunday and to deliver every fortnight my three theological lectures. I am nearing the end of my course, with my spirit as much as possible on high."

Eight years before his death a young ecclesiastic of noble family and personal celebrity sought to effect Beza's return to the Church of Rome. The future St. Francis of Sales, who had been successful in proselytising on a wholesale scale, tried his arts of persuasion upon the Protestant champion of Geneva. Several visits were paid to the aged Reformer, and on all these occasions a courteous reception was extended. The remark of the Reformer, "As for myself if I am not in the right way, I pray God every day that He will lead me into it," emboldened the papal agent to assure Beza that he need not hesitate to return to the pale of the Church from any fear of loss of means or of comforts, for he might depend upon it that the Holy Father at Rome would provide a pension with compensation at his own valuation for furniture and books parted with. This was too much for the venerable Protestant. He pointed to the shelves of his bookcase empty of books which had been sold to enable their owner to support French refugees, and then showed the visitor to the door, taking leave of him with the cutting words: "Get thee behind me, Satan."

On the long dark night of December 21, 1602, a force of Savoyards, eight thousand strong, attempted to capture Geneva. The advance guard had raised their scaling ladders and begun to climb the fortifications; two hundred men stood on the ramparts; a few forerunners had actually entered the city. Just in time an alarm was given to the inhabitants, the portcullis was let fall, those who had scaled the fortifications were encountered by the citizens and put to death, while the bulk of the besieging army took flight.

When the city was once more in safety and peace, the people flocked to the Church of St. Pierre for a thanksgiving service. Beza presided, and commenced the service by giving out to be sung the grand words of the One Hundred Twenty-fourth Psalm in the French version, which he himself had executed half a century earlier. On the bas-reliefs of a fountain erected in 1857, in the Rue des Allemands, styled the Monument of the Escalade, there is a representation of Beza in the act of returning thanks to God.

What a place Geneva had in the Frenchman's thoughts and affections can be gathered from the fact that on Sunday, October 13, 1605—the last day of his earthly life—he asked, "Is the city in full safety, and quiet?" When he received an assuring answer he sank back, lost consciousness, and in the course of a few minutes passed from friends surrounding him to the company of the glorified.*

✛

LORD, TAKE THOU THE REINS TO THEE

ZURICH was the first center of the Swiss Reformation, and its first leader was Huldreich Zwingli (1484-1531). From Zurich, preachers of the gospel fanned out to neighboring cantons where the Roman Catholic faith was still dominant. One of these preachers, Jacob Kaiser, was arrested in the canton of Schwyz and burned at the stake as a heretic on May 29, 1529. Zurich declared war against the offending cantons, but before battle was joined the two Swiss parties agreed on a treaty of peace. The pact guaranteed freedom for the preachers, but Zwingli felt troubled about the future. In a mood of despair suffused with Christian hope he wrote the words and music of this hymn.

Zwingli pictures the Church of Christ as a chariot surrounded by its enemies. The merely human wisdom, the puny political and military strength of those who love the Church and seek its reformation, will not avail now. So he prays that Christ will take the reins and conduct the chariot to safety, driving back her enemies and restoring her original faithfulness.

---

* From Beza's "Icones": Contemporary Portraits of Reformers by C. C. McCrie, pp. 3-13. Published in 1909 by The Religious Tract Society. Used by permission of Lutterworth Press.

Lord, Take Thou the Reins to Thee*

HULDRYCH ZWINGLI (1484-1531).

Herr, nun selbst den Wa - gen halt, Bald ab-
No - tre barque est en dan - ger : Prends Sei-
Lord, take Thou the reins to Thee Else our

seit geht sonst die Fahrt, Das brächt Freud dem Wi - der-
gneur la barre en main. A toi sont nos len - de-
course un - stead - y goes, Bring - ing glad - ness to Thy

part, Der dich ver - acht so fre - vent - lich.
mains ; Toi seul peux vrai - ment nous pro - té - ger.
foes That de - ride Thee thus de - spite - ful - ly.

2.
Gott, erhöh deins Namen's Ehr,
   Wehr und straf der Bösen Grimm,
   Weck die Schaf mit deiner Stimm,
Die dich lieb haben inniglich.

3.
Hilf, dass alle Bitterkeit
   Scheid, O Herr, und alte Treu
   Wiederkehr und werde neu,
Dass wir ewig lobsingen dir.

HULDRYCH ZWINGLI (1529).

This is a beautiful hymn of surrender to the leadership of Christ, whether we think of the Church or of our own personal need. In it we pray to our Lord to take the reins, the steering-wheel, the rudder. Indeed, the French translation changes the figure from that of a chariot to that of a little boat; so the prayer becomes essentially that of our well-loved English hymn of Edward Hopper:

> Jesus, Saviour, pilot me
> Over life's tempestuous sea.

The first stanza appears in the music score on p. 457. The second and third stanzas are:

> Thy most glorious name extol,
>   Bring the powers of ill to fall,
>   Rouse Thy people with Thy call
> That exalt Thee with their heart and soul.

> Help us banish disaccord,
>   And restore old kindliness,
>   That we evermore may bless
> And adore the name of God our Lord.

✠

WE GATHER TOGETHER

In its first hundred years the Reformation spread over much of Europe. The Protestant faith proclaimed by Luther was triumphant in many parts of Germany and in the Scandinavian countries. The Reformed faith preached by Zwingli and Calvin flourished in certain cantons of Switzerland and farther afield in the Netherlands, Scotland, Hungary, and parts of Germany. It become a vigorous minority movement in France (the Huguenots) and in England (the Puritans), and was transplanted from there to New England to become a dominant force in determining the early American character.

In the Netherlands, as in other countries, the struggle of the Protestants for the triumph of their faith became linked with a fight for political freedom. During the sixteenth century the King of Spain became Holy Roman Emperor and hereditary ruler over the Low Countries. Dutch patriots resisted his attempt to govern them from a distance, especially after he concentrated power in the hands of Cardinal de Granvelle, who did not speak their language nor understand them. Prince William of Orange led the rebellion against the Spaniards and the Dutchmen opened their dikes to flood their lands against the foreign troops. After a gallant struggle, they won their independence, and in 1574 the Synod of Dordrecht adopted the Reformed faith as the official religion of the country.

The stirring memories of the heroic days when they won their political

We Gather Together*

*Where two or three are gathered together in My name,
there am I in the midst of them.*

MATTHEW 18:20

KREMSER. 12. 11. 12. 11.

Anonymous

Old Netherlands melody in
The Collection by Adrianus Valerius, 1625

1. We gath - er to - geth - er to ask the Lord's bless - ing;
2. Be - side us to guide us, our God with us join - ing,
3. We all do ex - tol Thee, Thou Lead - er tri - um - phant,

He chas - tens and has - tens His will to make known.
Or - dain - ing, main - tain - ing His king - dom di - vine,
And pray that Thou still our De - fend - er wilt be.

The wick - ed op - press - ing now cease from dis - tress - ing;
So from the be - gin - ning the fight we were win - ning:
Let Thy con - gre - ga - tion es - cape trib - u - la - tion:

Sing prais - es to His name: He for-gets not His own.
Thou, Lord, wast at our side, all glo - ry be Thine!
Thy Name be ev - er praised! O Lord, make us free! A - men.

*From *Christian Hymns*, No. 43. Copyright 1945 by The Christian Foundation.

freedom from Spain and their religious freedom from Rome flamed in the hearts of the people of the Netherlands and found expression in the triumphant hymn, "We Gather Together to Ask the Lord's Blessing." The author is unknown; the tune is that of a folk song, published about 1625, the year when Prince William's youngest son, Frederick Henry, became the leader of the Dutch republic. The hymn recalls the perils through which the people have passed: "The wicked oppressing now cease from distressing." It affirms the prophetic faith of the Bible that in the afflictions which come upon the people divine judgment is executed upon their sins: "He chastens." At the same time it gives credit to God for the survival of His people: "He forgets not His own" and "Thou Lord, wast at our side." The final stanza is a glorious paean of praise, rising to a thrilling climax in the prayer, "O Lord, make us free!"

While this hymn will obviously stir the religious and patriotic emotions of the people of the Netherlands, it has rich meaning for the rest of us also. It expresses the great Biblical faith that God is at work in history, as does the American hymn, "Mine eyes have seen the glory of the coming of the Lord." And it celebrates the intimate relation between political and religious freedom which is so apparent wherever the Reformed faith has gone. "Stand fast therefore in the liberty wherewith Christ hath made us free" (Gal. 5:1).

CONTENTS

PART IV   SECTION 3

THE REFORMATION REACHES GREAT BRITAIN

—✛—

Fight the good fight of faith, lay hold on eternal life, whereunto thou art also called, and hast professed a good profession before many witnesses.—I TIMOTHY 6:12

—✛—

PICTURES: PAGE
  Interpretation: Canterbury Cathedral 462
  Picture: Canterbury Cathedral 463
  Interpretation: William Tyndale—*Boehm* 465
  Picture: William Tyndale—*Boehm* 467
  Interpretation: "And When Did You Last See Your Father?"—*Yeames* .. 468
  Picture: "And When Did You Last See Your Father?"—*Yeames* 469

POETRY:
  A Hymn to God the Father—*Donne* 471
  Teach Me, My God and King—*Herbert* 472
  On His Blindness—*Milton* 472
  Lord, It Belongs Not to My Care—*Baxter* 473
  The First Psalm—*Scottish Psalter* 473
  The Valiant Pilgrim—*Bunyan* 474
  Glory to Thee, My God, This Night—*Ken* 474
  In Lincoln Cathedral—*Clark* 475

STORIES:
  A Bible for Plowboys and Poets—*Goodspeed* 475
  Man with a Twa-Handed Sword—*Hutchinson* 478
  Pilgrim's Journey—*Bunyan* 481

MUSIC:
  Interpretation: We Praise Thee, O God; We Acknowledge Thee (Te
    Deum Laudamus)—*Nicetas of Remesiana* (?) 484
  Music: We Praise Thee, O God; We Acknowledge Thee (Te Deum
    Laudamus)—*Lawes, Cooke* 486
  Interpretation: I to the Hills Will Lift Mine Eyes (Psalm 121)—
    Scottish Psalter 487
  Music: I to the Hills Will Lift Mine Eyes (Psalm 121)—*Scottish
    Psalter* 488

CANTERBURY CATHEDRAL

To stand at Canterbury, to gaze at the towers of the famed cathedral, to survey each detail of the complex maze of buildings, to ponder the rich symbolism of the statuary and the windows—all this is to enter appreciatively into one of the noble achievements of medieval architecture. (See photo on p. 463.) It is more. It is to find oneself where many stirring events of the Christian story in England have occurred and at the ecclesiastical center of a great nation today.

The earliest church in this place was built in Roman times, when Britain was one of the outposts of empire and the faith was brought to the northern island by soldiers in the legions and perhaps by merchants and officials of the imperial government. Here at Canterbury they built a church dedicated to St. Martin. But in time the power of Rome diminished, the legions were withdrawn, the Anglo-Saxon invaders with their wild, heathen faith overran Britain, and the church fell upon desolate days.

A new opening was made for the gospel when King Ethelbert of Kent married a Christian princess from Paris, whose name was Bertha. Her husband gave her the ancient church as a place of worship. Then in the year 597, a company of missionaries from Rome, under the leadership of St. Augustine, arrived in England. Bearing before them a silver cross and a picture of the Christ as banners, they drew near to Canterbury chanting the litany: "We beseech thee, O Lord, in all thy mercy, that thy anger and wrath be turned away from this city, and from thy holy house, because we have sinned. Hallelujah." For the sake of his wife, the king granted them permission to meet in the ancient church, "to sing, to pray, to say mass, to preach, and to baptize."

Soon the king was converted, and then many of his people. Pope Gregory made St. Augustine Archbishop of Canterbury, the spiritual head of the Church of England. The archbishop rebuilt the ancient Roman church, but after four and a half centuries it was destroyed, along with much of the city, in the fire of 1067. The Archbishop Lanfranc, who had come to England with William the Conqueror, built a new church, but it also went up in flames in 1174. Work then began on the present cathedral and continued generation after generation for more than three hundred years. The central tower was not completed till 1495. Canterbury Cathedral stands on this spot as a reminder of the devotion of many generations of Christians—Roman, Briton, Saxon, Norman, English.

Canterbury has had many heroes, its most famous being Thomas à Becket. A youthful companion of King Henry II, he was elevated as archbishop in 1162; thereafter he abandoned his gay and frivolous ways and gave himself seriously to his ministry. Refusing to permit his old friend the king to dominate the church, Becket went into exile for some years. Then he returned to Canterbury where he soon received threats from the henchmen of the king. On December 29, 1170, he was assassinated as he knelt before the altar. He

CANTERBURY CATHEDRAL

was soon being venerated as an English martyr, and in 1173 the pope canonized him as a saint. Thereupon the cathedral became a place of pilgrimage; Chaucer's *Canterbury Tales* tells of one company of late medieval travelers on their way to the shrine.

When Henry VIII and his Parliament led the Church of England out of the Roman Catholic Church, they were acting as patriotic Englishmen who resented the power of a "foreign" ecclesiastical institution; they renounced the authority of Rome without rebelling as violently as the Reformers on the continent against all the practices of medieval religion. Nevertheless, in 1539 Henry VIII took Canterbury Cathedral from the monks who resided there and had it reconsecrated as a church for the populace at large, and he confiscated the monastic treasures of jewelry and gold which were carried away by seven or eight men and twenty-six carts. In the days of the Puritans, an iconoclast with a pike shattered some of the great stained-glass windows, irreplaceable masterpieces of medieval art.

In spite of such extreme actions, however, the Church of England maintained its sense of continuity with the Christian generations who had gone before. The liturgy was purged of some offensive elements and translated into the majestic English of the *Book of Common Prayer*. (See "We Praise Thee, O God," p. 486.) Priests and bishops continued to wear the symbolic vestments developed through long centuries of ceremonial use. The Church of England has a rich sense of tradition and takes pride that the Cathedral is the burial place of St. Augustine, St. Anselm, St. Thomas à Becket, the Black Prince, and many another famous name in English history.

Today the Archbishop of Canterbury is primate of all England and presides over the coronation of the British monarch. He is in an important position to speak for the Christian conscience to the English nation, in pointing out the meaning of Christian principles for economic life, education, international problems, and other areas of public affairs. He also serves as chairman of the Lambeth Conference, the meeting of Anglican (Episcopal) bishops from all over the world. Recent archbishops have given important leadership to the ecumenical movement. Dr. Geoffrey Francis Fisher, ninety-ninth Archbishop of Canterbury, who was elevated to that office in 1945, served as one of six co-presidents of the World Council of Churches from 1946 to 1954.

What a tradition of praise hallows this place! Day after day, year after year, century after century, since the time of Queen Bertha and St. Augustine, prayers of adoration have been chanted here. This passage from the canticle *Benedicite* may be considered the song of the Christian ages, ringing up to the highest arches of the venerable cathedral of Canterbury:

O let Israel bless the Lord: praise him, and magnify him for ever.
O ye Priests of the Lord, bless ye the Lord: praise him, and magnify him for ever.
O ye Servants of the Lord, bless ye the Lord: praise him, and magnify him for ever.
O ye Spirits and Souls of the Righteous, bless the Lord: praise him, and magnify him for ever.

O ye holy and humble Men of heart, bless ye the Lord: praise him, and magnify him for ever.

Let us bless the Father, and the Son, and the Holy Ghost: praise him, and magnify him for ever.

✠

WILLIAM TYNDALE

J. E. Boehm

ON the Victoria Embankment in London a statue of William Tyndale stands looking out on the English scene with a sense of serenity, dignity, and fulfilled purpose. At Tyndale's side is a printing press, with an open Bible resting beneath his hand, symbolic of the gift that he gave to the English-speaking people along with his love and his life. On the pedestal at the base of the statue are inscribed these words:

> "THY WORD IS A LAMP TO MY FEET, AND
> A LIGHT TO MY PATH"—"THE ENTRANCE
> OF THY WORDS GIVETH LIGHT."
> PSALM CXIX 105. 130.

> "AND THIS IS THE RECORD THAT GOD HAS
> GIVEN TO US ETERNAL LIFE, AND THIS LIFE
> IS IN HIS SON." I. JOHN V. 11.

In 1883, three and a half centuries after Tyndale's death, the people of England paid tribute to his genius and his service through the dedication of this statue by J. E. Boehm. (See p. 467.)

Little is known of the childhood and early youth of William Tyndale. Tradition gives the time and the place of his birth in Gloucestershire near the borders of Wales about the year 1494. While yet young, Tyndale went to Oxford for his schooling. He remained there until he received his degree, then went to Cambridge, where the great Erasmus [see Part IV, Section 1] had taught. Cambridge was becoming a new center of learning, and Tyndale was drawn to the more liberal atmosphere. Here he possibly had the opportunity to study Erasmus' new version of the Greek New Testament and to become better prepared for his own life's work of translating the Scriptures into English. Sometime during these student days he was ordained a priest, but where he preached is not recorded. In his final days at Cambridge he must have been a witness to the burning of Martin Luther's writings at the university. As the young man watched the flames lick at the books, was there any premonition of the flames that would one day burn his books and eventually his body?

Following his scholastic training, Tyndale took a position as a chaplain and teacher in the home of a country squire at Little Sodbury Manor. The children were young and required little time and his chaplain's duties were not rigorous;

so there was much time left for Tyndale to further his study of Greek and Latin. In this rural setting there must have come a growing awareness of the vast difference between the simple beauty of the New Testament words when translated into English and the overpowering scholarly terms used to expound upon the New Testament in Latin which had no relevance to the life of the common people. Many of the priests knew only enough Latin to conduct services and were unable themselves to read the Scriptures. Since many churchmen visited the home of Sir John Walsh, the young chaplain had ample opportunity to express his views.

From these conversations arose the conviction that was to lead Tyndale to the stake, the conviction that the Scriptures must be translated into English. This was a heretical view in these days, but in the heat of an argument with a leading churchman Tyndale earnestly declared, "If God spare my life, ere many years I will cause a boy that driveth the plough shall know more of the Scripture than thou dost." Tyndale did not stay long after this in the countryside, but left for London to look for a sponsor for his work of translation.

The Renaissance had brought new movements of life and thought to England in those days. New horizons were opening, merchants were moving freely from country to country, books were being printed, and men's minds were aflame with new ideas kindled by Martin Luther. Henry VIII was quarreling with the Pope, and the country was in a state of unrest. Tyndale spent a futile year in London looking for a place and opportunity to begin his translation.

At the age of thirty Tyndale went into voluntary exile to the continent so that he might do his work in greater freedom, taking with him his few belongings, his Latin and Greek New Testaments, and other books. Germany with its great universities was his destination. Part of his work was done at Hamburg, and there is reason to believe that he went to Wittenberg to use its library and possibly to meet Martin Luther and share his dream of an English translation. In this atmosphere of learning, Tyndale brought the full force of his scholarship to bear upon the translation of the Greek New Testament into contemporary English. By this time he had become well versed in seven languages, and this knowledge brought a richness and depth to his work.

When the translation was completed he journeyed to Cologne to find a printer who would do the job secretly. Arrangements were made for the copies to be taken to England, and the actual printing had begun, when he was betrayed. Tyndale managed to escape to Worms with some of the completed sheets and, after some delay, in 1526 the first printed English New Testament in translation from the original Greek was finished. Once the New Testament was in print, it was smuggled into England in bales of merchandise and found its way into the hands of the people. When copies reached the hands of the church authorities, they were burned at St. Paul's Cross in London. This type of publicity only increased the value of the book, and little groups of people gathered together to read God's Word in their own tongue. Copies were confiscated and burned by the authorities when they were found, but other copies came flooding into England to take their place.

WILLIAM TYNDALE—*BOEHM*

These were not easy years for Tyndale, who was forced to remain in hiding, but he managed to translate major portions of the Old Testament from the original Hebrew. His revision of his own New Testament in 1534 corrected some errors and is the actual foundation of much of the structure of our New Testament. The earlier translations from the Latin had been stilted and difficult to read.

The foes of Tyndale kept tracking him down and he eventually was betrayed by a supposed friend in the city of Antwerp. He was taken to the Castle of Vilvorde near the city of Brussels in May, 1535, and was kept there until his death on October 6, 1536. Even with the prospect of death before him, Tyndale continued to work on the translation. In a letter written to the governor of the castle where he was imprisoned, he asked for a warmer cap, some cloth to patch his leggings, a warmer coat (for he was suffering from a bad cough), and a lamp to use in the long evenings. He also begged permission to have the Hebrew Bible, the Hebrew grammar, and the Hebrew dictionary, that he might pass the time in study.

At his trial Tyndale was condemned as a heretic, stripped of his priestly office, and handed over to the civil authorities to be executed. His last words before he was strangled and his body burned at the stake were, "Lord! Open the King of England's eyes." His prayer was granted. Within a year it was possible to buy the New Testament in English in Tyndale's native land.*

✠

"AND WHEN DID YOU LAST SEE YOUR FATHER?"

W. F. Yeames

THIS is not a pretty picture. For war is not pretty, least of all civil war. Brainwashing is not pretty. The use of children as informers against their parents is not pretty. Religious persecution is not pretty. Indeed, all these involve crimes against mankind. And they cannot be excused simply because those who perpetrate them are "good" men, on "our" side.

The picture (p. 469) tells a graphic story. It is set during the Civil War in England (1642-1651) between the Cavaliers or Royalists and the soldiers of Parliament, called Roundheads, many of whom were Puritans. There was no clear division of the country on geographical lines; thus one's enemies might suddenly appear near at hand. In the picture, Roundhead troops have just succeeded in taking over a great house belonging to a wealthy Cavalier family. The father has fled, perhaps to save his life, more likely to rally Royalist forces. The victors in the most recent skirmish are determined to discover his whereabouts; it is an important item of military information. The stern Puritan gentlemen behind the table have set up a court of inquiry to interrogate each member of the family.

The presiding officer, who leans forward with his chin resting on the back

* This interpretation was prepared especially for the present anthology by Evelyn R. Wagner.

"AND WHEN DID YOU LAST SEE YOUR FATHER?"—YEAMES

of his hand, apparently does not like this piece of business; nevertheless he must see it through. The little boy stands erect upon the footstool facing his questioners; he is respectful, but bravely determined not to betray his father. His sister has already begun to sob, while the women of the household look on with grave and helpless concern.

The artist has made no effort to conceal his sympathies. Born nearly two centuries after the Civil War, W. F. Yeames (1835-1918) liked to paint historical incidents, and in this instance he pictures the Roundheads at considerable disadvantage. The situation is ironical, for once the Parliamentary army had secured its victory and pacified the country, Oliver Cromwell who ruled England from 1651 to 1660 as Lord Protector, extended to the various sects a greater degree of religious toleration than his country had yet known. But it cannot be denied that while the armies of Parliament were seeking to advance the Puritan cause, they persecuted Anglicans, Independents, and Baptists. And there is no more to be said for religious persecution when practiced by "our" side than when it is practiced against "us."

It took the Christian world a long time to learn the lesson of religious toleration. The earliest disciples were persecuted both by Jews and by the Roman government, but once the faith had become established, Christians turned the power of government against pagans and heretics. One of the blackest pages in church history is the record of the Inquisition in the late Middle Ages, which submitted suspected heretics to torture and sentenced many to be burned at the stake. In their denunciations of Rome, Protestants recounted many of these stories with righteous indignation. Yet Protestantism also launched its persecutions, such as the burning of Servetus in Geneva, with Calvin's approval.

In England the struggle between Catholic and Protestant, Anglican and Puritan, was embittered by official cruelty. Anglican King Henry VIII executed a noble Catholic like Sir Thomas More (1535), but when Henry's Catholic daughter came to the throne (1553-1558), she put Protestants to death at such a rate as to earn for herself the hated name, "Bloody Mary." Under her younger sister Queen Elizabeth (1558-1603) the Church of England was firmly established in the laws of the nation, but the more thoroughgoing Protestants known as Puritans, who wanted English religious institutions reconstructed after the pattern of the Reformed churches in Geneva, Scotland, and the Netherlands, continued their agitation into the seventeenth century.

Under King Charles I (1625-1649), Archbishop Laud ruthlessly sought to enforce uniformity; a Scottish physician and preacher named Alexander Leighton who wished to do away with bishops in the church was publicly whipped, mutilated by having his nostrils slit and one ear cut off, and branded in the face with the letters "S.S." (sower of sedition). The Long Parliament retaliated by condemning the archbishop to death without a trial (1645). And a few years later (1649) the king himself was sent to the block, for mingled political and religious reasons. Then the Puritan captain, Oliver Cromwell, ruled England as Lord Protector. But when he died, Charles II came back as king (1660-1685), and he renewed the policy of oppression, seeking religious uniformity and putting dissenters to death.

At length England wearied of all this inhumanity and blood-letting in the name of Christ. After the Glorious Revolution (1688) brought William and Mary to the throne, Parliament passed the Toleration Act of 1689, permitting Dissenters to worship in good conscience, though Roman Catholics were not admitted to public office till 1829. The new spirit of toleration passed to the English colonies in America. In 1785 the legislature of Virginia adopted the Statute of Religious Freedom written by Thomas Jefferson, and in 1789, when the Constitution of the United States of America was adopted, the first article in the Bill of Rights provided that "Congress shall make no law respecting an establishment of religion, or prohibiting the free exercise thereof." The guarantee of religious liberty is a political achievement which did not come easily.

Back to our picture. It is a scene to trouble our consciences. Whatever our background, Catholic or Protestant, Anglican or Puritan, we must penitently confess that our fathers in their zeal not to deny the faith sometimes denied the spirit of Christ. Ours is the difficult task of sustaining great convictions while maintaining the generous spirit of toleration toward others. But though our picture is not pretty, it can awaken us to thanksgiving. We can indeed be grateful that the descendants of the two parties here represented learned the lesson of religious liberty. As we think of this important victory, we may pray that the other evils represented in the picture—war, brainwashing, the exploitation of children—may also be banished some day from the common life of mankind.

✢

A HYMN TO GOD THE FATHER

I

Wilt thou forgive that sin where I begun,
  Which was my sin, though it were done before?
Wilt thou forgive that sin through which I run,
  And do run still, though still I do deplore?
    When thou hast done, thou hast not done,
    For I have more.

II

Wilt thou forgive that sin which I have won
  Others to sin, and made my sin their door?
Wilt thou forgive that sin which I did shun
  A year or two, but wallowed in a score?
    When thou hast done, thou hast not done,
    For I have more.

III

I have a sin of fear, that when I have spun
  My last thread I shall perish on the shore;
But swear by thyself, that at my death thy son
  Shall shine as he shines now, and heretofore;
    And, having done that, thou hast done;
      I fear no more.

                      —*John Donne (1572-1631)*

TEACH ME, MY GOD AND KING

    Teach me, my God and King,
      In all things thee to see;
  And what I do in anything
      To do it as for thee!

    A man that looks on glass,
      On it may stay his eye;
  Or if he pleaseth, through it pass,
      And then the heavens espy.

    All may of Thee partake;
      Nothing can be so mean,
  Which with this tincture, "for thy sake,"
      Will not grow bright and clean.

    A servant with this clause
      Makes drudgery divine;
  Who sweeps a room, as for thy laws,
      Makes that and the action fine.

    This is the famous stone
      That turneth all to gold;
  For that which God doth touch and own
      Cannot for less be told.

                    —*George Herbert (1593-1632)*

ON HIS BLINDNESS

When I consider how my light is spent,
Ere half my days, in this dark world and wide,
And that one talent, which is death to hide,
Lodged with me useless—though my soul more bent
To serve therewith my Maker, and present
My true account, lest He, returning, chide—
"Doth God exact day-labor, light denied?"
I fondly ask: But Patience, to prevent

That murmur, soon replies, "God doth not need
Either man's work or His own gifts: who best
Bear His mild yoke, they serve Him best: His state
Is kingly: thousands at His bidding speed,
And post o'er land and ocean without rest:
They also serve who only stand and wait."

—*John Milton* (*1608-1674*)

LORD, IT BELONGS NOT TO MY CARE

Lord, it belongs not to my care
  Whether I die or live;
To love and serve Thee is my share,
  And this Thy grace must give.

If life be long I will be glad
  That I may long obey;
If short—yet why should I be sad
  To soar to endless day?

Christ leads me through no darker rooms
  Than He went through before;
He that into God's kingdom comes
  Must enter by His door.

Come, Lord, when grace hath made me meet
  Thy blessed face to see;
For if Thy work on earth be sweet,
  What will Thy glory be?

Then shall I end my sad complaints
  And weary, sinful days;
And join with the triumphant saints
  To sing Jehovah's praise.

My knowledge of that life is small,
  The eye of faith is dim;
But 'tis enough that Christ knows all,
  And I shall be with Him.

—*Richard Baxter* (*1615-1691*)

THE FIRST PSALM

That man hath perfect blessedness
  Who walketh not astray
In counsel of ungodly men,
  Nor stands in sinners' way,
Nor sitteth in the scorner's chair;
  But placeth his delight
Upon God's law, and meditates
  On His law day and night.

He shall be like a tree that grows
  Near planted by a river,
Which in his season yields his fruit,
  And his leaf fadeth never;

And all he doth shall prosper well.
  The wicked are not so;
But like they are unto the chaff,
  Which wind drives to and fro.

In judgment therefore shall not stand
  Such as ungodly are;
Nor in the assembly of the just
  Shall wicked men appear.

For why, the way of godly men
  Unto the Lord is known,
Whereas the way of wicked men
  Shall quite be overthrown.

          —*Scottish Psalter*

THE VALIANT PILGRIM

Who would true valor see,
  Let him come hither;
One here will constant be,
  Come wind, come weather;
There's no discouragement
Shall make him once relent
His first avowed intent
    To be a pilgrim.

Who so beset him round
  With dismal stories
Do but themselves confound;
  His strength the more is.
No lion can him fright,
He'll with a giant fight,
But he will have a right
    To be a pilgrim.

Hobgoblin nor foul fiend
  Can daunt his spirit;
He knows he at the end
  Shall life inherit.
Then fancies fly away,
He'll fear not what men say;
He'll labor night and day
    To be a pilgrim.

        —*John Bunyan (1628-1688)*

GLORY TO THEE, MY GOD, THIS NIGHT

Glory to thee, my God, this night
For all the blessings of the light;
Keep me, O keep me, King of Kings,
Beneath thy own almighty wings.

Forgive me, Lord, for thy dear Son,
The ill that I this day have done,
That with the world, myself, and thee,
I, ere I sleep, at peace may be.

Teach me to live, that I may dread
The grave as little as my bed;
Teach me to die, that so I may
Rise glorious at the awful day.

O may my soul on thee repose,
And with sweet sleep mine eyelids close,
Sleep that may me more vigorous make
To serve my God when I awake.

When in the night I sleepless lie,
My soul with heavenly thoughts supply;
Let no ill dreams disturb my rest,
No powers of darkness me molest.

Praise God from whom all blessings flow,
Praise him all creatures here below,
Praise him above, ye heavenly host,
Praise Father, Son, and Holy Ghost.
                    —*Thomas Ken (1637-1711)*

IN LINCOLN CATHEDRAL

While lordly braggarts stir the world to arms,
    And statesmen preach the gospel of defense,
In this dear place I hide from all alarms;
    This quiet hour is ample recompense
For years of noisy arguments of men
    Who, faithless, prophesy a coming doom—
The frightened nations gripped by war again,
    The world collapsing in a sea of gloom.
Yet here is peace. For centuries meek souls
    Have walked these aisles and given God the praise
For life and love and beauty's lofty goals.
    Faith stirred their hearts, trust fortified their days.
For me, this hour, the woes of empires cease:
    At this still altar I have found God's peace.*
                    —*Thomas Curtis Clark*

✝

A BIBLE FOR PLOWBOYS AND POETS
Edgar J. Goodspeed

WILLIAM TYNDALE was a young Englishman who had come to the conclusion that it was "impossible to establish the lay people in any truth except the scripture were plainly laid before their eyes in their mother tongue"—"which thing only," he added, "moved me to translate the New Testament."

Failing to find church support for himself while he should make the translation, he went abroad and began printing at Cologne in 1525. But

* *The Christian-Evangelist* (November 12, 1936). Published by Bethany Press. Used by permission of the author and the publisher.

Catholic agents learned of the enterprise and broke up the work and Tyndale fled to Worms, where the printing was completed before the end of the year. The translation was made from the original Greek, as published by Erasmus in 1522.

Copies of Tyndale's translation reached England early in 1526. They were eagerly welcomed by people interested in the Reformation, but rigorously proscribed and sought out for destruction by the church authorities. Only one copy of the Worms octavo is now known to be in existence.

Tyndale's spelling is very different from ours; in his day there were a dozen ways of spelling "it"; but his language strongly colored all the succeeding revisions of the New Testament, and ninety-two per cent of the King James Version of it is still just as William Tyndale wrote it, more than four hundred years ago.

He proposed to use the familiar spoken English of his day. He declared that he would make a version a plowboy could read and understand.

Tyndale went on to learn Hebrew, and set about translating the Old Testament. His financial backers were a group of English merchants, who held reformed views. But in 1535 his enemies finally overtook him; he was imprisoned near Brussels, and the following year he was executed.

But he had set the English Bible on its way; and it went rapidly forward. In 1535, when Tyndale was in prison, Myles Coverdale put out the first printed English Bible. No one knows its printer's name or even where it was actually published. Somewhere on the Continent; certainly not in England! Coverdale hesitated to tell who had helped his project.

Only two years elapsed before another English Bible made its appearance, bearing the name of Thomas Matthew. This is generally believed to have been a pen name for John Rogers, who had been Tyndale's last friend, and possessed his translation of the first half of the Hebrew Old Testament. He also had Tyndale's last revision of the New Testament. His Bible was therefore half the work of Tyndale.

The feeling of English churchmen about the Bible in English had by this time so far altered that Archbishop Cranmer now wrote to secure a license from the king for Rogers' Bible, and so it became the first licensed English Bible, and could be bought and sold, owned and read without danger of molestation by the authorities. The English Bible had won its victory over the State.

But the victory over the Church remained to be won, and two years later the Bible won that victory too. Cranmer and the bishops at last agreed that there must be an English Bible for use in public worship, and they invited Coverdale to revise the John Rogers Bible. So arose the first authorized English Bible, the famous Great Bible—authorized by the church for use in public worship.

The Great Bible was called Great because it was a huge book, intended to lie on a church lectern or pulpit; it was what we call a "pulpit Bible." Now for the first time Englishmen began to hear the Bible read in church not in

Latin but in English, the language they could all understand. The Great Bible was warmly welcomed. In every parish church a copy of it was set out, to be read by anyone who wished to do so. It was secured by a chain so that it could not be stolen, and so became the famous Chained Bible of English church history. But it was chained not to prevent its being read but to facilitate it. Many grown people learned to read, it is said, in order to read the English Bible, which now for the first time was made really accessible to them.

The *Book of Common Prayer,* which appeared in 1549, contained the Psalms in English, for reading and chanting in church. This Psalter was taken from the Authorized Bible, the Great Bible of 1539. To this day the Psalter in the Prayer Book is the Psalter of the Great Bible, as first translated and then revised by Myles Coverdale.

The other event of those years was the invention of the verses. These four early Bibles had no verse numbers or divisions. It remained for Robert Etienne, the French printer, to devise the verse numbering of the New Testament, which he introduced into his 1551 edition of the Greek Testament. He was making a concordance of the Greek Testament and needed a more convenient unit of reference than the old chapters. Unfortunately, Etienne made every verse a paragraph, and this led people to think each verse had the completeness of a proverb, which was very far from true.

His ingenious system was speedily adopted by the Puritan refugees in Geneva, who were busying themselves with the revision of the Bible. The Geneva Bible (1560) was a book of moderate size—obviously not a pulpit but a fireside Bible. It was printed not in the old black-letter, but in the elegant new Roman type, which was just coming into fashion—the type that is in universal use today.

The Geneva Bible, generally known as the Breeches Bible, because it reads in Genesis 3:7, "And they sewed figtre leaves together, and made themselves breeches," had a great history. It passed through more than a hundred editions; it was the Bible of Shakespeare, of Cromwell and his Ironsides, of the Pilgrim Fathers and the Mayflower Compact. It was also an important contribution to a better English Bible, for its makers knew Hebrew and Greek, and were able to make much needed improvement in translation.

It was soon followed by a revision of the Great Bible. Englishmen heard that Bible read in church, but at home they read the smaller Geneva Bible, with its convenient little verses. So Archbishop Parker organized a revision of the then Authorized Bible (the Great Bible), and in 1568 appeared the second Authorized English Bible, called the Bishops', because so many bishops worked on the revision.

English Catholics had no English Bible as yet, but in their English College then at Rheims, in France, Gregory Martin set about the translation of the Latin Bible into English. He proceeded, it is said, at the rate of two chapters a day, and completed the whole Bible within four years. His New Testament came out in 1582, the Old Testament (including the Apocrypha) waiting until 1610. By that time the College had removed to Douai, so that the whole translation came to be called the Douai Bible.

The climax of all this great period of Bible translation and revision was reached when in 1604 King James summoned a conference of high and low churchmen to consider "things pretended to be amiss in the church." John Reynolds, the leader of the Puritans, moved that they retranslate the Bible. King James took up the suggestion and named the committees to which the work was referred. So arose in 1611 the King James Version, a very cautious revision of the Bishops' Bible of 1568. It was the third authorized English Bible.

English had made great advances as a literary language since Tyndale published his New Testament in 1525; Shakespeare and the Elizabethans had done their work; and this progress is reflected in the King James Version. It is a standard piece of English literature and a treasure of Christian liturgy and it brought the heroic period in the history of the English Bible to a noble conclusion.*

✠

MAN WITH A TWA-HANDED SWORD
Paul Hutchinson

THE man's name was Knox—plain John Knox. Everything about him was as plain as his name. His robe was the plain black gown which had been adopted by the reforming preachers of Geneva. His presence was the plain but self-respecting dignity of the bra' Scot who trembles before neither man nor devil. His speech was plain. And almost from the hour of his first speaking, all Scotland had listened to John Knox.

Some day, let us hope, a movie magnate, seeking for a scenario more thrilling than any concocted by fiction writers, will see the possibilities in the career of Knox. List the requirements of the successful films—adventure, suspense, struggle, humor, tragedy, the sex element, and final victory snatched out of the jaws of defeat—and you can find every one present in heaping measure in the life of Scotland's great reformer.

We would see, first of all, the gaunt, gawky, coarsely clad young lowlander coming to the gates of one of the proud Scottish universities seeking the education which is already the highest desire of Scotland's youth. But he does not stay there long. Perhaps his poverty makes it impossible. He leaves the university to enter the priesthood of the ancient church. It is a troubled time. A Luther, a Zwingli, a Calvin have set afoot movements which men already speak of as a reformation. The young priest meets an older priest, Wishart. This man has studied the new teaching in Germany and in Switzerland. He has come back to Scotland, intent that the new truths shall be given to his own countrymen. The young priest hears, believes, follows.

* Abridged from *How Came the Bible?* by Edgar J. Goodspeed, pp. 97-107. Copyright 1940 by Edgar J. Goodspeed. Published by Abingdon Press. Used by permission of the publisher.

Then, swiftly, the picture builds toward catastrophe. The churches close their doors to the reforming preachers. Barred from the pulpits, Wishart takes to the fields. Knox stands at his side. A band of hardy, resolute men surround him. But the great Cardinal Beaton shows his power. Wishart is captured, convicted of heresy, burned at the stake. Three months later, the cardinal is assassinated.

French troops are quickly supplied to hunt down the reformers who have defied the throne and killed the cardinal. These bold men, knowing that their lives are at stake, fling themselves into the castle of St. Andrews.

The castle falls. Most of the defenders are slain; the rest are taken into captivity. And now for nineteen months John Knox is a galley slave chained to his oar as the lash of his French captors falls upon his shoulders.

Suddenly, freedom. England has a Protestant king, the young Edward VI, who asks for the release of many of the Protestant prisoners in French hands. Almost overnight, the young Scot who has been in chains finds himself a chaplain to the king, the intimate of Cranmer, Latimer, Ridley, and the other leaders of the English Reformation. He even has a large part in the writing of a new English prayer book.

Five years, and again, without warning, Knox is fleeing for his life. The young king dies. He is succeeded by his half-sister, Mary, a fierce Catholic, whose proscriptions and persecutions have gained for her the sobriquet of "Bloody Mary." But Knox finds refuge in Switzerland and Germany.

It is at Geneva that the reformer meets Calvin and comes under his sway. There he obtains the theological opinions which he is to hold tenaciously for the rest of his life; there, more important, he obtains the ideas of a proper form of Church and State government with which he is to remake Scotland. From this time, the Reformation in Scotland is largely the mind of John Calvin working itself out through the relentless energy of John Knox.

Three years Knox stays with Calvin in Geneva; probably the happiest years of his life. Then word comes to him that the political situation in Scotland has completely changed. Knox feels that the moment for action has arrived. Bidding farewell to Geneva, he returns to his homeland for the crowning years of his life.

In less than a year a Scottish Parliament met; the old Church was disestablished; in its place there was put a Reformed Church, patterned on the model Knox had brought back with him from Geneva. This new Church acknowledged no papal authority, and no bishops. It was ruled by its own elders, or presbyters, as the older Greek word had it. And because it was the Church ruled by presbyters, it soon came to be known as the Presbyterian kirk.

Then Knox had to face the great antagonist of his life—Mary Stuart, Queen of Scotland and claimant to the throne of England, reputed to be the most beautiful woman of her time and certainly one of the most gifted. Mary gave every indication of being willing to let Knox alone, but Knox had no intention of leaving her alone. He did not trust her for an instant, and he took great pains to tell her so.

There she was, young, beautiful, brilliant, and obviously using every femi-
nine art to dazzle and overwhelm the reformer. And there he was, grizzled,
rough-maned, uncouth, pitting his prophetic zeal against his queen's personal
charm. His first remark when meeting the sovereign was that he regarded
living under her reign as Paul must have regarded living under that of Nero!

Unable to win over Knox to her side, Mary concentrated her arts on the
Protestant nobility, and with considerable success. Although she retained her
own private practice of Catholic rites—to the accompaniment of Knox's
constant denunciation from the pulpit of St. Giles—the queen persuaded
many of the most powerful nobles that she had no intention of interfering
with the newly established reformed religion of the realm. Knox was forced
to give up preaching in Edinburgh, and retire into comparative privacy.

Then, by a series of incredible blunders, Mary threw away all the advantage
she had gained. Her marriage with Darnley was followed by sordid intrigue,
first with her Italian secretary and later with the libertine Earl of Bothwell.
Darnley was murdered under circumstances which pointed toward Bothwell
and Mary. When the two were married soon thereafter, Knox came forth
preaching a new crusade. The nobles forced the queen to abdicate, placing her
infant son upon the throne.

Knox held an almost undisputed grip on Scotland from the day when Mary
fled the country until the day, five years later, when he died. To the very end,
the fire burned within him. Sick, burdened with many cares, he yet managed
to ascend the pulpit. It required a servant to hold him up to begin to preach.
But the famous record tells us that "ere he was done with his sermon, he was
so active and vigorous that he was lyke to ding the pulpit in blads and flie
out of it." Preaching, with John Knox, was always a case of dinging the pulpit
in blads.

Knox was not noted for his affability. When he warmed up, it was for the
purpose of putting somebody to sizzling over the fire of his wrath. It struck
him that there were too many women rulers doing everything they could to
restore the authority of the Pope. So Knox wrote a pamphlet to which he gave
the title, "First Blast of the Trumpet against the Monstrous Regiment of
Women."

He was hopelessly one-sided. He believed that he was on the side of God.
So it followed that any who opposed him were on the side of the devil. He
made it a practice, he tells us, to bear before him a "twa-handed sword."

If there grew up, not only in Presbyterianism but in Protestantism generally,
a conception of the saint as a man who never lost sight of the seriousness of
life, and of the ministry as the most funereal of callings, John Knox contributed much to that idea. A smile was almost equivalent to confession of sin.
Knox always thundered; he never smiled. One cannot resist the feeling that it
was more because of her love of laughter than of her love of the Pope that
Knox fought Mary so relentlessly.

Yet the man compels admiration. There was granite in him. In a time
when too many allowed their opinions to be made by the prince who happened

to be reigning, it was truly said of him that he "never feared nor flattered any flesh."

When he became the disciple of Calvin at Geneva, Knox found under way there the first actual attempt ever made to govern a city fully in accord with the will of God. The question grew within his mind, "If a city can be governed for God, why not a kingdom? If Geneva, why not Scotland?"

From one of the rudest states in Europe, he set Scotland on the road to becoming one of the most cultured kingdoms known to history. In the place of a Church that had sunk into a dead formalism, he raised up a Church that has given stamina to a whole people, while it has proved the prolific source of new spiritual life on every continent.

John Knox is entitled to honor, not only as the father of a great branch of Protestantism, but as the father of all those who will not be content until the rule of God embraces all the affairs of men.*

✢

PILGRIM'S JOURNEY
John Bunyan

As I walked through the wilderness of this world, I lighted on a certain place where was a den, and laid me down in that place to sleep; and, as I slept, I dreamed a dream. I dreamed, and, behold, I saw a man clothed with rags, standing in a certain place, with his face from his own house, a book in his hand, and a great burden upon his back. I looked, and saw him open the book, and read therein; and, as he read, he wept and trembled; and not being able longer to contain, he broke out with a lamentable cry, saying, "What shall I do?"

I looked then, and saw a man named Evangelist coming to him, and asked, Wherefore dost thou cry? He answered, Sir, I perceive by the book in my hand that I am condemned to die, and after that to come to judgment; and I find that I am not willing to do the first, nor able to do the second.

Then said Evangelist, Why not willing to die, since this life is attended with so many evils? The man answered, Because I fear that this burden that is upon my back will sink me lower than the grave, and I shall fall into Tophet. And, sir, if I be not fit to go to prison, I am not fit, I am sure, to go to judgment, and from thence to execution; and the thoughts of these things make me cry.

Then said Evangelist, If this be thy condition, why standest thou still? He answered, Because I know not whither to go. Then he gave him a parchment roll, and there was written within, "Fly from the wrath to come."

The man therefore read it, and looking upon Evangelist very carefully,

* Abridged from *Men Who Made The Churches* by Paul Hutchinson, pp. 59-77. Copyright 1930 by Lamar & Whitmore. Used by permission of Abingdon Press.

said, Whither must I fly? Then said Evangelist, pointing with his finger over a very wide field, Do you see yonder Wicket-gate? The man said, No. Then said the other, Do you see yonder shining light? He said, I think I do. Then said Evangelist, Keep that light in your eye, and go up directly thereto; so shalt thou see the gate; at which, when thou knockest, it shall be told thee what thou shalt do.

So I saw in my dream that the man began to run. Now he had not run far from his own door, but his wife and children, perceiving it, began to cry after him to return; but the man put his fingers in his ears, and ran on, crying, Life! Life! eternal life! So he looked not behind him, but fled towards the middle of the plain.

The neighbors also came out to see him run; and as he ran, some mocked, others threatened, and some cried after him to return; and among those that did so, there were two that resolved to fetch him back by force. The name of the one was Obstinate, and the name of the other Pliable. Now, by this time, the man was got a good distance from them; but, however, they were resolved to pursue him, which they did, and in little time they overtook him. Then said the man, Neighbors, wherefore are you come? They said, To persuade you to go back with us. But he said, That can by no means be.

Now as Christian (for that was the man's name) was walking solitarily by himself, he espied one afar off come crossing over the field to meet him; and their hap was to meet just as they were crossing the way of each other. The gentleman's name that met him was Mr. Worldly-Wiseman; he dwelt in the town of Carnal-Policy, a very great town, and also hard by from whence Christian came. This man then meeting with Christian, and having some guess of him, by beholding his laborious going, by observing his sighs and groans, and the like, began thus to enter into some talk with Christian.

WORLDLY–WISEMAN. How now, good fellow, whither away after this burdened manner?

CHRISTIAN. A burdened manner indeed, as ever I think poor creature had. And whereas you ask me, Whither away? I tell you, sir, I am going to yonder Wicket-gate before me; for there, as I am informed, I shall be put into a way to be rid of my heavy burden.

WORLDLY–WISEMAN. Why, in yonder village (the village is named Morality) there dwells a gentleman, whose name is Legality, a very judicious man, and a man of a very good name, that has skill to help men off with such burdens as thine are, from their shoulders; yea, to my knowledge he hath done a great deal of good this way; aye, and besides, he hath skill to cure those that are somewhat crazed in their wits with their burdens. To him, as I said, thou mayest go, and be helped presently. His house is not quite a mile from this place.

Now was Christian somewhat at a stand, but presently he concluded: If this be true which this gentleman hath said, my wisest course is to take his advice. So Christian turned out of his way to go to Mr. Legality's house for help; but behold, when he was got now hard by the hill it seemed so high, and also that side of it that was next the wayside did hang so much over, that Christian was afraid to venture further, lest the hill should fall on his head; wherefore there he stood still, and he wot not what to do. Also his burden, now, seemed heavier to him than while he was in his way. There came also flashes of fire out of the hill, that made Christian afraid that he should be burned. Here therefore he sweat, and did quake for fear. And now he began to be sorry that he had taken Mr. Worldly-Wiseman's counsel. And with that he saw Evangelist coming to meet him; at the sight also of whom he began to blush for shame. So Evangelist drew nearer and nearer; and coming up to him, he looked upon him with a severe and dreadful countenance, and thus began to reason with Christian.

EVANGELIST. What doest thou here, Christian? said he; at which words Christian knew not what to answer; wherefore at present he stood speechless before him. Then said Evangelist further, Art not thou the man I found crying without the walls of the City of Destruction?

CHRISTIAN. Yes, dear sir, I am the man.

EVANGELIST. Did not I direct thee the way to the little Wicket-gate?

CHRISTIAN. Yes, dear sir, said Christian.

EVANGELIST. How is it then that thou art so quickly turned aside? for thou art now out of the way.

CHRISTIAN. I met with a gentleman so soon as I had got over the Slough of Despond, who persuaded me that I might, in the village before me, find a man that could take off my burden.

Then Evangelist proceeded, saying, Give more earnest heed to the things that I shall tell thee of. I will now show thee who it was that deluded thee, and who it was also to whom he sent thee. The man that met thee is one Worldly-Wiseman, and rightly is he so called; partly, because he favoreth only the doctrine of this world (therefore he always goes to the town of Morality to church); and partly, because he loveth that doctrine best, for it saveth him from the Cross. And because he is of this carnal temper, therefore he seeketh to pervert my ways, though right.

Then said Evangelist to him, Thy sin is very great, for by it thou hast committed two evils; thou hast forsaken the way that is good, to tread in forbidden paths; yet will the man at the gate receive thee, for he has good will for men; only, said he, take heed that thou turn not aside again, "lest thou perish from the way, when his wrath is kindled but a little." Then did Christian address himself to go back; and Evangelist, after he had kissed him, gave him one smile, and bid him God-speed. So he went on with haste.

Now I saw in my dream that the highway up which Christian was to go, was fenced on either side with a wall, and that wall is called Salvation. Up this way therefore did burdened Christian run, but not without great difficulty, because of the load on his back.

He ran thus till he came at a place somewhat ascending, and upon that place stood a Cross, and a little below in the bottom, a Sepulcher. So I saw in my dream, that just as Christian came up with the Cross his burden loosed from his shoulders, and fell from off his back; and began to tumble, and so continued to do, till it came to the mouth of the Sepulcher, where it fell in, and I saw it no more.

Then was Christian glad and lightsome, and said with a merry heart, He hath given me rest by his sorrow, and life by his death. Then he stood a while to look and wonder; for it was very surprising to him, that the sight of the Cross should thus ease him of his burden. Now as he stood looking and weeping, behold three Shining Ones came to him and saluted him with "Peace be to thee." So the first said to him, "Thy sins be forgiven"; the second stripped him of his rags, and clothed him with change of raiment; the third also set a mark in his forehead, and gave him a roll with a seal upon it, which he bid him look on as he ran, and that he should give it in at the Celestial Gate. So they went their way. Then Christian gave three leaps for joy, and went on singing.*

✝

WE PRAISE THEE, O GOD; WE ACKNOWLEDGE THEE
(*TE DEUM LAUDAMUS*)

THE mood of the Reformation in England was less radical than that in Germany and Switzerland; the Church of England managed to break its connection with Rome without severing the ties of tradition which bound it to the long Christian past. The canticle before us, "We Praise Thee, O God," is a case in point. One of the most ancient of existing Christian hymns, it was published in English in the *Book of Common Prayer* (1549) and since 1552 has been chanted daily in Anglican (Episcopal) worship. Its various qualities —its antiquity, its continued use through the centuries, its sense of identification with the people of God in earlier generations ("Apostles," "Prophets," "Martyrs"), and its place in the service of the prayer book—combine to make it an especially fitting representative of the Anglican spirit.

The *Book of Common Prayer* was issued to give the English churches a standard for public worship which would continue the rich spiritual tradition of the Christian centuries and would at the same time deliver popular devotion from various corruptions which the Reformers considered contrary to the gospel. The basic structure of its services for morning and evening prayer continues patterns of worship from ancient and medieval times, and it contains English translations of hymns and prayers from the piety of many generations. Not only is this material rich in content, but it is phrased in language of rare beauty. Thomas Cranmer, Archbishop of Canterbury, who directed the work of compilation, was one of the great masters of English prose. His work is a literary classic and a spiritual treasury. It is closely followed to the present day

---

* Abridged from *The Pilgrim's Progress* by John Bunyan.

in the worship of the Episcopal Church, and is used to a remarkable degree in the prayer and praise of a large part of British and American Protestantism.

Whereas the Continental and Scottish Reformers emphasized the congregational hymn and metrical psalm in worship, the *Book of Common Prayer* brought over into English a number of canticles which the church had chanted for generations. These are still commonly known by their Latin names, though they are sung in English: *Benedictus es, Benedicite,* and *Te Deum Laudamus.* The canticle is less rigid in form than the modern hymn, which has both rhyme and meter (a regular pattern of accented syllables). The rhythm of the canticle is like that of the Psalms and other poetic passages in our Bible, a rhythm of ideas or similar phrases:

> To Thee all Angels cry aloud;
>   the Heavens,
>   and all the Powers therein;
> To Thee Cherubim and Seraphim continually do cry.

Such a composition cannot be sung to a rigid musical pattern like our metrical hymn tunes. Instead it is chanted to a melodic scheme which can be freely adapted to the varying length of the lines, yet which by the repetition of the simple musical pattern gives a sense of wholeness. To those who are accustomed only to the hymn, chanting may seem a bit awkward at first, but it is the manner in which the vast majority of believers have sung their praises to God through most of the Christian centuries.

Many composers have provided musical arrangement for the *Te Deum,* including Sir John Stainer and Samuel Wesley. The basic setting used here was written by Henry Lawes (1596-1662), a gentleman of the Chapel Royal of King Charles I. He composed music for Robert Herrick's *Hesperides* and John Milton's *Comus,* and Milton expressed his satisfaction by celebrating Lawes as that

> Harry, whose tuneful and well-measured song
> First taught our English music how to span
> Words with just note and accent.

Lawes also wrote an anthem, "Zadok the Priest," for the coronation of King Charles II in 1660. The variation for the second part of the canticle was written more than a century later by Robert Cooke (1768-1814), organist at the famous London church of St. Martin's-in-the-Fields and later organist and master of the choirboys at Westminster Abbey.

Nicetas of Remesiana is believed to have composed the *Te Deum* in Latin in the fourth century. The present arrangement emphasizes its three stanzas. Stanza one (verses 1-13) is a prayer of praise to the Trinity: the whole earth, the hosts of heaven, the saints of preceding generations, and "the holy Church throughout all the world" unite in homage before Father, Son, and Holy Spirit. Stanza two (verses 14-21) is a prayer addressed particularly to Christ and is a confession of faith in Him which follows the basic outline of the

We Praise Thee, O God; We Acknowledge Thee
(Te Deum Laudamus)

H. Lawes (1596—1662).

1 We *praise* | Thee O | God ‖ we ac*know*ledge | Thee to | be the | Lord.
2 All the *earth* doth | wor-ship | Thee ‖ *the* | Fa-ther | ev-er- | lasting.
3 To Thee all *Angels* | cry a- | loud ‖ the *Heavens* and | all the | Powers there- | in
4 To Thee *Cherubim* and | Ser-a- | phim ‖ *con-* | tin-ual- | ly do | cry,
5 *Holy* | Ho-ly | Ho-ly ‖ *Lord* | God of | Sab-a- | oth;
6 Heaven and earth are *full* of the | Maj-es- | ty ‖ *of* | Thy — | Glo- — | ry.
7 The glorious *company* | of ˙ the A- | postles ‖ *praise* | — — | — — | Thee.
8 The goodly *fellow*ship | of the ˈ Prophets ‖ *praise* | — — | — — | Thee.
9 The *noble* | army ˙ of | Martyrs ‖ *praise* | — — | — — | Thee.
10 The holy *Church* throughout | all the | world ‖ *doth* | — ac- | knowl-edge | Thee:
11 *The* | Fa- — | ther | *of* an in- ˙ finite | Maj-es- | ty;
12 *Thine* a- | dor- ˙ able, | true ‖ *and* | on- — | — ly | Son;
13 ✻ *Also the* | Holy | Ghost ‖ *the* | com- — | fort- — | er.
14 *Thou* art the | King of | Glory ‖ *O* | — — | — — | Christ.
15 Thou art the *ever-* | last-ing | Son ‖ *of* | — the | Fa- — | ther.

✻ Last half of Chant.

R. Cooke (1768—1814).

16 When Thou tookest upon *Thee* to de- | liv-er | man ‖ Thou didst humble Thy*self* to be | born — |
of a | Virgin.
17 When Thou hadst over*come* the | sharpness ˙ of | death ‖ Thou didst open the *King*dom of |
Heaven ˙ to | all be- | lievers.
18 Thou sittest at the *right* | hand of | God ‖ *in* | the | Glo-ry | of the | Father.
19 We be*lieve* that | Thou shalt | come ‖ *to* | be — | our — | Judge.
20 We therefore *pray* Thee | help Thy | servants ‖ whom Thou hast re*deem*ed | with Thy | pre-cious |
blood.
21 Make them to be *numbered* | with Thy | Saints ‖ *in* | glo-ry | ev-er- | lasting.
22 O *Lord* | save Thy | people ‖ *and* | bless Thine | her-it- | age.
23 *Gov-* | — ern | them ‖ *and* | lift them | up for- | ever.

Return to chant in B♮ at the top of page

24 *Day* | by — day ‖ *we* | mag-ni- | fy — | Thee;
25 *And* we | worship ˙ Thy | Name ‖ *ever* | world with- | out — | end.
26 *Vouch-* | safe O | Lord ‖ *to* keep *us* this | day with- | out — | sin.
27 O *Lord* ˙ have | mercy ˙ up- | on us ‖ *have* | mercy ˙ up- | on — | us.
28 O Lord, let Thy *mercy* | be up- | on us ‖ *as* our trust — | is in | Thee
29 O Lord, in *Thee* | have I | trusted ‖ *let* me | nev-er | be con- | founded.

gospel as suggested in the great creeds. Stanza three (verses 22-29), while still maintaining the note of praise, asks the help of God in our various spiritual needs; it includes a number of familiar phrases from the Psalms.

The *Te Deum* is not only one of the oldest but also one of the most majestic of Christian hymns. It has been sung on many a great occasion of solemn rejoicing throughout Christian history. Its words are unsurpassed for the joyful and reverent praise of the Eternal God.

✠

I TO THE HILLS WILL LIFT MINE EYES (Psalm 121)

AMONG all the nations which embraced the Reformation, none took the Psalter more to its own heart or made a larger place for the singing of the Psalms than did Scotland.

Luther wrote "A Mighty Fortress Is Our God" as a metrical version of Psalm 46, and in Switzerland Marot and Beza compiled the Geneva Psalter. English Protestants who came to the city of Calvin and then returned home brought the practice of Psalm-singing with them, and it was reported that crowds numbering as high as six thousand gathered outside St. Paul's Cathedral in London to praise God with the Psalms. Devout Protestants sought to popularize these in preference to the love songs and bawdy tunes often heard in those days, but Queen Elizabeth dismissed them contemptuously as "Geneva jiggs." As early as 1549 an Englishman named Thomas Sternhold published a collection of nineteen metrical Psalms. The first book to be printed in New England was the *Bay Psalm Book,* issued for Puritan worship in 1640.

The General Assembly of the Church of Scotland first authorized a metrical Psalter in 1564, and new editions were approved from time to time. Finally in 1650 the standard edition appeared, which replaced the earlier versions and has stood for more than three hundred years. Some of the Psalms were taken from various renditions published in England, some were adapted from the Geneva Psalter, some were borrowed from the *Bay Psalm Book,* some were revised from earlier Scottish editions, and many were prepared especially for this edition by the committee appointed for the task. For only a few of the one hundred and fifty Psalms have we the name of an individual poet.

The Psalter became the voice of congregational praise in the Kirk of Scotland. Until 1780 no other hymns were permitted, and it would be a strange Sunday in a Scottish church yet today if none of the Psalms were sung. The "Psalms of David in Metre" were bound in the back of Scottish Bibles as a matter of course; so the churchgoer had his Scripture and his hymnal all in one book.

The Scottish Psalms are simple, sturdy, rugged, devout, utterly sincere, and wholly without adornment. They were sung to common tunes of the

I to the Hills Will Lift Mine Eyes**

DUNDEE.* (C.M.)   PSALM 121.   *Scottish Psalter,* 1615.

Unison or Parts

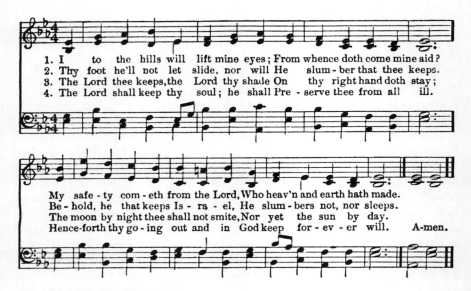

1. I   to   the hills will   lift mine eyes; From whence doth come mine aid?
2. Thy foot he'll not let   slide, nor will He   slum-ber that thee keeps.
3. The Lord thee keeps,the Lord thy shade On   thy right hand doth stay;
4. The Lord shall keep thy soul; he shall Pre - serve thee from all   ill.

My safe-ty com-eth from the Lord,Who heav'n and earth hath made.
Be-hold, he that keeps Is - ra - el, He slum-bers not, nor sleeps.
The moon by night thee shall not smite,Nor yet the sun by day.
Hence-forth thy go-ing out and in God keep for - ev - er will.   A-men.

* Known as *French* in Scotland.

**From *The Three Hundredth Anniversary of the Scottish Psalter, 1650-1950.* Published 1950 by The Hymn
Society of America.

same character; words and music were readily memorized by the people and
became a part of their national heritage. The typical qualities of the Scottish
Psalter are evident in "I to the Hills Will Lift Mine Eyes." Observe its simplicity; in the third stanza there is not a word of more than one syllable.
It is a song of trust in God, but is in no sense sentimental; compare it, for
example, with "Leaning on the Everlasting Arms" or "Close to Thee." It is
faithful to the original text; a careful matching with the English Bible will
show that the thought of each verse is faithfully presented with only an
occasional change in the order of phrases; yet for this Psalm the King James
Version uses one hundred ten words of prose, the Scottish Psalter only one
hundred, and this in spite of the demands of fitting the thought into a rhyme
scheme! The tune "Dundee" (also known as "French") is used for various
Psalms, and is the tune most commonly sung in the Scottish churches.

Because the original Psalter in the Old Testament gave expression to such a rich variety of experiences, public and private, the Scots can find an appropriate Psalm to sing on almost any occasion in the life of Church or State, almost any event in personal experience, whether joy or sorrow.

It is a far cry from the hills of Judea to the braes of Caledonia, from the desert heat and the stinging sands of Palestine to the mists and the moors of Scotland. But both lands have their devout believers. And in both lands, men of faith have sung with gladness of the faithfulness of their God.

CONTENTS

PART IV SECTION 4

THE REFORMATION CONTINUES

Wherefore seeing we also are compassed about with so great a cloud of witnesses, let us lay aside every weight, and the sin which doth so easily beset us, and let us run with patience the race that is set before us, looking unto Jesus the author and finisher of our faith.—HEBREWS 12:1-2

PICTURES: PAGE

Interpretation: Old Woman at Prayer—*Maes* 491

Picture: Old Woman at Prayer—*Maes* 493

Interpretation: John Wesley—*Salisbury* 492

Picture: John Wesley—*Salisbury* 495

Interpretation: Pestalozzi and the Children—*Lanz* 496

Picture: Pestalozzi and the Children—*Lanz* 499

POETRY:

A Prayer for the Church—*Löwenstern* 500

Give to the Winds Thy Fears—*Gerhardt* 500

Jesus, Priceless Treasure—*Franck* 501

The Heavens Declare Thy Glory, Lord—*Watts* 502

Glory to God, Whose Witness Train—*Zinzendorf* 502

The Church of Christ—*Spangenberg* 503

Robert Raikes—*Tappan* 503

STORIES:

Handel's Messiah—*Flower* 504

Robert Raikes and His Ragged Schools—*Harris* 507

Prisons—and the Golden Rule—*Marchant* 509

MUSIC:

Interpretation: O Sacred Head, Now Wounded—*Author Unknown* 512

Music: O Sacred Head, Now Wounded—*Hassler;* harmonization by
J. S. Bach 513

Interpretation: Ye Servants of God, Your Master Proclaim—*C. Wesley* ... 514

Music: Ye Servants of God, Your Master Proclaim—*J. M. Haydn* 515

OLD WOMAN AT PRAYER

Nicolas Maes

THE influence of Rembrandt upon the artist is immediately sensed as one looks at this picture (p. 493). Christian teachings translated into light patterns and colors are here. In jewel-like tones everything—the loaf of bread as well as the woman's face—glows as if from a light within. Out of each shadow light seems to emerge. Each object in the picture is painted with an attention to detail that surrounds with love and meaning the common articles of everyday living. The uncommon light pervades every common thing. All of life has become holy.

Worker, worshiper, and priest are one. The woman in the picture is all three. Seated as she is before a table, her daily labor as well as her bread is spread before her. In front of her are the soup and fish she has prepared and the loaves of bread she has baked, for which she has perhaps ground the flour and even gathered the harvest. The hands folded in prayer are scarred and callused with hard labor.

The face bowed forward is not young. Thin, hollow-cheeked, lined, it is a face that unfolds a life of drudgery, labor, poverty, and deep devotion. Even the tugging of the tablecloth by the playful kitten does not distract her from her prayer of thanksgiving. How very rich the intentness of gratitude on her face, as she prays, makes her seem.

Although simply furnished, the room is clean and well ordered. Out of much experience has come the present arrangement, so carefully planned and done, so as to save steps. There is a place for everything. The peg on which the keys are hung is within easy reach. Accessible from the table are the lamp, a funnel (perhaps for straining the milk), an open book (the almanac?), the hourglass, and the Bible. Perhaps the woman's birth was registered in this Bible by one who could scarcely write. And perhaps this same Bible had been her own primer from which she learned to read.

While the sand trickles through the hourglass, arguments about the nature of the sacraments falls away. The evening meal has become, through the sincere devotion of an elderly woman at prayer, the sacrament. The common ventures of life have become, through the woman's relationship with God, the means of God's grace. In a little room, the history of the Church is unfolded; for God is present, sustaining a life for which He has provided. So it has been from the beginning, down through the ages, and so it will always be. Through the quality of everyday living and the prayers of the faithful are the power and majesty of the living God realized. How one feels toward God and life and how that feeling is expressed becomes the reality, not why.

The woman who at her table bows in quiet and genuine devotion would listen with rapt attention and reverent appreciation to the learned scholar of religion and interpreter of her beloved Bible. Would that they could also listen with as rapt attention and reverent wonder to the whispering of His spirit in the quiet devotion of her prayers and life.

As wise men knelt of old at a manger, let wise men here also bow in this simple room, and let this faithful member of Christians Anonymous be to them an expression of His presence.

To paraphrase the poet, "they also serve who sit and pray." What divine mysteries are unlocked and made manifest in human affairs by the act of prayer, no one can measure. What communications of the Living Word take place in the fulfillment of the daily tasks of living! What revelations of the Scripture occur through the faltering study of those who are led by their trust in God and faith that truth is contained in the Book! Again, no man can draw the boundaries, nor foretell the measure.

If the nature of this universe is spirit as we believe and confess, we can but be humble in our knowledge about the power that is released through prayer and the extent of its influence.

When all has been explored, analyzed, and expressed we have but found other ways growing out of our need and experience—to love, trust, and obey.

There is no argument for God like the serenity of the life committed to His presence. Our logic is as confounded by simple trust and goodness as it is by evil and suffering. Confronted by the face of one caught up in a prayer of trust and thanksgiving, we too hear the ancient admonition: "Be still and know that I am God."

Through prayer the realization becomes ours that we are not so much reformers, as reformed; not so much changemakers, as changed. We are transformed and renewed from within. God is not yet finished with creation. We are not yet finished.*

✛

JOHN WESLEY
Frank O. Salisbury

JOHN WESLEY, the founder of Methodism, did not possess the physique of a large man. He was only five feet six inches tall and probably never topped one hundred and twenty pounds. In his outdoor preaching, he was often beset by mobs wild enough to frighten the most ardent Christian. Yet his self-control was such that he never gave a sign of fear and soon had the violent mob under his influence. It is difficult to imagine what would have happened to him had he not exercised such superb self-mastery.

The spirit of the man shone from his steadfast eyes. His self-control was obvious in them, more than in any other feature of his face or part of his body. He knew that in order to tame wild animals one must look directly into the eyes of the beasts, and when he appeared before a mob he would gaze squarely into the eyes of his hecklers. This must have been a major reason for

* This interpretation was prepared especially for the present anthology by Harold Johnson.

OLD WOMAN AT PRAYER—*MAES*

his control of them; perhaps this characteristic exerted a sort of hypnotic power. In any case, it must have been quite confusing to the rowdies to have someone look at them with a Godlike compassion. Wesley had a message to give to those unruly rustics who needed something to fill their spiritual void.

The methodical habits of John Wesley are well known. The firm jaw, the determined lip, the strong nose, the high forehead reflect his strength of purpose and resoluteness of character. The celebrated modern portraitist, Frank O. Salisbury, has caught not only Wesley's features, but also his spirit. (See portrait on p. 495.) Here is a man whose whole bearing seems to say, "I must fulfill my destiny," a man who by his steadfast purpose and methodical means turned a considerable portion of the world upside down.

A natural question is, "How did he get that way?" Much of his determination and his methodical temperament can be attributed to his early training. His mother was a major force in his life, and Susanna Wesley was the personification of system. How else could she have accomplished all that she did? Great mothers produce great sons, and she was one of the world's great mothers. John's father also was a man of orderliness. Samuel Wesley brought devotion and careful procedure to his tasks as a clergyman.

John Wesley became an organizer of the first caliber. His skill in organizing and guiding persons in the Christian life was at the very heart of his success as a great Christian leader. "Scriptural holiness" was his objective, but he knew that unless efficient methods were used, the objective would remain no more than an ideal.

It is true that he could be dictatorial, as men in high and responsible positions have sometimes been. Wesley was determined to keep the authority over his preachers and his societies firmly in his grasp. We can see the firmness in practically every feature of this magnificent painting. Yet it is important for us to remember Wesley's viewpoint. He was not the head of an established church, nor could he think of himself in such a capacity. He headed a religious and reforming society. Such a task required tenacity of purpose on the part of the leader and discipline among the members. His society has grown into an efficient and well-organized branch of the church.

For all Wesley's gifts as an organizer, one flaw in his leadership showed itself near the end of his career. His own autocratic direction of the societies would be terminated by his death, and he knew it; yet he had no one prepared to take his place as their leader. He seemed to lack the quality of inspiring a strong man to serve as his lieutenant for any length of time; even his brother Charles was no exception. As a last resort a group of one hundred preachers was selected to take the place of John Wesley. Yet from their labors has risen the mighty Methodist Church, marked by Wesley's own righteous zeal.

In Wesley we also note the God-given qualities of compassion and simplicity. His God was a God of compassion; in the fateful prayer meeting at Aldersgate, Wesley's heart was "strangely warmed" by the realization of His grace. Thereafter this Methodist of Methodists often implored Him for the

JOHN WESLEY—*SALISBURY*

love that grows from such a realization. If the Aldersgate experience had never occurred, we should probably be viewing a man who evidenced only a steely, military firmness. Instead we see in John Wesley the attitude of the believer who says, "I determined not to know anything, save Jesus Christ and Him crucified."

One of the best examples of both his simplicity and compassion is found in a letter to William Wilberforce. At about the time of Wesley's death (1791), Wilberforce was fighting almost single-handedly in England the war against slavery. The preacher encouraged the great statesman:

Unless the divine Power had raised you up to be as Athanasius "contra mundum" [against the world], I do not see how you can go through your glorious enterprise, in opposing that execrable villainy, which is the scandal of religion, of England, and of human nature. Unless God has raised you up for this very thing, you will be worn out by the opposition of men and of devils; but if God be for you, who can be against you? Are all of them together stronger than God? O! Be not weary in well-doing. Go on in the name of God, and in the power of His might, till even American slavery, the vilest that ever saw the sun, shall vanish before it.

He did not present an essay on the evils of slavery. He did state succinctly and compassionately a need for the eradication of that horrendous evil.

Discipline, leadership, compassion, simplicity—these were the jewels that John Wesley possessed.*

✛

PESTALOZZI AND THE CHILDREN
Karl Alfred Lanz

ON THE southern end of Lake Neuchâtel in Switzerland, the market town of Yverdon gazes down on the calm waters and ponders the quiet of the vine-clad valley. To the west, the Jura Mountains stretch their varied beauty of forest and ravine, pasture and rock, while the distant Alps tower in the south and gather their snow-covered shoulders around Mont Blanc. Springing from a lake hidden beneath the high rocks, the River Orbe flows over a cliff and winds its way through the valley. The scene is one of loveliness and tranquility.

Yet it is not the inspiring beauty alone that calls our attention to Yverdon. Memories of a life which attracted the attention of all Europe are stirred by the statue in the city square (see p. 499), and the people of Yverdon speak with pride concerning their part in a movement that has led to many of the practices in our schools of today. Such was the fruitful harvest from the sowings of John Henry Pestalozzi.

Born in 1746, the grandson of a Swiss Reformed pastor, Pestalozzi was brought up by his widowed mother. As a young man he studied for the

---

* This interpretation was prepared especially for the present anthology by Donald C. Lacy.

ministry and then for law. Then seeing the urgent needs of the impoverished masses, he turned to teaching. He and his wife opened their home for a small school. They gathered together the poor children of their community for training in the basic rudiments as well as in weaving, farming, and similar vocational activities. Success brought more and more children and also greater expenses, until finally they were forced to abandon the venture. With the assistance of friends, however, he began again, with zeal and Christian idealism, to stretch out his hand to the children he loved—to the abandoned, the neglected, the poor, to all who sought to improve themselves.

Gradually Pestalozzi attained fame as an educator. After a fruitful life, he came in 1805 to Yverdon. In a thirteenth-century castle at the heart of town he opened a school that for twenty years drew the leaders of Europe to its doors and sent them away enlightened and challenged by ideas that would affect their schools and churches for years to come. With his assistants, he taught his pupils in new ways that departed from the traditional memorization, the reciting of words, and the strict discipline which the common schools required. Filled with reverence and love for his children, he sought to lead them in experiences that were in keeping with their stages of natural development. Each boy was seen as an individual person, with his own hopes and fears, loves, and needs. Each was guided in self-activity that would result in the harmonious growth of the whole child—his mind, his heart, his spirit, and his body.

Pestalozzi had long been sensitive to the lessons of nature and here, amidst the beauties of Yverdon, he aroused the spirit of observation in his pupils, stimulating their thought and expression. Walks on the sunny hills during the summer and the panoramic views of the wintry snow brought contemplation of nature and her laws. Language and composition made use of words from such meaningful experience rather than dealing with unrelated themes. Mathematics was taught according to the readiness of the pupil, and history was investigated with an understanding that went beyond mere dates and names.

Realizing the importance of a healthy body for a healthy mind, Pestalozzi insisted on regular exercise for every student, particularly in gymnastics. Specific duties were also required of each boy to help in developing good work habits and to enable him to earn at least part of his expenses. To these activities were added the thrill of games and the joy of singing that bound both students and teachers together in wholesome unity.

Throughout all of these activities, Pestalozzi breathed continually his unaffected love in a way that inspired each boy and each teacher to offer his best. Religious training permeated the entire life of the school; not the formal dogmas which most churches emphasized, but a Christianity of faith and love that prepared the children for a life of godliness. Words went often unspoken, but the witness he gave in love, understanding, gratitude, and humility was a constant sermon on his Christian faith.

At Yverdon, Pestalozzi achieved his greatest success. He brought in boys from all parts of Europe, regardless of their ability to pay board or tuition.

Poverty was not new to this slender man; like St. Francis, he had wedded him-self to the poor, lived amongst them, and learned their miseries. At Yverdon, he was able to demonstrate his concern and his theories for their betterment in a practical way. He found his greatest reward in seeing young men, once his boys, fill positions of trust, responsibility, and service.

So effective was he in lifting his pupils that educators from all Europe came to observe the school and to study under Pestalozzi. In most countries, only the children of the wealthy obtained a decent education while the masses were left in ignorance and poverty. The few common schools that existed practiced traditional methods and rigid discipline. Teachers were selected at random and regardless of training. Often, villages had to content themselves with only the very basic instruction by a widow or servant who would teach the children for an hour or two on Sunday.

At Yverdon, however, the visiting educators found a new concept and a new challenge: the right of every child, rich or poor, to an education that would enable him to help in making a better world. Returning to their own countries, they began schools using the Pestalozzian methods and they trained teachers to serve in them. Universal education became their cry and, echoing the sound of Reformation days, the dignity of every man became their creed. Luther, Calvin, Knox, and other Reformation leaders had realized the im-portance of every individual man to God and to the world and had struggled for freedom of thought. Under Pestalozzi's guidance, men now realized that these cries must sound beyond the walls of the church proper and must sum-mon the best from all that man is. His mind must be led in paths of under-standing that progresses as he matures; his body must be nourished in healthy growth that strengthens all of his resources; his heart must be filled with a love that reaches out to other men; his spirit must be nurtured with the faith in God that undergirds life and all its meaning; his hands must be guided in practical skills that bring satisfaction, helpfulness, and peace.

Is it any wonder, then, that the people of Yverdon look with pride at the statue of their great schoolmaster who walked in the steps of the Teacher of Galilee? Erected in the period 1887-1890, the work of the Swiss sculptor Karl Lanz, the statue rises from the very hub of the city in front of the same castle of Peter of Savoy that was once the Institution. Bending his head lovingly toward the children, the great man gently rests his hand on the boy's shoulder while the little girl clings trustingly to his coat. The trace of a tender smile is on his lips and his eyes are deep and direct. His hand is lifted as if in patient explanation, and we can hear him say, as he often did, "You, too, mean to be wise and good, don't you?"*

* This interpretation was prepared especially for the present anthology by Joe H. Bragg, Jr.

PESTALOZZI AND THE CHILDREN—*LANZ*

A PRAYER FOR THE CHURCH

Lord of our life, and God of our salvation,
Star of our night, and Hope of every nation,
Hear and receive thy Church's supplication,
Lord God Almighty.

See round thine ark the hungry billows curling;
See how thy foes their banners are unfurling;
Lord, while their darts envenomed they are hurling,
Thou canst preserve us.

Lord, thou canst help when earthly armor faileth,
Lord, thou canst save when deadly sin assaileth;
Christ, o'er thy Rock nor death nor hell prevaileth;
Grant us thy peace, Lord.

Peace in our hearts, our evil thoughts assuaging;
Peace in thy Church, where brothers are engaging;
Peace, when the world its busy war is waging:
Calm thy foes' raging.

Grant us thy help till backward they are driven,
Grant them thy truth, that they may be forgiven;
Grant peace on earth, and, after we have striven,
Peace in thy heaven.*
—*Matthäus Appeles von Löwenstern (1594-1648)*

GIVE TO THE WINDS THY FEARS

Give to the winds thy fears,
Hope and be undismayed;
God hears thy sighs and counts thy tears,
God shall lift up thy head;
Through waves, and clouds, and storms,
He gently clears thy way;
Wait thou His time, so shall the night
Soon end in joyous day.

He everywhere hath way,
And all things serve His might,
His every act pure blessing is,
His path unsullied light;
When He makes bare His arm,
What shall His work withstand?

* Translated by Philip Pusey (1799-1855). Von Löwenstern wrote during the tragic years of the Thirty Years' War, when the future of Protestantism was clouded with uncertainty.

When He His people's cause defends,
Who, who shall stay His hand?

Leave to His sovereign sway
To choose and to command,
With wonder filled thou then shalt own
How wise, how strong His hand;
Thou comprehend'st Him not,
Yet earth and heaven tell,
God sits as sovereign on the throne,
He ruleth all things well.

Thou seest our weakness, Lord,
Our hearts are known to Thee,
Oh lift Thou up the sinking hand;
Confirm the feeble knee;
Let us, in life and death,
Boldly Thy truth declare,
And publish with our latest breath
Thy love and guardian care.*

—*Paul Gerhardt (1607-1676)*

JESUS, PRICELESS TREASURE

Jesus, priceless treasure,
Source of purest pleasure,
    Truest Friend to me;
Long my heart hath panted
Till it well-nigh fainted,
    Thirsting after Thee.
Thine I am, O spotless Lamb,
I will suffer nought to hide Thee,
    Ask for nought beside Thee.

In Thine arm I rest me;
Foes who would molest me
    Cannot reach me here.
Though the earth be shaking,
Every heart be quaking,
    God dispels our fear;
Sin and hell in conflict fell
With their heaviest storms assail us:
Jesus will not fail us.

Hence, all thoughts of sadness!
For the Lord of gladness,
    Jesus, enters in:
Those who love the Father,
Though the storms may gather,
    Still have peace within;
Yea, whate'er we here must bear,
Still in Thee lieth purest pleasure,
Jesus, priceless treasure!**

—*Johann Franck*

* Translated by John Wesley, 1739 (altered). From the *Hymnal and Liturgies of the Moravian Church (Unitas Fratrum)*. Used by permission of the Provincial Elders Conference.
** From *Cantate Domino*. Translated by Catherine Winkworth (1829-1878).

THE HEAVENS DECLARE THY GLORY, LORD

The heavens declare Thy glory, Lord;
In every star Thy wisdom shines;
But when our eyes behold Thy Word,
We read Thy name in fairer lines.

The rolling sun, the changing light,
And night and day, Thy power confess;
But the blest volume Thou hast writ
Reveals Thy justice and Thy grace.

Sun, moon, and stars convey Thy praise,
Round the whole earth, and never stand;
So when Thy truth began its race,
It touched and glanced on every land.

Nor shall Thy spreading gospel rest
Till through the world Thy truth has run;
Till Christ has all the nations blest
That see the light, or feel the sun.

—Isaac Watts

GLORY TO GOD, WHOSE WITNESS TRAIN

Glory to God, Whose witness train,
   Those heroes bold in faith,
Could smile on poverty and pain,
   And triumph e'en in death.

Scorned and reviled as was their Head,
   When walking here below,
Thus in this evil world they led
   A life of pain and woe.

With the same faith our bosom blows,
   Wherein those warriors stood,
When in the cruel hands of those
   Who thirsted for their blood.

God Whom we serve, our God can save,
   Can damp the scorching flame,
Can build an ark, or smooth a wave,
   For such as fear His Name.

If but His arm support us still,
   If but His joy our strength,

We shall ascend the rugged hill,
And conquerors prove at length.*
—*Nicholaus L. von Zinzendorf*

THE CHURCH OF CHRIST

The Church of Christ, which He hath hallowed here
To be His house, is scattered far and near,
In North, and South, and East, and West abroad;
And yet in earth and heaven, thro' Christ, her Lord,
The Church is one.

One member knoweth not another here,
And yet their fellowship is true and near;
One is their Saviour, and their Father one;
One Spirit rules them, and among them none
Lives to himself.

They live to Him Who bought them with His blood,
Baptized them with His Spirit, pure and good;
And in true faith and ever-burning love,
Their hearts and hopes ascend, to seek above
The eternal good.

O Spirit of the Lord, all life is Thine;
Now fill Thy Church with life and power divine,
That many children may be born to Thee;
And spread Thy knowledge like the boundless sea,
To Christ's great praise.**
—*Augustus G. Spangenberg (1704-1792)*

ROBERT RAIKES

And who is he that's seeking,
With look and language mild,
To heal the heart that's breaking,
And glad the vagrant child?

He searches lane and alley,
The mean and dark abode,
From Satan's hosts to rally,
The conscripts due to God.

* Translated M., 1808. From the *Hymnal and Liturgies of the Moravian Church (Unitas Fratrum)*. Used by permission of the Provincial Elders Conference.
** Translated by Catherine Winkworth, 1858. A Prussian, Spangenberg became a Moravian in 1733. He taught at Halle and later ministered in England and North America, where he was made a bishop. *Ibid.*

With words of kindly greeting,
    Warm from an honest heart,
He's ignorance entreating,
    In knowledge to have a part.
With Charity unfailing,
    He patiently doth take
Rebuke and sinful railing
    For Christ the Shepherd's sake.

He wins from vicious mothers,
    The children of neglect;
The sisters and the brothers
    From households sadly wrecked
And these, the truth impressing,
    Beneath his gentle rule,
Have called on him a blessing,
    Who formed the Sunday school.

I'd rather my life's story
    Should have such episode,
Than all the gorgeous glory
    Napoleon's history showed.
For when no more war's banner,
    With shouting is unfurled,
Those children's sweet hosanna
    May shake the upper world.*

—*William B. Tappan*

✛

HANDEL'S MESSIAH

Newman Flower

WHEN the spring of 1741 came Handel was broken. London had buried him. He had only the remnants of a following. His health was beating him down. He never slept. He was shunned in the street. Friends left and he sealed his lips. The pains of an unhealthy body tore him, tortured him, but the beauty of all things never faltered in his notes.

Out of this welter of suffering came the glorious *Messiah*.

At this juncture Charles Jennens came boldly into Handel's orbit by sending him the selected words from the Scriptures which were to be the basis of *Messiah*. At the end of August, Handel sat down to the work of composition in the little front room of the house in Brook Street. He completed the first part in seven days, the second part in nine days, the third part in six days, filling in instrumentation in two days. The whole of *Messiah* from beginning to end was set upon paper in twenty-four days. Considering the immensity of

* From *Robert Raikes: His Sunday Schools and His Friends.*

the work, and the short time involved, it will remain perhaps forever, the greatest feat in the whole history of musical composition.

It was the achievement of a giant inspired—the work of one who, by some extraordinary mental feat, had drawn himself completely out of the world, so that he dwelt—or believed he dwelt—in the pastures of God. Handel was unconscious of the world during that time, unconscious of its press and call; his whole mind was in a trance. He did not leave the house; his manservant brought him food, and as often as not returned in an hour to the room to find the food untouched, and his master staring into vacancy. When he had completed Part II, with the "Hallelujah Chorus," his servant found him at the table, tears streaming from his eyes. "I did think I did see all Heaven before me, and the great God Himself!" he exclaimed. Of a certainty, Handel was swept by some influence not of the world during that month—an influence not merely visionary. Never in his life had he experienced the same emotional sense, and he never experienced it again. For twenty-four days he knew those uplands reached only by the higher qualities of the soul.

Music—and music that was on a scale of grandeur not often attained—was rushing from him like a flood.

He had no thought for production. The work as it was completed was put away. *Messiah* went into a drawer for seven weeks. Then an invitation came to him from the Lord-Lieutenant of Ireland to go to Dublin. Handel left London at the beginning of November. In Dublin he took a house in Abbey Street. William Neal, a music publisher, had built a new music hall in Fishamble Street, and he placed the building at the disposal of the master.

Handel opened his season with a performance of *L'Allegro* two days before Christmas. The piece which had failed in London, was acclaimed in Dublin. The moral effect of this success was soon evident in him; it proved that his work had failed in London not because of quality.

The old despairs departed. Never had he known such ecstasies at the organ. The whole spirit of the man was uprising as a root may yield new freshened life after the surge of winter. Not for many years had Handel loved his life so much.

It was not until March, 1742, that any announcement was made regarding *Messiah*. The first performance was billed for April 13.

Seven hundred people crowded into the music hall on that Tuesday when *Messiah* was first given to the world; hundreds more waited in the street. "Words are wanting to express the exquisite Delight it afforded to the admiring crowded Audience," wrote *Faulkner's Journal* next day. Dubourg, the violin maestro, who had for years resided in Dublin, was in charge of the band. The choirs of two cathedrals had been trained to the greatest perfection in the choruses. Mrs. Cibber put more than the art of the singer into her part in *Messiah*. She understood, perhaps no less than Handel, the meaning of every note he had written. So wonderful was her rendering of "He was despised," that Dr. Delany, who was present, exclaimed: "Woman! for this thy sins be forgiven thee!"

Handel returned to London unannounced. He did not appear in public; he gave no concerts. But London was in a mood to receive him. Pope had published a volume in which he extolled the greatness of Handel, and spoke of him as the man to save music from the serfdom of the Italian opera. He wrote of the wonder of his choruses, of his sense of sound which made him project new instruments into a chorus to gain effect.

Pope had, in fact, changed that weathercock thing—public opinion—into an appreciation of Handel such as he had never had in London before. He convinced London that in Handel it had a genius.

Handel then decided to produce *Messiah*. But difficulties with the Church broke out. The religious controversy kept many people away; they argued that any work about the Omnipotent should never be performed in a playhouse. For years the storm about performing a work of this nature in a playhouse rolled on. The clergy called the oratorio sacrilege and Handel a heretic. There was nothing about *Messiah* that appealed to the age. A few hailed it as a masterpiece in religious thought, but they were lone voices crying in the wilderness.

The king attended one performance, and was so moved by the fervor of the "Hallelujah Chorus" that he rose to his feet and remained standing till the last chords had dropped to silence. But no one really understood *Messiah*. No one wanted to understand it. The few who did understand it failed to convince the others. Miss Talbot wrote:

"I have been to hear the *Messiah*, nor can there be a nobler entertainment. I think it is impossible for the most trifling not to be the better for it. I was wishing all the Jews, Heathens and Infidels in the world (a pretty full house you'll say!) to be present. The Morocco Ambassador was there, and if his interpreter could do justice to the divine words (the music anyone that had a heart must feel) how must he be affected, when in the grand choruses the whole audience solemnly rose up in joint acknowledgment that He who for our sakes had been despised and rejected of men, was their Creator, Redeemer, King of Kings, Lord of Lords! To be sure the playhouse is an unfit place for such a performance, but I fear I shall be in Oxfordshire before it is heard at the Foundling Hospital."

One questions whether Handel ever had any thought of making money out of *Messiah*, and, since London did not seem to want it, he withdrew it. From time to time he revived it for a single performance. He associated it with all his later charity for the Foundling Hospital, and, during his lifetime, he raised eleven thousand pounds for the Hospital by its performance.

As a work, *Messiah* was his one creation that ever pleased him, and which he never heavily altered. *Messiah* remained to him the one beautiful thing that held in it all those vagrant thoughts he had ever had of religion and its influence.

After *Messiah* had been produced in London, he happened to call upon Lord Kinoul, who had heard the work and complimented Handel upon it. "My lord," replied Handel, "I should be sorry if I only entertained them; I wished to make them better."

Happy soul! He knew, as few creators do, that he had done something for humanity. He at least realized what he had given.*

✠

ROBERT RAIKES AND HIS RAGGED SCHOOLS
J. Henry Harris

ROBERT RAIKES was forty-four years of age when he began a new "experiment." He was already old in effort, having for nearly a quarter of a century studied life in the prisons and the streets, with the view of creating what he termed "a new race." He commenced with adults, and failed; and then he changed his method. Having failed with the adult he tried the child. He began to study child life at close quarters, and he very soon found that he was on the right track.

The condition of the children of the working classes in 1780 was a problem which required courage to face. Listen to what a poor woman said to Mr. Raikes about the state of things on Sundays:

"The street is filled with multitudes of these *wretches,* who, released on that day from employment, spend their time in noise and riot, playing at 'chuck,' and cursing and swearing in a manner so horrid as to convey to any serious mind an idea of hell rather than any other place."

This was no news to Mr. Raikes, because the same thing went on under the window of his office, and disturbed him when reading "proofs" and writing for his newspaper. His old prison experiences came to his aid. He knew the parents of these children, and the habits of their class, and he said both of parents and children that neither they nor their ancestors had ever entered the house of God for the purpose of worship! It was no good for him to appeal to such parents. George Whitefield had also tried his hand on the masses in Gloucester and failed. The Wesleys and Howel Harris, and such men, were stirring the souls of men everywhere, but here was a new field for Robert Raikes—begin with the child.

Vice is preventable. Begin with the child.

Nothing simpler since the days of the apostles ever crossed the mind of man.

Certainly to all outward seeming these children were wretched. They were in groups—bright-eyed and intelligent; full of fun and frolic and mischief; uncombed, unwashed, ragged, and disgusting. Of such was the new generation on which England must depend for her greatness and supremacy, for the throb of the steam-engine had been felt, and some men, like Adam Smith, had already seen that this child "waste" contained the vital reserve of national supremacy. This "waste," which society treated as though only fit for hanging, contained invention, art, science, poetry, language, enterprise—everything which marks the highest civilization. All it wanted was development.

* Abridged from *George Frederic Handel* by Newman Flower, pp. 284-302. Published in 1959 by Cassell and Company Ltd., Publishers. Used by permission of the publisher.

Robert Raikes had seen this "waste" for years, and looked on it with despair.

Whilst he was thinking over these things, the simple word "try" came into his mind. He had been during all his manhood, trying in the face of opposition and ridicule, and made but little progress. Some men would have given up, but not so Robert Raikes. To elevate the people! Here was a mission! Here was a chance for the close imitation of Christ!

At the right moment, while these ideas were taking shape, he met the right man to help him. The Reverend Thomas Stock, Vicar of St. John the Baptist, and Headmaster of the Cathedral School, "chanced" to be walking in the same street. They talked the matter over. They agreed to do something, and they did it. They found some poor, but respectable, women who would teach children on Sundays, and then they visited some parents in the city slums, and induced them to send their children to these good women instead of turning them into the streets to riot and play at "chuckfarthing."

Mr. Raikes's first idea of a Sunday school was what is known as a Ragged School, kept on Sundays by women paid one shilling per week, and extra for coals in winter. At that moment were laid the foundations of an institution which would become national and world-wide. Very many good people had gathered children together, and taught them their catechism and prayers long before Mr. Raikes was born, and when they grew tired, or old, or died, there was an end of effort, and the world seemed little better than before. Here was the real difference between the Gloucester movement and all which had gone before. Mr. Raikes collected ragamuffins as wild as colts and tamed them, and humanized them, until they became to him children who brought him much joy.

The first school which Mr. Raikes started was in Sooty Alley. The mistress over this school was Mrs. Meredith, who kept a Dame, or "Mam" School, to use the local word. This school was kept in the kitchen, and Mrs. Meredith's spinning wheel was in one corner. On Sundays the children sat on forms or stools, but learned little, and poor Mrs. Meredith's patience was soon worn out with trying to keep them in order.

One of her pupils was Charles Cox, five years old, and when he was a hale old man of eighty-seven, he said he did not learn much "except perhaps to sit still, which the older boys found it very hard to learn." He also said the boys were "terrible bad," which, in Gloucester, meant as bad as they could be made. Poor Mrs. Meredith had a very hard time of it, and gave up her post after a few month's trial.

Mr. Raikes found a woman better fitted for his purpose in Mrs. Mary Critchley, and she took Mrs. Meredith's pupils into her house in the Southgate Street. It was near to Mr. Raikes's house.

The nearness of Mr. Raikes was a great moral support to the teacher, for some of the boys continued to be "terrible bad." He sometimes birched them with his own hands, and sometimes marched them home and insisted on their parents "leathering" them, stopping to see it done, and then marching them back to school again. Before those poor children could be taught anything they had to be disciplined, and this made the first step more tedious and difficult.

Mr. Raikes gave the experiment a three years' trial, from 1780 to 1783, before he ventured to let the world know anything about it. When he first took the children to church, they did not know how to behave, and he taught them to bow, as a sign of reverence, on entering a holy place. When he found that they stuck pins into one another, and fought, and swore, and were turned out by the parish "beadle," then he sat very close to them, and, in time, got them under control. Some persons thought the dandy and rich Mr. Raikes—the poor people always referred to him as a rich man—very soft and very foolish, and a little "cracked" over his new fad about dirty children, and they called him, playfully, or by way of derision, "Bobby Wild Goose"!

During these three years seven or eight Sunday schools were opened in the city by Mr. Raikes, the Reverend Thomas Stock, and the Vicar of St. Nicholas, with an average of thirty scholars in each. By means of the children a new atmosphere was brought into the squalid homes of these little ragamuffins, who even began to reform their own parents!

The rule on which mankind had acted for ages was reversed. This new rule was: the child first! The pyramid stood on its apex and did not topple over, and those who watched, marveled.*

✠

PRISONS—AND THE GOLDEN RULE
Sir James Marchant

IN THE days when Clapton was a country village in the vicinity of London, John Howard was born there in 1727, his father being a rich upholsterer. A philanthropist in the best sense of the word, his name will always be associated with the amelioration of prison conditions, in which he did heroic work, till his death in 1790. How he took up that work is a romance in itself.

Howard was a quiet man, and very religious. He lived among his books on a small estate where he studied astronomy and questions about heat and cold, and when only twenty-nine was elected a Fellow of the Royal Society. Medicine always interested him.

In spite of his quiet ways, Howard had a passion for traveling. He determined to go to Lisbon, then lying in ruins after the recent earthquake. Before his ship was out of the English Channel it was attacked and overpowered by a French privateer, and both crew and passengers were left without anything to eat or drink for nearly two days. They were then taken to the prison at Brest, thrown into a dark and horribly dirty dungeon, and apparently forgotten. Besides hunger and thirst they went through terrible pangs, fearing lest they were to be left to starve; but at length the heavy bolts of the iron door were shot back, and a leg of mutton was thrust inside. They sprang on the food like wolves and gnawed it like dogs.

* Abridged from *The Story of Robert Raikes for the Young* by J. Henry Harris, pp. 46-60.

For a week they all remained in their dungeon, and then Howard was allowed to leave it. In two months he was sent to England. His captivity in France first gave him an idea of the state of prisons and the sufferings of prisoners, but eighteen years were to pass before the improvement of their condition became the business of his life.

Mr. Howard was appointed high sheriff for the county of Bedford, 1773, and as such had the prisons under his charge. He at once visited the county prison in Bedford, and the misery that he found there was repeated almost exactly in nearly every prison in the British Isles. The jailer in Bedford—and in many other places—had no salary paid him, and therefore screwed all he could out of his prisoners; and no matter if a man were innocent or guilty, if a jury had condemned him or not, he must pay fifteen shillings and fourpence to the jailer, and two shillings to the warder who brought him his food—when he had any—before he was set free. If, as often happened, the prisoners could not find the money, they were locked up till they died, or till the fees were paid.

When Howard informed the magistrates of what he had found, they were as much shocked as if it had not been their business to have known all about it. "Yes, certainly, the criminals and those who had been confined for debt alone ought to be placed in different parts of the prison, and the men and women should be separated, and an infirmary built for the sick. But the cost would be very heavy, and the people might decline to pay it, unless the high sheriff could point to any other country which supported its own jail!"

Howard at once started on a visit to some of the county prisons, but did not discover *one* in which the jailer was paid a fixed salary. And the more he saw of the prisons, the more he was grieved at their condition. Almost all had dungeons for criminals built underground, dark, damp, and dirty, and sometimes as much as twenty feet below the surface; and often these dungeons were very small and very crowded. Mats, or in a few of the better-managed prisons, straw, was given to the prisoners to lie on, but no coverings; and those who were imprisoned for debt were expected to pay for their own food or go without.

Having satisfied himself of the state of the English prisons, and done what he could to improve them, Howard determined to discover how those in foreign countries were managed. Paris was the first stop. Howard called on the head of the police, who received him politely and gave him a written pass to the chief prisons. These he found very bad, with dungeons "beyond imagination, horrid and dreadful."

The prisons in Belgium with scarcely an exception, were "all fresh and clean; no jail distemper; no prisoners in irons." When Howard passed from Belgium to Holland he found the same care. From Holland he traveled to Germany, where, as a whole, the same sort of rules prevailed.

After three months Mr. Howard returned home and inspected the prison at Dover, to find to his dismay everything exactly as before; and when, after a little rest, he set out on a second English tour, scarcely anywhere did he perceive an improvement. Again and again Howard paid out of his own pocket the debts of many of those miserable people which sometimes began by being no more than a shilling, but soon mounted up, with all the fees, to several pounds.

Howard's journeys included Italy, Russia, Turkey, Germany, France, and Holland. In most of the great seaport towns along the Mediterranean, lazarettos, or pesthouses were built, so that passengers on arriving from plague-stricken countries should be placed in confinement for forty days, till there was no fear of their infecting the people. Howard felt that the time had come when he should first visit the lazarettos, and then go through the forty days' quarantine himself.

In Italy there were several that were extremely well managed, especially in the dominions of the Grand Duke of Tuscany; but he had made up his mind that when the moment came for his quarantine it should be undergone in Venice, the most famous lazaretto of them all. He took a ship eastwards, to Smyrna, and then changed to another vessel bound for Venice, which he knew would be put in quarantine the moment it arrived in the city.

At length, after two months, Venice was reached, and as a passenger on board a ship from an infected port, Howard was condemned to forty days' quarantine in the new lazaretto. His cell was as dirty as any dungeon in any English prison, and had neither chair, table nor bed. His first care was to clean it, but it was so long since anyone had thought of doing such a thing that it was nearly as long before the dirt could be made to disappear, and meanwhile he was attacked by the same headache which always marked his visit to such places, and in a short time became so ill that he was removed to the old lazaretto. He was rather worse off than before, for the water came so close to the walls that the stone floor was always wet, and in a week's time he was given a third apartment, this time consisting of four rooms, but all without furniture and as dirty as the first.

By the help of the English consul he was allowed to have some brushes and lime, which by mixing with water became whitewash. He then brushed down the walls without hindrance from anyone, though he had made up his mind that if the guard tried to stop him, he would lock him up in one of his rooms. Almost directly he grew better, and was able to enjoy his tea and bread once more.

On November 20, Howard was set free, his health having suffered from the lack of air and exercise. However, he still continued his tour of inspection, and it was not till February, 1787, that he reached home.

After a short time given to his own affairs he was soon busily employed in putting a stop very vigorously to the erection of a statue in his honor. The subscriptions to it had been large, for everybody felt how much the country owed to his unwearied efforts in the cause of his fellow men, carried out entirely at his own cost. But Howard would not listen to them for one moment.

"The execution of your design would be a cruel punishment to me," he says in a letter to the subscribers. "I shall always think the reform now going on in several of the jails of this kingdom, which I hope will become general, the greatest honor and most ample reward I can possibly receive."*

* Abridged from *Deeds Done for Christ* by Sir James Marchant, pp. 81-88. Copyright 1928 by Harper & Brothers. Used by permission of the publisher.

O SACRED HEAD, NOW WOUNDED

MANY strands of spiritual tradition, artistic talent, and personal devotion sometimes converge in a single hymn which a congregation may sing in less than five minutes; there is no better example of the wealth of tradition carried by one sacred song than "O Sacred Head, Now Wounded." The words come to us from a medieval monk, a Lutheran pastor, and an English clergyman— men of the fourteenth, the seventeenth, and the nineteenth centuries respectively. The tune was first written about 1600 for a German love song, then revised and harmonized four generations later to become the carrier of most profound and solemn religious emotion.

The lyric deserves a high place in the hymnody of the continuing Reformation, both in its own right and as a representative of the many hymns written by Paul Gerhardt (1606-1676). This best beloved of German hymn writers knew a long struggle against poverty and misfortune. Nevertheless, as a village pastor he began to publish his hymns, and by his death had won a place in the hearts of German Christians.

Gerhardt rebelled against the contentious spirit of the time which gloried in religious argument; instead he celebrated the love of God and poured out the offering of a grateful heart. We know him as the author of "All My Heart This Night Rejoices," "Give to the Winds Thy Fears," and "Jesus, Thy Boundless Love to Me." He found his inspiration for the present hymn in a medieval poem of devotion to the crucifix, probably written in the fourteenth century, though attributed by tradition to St. Bernard of Clairvaux. Gerhardt did not, however, simply translate the older work; he wrote in his own language and in the Protestant spirit a moving poem which some consider superior to the original. Our English translation is adapted from a rendition made about a century ago.

The spiritual impact of this hymn also owes much to the arrangement of the music by Johann Sebastian Bach, whose compositions along with those of Handel and Haydn made the eighteenth century an age of glorious Christian music. Bach was organist and choirmaster at Leipzig, Germany, and composed with a deep sense of stewardship: his work was an offering to God. He often wrote in the margins of his manuscripts the initials "J. J." (*Jesu juva*—Jesus, help me) or "S. D. G." (*Sola dei gloria*—to God alone be praise). He has been called the greatest of Protestant composers and even—because of the spiritual earnestness and clarity of his music—the greatest of preachers.

The musical setting for this hymn comes from the "Passion Chorale" in Bach's *St. Matthew Passion*. This great work, first performed in 1729, follows the Gospel According to St. Matthew in telling the story of the betrayal, arrest, crucifixion, death, and burial of Jesus Christ. Arranged for soloists, chorus, and orchestra, it uses the very words of Scripture, interspersed with chorales, to express the wonder of Christians at the love of God and their devotion to the Saviour. The entire work requires three hours and forty minutes to produce.

O Sacred Head, Now Wounded*

PASSION CHORALE. 7. 6. 7. 6. D.

Authorship uncertain
Tr. by Paul Gerhardt, 1607-1676
Tr. by James W. Alexander, 1804-1859

Hans L. Hassler, 1564-1612
Harmonized by J. S. Bach, 1685-1750

1. O   sa - cred Head, now wound-ed, With grief and shame weighed down,
2. What Thou, my Lord, hast suf - fered Was all   for sin - ners' gain:
3. What lan - guage shall I bor - row To thank Thee, dear - est Friend,

Now   scorn-ful - ly sur - round-ed With thorns, Thine on - ly crown;
Mine,   mine was the trans - gres - sion, But Thine the dead - ly pain.
For   this Thy dy - ing sor - row, Thy pi - ty with - out end?

How   pale Thou art with an - guish, With sore a - buse and scorn!
Lo,   here I fall, my Sav - iour! 'Tis I de - serve Thy place;
O   make me Thine for - ev - er; And should I faint - ing be,

How does that vis - age lan - guish Which once was bright as morn!
Look on me with Thy fa - vor, Vouch - safe to me Thy grace.
Lord, let me nev - er, nev - er Out - live my love to Thee. A - men.

Recurring throughout the work, the "Passion Chorale" is heard five times, set to different words on each occasion. It is profoundly moving music, appropriate to the mood of the humble Christian bowed before the cross. Bach's genius as a religious composer is here revealed, for the tune which he uses he took from a popular love song by Leo Hassler which was sung in the beer gardens, a sort of seventeenth-century blues. Bach altered the tune, provided the rich and sorrowful harmony, and gave to worshiping Christians one of their supreme expressions of devotion.

When reverently sung, this hymn brings the worshiper to the mood of gratitude, humility, and love for God with which Bach closes the *St. Matthew Passion* as the body of the Crucified Saviour is laid in the tomb:

> At Thy grave, O Jesu blest,
> May the sinner, worn with weeping,
> Comfort find in Thy dear keeping,
> And the weary soul find rest.
> Sleep in peace,
> Sleep Thou in the Father's breast.

✦

YE SERVANTS OF GOD, YOUR MASTER PROCLAIM

THE words of this hymn are so stately, so majestic, so admirably suited to worship, that they might seem to have been written for a great choir in a magnificent church. What more adequate vehicle could we find to express adoration as a congregation before God? But the glory of this hymn and the courage of its author tell a story of wild excitement and steadfast faithfulness which we ought not forget. As first published, this hymn carried the directions, "To be sung in a tumult."

The preaching of the Wesleys had stirred up just that. They came upon the scene in a day of social unrest, violence, and popular ignorance; in the first ugly developments of the Industrial Revolution thousands of rural people were leaving their cottage homes and flocking to the smoking, crowded factory towns. The Church of England was for the most part cold and formal and disinterested in the common rabble, and they in turn hesitated to come to the churches.

So George Whitefield and then the Wesleys went out to the people, to the pit heads at the mines, to the open fields near the cities, and preached to thousands. We can scarcely imagine the violence of the opposition. Sometimes it came from the "decent people of the community," who did not think that religion should be "desecrated" in this way, and sometimes it came from the rowdy and the ignorant; in any case, the preachers and their supporters were often attacked with sticks, stones, eggs, and other flying objects. But they stood their ground, and England was swept by revival.

This hymn, "to be sung in a tumult," was a song of battle, a rallying cry for

Ye Servants of God, Your Master Proclaim*

LYONS. 10. 10. 11. 11.

Charles Wesley, 1707-1788

Johann Michael Haydn, 1737-1806

1. Ye serv-ants of God, your Mas-ter pro-claim,
2. God rul-eth on high, al-might-y to save;
3. Sal-va-tion to God who sits on the throne!
4. Then let us a-dore, and give Him His right,

And pub-lish a-broad His won-der-ful Name;
And still He is nigh— His pres-ence we have!
Let all cry a-loud and hon-or the Son:
All glo-ry and power, and wis-dom and might,

The Name, all-vic-to-rious, of Je-sus ex-tol;
The great con-gre-ga-tion His tri-umph shall sing,
The prais-es of Je-sus the an-gels pro-claim,
All hon-or and bless-ing, with an-gels a-bove,

His king-dom is glo-rious, and rules o-ver all.
As-crib-ing sal-va-tion to Je-sus our King.
Fall down on their fac-es and wor-ship the Lamb.
And thanks nev-er ceas-ing, and in-fi-nite love. A-men.

the faithful when their opponents would scare them into flight. It is a trumpet call to the whole Christian flock to stand fast before the world and to make their glorious message known. Note how eminently fitting every word is to the situation for which the hymn was written. Perhaps a knowledge of the circumstances will put iron into our souls the next time we sing it.

Quite beyond the colorful circumstances of its composition, the hymn wonderfully represents Charles Wesley, whose whole life was given to the proclamation of his Master. He is the supreme hymn writer of Protestantism, having composed more than sixty-five hundred sacred songs: it has been said that he scarcely missed a day writing a religious poem in fifty years. Naturally, not all his compositions have remained in use, but an American hymnal published in the twentieth century contained more than one hundred twenty of them, and it would be a rare hymnal indeed that had none of them. Among those better known are the following: "O For a Thousand Tongues to Sing," "Love Divine, All Loves Excelling," "Jesus, Lover of My Soul," "Hark! the Herald Angels Sing," "Christ the Lord Is Risen Today," "Come, Thou Long-Expected Jesus," "Soldiers of Christ, Arise," and "A Charge to Keep I Have."

Wesley wrote hymns in many different meters, and they are sung to tunes from various sources. One of his converts was an actress, Mrs. Rich, who introduced him to her daughters' music teacher; he was George Frederick Handel, composer of the *Messiah*. The great musician wrote four tunes for the hymnist. Wesley also converted John Frederick Lampe, a composer of operas, who thereafter began to do hymn tunes and provided the music for one of Wesley's hymnals. Two of Charles Wesley's sons, Charles and Samuel, became musicians and composed tunes for their father's poetry.

The hymn tune, "Lyons," is eminently stately and singable, with a warm, triumphant quality that accords well with Wesley's words. It also represents the contributions to our hymnal from a distinguished musical family of Austria. Franz Josef Haydn (1732-1809) composed famous oratorios (*Creation, Tobias*) and melodies for some of our hymns. But, as in the case of the Wesley family, this hymn comes from the younger brother who is perhaps not quite so well known. Johann Michael Haydn (1737-1806) was choirmaster at Salzburg for forty-three years, during which time he wrote more than three hundred sixty compositions for the church. What a wealth of tribute Charles Wesley and Michael Haydn offered to their Lord from the talents with which He endowed them!

CONTENTS

PART IV SECTION 5

THE UNFINISHED REFORMATION

✠

And other sheep I have, which are not of this fold: them also I must bring, and they shall hear my voice; and there shall be one fold, and one shepherd.—JOHN 10:16

✠

PICTURES: PAGE
  Interpretation: The Good Samaritan—*Van Gogh* 518
  Picture: The Good Samaritan—*Van Gogh* 519
  Interpretation: Arnoldshain Altar—*Moroder* 520
  Picture: Arnoldshain Altar—*Moroder* 523
  Interpretation: Head of Christ—*Barosin* 524
  Picture: Head of Christ—*Barosin* 525

POETRY:
  Jerusalem—*Blake* 527
  New Every Morning Is the Love—*Keble* 527
  Abou Ben Adhem—*Hunt* 528
  East London—*Arnold* 528
  Recessional—*Kipling* 529
  Indifference—*Studdert-Kennedy* 530

STORIES:
  "Attempt Great Things for God"—*McLean* 530
  His Mother's Sermon—*Watson (Maclaren)* 533
  God in the Slums—*Redwood* 536

MUSIC:
  Interpretation: Through the Night of Doubt and Sorrow—*Ingemann* 538
  Music: Through the Night of Doubt and Sorrow—*Bambridge* 539
  Interpretation: Thine Is the Glory—*Budry* 540
  Music: Thine Is the Glory—*Handel* 541

THE GOOD SAMARITAN
Vincent Van Gogh

THE Parable of the Good Samaritan is familiar to every Christian, and its message of love and deliverance speaks clearly to all men. For one who had given himself impulsively to others and yet, within the depths of his being, yearned for friendship and love to fill his lonely life, as had Vincent Van Gogh, this theme was particularly meaningful.

Born in 1853, the son of a Dutch clergyman, Van Gogh went to work for an art dealer in The Hague at the age of sixteen. Four years later he determined to follow his father's path in service to God. The necessary university training seemed tedious and often irrelevant to him, and he longed to be out in practical service. He was a restless man, impetuous in his actions, and in constant struggle with himself to express his feelings. Finally, leaving the university, he secured a post as lay preacher in the miserable coal-mining towns of the Borinage in Belgium.

He set about his work with eagerness. His sermons were awkward and poorly delivered, but they resounded with the love that he had for men. He taught Bible classes, visited the sick, and sought earnestly to identify himself with his people. He went down into the coal mines, sharing their work and dirt. He moved from his comfortable housing into a hut of squalor, feeling their pain and cold. So strong was his devotion that he gave away his clothes, his food, his meager pay, and even his bed. For almost two years, Van Gogh lived among these people, loving them and being loved in return. But soon the disapproval of the evangelical authorities in Brussels forced him to leave the career that was absorbing him body and soul.

Empty-hearted and lost, he turned to painting and quickly became engrossed in its study. First one school and then another made its impact on him, but in a few short years he evolved his own style. He had always been acutely sensitive to the world about him, and now he expressed this awareness with emotion and power. His colors were vivid and often set in extreme contrasts, and his technique captured the subject in its grasp and swirled it into motion.

Still consumed with passionate love for humanity and with almost insane devotion and zeal, Van Gogh painted with an intensity that paralleled his inner life. His works are radiant in bold colors and alive with the movement of forms. There is a thrilling yet mystical quality about them that seems to convey the exciting unfathomable mystery of life and its creation.

While convalescing from mental fatigue in an asylum at St. Remy, Van Gogh made numerous copies of works by some of his most admired painters. To him, these copies were like interpretations of music. When a person plays Beethoven, he adds his personal interpretation. To the paintings he posed, Van Gogh improvised his own color and his own peculiar style of brushwork. "And then," he wrote his brother Theo, "my brush goes between my fingers as a bow would on the violin and absolutely for my pleasure."

THE GOOD SAMARITAN—*VAN GOGH*

He had long admired the work of Delacroix for its dramatic color and composition and had earlier copied his painting of Christ and the Virgin Mary. Turning to "The Good Samaritan," he followed the general pattern of Delacroix's drawing, but increased the visible brush strokes to passionate movement. The rippled sky of muted blues and browns is set as a background for the brilliant yellow and blue garb of the figures. Subdued green and neutral tones cover the ground in broken but harmonious lines. Rich and dynamic in its color, the painting pulsates with an intense rhythm that lifts the parable to dramatic heights.

This was no mere exercise to Van Gogh. The theme was one that spoke from the core of his being and cried out the suffering of his loneliness. Here was a man willing and eager to share his life with someone else, yet able to express his need only in the turbulence of his art. Terribly aware of his own personal conflicts and of those in the life of his society, he saw the vital significance of love as the motivating force behind all meaningful existence. Yet here was a man alone and distraught, reaching but abandoned.

In 1883, a few years before his death, Van Gogh wrote his brother: "Love is something eternal—the aspect may change, but not the essence. There is the same difference in a person before and after he is in love as there is in an un-lighted lamp and one that is burning. The lamp was there and it was a good lamp, but now it is shedding light, too, and that is its real function. And love makes one calmer about many things, and in that way, one is more fit for one's work." *

✠

ARNOLDSHAIN ALTAR
Siegfried Moroder

As a people's movement, the Reformation profoundly influenced daily life in the Protestant lands. The doctrine of vocation which held that every Christian was divinely called in his work made for a sense of comradeship with God in doing it well. The doctrine of the universal priesthood emphasized every Christian's obligation to pray on behalf of himself and his neighbor. So Protestantism brought a meaningful revival of religion as its message was understood and put into practice by the people.

But as centuries passed the world changed. New philosophies, new science, new inventions, new nations, new political movements, new wars altered the character of European life, and in large measure the churches lost touch with the people of the new industrial civilization. Luther spoke of the shoemaker and Tyndale of the plowboy, and Protestantism had meaning for the craftsman

* The letters quoted here are reprinted from *The Complete Letters of Vincent Van Gogh* by permission of the New York Graphic Society, Greenwich, Conn. This interpretation was especially prepared for the present anthology by Joe H. Bragg, Jr.

or the peasant in the sixteenth century. But what had it to say to the factory worker on an assembly line, to the atomic scientist, to the mass man lost in the vast cities of the twentieth century? Many began to feel that the gospel had no relevance for the new age. To millions the Church seemed a mere relic from the past. Men began to speak of "post-Christian Europe."

A vivid parable of this situation is the historic Church of St. Katherine in the industrial city of Frankfurt. During World War II Allied bombers obliterated the heart of the great city, and it has been built anew. As one enters the area that was bombed he suddenly finds himself in a gleaming crater of modernistic offices and shops, all plate glass and stainless steel. Everything is new—everything but the church. Its exterior was carefully rebuilt as a monument, its gray lines standing out in sharp contrast against the shining glass and steel of its surroundings. To many a passerby in post-Christian Europe, it must seem that this is indeed the Church, a museum piece from the past which no longer fits on the modern scene.

But the traveler who takes time to enter the Church of St. Katherine will discover that all is not as it was in centuries past. The interior is bright. Its stained-glass windows and altarpieces are new, done by contemporary artists in the idiom of our own time. There is no question here that the Church is still a living force, with a message for modern man in the midst of the twentieth century. But how can the Church convey this fact to the man on the outside, who comes only to be married, or to have his children baptized, or to attend the funeral of a friend? How does the Church speak the gospel compellingly to modern man?

One answer of the Church in Germany is the Evangelical Academy. This is a cutting-edge of the Church, where it meets the world. It is a conference center, but not primarily a place for those who are already active Christians to sing hymns and say prayers; rather it is a meeting-ground where keen-minded leaders in modern life who may have lost touch with the Church are willing to come and discuss the problems of our day with well-informed Christian thinkers. Week after week the academy conducts consultations for particular vocational or professional groups—newspapermen, labor leaders, lawyers, prison officials, physicians and nurses, kindergarten teachers, scientists, students. Every such group confronts its major problems and then looks at them in the light of the gospel. So the realization is growing that the Christian faith is meaningful for twentieth-century man, and the Reformation doctrine of vocation is taking on vitality once again.

Not far from Frankfurt is the academy of the Evangelical Church in Hesse-Nassau, the church of which Martin Niemöller is president. Located just outside the village of Arnoldshain, it stands in a clearing on a wooded hillside, commanding a view of a fertile valley and of impressive hills beyond. As seen from the highway, its buildings present an imposing sight. Erected after World War II, they are done in the clean, functional, contemporary style. Professor Theo Pabst, a teacher of architecture in Darmstadt, designed the buildings to take full advantage of the hillside setting. They spread out over the ample campus so that every dormitory room and every meeting room has a large picture window opening on to the magnificent scenery.

The chapel is an important place at the academy. Here the members of the various conferences come for daily prayers, for a sermon, for a service of Holy Communion. Professor Pabst has given it a design distinctive from the rest of the buildings. Its appearance is strikingly contemporary, yet somehow reminiscent of medieval times, as though to say that the Church indeed belongs to our time and to all the ages. The living Church is also the Church of our fathers. The chapel is octagonal in shape, with copper roofing. Its sturdiness of appearance alongside the lightness of the other buildings with their abundant use of glass suggests once more the stability of the Church.

The art used in the chapel is contemporary in form and Christian in spirit. On the main door, panels of hammered metal represent major scenes of the Biblical story. The interior is intimate and colorful, with the natural red wood of the ceiling, the gray wall, the brightly painted blue pews. The pulpit is painted in a contemporary abstract motif by Eberhard Schlotter of Darmstadt. The candlesticks, as well as the Communion chalice and plate, were designed by Walter Schoenwandt of Burg Nordeck.

The center of attention is the altar, designed by the architect, with its cross and pictorial walls by the sculptor, Siegfried Moroder of Munich (p. 523). Moroder comes from an old family of wood carvers in South Tirol and has done a number of pieces for churches. Until he was commissioned to do the work for the Arnoldshain chapel, all his sculpture had been in wood, but Professor Pabst suggested that he undertake a new metal-technique embossing figures "negatively" on sheet-brass, to produce a simple outline sketch. His use of this medium was so successful that he has employed it frequently since that time.

Moroder's sketches, embossed on the softly gleaming brass, bear effective witness to the faith. At the ends of the altar (in panels not visible in this picture) appear the apostles, the messengers of God. In the three panels on the front of the altar are represented in turn the birth of Jesus, His baptism (with the Holy Spirit descending as a dove), and His Resurrection: thus are proclaimed three great elements in the testimony to Christ—the Incarnation, the Epiphany (the manifestation of God), His Eternal and abiding glory. Dominating all, of course, is the figure of the Saviour, crucified by the sins of mankind, offering Himself for the world's redemption.

It is appropriate to the spirit of the Evangelical Academy that the center of worship is framed by a window, for the disciple with a concept of vocation must ever be conscious of the world outside as he makes his devotion to Christ. And when the Christian looks upon the world, he must ever see it through the cross.

ARNOLDSHAIN ALTAR—*MORODER*

HEAD OF CHRIST
Jacques Barosin

JACQUES BAROSIN'S interest in Biblical and religious art stems from a strong artistic background in his early life and a strange combination of circumstances which culminated in his seeking and finding asylum in the United States.

During his early life young Jacques moved with his family from his birthplace in Latvia, to Berlin, Germany, where he went to high school and later to an art school. Still later came the University of Berlin and the degree of Doctor of Philosophy in the history of art from the University of Freiburg. In 1932, now boasting the acquisition of a wife, he moved to France, maintained a studio, and painted professionally until his enlistment in the French army.

After his discharge in 1940, the Barosins lived comfortably in Nice, in unoccupied France, but it was not long before he was detained by the authorities because of his Jewish blood and background. After a year in a forced labor camp he was discharged, only to be re-arrested in 1943 under the German occupation. He was destined for deportation to Auschwitz. However, before he could be deported, he escaped from the concentration camp and joined his wife in a little mountain village in southern France. Here their fairy godmother was Mrs. Simone Serriere, a French Protestant schoolteacher. One can gauge the size of the village, and the unsettled local conditions, by the fact that the school had only four pupils—all boys. Luckily for Jacques and his wife, there was an unoccupied room on the second floor of the schoolhouse where they could stay, but to protect themselves and Mrs. Serriere it was necessary to avoid all semblance of their presence in the building. They didn't dare light a fire for cooking or illumination, and they had to avoid any unnecessary movement that might attract attention, for no one but the schoolteacher and the minister of a French Reformed Church were to know they were there.

It was to good Pastor Gall that they were indebted for their daily bread. Pastor Gall had for some time, at the risk of his own and his family's lives, been active in the feeding and helping of escaped prisoners. And it was Pastor Gall and his associates in the underground who were instrumental in procuring safe conduct for the Barosins to a refuge near Paris, when some of the villagers discovered their schoolhouse hideaway.

It was in their cramped schoolhouse quarters, with no money, no identification papers, and a price on their heads at the Gestapo headquarters only five miles away, that their most valuable possession was an old French Bible which Mrs. Serriere, the daughter of a Christian minister, put into their hands. Time hung heavy on their hands, and the Barosins read every word of it—Old and New Testaments—in muted voices so that the pupils in Mrs. Serriere's classroom below them would not hear. And a new strength and renewed hope came to them. And it was there that Jacques made his resolution to put into pictures the wonderful story of Jesus as revealed to him in that little French Bible.

HEAD OF CHRIST—*BAROSIN*

"If we ever get out of this spot alive," said Jacques Barosin to his wife before leaving their schoolhouse retreat, "I will illustrate the greatest book ever written."

After their return to Paris, Mr. Barosin received and executed some portrait commissions. Some of the American officers at the First General Hospital suggested that the artist come to the United States. He and his wife arrived at the end of 1947. It was just two years later that the artist had his first exhibit in New York City.

For a number of years the Board of Christian Education of the Evangelical and Reformed Church and the Division of Christian Education of the Congregational Christian Churches had felt the need of pictures to supplement their integrated course of study in their church schools. It was at this time that artist Barosin appeared on the scene and was, after due deliberation, commissioned to paint the pictures.

The seventy-five paintings in vivid water colors depict Jesus' life from the Annunciation, the Journey of the Wise Men, the Flight into Egypt, through the familiar scenes of his childhood and youth, His Baptism by John, the Sermon on the Mount, the Transfiguration, many of the miracles, the parables, the Last Supper, the Betrayal and Arrest, Before Pilate, the Crucifixion, and the Resurrection.

Asked how he happened to paint Jesus as he did, Mr. Barosin said:

"A man whose impact on His contemporaries was so strong and whose teachings had so far-reaching consequences must have been a powerful personality. In times like those of the first century, when the enemy occupies one's country, when the nation is split into many parties, when all the people live under a terrible moral and physical strain, no weakling or teacher of soft theories could hope to be of any influence.

"Only an overwhelmingly strong personality whose goodness comes from strength and suffering, whose human ideals were accepted by the oppressed and persecuted of *His* time and by men of good will in centuries *to come,* was able to stand up and teach people how to live.

"But my task to depict Jesus would not have been accomplished if I had seen Him only in His historical surroundings. He had to be a leader of all times and of our time as well. I had to find a face which would look acceptable in our times, which we would like to meet, which reveals supreme intelligence and goodness, and an ardent love of all humanity, powerful and realistic at the same time." He paused and then continued, "I leave it to the public to decide if I succeeded."

People react in different ways to the pictures. There were those with whose preconceived notion of the face of Jesus the pictures did not agree at all— concepts from early childhood, no doubt, culled from pictures in Sunday-school literature of long ago, from stained-glass windows. Who knows where such impressions come from? Most of the young people expressed much joy and satisfaction with the pictures; they were much more realistic, they said, than the ones they had been accustomed to. One man who came by himself seemed to be quietly meditating as he looked at the pictures one by one, and unashamedly gave way to tears.

There is no doubt that the pictures bring profound religious experience to those who see them.*

✠

JERUSALEM

And did those feet in ancient time
Walk upon England's mountains green?
And was the holy Lamb of God
On England's pleasant pastures seen?

And did the Countenance Divine
Shine forth upon our clouded hills?
And was Jerusalem builded here
Among these dark Satanic mills?

Bring me my bow of burning gold!
Bring me my arrows of desire!
Bring me my spear! O clouds unfold!
Bring me my chariot of fire!

I will not cease from mental fight,
Nor shall my sword sleep in my hand,
Till we have built Jerusalem
In England's green and pleasant land.
—*William Blake (1757-1827)*

NEW EVERY MORNING IS THE LOVE

New every morning is the love
Our wakening and uprising prove;
Through sleep and darkness safely brought,
Restored to life, and power, and thought.

New mercies, each returning day,
Hover around us while we pray;
New perils past, new sins forgiven,
New thoughts of God, new hopes of heaven.

If on our daily course our mind
Be set to hallow all we find,
New treasures still, of countless price,
God will provide for sacrifice.

* Abridged from "Life of Christ Pictures" by Helen E. Groninger in *Church Management* (June 1955). Used by permission of the author and the publisher.

Old friends, old scenes will lovelier be,
As more of heaven in each we see;
Some softening gleam of love and prayer
Shall dawn on every cross and care.

We need not bid for cloistered cell,
Our neighbor and our work farewell,
Nor strive to wind ourselves too high
For sinful man beneath the sky:

The trivial round, the common task,
Would furnish all we ought to ask—
Room to deny ourselves, a road
To bring us daily nearer God.

Only, O Lord, in thy dear love
Fit us for perfect rest above;
And help us this and every day
To live more nearly as we pray.

                              —*John Keble (1792-1866)*

ABOU BEN ADHEM

Abou Ben Adhem—may his tribe increase—
Awoke one night from a deep dream of peace,
And saw within the moonlight in his room,
Making it rich like a lily in bloom,
An angel writing in a book of gold.
Exceeding peace had made Ben Adhem bold
And to the presence in the room he said:
"What writest thou?" The vision raised its head,
And with a look made all of sweet accord,
Answered: "The names of those who love the Lord."
"And is mine one?" said Abou. "Nay, not so,"
Replied the angel. Abou spoke more low,
But cheerly still; and said: "I pray thee, then,
Write me as one that loves his fellow-men."
The angel wrote, and vanished. The next night
It came again with a great wakening light,
And shewed the names whom love of God had blessed,
And lo! Ben Adhem's name led all the rest.*

                              —*Leigh Hunt (1784-1859)*

EAST LONDON

'Twas August, and the fierce sun overhead
Smote on the squalid streets of Bethnal Green,

* The son and grandson of Anglican clergymen, Leigh Hunt was an English poet and essayist.

And the pale weaver, through his windows seen
In Spitalfields, look'd thrice dispirited.

I met a preacher there I knew, and said:
"Ill and o'erwork'd, how fare you in this scene?"—
"Bravely!" said he; "for I of late have been
Much cheer'd with thoughts of Christ, *the living bread.*"

O human soul! as long as thou canst so
Set up a mark of everlasting light,
Above the howling senses' ebb and flow,

To cheer thee, and to right thee if thou roam—
Not with lost toil thou labourest through the night
Thou mak'st the heaven thou hop'st indeed thy home.
—*Matthew Arnold (1822-1888)*

RECESSIONAL

God of our Fathers, known of old,
Lord of our far-flung battle line—
Beneath whose awful hand we hold
Dominion over palm and pine—
Lord God of Hosts, be with us yet,
Lest we forget—lest we forget!

The tumult and the shouting dies—
The Captains and the Kings depart—
Still stands Thine ancient sacrifice,
An humble and a contrite heart.
Lord God of Hosts, be with us yet,
Lest we forget—lest we forget!

Far-called our navies melt away—
On dune and headland sinks the fire—
Lo, all our pomp of yesterday
Is one with Nineveh and Tyre!
Judge of the Nations, spare us yet,
Lest we forget—lest we forget!

If, drunk with sight of power, we loose
Wild tongues that have not Thee in awe—
Such boasting as the Gentiles use,
Or lesser breeds without the Law—
Lord God of Hosts, be with us yet,
Lest we forget—lest we forget!

For heathen heart that puts her trust
In reeking tube and iron shard—

All valiant dust that builds on dust,
And guarding calls not Thee to guard,
For frantic boast and foolish word,
Thy mercy on Thy people, Lord!

—*Rudyard Kipling (1865-1936)*

INDIFFERENCE

When Jesus came to Golgotha they hanged Him on a tree,
They drave great nails through hands and feet, and made a Calvary;
They crowned Him with a crown of thorns, red were His wounds and deep,
For those were crude and cruel days, the human flesh was cheap.

When Jesus came to Birmingham, they simply passed Him by,
They never hurt a hair of Him, they only let Him die;
For men had grown more tender, and they would not give Him pain,
They only just passed down the street, and left Him in the rain.

Still Jesus cried, "Forgive them, for they know not what they do,"
And still it rained the winter rain that drenched Him through and through;
The crowds went home and left the streets without a soul to see,
And Jesus crouched against a wall and cried for Calvary.*

—*G. A. Studdert-Kennedy*

✣

"ATTEMPT GREAT THINGS FOR GOD"
Archibald McLean

WILLIAM CAREY, the father of modern missions, was born in Paulerspury,
England, in 1761. His father was a schoolmaster. On this account he had some
advantages that were not enjoyed by many of his playmates. He took naturally
to books. Whatever he began he finished. No difficulties discouraged him. He
was fond of drawing and painting as well as collecting birds and insects. He
filled the house with specimens. On account of the poverty of his family
he was apprenticed to a shoemaker at the age of fourteen. From that time he
depended on his own efforts for support. His master dying after two years,
he bought his time and started in business for himself. At the age of twenty
he married.

His parents belonged to the Established Church, but through the influence
of a fellow worker he was led to attend a Dissenting Chapel. Under the
stirring preaching there he was persuaded to give himself in love and trust to
the Lord. He was baptized in the River Nen, October 5, 1783. Soon after his
baptism he was invited to speak in public. For three years he ministered to the
little church in Barton, walking six miles for that purpose Sunday morning

and returning in the evening. Having no acquaintance with ministers, he said, "I was obliged to draw all from the Word of God."

Carey was a born linguist. A friend loaned him a Latin grammar. In six weeks he mastered it and was able to read Latin easily. In an incredibly short time he acquired Dutch. He learned Greek and Hebrew without a teacher. Within seven years he read the Bible in six or seven tongues. He bought a French book. In three weeks he was able to read it with great satisfaction. It was only his spare hours that he devoted to his linguistic studies.

The reading of Cook's *Voyages* led Carey to think of the nations that are without hope because they are without God. As he worked at his bench he thought of these nations and resolved to do something for the betterment of their condition. He made a globe of leather to help him in teaching geography. As he would point out the different nations he would say to his pupils, "These are Christian; these are Mohammedans; and these are pagans." As he uttered the word "pagan" his lips quivered and his eyes filled with tears. That humble shoemaker's shop was the birthplace of modern missions. Many years afterwards, in the English House of Parliament, Wilberforce said that he did not know of a finer instance of the moral sublime than that a poor cobbler working in his stall should conceive the idea of converting the Hindus to Christ. "Why, Milton's planning his 'Paradise Lost' in his old age and blindness was nothing to it."

At a ministerial meeting he was attending, Carey proposed as a suitable topic of discussion this, "The duty of the Church to attempt to send the gospel to the heathen." The presiding officer heard the proposal with surprise and anger and said, "Young man, sit down; when it will please the Lord to convert the heathen, He will do it without your aid or mine." He sat down, but he could not refrain from pleading in public and in private on behalf of this cause which he had so much at heart. In time, others were convinced. The next year he preached the opening sermon to the conference. His sermon was based on Isaiah 54:2-3. The main divisions were, "Expect great things from God"; "Attempt great things for God." A collection amounting to thirteen pounds, two shillings and sixpence was taken up.

One result of that sermon was the organization of a society for propagating the gospel among the heathen. At that time Dr. Thomas, a young surgeon who had gone out under the East India Company, was in London seeking to secure funds to pay his way back and looking for a companion. He was appointed the first agent of the new society. Someone said, "There is a gold mine in India, but it seems as deep as the center of the earth; who will go down and explore it for us?" Carey promptly replied, "I will go, but remember you must hold the ropes." He was appointed to go with Dr. Thomas to India.

At first, Mrs. Carey refused to go. The East Company opposed his going and refused him a passage on any of their ships. When he reached India on a Danish ship they objected to his settling in any part of the country under their control. The society that sent him out did not care very much what became of him. He was reduced to absolute destitution. Very unexpectedly and very fortunately he was offered the superintendence of an indigo factory. This position afforded him a good living. At once he relieved the society of his support. He discharged his duties to his employer with the utmost fidelity. His spare hours were devoted to gardening and to the study of the language. As he found time he went out into two hundred villages in his district and preached to the natives.

Many of the people of India had been reached by the preaching and by the circulation of parts of the Bible and other religious works. Seven years after the mission was opened, Carey baptized his first Hindu convert. His name was Krishna-Pal. The same day he baptized his own son, Felix. Krishna-Pal lived for twenty years to preach the gospel with great ability and success. His baptism marked an epoch in the history of the work. Another event of capital importance was the publication of the Bible in Bengali. The news of this translation was received in England with great joy. One merchant collected a thousand pounds to show his sympathy. In Philadelphia five thousand dollars was raised and added to this sum. Before Carey's death 212,000 copies of the Scriptures in forty different languages were issued. The Word of God was thus brought within the reach of three hundred million human beings. He and his associates did more to spread the knowledge of the Scriptures among the heathen than all the world besides.

The work he did as a translator of the Bible was only part of what he accomplished. He prepared grammars and lexicons in several languages. These were elaborate works. He was one of the foremost botanists and horticulturists of his age. He sought to serve his adopted country in these capacities. When the government founded a college in Fort William, Carey was selected as one of the teachers. He was the ablest living linguist and was chosen for that reason. He preached constantly. Carey and Marshman and Ward earned and paid $250,000 to the treasury of the mission. They said, "Let us never think of our time, our gifts, our families, or even the clothes we wear as our own. Let us sanctify them all to God and His cause."

He had his trials. He was denounced by theologians, by traders, by politicians. He was said to be engaged in the maddest, most extravagant, the most unwarrantable project that ever entered the brain of a lunatic enthusiast. He was called a fool, a tinker, a schismatic. His great printing establishment was destroyed by fire. In an hour the labors of many years were consumed. The loss was estimated at seventy thousand rupees. Important manuscripts perished. It required twelve months of hard labor to replace what had been destroyed.

Before his death, he won the confidence and esteem of all good men. He was a welcome guest and a trusted adviser in the viceregal palace. Learned societies delighted to admit him to their fellowship. When he died the flags were hung at half-mast. The burning of the printing press was a gain rather than a loss. Sympathy was excited. Money was raised to replace what had been destroyed. The mission became more widely known. A mighty impetus was given to the work of Bible translation.

This man who was sneered at as low-born and low-bred made all nations his beneficiaries. He did a work that will tell on ages and that will tell for God.*

✠

HIS MOTHER'S SERMON
John Watson (Ian Maclaren)

HE WAS an ingenuous lad, with the callow simplicity of a theological college still untouched, and had arrived on the preceding Monday at the Free Kirk manse with four cartloads of furniture and a maiden aunt. For three days he roamed from room to room in the excitement of householding, then he shut himself up in his study to prepare the great sermon, and his aunt went about on tiptoe. During meals on Friday he explained casually that his own wish was to preach a simple sermon, and that he would have done so had he been a private individual, but as he had held the MacWhammel scholarship a deliverance was expected by the country. He would be careful and say nothing rash, but it was due to himself to state the present position of theological thought, and he might have to quote once or twice from Ewald.

His aunt was a saint, with that firm grasp of truth, and tender mysticism, whose combination is the charm of Scottish piety, and her face was troubled. While the minister was speaking in his boyish complacency, her thoughts were in a room where they had both stood, five years before, by the deathbed of his mother.

His mother, brave and faithful to the last, was bidding him farewell.

"I cannot see ye noo, John, but I know ye're there, and I've just one wish. If God calls ye to the ministry, ye'll no refuse, and the first day ye preach in your own kirk, speak a good word for Jesus Christ: an' John, I'll hear ye that day, though ye'll no see me, and I'll be satisfied."

Five years had passed, crowded with thought and work, and his aunt wondered whether he remembered that last request.

"What's the matter, auntie?"

"Do not be angry with me, John, but I'm concerned aboot Sabbath, for I've been prayin' ever since ye were called to Drumtochty that it might be a great day, and that I might see ye comin' to your people, laddie, with the beauty o' the Lord upon ye."

"Go on, auntie, go on," he whispered.

"It's no for me to advise you, who am only a simple old woman, who knows nothin' but her Bible and the Catechism; and it's not that I'm feared aboot your faith, but it's the folk, John, I'm anxious aboot; the flock o' sheep the Lord has given ye to feed for Him."

She could not see his face but she felt him gently press her hand, and took courage.

* Abridged from *Epoch Makers of Modern Missions* by Archibald McLean, pp. 58-64. Copyright 1912 by Fleming H. Revell Company. Used by permission of the publisher.

"Ye must mind, laddie, that they're no clever and learned like what ye are, but just plain country folk, each one wi' many cares o' this world. They'll need a clear word to comfort their hearts and show them the way everlastin'. Ye'll say what's right, no doubt o' that, and everybody'll be pleased wi' ye, but oh, laddie, be sure ye say a good word for Jesus Christ."

The minister's face whitened, and his arm relaxed. He rose hastily and went to the door, but in going out he gave his aunt an understanding look. The son had not forgotten his mother's request. He asked his aunt to have worship with the servant, for he must be alone in his study.

It was a pleasant room and the light of the lamp fell on the books he loved. But his books went out of mind as he looked at the sermon shining beneath the glare of the lamp, and demanding judgment. He had finished its last page with honest pride that afternoon, and had declaimed it, facing the southern window, with a success that amazed himself. Now he lifted the sheets with fear. The brilliant opening, with its historical parallel, this review of modern thought reinforced by telling quotations, that trenchant criticism of old-fashioned views, would not deliver. For the audience had vanished, and left one careworn but ever beautiful face, whose gentle eyes were waiting with a yearning look. Twice he crushed the sermon in his hands, and turned to the fire, and twice he repented and smoothed it out. What else could he say now to the people? and then in the stillness of the room he heard a voice, "Speak a good word for Jesus Christ."

Next minute he was kneeling on the hearth, and pressing the magnum opus that was to shake Drumtochty into the heart of the red fire, and he saw the impressive words shrivel up and disappear. Very likely it was no masterpiece, but only the crude production of a lad who knew little of letters and nothing of the world. Very likely it would have done neither harm nor good, but it was his best, and he gave it for love's sake, and there is nothing in a human life so precious to God, neither clever words nor famous deeds, as the sacrifices of love.

His prayer next morning was very short, but afterwards he stood at the window for a space, and when he turned, his aunt said:

"Ye'll get your sermon, and it'll be worth hearing."

When he shut himself into the study that Saturday morning he heard her go into her room above, and he knew she went to intercede for him.

Hours later—for still she prayed and watched in faithfulness to mother and son—she observed him come out and wander round the garden in great joy. Then she knew that his heart was full of love, and that it would be well on the morrow.

When the bell began to ring, the minister rose from his knees and went to his aunt's room to be robed. His gown was spread out in its silken glory. When she had given the last touch, and he was ready to go, a sudden seriousness fell upon them.

"Kiss me, auntie."

"For your mother, and her God be with you," and then he went through the garden and underneath the honeysuckle and into the kirk, where every Free Kirker in Drumtochty that could get out of bed, and half the Established Kirk, were waiting in expectation.

I sat with his aunt in the minister's pew, and shall always be glad that I was at that service. In my time I have seen many religious functions. I have been in Mr. Spurgeon's Tabernacle, where the people wept one minute and laughed the next; have heard Liddon in St. Paul's, have seen High Mass in St. Peter's and stood in the dusk of the Duomo at Florence when Padre Agostino thundered against the evils of the day. But I never realized the unseen world as I did that day in the Free Kirk of Drumtochty.

We thought none the worse of him that he was nervous, and two or three old people who had suspected self-sufficiency, took him to their hearts when the minister concluded the Lord's Prayer hurriedly, having omitted two petitions. His youth commended him, since he was also modest, for every mother had come with an inarticulate prayer that the "puir laddie would do weel on his first day, and him only twenty-four." Texts I can never remember, nor, for that matter, the words of sermons; but the subject was Jesus Christ, and before he had spoken five minutes I was convinced that Christ was present. The preacher faded from before one's eyes, and there arose the figure of the Nazarene, best lover of every human soul, stretching out His pierced hands to old folk and little children as He did, before His death, in Galilee. His voice might be heard any moment, as I have imagined it in my lonely hours by the winter fire or on the solitary hills—soft, low and sweet, penetrating like music to the secret of the heart, "Come unto me . . . and I will give you rest."

During a pause in the sermon I glanced up the church, and saw the same spell held the people. The women were weeping quietly, and the rugged faces of our men were subdued and softened, as when the evening sun plays on the granite stone.

The elders, one by one, gripped the minister's hand in the vestry, and, though plain, homely men, they were the godliest in the Glen; but no man spake save Burnbrae.

"I lost one fairm for the Free Kirk, and I would have lost ten to be in the kirk this day."

His aunt could only meet him in the study, and when he looked on her his lip quivered, for his heart was wrung with one wistful regret.

"Oh, auntie, if she had only been spared to see this day, and her prayers answered!"

But his aunt flung her arms around his neck.

"Do not be cast doon, laddie, nor be unbelievin'. Your mither has heard every word, and is satisfied, for ye did it in remembrance o' her, and yon was your mither's sermon."*

---

* Abridged from *Beside the Bonnie Brier Bush* by John Watson (Ian Maclaren), pp. 26-31.

GOD IN THE SLUMS

Hugh Redwood

THERE is a hospital matron somewhere in England who owes her life as well as her position to an officer of the slums. They live their busy lives far removed from each other; the one in dignity and power, with the hush of the wards about her, the other in strenuous responsibility at a post of the Salvation Army. But once they met and strove together on the very brink of death.

The place of their meeting was a dark and dirty room. The officer had been summoned thither by a half-intoxicated woman who had run screaming to her quarters with word that her lodger was going to commit suicide and was threatening to kill anyone who interfered with her. It being part of the slum officer's ordinary round to prevent suicide and murder, she put on her hat and hurried through the rain to the address given. The door at the top of a bare and rickety stair was locked, but there was a scurrying behind it when she tapped, and then a silence. She tapped again.

"Who is it?" asked a woman's voice.

"Only me," said the slum officer. Tactful, perhaps, but hardly more informative than grammatical. The occupant of the room, in very unpleasant tones indeed, demanded to know more.

"It's the Salvation Army," vouchsafed the officer—who was frightened and could not think of any less comprehensive way of describing herself.

At once the door opened. "If it's the Army you can come in," said the voice, but with no kinder accent. And its owner, as soon as the officer had crossed the threshold, darted from some unseen lurking-place and turned the key in the lock behind her. "Now what's your business?" she shouted.

It was clear to the officer that she was in genuine danger. The woman had been drinking heavily and was more than half demented, but she was still able to think quickly. The direct method was the only safe way of dealing with her, so the truth was told without dissembling. "I called to see you because I was told you were going to kill yourself," said the officer.

The woman came forward to the table. There were some scraps of food upon it and a long, thin-bladed knife, like those so deftly wielded by the proprietors of ham-and-beef shops. The visitor noticed the knife just a second too late: the woman's grip had already closed upon its handle. "That's right," she said, dropping her voice for the first time. "I'm going to die, and I'm going to die now. I've had more than enough of life, and this is going to be the end of it. Why shouldn't you die too? Why shouldn't we go together?"

Not by so much as a shake in her voice did the officer betray the alarm she felt. She knew that she must keep her self-control and play for time.

"Well," she replied, as if weighing the proposal, "if I had to die tonight I should at least be ready for it. What about you? Are you quite sure you are ready also?"

It was a queer setting for a confessional. The traffic of the Tower Bridge rattled on its way at the distance of a street or two; the sounds and smells of the slums drifted sluggishly into the room on a tide of stale, damp air. The gaslight looked as if it also might be meditating self-extinguishment.

A questioning look crept into the woman's sullen face. The officer saw it, and was quick to press her advantage. "Couldn't we pray?" she asked. "It wouldn't be nice to die without trying to say a prayer, would it?" And praying already in silence she went upon her knees by the table. The other, after a few seconds of hesitation, knelt beside her. The knife was still clasped in her right hand, and the officer's left hand, falling softly but strongly upon her wrist, held it fast. So they prayed, and perhaps a stranger prayer was never offered. Words came with difficulty at first, because of the distraction of listening for steps upon the staircase, but gradually the petition took life, and as it did so fear withdrew. Then, in a flood of simple words, the wonder of an understanding Christ was told to a soul in torment. She, who for years had carried her secrets in her own heart, for shame of sharing them and want of a friend to share them with, heard how already they were known and sorrowed over. To her own amazement she found herself believing it. This was prayer as she had never heard it before; prayer with so vivid a sureness about it that it became impossible to doubt the presence of the Person addressed. Her grasp of the knife handle relaxed, and the weapon fell to the floor. The slum officer knew that victory was in sight.

When they arose, her arm was about the woman's waist and tears were upon their faces. Ten minutes earlier one of them had contemplated murder and suicide: now she sank back in a chair, shaking but sober, and the woman she would have killed bent over her and kissed her.

A kiss—and a cup of tea. The one to warm the heart; the other to stop the shivering of a body in the throes of a violent reaction. The two in combination to draw out as sad a story as well could be imagined.

The woman who sat there telling it, unkempt and gross of body, with clothes so ragged and scanty that it was impossible for her to go out until the slum officer had fetched additional garments, was of good birth and education. She had trained as a nurse and had risen to the rank of sister in a London hospital. Then, as the consequence of an unfortunate companionship, she had developed a craving for whisky. There came a day when she should have been present at an operation upon a distinguished patient, but was so fuddled that she had to be relieved of her duties. For this unforgivable offense she was instantly dismissed, with a career that had promised to be brilliant in ruins. She could not face her friends and she had spent all her money: in this extremity she was reduced to seeking help from one of the ward maids, who sent her to her own mother, a drunkard herself. The two women lived together, each holding the other down, until the night when one of them broke out in suicidal frenzy and the other ran to the slum post for assistance.

The slum officer told her what she never could have credited, had it not been for the strange conviction which had seized her as they knelt in prayer. Believing herself so hopelessly in the toils of her craving that suicide offered the only escape, she heard a doctrine expounded to her which in an astonishing manner pointed her back to life. As if in a dream, she assented to the officer's proposition that she should enter one of the Army's homes for inebriates; and out of that home, in due course, there came a recreated being. Eventually she was able to return to her former profession and to succeed in it.

Slum officers are few who have not at some time or other risked their lives, as this one did.*

✠

THROUGH THE NIGHT OF DOUBT AND SORROW

OUR hymnal is an ecumenical (world-wide) book. In any given service we may sing an ancient Christian response, a song of praise by an eighth-century Greek priest, a meditation by a twelfth-century Latin monk, a Scottish metrical version of a Hebrew Psalm, a modern hymn by an Anglican, Baptist, Congregationalist, Disciple, Evangelical, Friend, Holiness, Independent, Lutheran, Moravian, Orthodox, Presbyterian, Quietist, Roman Catholic, Universalist, or Wesleyan from any of the inhabited continents. Our hymnals, of course, draw most largely on British and American sources, with Germany probably coming next. One of the countries least represented is Denmark, which has a splendid body of hymnody, but a language not too widely known. This hymn and "That Cause Can Neither Be Lost Nor Stayed" are probably the best-known Danish hymns in America.

Bernhard Severin Ingemann (1789-1862), the author of "Through the Night of Doubt and Sorrow," was a professor literature at Soroe, a novelist, and a poet, who wrote many hymns and who edited the Danish hymnbook. He was the son of a rural minister. This hymn was particularly fortunate in its translator, the Reverend Sabine Baring-Gould (1834-1924), an Anglican rector who had a special gift for writing liturgical marching-songs; his best-known hymn is "Onward Christian Soldiers," and his beautiful evening recessional, "Now the Day Is Over," is also widely loved. (Two of the Reverend Baring-Gould's writings appear on p. 196 and 279.)

"Through the Night of Doubt and Sorrow" beautifully expresses the ecumenical spirit of the "Unfinished Reformation." It pictures the Church on the march, toward the fulfillment of the divine purpose, an image derived from the Exodus of the Hebrew slaves out of Egypt under Moses, God's

* Abridged from *God in the Slums* by Hugh Redwood, pp. 45-48. Published 1930 by Hodder & Stoughton, Ltd. Used by permission of the publisher.

Through the night of doubt and sorrow

B. S. INGEMANN
Tr. by SABINE BARING-GOULD

ST. ASAPH

WILLIAM S. BAMBRIDGE

1 Thro' the night of doubt and sor-row On-ward goes the pil-grim band,
2 One, the light of God's own pres-ence, O'er His ran-somed peo-ple shed,
3 One, the strain which lips of thou-sands Lift as from the heart of one;
4 On-ward there-fore, pil-grim broth-ers, On-ward, with the cross our aid;

Sing-ing songs of ex-pec-ta-tion, March-ing to the prom-ised land.
Chas-ing far the gloom and ter-ror, Bright'ning all the path we tread:
One the con-flict, one the per-il, One, the march in God be-gun:
Bear its shame, and fight its bat-tle, Till we rest be-neath its shade.

Clear be-fore us thro' the dark-ness Gleams and burns the guid-ing light;
One, the ob-ject of our jour-ney, One, the faith which nev-er tires,
One, the glad-ness of re-joi-cing On the far e-ter-nal shore,
Soon shall come the great a-wak-ing; Soon the rend-ing of the tomb;

Broth-er clasps the hand of broth-er, Stepping fear-less thro' the night.
One, the ear-nest look-ing for-ward, One, the hope our God in-spires.
Where the One Al-might-y Fa-ther Reigns in love for-ev-er-more.
Then, the scatt'ring of all shad-ows, And the end of toil and gloom. A-MEN.

540 THE CHURCH AND THE FINE ARTS

appointed deliverer. Here are the familiar incidents in that story: the songs, the pillar of fire, the battles, the hope of the Promised Land. But Christians have long seen in the Exodus a manifestation of God's way of dealing with His people and a pageant of our salvation. So the pilgrim band in the hymn is the company of faithful Christians, bound to one another as brothers under the banner of the cross.

This hymn reminds us that we are a "pilgrim band." Many Christians have seen in the wanderings of Abraham and in the long journey of the Israelites under Moses a true picture of the Church's calling: our home is not here, we are not to settle down in ease with the world as it is, our duty is to press on toward God's purpose for us. One of the stirring themes of Christian heroism has been that of the pilgrim. Some have distorted this doctrine to the point of renouncing any Christian concern for the world or any appreciation of the good things of this life. But as set forth in this hymn, it is a call to heroism, the peal of trumpets rousing the company of disciples for another day's march.

✠

THINE IS THE GLORY

THE French-speaking Protestant community is small in numbers, but its influence in world Protestantism has been large from the beginning. Calvin was a Frenchman and Geneva is a French-speaking city. Calvin's *Institutes,* the Geneva Psalter, the Geneva Bible became major instruments of the Reformation. The Huguenots, as the Protestants of France were called, inspired their co-religionists in other lands by their zeal and their steadfastness under persecution. The Reformed theological faculties in France and Switzerland have furnished able scholars and leaders for their own churches and for the ecumenical movement. Pastor Marc Boegner was one of the first presidents of the World Council of Churches. The headquarters of that body are located in Geneva, and its ecumenical Institute is in nearby Céligny. And the hymn which now seems to have emerged as the clear favorite at ecumenical meetings is French—"A Toi la Gloire," translated into English as "Thine Is the Glory."

The hymn is a triumphant ascription of praise to the resurrected Christ. The references throughout the first half are to the first Easter morning—the angels in shining garments, the stone that was rolled away, the Risen Lord greeting His disciples. Then midway through the hymn the scene shifts from Jerusalem in the first century to the Church of Christ in our time. We who sing become one with the first believers in our joy and in our glorious proclamation of the resurrection faith. Armed with the strength of the Prince of Life, the divine Conqueror over death, we sing our song of hope and gladness.

It is fitting that this hymn should have exceeded others as an expression

Thine is the Glory*

5. 5. 6. 5. 6. 5. 6. 5. with Refrain

Edmond Budry, 1884
Translated by R. Birch Hoyle, 1923

George Frederick Handel, 1685-1759

1. Thine is the glo - ry, Ris - en, con-qu'ring Son; End-less is the
2. Lo! Je - sus meets thee, Ris - en from the tomb; Lov-ing - ly he
3. No more we doubt thee, Glo - rious Prince of Life! Life is nought with -

vic - t'ry Thou o'er death hast won. An - gels in bright rai - ment
greets thee, Scat-ters fear and gloom; Let his church with glad - ness
out thee; Aid us in our strife; Make us more than con-qu'rors,

Rolled the stone a - way, Kept the fold - ed grave - clothes
Hymns of tri - umph sing, For her Lord now liv - eth;
Through thy death-less love; Bring us safe through Jor - dan

REFRAIN

Where thy bod - y lay.
Death hath lost its sting. Thine is the glo - ry, Ris - en, con-qu'ring Son;
To thy home a - bove.

End - less is the vic - t'ry Thou o'er death hast won. A - MEN.

*From *Cantate Domino*, No. 28. Copyright 1951 by World's Student Christian Federation. Used by permission of the publisher.

of ecumenical worship. For while one might have expected a hymn like "The Church's One Foundation" to gain greatest favor, the heart of the gospel is not the Church, but Christ. The Church is the divinely created fellowship, brought into being by the gospel, commissioned to make that good news known to all mankind. But He is the message. "For we preach not ourselves, but Christ Jesus the Lord; and ourselves your servants for Jesus' sake" (II Cor. 4:5). So when Christians come together from all the nations and the various Protestant and Orthodox confessions, this is their song that expresses the loyalty of every heart.

Ours is a faith in a living Christ. He meets us this day in our deepest need, and He brings us victory. Then He sends us forth in His name.* And as we go, we unite in that ancient cry of adoration, "Glory be to thee, O Christ."

Edmond L. Budry (1854-1932) composed a number of hymns, and, with one or two possible exceptions, ranks as the largest contributor since the days of the Reformation to the parish hymnal in the French language. None of his other hymns seems to have become well known in English. The music from Handel's *Judas Maccabaeus* gives a particularly stirring setting to the lyrics, and the refrain marks the hymn with a recurring crescendo of triumph.

---

* See "Head of Christ," by Barosin, in this section, a representation of Christ giving the Great Commission, by an artist who was led to the Christian faith in a French Protestant community.

PART V

THE PROTESTANT CHURCH
IN NORTH AMERICA

by

ALFRED T. DEGROOT

1. THE CHURCH IN THE COLONIAL ERA ..... *page* 544

2. THE CHURCH ON THE FRONTIER:
   THE EARLY WEST .... *page* 564

3. THE CHURCH ON THE PLAINS AND
   IN THE SOUTHWEST .... *page* 587

4. CHURCH DEVELOPMENT ON THE
   PACIFIC COAST .... *page* 612

5. THE CHURCH CROSSES CANADA AND ALASKA *page* 633

6. THE CHURCH IN THE MODERN ERA ...... *page* 661

7. CHRISTIANITY AND EDUCATION .... *page* 686

CONTENTS

PART V   SECTION 1

THE CHURCH IN THE COLONIAL ERA

—✠—

Therefore they that were scattered abroad went every where preaching the word.—ACTS 8:4

—✠—

PICTURES: PAGE
   Interpretation: Old Brick Church, Smithfield, Virginia 545
   Picture: Old Brick Church, Smithfield, Virginia 547
   Interpretation: Trinity Church, New York City 546
   Picture: Trinity Church, New York City 549
   Interpretation: Fan Tracery, Unitarian Church, Charleston, S. C. 550
   Picture: Fan Tracery, Unitarian Church, Charleston, S. C. 551

POETRY:
   Petition—*Pugh* 553
   The Word of God to Leyden Came—*Rankin* 553
   Landing of the Pilgrim Fathers—*Hemans* 554
   God Makes a Path—*Williams* 555
   An Epitaph on My Dear and Ever Honoured Mother—*Bradstreet* 556
   The Nameless Saints—*Hale* 556
   New England Spires—*Clark* 557
   The Quiet Hour—*Pugh* 558

STORIES:
   The Story of the Mayflower Compact—arr. by *Snyder* 558
   Quaker Individualism—*Penn* 559
   The Search for a Personal God—*Williams* 560

MUSIC:
   Interpretation: O God, Beneath Thy Guiding Hand—*Bacon* 561
   Music: O God, Beneath Thy Guiding Hand—*Hatton* 562
   Interpretation: The Lord's My Shepherd—*Scottish Psalter* 562
   Music: The Lord's My Shepherd—*Havergal* 563

OLD BRICK CHURCH, SMITHFIELD, VIRGINIA

THE importance of St. Luke's Church, near Smithfield, Virginia, as a relic and as a symbol of America's religious heritage, can scarcely be overstated. It is the nation's oldest church.

America's national history began with the establishment of the first permanent colony at Jamestown, Virginia, in 1607. From this experiment the fundamental principles of religious faith and of English law and liberty were introduced into the New World. Democracy "sounded its barbaric yawp across the roof of the world" here in 1619 with the establishment of the House of Burgesses. "The most convenient place we could find to sit in," say the minutes of this meeting, "was the choir of the church where Sir George Yeardley, the governor, being set down in his accustomed place, those of the Council of State sat next to him."

Unfortunately, except for one ruined tower (itself younger than the Old Brick Church), all of the buildings of Jamestown Colony have disappeared. But, twenty-seven miles away, down and across the James River in the spreading settlement, there arose a monument to Christian faith in the form of a house of worship. "It is," said Thomas E. Tallmadge, "in many respects the most precious building in America."

The church was to serve Warrosquyoake Parish, in what is now Isle of Wight County, and is near present-day Smithfield. Its worshipers may have included some who remembered the baptism of Pocahontas in 1613, "The first fruits of the church in Virginia." There is a memorial window to the Reverend Alexander Whitaker, who administered the baptism and who married her to John Rolfe. Another window speaks of the Reverend Robert Hunt, who came over with the colonists and held the first service at Jamestown. Part of the original congregation probably consisted of survivors of the Indian massacre of 1622 that wiped out nearly one third of the Virginia setttlers and permanently affected the subsequent governmental and missionary policy of the Colonies.

The building went undamaged through Bacon's Rebellion in 1676. Following disestablishment of the Church of Virginia in 1785 it was used only occasionally. Around 1821 it was repaired and acquired its present name of St. Luke's. Later it was abandoned.

A summer storm in 1887 proved to be a blessing in disguise. Modern residents had come to doubt the antiquity of St. Luke's and its claim to be the nation's oldest church. Repairs of the heavy storm damage turned up two bricks, from the debris of the east gable, incised with the numerals 1632. These confirmed the recorded memory of Nathaniel Young, Clerk of the County, who had read of the construction in this year in the original vestry book. This and a second vestry book were buried for safekeeping during Lord Cornwallis' Virginia campaign, and the oldest volume perished in the damp. Among entries in the second book, well preserved, is one under date of October 11, 1737, authorizing that "Peter Woodward do re-shingle the Old Brick Church with good Cypress shingles of good substance and well nailed, for seven hundred pounds of tabacco [sic]."

A restoration campaign from 1887 to 1894 preserved the structure, and another beginning in 1954 prepared it for participation in the three hundred and fiftieth anniversary Jamestown Festival of 1957.

In artistic form, Old St. Luke's ties America's heritage firmly to the ideals of the English settlers. George Carrington Mason, historiographer of the Diocese of Southern Virginia and author of *Colonial Churches of Tidewater Virginia* (1945), depicts it as "Undeniably the only Gothic Colonial church in the United States." (See picture on page 547.) It reminds the traveler of some of the smaller sixteenth-century churches of England, particularly the one at Woodham Walter in Essex.

It is evident from this example that the first Virginia colonists designed their modest churches as much as possible in the image of the ones they had left at home. In that day the medieval style lingered as a living tradition. The builders of St. Luke's were either ignorant of Renaissance innovations or deliberately rejected them.

Typical Gothic buttresses support the walls of St. Luke's. The windows of the nave and tower show pointed arches and brick tracery. The square tower, Norman in its proportions, was probably battlemented at its crown; the abutting wall still retains this form of decoration. In his book, *Early American Architecture,* Hugh Morrison perceptively calls St. Luke's "The most convincingly Gothic church of the colonial period, its every detail speaking of the small parish churches of the late medieval period in England." The Old Brick Church on the Isle of Wight, off the south coast of England, was considered so typical an example of medieval religious architecture that it was used as the model of the Jamestown Brick Church which was reconstructed in 1907.

✠

TRINITY CHURCH, NEW YORK CITY

THE most venerable site devoted to the worship of God in New York City, and still in use, is that of Trinity Church, of which the original building was chartered in 1697 and the present structure, the third on the same spot, consecrated in 1846. Trinity Church still operates under the charter granted by King William III in 1697. "Old Trinity," as it is affectionately called, has played a leading part in the spiritual life of the changing city from colonial times to the present day.

Verrazano discovered New York's fine harbor in 1524, but Henry Hudson, who in 1609 explored the great river emptying into it, has given his name to the river. Peter Minuit, the director-general of New Netherland, as the territory was then called, is said to have given twenty-four dollars' worth

Photo by Samuel Chamberlain

OLD BRICK CHURCH, SMITHFIELD, VIRGINIA

of trinkets to the Indians in exchange for Manhattan Island in 1626, and the city of New Amsterdam was begun eight years later. The Dutch churches established in the next few years have now left lower Manhattan for new sites uptown.

When in 1664 the English took the city from the Dutch, and renamed it New York, they brought the Church of England with them, the early services for troops and settlers being held by army chaplains in the garrison church and the Dutch church. By 1696 the English inhabitants had started to erect a civilian church of their own just outside the city wall, and the next year procured for it a charter in which it is described as "a certaine church and steeple that hath been lately built within our said city of New Yorke, together with a certaine piece or parcell of ground, thereunto adjoyning scituate lyeing and beeing in or neere to a streete without the north gate of our said city commonly called and knowne by the name of the Broadway."

It was opposite what is now Wall Street, the present financial center, that the original sanctuary was erected—the site still occupied today. The Church faced the Hudson River. Its corporate organization was modeled upon that of St. Mary-le-Bow, London. Costs were met by popular subscription, supplemented in part by a patent or privilege "for certain wrecks and drift whales" from Governor Fletcher to the churchwardens. Still well within the colonial period, in 1737, the building was enlarged to the form shown in our picture (p. 549). Its "noble spire" was one hundred eighty feet in height, dominated the skyline from the river, and lasted until ravaged by fire during the Revolution in 1776, a fateful date.

The first rector, the Reverend William Vesey, served here over forty-eight years, the longest pastorate in Trinity's venerable history. This pattern of lengthy pastorates still holds, the rector in 1960 being only the thirteenth in over two hundred sixty years of history. Among precious antiquities is a silver "Baptismal Bason" given by their majesties William and Mary. It is now entering its second quarter of a millennium of use. Queen Anne gave the church a farm that is now invaluable city property, and its income across the years has financed incalculable good deeds and causes.

After the restoration and enlargement of Trinity Church in 1737 and the addition of a tall steeple, it was one of the largest in the Colonies, and although very plain, reflected some of the feeling for churchliness brought from England in this period of generally impoverished ecclesiastical architecture. Rich communion plate, to the number of seven pieces, was provided by Queen Anne in 1709 and is cherished today.

St. Paul's Chapel, opened in 1766 as the second daughter of Trinity Church, remains an unaltered example of the "Wren" type of building used after the Great Fire in 1666 in London, and so generally adopted in the new country that it is called "colonial." This chapel is the oldest public building of any kind in New York City, and a valuable relic of pre-Revolutionary architecture, made yet more interesting by the fact that it was used as the

TRINITY CHURCH, NEW YORK CITY

parish church from 1776 to 1790, and thus was regularly attended by George Washington as first President.

The second edifice for Trinity Church was built on the old site in 1790 in another variation of colonial architecture, but, proving too small and insecure, it was removed in 1840.

The third and present building, designed by Richard Upjohn, and completed in 1846, is one of the most successful attempts to return to true Gothic architecture, with the earliest ecclesiastical glass made in America. Memorials and extensions have enriched it as the years have passed.

The tall spire of Trinity Church in its colonial period cast a shadow of magnificent accomplishments which seems to grow with the years as later generations augmented the early beginnings. The founding of St. George's Chapel in 1752 (now St. George's Church, Stuyvesant Square), St. Paul's Chapel at Fulton Street and Broadway, Trinity School, King's College (now Columbia University), the French Église du St. Esprit, all in colonial days, and a dozen other chapels since then, as well as the responsibility for numbers of institutions and churches throughout the city and state, show Trinity Church's broad and developing interest in the community.

Meanwhile, though isolated in the downtown business area of New York, "Old Trinity" remains an active parish church with a ministry both to the people who work there during the week and to people who come in on Sundays from all parts of the city. It is the largest Episcopal Church parish in the nation, with more communicants, more clergy, more church buildings, more wealth, and more Sunday and weekday services than any other parish—or some whole dioceses. Past and present are joined in a slogan that aptly expresses the spirit of Trinity Church, "Evangelical Truth, Apostolic Order, and Ecumenical Concern."

✝

FAN TRACERY, UNITARIAN CHURCH, CHARLESTON, S. C.

BEFORE the colonial era reached its end with the Declaration of Independence, the Unitarian Church in historic and cultured Charleston, South Carolina, erected a building with features of artistic embellishment unknown in America in that day. The original church structure arose about 1772. Some uncertainty surrounds the date, because during the Civil War (1861-65) records were taken to Columbia in an effort at safekeeping, only to be lost when the tragedy of conflict resulted in the burning of that city.

The exterior of the building of today presents a somewhat quaint and even somber appearance, for the new portions are themselves well over a century old and many elements are original. Important for our concern is the fact, recorded in the *Charleston Courier* of April 3, 1854, that the existing structure retains the principal features of the building of the colonial era, "due to a natural regard and respect for time-honored associations, rather than

Courtesy The Vestry of the Unitarian Church, Charleston, S. C.

FAN TRACERY, UNITARIAN CHURCH, CHARLESTON, S. C.

to any considerations of mere economy. . . ." Indeed, only deep devotion has preserved for us today this unique example of elaborate architectural beauty in the service and praise of God, for the record says, "The difficulties surmounted in perforating the faithful old masonry to admit the new and lofty windows, and of encompassing the ancient massive tower to build one far more lofty and imposing" were great.

Our picture (page 551) portrays the most striking feature, the ceiling of the nave. It is an inspiring example of that peculiar Gothic work styled "fan tracery." Here delicate enrichments of almost numberless arches intersecting each other in every direction, and gracefully falling pendants, are filled with the richest tracery, imparting to the whole interior an exceedingly gorgeous appearance.

The groins of the ceiling are supported by shafts attached to the sturdy but delicate-appearing columns. Between these columns at the end are flat arches, the spandrels of which are filled with cusped work, surmounted by a light cast-iron railing of related design. This rail (see bottom of picture) forms the gallery front.

The over-all style is Gothic Perpendicular, and the most notable feature of the exterior is the buttressed tower, through the base of which is the principal entrance to the church. The form of it is square, with eight buttresses rising in successive stages, paneled and surmounted with pinnacles richly covered with crockets (ornaments resembling curved foliage). Above the entrance spacious stained-glass windows open on the organ loft. Succeeding tiers of windows with richly decorated heads mount the tower. At the four angles of the summit rise lofty pinnacles crowned with enriched crockets and finials; each finial bears a vane in the shape of a pennant, a form frequently used in English churches of the period.

The beautiful tracery pattern extends to every principal area of the church. A tall archway opens upon the pulpit recess, the splayed jambs of which are filled with this Gothic design. In the rear of this recess is the great east window.

The furniture of the church from the time of its completion was in conformity with the rich artistry already depicted. The pulpit was old solid walnut; the pews, fallery, rail, and other features were capped with the same wood. A reporter proudly recorded, at that time, "The whole church is lit with gas."

One cannot look upon the startling wizardry of this house of worship and fail to have his thoughts made akin to the reach, the beauty, and noble purpose which it portrays.

PETITION

Thou compassionate Creator,
Help me to be understanding
Of those I meet
And to listen quietly
To those who have to share
Their burdens
With someone.

Help me to remember
To learn why
People are troubled
Rather than to be critical of them
Because they are.

It is so easy to forget,
It is also easy to call on Thee.
Grant me strength
And understanding
This day,
Dear Lord.*

Amen.

—*Samuel F. Pugh*

THE WORD OF GOD TO LEYDEN CAME

The word of God to Leyden came,
    Dutch town by Zuyder Zee:
Rise up, my children of no name,
    My kings and priests to be.
There is an empire in the West,
    Which I will soon unfold;
A thousand harvests in her breast,
    Rocks ribbed with iron and gold.

Rise up, my children, time is ripe!
    Old things are passed away.
Bishops and kings from earth I wipe;
    Too long they've had their day.
A little ship have I prepared
    To bear you o'er the seas;
And in your souls my will declared
    Shall grow by slow degrees.

Beneath my throne the martyrs cry;
    I hear their voice, How long?
It mingles with their praises high,
    And with their victor song.
The thing they longed and waited for,
    But died without the sight;

* From *Between-Time Meditations* by Samuel F. Pugh, p. 24. Copyright 1954 by Bethany Press. Used by permission of the author and the publisher.

So, this shall be! I wrong abhor,
   The world I'll now set right.

Leave, then, the hammer and the loom,
   You've other work to do;
For Freedom's commonwealth there's room,
   And you shall build it too.
I'm tired of bishops and their pride,
   I'm tired of kings as well;
Henceforth I take the people's side,
   And with the people dwell.

Tear off the miter from the priest,
   And from the king, his crown;
Let all my captives be released;
   Lift up, whom men cast down.
Their pastors let the people choose,
   And choose their rulers too;
Whom they select, I'll not refuse,
   But bless the work they do.

The Pilgrims rose, at this, God's word,
   And sailed the wintry seas:
With their own flesh nor blood conferred,
   Nor thought of wealth or ease.
They left the towers of Leyden town,
   They left the Zuyder Zee:
And where they cast their anchor down,
   Rose Freedom's realm to be.*

                    —*Jeremiah Eames Rankin*

LANDING OF THE PILGRIM FATHERS

The breaking waves dashed high
   On the stern and rock-bound coast,
And the woods, against a stormy sky,
   Their giant branches tossed;

And the heavy night hung dark
   The hills and waters o'er,
When a band of exiles moored their bark
   On the wild New England shore.

Not as the conqueror comes,
   They, the true-hearted, came:
Not with the roll of the stirring drums,
   And the trumpet that sings of fame;

Not as the flying come,
In silence and in fear,—
They shook the depths of the desert's gloom
With their hymns of lofty cheer.

Amidst the storm they sang,
And the stars heard, and the sea;
And the sounding aisles of the dim woods rang
To the anthem of the free!

The ocean-eagle soared
From his nest by the white wave's foam,
And the rocking pines of the forest roared:
This was their welcome home!

There were men with hoary hair
Amidst that pilgrim band;
Why had they come to wither there
Away from their childhood's land?

There was woman's fearless eye,
Lit by her deep love's truth;
There was manhood's brow, serenely high,
And the fiery heart of youth.

What sought they thus afar?
Bright jewels of the mine?
The wealth of seas, the spoils of war?—
They sought a faith's pure shrine!

Aye, call it holy ground,
The soil where first they trod!
They have left unstained what there they found—
Freedom to worship God!*

—*Felicia Hemans*

GOD MAKES A PATH

God makes a path, provides a guide,
And feeds in wilderness!
His glorious name while breath remains,
O that I may confess.

Lost many a time, I have had no guide,
No house, but hollow tree!
In stormy winter night no fire,
No food, no company:

* *Ibid.,* pp. 57-58.

In him I found a house, a bed,
  A table, company:
No cup so bitter, but's made sweet,
  When God shall sweet'ning be.*

—*Roger Williams*

AN EPITAPH ON MY DEAR AND EVER HONOURED MOTHER

Mrs. Dorothy Dudley, Who Deceased December 27, 1643, and of Her Age 61

Here lies

A worthy matron of unspotted life,
A loving mother, and obedient wife,
A friendly neighbor, pitiful to poor,
Whom oft she fed and clothèd with her store;
To servants wisely awful, but yet kind,
And as they did so they reward did find;
A true instructor of her family,
The which she ordered with dexterity;
The public meetings ever did frequent,
And in her closet constant hours she spent;
Religious in all her words and ways,
Preparing still for death till end of days;
Of all her children children lived to see,
Then dying, left a blessed memory.**

—*Anne Bradstreet*

THE NAMELESS SAINTS

I

What was his name? I do not know his name.
I only know he heard God's voice and came,
  Brought all he had across the sea
  To live and work for God and me;
    Felled the ungracious oak;
    Dragged from the soil
    With horrid toil
  The thrice-gnarled roots and stubborn rock;
With plenty piled the haggard mountain-side;
And at the end, without memorial, died.
No blaring trumpets sounded out his fame,
He lived—he died—I do not know his name.

* *Ibid.,* p. 72.
** From *American Poetry and Prose,* edited by Norman Foerster, pp. 38-39. Copyright 1934 by Houghton Mifflin Company. Used by permission of the publisher.

II

No form of bronze and no memorial stones
Show me the place where lie his mouldering bones.
 Only a cheerful city stands
 Builded by his hardened hands.
  Only ten thousand homes
   Where every day
   The cheerful play
 Of love and hope and courage comes.
These are his monument, and these alone.
There is no form of bronze and no memorial stone.

III

And I?
Is there some desert or some pathless sea
Where Thou, Good God of angels, wilt send me?
 Some rock for me to rend; some sod,
  Some rock for me to break;
  Some handful of His corn to take
  And scatter far afield,
  Till it, in turn, shall yield
   Its hundredfold
   Of grains of gold
 To feed the waiting children of my God?
Show me the desert, Father, or the sea.
Is it Thine enterprise? Great God, send me.
And though this body lie where ocean rolls,
Count me among all Faithful Souls.*

—Edward Everett Hale

NEW ENGLAND SPIRES

 England grew small for them and cramped,
 These Pilgrims by a dream possessed,
 Who followed over alien lands
 The soul's inexorable quest.
 Bleak their lot and gaunt, yet, still
 Upon the shores they trod,
 Unwavering, their steeples point
 To far frontiers of God.**

—Leslie Savage Clark

---

* From *The World's Great Religious Poetry* by Caroline Hill, p. 631. Copyright 1923 by The Macmillan Company. Used by permission of the publisher.
** From *The Christian Century.* Used by permission of the author and Christian Century Foundation.

THE QUIET HOUR

The secret place is a holy place
    Where God and man commune,
Where if we see him face to face
    He puts each life in tune.

The quiet hour is a lovely hour,
    Apart from noise and din,
As we talk with him we find new power,
    And rid our lives of sin.

The morning time is a timely time
    To set one's tastes a-tone
So what we do all day will rhyme
    With God—and God alone.

The evening prayer is a sacred prayer,
    A time to reminisce,
Evaluate, then lay each care,
    On Him—and sleep in bliss!*

—Samuel F. Pugh

✠

THE STORY OF THE MAYFLOWER COMPACT
Karl E. Snyder

SEATED around the oaken table in the great cabin of the *Mayflower,* the group of men stirred and shifted with relief. At the head of the table sat Master John Carver, governor of the colony, gathering together a sheaf of papers, sanding them to dry the ink. Elder Brewster, sitting on the governor's right, cleared his throat and gently spoke.

"Methinks we ought at this time to thank God for being with us in our deliberations bearing so weightily on the future of our colony. Let us then bow our hearts before the Almighty in silent thanksgiving for His guidance in the preparation of our charter."

The men of the Pilgrims followed the gentle admonition of the well-loved Elder, each in his place around the table. Beside Elder Brewster sat Samuel Fuller, the physician of the company. Next to him was Master Hopkins. At the foot of the table sat the armed protector of the band, Captain Miles Standish. On the other side of the table were John Alden, Gilbert Winslow, and William Bradford, the lieutenant-governor of Plymouth.

As the Elder spoke "Amen," Carver leaned toward Bradford saying,

* From *Between-Time Meditations* by Samuel F. Pugh, p. 59. Copyright 1954 by Bethany Press. Used by permission of the author and the publisher.

"Prithee read aloud to us once more, Master Bradford, our compact in its final form."

Bradford, in whose hand the paper was written, inclined his head to the governor, rose from his seat, took the paper, and read:

"In the name of God, Amen. We whose names are underwritten, the loyall subjects of our dread soveraigne Lord, King James, by the grace of God, of Great Britaine, France, and Ireland, king, defender of the faith, etc., haveing undertaken, for the glorie of God, and advancemente of the Christian faith, and the honour of our king and countrie, a voyage to plant the first colonie in the Northerne parts of Virginia, doe by these presents solemnly and mutualy in the presence of God, and one of another, covenant and combine our selves togeather into a civill body politick, for our better ordering and preservation and furtherance of the ends aforesaid; and by virtue hereof doe enact, constitute, and frame, such just and equal lawes, ordinances, acts, constitutions, and officies, from time to time, as shall be thought most meete and convenient for the generall good of the Colonie, unto which we promise all due submission and obedience. In witnes whereof we have hereunto subscribed our names at Cap-Codd the 11. of November, in the year of the raigne of our soveraigne lord, King James, of England, France, and Ireland, the eighteenth, and of Scotland the fiftie fourth. Ano: Dom. 1620."*

As he closed his reading, Master Carver spoke. " 'Tis a worthy piece of work. Let us hope that it lives long to direct the ways of our colony under God's rule."

✛

QUAKER INDIVIDUALISM
William Penn

William Penn, dressed in the quiet Quaker gray, sat staring meditatively out through the narrow barred window of his cell in the Tower of London. In 1675 it was not considered proper to oppose the Established Church either in the performance of its ceremonious rites or in the articles of its faith. But Penn had done both and was in prison.

Before him on his rough table lay a few sheets of paper; his quill pen stood in the shot box beside the inkpot and the sand shaker. The paper held jotted exercises of his solitude, the beginnings of an interpretation and defense of his doctrine that combined, in a peculiarly Quaker way, common sense with spiritual elevation.

As Penn picked up the first of the loose sheets, he read:

NOTHING more shows the low condition man is fallen into than the unsuitable notion we must have of God, by the ways we take to please him. As if it availed anything to him that we performed so many ceremonies and external forms of devotion, who never meant more by them than to try our obedience,

* The text of this famous document, here given exactly, is available in many histories.

and, through them, to show us something more excellent and durable beyond them. Doing, while we are undoing, is good for nothing.

Of what benefit is it to say our prayers regularly, go to church, receive the sacraments, and maybe go to confessions too; ay, feast the priest, and give alms to the poor, and yet lie, swear, curse, be drunk, covetous, unclean, proud, revengeful, vain and idle at the same time? Can one excuse or balance the other? Or will God think himself well served, where his law is violated? Or well used, where there is so much more show than substance?

'Tis a most dangerous error for a man to think to excuse himself in the breach of a moral duty, by a formal performance of positive worship; and less when of human invention.

Our Blessed Saviour most rightly and clearly distinguished and determined this case when he told the Jews that they were his mother, his brethren and sisters, who did the will of his Father.*

✢

THE SEARCH FOR A PERSONAL GOD
Roger Williams

Roger Williams, harried from the Massachusetts Bay Colony by a theocratic government which demanded unquestioning obedience to its dictates, found his refuge in the wilderness where he could meet with his God in a completely personal relationship. His attempts to work out his spiritual foundation were recorded in letters to a friend of long standing. These private meditations so moved his friend that they were made public and received with enthusiasm. Williams was then persuaded to record his search for God in a book so that his individual approach to God could benefit other persons. In the introductory letter to this book, Williams addresses the reader concerning his experiments in search of the spiritual life:

As it is in the earthly, so it is in the heavenly marriage of a poor sinner to his Maker. There is first a private kindling of love and a private consent and promise, which sometimes are long, before the open solemnity and the public profession of a married life together. This is my present design, not to controvert the matters of public order and worship, but to present some poor experiments of those personal excellencies of each true believing soul and spirit.

'Tis true all public and private Christian spirits pretend the spirit of holiness; yea, how great a part of the world pretend to be Christendom, the Christian world that is anointed with the Spirit of Christ Jesus. But if it was death in Moses' rites to counterfeit that ceremonial and figurative ointment, what shall it be to counterfeit the Spirit of life and holiness itself? What I believe, therefore, as David and Paul once spake, I freely speak. Yea, who can but speak, saith Peter and John, the things they have seen and heard?

* Abridged by Karl E. Snyder from *More Fruits of Solitude* by William Penn. *The Harvard Classics,* Vol. I, pp. 405-406. Copyright 1910 by P. F. Collier & Son.

My scope is to fill each truly Christian soul with triumphing and rejoicing. I speak peace and joy to the weakest lamb and child in Christianity that is so low, so weak, so little, so poor in its own eyes, that it sometimes saith it hath no Christ, no Spirit, no faith, no love, no, nor true desire in itself. To this poor weak one I speak peace and joy, and say that this spiritual poverty is blessed and is the first step or round of that spiritual ladder, "Blessed are the poor in spirit, for theirs is the kingdom of heaven." Secondly, I sound joyful alarms of encouragement to the strong to grow, as Peter exhorteth, in the grace and knowledge of the Lord Jesus.

I end, dear Christian, with the proposal of two Christian knots or riddles, not unsuitable to these present times and spirits. First, why is the heart of a David himself more apt to decline from God upon the mountain of joy, deliverance, victory, prosperity, than in the dark vale of the shadow of death, persecution, sickness, adversity? Secondly, why is it, since God worketh freely in us to do and to will of his own good pleasure, that yet he is pleased to command us to work out our own salvation with fear and trembling? Let us all humbly beg the Spirit of the Lord to untie these knots for us.*

✠

O GOD, BENEATH THY GUIDING HAND

THIS is a hymn which with swift and sure understanding gives vivid expression to the splendor of our Pilgrim heritage. Here is felt the pathos, the daring, the devoutness of "our exiled fathers" as, guided by God, they crossed the sea and established themselves on this "wintry strand." Here, too, is the sturdy conviction that prayer and praise must forever be central in the heart of America. The first gifts our fathers gave us—laws, freedom, truth, faith in God—are still the best gifts. It must be the hope and prayer of every generation of Americans that their great people shall adore His name "Till these eternal hills remove, and spring adorns the earth no more."

The author of the hymn, the Reverend Dr. Leonard Bacon (1802-1881) was himself of pioneering stock. His father had trekked from Connecticut to Detroit, leading his seventeen-year-old wife on horseback, to preach to the Indians of Michigan. After the father's untimely death, Leonard returned to New England and put himself through Yale College and Andover Theological Seminary. Throughout his life he maintained interest both in missionary work and in hymns. In 1823, while still a student in Andover, he published a small collection of *Hymns and Sacred Songs,* the first effort in America to provide missionary hymns for use in the rapidly expanding activities of the evangelical churches.

His great work on hymns, published in 1845, was called *Psalms and Hymns, for Christian Use and Worship.* This massive work contained 705 hymns and 498 metrical Psalms. Dr. Bacon was chairman of the editorial committee and

* Abridged by Karl E. Snyder from *Experiments of Spiritual Life and Health* by Roger Williams, pp. 39-41. Published 1951 by Westminister Press.

O God, Beneath Thy Guiding Hand*

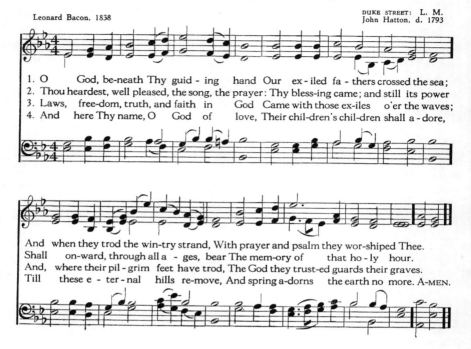

Leonard Bacon, 1838

DUKE STREET: L. M.
John Hatton, d. 1793

1. O   God, be-neath Thy guid - ing   hand Our ex - iled fa - thers crossed the sea;
2. Thou heardest, well pleased, the song, the prayer: Thy bless-ing came; and still its power
3. Laws,   free-dom, truth, and faith in   God Came with those ex-iles   o'er the waves;
4. And   here Thy name, O   God of   love, Their chil-dren's chil-dren shall a - dore,

And when they trod the win-try strand, With prayer and psalm they wor-shiped Thee.
Shall   on-ward, through all a - ges, bear The mem-ory of   that ho - ly hour.
And, where their pil - grim feet have trod, The God they trust-ed guards their graves.
Till   these e - ter-nal   hills re-move, And spring a-dorns the earth no more. A-MEN.

*From *The Hymnbook*. Used by permission of Westminster Press.

wrote five of the hymns. This book became the true successor to Timothy Dwight's 1801 edition of Isaac Watts' *The Psalms of David*.

"O God, Beneath Thy Guiding Hand" was written in 1833 for the two hundreth anniversary of the founding of the city of New Haven, celebrated in 1838 in the Center (Congregational) Church, New Haven, of which he was minister from 1825 to 1866. From 1866 to 1881 he was professor and lecturer in Yale Divinity School.

The familiar tune, "Duke Street," to which other words are sometimes sung, first appeared in 1793 in *A Select Collection of Psalm and Hymn Tunes*, Glasgow. John Hatton, the composer, gave the tune the name of the street on which he lived in the English town of St. Helens.

✠

THE LORD'S MY SHEPHERD

THAT the first book printed on the American continent north of the Rio Grande should have been the *Bay Psalm Book* of 1640, indicates the importance of the Metrical Psalter in Christian worship in the early history of America. Indeed, for nearly a century and a quarter, only Psalms were sung for church worship in the English-speaking colonies. In the churches which followed the train of the Reformers, the Lutherans used free hymns.

John Calvin, however, had insisted that only words of Scripture be used in song, and that the translations should be as close and accurate as possible. The result was that whether in Scotland, England, or in the Colonies, the Reformed Churches became Psalm-singers. Even in the Church of England the metrical psalms were commonly bound up with copies of the Bible and

The Lord's My Shepherd*

From Psalm 23
Scottish Psalter, 1650

EVAN: C. M.
William H. Havergal, 1846

1. The Lord's my Shep-herd, I'll not want; He makes me down to lie
2. My soul He doth re - store a - gain; And me to walk doth make
3. Yea, though I walk in death's dark vale, Yet will I fear none ill;
4. My ta - ble Thou hast fur - nish - ed In pres-ence of my foes;
5. Good-ness and mer - cy all my life Shall sure - ly fol - low me;

In pas-tures green; He lead-eth me The qui - et wa - ters by.
With - in the paths of right-eous-ness, E'en for His own name's sake.
For Thou art with me; and Thy rod And staff me com - fort still.
My head Thou dost with oil a-noint, And my cup o - ver-flows.
And in God's house for - ev-er-more My dwell-ing place shall be. A-MEN.

*From The Hymnbook. Used by permission of Westminster Press.

the *Book of Common Prayer*. So well-established was psalm-singing in New England, that the *Bay Psalm Book* reigned supreme for more than a century.

Since most current hymnbooks print such a small number of metrical psalms, they effectively conceal the importance of the Psalter in the colonial period of American history. A true understanding of the Church in the Colonies, however, can only be had through awareness of this fascinating and important chapter in American Church history.

The Psalm selected to represent this period is the favorite metrical version of the Twenty-third Psalm, first printed in the Scottish Psalter of 1650. It is easy to see why the early settlers delighted in this version: the poetry is almost prose; only slight changes have been made in the order of words, leaving the text almost as we have learned it in the Bible; it is "close-fitting," that is, there is no profane tinkering with the sacred text; it is Bible as Bible, and therefore truly inspired.

The tune "Evan" was made by Lowell Mason from a longer one by William Henry Havergal, an English clergyman and musician (1793-1870).

CONTENTS

PART V SECTION 2

THE CHURCH ON THE FRONTIER: THE EARLY WEST

───────────────────✠───────────────────

Herein is my Father glorified, that ye bear much fruit; so shall ye be my disciples.—II JOHN 15:8

───────────────────✠───────────────────

PICTURES: PAGE
Interpretation: Congregational Meetinghouse, Oberlin, Ohio 565
Picture: Congregational Meetinghouse, Oberlin, Ohio 567
Interpretation: Quaker Meetinghouse, Richmond, Indiana—*Mote* 566
Picture: Quaker Meetinghouse, Richmond, Indiana—*Mote* 569
Interpretation: Wood Carving of The Last Supper, St. Louis, Missouri
  —*Lang* 570
Picture: Wood Carving of The Last Supper, St. Louis, Missouri—*Lang* .. 571

POETRY:
Why?—*Pugh* 572
To a Waterfowl—*Bryant* 573
My Church—*Author Unknown* 573
The Problem—*Emerson* 574
A Forest Hymn—*Bryant* 575
I Never Saw a Moor—*Dickinson* 576
Evening—*Doane* 576

STORIES:
Winter, Stoves, and the Meetinghouse—*Goodrich* 576
Prayer and Creeds—*Emerson* 578
Move to Indiana—*Tippy* 579

MUSIC:
Interpretation: My Faith Looks Up to Thee—*Palmer* 582
Music: My Faith Looks Up to Thee—*Mason* 583
Interpretation: Saviour! Thy Dying Love—*Phelps* 584
Music: Saviour! Thy Dying Love—*Lowry* 585

CONGREGATIONAL MEETINGHOUSE, OBERLIN, OHIO

THE embargo of 1808 and the War of 1812 created a depression which sent settlers in swarms seeking a new life in the West. The roads thronged with people and their possessions. A record in one village of Pennsylvania which lay on the road to Pittsburgh states that in a single day in 1811 there passed through it enroute to Ohio 236 wagons and 600 Merino sheep. Old settlers in central New York declared that they had never seen "so many teams, and sleighs loaded with women, children, and household goods" on their way to Ohio as in the winter of 1814. "All America," said a European observer in 1817, "seems to be breaking up and moving westward." Indiana was admitted to the Union in 1816 with a population of 63,897—42,000 of whom arrived in that year!

The Ohio River was the greatest highway westward, filling southern Ohio; but the New England peoples pushed along the shores of Lake Erie to occupy the "Western Reserve." The Buckeye State in 1820 was fifth in population in all the nation.

The solid homogeneity of Congregationalism as a church system in New England enabled many Western Reserve towns to assume that one church would serve all the religious needs. "The Congregational Church of Christ at Oberlin," formally established in 1834, was the only religious society there until the fifties. The famous Eastern revivalist, Charles G. Finney, was called as pastor and remained to serve not only in this capacity but also as the developer of Oberlin College.

The center and capitol of the community, and the most important college building, was the "meetinghouse." It housed the church, but it was not alone a church; it was the gathering place for all members of a fully integrated society such as is seldom seen today, for it was the symbol of the high moral purpose which dominated the town.

The meetinghouse, when erected in 1842, was the largest public building west of the Allegheny Mountains. In both design and construction it was an amazing demonstration of practical democracy. An architect's plan was contributed by a Boston friend, but it was liberally revised by vote of the church members. They decreed that the tower should follow a certain drawing in "Benjamin's Architect."

As with medieval cathedrals, the meetinghouse was built with the offerings of material and labor from the people of the community. Oberlin masons, teamsters, blacksmiths, tinsmiths, carpenters, and cabinetmakers donated part or all of their time. Others gave bricks, stone, timber, hardware, and paint. The acknowledgments of gifts list money (usually a dollar or two from each person) and also twelve pounds of nails, a hat, a cheese, four bushels of apples, a barrel of flour, a one-horse wagon, and two cows from residents of Medina. Most of these articles, of course, would have to be sold or exchanged in order to apply them on the building. This was not impractical, for old records show

that, on one occasion, the college paid "one hat" to have a stone quarried and delivered.

There were two preaching services every Sunday, one in the morning and one in the afternoon. All the people came, Negro and white, and filled the house to overflowing. Many families sat in their assigned pews between the great black stoves that stood sentry on either side near the windows. College students crowded the circling balcony. The sermons might last an hour or two, prayers perhaps half as long. The bass viol or the organ (after 1855) accompanied the hymns from Mason's and Hastings' songbooks.

Commencement exercises were held here, as were affairs of the Oberlin Musical Association. An ambitious oratorio was performed in 1852, the accompaniment including a piano, a melodeon, two flutes, two violins, a cello, a violone, a horn and a drum. Panoramic paintings were displayed here —one of Niagara Falls in 1853. The community fire engine was housed in the basement. Oberlin was a center of anti-slavery sentiment and a station on the underground railroad. Of twenty-one Oberlin citizens jailed at Cleveland in 1859 for assisting a fugitive slave, one was the superintendent of the Sunday school and another the college professor of moral and mental philosophy.

The meetinghouse today (see page 567) is the only building remaining from Oberlin's first generation. It continues to re-echo to the call to sacrificial service and human justice. At a stone's throw stands a beautiful memorial arch to the fourteen Oberlin College students who lost their lives while serving as Christian missionaries at the time of the Boxer Rebellion.

A professor of history at Oberlin College writes, "The voice of Oberlin-in-its-youth still echoes from the walls of the old meetinghouse. It is a decisive voice with no captious quaverings, a voice of hope and not of cynicism, a brave voice, a fighting voice, a voice that speaks in no uncertain terms for decent justice for all humanity, for a righteousness unlimited by convenience, for the brotherhood of all races and all colors of mankind. It is not a voice of consolation but a voice of alarm. It cries out in indignant anger against all tyrants and all forms of slavery."

✛

QUAKER MEETINGHOUSE, RICHMOND, INDIANA
Marcus Mote

WITH inspired art equal in accuracy to a photography at that time not yet invented, this painting depicts an annual gathering of Quakers in the Midwest.

The painting, its maker, and his fellow church members must be considered together. The Society of Friends (the proper name for Quakers) with a belief in the Inner Light as their basic principle, appealed for simplicity in religion.

CONGREGATIONAL MEETINGHOUSE, OBERLIN, OHIO

Dress, food, deportment, as well as church worship and properties, were to be "plain." Art and embellishment were temptations to the frivolous in man, dangerous to his spirit.

But the rich genius for art born in Marcus Mote, Quaker, was not to be denied. At the age of two and a half he drew a charcoal picture on the footboard of his parents' bed, a "mischief" deplored by them. With brushes he made from the hair of squirrel tails and color from the woods or his mother's bluing bag, he worked onward. All his life from the age of twenty-three he was a full-time professional artist—and almost always against the opposition of his Quaker companions, whom he loved and refused to leave.

When only twenty, Mote attended the Indiana Yearly Meeting of Friends at Richmond in 1837, making sketches of some leaders. Probably he never missed a yearly meeting thereafter. Established families, including Quakers, called on him for portraits over four decades. At the Yearly Meeting in 1844 he made the first version of the painting that we see on page 569. It preserves for us the Quaker demand for plainness in church construction, and complete lack of decoration. The variety of conveyances then in use is portrayed. Since the painting aroused a continuing interest, the artist did an enlarged version of it much later in life, in 1885. This later picture is now the property of Earlham College, Richmond, Indiana, from which the reproduction was made especially for this book.

The 1844 Meeting was a crucial one, with some of its abolitionist members withdrawing. In that year the Baptist and Methodist bodies split over slavery, soon to be followed in similar action by the Presbyterians. You see near the center of this painting a man in white breeches and white stockings. This was John Pease, a visiting English Friend who was sent to confer with American brethren on this volatile topic. The artist here shows him conversing with Elijah Coffin, Clerk of the Meeting, and the noted minister, Jeremiah Hubbard, said to be part Indian, who towers head and shoulders above them. While attention is caught by the characteristic costumes of the day, and the plain but adequate carriages of a not unprosperous Quaker community, the picture is dominated by the severely plain meetinghouse, symbol of man's unadorned nature.

The creator of this painting persisted in the "mischief" of his art despite the frowns of his plain Friends. When he was nominated as Clerk of the Quarterly Meeting at Waynesville, Ohio, the opposition to his un-Quakerly profession came to a focus. He would have been disowned but for the intercession of one weighty member. Gradually the opposition subsided and he continued to make a living from his art, principally through teaching and painting portraits.

Growing recognition came from four huge panoramas, a form of picture sequence which enjoyed a vogue in the latter half of the nineteenth century. His first work of this kind illustrated the popular book, *Uncle Tom's Cabin.* His next was in forty scenes, each nine by fifteen feet, on "Paradise Lost and

QUAKER MEETINGHOUSE, RICHMOND, INDIANA—MOTE

570 THE CHURCH AND THE FINE ARTS

Regained." Another of equal extent was on "The Geological History of
the Course of Creation," an effort to reconcile the Biblical account and
scientific discoveries. His last panorama was on "The Progress of Intemperance." Some of these were exhibited during Yearly Meeting and helped to
win favor for art among the Quakers.

Rhoda, his wife, with whom he had an un-Quakerly elopement (for which
both had to make "satisfaction" before their respective Monthly Meetings)
was first a Quaker and second his wife, thus having a deep inner conflict.
Marcus was first an artist and second a Quaker, the one eternally in opposition
to the other, each an indestructible part of his personality. Oddly enough,
except for his championing of art he was thoroughly conservative. He opposed
music in the church, a paid ministry, and evangelistic preaching. He aided
the temperance cause. Opal Thornburg, noted Quaker historian, says that
a final glimpse of him epitomizes the Quaker, the artist, and the "human
weakness." In his old age he would come down fom his Main Street studio
in Richmond in a gaudy coat such as he thought an artist might wear, topped
by a Quaker hat, and in his progress along the pavement he took sardonic
delight in greeting embarrassed Friends with a "How does thee do?"

✝

WOOD CARVING OF THE LAST SUPPER, ST. LOUIS, MISSOURI
Alois Lang

DEVOUT German Christians suffered much for their faith in the homeland
of the Reformation, and large numbers of them fled to colonial America,
aided by William Penn. When the first great western migration pressed
into what are now our Midwestern states, new wars in Germany drove out
more of her best people in a renewed search for freedom of worship. Today
great Midwestern cities like St. Louis, Cincinnati, and Milwaukee can be
known fully only if one understands the Germanic, largely Lutheran strain
which entered into their growth and culture.

High among the crafts, skills, and concerns of the gifted German people
was a love for art, especially in its plastic forms. Something about the north-
land gave significance to sculpture and carving. These were forms of expression appropriate and "at home" outdoors or within, solid representations
of a firm faith. Granite hills and heavy forests lent their very substance to
rugged but sensitive hands among these craftsmen, who dotted the hills of
northern Europe with massive stone castles and decorated them within
with beautiful wood carvings. The Midwest garnered the treasure of this
inheritance.

Early in the twentieth century the Mount Calvary Lutheran Church of St.
Louis, Missouri, found itself ready for the expansion of its facilities for
worship. It was only natural that thought should turn toward a fitting symbol
for the focus of all eyes—the altar. And what is the chief honor of the

WOOD CARVING OF THE LAST SUPPER,
ST. LOUIS, MISSOURI—LANG

Christian altar, if it be not the environs of Holy Communion? A search began for an appropriate emblem.

The Lang family of the Oberammergau region of Germany has long been identified with the Passion play enacted there about every decade. Alois Lang, nephew of Anton Lang, the "Christus" of the famous play, was in the United States at the time. He was prevailed upon to execute what became then only the third hand-carved "Last Supper" in this country. It was patiently and reverently done in solid oak, carved in full relief, seven and one-half feet long, thirty inches high, and nine inches deep.

The arrangement of the subject, of course, is that given by that monumental genius of art and engineering in the Renaissance, Leonardo da Vinci, whose famous fresco still draws its throngs daily to the refectory of the church of Santa Maria della Grazie in Milan. I suggest that as Michelangelo's Sistine ceiling may be the greatest "epic"—fit to be compared in literature to the work of Dante; and Raphael's *Sistine Madonna* the greatest "hymn"—comparable to the gifts of Shakespeare; so is da Vinci's art, essentially tragic (such as his *Medusa,* and his curious *Mona Lisa*—perhaps reflecting the enigma of his unlettered mother), to be compared only to Goethe in the field of writing. Goethe was himself the epitome of the qualities of the German-American people whose descendants chose this art subject, perhaps unconsciously but quite naturally, to express their adoration.

With consummate art (see page 571), Leonardo has divided the number of characters into four groups of three each, every attitude and every motion of each character being made a contributing factor to heighten the plot. For identification of each of the disciples, see Interpretation of "The Last Supper" Window, page 38.

✠

WHY?

I don't discern divinity
Or translate things divine.
But there's a voice that speaks to me
And says, "O child, you're mine."

Nor am I versed in languages
Of lands across the sea.
Yet every nation seems a part
Of one fraternity.

If hate and bloodshed rightly say
That man's of little worth,
Why then did God first put us here
To live on this, His earth?

Oh, man is made for brotherhood
For love and work and play
And service to our fellow-man
And worship day by day.*

—*Samuel F. Pugh*

TO A WATERFOWL

Whither, midst falling dew,
While glow the heavens with the last steps of day,
Far, through their rosy depths, dost thou pursue
Thy solitary way?

Vainly the fowler's eye
Might mark thy distant flight to do thee wrong,
As, darkly painted on the crimson sky,
Thy figure floats along.

Seek'st thou the plashy brink
Of weedy lake, or marge of river wide,
Or where the rocking billows rise and sink
On the chafed ocean side?

There is a Power whose care
Teaches thy way along that pathless coast—
The desert and illimitable air—
Lone wandering, but not lost.

All day thy wings have fanned,
At that far height, the cold, thin atmosphere,
Yet stoop not, weary, to the welcome land,
Though the dark night is near.

And soon that toil shall end;
Soon shalt thou find a summer home, and rest,
And scream among thy fellows; reeds shall bend,
Soon, o'er thy sheltered nest.

Thou'rt gone, the abyss of heaven
Hath swallowed up thy form; yet, on my heart
Deeply hath sunk the lesson thou hast given,
And shall not soon depart.

He who, from zone to zone,
Guides through the boundless sky thy certain flight,
In the long way that I must tread alone,
Will lead my steps aright.

—*William Cullen Bryant*

MY CHURCH

On me nor Priest nor Presbyter nor Pope,
Bishop nor Dean may stamp a party name;

But Jesus, with His largely human scope,
    The service of my human life may claim.
Let prideful priests do battle about creeds,
    The church is mine that does most Christlike deeds.*

                         —Author Unknown

THE PROBLEM

I like a church; I like a cowl;
I love a prophet of the soul;
And on my heart monastic aisles
Fall like sweet strains, or pensive smiles;
Yet not for all his faith can see
Would I that cowlèd churchman be.
Why should the vest on him allure,
Which I could not on me endure? . . .
Out from the heart of nature rolled
The burdens of the Bible old; . . .
The hand that rounded Peter's dome
And groined the aisles of Christian Rome
Wrought in a sad sincerity:
Himself from God he could not free;
He builded better than he knew;—
The conscious stone to beauty grew. . . .

O'er England's abbeys bends the sky,
As on its friends, with kindred eye;
These wonders rose to upper air;
And Nature gladly gave them place,
Adopted them into her race. . . .

These temples grew as grows the grass;
Art might obey, but not surpass.
The passive Master lent his hand
To the vast soul that o'er him planned;
And the same power that reared the shrine
Bestrode the tribes that knelt within.
Ever the fiery Pentecost
Girds with one flame the countless host,
Trances the heart through chanting choirs,
And through the priest the mind inspires.
The word unto the prophet spoken
Was writ on tables yet unbroken; . . .
One accent of the Holy Ghost
The heedless world hath never lost.
I know what say the fathers wise,—
The Book itself before me lies,

* From *Masterpieces of Religious Verse*, edited by James Dalton Morrison, p. 485. Published in 1948 by Harper & Brothers.

Old *Chrysostom,* blest Augustine,
And he who blent both in his line,
The younger *Golden Lips* or mines,
Taylor, the Shakespeare of divines.
His words are music in my ear,
I see his cowlèd portrait dear;
And yet, for all his faith could see,
I would not the good bishop be.*

—*Ralph Waldo Emerson*

A FOREST HYMN

The groves were God's first temples. Ere man learned
To hew the shaft, and lay the architrave,
And spread the roof above them—ere he framed
The lofty vault, to gather and roll back
The sound of anthems; in the darkling wood,
And offered to the Mightiest solemn thanks
And supplication. For his simple heart
Might not resist the sacred influences
Which, from the stilly twilight of the place,
And from the gray old trunks that high in heaven
Mingled their mossy boughs, and from the sound
Of the invisible breath that swayed at once
All their green tops, stole over him, and bowed
His spirit with the thought of boundless power
And inaccessible majesty. Ah, why
Should we, in the world's riper years, neglect
God's ancient sanctuaries, and adore
Only among the crowd, and under roofs
That our frail hands have raised? Let me, at least,
Offer one hymn—thrice happy, if it find
Acceptance in His ear.

Father, thy hand
Hath reared these venerable columns, thou
Didst weave this verdant roof. Thou didst look down
Upon the naked earth, and, forthwith, rose
All these fair ranks of trees. They, in thy sun,
Budded, and shook their green leaves in thy breeze,
And shot toward heaven. The century-living crow
Whose birth was in their tops, grew old and died
Among their branches, till, at last, they stood,
As now they stand, massy, and tall, and dark,
Fit shrine for humble worshiper to hold
Communion with his Maker.**

—*William Cullen Bryant*

* From *American Poetry and Prose,* edited by Norman Foerster, p. 444. Copyright 1934 by Houghton
Mifflin Company. Used by permission of the publisher.
** Verses from *"A Forest Hymn."*

I NEVER SAW A MOOR

I never saw a moor,
I never saw the sea;
Yet know I how the heather looks,
And what a wave must be.

I never spoke with God,
Nor visited in heaven;
Yet certain am I of the spot
As if the chart were given.*

—*Emily Dickinson*

EVENING

Softly now the light of day
Fades upon my sight away;
Free from care, from labor free,
Lord, I would commune with Thee:

Thou, whose all-pervading eye,
   Naught escapes, without, within,
Pardon each infirmity,
   Open fault and secret sin.

Soon, for me, the light of day
Shall for ever pass away;
Then, from sin and sorrow free,
Take me, Lord, to dwell with Thee:

Thou, who, sinless, yet hast known
   All of man's infirmity;
Then, from Thine eternal throne,
   Jesus, look with pitying eye.

—*George Washington Doane*

✣

WINTER, STOVES, AND THE MEETINGHOUSE
Samuel Griswold Goodrich

ONE thing strikes me now with wonder, and that is, the general indifference, in those days, to the intensity of the winter. No doubt, as I have said before, the climate was then more severe; but be that as it may, people seemed to suffer less from it than at the present day. Nobody thought of staying at home from church because of the extremity of the weather. We had no thermometers, it is true, to frighten us with the revelation that it was twenty-five degrees below zero. The habits of the people were simple and hardy, and

* From *Masterpieces of Religious Verse,* edited by James Dalton Morrison, p. 380. Published in 1948 by Harper & Brothers.

there were few defenses against the assaults of the seasons. The houses were not tight; we had no stoves, no Lehigh or Lackawanna coal; yet we lived, and comfortably too; nay, we even changed burly winter into a season of enjoyment.

Let me tell you a story, by the way, upon the meetinghouses of those days. They were of wood, and slenderly built, of course admitting somewhat freely the blasts of the seasons. In the severe winter days, we only mitigated the temperature by foot-stoves; but these were deemed effeminate luxuries, suited to women and children. What would have been thought of Deacon Olmstead and Granther Baldwin, had they yielded to the weakness of a foot-stove!

The age of comfortable meetinghouses and churches, in county towns, was subsequent to this, some twenty or thirty years. All improvement is gradual, and frequently advances only by conflict with prejudice, and victory over opposition. In a certain county town within my knowledge, the introduction of stoves into the meetinghouse, about the year 1830, threatened to overturn society. The incident may be worth detailing, for trifles often throw light upon important subjects.

In this case, the metropolis, which we will call H., had adopted stoves in the churches, and naturally enough some people of the neighboring town of E. set about introducing this custom into the meetinghouse in their own village. Now, the two master-spirits of society—the Demon of Progress and the Angel of Conservatism—somehow or other had got into the place, and as soon as this reform was suggested, they began to wrestle with the people, until at last the church and society were divided into two violent factions— the Stove Party and the Anti-stove Party. At the head of the first was Mrs. Deacon K. and at the head of the latter was Mrs. Deacon P. The battle raged portentously, very much like the renowned tempest in a teapot. Society was indeed lashed into a foam. The minister, between the contending factions, scarcely dared to say his soul was his own. He could scarcely find a text from "Genesis to Jude," that might not commit him on one side or the other. The strife—of course—ran into politics, and the representative to the assembly got in by a happy knack at dodging the question in such wise as to be claimed by both parties.

Finally, the progressionists prevailed—the Stove Party triumphed, and the stoves were accordingly installed. Great was the humiliation of the Antistoveites; nevertheless, they concluded to be submissive to the dispensations of Providence. On the Sabbath succeeding the installation of the stoves, Mrs. Deacon P., instead of staying away, did as she ought, and went to church. As she moved up the broad aisle, it was remarked that she looked pale but calm, as a martyr should, conscious of injury, yet struggling to forgive. Nevertheless, when the minister named his text—Romans 12:20—and spoke about heaping coals of fire on the head—she slid from her seat, and subsided gently upon the floor. The train of ideas suggested was, in fact, too much for her heated brain and shattered nerves. Suddenly there was a rush to the pew, and the fainting lady was taken out. When she came to the air, she slightly revived.

"Pray what is the matter?" said Mrs. Deacon K., who bent over her, holding a smelling-bottle to her nose.

"Oh, it is the heat of those awful stoves," said Mrs. Deacon P.

"No, no, my dear," said Mrs. Deacon K.; "that can't be: it's a warm day, you know, and there's no fire in them."

"No fire in the stoves?" said Mrs. Deacon P.

"Not a particle," said Mrs. Deacon K.

"Well, I feel better now," said the poor lady; and so bidding her friends good-by, she went home, in a manner suited to the occasion.*

✛

PRAYER AND CREEDS
Ralph Waldo Emerson

IN WHAT prayers do men allow themselves! That which they call a holy office is not so much as brave and manly. Prayer looks abroad and asks for some foreign addition to come through some foreign virtue, and loses itself in endless mazes of natural and supernatural, and mediatorial and miraculous. Prayer that craves a particular commodity, anything less than all good, is vicious. Prayer is the contemplation of the facts of life from the highest point of view. It is the soliloquy of a beholding and jubilant soul. It is the spirit of God pronouncing his works good. But prayer as a means to effect a private end is meanness and theft. It supposes dualism and not unity in nature and consciousness. As soon as the man is at one with God, he will not beg. He will then see prayer in all action. The prayer of the farmer kneeling in his field to weed it, the prayer of the rower kneeling with the stroke of his oar, are true prayers heard throughout nature, though for cheap ends. Caratach, in Fletcher's *Bonduca,* when admonished to inquire the mind of the god Audate, replies,

> His hidden meaning lies in our endeavors;
> Our valors are our best gods.

Another sort of false prayers are our regrets. Discontent is the want of self-reliance: it is infirmity of will. Regret calamities if you can thereby help the sufferer; if not, attend your own work and already the evil begins to be repaired. Our sympathy is just as base. We come to them who weep foolishly and sit down and cry for company, instead of imparting to them truth and health in rough electric shocks, putting them once more in communication with their own reason. The secret of fortune is joy in our hands. Welcome evermore to gods and men is the self-helping man. For him all doors are

* From *Recollections of a Lifetime* by Samuel Griswold Goodrich.

flung wide; him all tongues greet, all honors crown, all eyes follow with desire. Our love goes out to him and embraces him because he did not need it. We solicitously and apologetically caress and celebrate him because he held on his way and scorned our disapprobation. The gods love him because men hated him. "To the persevering mortal," said Zoroaster, "the blessed Immortals are swift."

As men's prayers are a disease of the will, so are their creeds a disease of the intellect. They say with those foolish Israelites, "Let not God speak to us, lest we die. Speak thou, speak any man with us, and we will obey." Everywhere I am hindered of meeting God in my brother, because he has shut his own temple doors and recites fables merely of his brother's, or his brother's brother's God. Every new mind is a new classification. If it prove a mind of uncommon activity and power, a Locke, a Lavoisier, a Hutton, a Bentham, a Fourier, it imposes its classification on other men, and lo! a new system. In proportion to the depth of the thought, and so to the number of the objects it touches and brings within reach of the pupil, is his complacency. But chiefly is this apparent in creeds and churches, which are also classifications of some powerful mind acting on the elemental thought of duty and man's relation to the Highest. Such is Calvinism, Quakerism, Swedenborgism. The pupil takes the same delight in subordinating everything to the new terminology as a girl who has just learned botany in seeing a new earth and new seasons thereby. It will happen for a time that the pupil will find his intellectual power has grown by the study of his master's mind. But in all unbalanced minds the classification is idolized, passes for the end and not for a speedily exhaustible means, so that the walls of the system blend to their eye in the remote horizon with the walls of the universe; the luminaries of heaven seem to them hung on the arch their master built. They cannot imagine how you aliens have any right to see—how can you see; "It must be somehow that you stole the light from us." They do not yet perceive that light, unsystematic, indomitable, will break into any cabin, even into theirs. Let them chirp awhile and call it their own. If they are honest and do well, presently their neat new pinfold will be too strait and low, will crack, will lean, will rot and vanish, and the immortal light, all young, and joyful, million-orbed, million-colored, will beam over the universe as on the first morning.*

✛

MOVE TO INDIANA
Worth M. Tippy

WHEN the bishop [Robert R. Roberts of the Methodist Church] and his wife Elizabeth came from Philadelphia in the summer of 1816, they had settled upon Shenango as their permanent home; but a long journey to

* Abridged by Karl E. Snyder from *Self-Reliance*, as found in *American Poetry and Prose*, edited by Norman Foerster, pp. 512-13. Published 1934 by Houghton Mifflin Company.

the South convinced him that the future of the Church lay much farther
west and south, and that Shenango was too far north for the work he had to
do. It was near the Canadian border, at the foothills of the Allegheny Mountains and on the eastern border of the Mississippi Valley. Southern Indiana
was better located for his episcopal duties.

But he had other reasons. The soil at Shenango was not as fertile as he
had thought it to be. Southern Indiana was a bluegrass country, the growing
season was longer, and land was plentiful and cheap.

We know little except by inference of the long and anxious discussions
which led to the final decision to move to Indiana. It must have seemed to
Elizabeth that she should never have a settled home. When the fall conferences of 1817 were over, he and Elizabeth made a quick trip to Lawrence
County, Indiana, for her to see the country. They traveled on horseback and
took the southern route to the falls of the Ohio, and then the Vincennes
Trace to Mitchell.

After riding over the area, they selected a tract of land in the extreme
southeast corner of Lawrence County. It lay among the hills five miles
southwest of Bono. The village of Lawrenceport was not then in existence.
He could hardly have found a more out-of-the-way place, but it was good
land and in the most beautiful part of Indiana. Bono was an ambitious community from which produce was already being shipped by flatboat down the
White River to New Orleans.

A small stream called Fishing Creek ran through the land he bought, providing running water and bottom fields. The country to the north was
gently rolling and promised well. All was covered with magnificent poplars
and hardwoods.

Having bought the land and fixed the location of the cabin, they rode back
to Shenango; but nearly two years elapsed before he could arrange his affairs
and find time from the pressure of episcopal duties.

His schedule of conferences in 1818 was unusually heavy: Norfolk, in
February; Baltimore, in March; Philadelphia, in April; New York, in May;
Hallowell, Maine, in June; and Lansing, Cayuga County, New York, in
July.

Roberts was absent from home six months on this round of conferences.
The labor was exacting, but involved much less exposure and danger from
sickness than his trip the previous year. His travels were mostly in a settled
country with good inns and comfortable houses. He had one night out when
he lay with his head on the saddle and held the lead rope of the horse while
he slept. He had also three days without food, except wild berries, when he
rode from the conference at Lansing through southern New York to Shenango.

Another year elapsed before they could get away. He probably took the
Ohio, Missouri, and Tennessee conferences in the fall of 1819, and then
hurriedly returned to Shenango for the long-awaited move to Indiana.

They finally started the first week in November of 1819. They took along
their niece, Esther, and three nephews, George, Thomas, and Robert. They

had two horses for the carriage and two for riding. Esther rode one of the horses, with the twelve-year-old George either behind her or riding in the carriage with his uncle and aunt. The two young men alternately rode the other horse and walked. The carriage was packed with baggage, and the saddle horses carried packs. They spent the first two nights out with friends, but after that stopped mostly at inns. These were rough log houses where they could get shelter and provender for the horses, but often in good weather they camped out.

The journey across Ohio and Indiana was slow because the roads were new. The bishop and his wife often preferred to walk over the worst places. A highway had been cut across Ohio from Pittsburgh to the Indiana border at Laurel, where it was met by the Whetzel Trace, a rough sort of wagon road cut through the year before by Jacob Whetzel, his son Cyrus, and four axmen. It led from Laurel to a junction with the Berry Trace near Franklin and then continued south to the falls of Ohio.

The Roberts' caravan reached their land on November 28. They came out of the forest toward evening and drove down the hill to the cabin where they were to live. They were tired, and what they saw must have been depressing: only the skeleton of a log cabin—no door, no windows, no chimney, no fireplace, no floor; only log walls and a clapboard roof. Below in the flats lay a small clearing in which ripened corn was standing, but elsewhere thick woods hemmed them in on all sides.

When Elizabeth started to get supper, only potatoes were left from their provisions! Roberts built a fire and roasted the potatoes in the hot ashes. Then he laid them on a sill and said grace, as if they were sitting down to a feast. Probably he was amused as well as serious. But Esther, who was only fourteen and hungry, confided to the boys that she did not "see why uncle should ask a blessing and return thanks, for a supper of nothing else in the world but roasted potatoes."

When night fell Elizabeth made beds as best she could on puncheon boards. The children were awakened by wolves howling in the woods nearby. Esther remembered that wolves had once killed one of their horses at Shenango. Her uncle assured her that wolves were afraid of fire and that he would keep the hearth blazing all night.

They awakened in the morning with their fears forgotten. They were starting from scratch. It was as if the world they had known had vanished in the night. They had only the frame of a house, their horses, a few tools, the simplest household equipment, and their strong and willing hands. About them endless woods.

Breakfast over, the three men went to work on the cabin: fireplace, floor, door, windows, a half attic where the boys could sleep. It was a little cabin; Roberts expected to build a larger one soon, but they were to live in this shelter three years. The men worked fast, and in a few days the cabin was snug for the winter. While they were building, Elizabeth cooked out-of-doors and sat on a log while she knitted and mended.

The bishop's salary was but two hundred dollars and traveling expenses, and an additional allowance for the family, which he now accepted. They had accumulated savings, but these had mostly gone into the journey from Shenango and purchase of the farm. The property at Shenango had been sold for six hundred dollars, but he realized little cash. The proceeds from hunting, slight as they were except for meat, were greatly needed. His neighbors thought little about his hunting except to admire his skill with the rifle. They listened to him preach with greater interest, but always with a touch of deference because of his exalted position.

The big job was the clearing of land. It was imperative that they should be self-sustaining as quickly as possible and that fields should be ready for spring planting. As soon as the cabin and barn were finished, the men began on the land. They worked every moment of daylight because Roberts had to leave in March for the spring conferences, and so much had to be done before he left.

First they cleared a ten-acre field for corn, leaving three acres for flax and a garden. Elizabeth wanted flax for spinning and weaving. They girdled the larger trees, leaving them to be cut down later. They cut down and burned smaller trees and grubbed out undergrowth. Esther and George, and even Elizabeth, helped the men with the brush and burning, for they were working against time. Of evenings the men built furniture from puncheon boards by candlelight—a table, stools, and one chair so heavy that Esther and George could not lift it, but had to push it over the floor.

Roberts left for the Baltimore Conference on the eighth of March. When he had ridden away, Elizabeth took over. The two young men plowed and dug up the fields. George was old enough to furrow a field for corn. Elizabeth, with one arm in a sling (she had an infected finger) and corn in a bag, dropped seed in the furrows, and Thomas and Robert covered them with hoes. When the bishop came back in July they had reaped a fair crop of wheat, and there was a good stand of corn. The garden also was flourishing and the field of flax was well advanced.

They were now over the hard beginnings. When the crops were in that fall and Roberts had secured an abundance of meat from the forest, they were largely self-sustaining. Long afterward they looked back to this first winter in Indiana, hard as it was, with peculiar pleasure.*

✢

MY FAITH LOOKS UP TO THEE

WITH the westward trek of the American people, the mid-nineteenth century saw swift increase in the making of distinctly American hymns. So typical of this period is "My Faith Looks Up to Thee" that the hymn has been called "a

*Abridged from *Frontier Bishop* by Worth M. Tippy, pp. 120-29. Copyright © 1958 by Abingdon Press. Used by permission of the publisher.

perfect expression" of the American Christianity of the century. And this is true both of the hymn and the tune.

Ray Palmer, the author, was a Congregational minister. He served churches in Bath, Maine, and Albany, New York, and was later secretary of the American Congregational Union, New York. His life (1808-1887) well covered the century.

Mr. Palmer had written "My Faith Looks Up to Thee" shortly after graduation from Yale in 1830. He had copied it in a small morocco-covered book which he was accustomed to carry about in his pocket. One day on the street he met Lowell Mason, who asked him if he had any hymns to contribute to a new hymnal which Mason and Thomas Hastings were collaborating to publish. Palmer promptly produced the hymn from his pocket. Mason received it with delight and at once wrote the tune "Olivet," which has been in no small way responsible for helping Mason's prophecy to come true: "Mr. Palmer, you

My Faith Looks Up to Thee

Ray Palmer, 1830

OLIVET: 6. 6. 4. 6. 6. 6. 4.
Lowell Mason, 1832

1. My faith looks up to Thee, Thou Lamb of Cal - va - ry,
2. May Thy rich grace im - part Strength to my faint - ing heart,
3. While life's dark maze I tread, And griefs a - round me spread,
4. When ends life's tran - sient dream, When death's cold, sul - len stream

Sav - iour di - vine: Now hear me while I pray, Take all my
My zeal in - spire; As Thou hast died for me, O may my
Be Thou my Guide; Bid dark - ness turn to day, Wipe sor - row's
Shall o'er me roll, Blest Sav - iour, then, in love, Fear and dis -

guilt a - way, O let me from this day Be whol - ly Thine!
love to Thee Pure, warm, and change - less be, A liv - ing fire!
tears a - way, Nor let me ev - er stray From Thee a - side.
trust re - move; O bear me safe a - bove, A ran - somed soul! A-MEN.

may live many years and do many good things, but I think you will be best known to posterity as the author of 'My Faith Looks Up to Thee!' "

Palmer wrote three other widely enjoyed hymns: "Jesus, Thou Joy of Loving Hearts," a rich translation of a section of a medieval Latin hymn; "Come, Holy Ghost, in Love," founded on the twelfth- or thirteenth-century Latin, *Veni, Sancte Spiritus;* and "Jesus, These Eyes Have Never Seen."

Lowell Mason (1792-1872) has been called the greatest musical figure in American hymnody. He spent a lifetime of tireless devotion to music in church and in education. He is noted as primarily responsible for obtaining a place for music in the curriculum of the public schools. Although his many hymn tunes are plain, simple, and undistinguished, they have been generally easily learned and sufficiently sentimental to be popular. They are therefore still widely printed, and a number of them will be found in this book. "Olivet" is a good example of a type of tune quickly and eagerly learned in a pioneering era.

"My Faith Looks Up to Thee" has given expression to the faith of countless persons in these more than a hundred years since its appearing. As we come before God acknowledging our guilt, we know that His love for us has been set out sacrificially in the "Lamb of Calvary." This "rich grace" strengthens and inspires us and in response to God's love, love awakens in us—"pure, warm, and changeless." Living and dying in this love redeems us from "fear and distrust" even while we live in "life's dark maze."

✠

SAVIOUR! THY DYING LOVE

FOR a hundred years, Christian people have offered themselves in glad, warm devotion inspired by the fervent language of this hymn. Sylvanus Dryden Phelps (1816-1895), father of the late William Lyon Phelps, distinguished professor of English literature at Yale University, was a Baptist minister. Although the hymn was written and published in 1862, it was first given wide publicity when published by Robert Lowry, to his tune, "Something for Jesus," in a Sunday-school collection of 1871 called *Pure Gold.* Over a million copies of this hymnal were sold. Circulation of the hymn further increased when it was taken up in the Moody revival and printed in the Sankey-Bliss *Gospel Hymns,* Number 1, of 1875. From that day to this it has been beloved by many people.

In simple statement and humble prayer, the Christian's life is set forth as a glad response in service. God's love, made plain in Christ's "dying love," summons man to give his all gladly and in utter consecration. To fulfill this responsibility adequately the Christian prays that each day "may see some work of love begun, some deed of kindness done, some wanderer sought and won." Since all life is God's gift to us, our lives fulfill their destinies when we give them back to Him from whom we come and to whom we belong.

Saviour! Thy Dying Love*

Sylvanus D. Phelps, 1862

SOMETHING FOR JESUS: 6. 4. 6. 4. 6. 6. 6. 4.

Robert Lowry, 1871

1. Sav - iour! Thy dy - ing love Thou gav - est me,
2. At the blest mer - cy seat, Plead - ing for me,
3. Give me a faith - ful heart, Guid - ed by Thee,
4. All that I am and have— Thy gifts so free—

Nor should I aught with - hold, Dear Lord, from Thee:
My fee - ble faith looks up, Je - sus, to Thee;
That each de - part - ing day Hence - forth may see
In joy, in grief, through life, Dear Lord, for Thee;

In love my soul would bow, My heart ful - fill its vow,
Help me the cross to bear, Thy won - drous love de - clare,
Some work of love be - gun, Some deed of kind - ness done,
And when Thy face I see, My ran - somed soul shall be,

Some of - fering bring Thee now, Some - thing for Thee.
Some song to raise, or prayer, Some - thing for Thee.
Some wan - derer sought and won, Some - thing for Thee.
Through all e - ter - ni - ty, Of - fered for Thee. A - MEN.

In part the popularity of the hymn is due to the simple tune of Robert Lowry (1826-1899). Lowry was a Baptist minister who was long active in promotion of the gospel-song movement. Since he was concerned only to produce music which was popularly effective, his tunes are not musically important. Nevertheless, by being simple, straightforward, and catchy, they have been and still are enjoyed by large numbers of people. As the original and persistent setting for this hymn, the melody "Something for Jesus" has warmed many hearts.

CONTENTS

PART V   SECTION 3

THE CHURCH ON THE PLAINS AND IN THE SOUTHWEST

In him was life; and the life was the light of men.—JOHN 1:4

PICTURES: PAGE
  Interpretation: First Presbyterian Church, Bellevue, Nebraska 588
  Picture: First Presbyterian Church, Bellevue, Nebraska 589
  Interpretation: Pulpit, St. Martin's Evangelical Church, Austin, Texas 590
  Picture: Pulpit, St. Martin's Evangelical Church, Austin, Texas 591
  Interpretation: Altar View, St. Philip's in the Hills, Tucson, Arizona 592
  Picture: Altar View, St. Philip's in the Hills, Tucson, Arizona 593

POETRY:
  Prairie Woman's Prayer—*Thompson* 594
  Circuit Rider—*Gillis* 595
  The Church Universal—*Longfellow* 595
  Song of Myself—*Whitman* 596
  R.I.P.—*Sampley* 597
  A Ballad of Trees and the Masters—*Lanier* 597
  Christmas in the Ozarks—*Marinoni* 597
  Litany for New Mexico—*Austin* 598

STORIES:
  Music on the Muscatatuck—*West* 599
  The Ministry of Friendship—*Osborn* 603
  A Spire on the Horizon—*Hyde* 606

MUSIC:
  Interpretation: God of the Prairies—*Richardson* 608
  Music: God of the Prairies—*Vaughan Williams* 609
  Interpretation: City of God—*Johnson* 610
  Music: City of God—*Haweis* 611

FIRST PRESBYTERIAN CHURCH, BELLEVUE, NEBRASKA

"LA BELLE VUE," cried Manuel de Lisa, a Cuban trader of St. Louis, when he first saw this happy situation on the banks of the Missouri River in 1805. Its beauty was celebrated in England and on the Continent before most people of the Americas knew of it, for Bradbury, the English naturalist, stopped here in 1819 and published his pen picture of the place; and in 1833 Prince Maximilian of Prussia visited the village and wrote concerning the fertility of its soil. Dr. Marcus Whitman, of Oregon fame, stopped here two years later en route to his labors, fought down a local siege of cholera, and prevailed upon the settlers to relocate on the more salubrious higher ground. In 1846 Mormons on their heroic trek sheltered in the town ravine.

The day after Christmas, 1850, five faithful Presbyterians "associated themselves together for the worship and service of Almighty God" under the guidance of the Reverend Edmund McKinney. Thus was begun the oldest church in Nebraska. The pastor had arrived in Bellevue four years earlier to do mission work among the Pawnees, Otoes, and Omahas. The organization was reconstituted in 1855 and the following year its first church building was erected—the structure still in use after a century, shown on page 589.

The only significant change in its form was occasioned by the tornado of Easter, 1908, when the graceful spire was blown down and replaced by a parapet. The pews were hand-built by Joseph Betz, ready for opening day, and descendants of his family continued to use them for nearly a century. As one commentator notes, the building "was erected in 1856 and has since withstood Indians, woodpeckers, tornado and debt, but not the onslaught of modern Bellevue's population increase"; for a new building is under construction. The reference to woodpeckers concerned an only too real problem, for church minutes reveal that in 1875 a "redhead shoot" was held, to reduce the birds before they reduced the steeple!

Nebraska became a state in 1869. In the same year there was appointed as Superintendent of Missions in this area one of the greatest figures of all Western church expansion—Sheldon Jackson. It was he who had church buildings fashioned in Chicago and delivered by rail to the almost treeless Great Plains. He had left us a description of another early problem in this area.

At Grand Island, a swarm of mosquitoes interfered with the regular order of service, and well-nigh baffled the attempt to organize a church. The meeting for this purpose as previously announced was held in a schoolhouse. To guard against the interference of these pests of the lowlands—which for a time disputed, with claims of the early settlers, to the possession and occupancy of the land—a man was sent an hour before the time of assembly to build a smudge before the door. He did his work well but despite the smoke the mosquitoes gathered in such numbers that it "was not deemed expedient to preach." The assembly remained long enough . . . to organize a church and elect two good elders, after which the congregation beat a hasty retreat.

FIRST PRESBYTERIAN CHURCH, BELLEVUE, NEBRASKA

Bellevue's church was a fairly ambitious undertaking for its day—as witnessed by the fact that it struggled under a mortagage for seventy-five years! Most early residences and some churches were built from sod, erected in thick walls. Logs were a privileged step upward in quality, and sawed lumber, as at Bellevue at this early date, was another advance. Our picture shows the decorative cornices provided over each window and the fact that a simple form of colored glass added to the artistic effect. Upon the rolling ground adjacent to the river but amid the vast expanse of the grassland plains, its courageous spire gave clear index of the direction to which its people aspired in affairs of the spirit.

✢

PULPIT, ST. MARTIN'S EVANGELICAL CHURCH, AUSTIN, TEXAS

THE modest, inexpensive pulpit dominated by straight lines and a few symbolic wood carvings seems utterly prosaic as it serves its purpose in St. Martin's Evangelical Lutheran Church, Austin, Texas. Its simplicity is further accentuated because it stands but a few feet from a truly impressive altar, intricately carved from massive white oak, and acknowledged as one of the finest examples of its kind in the South. Sixteen magnificent windows, each thirty-six feet high, original in design and telling the Bible story from the creation of man to the final glorification of the Church, further overshadow the simple pulpit. Yet it regains the visitor's attention, for it embodies much of the genius, the artistic longing, and the devotion of the German-Americans and their solid contributions to the development of Texas.

Unhappy conditions in Germany at the beginning of the nineteenth century impelled many of its people to leave, and in the period of a few years some five thousand of them arrived in Texas, via Indianola, founded New Braunfels, and expanded along the Pedernales River. Many were poor and without pastors except as these were sent by mission societies in the homeland and in Switzerland.

The First German Evangelical Lutheran Synod of Texas was organized at Houston in 1851. San Antonio at this time had a population of some four thousand Mexicans, three thousand Germans, two thousand Frenchmen, and two thousand of other nationalities. A spirit of independence, even of antagonism, characterized many of the German settlers in their memory of the tightly ruled church of their homeland, and in their new freedom they often rejected the religious ministrations of the itinerant pastors. There are many tales of privation, hunger, sickness, and neglect on the part of some of the heroic early ministers. Later the work achieved solid foundations.

Education has ever been a concern of the German people, and around this fact an important work was undertaken in Austin, state capital and site of the state university. A young man named F. G. Roesener from Wartburg

PULPIT, ST. MARTIN'S EVANGELICAL CHURCH, AUSTIN, TEXAS

Seminary in Iowa accepted a call to the church in Austin in 1913. He prevailed upon his Synod in 1919 to assist in erecting an attractive church adjacent to the state capitol, but had to accomplish most of the financing by personal solicitation. The winning argument was the need of college students for the ministry of the church in their crucial days of higher learning. Paying for a sanctuary costing nearly $150,000 was no small accomplishment!

Happy occupation of the beautiful new church was achieved just as the depression broke, in 1929. Much money had been committed to the beautiful windows, the splendid altar, and other major appointments. The Reverend Roesener had planned and designed most of the adornments amid the benefits of a happier financial period. The pulpit was the remaining item needed.

In the old first church erected in 1884 was a comparatively plain, pine pulpit of octagonal design, painted white to match the old church interior. The paint was removed, and oak panels were substituted, the better to match the beauty and the material of the lovely altar. Three carved figures were obtained and installed on the major panels. These represented God the Father (the creating hand), God the Son (the Lamb with flag, resting on the Bible), and God the Holy Spirit (the dove).

St. Martin's Church with its contingent of youthful students was not to be denied a pulpit which would preach artistically and by way of symbolic representation even if the times were strait! Indeed, said the pastor to his people, "It shows how old things can be made into new things, just as the gospel does with us."

✠

ALTAR VIEW, ST. PHILIP'S IN THE HILLS, TUCSON, ARIZONA

THE earliest attempt of white men to settle within the present boundaries of the United States was in the highlands of the Southwest. The elevated plains were hot and dry by day, but cool at night and adequately watered by mountain streams. Their fame for health-giving sunshine, crisp atmosphere, and glorious color abounding everywhere reaches back as far as records go.

Friars began explorations in this area, out of Mexico, in 1539. Religious missions were established while soldiers searched for fabled cities of gold, and a report to the King of Spain within a century boasted of worshiping communities among eighty thousand Indians of ninety pueblos. When the military forces were withdrawn, the work of the missions also ceased, and Christianity had to wait for a new planting by agencies moving in from the east and west coasts.

In our generation the Southwest is once more being rediscovered as a place with many ideal conditions for health, work, and all normal living. Benign

ALTAR VIEW, ST. PHILIP'S IN THE HILLS, TUCSON, ARIZONA

blue skies overarch a region rich in beauty, natural resources, and growing appeal. At places great mountains thrust their peaks sharply up from a vast surrounding plain, so that within an hour's drive one may move from sunny summer to crisp spring.

Among the originally uncrowded settlers along desert sand roads that led out from the modern city of Tucson, the Episcopal Church planted a haven for worship in 1936. With an eye and a spirit for the beautiful in nature, its members desired to gather at a point enough removed from the signs of a city so that the evidences of God's handiwork would dominate. In particular, the church was situated so that the worshipers might look between the altar appointments through a clear window upon the desert near at hand but also upon the glorious Catalina Mountains as a focal point, rising over eight thousand feet toward the sky. It is believed that this was the first parish church to conceive of this aid to reverent devotion. Appropriately, the church was named St. Philip's in the Hills.

The appeal of the little parish church grew. A neighbor artist added a contribution in the form of an original tile design of Our Lady of Guadalupe, to be seen on the wall of one patio. Its humble excellence is almost overshadowed, however, by gifts of sixteenth-century art treasures from Europe, including six marble Lombard reliefs depicting scenes from the birth of Christ.

By the summer of 1957 it became necessary to enlarge the sanctuary in order to accommodate the growing parish services. While other changes were permitted, all agreed on the retention in its original place for the window, twelve feet wide, as the rear dais for the altar.

Upon the altar in the foreground of the picture on page 593 may be seen candlesticks and a cross made of ironwood, a rare growth occasionally to be found in the dry washes of isolated desert areas. Its beautiful texture escapes us in a picture which purposely focuses on the distant view. The centuries are spanned and united by the sixteenth-century ivory crucifix of Flemish craftsmanship—made at the very time the Southwest first received the Good News.

St. Philip's nestles today among its chosen hills, a beautiful example of colonial Spanish architecture embracing three landscaped patios, echoing an ancient faith amid its more than a thousand communicants of an established Episcopal parish, as well as the growing train of visitors who are refreshed by its reverent beauty.

✣

PRAIRIE WOMAN'S PRAYER

Dear Lord, give me strength to love
The taste of grit when dust storms blow
A grinding blanket, choking, gray,
Into my heart. And let me know

An overwhelming sense of hope
When torrid suns beat blinding rays
Of burning, incandescent heat
Across my brow. Nor let the haze
Make me forget the blessed calm
That follows in the sordid wake
Of black tornado, slashing, mad,
Across my land. But let me take
The dust, the heat, the constant wind
And make me hard as Thy will can,
That strangers passing by in years
May say, "She wed a Prairie Man."*
—*Mary Agnes Thompson*

CIRCUIT RIDER

They called him "fightin' parson," he could fight
As well as he could paint a sinner black.
On circuit rounds he carried in his pack
The Word of God (with which to preach the light),
And shooting arms, to prove he had the right
To preach just *where* he pleased. He had a knack
Of stopping short the usual attack
From rowdies on the Sunday meeting night.

It riled him though, to have to leave his wife
For months on end in circuit, take just what
Small pay his hearers gave him; and a life
Of riding every day would, like as not,
Cut ten years off his natural days; but yet
He'd not have traded jobs on any bet!**
—*Everett Gillis*

THE CHURCH UNIVERSAL

One holy Church of God appears
Through every age and race
Unwasted by the lapse of years,
Unchanged by changing place.

From oldest time, on farthest shores,
Beneath the pine or palm,
One Unseen Presence she adores,
With silence or with psalm.

* From *Southwester Anthology,* edited by Elsie Smith Parker and Miriam G. Beaird, p. 16. Published 1937 by American Poetry Association, Inc. Used by permission of the author.
** *Ibid.,* p. 46. Used by permission of the author.

Her priests are all God's faithful sons,
To serve the world raised up;
The pure in heart her baptized ones;
Love, her communion-cup.

The truth is her prophetic gift,
The soul her sacred page;
And feet on mercy's errands swift
Do make her pilgrimage.

O living Church! thine errand speed;
Fulfill thy task sublime;
With bread of life earth's hunger feed;
Redeem the evil time!

—*Samuel Longfellow*

SONG OF MYSELF

(Section 48)

I have said that the soul is not more than the body,
And I have said that the body is not more than the soul,
And nothing, nor God, is greater to one than one's self is,
And whoever walks a furlong without sympathy walks to his own funeral,
    dressed in his shroud,
And I or you pocketless of a dime may purchase the pick of the earth,
And to glance with an eye or show a bean in its pod confounds the learning
    of all times,
And there is no trade or employment but the young man following it may
    become a hero,
And there is no object so soft but it makes a hub for the wheeled universe,
And any man or woman shall stand cool and supercilious before a million
    universes.

And I call to mankind, Be not curious about God,
No array of terms can say how much I am at peace about God and about death.

I hear and behold God in every object, yet I understand God not in the least.
Nor do I understand who there can be more wonderful than myself.

Why should I wish to see God better than this day?
I see something of God each hour of the twenty-four, and each moment then,
In the faces of men and women I see God, and in my own face in the glass;
I find letters from God dropped in the street, and every one is signed by
    God's name,
And I leave them where they are, for I know that others will punctually come
    forever and ever.*

—*Walt Whitman*

* From *Walt Whitman's Poems*, edited by Gay Wilson Allen and Charles T. Davis, p. 123. Copyright
1955 by New York University Press. Used by permission of the publisher.

R. I. P.

Lo this man fought for God and right,
They slew each other in one night
   And lie beneath one sod.
   And this for right and God;

Here prostrate now they worship long
   The God whom all men trust,
And weigh uncertain right and wrong
   In scales of certain dust.*

                    —Arthur M. Sampley

A BALLAD OF TREES AND THE MASTER

Into the woods my Master went,
Clean forspent, forspent.
Into the woods my Master came,
Forspent with love and shame.
But the olives they were not blind to Him,
The little gray leaves were kind to Him:
The thorn-tree had a mind to Him
When into the woods He came.

Out of the woods my Master went,
And He was well content.
Out of the woods my Master came,
Content with death and shame.
When Death and Shame would woo Him last,
From under the trees they drew Him last:
'Twas on a tree they slew Him—last
When out of the woods He came.**

                    —Sidney Lanier

CHRISTMAS IN THE OZARKS

The sky is gray,
Gray like the thin mare nosing above the grassless field,
Gray as the unpainted shack and its hingeless door,
And its cardboard-patched north window—
And its south and west windows too.
Gray as the dusty road, the barren trees, and the blackberry bushes.

* From *Signature of the Sun*, edited by Mabel Major and T. M. Pearce, p. 219. Copyright 1950 by University of New Mexico Press. Used by permission of the author.
** From *Poems of Sidney Lanier*, edited by Mrs. Sidney Lanier, p. 141. Copyright 1915 by Charles Scribner's Sons. Used by permission of the publisher.

The corn stubble nodding in the wind is also gray
Like the cowless barn that slants northward revealing its ribs.
The headless scarecrow is gray,
And the snow, fast-frozen on the useless trough, is gray.

But at the east window,
The only one with a glass pane in it,
There hangs a bright Christmas wreath
Made of tiny, red paper stars caught on a twisted wire.*

—*Rosa Zagnoni Marinoni*

LITANY FOR NEW MEXICO

Bless God for the day!

Bless Him for the wide clear-flowing
New Mexico morning,
Poured round the shadow pools,
Gilt on the cumbres.[1]
Bless Him for the nooning,
When the white thunderheads with sails full blowing
Sleep on the three wind rivers.
Bless God and praise Him
For the west-sloping hour of siesta
Under domed cottonwoods,
That in a rainless land make ever the sound of rain.

Bless Him for the evening;
For the releasing cool hands of the wind
On the flushed headlands;
For the lilac and larkspur veils
Let down by the mothering mountains
Between the work that fails and the dream that lingers.
Bless Him for home-coming sounds—
The window-shine on the loma,[2]
For the welcoming flame and the savory smell
And the snuggling cry of the children.

Bless God for the night!
Bless Him for the keen curled sickle that reaps
The saffron meadows of the sun's late sowing;
For the full-shaped globes of wonder,
Pacing the eastern ranges.
Oh, bless Him more than all
For the ever-recurrent orb that emerges
Between the light that goes and earth's oncoming shadow.

* From *Signature of the Sun,* edited by Mabel Major and T. M. Pearce, p. 149. Copyright 1950 by University of New Mexico Press. Used by permission of the author.
1 Mountain crests.
2 Broad-topped hill.

Bless Him for shared sleep,
For the midnight's healing fountain,
For the companionable cock-crown warning
The sleeper back from dreams to the pastures of morning.

Bless God for the dawning,
For the earth collecting
Darkness again to her breast,
For the hills resounding
Clarion blue to the sun's reluctance.

Bless God and praise Him
With exceeding thanksgiving
For His gift of the day and the night!*

—*Mary Austin*

✠

MUSIC ON THE MUSCATATUCK

Jessamyn West

NEAR the banks of the Muscatatuck where once the woods had stretched, dark row on row, and where the fox grapes and wild mint still flourished, Jess Birdwell, an Irish Quaker, built his white clapboard house. Here he lacked for very little. On a peg by the front door hung a starling in a wooden cage and at the back door stood a spring-house, the cold spring water running between crocks of yellow-skinned milk. At the front gate a moss-rose said welcome and on a trellis over the parlor window a Prairie Queen nodded at the roses in the parlor carpet—blooms no nurseryman's catalogue had ever carried and gay company for the sober Quaker volumes: Fox's *Lives,* Penn's *Fruits of Solitude,* Woolman's *Journal,* which stood in the parlor secretary.

Jess had a good wife, a Quaker minister, Eliza Cope before she was wed, and a houseful of children. Eliza was a fine woman, pious and work-brickel and good-looking as female preachers are apt to be: a little, black-haired, glossy woman with a mind of her own.

Yet, in spite of his content, Jess wasn't completely happy, and for no reason anyone could have hit upon at first guess. It certainly wasn't having Eliza ride every First Day morning to the Grove Meeting House, there to sit on the elevated minister's bench and speak when the spirit moved her. Jess knew Eliza had had a call to the ministry and was proud to hear her preach in her gentle way of loving-kindness and the brotherhood of man.

No, it wasn't Eliza's preaching nor any outward lack the eye could see that troubled Jess. It was music. Jess pined for music, though it would be hard to say how he'd come by any such longing. To the Quakers music was a popish dido, a sop to the senses, a hurdle waiting to trip man in his upward struggle.

* *Ibid.,* p. 252. Used by permission of the author.

They kept it out of their Meeting Houses and out of their homes, too. Oh, there were a few women who'd hum a little while polishing their lamp chimneys, and a few men with an inclination to whistle while dropping corn, but as to real music, sung or played, Jess had no more chance to hear it than a woodchuck.

Jess hadn't a notion in the world of buying an organ when he went into Payson and Clarke's Music Store. He'd got the cherry stock he'd come after, had had a nice visit with his mother, and was ready to start homeward when he thought he'd as well hear "The Old Musician and His Harp," on a Payson and Clarke organ. That was the way he had it figured out to himself before he went in, anyway.

When he'd walked out, the organ was his. He didn't know what he'd do with it; he didn't think Eliza would hear to keeping it; he thought he'd like as not slipped clean away from grace, but he had the papers for the organ in his pocket. He'd paid half cash, the rest to be in nursery stock. Clarke of Payson and Clarke was an orchardist.

So that's the way it was done. The organ was put in the attic and from there it could be heard downstairs, but not in any fullbodied way. It took the gumbo out of it—having it in the attic—and besides Jess was careful not to play it when anyone was in the house. He was careful, that is, until the day the Ministry and Oversight Committee called. He was careful that day, too; it was Mattie who wasn't careful, though unlucky's more the word for it.

Jess had noted right off that Mattie had a musical turn. She'd learned to pick out "The Old Musician" by herself, with one hand, and when Jess discovered this, he taught her the bass chords so that she could play for him to sing. That was a bitter pill for Eliza to swallow, and just what she'd feared: the children becoming infected with Jess' weakness for music. Still, she couldn't keep herself from listening when the deep organ notes with Jess' sweet tenor flying above them came seeping down through the ceiling into the sitting-room below.

But in spite of Jess' being careful, in spite of Eliza's being twice as strict as usual, and speaking at the Hopewell Meeting House with increased gravity, the matter got noised about. Not that there was an organ at Birdwell's: there wasn't anything definite known, anything you could put your finger on. It was just a feeling that Friend Birdwell wasn't standing as squarely in the light as he'd done at one time. Perhaps someone had heard a strain of organ music coming out of an attic window some spring evening, but more than likely it was just the guilty look Eliza had.

However that may be, the Ministry and Oversight Committee came one night to call. It was nearing seven; supper had been over for some time, the dishes were washed and the table was set for breakfast. Jess and Eliza were in the sitting-room resting after the heat and work of the day and listening to the children who were playing duck-on-rock down by the branch.

The Committee drove up in Amos Pease's surrey, but by the back way, leaving the rig at the carriage-house, so that the first sign Jess and Eliza had of visitors was the smell of trodden mint. Amos Pease wasn't a man to note where he put his feet down when duty called.

Eliza smelled it first and stepped over to the west window to see who was coming. She saw, and in a flash she knew why. "It's the Ministry and Oversight," she said, and her voice shook, but when Amos Pease knocked at the door she was sitting in her rocker, her feet on a footstool, one hand lying loose and easy in the other.

Jess answered the knock. "Good evening, Amos. Good evening, Ezra. Good evening, Friend Hooper."

The Committee said its good evenings to Jess and Eliza, found chairs, adjusted First Day coat-tails—it wasn't First Day, but they'd put on their best since what they had to do was serious. But before they could even ease into their questions with some remark upon the weather or how the corn was shaping up—Jess heard it—the faint kind of leathery sigh the organ made when the foot first touched the bellows. That sound was like a pain hitting him in the heart and he thought, I've sold my birthright for a mess of pottage. For Jess was a Quaker through and through, no misdoubting that. For two hundred years his people had been Quakers, sometimes suffering for that right, and now he thought, I've gone and lost it all for a wheezing organ.

It was Mattie at the organ and Jess knew her habits there: they were like his own. She never began to play a piece at once, but touched the organ here and there, slowly pumped in the air, then lovingly laid her fingers across the keys. After that the music. Jess looked across at Eliza and he saw by the way her hands had tightened round each other that she'd heard too. I'm a far worse man than Esau, he thought, for he sold only his own birthright, and I've sold my wife's as well as my own.

Jess remembered how Eliza loved to bring the Lord's message to the Lord's people and how his own love for pushing air through a set of reeds was going to lose her all this. And before his lips moved his heart began to pray, "Lord, deliver thy servant from the snare of his own iniquity."

By the time Mattie was ready to touch the first key he was on his feet saying, "Friends, let us lift our hearts to God in prayer." This was nothing startling to a gathering of Quakers. They'd any of them take to praying at the drop of a hat. So some knelt and others didn't, but all bowed their heads and shut their eyes.

All except Jess. He stood with face uplifted to the ceiling, facing his God and his sin. By the time Mattie had got into "The Old Musician," and a few faint wisps of music were floating into the room, Jess was talking to God in a voice that shook the studding. He was talking to Him in the voice of a man whose sins have come home to roost. He was reminding Him of all the other sinners to whom His mercy had nevertheless been granted.

He went through the Bible book by book and sinner by sinner. He prayed in the name of Adam, who had sinned and fallen short of grace; of Moses, who had lost the Promised Land; of David who had looked with desire on another man's wife. He prayed in the name of Solomon, his follies, of Abraham and his jealousies, and Jephthah, who kept his word in cruelty; he made up a music of his own out of his contrition; his revulsion mounted up in melody.

He left the Old Testament and prayed for them all, sinners alike, in the name of Paul, who, what he would not, he did; and of Peter, who said he knew the Man not, and of Thomas who doubted and Judas who betrayed and of that Mary who repented.

He stood with his red head lifted up while his long Irish lip wrapped itself around the good Bible names. He prayed until the light had left the room and his hair in the dark had become as colorless as Amos Pease's dun thatch. He prayed until all the mint smell had left the room and the only smell left was that of a penitent man seeking forgiveness.

Now Jess was no hypocrite and if his prayer swelled a little, if it boomed out a little stronger when Mattie pulled the fortissimo stop, it was through none of his planning; it was the Lord's doing entirely. And if his prayer wasn't finished until Mattie'd finished playing after going five times through "The Old Musician," that was the Lord's hand, too, and nothing of Jess' contriving.

Finally, when he'd made an end, and the visiting men had taken their faces out from behind their hands and looked around the dark room with dazed eyes, Jess dropped down into his chair and rubbed his forefinger across his lips, the way a man will when he's been speaking. Eliza lit them a candle, then went out to bring in the lamps.

Amos Pease picked up the candle and held it so the light fell on to Jess' face. "Friend," he said, "thee's been an instrument of the Lord this night. Thee's risen to the throne of grace and carried us all upwards on thy pinions. Thy prayer carried us so near to heaven's gates that now and again I thought I could hear angel's voices choiring and the sound of heavenly harps."

And with that he set the candle back down, put his hat on his head and said, "Praise God." Friend Griffith and Friend Hooper said, "Amen, brother. Amen to that," and with great gravity followed Amos Pease out of the door.

When Eliza came back in with the lamp, Jess was sitting there alone in the candlelight. There was a smell of trod-on mint again in the room and the children had stopped playing duck-on-rock and were whooping after lightning-bugs to put in bottles. Jess was huddled over, his eyes shut, like a man who has felt the Lord's hand between his shoulder blades. But before Eliza could clear her throat to say "Amen" to the edifying sight he made, down from the attic floated "The Old Musician" once again, and Jess' foot began to tap:

> Tap, tap—the riverside,
> Tap, tap—upon its tide.*

* Abridged from *The Friendly Persuasion* by Jessamyn West, pp. 3-17. Published 1945 by Harcourt, Brace & Company. Used by permission of the publisher.

THE MINISTRY OF FRIENDSHIP

Ronald E. Osborn

THE frontier was a place of desperate loneliness. The pioneer found himself isolated by distance from the scenes of his youth, from loved ones, often from anyone. Day after day he looked out on the bleakness of the prairie—hopeful enough in spring and summer, but depressing in autumn rains, and only a white blank through the long winter months. A friend of mine talked with an old settler in the Dakotas who had been there "in the early day." After a trying winter he took his wagon and drove for miles, returning with young trees to set around the house; he feared that his wife would lose her mind if she should pass another winter with nothing to be seen in any direction but the drifting snows swirling across the flat and barren plains until all was blurred in the distant gray horizon.

The drabness of poverty was the frontiersman's lot. There was little money in circulation and little that money could buy. He had his land, he struggled to improve it, but his life was hard and his fare was meager. The cultural barrenness was even more depressing; it is difficult to imagine the intellectual and spiritual hunger of cultivated and sensitive spirits. That hunger still prevails in small communities where distance from larger centers is a factor. The novelist Sinclair Lewis analyzed it a generation ago in *Main Street,* his depressing picture of life in Gopher Prairie, Minnesota.

The spiritual desolation of the pioneers was hardest of all to bear. What loneliness can be compared to that of the sinner who clung to his sin, of the sinner under conviction and seeking assurance of forgiveness, of the Christian who longed for spiritual fellowship with others of like mind? One wonders at the pathetic isolation and the bravery of a single family that regularly kept the Lord's Supper about their own table on the Lord's Day, because there were no others with whom they could join.

The work of the frontier churches was a gracious ministry to this loneliness. Here along the trail comes the circuit rider or evangelist. He stops at an isolated cabin and takes a meal or even stays overnight. There is talk by the fireside—and news. Week before last he saw someone you know. Three months ago he was in Cincinnati for a convention. He is here because he is interested *in you.*

Today there is preaching at Oak Grove. From the whole neighborhood people are coming together, lots of folks. Much friendly visiting ensues, and between the morning and afternoon services the ladies spread out a basket dinner. In such a setting of reunion after loneliness the handshake becomes a sacramental act, truly the "right hand of fellowship." It is even celebrated in an old frontier hymn, now long forgotten, to be accompanied by the appropriate action:

> Take your companion by the hand,
> And all your children in the band.*

Singing, too, becomes an act of fellowship. It is easy for a later generation to criticize their hymns from an aesthetic or even a theological standpoint. But in a lilting song that made people pat their feet to the rhythm they were caught up in the spirit of the group. If there was a bouncy refrain and the men could come out with extra words in the bass, it met an elemental hunger—to belong, to be needed.

Later on, in better-established rural communities, the same ministry continued. The Sunday services, the revival meeting, the prayer meeting, the annual reunion brought human beings together in the name of Christ. All this was not mere gregariousness. (But why are Americans gregarious? Why do they want to be liked? May it not be because the corporate memory is still haunted by a recollection of loneliness, of an isolation which perhaps the Englishman seeks by his reserve?) This was friendship given a spiritual quality. It expressed itself in the "circle of prayer," an intimate act of worship in which each believer in turn offered up his thanksgiving and supplications to God. It took on moral sternness. Neighbors who became estranged knew that they could not approach the sacred things of God until they were right with each other; in many a simple rural church penitent farmers confessed their sin in the presence of the congregation and standing before the Table of the Lord extended to one another the right hand of reconciliation. A stanza written by an English clergyman, but sung often in America, speaks clearly of the friendship prevailing among the people of God:

> Blest be the tie that binds
> Our hearts in Christian love;
> The fellowship of kindred minds
> Is like to that above.

The ministry of friendship remains an important part of the Church's service to modern America. For there is loneliness still—in the crowded city, where so often men and women cease to be regarded as persons; in factories and offices, where one confronts machines rather than people; in the overgrown smooth-running institutions which many of our schools and hospitals have become. The most common advertisement of a congregation is that it is "a friendly church." Newcomers seldom return to a church if it seems "cold," if no one speaks to them. More often than not there are ushers at the door to greet worshipers as they arrive, and the minister is there to shake hands as they leave. Many of our groups in the Church—for men, for women, for young people, even many of our church-school classes—center their work largely in Christian friendship and its transforming power.

The concept of *fellowship*, which bulks so large in American Christianity, means to us a human togetherness, a belonging to one another, which is created

* From *Protestantism in America*, p. 111. Westminster Press, 1953.

by God's grace. But it is not just to one another that we belong. It is to Him. That is why we can be together. The contagion of such a fellowship is a major element in our evangelism. Men and women searching for companions, groping dimly after a better life, are drawn into the circle of some group within the Church, doubtless on a purely human level first of all. But as they enter more intimately into the life of the group they are brought into encounter with Him who is the source of this togetherness; they are confronted by the Friend of publicans and sinners, and they yield their lives to Him. . . . All this can be criticized, and sometimes is, by the spiritually elite, who imagine that they do not need the love of a brother. Certainly the New Testament concept of Christianity is not exhausted by such an interpretation. . . . The Apostolic Church was a fellowship which could draw men to Christ, which upheld them in the rigorous ethical demands of discipleship, and in which the Christian life could actually be realized.

A striking characteristic of congregational life in America is the large number of men, women and young people who are actively engaged in carrying on the work of the Church. In many of our congregations laymen assume responsibilities which in other parts of the world are reserved to the ministry or the priesthood.

Our peculiar history has affected this situation. Our churches came into being in an atmosphere of fierce democracy; there was no feudal tradition to elevate either the clergy or a noble class as the ruling element in congregational life. A fact against which there was no good theoretical answer was the sheer lack of ministers on the frontier. Those communions whose life centers in the sacraments as administered by an episcopally ordained priesthood just could not keep up with the westward-moving population, because they lacked priests. Heroic missionaries carried Roman Catholicism into the West, but their numbers were too few to provide their scattered people with a continuing sacramental life. For a while they experimented with lay preachers, but these men could not say Mass, and without it Roman spirituality cannot live. The Protestant Episcopal Church required a generation or more after our national independence to recover from the separation from England, to establish its own episcopal institutions, and to recruit a ministry. It was destined to play a much larger role later in our history than it did in the days of the western migrations. If the sacraments were administered with any frequency, it was at the hands of laymen.

In early Pennsylvania in the 1720's John Philip Boehm was prevailed upon to preach and to baptize among the German Reformed people, though he had not received ordination. The situation was reported to the Classis of Amsterdam, which recognized the validity of what he had done, but insisted that he now be ordained. The doctrine of the sacraments held by most churches recognizes a situation of emergency in which a layman may lawfully administer them. On the frontier that emergency was a continuing condition.

The priesthood of believers was bound to be emphasized in such circumstances, sometimes in radical fashion. The farmer-preacher of the Baptists and the Disciples, or the lay exhorter of the Methodists, usually lacked the rudiments of divinity. But he had the respect of his neighbors who knew that he earned his living with his hands, as they did. He had sufficient zeal to leave his own work, and to forget his own comfort for the sake of others. He had a working knowledge of the English Bible and a devotion to the Christ whom he served. So he gathered the congregations and instructed them in the nurture and admonition of the Lord. James A. Garfield, before he entered politics, eventually to become president of the United States, was a teacher-preacher who served the Disciples of Christ in rural Ohio in such a spirit.

Lay leadership today does not center primarily in the work of the ministry. The farmer-preacher emerged in a peculiar environment and served the needs of his time, but no sizable American denomination today takes a dogmatic stand against a paid ministry; it long ago became apparent that if a congregation was to survive it must have a well-qualified, full-time leader. But the layman still renders large and significant service in the church school, the board of officers, various committees, men and women's work, evangelistic calling, and the like. In the work of the denominations he also has an important place. The Methodist Church, for example, has in its national conference a house of lay delegates corresponding to the house of clergy.

The outstanding American layman probably spends much more time in the work of the Church as an institution, less in exploring deeply the Christian implications of his vocation in the world, than his European counterpart. Yet our tradition of lay leadership has given to the Christian world such men of influence as Dwight L. Moody, Robert E. Speer, and John R. Mott. It has saved us from that abysmal gulf which yawned between priest and people in the Middle Ages and has helped us, at least in our congregation, to realize that wholeness of the Church which the Reformation arose to proclaim.*

✝

A SPIRE ON THE HORIZON
William J. Hyde

IMPERCEPTIBLY Minnesota faded into Dakota Territory. It was early summer; swales still held a little water; otherwise, the eye was met with green prairie grass extending as far as one could look—in any direction. We were in the Dakota prairie.

The infrequent small towns were dusty, buildings weather beaten; storm and wind had left them defeated. Occasionally a building newly painted stood out in glaring contrast. From the train window we saw a line of covered wagons in the distance.

* Abridged from *The Spirit of American Christianity* by Ronald E. Osborn, pp. 93-100. Copyright 1958 by Ronald E. Osborn. Published by Harper & Brothers. Used by permission of the author and the publisher.

And so we arrived in Aberdeen. On a Saturday in June, 1886, I [a young Methodist minister] set foot for the first time on Dakota Territory.

Each day brought its new experiences. I helped a family build its first sod house. By eight o'clock on the morning of the appointed day the neighbors were arriving from miles around—whole families. They brought their implements and tools with them. Two plows turned up the sod in long strips which the men cut into rectangular slabs. The location for the house was staked out by another group and the corner uprights were put into place. A few more two-by-fours were set in between these uprights and the plate laid across. With the framework up, the sod slabs were then laid, the slabs of one layer laid over the cracks of the layer below; then the cracks were chinked with damp earth forming a thick, solid wall. Space was left for a door and two small windows. As soon as the frame was secure the carpenters moved to the roof. Rough boards were laid, sloping gently from the front of the house to the back, assuring drainage Then the roof surface was covered with a sod thatch.

It was good to share the social gatherings of the people but I realized that I must know them individually before I could really serve them. For instance, one night when I was caught in a bad storm and had to spend the night at the Perkins house Mrs. Perkins told me about her first reaction to the great prairie. For the first six months her husband had tried to work in Aberdeen, while she stayed on the claim to satisfy the requirements of the law. She said she used to stand at the doorway and pray for a "miracle of shape."

" 'God, let just one thing rise up and have some shape!' I used to pray. Everything was so flat and stationary! Couldn't God raise up a tree? Couldn't He heave the earth into just the smallest hill? But the land lay there motionless and flat. The only thing that ever rose was the horizon, and when it began to weave you knew you better look away before you went mad. Back east in Wisconsin I used to be alone but there it's different. Here it isn't so much that you *are* alone as that you *feel* yourself alone." After a little pause she added, "But if you live it out long enough you come to like it."

When spring came we moved out of the G.A.R. hall and into a tent for our services. It was much better during the hot summer weather. Harvest came early that year—perhaps the most exciting harvest of my life in Dakota. It helped me harvest a church! As I watched the constant procession of wagons loaded with wheat pull up to the elevators I realized that here was the wealth of the country. Many times I jumped up on the wagon seat beside the owner and told the farmer that we were going to build a church, that the church would make the community a better place for him and his family. Everyone knew this was so true that not one man turned me down. I had to work fast but I found I had the best product in the world to sell.

We continued to hold services in the tent while the building got under way. A frame structure, forty by forty-five feet, had been decided on. There would be a large room for worship; a smaller lecture room for prayer meetings; downstairs a kitchen, dining room and Sunday School rooms; and rising above it all a belfry with a spire. A stone foundation, of course.

The nearest stones were twelve miles away, out across the prairie. I borrowed a horse to team with [my own horse] Prince, hitched them to an old wagon and we spent most of the summer under a blistering July sun. There never was a sun as hot as the Dakota sun of 1887. I was thankful it wasn't the walls of Jericho I had contracted for! By October the foundation had begun to rise upon these stones and we had raised all but eight hundred dollars of our share to match the equal amount from the Extension Society.

That winter a store was vacated which we promptly hired for a church until ours should be completed. Our membership kept growing. I held another revival meeting that year. A series of meetings keeps the church constantly in the minds and prayers of its members. It is the best way of working the field unto the harvest.

Almost feverishly we rushed toward the completion of the building, still carrying on all our services and other work. Finally it was near enough completion so that only the few last details remained to be done.

That afternoon I took Prince and drove the twelve long miles to the rise of ground from which our foundation stones had come. Arriving at the familiar spot Prince stopped of his own accord and I got out of the buggy. I was looking off toward the west. The Psalmist had once sung, "I will lift up mine eyes unto the hills." Here I had no hills but I had the long, long view to the rim of the world where the sun set. To myself I repeated:

> So be my passing
> My task accomplished and the long day done,
> My wages taken, and in my heart
> Some late lark singing,
> Let me be gathered to the quiet west,
> The sundown beautiful and serene.*

✛

GOD OF THE PRAIRIES, BY THY BOUNDLESS GRACE

THE very phrase "the Great Plains" pushes out the soul into the vast expanses of time and eternity. For here the uninhibited eye sees for the first time the active ennobling sky, the incessant movement of clouds; and the mind is moved to contemplate the eternal vastness which surrounds and encompasses our life. Here the earth stretches out before us, offering to man its fruitfulness, waiting to be plowed, tilled, and irrigated—even the deserts wanting to blossom as a rose.

Cyril C. Richardson's fine hymn, "God of the Prairies," is a prayer that in

* Abridged from *Dig or Die, Brother Hyde* by William J. Hyde, pp. 30-31, 65-67, 95-100. Copyright 1954 by Harper & Brothers. Used by permission of the publisher.

God of the Prairies, By Thy Boundless Grace*

MAGDA 10 10 10 10   R. Vaughan Williams, 1872-1958

A - men.

God of the prairies, by Thy boundless
grace,
Give us the strength to build a worthy race,
That shall not lose its steadfast faith in
Thee,
Through all the winds and hails of destiny.

2 Here shall Thy seed fall on no untilled soil,
For we have pledged unwearying hands to
toil,
Till through the miles of myriad wheat is
heard
The whispering voice of Thine Almighty
Word.

3 Teach us to seek our happiness in Thee,
To know the joys of simple purity:
Clean laughter's ring and all the ample
wealth
Of youthful strength and vigorous life and
health.

4 Grant us such breadth of vision that our
eyes,
Scanning the wheat that meets the flaming
skies
Far in the West, may never be made blind
Through selfish aims or narrowness of
mind.

5 God of the prairies, by Thy boundless grace,
Give us the strength to build a worthy race,
That shall not lose its steadfast faith in Thee,
Through all the winds and hails of destiny!

Cyril C. Richardson, 1938

*From *The English Hymnal*. Words used by permission of Cyril C. Richardson. Music used by permission of Oxford University Press, London.

God's grace, as boundless as the prairies, a race of men may be raised up who
see the fruitful earth as God's gift, and ourselves as those whose lives are
made rich and strong by gratitude which expresses itself in unwearied toil, in
the "joys of simple purity" and in "clean laughter." Who else should have
"breadth of vision" but those whose eyes are feasted on billowing fields of
wheat? As here man stands in the presence of this infinity, how can he help
but see himself as in and under God? Surely here, man ought not to be made
blind by "selfish aims or narrowness of mind." For here is wholeness, which is
holiness and health.

Dr. Richardson is professor of Church History in Union Theological Seminary, New York City. Born in London, Professor Richardson came to America as a young man and was educated in the higher schools of Canada and
the United States. He is a minister of the Protestant Episcopal Church. The
hymn was written in 1938.

The tune "Magda" was written by the distinguished English composer,
the late Ralph Vaughan Williams, for the original edition of *Songs of Praise,*
published in 1925.

✛

CITY OF GOD

THERE are two characteristics of the Great Plains and the Southwest of which
the dwellers in this land are always aware: one is the vast extent of this widely
spreading area; the other is its youthful vigor, its sense of walking with bold
and eager step into the sunrise. If, on the one hand, its geographical foundations seem primeval and enduring, if its contacts with the red earth are direct
and vital, yet, on the other hand, it knows that its future lies before it: it lives
always in the presence of great expectations.

In the context of the Great Plains and the Southwest, therefore, Samuel
Johnson's hymn, "City of God, How Broad and Far," seems peculiarly at
home. No hymn has more richly captured the sense of spaciousness and the
fact of the fundamental oneness of the Church, God's city on earth. If the
walls of the Church are all-capacious, if there is room for all, yet those who
dwell within are not a characterless crowd; rather, they are "one army strong
. . . one working band." The Church, too, is an empire—an empire of "freedom, love, and truth." And how grandly this empire has grown! How its
towers, still in building, rise "serene and bright to meet the dawning day!"

The author was a Unitarian minister, pastor of the Independent Church,
Lynn, Massachusetts, from 1853-1870—a church which he himself organized.
He collaborated with Samuel Longfellow, brother of the well-known poet, to
produce two hymnals: *Book of Hymns* (1846) and *Hymns of the Spirit*
(1864). "City of God" was written in 1860 but was first published in the
1864 Hymnal. Based on John's vision of the New Jerusalem (Rev. 21:2, 27),
the hymn sees the Church as "the eternal city" even now standing "unharmed

upon th' eternal rock," the rock on which God has built His Church.

The hymn was introduced into England by Percy Dearmer, who printed it in *The English Hymnal* of 1906. Set to the tune of "Richmond," the hymn has seen notable uses in England. In 1924 it was sung by the massed choirs in the new cathedral at Liverpool after the words of consecration had been spoken. It was sung in Westminster Abbey in 1935 at the great service for the League of Nations. It was chosen to be sung at the jubilee service for the twenty-fifth anniversary of the coronation of George V. The Archbishops of Canterbury and York selected it to be one of seven hymns to be sung throughout England at the time of the coronation of King George VI.

The tune "Richmond" first appeared in a book called *Carmina Christo* in 1792, edited by Thomas Haweis (1734-1820). Haweis wrote both tunes and hymns, and originally published this tune to his own words. The tune was adapted by Samuel Webbe, Jr., and named by him for the composer's friend, Leigh Richmond. Haweis was a minister of the Church of England. In 1768 he became chaplain to the Countess of Huntingdon and superintended the college she established at Trevecca in Wales.

City of God *

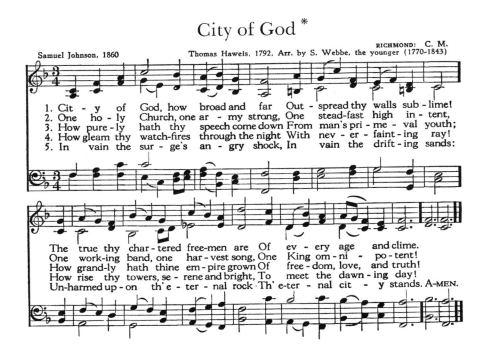

*From *The Hymnbook*. Used by permission of Westminster Press.

CONTENTS

PART V   SECTION 4

CHURCH DEVELOPMENT ON THE PACIFIC COAST

---·I·---

This is the covenant that I will make . . . , saith the Lord, I will put my laws into their hearts, and in their minds will I write them.—HEBREWS 10:16

---·I·---

PICTURES: PAGE
Interpretation: Children's Chapel, Pasadena, California 613
Picture: Children's Chapel, Pasadena, California 615
Interpretation: Christ and the Children of the World, Redlands,
    California 614
Picture: Christ and the Children of the World, Redlands, California 617
Interpretation: The Wayfarers' Chapel, Palos Verdes, California—
    Wright 616
Picture: The Wayfarers' Chapel, Palos Verdes, California—*Wright* 619

POETRY:
The Mountain Cemetery—*Bowers* 620
The Wise Men—*Bowers* 621
To My Father—*Drummond* 621
Sonnet for a Marriage—*Hayes* 622
Lord, Must I Climb?—*Pugh* 622
Doubt—*Jackson* 623
A Prayer to Make Your Own—*Bryant* 623

STORIES:
The Faith Healer—*Moody* 624
The Temperance Pledge—*Marshall* 625
American Home Missionary Society and Oregon—*Goodykoontz* 626

MUSIC:
Interpretation: "Thy Kingdom Come," on Bended Knee—*Hosmer* 628
Music: "Thy Kingdom Come," on Bended Knee—*Day's Psalter* 629
Interpretation: God of Grace and God of Glory—*Fosdick* 631
Music: God of Grace and God of Glory—*Smart* 630

CHILDREN'S CHAPEL, PASADENA, CALIFORNIA

"A LITTLE child shall lead them," said the Master, and this has been true for the Neighborhood Church of Pasadena. Its original sanctuary, erected in 1887, reflected the forms of church building in that day. The adjoining spaces were cluttered with fences and service buildings, lending no dignity to the giant Pittosporum tree that loomed over the area.

Today the church park or campus lies peacefully under and around the great tree, whose pattern of filtered sunlight has been captured in the grille at the front of the Children's Chapel, the designing of which revolutionized the whole aspect of the church properties. The expansive patio welcomes family throngs whose children go to worship in their own chapel, and following the services the people return to the shaded grounds for "coffee hour" and fellowship. Here art and nature complement each other and combine to encourage the worship of God, the Creator.

When Mrs. William C. Free offered to make a gift for children, she was asked, Is it to be a memorial? She replied, "It is not. I only wished to do my part in helping our children have an opportunity to find more hope, courage, faith, and love—in this, their chapel. The children of our churches today are the Christian leaders of tomorrow; and our future depends in large measure on their leadership. I hope this chapel may be a place where they can build a Christian faith which they can hold through life, and that through their worship here a clearer image of God may grow in their minds and hearts."

An immediate problem was what style of architecture to use. Spanish mission forms were indigenous to California, and even stately Gothic or New England meetinghouses were types accepted by tradition. The committee asked, Why should we go to the forms of the past to express our religion today? Even Byzantine was "modern" in its day. In every creative age of history builders have tried to do the same thing: to use the materials they possessed in a natural way, and to express in form what they felt in the depths of their own souls.

One notable feature of the Children's Chapel is the wooden tracery covering the entrance end, which is enclosed by clear glass. Inside, another huge glass window looks out onto a planted area, backed by an ivy-covered wall. In warm weather the window wall is opened, making the garden a part of the chapel itself. In evening, or whenever desired, a curtain is drawn across the window wall, closing out the garden.

Music, poetry, architecture, the graphic and plastic arts, nature's planting— all pay tribute to the chapel and its program. Since it was designed to serve young children, in the first six grades, their interests were made dominant.

Several figures and designs carved in ash are secured to the outside of the dark redwood entrance doors. These show a little child admiring the objects of nature; the planets, sun, clouds, and stars; a Mother and Child; a figure depicting the prodigal son; and a figure with upstretched hands, suggesting worship. These represent, in terms a child can understand, the Creation, the love of God, the quality of forgiveness, and the universal upreach of the human soul for contact with its Maker.

Inside, on an altar, is a white cross which was made in Sweden. Between the arms of this cross are thin radii of wood, coming out from the center like the rays of the sun. The children find this a meaningful symbol, combining the traditional Christian cross with the thought of light. A pair of delicate three-taper candlesticks of brass and a bowl of flowers set on an Italian lace tablecloth complete the altar arrangement.

The inside of the chapel has been designed for beauty, quietness, and light. Everything is a symphony of browns—from the light browns of the chancel carpet and draperies through the medium browns of the walls and cork floor to the darker browns of the woodwork and pews. Even the windows, which are narrow vertical strips of stained glass, blend with this color scheme. An acoustic-tile ceiling and cork floor make for quietness. The carpet was hand-woven and imported from Puerto Rico. To complete the mood of worship, there is a little organ.

The entire chapel was conceived in response to the divine injunction: "Let the children come unto me, and forbid them not; for of such is the Kingdom of God."

✝

CHRIST AND THE CHILDREN OF THE WORLD, REDLANDS, CALIFORNIA

THE first Christian worship service in the English language on the North American mainland was held on the West Coast. The Reverend Francis Fletcher was chaplain to Sir Francis Drake, and when his ship, the *Golden Hind,* anchored in Drake's Bay, Marin County, California, in 1579, Fletcher went ashore and conducted services of worship according to the rites of the Church of England.

The golden crown of righteousness was earnestly sought in California before metallic gold was discovered at Sutter's Mill in 1847. Among early workers for the Christian faith was Ezra Fisher of Oregon fame, representing the Baptists. Osgood Church Wheeler heard his call, sailed to the Isthmus of Panama and up the coast on the *California,* first steamship to enter the Golden Gate. Wheeler saw to the erection of the first Protestant Church building in California, dedicated at San Francisco on August 5, 1849. The first free public school in the West was begun in this church the same year.

Location, climate, and natural resources destined California to become a vast melting pot of nationalities and races. Native American Indians were forced west, and peoples of Mexico long had moved back and forth to the West Coast. A fascinating chapter in coastal history is the movement of Russians

Courtesy Smith & Williams, Architects, Pasadena, Calif.
Photo by Julius Shulman, Los Angeles, Calif.

CHILDREN'S CHAPEL, PASADENA, CALIFORNIA

across the Bering Strait, bringing their form of the Christian faith through Alaska and southward. Orientals of many origins swarmed in at the time of mining and industrial development. Every species of American, free and slave, was to be found among the burgeoning throngs seeking fortune in the beckoning West.

Here was a situation loaded with peril and with opportunity. Many a minor explosion of human jealousy, fear, and misunderstanding erupted between the unacquainted, varied peoples as they settled into closer and closer proximity. Only a strong conviction about American democracy, built upon a deep foundation of religious faith concerning God, the Creator of all men, could possibly ensure peace in this Paradise of nature.

Typical of the response of the Church to this condition of man was the message first preached and then made majestically material in the window of the First Baptist Church, Redlands, California (see page 617). The title of the portrayal is "Christ and the Children of the World." Receiving the blessing and compassion of the Saviour are (counterclockwise, from the left) children of the Negro, Chinese, Mexican, and Caucasian people. Situated in the east transept of the sanctuary, the window looks out toward the education unit of the church, symbolizing the conviction arising in worship which issues in equal education and fellowship for all whom a common Father has made.

This church, organized in 1887, is one of the earliest built by the Baptists in Southern California. The University of Redlands is sponsored by the same denomination. The church is rich in other art works and symbols. Great windows portray many episodes in the life of Christ. The past is made present by a unique window entitled "Christ over Redlands." The dedication message of the pastor, Dr. Frank B. Fagerburg, said, "This sermon in glass and color says, 'The Living Christ is at your side in each moment of common life—on the campus, in the classroom, in the orchard, field, shop, store, and home.' We are not to forget that we serve Him best as we serve Him in our daily work. No more vicious idea possesses us than that which is held by so many people: that worship is something we do only in church, all unmindful of the fact that worship—expressing the worth of God in our lives—is something which we do mostly at the plow, the counter, the kitchen sink, the typewriter, or desk."

✝

THE WAYFARERS' CHAPEL, PALOS VERDES, CALIFORNIA

> Then are they glad because they be quiet;
> So he bringeth them into their desired haven.

THESE words from Psalm 107:30, placed in stone at an entrance way, generate a reverent mood among the throngs, averaging over ten thousand persons each week, which seek a spiritual ministry at the Wayfarers' Chapel. Only a dozen years ago there was only a dream in the mind of Mrs. F. F.

CHRIST AND THE CHILDREN OF THE WORLD,
REDLANDS, CALIFORNIA

Schellenberg; quickly a series of minor miracles has created a quiet haven of devotion here, looking out upon the blue Pacific.

Swept by fresh breezes from the sea, strewn in the spring with a magic carpet of wild flowers, bathed in the health-giving rays of a benevolent sun, the Rancho San Pedro saw herds of cattle and sheep on its broad hills far into the present century. But the good lady who drove over its natural paths visualized a shrine on this promontory where the wayfarer might pause in his haste to drink in the calm and peace of the scene, hear some phrase or echo of the Holy Word, realize the bounty of our Father and our too-often casual acceptance of His gifts.

The dream was made reality through the responsive imagination of Mr. and Mrs. Frank A. Vanderlip of New York, owners of a large portion of the original Spanish grant to this land. First plans contemplated a mission-type structure. Lloyd Wright, famous son of an eminent father, asked to meet members of the chapel committee on the site in order to suggest a change to a design he had long wished to realize.

He had, at times, stood in the solemn and silent grandeur of the giant redwoods and had been convinced that here was the true temple where man should worship. Instead of a church turned into a cave by sepulchral stone vaults, he planned a minimum of interference with the grove that he would plant for growth, a glass shelter over and around an altar, interweaving inner sense outward to infinite space, and emphasizing the correspondence of all things. This was of a piece with the religious philosophy of Emanuel Swedenborg, eighteenth-century scientist, statesman, and mystic, upon whose teachings regarding the Lord and His word the Church of the New Jerusalem was established, of which Mrs. Vanderlip was a member. The National Convention of the Church subscribed to these plans and met for the laying of the cornerstone in 1949 on berm walls of native rock.

Everywhere, in stones, in over-all layout, in the glass sections, the triangle is used, signifying the threefold nature of the spiritual life in the Holy Trinity. Redwood trusses rear support for steel frames enclosing plate glass as walls and roof. Delicate flowering vines which rise from inside planters entwine overhead, forming exquisite patterns against the roof. From the tower a cloister leads to an educational building containing the Wayfarers' reception room and library, overlooking the ocean on one side and a restful garden on the other. In a climate similar to that of the Holy Land, the garden provides Biblical trees and flowers.

Here lives today a continuation of the remarkable ministry of Emanuel Swedenborg, member of the Royal Swedish Academy of Sciences, nobleman, Member of Parliament, mathematical pioneer, metallurgist and mining engineer, neurologist, astronomer, inventor, and mystic. Hardly another person in the world's history has encompassed in himself so great a variety of useful knowledge or has written competently on so vast a range of practical subjects. From his fifty-fifth year Swedenborg concentrated his writings on Biblical interpretation and theology, providing a mine of materials still being explored.

THE WAYFARERS' CHAPEL, PALOS VERDES, CALIFORNIA—*WRIGHT*

Unending pilgrimages and visitations bring throngs to this lovely chapel each day, for rest, meditation, and prayer. Seated, they face a great stone altar, the three broad steps to which bear the inscriptions "Hallowed be Thy Name," "Thy Kingdom come," and "Thy will be done"—signifying man's three steps of regeneration. A child may ask that the fragrant gardenia in her hand be laid on the altar for her grandmother. Congregations gather for the Sunday morning and sunset services. A hidden instrument provides organ accompaniment for the hymns, and reverberates the *Solo Sanctus, Gloria,* and *Nunc Dimittis.* Weekly recitals of the world's finest religious music are another ministry.

Truly the Wayfarer finds here a haven of refreshment.

✛

THE MOUNTAIN CEMETERY

With their harsh leaves old rhododendrons fill
The crevices in grave plots' broken stones.
The bees renew the blossoms they destroy,
While in the burning air the pines rise still,
Commemorating long forgotten biers,
Whose roots replace the semblance of these bones.

The weight of cool, of imperceptible dust
That came from nothing and to nothing came
Is light within the earth and on the air.
The change that so renews itself is just.
The enormous, sundry platitude of death
Is for these bones, bees, trees, and leaves the same.

And splayed upon the ground and through the trees
The mountain's shadow fills and cools the air,
Smoothing the shape of headstones to the earth.
The rhododendrons suffer with the bees
Whose struggles loose ripe petals to the earth,
The heaviest burden it shall ever bear.

Our hard earned knowledge fits us for such sleep.
Although the spring must come, it passes too
To form the burden suffered for what comes.
Whatever we would give our souls to keep
Is only part of what we call the soul;
What we of time would threaten to undo.

All time in its slow scrutiny has done.
For on the grass that starts about the feet
The body's shadow turns, to shape in time,

Soon grown preponderant with creeping shade,
The final shadow that is turn of earth;
And what seems won paid for as in defeat.*

—*Edgar Bowers*

THE WISE MEN

Far to the east I see them in my mind
Coming in every year to that one place.
They carry in their hands what they must find,
In their own faces bare what they shall face.

They move in silence, permanent and sure,
Like figurines of porcelain set with gold,
The colors of their garments bright and pure,
Their graceful features elegant and old.

They do not change: nor war nor peace define
Nor end the journey that each year the same
Renders them thus. They wait upon the sign
That promises no future but their name.**

—*Edgar Bowers*

TO MY FATHER

The strong grow stronger in their faith
And from their strength their faith grows strong.
And you who fastened on a wraith
Which moved John Wesley were not wrong

To fix your being to that rock
From which the purest water flowed,
Allying pity to the stock
Whom Calvin fired into a goad

Which pricked old kings and cardinals
To fury, and whose faith subdued
The Plymouth winter, and the calls
Of flesh which tore the multitude,

Who built a solitary state
Upon the bare Laurentian soil,
Who looked on slothfulness with hate
That moment they were hating toil.

* From *Poets of the Pacific*, edited by Yvor Winters, 2d series, p. 13. Published in 1949 by Stanford University Press. Used by permission of the publisher.
** *Ibid.*, p. 14. Used by permission of the publisher.

You were not wrong to scorn the man
Who scorning, turned the other cheek,
Nor with your grave religious scan
To seek the best which men can seek.

And you may challenge, not condemn
The risk each generation runs:
That faith from which your being stems
Prove insubstantial to your sons.*

—*Donald F. Drummond*

SONNET FOR A MARRIAGE

If quiet after music is more still
For sounds that linger yet within the air,
How quiet then the church: the bridal pair
Are met in echoes of processional.
Riches of grace be on them! For they will
To enter an estate that God made fair,
And humbly, in His presence Who was there
At rites in Cana, and did miracle.
Let quietness of marriage flow from grace,
With joy in doing that they ought to do,
With hope of God in all humility.
Let two be one, and in His sight embrace,
And in communion feel His love renew
God's blessing on them and His Charity.**

—*Ann Louise Hayes*

LORD, MUST I CLIMB?

Lord, must I climb to some far peak,
    Or sit alone by rippling stream
To be aware of thy still voice
    And know my Master's noble dream?

Lord, must I sail to distant ports
    And see the children still unfed
Before there is a deep concern—
    Before a single word is said?

Lord, must I wait for ideal time
    When every mood and whim are right
Before I know the splendid joy
    Of fellowship through day and night?

* *Ibid.*, p. 42. Used by permission of the publisher.
** *Ibid.*, p. 74. Used by permission of the author.

Lord, grant that noise and tensions may
  Be signals of my need for thee;
Oh, help me find in all thy earth
  A pathway to serenity.*

—*Samuel F. Pugh*

DOUBT

They bade me cast the thing away,
They pointed to my hands all bleeding,
They listened not to all my pleading;
  The thing I meant I could not say;
  I knew that I should rue the day
    If once I cast that thing away.

  I grasped it firm, and bore the pain;
The thorny husks I stripped and scattered;
If I could reach its heart, what mattered
  If other men saw not my gain,
  Or even if I should be slain?
  I knew the risks; I chose the pain.

  O, had I cast that thing away,
I had not found what most I cherish,
A faith without which I should perish—
  The faith which, like a kernel, lay
  Hid in the husks which on that day
  My instinct would not throw away!**

—*Helen Hunt Jackson*

A PRAYER TO MAKE YOUR OWN

Look from thy sphere of endless day,
  O God of mercy and of might;
In pity look on those who stray,
  Benighted, in this land of light.

In peopled vale, in lonely glen,
  In crowded mart, by stream or sea,
How many of the sons of men
  Hear not the message sent from Thee!

Send forth thy heralds, Lord, to call
  The thoughtless young, the hardened old,

* From *Between-Time Meditations* by Samuel F. Pugh, p. 10. Copyright 1954 by Bethany Press. Used by permission of the author and the publisher.
** From *The World's Great Religious Poetry*, edited by Caroline Hill, p. 197. Copyright 1923 by The Macmillan Company. Used by permission of the publisher.

A scattered, homeless flock, till all
  Be gathered to thy peaceful fold.

Send them thy mighty word to speak,
  Till faith shall dawn, and doubt depart,
To awe the bold, to stay the weak,
  And bind and heal the broken heart.
                                    —*William Cullen Bryant*

✢

THE FAITH HEALER
William Vaughan Moody

The phenomenon of the faith healer is an integral part of the evangelistic movement of Protestantism in the Middle and Far Western United States. A most
moving portrayal of the character of the healer is found in William Vaughan
Moody's *The Faith Healer,* a drama of American life in 1910. After a period of
anguish and doubt, during which the healer feels that his power to do good for
others has left him, the healer regains his belief in himself and his mission. At the
close of the play he says:

ONE should not lose hope, for there is always hope. That is the meaning of
the sweetness in the air. It is not the perfume of lilacs nor of lilies, though
both are blooming outside the open window. It is not the scent of real flowers
at all. It is like some kindness in the air, some newborn happiness, or a
new hope rising. There is a perfume about us this beautiful Easter. The
woman in the wheelchair feels it with senses which suffering and a pure soul
have made fine beyond the measure of woman. There is a kindness in the air,
newborn happiness, and new-risen hope. It rises from any heart which can
shake off its burden through faith in the mercy of God. Lay your suffering
and your sickness from you as an outworn garment. Rise up. It is Easter
morning. The power of faith comes when one finally realizes that man
does not need to sacrifice one kind of love to another, but that God intends
us to use all kinds of love. God does not deny love to any of His children,
but gives it as a beautiful and simple gift to them all. Upon the head of each
be the use He makes of the gift of love! Let us go forward, step by step,
from faith to faith, from strength to strength; for depths of life open and
heights of love come out never dreamed of before and faith delivers all
prisoned human souls—the faith which makes all things possible, which
brings all things to pass.*

* Abridged by Karl E. Snyder from *The Faith Healer,* Act III, in *Representative American Plays,* published 1953 by Appleton-Century-Crofts, Inc. by permission of Mrs. Harriet C. Moody and Frederick J.
Fawcett II, and by special arrangement with Houghton Mifflin Company.

THE TEMPERANCE PLEDGE
Thomas Francis Marshall

One of the most influential and far-reaching movements in the religious and social life of the United States in the nineteenth century was the temperance movement. From the mass of writing of all types produced by this movement, the following is chosen as a typical example of the feeling about what temperance could accomplish. One should always remember that this feeling of what decision can achieve in this field is very much with us today in modern organizations like Alcoholics Anonymous.

It does appear to me that, if the loftiest among the lofty spirits which move and act from day to day in this hall—the proudest, the most gifted, the most fastidious here—could hear the tales I have heard, and see the men I have seen, restored, by the influence of a thing so simple as this temperance pledge, from a state of the most abject outcast wretchedness, to industry, health, comfort, and, in their own emphatic language, to "peace," he could not withhold his countenance and support from a cause fraught with such actual blessings to mankind. I have heard unlettered men trace their own history on this subject through all its stages, describe the progress of their ruin and its consequences, paint without the least disguise the utmost extent of degradation and suffering, and the power of appetite, by facts which astonished me—an appetite which triumphed over every human principle, affection and motive, yet yielded instantly and forever before the simple charm of this temperance pledge.

It is a thing of interest to see and to hear a free, bold, strong-armed, hard-fisted mechanic relate, in his own nervous and natural language, the history of his fall and his recovery; and I have heard him relate how the young man was brought up to labor, and expecting by patient toil to support himself and a rising family, had taken to his bosom in his youth the woman whom he loved—how he was tempted to quit her side, and forsake her society for the dram-shop, the frolic, the midnight brawl—how he had resolved and broken his resolutions, till his business forsook him, his friends deserted him, his furniture was seized for debt, his clothing pawned for drink, his wife broken-hearted, his children starving, his home a desert, and his heart a hell.

And then, in language true to nature, they will exultingly recount the wonders wrought in their condition by this same pledge: "My friends have come back—I have good clothes on—I am at work again—I am giving food and providing comforts for my children—I am free, I am a man, I am at peace here. My children no longer shrink cowering and huddling together in corners, or under the bed, for protection from the face of their own father. When I return at night they bound into my arms and nestle in my bosom. My wife no longer with a throbbing heart and agonized ear counts my steps before she sees me, to discover whether I am drunk or sober—I find her now singing and at work." What a simple but exquisite illustration of a woman's love, anxiety, and suffering! The fine instinct of a wife's ear detecting, from the intervals of his footfall before he had yet reached his door, whether it was the drunken or the sober step, whether she was to receive her husband or an infuriated monster in his likeness.

I say, sir, these things have an interest, a mighty interest for me; and I deem them not entirely beneath the regard of the proudest statesman here. On my conscience, sir, I speak the truth when I say that, member of Congress as I am—(and no man is prouder of his commission)—member of Congress as I am, if, by taking this pledge, it were even probable that it would bring back one human being to happiness and virtue, no matter what his rank or condition, recall the smile of hope, and trust, and love, to the cheek of one wife, as she again pillowed it in safety, peace, and confidence upon the ransomed bosom of her reclaimed and natural protector, sent one rosy child bounding to the arms of a parent whence drunkenness had exiled it long, I would dare all the ridicule of all the ridiculous people in the world, and *thank God that I had not lived in vain*. And sir, I have had that pleasure.*

✠

AMERICAN HOME MISSIONARY SOCIETY AND OREGON
Colin Brummit Goodykoontz

MINISTERS of the gospel were among the earliest pioneer settlers in Oregon, but since they were interested primarily in Indians they were regarded as foreign and not home missionaries. In this instance foreign missions helped open the way for white settlement, and white settlement called for home missions.

Between 1840 and 1850 several thousand persons from the East and the Middle West sought homes "where rolls the Oregon." Their motives were first of all economic, but political and religious considerations were also of importance. In the Mississippi Valley states and territories the home market for agricultural produce had so completely broken down by 1840 that farmers could not sell what they raised; in Oregon they hoped to find a market for their crops among the fur traders and whalers.

The ownership of Oregon was in dispute with Great Britain; it was thought that settlers would strengthen the claims of the United States. And then there were the heathen, some of whom, so the story went, had gone to St. Louis in search of the white man's Book to Heaven; a few of the men and women bound for Oregon may have had rather vaguely in mind the

* From an address before the Congressional Total-Abstinence Society. Abridged by Karl E. Snyder from *A Library of American Literature*, p. 38.

presumptive salutary effect of their presence upon the benighted inhabitants of the region. In addition, Oregon, with its mild climate, its rich soil, its pleasant streams, and its stately trees, was pictured as an earthly paradise. So the "Oregon fever" swept over the Middle West.

Where the settlers went the Church must go too. The first missionary sent to Oregon by the American Home Missionary Society was George A. Atkinson, who, with his wife, reached Oregon City in June, 1848, after a nine-months' trip around the Horn.

Moving from New England to Oregon in 1847-48 by way of the tip of South America was no light undertaking. There were supplies for the mission and household to be assembled; some food for the journey, eight or nine months in length, must be secured; a supply of medicines must not be forgotten; insurance must be arranged for.

In one very important respect Mr. Atkinson was prepared for his Oregon mission; he had a wife. His classmate at Andover, Horace Lyman, who had planned to go to Oregon with him, was not married but had been strongly advised by his friends not to go to a region so distant without a helpmeet. The basic cause of his difficulty was that perforce he had to be a hasty wooer if he were to find a wife before the boat sailed. In September, 1847, with the date of the Atkinsons' departure set for October, he wrote: "I have not yet been able to make any definite arrangement in the matter of securing a companion to go with me. I cannot now definitely tell when I shall be ready to sail."

Later Lyman wrote to admit another defeat: "I have been disappointed *unexpectedly* in regard to my expectations of securing the lady to whom I have before referred, as my companion. The difficulties of my field seem to have dissuaded her. Ought I to make ready to sail next month, in the vessel then going, or ought I to delay till Spring, & make still further efforts for securing one to go with me?" Fortunately for Horace Lyman he took his time and found a suitable "companion," with whom he arrived in Oregon in 1849.

Messrs. Atkinson and Lyman began their work in Oregon under trying circumstances. White settlers and the Indians were in a state of excitement. Religious animosities had been intensified because of the charges made by rabid foes of Rome that Catholics had stirred up the Indians to attack the Protestant missionaries. Oregon was in a state of transition from provisional to regular territorial government. The California gold fever, which broke out shortly after Atkinson's arrival in Oregon, occupied men's minds to the exclusion of religious considerations.

In addition to the usual difficulties of carrying on religious work in the midst of many men who were given to intemperance, gambling, and profanity, the representatives of the Society, some of whom were Congregationalists from New England, faced special problems. The population was not only heterogeneous, but there was also a considerable number of persons of Southern background or sympathies who were prejudiced against New

Englanders. In pre-Civil War days there were sharp clashes in Oregon between the foes and friends of slavery. The uncompromising stand of the New England men rendered them unpopular with certain groups who denounced them as abolitionists, "black Republicans," "grannies," and the "beneficiaries of Old Women's Sewing Circles."

A homely phase of missionary life in Oregon involved wearing apparel. To the officers of the Society in New York City came requests from time to time that such purchases as these be made on account of some particular missionary: "3 pairs best French kid walking shoes for Mrs. L. sise 4½ & 2 pairs of good pegged boots (calf) & 2 pegged shoes, sise smallish No. 9s for myself. 2 good hats, circumference (I do not know No.) at the band on the outside 22¾ inches & 1 cloth cap. 1 good Summer straw bonnet good sise, lined and trimmed"; or "1 Thick, well lined overcoat, loose fit, dark, pilot cloth if not too coarse. 1 India Rubber overcoat with leggins & cap, not a comical one. I wish this to wear over others but to button, in surtout form. 4 pairs of shoes for a little boy, 1, 2, & 3 years old. 4 pairs of shoes for a girl 9 and 10 years old—small sise." What a boon to these remote frontiersmen a Montgomery Ward or Sears-Roebuck catalogue would have been!*

✢

"THY KINGDOM COME," ON BENDED KNEE

ONE of the most exciting sagas in American history is the story of the westward movement. The covered wagon and the stagecoach, the wild frontier town, the relentless pushing toward new frontiers, on through deep gorges and over high mountain passes, and finally the railroads—all these stand for the conquest of the rugged barriers which separated the Pacific from the Atlantic. In imagination one can still hear the thud of eager feet and feel the shudder of the iron horses on the rails as a long procession of men sought new lands and new wealth, and as they set out to build a new civilization in the far west.

Frederick Lucian Hosmer's hymn, " 'Thy Kingdom Come,' on Bended Knee," gives rich expression to man's ardent and patient hope that the pilgrimage of history will issue into a splendid fulfillment here and now, that the prayer of the ages, "Thy Kingdom Come," will find immediate realization. This is the desire of all pilgrim souls who desire a better country.

The hymn devoutly sees that even as man must wait through "the slow watches of the night," yet these too belong to God, and that when men are disobedient and rebellious to frustrate the right, yet the "silent stars" fight from heaven and the cause is not really lost.

Yet as the hymn moves, hope flares brightly: "Already on the hills the

* Abridged from *Home Missions on the American Frontier* by Colin Brummit Goodykoontz, pp. 272-78. Copyright 1939 by The Caxton Printers, Ltd. Used by permission of the publisher.

flags of dawn appear." God is bringing in His day, the day when justice "shall be clothed with might, and every hurt be healed." God's promised day of perfect righteousness will come.

Dr. Hosmer (1840-1929) wrote the hymn in 1891, for the commencement exercises of the Meadville Theological School, Meadville, Pennsylvania. It was first published in 1894. Born in Framingham, Massachusetts, Mr. Hosmer entered the Unitarian ministry after graduation from Harvard Divinity School. After serving pastorates in Massachusetts, Illinois, Ohio, and Missouri, he finally moved to Berkeley, California, in 1900, where he spent the rest of his life.

Highly productive in the writing of hymns, Dr. Hosmer has been called the foremost American hymn writer of the turn of the century. Some thirty-five of his hymns have come into use, and the best of them are included in many hymnals both in America and in England.

The tune "St. Flavian" is the first half of the tune which first appeared in the *English Psalter* of 1562 and set to Psalm 132. This Psalter was popularly known as *Day's Psalter* from the name of the printer. The present form seems to be due to Richard Redhead's *Ancient Hymn Melodies* (1853).

"Thy Kingdom Come," on Bended Knee *

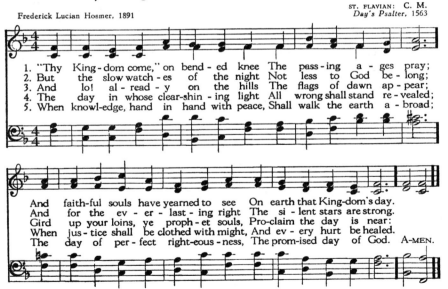

*From *The Hymnbook*. Used by permission of Westminster Press.

God of grace and God of Glory *

REGENT SQUARE   8.7.8.7.8.7.

Harry Emerson Fosdick, 1930

Henry Smart, 1867

1 God of grace and God of glo - ry, On thy peo - ple
2 Lo! the hosts of e - vil round us Scorn thy Christ, as -
3 Cure thy chil - dren's war - ring mad - ness, Bend our pride to
4 Set our feet on loft - y plac - es; Gird our lives that

pour thy power; Crown thine an - cient church's sto - ry;
sail his ways! From the fears that long have bound us
thy con - trol; Shame our wan - ton, self - ish glad - ness,
they may be Ar - mored with all Christ - like grac - es

Bring her bud to glo - rious flower. Grant us wis - dom,
Free our hearts to faith and praise: Grant us wis - dom,
Rich in things and poor in soul. Grant us wis - dom,
In the fight to set men free. Grant us wis - dom,

grant us cour - age, For the fac - ing of this hour.
grant us cour - age, For the liv - ing of these days.
grant us cour - age, Lest we miss thy king - dom's goal.
grant us cour - age, That we fail not man nor thee.

GOD OF GRACE AND GOD OF GLORY

AMONG the hymns which have traveled from East Coast to West Coast and which have moved north and south and across all lands is the widely sung and deservedly popular hymn of Harry Emerson Fosdick, "God of Grace and God of Glory." The hymn represents significantly the way in which Dr. Fosdick so richly gathered together the most forward-looking and vital concerns of American Christianity at its best as they pushed for expression in the first half of the twentieth century. Dr. Fosdick symbolizes an era in the history of American Christianity, and his lifelong concerns come to splendid expression in this hymn.

The hymn was written during the summer of 1930 in anticipation of the opening of the great Riverside Church in New York City; it was first sung at the opening service, October 5, 1930, and again at the dedication, February 8, 1931.

The opening line brings us a tremendous and unforgettable description of God in the great Biblical terms of grace and glory, numinous words which split the heavens open. There follows the prayer for power, as if a new Pentecost might be granted the Church, a Pentecost in which again all men would hear in their own tongue the mighty works of God. How well our time knows the "hosts of evil" which assail man and enslave him to unfaith and to the ruin of his times!

The constant prayer is for wisdom and courage "for the facing of this hour," "for the living of these days." And if you ask, which hour? what days? Dr. Fosdick replies, days when men are literally mad for war, insolent in pride, self-centered and wanton, "rich in things and poor in soul." But the Christian warrior who girds himself for this our battle must be the happy warrior, "armored with all Christlike graces." Unless the Christian warrior is Christian in his strife, he will fail both man and God.

The fifth stanza pleads for an active faith, undaunted by the strength of the enemy, and which sees its glory in man's search for God's salvation:

> Save us from weak resignation
> To the evils we deplore;
> Let the search for Thy salvation
> Be our glory evermore.
> Grant us wisdom,
> Grant us courage,
> Serving Thee whom we adore.

The tune "Regent Square" was written for *Psalms and Hymns for Divine Worship,* a book published in 1867 for use among English Presbyterians. The name of the tune was taken from the Regent Square Church, the most

prominent Presbyterian Church in London. Henry Smart, the composer
(1813-1879), was one of the most important English church musicians. As
organist, composer, and editor of hymnals, he served the church of his
day with great devotion and effectiveness.

CONTENTS

PART V SECTION 5

THE CHURCH CROSSES CANADA AND ALASKA

✝

Yea, so have I strived to preach the gospel, not where Christ was named, lest I should build upon another man's foundation.—ROMANS 15:20

✝

PICTURES: PAGE

Interpretation: St. Paul's Church, Halifax, Nova Scotia—*Fougeron* 634
Picture: St. Paul's Church, Halifax, Nova Scotia—*Fougeron* 635
Interpretation: Communion Table, Lakeview United Church, Regina,
   Saskatchewan 636
Picture: Communion Table, Lakeview United Church, Regina,
   Saskatchewan 637
Interpretation: Moosehide Altar, Fort Yukon, Alaska 639
Picture: Moosehide Altar, Fort Yukon, Alaska 641

POETRY:

Harvest Hymn—*Sangster* 642
Standing on Tiptoe—*Cameron* 643
The Builder—*Scott* 643
Far Music—*Marlatt* 644
The Wayside Cross—*Scott* 645
Sea Lavender—*Bowman* 645
Mountain Communion—*Marlatt* 646

STORIES:

The Tumult of Her Birth—*Silcox* 646
The Winter of the Cross—*Robins* 649
Eskimo Preacher—*Agnew* 652

MUSIC:

Interpretation: O North, With All Thy Vales—*Bryant* 656
Music: O North, With All Thy Vales—*Schein* 657
Interpretation: My Faith It Is an Oaken Staff—*Lynch* 658
Music: My Faith It Is an Oaken Staff—*Folk Melody* 659

ST. PAUL'S CHURCH, HALIFAX, NOVA SCOTIA

HALIFAX in the eighteenth century was the center of the great English naval and military activities in connection with the capture and settlement of Canada. Its harbor, one of the finest in the world, formerly known as Chebucto, was named for the Earl of Halifax and the town was established in 1749.

The Reverend William Tutty was a missionary sent by the Society for the Propagation of the Gospel along with the founding governor. The first divine worship was held in the dining room of the governor's home, and the next in a warehouse. But a place for a church building was included in the original plan for the town, a document still to be seen in the British Museum. Its frame, modeled on St. Peter's in London, was shipped from Boston and erected in 1750—the first Protestant church in Canada. The oak and pine beams enclosed a sanctuary ninety by fifty-six feet. In 1930 when renewal work was done, these beams were still perfectly sound. Planned by the architect, Fougeron, in the style of Sir Christopher Wren's many churches, it was named after his masterpiece in London, St. Paul's, and situated on "the Parade." The original local sponsor in 1750 was the Honorable Edward Cornwallis, Royal Governor of Nova Scotia. He was a twin brother of the Archbishop of Canterbury, and uncle of Lord Charles Cornwallis of Yorktown note.

A historic deed refers to the church as a Royal Foundation, in honor of the original benefactions and endowments from His Majesty King George II. As such it was for some generations not subject to any bishop or ecclesiastical court. As the "garrison church," for nearly a century it was the one to which the regiments on duty in Halifax paraded to join with the civilian congregation in divine service. Here was announced the final debacle and surrender at Yorktown in 1781.

Here, too, during the War of 1812, were announced the tidings of the burning of Washington by British troops. And here, one Sunday morning in June, 1813, just as the rector had begun his sermon, someone tiptoed into the church to whisper to friends seated near the door that the British ship, *Shannon,* fresh from her duel off Boston, had arrived in the harbor convoying her adversary, the captured *Chesapeake,* whose gallant captain, Lawrence, lay with other dead and dying of his heroic ship's company on the shattered and bloodstained deck. The church, we are told, was emptied in record time, only the rector remaining at his post. And since the age of chivalry was not yet over, the young enemy commander whose last order had been "Don't give up the ship," was buried from St. Paul's two days later, with full naval, military, and civil honors.

Some thirty thousand Loyalists fled the American Revolution and settled in Nova Scotia, with Halifax and St. Paul's Church receiving a large share of this new population.

ST. PAUL'S CHURCH, HALIFAX, NOVA SCOTIA—FOUGERON

During the first fifty years of the church's history, attendance at divine service in the winter months called for courage and hardihood, for the building was not heated in any way. Worshipers brought with them foot-warmers, consisting of iron boxes filled with burning charcoal, or wooden boxes containing heated bricks; others took their dogs to church to serve a similar purpose; everyone kept on his fur coat.

Music was also sometimes a problem in the early days. At a meeting of the Vestry, held July 24, 1770, it was voted that: "Whereas the Anthems sung by the Clerk and others in the Gallery, during divine service, have not answered to the Honour and Glory of God, inasmuch as the major part of the congregation do not understand either the words or the music, and cannot join therein; Therefore, for the future, the Clerk has express orders not to sing any such Anthems, or leave his usual Seat without direction and leave first obtained from the Rev. Mr. Breynton."

In the possession of St. Paul's is a priceless silver Communion service bearing faint traces of the monogram of its Royal donor, Queen Anne, and the date 1713. An early organ was a prize of war between Britain and Spain in 1763. Tradition says that a captured Spanish ship, on her way to South America, was brought into harbor as a prize, and that among the articles composing her cargo was an organ made of excellent material. The organ, as the other goods on board, was offered for sale and the church-wardens of St. Paul's became its purchasers.

This church has the oldest Sunday school in North America, with a continuous history unbroken since 1783. One pew in this historic church has been occupied by successors in a single family, by the name of Almon, through five generations from 1786 to the present day.

St. Paul's was the first cathedral of the Church of England in the overseas Empire. Within its venerable walls were held the first episcopal visitation, the first confirmation, and the first ordination in Canada, all solemnized by Bishop Charles Inglis. One of its assistant rectors was the Reverend Aaron Cleveland, ancestor of a President of the United States.

Today the church bears the proud title of "The Westminster Abbey of Canada," a treasure house of interest unrivaled in Canadian church history; flags, brasses, hatchments, mural tablets, fonts, pulpit, lectern, Holy Table, portraits, windows, arches, all bear witness to its long association with the Province, the Dominion, and the Empire.

✠

COMMUNION TABLE, LAKEVIEW UNITED CHURCH, REGINA, SASKATCHEWAN

THE Lakeview United Church, at Regina, is more than a phenomenally successful local church; it is a symbol of a fond ideal—the dream of a united church, the One Body of Christ, foretold by the primitive apostles.

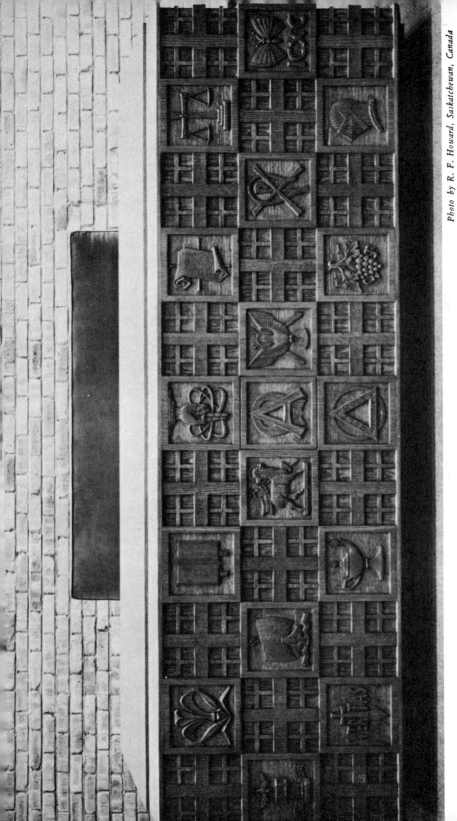

COMMUNION TABLE, LAKEVIEW UNITED CHURCH, REGINA, SASKATCHEWAN

When four great communions in Canada merged in 1925, a witness said the year became "a monumental date in ecclesiastical history" because it marked "the first large-scale achievement of organic union since the Protestant Reformation." The second largest country in the world, Canada presented vast areas, sparsely populated, with a varied people speaking twenty-five languages in the scattered settlements. No one church was equal to the missionary task. Christian challenge overcame denominational pride and the Methodist, Presbyterian, Congregational, and local union bodies cast their lots as one. But this was only the capstone of a series of previous successes in merger, for experts have computed that the United Church of Canada has gathered into itself forty distinct Christian bodies, in nineteen separate acts of church union. (See "The Tumult of Her Birth," p. 646.)

In the western prairies was Regina, whose growing Lakeview area presented a challenge to Christian adventure. A community Sunday school had previously served the young community, but rapid growth showed need of a church. In 1947 it was organized, in 1951 it occupied its Church Hall, and in 1956 the beautiful sanctuary was dedicated. Modern art in the service of an ancient faith had reared its symbolic House on the western plains.

Built of brick and stone, this contemporary assembly of worship facilities is dominated by a seventy-foot tower on which is mounted a metal cross. One view from the mahogany-paneled narthex reveals the small chapel, which is hushed beneath a mural depicting the life of Christ, including scenes of the Nativity, the Crucifixion, and the Resurrection. Turning, one sees the nave, walled with oak and brick, under lights small and starlike. Fine wood carvings adorn the pulpit, lectern, baptismal font, choir screen— and the Communion Table, whose impressive symbolism captures the attention.

The Table (see below) is designed to tell the story of the Christian life in graphic representation. The chart at the conclusion of this paragraph is a key to the message. Through Baptism (1), we receive the gift of Purity (2), and the Sword of Truth (3), and are initiated into the fellowship of the Church portrayed by the "navis" or ship (4). As members of the Church we are instructed in the Holy Bible (5), and Christian doctrine (6). The life of the Christian and the Church is centered in God the Father (9), in God the Son, the Alpha and Omega (8) and Victorious Lamb (7), and God the Holy Spirit (10), the Blessed Trinity (11). Our names are added to the scroll of the Church (12); we are privileged to partake of Holy Communion (13) and to be followers of Christ the Good Shepherd (14). We receive the Helmet of Salvation (16), anticipate the Judgment (15), and the gift of Everlasting Life (17).

Thus, within the span of less than one decade, it was demonstrated that the power of a united church could work wonders among conditions previously almost impervious to the weaker witness and action of divided denominations. The art form of the Lakeview Church is contemporary, consonant with the ecumenical movement of which it is a part—for it is the twentieth century which seems destined to go down in history as the era of the Ecumenical Reformation.

✠

MOOSEHIDE ALTAR, FORT YUKON, ALASKA

In the long ago of Russian Alaska, "servants" of the Hudson's Bay Company in search of better furs and trading facilities portaged from the Mackenzie River in the far northwest of Canada to the Bell River; down that river to the Porcupine; and down the Porcupine River to the mighty Yukon. Near the confluence of these two rivers they established, in 1847, a fort and trading post which they named Fort Yukon.

Although one hundred twenty miles west of the then unsurveyed Alaska-Canada border, it is debatable whether or not the founders of Fort Yukon realized that they were on foreign soil. However, Russia either ignored or was ignorant of the presence of the fort in her territory and, being fully occupied with her region about the lower Yukon, sent neither traders, soldiers, nor missionaries to the region served by the Hudson's Bay Company.

Aware of this situation, missionaries of the Church Missionary Society in England and of the Church of England in Canada followed the trails of the H.B.C. servants to bring the gospel and sacraments to the primitive Indians who constantly migrated about the region and came to the fort to trade furs for supplies.

Among the first of these daring servants of the Cross was the Venerable Archdeacon McDonald, D.D., who, about 1870, came into the region from the Canadian Northwest Territory. Having learned the very difficult native tongue (Takudh) from the Athapascan Indians at Fort McPherson, Canada, he reduced it to a written language by using his own system of phonetic spelling. He then prepared a grammar and dictionary and accomplished the heroic task of translating the entire Holy Bible, the *Book of Common Prayer,* and several hymns into this written form and proceeded to teach the people to read their own language. To date, his translations are the only ones which have been made and they are used today whenever church services are conducted in the native tongue in the Yukon region.

At noon on August 8, 1869, the Union Jack of England was lowered from its mast over the fort and the Stars and Stripes of the United States was raised in its place. By this simple ceremony the Hudson's Bay Company acknowledged the purchase of Alaska by the United States from Russia on October 18, 1867. Almost two years had elapsed since the purchase, but the Company had remained at Fort Yukon until a boundary survey definitely established the fact that it was in Alaska and not Canada.

Immediately the Company withdrew up the Porcupine River into Canada. The mission which had been established at Fort Yukon was also withdrawn at this time and re-established at Old Rampart House on the Porcupine. Later, however, the Canadian missionaries traveling by boat in summer and dog team in winter followed the Yukon and Porcupine Rivers once again into the region and continued to bring the gospel and sacraments to the people until the Protestant Episcopal Church in the United States of America was able to station a priest permanently at Fort Yukon in 1898. Even after this date they continued to serve the region in conjunction with the Episcopal Church for several years.

Fort Yukon is located at the northernmost bend of the Yukon River about eight and one-half miles north of the Arctic Circle in the center of a vast valley known as the Yukon flats. In this flat region the Yukon broadens to a point about a mile wide at Fort Yukon and drains a marshy plain some two hundred miles long and one hundred miles wide. From the character of this region the Indian people received their tribal name of Kutcha Kutchin, meaning "People of the Flat Lands." Although monotonous and unvaried in topography the region is extremely varied climatically, the temperature ranging from almost a hundred degrees above zero in the summer to seventy-eight below in the winter. The population of Fort Yukon is now approximately seven hundred Athapascan Indians and fifty Caucasians, and an additional five hundred Indians are served by the mission and its clinic in their isolated villages located fifty to two hundred miles away from Fort Yukon.

Prior to the coming of the white man, the Indians used beads primarily for money and not for decoration. Such "trade-beads" were large in size and, if used for ornamentation, were simply sewn on the ends of strands attached to the outer garments. "Jewelry," a sign of wealth and position, was made of dentalium shells, beads, and porcupine quills in the form of necklaces.

Because of the dreary monotony of the region, especially in winter when "black" spruce trees and white snow are almost the only colors, the people needed color and design to brighten their lives. Yet being what the historian Arnold Toynbee would call an "arrested civilization" they had been too busily engaged in the struggle to survive to have time to develop an art or design. Thus the introduction of small, brightly colored beads, the coming

Courtesy St. Stephen's Episcopal Church, Fort Yukon, Alaska

MOOSEHIDE ALTAR, FORT YUKON, ALASKA

of a less migratory life owing to the supplies available at the trading post, and the use of rifles for hunting provided a new craft for these people and they were soon so skillful in the creation of bead-worked objects that they are still unequaled in the other regions of the territory. In time they had created a floral design which has become known as the "Fort Yukon Rose."

In 1921, eight Indian women under the direction of Archdeacon Hudson Stuck invested their unique talents in the making of an altar frontal and superfrontal from unsmoked moosehide as a thank offering to God for His mercies. The moosehide was first cleaned and prepared by soaking; then, constantly wetted, it was scraped with sharp knives until all hair and flesh had been removed and it was soft and pliable. After being dried and cut to shape, the superfrontal was covered with thousands upon thousands of beads forming a floral pattern against a white background. Similarly, the *IHS* symbol was then sewn on the frontal, and four solidly beaded strips were made to hang down over the frontal.

Such sewing is a long and tedious process. Two needles are used. The first lays down four or five beads and the second is used to place a stitch beside each bead to hold it securely in place. The long hours of sewing witness to the devotion and love of the women who made this unrivaled example of native American art earnestly devoted to the adoration of the Universal Father of Mercies.

When the first altar cloth had been completed, a duplicate was made and sent to the Cathedral of St. John the Divine, New York City, where it may be seen on an altar in a side chapel in the nave of that cathedral.

HARVEST HYMN

God of the Harvest, Thou, whose sun
  Has ripened all the golden grain,
We bless Thee for Thy bounteous store,
The cup of Plenty running o'er,
  The sunshine and the rain!

The year laughs out for very joy,
  Its silver treble echoing
Like a sweet anthem through the woods,
Till mellowed by the solitudes
  It folds its glossy wing.

But our united voices blend
  From day to day unweariedly;
Sure as the sun rolls up the morn,
Or twilight from the eve is born,
  Our song ascends to Thee.

Where'er the various-tinted woods,
  In all their autumn splendour dressed,

Impart their gold and purple dyes
To distant hills and farthest skies
    Along the crimson west:

The spirits of the golden year,
    From crystal caves and grottoes dim,
From forest depths and mossy sward,
Myriad-tongued, with one accord
    Peal forth their harvest hymn.*

—*Charles Sangster*

STANDING ON TIPTOE

Standing on tiptoe ever since my youth
    Striving to grasp the future just above,
I hold at length the only future—Truth,
    And Truth is Love.

I feel as one who being awhile confined
    Sees drop to dust about him all his bars:—
The clay grows less, and leaving it, the mind
    Dwells with the stars.**

—*George Frederick Cameron*

THE BUILDER

When the deep cunning architect
Had the great minster planned,
They worked in faith for twice two hundred years
And reared the building grand;
War came and famine and they did not falter,
But held his line,
And filled the space divine
With carvings meet for the soul's eye;
And not alone the chantry and thereby
The snowy altar,
But in every part
They carved the minster after his own heart,
And made the humblest places fair,
Even the dimmest cloister-way and stair,
With vineyard tendrils,
With ocean-seeming shells,
With filmy weeds from sea,
With bell-flowers delicate and bells,

---

* From *Canadian Poets and Poetry*, edited by John W. Garvin, p. 13. Published in 1916 by McClelland,
Goodchild & Stewart. Used by permission of the publisher.
  ** *Ibid.*, p. 103.

All done minute with excellent tracery.
Come, O my soul,
And let me build thee like the minster fair,
Deep based and large as air,
And full of hidden graces wrought
In faith and infinite thought,
Till all thy dimmest ways,
Shall gleam with little vines and fruits of praise,
So that one day
The consummate Architect
Who planned the souls that we are set to build,
May pause and say:
How curiously wrought is this!
The builder followed well My thought, My chart,
And worked for Me, not for the world's wild heart;
Here are the outward virtues true!
But see how all the inner parts are filled
With singular bliss:
Set it aside
I shall come here again at eventide.*

—*Duncan Campbell Scott*

FAR MUSIC

They have chanted their hymns
To Olympus
And the vales of Arcady;
They have clothed them with rifted clouds
And rainbow pageantry;
But Calvary . . . ?
Pagans may pipe of Pan,
Of Daphne,
Apollo and Aphrodite,
But I shall sing of God—
The God of Moses,
The God of Prophecy,
The God of Him,
Whose life and death were poems,
Singing, singing,
Down the measures of eternity
The motifs of love
And death
And life that carols on forever . . .
Amen.**

—*Earl Marlatt*

* *Ibid.*, p. 141.
** From *Cathedral: A Volume of Poems* by Earl Marlatt, p. 124. Copyright 1956 by Earl Marlatt. Published by Parthenon Press. Used by permission of the author and the publisher.

THE WAYSIDE CROSS

A wayside cross at set of day
Unto my spirit this did say—

"O soul, my branching arms you see
Point four ways to infinity.

"One points to infinite above,
To show the height of heavenly love.

"Two point to infinite width, which shows,
That heavenly love no limit knows.

"One points to infinite beneath,
To show God's love is under death.

"The four arms join, an emblem sweet
That in God's heart all loves will meet."

I thanked the cross as I turned away
For such sweet thoughts in the twilight grey.*
—*Frederick George Scott*

SEA LAVENDER

My Puritan grandmother!—I see her now,
With placid brow,
Always so sure
That no things but the right things shall endure!
Sombrely neat, so orderly and prim,
Always a little grim,
Austere but kind. . . .
Smooth-banded hair and smoothly-banded mind.

But let me whisper it to you today—
I know it now
That deep in her there was a flame at play.
Beneath that brow
The blue-grey eyes sought beauty, found it too
Most often by the ocean's passionate blue.
Her sea-beach treasures—shells and coloured weed
Gathered and hoarded with glad human greed—
They warm my heart today with insight new.
How vividly I see her, frail and old,

* From *The Book of Canadian Poetry,* edited by A. J. M. Smith, p. 209. Published in 1943 by University of Chicago Press. Used by permission of the publisher.

A tiny, black-clothed figure on the beach,
Compactly wrapped against the sea-wind's cold,
Patiently waiting till waves let her reach
Some sandy strip, where purple, amber, green,
Her lacy sea-weed treasures could be seen.
(She pressed and mounted them—frail tangled things!
Handled by her, fit to trim fairies' wings.)

So I recall her,
Searching salt-sea pools
For Beauty's shadow.
All her rigid rules,
And cold austereness with a storm-tossed child,
Melt into airs of evenings, warm and mild.
And I find revelation, sweet indeed,
In her dear treasures of sea shells and weed.*

—Louise Morey Bowman

MOUNTAIN COMMUNION

If you have once seen ripples
Upon a mountain lake,
You will not marvel that love can fill
Hearts until they break.

If you have once seen granite
Above the highest grass,
You will not grieve that fragile things
Blossom and seed and pass.

If you have once seen birches
Rise, star-lit, from the snow
You will not fear the white release
Beyond the afterglow.**

—Earl Marlatt

THE TUMULT OF HER BIRTH

(The Ecumenical Movement in Canada)

Claris Edwin Silcox

AFTER some twenty-five years of toil and careful preparation, the union of the Congregational, Methodist, and Presbyterian churches of Canada became a fact for the great majority of the communicants of the three denominations.

* *Ibid.*, p. 261.
** From *Cathedral: A Volume of Poems* by Earl Marlatt, p. 5. Copyright 1956 by Earl Marlatt. Published by Parthenon Press. Used by permission of the author and the publisher.

The narrative of the inauguration of this church union is a dramatic and soul-stirring story.

On June 10, 1925, the inaugural services were held in the Arena, the largest building in Toronto available for such a service, and holding eight thousand people. The order of service had been carefully worked out by a committee of men who had a rare flair for liturgical art and was most beautifully printed in a two-colored booklet of forty pages. Three hundred and fifty laymen—elders, stewards and deacons—had been mobilized to assist in the communion service. There was no organ in the Arena, and the music was led by a large orchestra and a choir of two hundred and fifty picked voices, under the leadership of Dr. H. A. Wricker, the conductor of the world-famous Mendelssohn Choir of Toronto. The official delegates of the three denominations met at a designated place and entered the hall in three different "streams" singing the processional hymn "The Church's One Foundation." The service that followed was divided into four parts:

(a) A Period of General Devotion, Praise and Intercession.
(b) The Hallowing of Church Union.
(c) Declaration of Church Union, with prayer constituting the General Council of the United Church.
(d) The Holy Communion.

A careful study of this service would well repay any who have the responsibility of planning a similar gathering. The hymns were purposefully selected to represent the contributions of various denominations—Presbyterian, Congregational, Methodist, Anglican and Moravian—to the hymnody of the Church Catholic; so, too, the collects were drawn from the *Book of Common Prayer,* the *Book of Common Order* (Presbyterian) and the *Book of Congregational Worship,* while some prayers were especially composed for the occasion.

In that part of the ritual dealing with the hallowing of Church Union the representatives of the various churches concisely expressed the special contributions of their denominations to the United Church in the manifestation of the spirit, thus:

Presbyterian: "In vigilance for Christ's kirk and covenant, in care for the spread of education and devotion to sacred learning."

Congregational: "In the liberty of prophesying, the love of spiritual freedom and the enforcement of civic justice."

Methodist: "In evangelical zeal and human redemption, the testimony of spiritual experience, and the ministry of sacred song."

Local Union: "In the furtherance of community-life within the Kingdom of God."

This part of the service concluded with a commemoration of the Faithful and an acceptance on the part of the people of the triple or quadruple inheritance thus received.

The Declaration of the Church Union involved the official signing of the covenant by the four officials especially designated for this purpose. Later, all the duly accredited members of the First General Council attached their signatures to this historic document, and some others also signed by error.

The Communion address was delivered by Dr. S. P. Rose on "The Cross at the Heart of Life," based on John 12:24-25. The sacramental service was significant not only in the spirit which prevailed but in the form used. In Congregational and Presbyterian churches, the elements had always been distributed by elders and deacons; the early custom in the Methodist churches had been inherited from the Anglican communion, where the communicants came to the altar rail and received the bread and wine from the hands of the officiating minister. As the individual cup came into vogue, however, the minister (sometimes assisted by visiting ministers) carried the elements through the congregation. Confronted with the necessities of administering communion to eight thousand persons and the difference in distribution practiced by the uniting churches, those entrusted with the details of this part of the service decided to use laymen.

As a result, this method is the one mostly used today throughout the United Church and to this extent the United Church has definitely moved away from the type of observance so dear to those who cherish the Catholic tradition—especially the Anglicans and the Lutherans. There are many former Methodists who feel here a distinct loss, and the Holy Communion does not mean as much to them now as it did before, when they went forward, humbly knelt and partook of the symbols of spiritual nurture offered by the representative of Christ. There are many who feel that the United Church of Canada should be broad enough to encourage in the same local church both types of distribution. The prevailing tendency, however, throughout the entire church, is for but four observances a year, and one detects the dominance of the Presbyterian attitude. At this point, however, the Methodist tradition is that which may have the greatest influence in preserving a spiritual nexus with those of the Anglican communion.

Thus, in a solemn act, and before an immense concourse of people, the United Church of Canada was dedicated to its high emprize. At the same time and at the same hour, all over the Dominion, community groups met together to vent their high enthusiasm and, in their own way, to share in this act of dedication. Visitors and fraternal delegations from churches all over the world occupied an honored place on the occasion, and later in more informal gatherings brought the good wishes of their respective communions. The day was graced by the initial appearance of the consolidated religious weekly, henceforth called *The New Outlook*. On its cover was the figure of a youth in classic dress, standing on an eminence overlooking a rolling country wherein was no sign of human habitation—but the arms were outstretched in hope as he surveyed the wide expanse before him. Thus, young Canada stood on one of its great peaks of achievement on June 10, 1925, and looked forward to the years with the thrill of hope and prayer.*

* Abridged from *Church Union in Canada, Its Causes and Consequences*, pp. 287-89. Copyright 1933 by Institute of Social and Religious Research. Used by permission of the publisher.

THE WINTER OF THE CROSS
Elizabeth Robins

Elizabeth and Raymond Robins were a remarkable brother and sister. She was a great actress, the first and possibly the best actress of Ibsen in English. Although an American, she numbered among her friends the cream of English political and intellectual society. Raymond Robins achieved fame as a social economist, being an important member of the Red Cross Mission to Russia during and after World War I, and a consistent worker for peace and improvement of social conditions in the 1920's. As a result of the following letter, Elizabeth journeyed to Nome in 1900, the first summer of the great Alaskan gold rush, to find her brother Raymond, as she thought, wasting his youth and his health as minister and friend to the hundreds of men and women who came to him in their distress. The letter is a fine example of the effect of an Arctic winter experience on the philosophical agnostic, leading him to the position of lay pastor of a Protestant Church in Nome at the turn of the twentieth century.

Yukon River, Alaska
Steamer *Sarah,* Aug. 31, 1899

SISTER MINE,

Much of what I am about to relate may seem strange, part may appear incomprehensible, yet in all "I speak the words of soberness and truth."

As a preface to what follows I would state that, whether from heredity or environment I shall not here enquire, certain it is, that from the dawn of my intellectual life I have felt a profound interest in questions of moral philosophy and religion. At the age of fifteen I had begun to dissent from the dogmas of current Theology; at nineteen I was an agnostic and an enthusiastic follower of Spencer and Huxley, and at twenty-one supposed I had sounded the depths of this matter and laid it upon the self. I had discovered in my arrogant ignorance that Jesus of Nazareth was simply a moral and religious reformer, and the Bible the mere history of an oriental people with a distinctly religious bias.

So denying God I began the worship of mammon. The motives and hopes of this period are indicated by a letter written you from Burnet, Texas. But owing to an innate love for the things that are more excellent, this faith was transitory, and I speedily found my God was a miserable image of clay. Then I slowly began to worship "Fame." Here at last was a God worth having and I determined to be great in the vulgar sense and for a time the applause of my fellows was as a Siren's song. The height of this dream with its vain ambitions is indicated by a letter written you from San Francisco. Yet not here might I find peace. From the argument of my first great law case I began to distrust my new Deity and it was this secret distrust, unexpressed and half denied even to myself, that together with another motive impelled my turning back once again to mammon's shrine in faraway Alaska.

So. . . . I gave up what the worldly-wise called a brilliant future and came to Alaska hunting the "Golden Fleece." There were, of course, other surface motives, but deep down these were controlling.

As I look back upon my first winter in Alaska, its hardship and suffering are appalling. There were times when I coveted death. And on the icebound snow-covered tundras with the north wind howling, miles from any human habitation, starvation possible, death imminent, my self-confident pride of intellect and skeptical philosophy was tried in the balance and found wanting. Do not misunderstand me. I am not easily alarmed and I have not been frightened into the Kingdom of God. As an agnostic I could have died fearlessly and been glad that the struggle was over. But to live an agnostic among such surroundings and be human, this was impossible. The deathlike stillness of the long Arctic night, the cold mocking sunshine of the quickly passing daytime, the constant presence of the Ice King eager to touch you into dreamless sleep, starvation staring at you with hollow eyes and sunken cheeks, so environed, you must either drug the senses into dullness with tobacco or whiskey, or realize that without faith in something not ourselves, we shall either turn demon or go mad.

In the midst of this never-to-be-forgotten journey over the ice and snow, we stopped for a night and a day at a Jesuit Mission on the Yukon. Here were four Priests of the Order, five sisters of St. Anne and two Brothers, teaching the Indians not only religion but the three R's and habits of domestic cleanliness and order; quietly and gladly wearing out their lives serving others, doing good without money and without price.

Yet not here, nor for many months to come, was I to understand the power of the Christian faith and the marvel of the life in Christ. I write of . . . the Mission of the Holy Cross because, while not convinced, I was deeply moved by the love and service of this consecrated Priest. My difficulty was an intellectual one and no amount of personal testimony nor example could have converted me from the error of my ways.

Another incident and I have done with this lengthy preface. In one of the darkest hours of our long journey we camped by the side of a gulch in the mountains, and prepared to rest for the night. It was bitterly cold. Not a breath of air stirred the loose snow in the gulch. The stillness was so oppressive I could not sleep. Rising I drew on my parka, mitts and moccasins, and slipping on my snowshoes went a short distance up the gulch. The night was terrible yet superb. As far as the eye could reach stretched the spotless coverlet of snow . . . the gorgeous streamers of the Aurora, shot from horizon to zenith, gleamed in all the colors of the rainbow, then flickered, rose again, faded and died away. Over all brooded the inexpressible silence of the Arctic night, full of awful menace, yet sublime.

As I walked slowly along the edge of the mountain I saw in the distance a snow-white cross. I thought I was going mad, turned and started for the camp. After walking a few rods I looked back. There stood the white cross, solitary, on the mountain side. I started towards it, expecting each moment it would fade away, but on getting nearer, I saw the end of a rude fence reaching above the snow and knew I was standing by an Indian grave. The cross was rudely fashioned from a birch sapling, and so covered with frost crystals as to appear to rise phantomlike from the surrounding snow. I stood there looking at this symbol of the Church militant and triumphant, over a hundred miles from any human habitation, alone amid that boundless expanse of snow and ice. And I thought of the simple carpenter's son, that was born in the village of Nazareth amid the hills of Galilee, nearly nineteen hundred years ago. I saw Him dressed in simple robes, teaching the multitudes on the Mount, as never man taught before. I saw His . . . [The rest of this paragraph is missing.]

. . . the State crucified Him. Still, since He uttered that Sermon on the Mountain, cast out the money-changers from the Temple, and said to the accusers of the fallen woman, "he that is without sin among ye let him cast the first stone," kingdoms have perished, nations have dropped out of history, eighteen centuries have come and gone. But firmer than the eternal hills, Christ's words and example live, inspiring to worthy purpose and high endeavor noble men and women in all the corners of the earth. And I said in my heart, Jesus of Nazareth was more than an ethical Teacher, the Bible is more than an historical moral code. That cross is more than the symbol of human superstition and vanity, more than the evidence of "morality touched with emotion."

The journey ended amid the rushing thousands of Dawson town, I began again the service of mammon, but the heart was gone from my work. Still I kept on, and was in a fair way to become rich.

Shortly after this came the crisis of my life. On the 17th of February, by merest chance, I began to read *Natural Law in the Spiritual World,* by Professor Drummond. Late in the night I finished the book. My hour had come. This book took possession of me. Day and night I thought of this wonderful revelation of the teachings of Jesus, and the life of the Spiritual World. Wherever I looked I saw the words "Except ye be born again ye cannot enter the Kingdom of God." "I am the way, the truth and the life." "And as many as received him to them gave he power to become the sons of God."

Here at last was an expression of the fundamental doctrines of the Christian faith, in the terms of the rest of our knowledge. Here at last was Christian dogma developed, explained and proven, by the scientific method.

At last the scales fell from my eyes. But the light was blinding. Since then until a few days ago I have been much like one in a dream. Slowly have I drawn away from my worldly interests until when I reached Dawson I found I was in debt. Then, for a time, a little regret seized me. At times I thought I was losing my mind.

But the night has passed away. Through the glorious dawning of a new life, I see the radiant face of the blessed Master, Jesus the Christ, Son of God, and Redeemer of Mankind.

That Christ is the Way, the Truth and the Life, and that to as many as receive Him to them gives He power to become the Sons of God, is no longer oriental imagery, but a profound spiritual truth. This new life has come but recently, yet now my highest hope is that I may so live that at the last I may be accounted worthy to obtain an inheritance in that other world, being one of the children of the resurrection. My desire now, as well as my duty, is no longer Wealth nor Fame, but simply to serve. If as the result of my living here, I can add to the sum of sweetness and light in this world, I shall not go empty-handed into the next. Like a worthy laborer, I would meet my Master in the harvest time, bringing in my sheaves. And having, by the mercy of God, been permitted to save my own soul alive, though buried in selfishness and vain ambitions, should I not turn to the many that know not God, and seek to discover to some at least, the glory of the Risen Lord and the mystery of Eternal Life? So, laying aside every weight that can be put away in honor, with serene and confident faith I have entered upon the work of a disciple of Him of Nazareth, firmly believing that what I have committed unto Him, He will preserve. . . . [The rest of this paragraph is missing.].*

✝

ESKIMO PREACHER
Edith J. Agnew

THE career of Eskimo Roy Ahmaogak, who started as a hunter and is now a Presbyterian minister, is linked in my mind with the poem, "Hound of Heaven," by Francis Thompson, which describes the writer's vain attempts to evade the call of Christ.**

For Ahmaogak hadn't wanted to be a minister. He didn't want to spend his time and energy translating the Bible into the unwritten Inupiat dialect. It was too hard.

Oh, he knew the work ought to be done. People were continually suggesting it to him—Dr. Greist and Mr. Klerekoper, the missionaries; that couple he met on a trip from Barrow to Demarkation Point, who begged for a few chapters of the Bible in their own language; Eskimo friends at Barrow; his wife; and that inner voice, insistent.

He had shut his ears and his mind to them all. No, he would do his Christian duty by interpreting for missionaries. He would quiet his conscience by translating a few hymns now and then. But at heart he was a hunter and always would be. And he always would have been, except for that other inescapable Hunter of men.

When he was born at Barrow (Ootkeavik), Alaska, in 1898 (he was never

* Abridged by Karl E. Snyder from *Raymond and I* by Elizabeth Robins, pp. 37-43. Published in 1956 by The Macmillan Company. Used by permission of the publisher.
** See page 387 of this book.

certain of the exact date), the village was altogether Eskimo except for the missionaries.

His father was, like all the neighboring men, a hunter and fisherman. His mother was homekeeper and a midwife. The life of the family was made up of the simple essentials of getting food, keeping warm, bringing up babies, and sharing in neighborhood episodes of births, marriages, deaths, privations in hard years, and celebrations over successful hunting in good years.

These were the things Roy knew as a boy: his own house, built of whalebone and sod, banked with blocks of ice in winter against the cold winds; the sand bar that pointed like a finger out into the ocean, with a tiny settlement at the tip of it known as Point Barrow; the ocean itself, where great cakes of ice cracked off from the ice shelf at the beginning of summer and piled up in ridges like mountains; animals of the far North—walruses, seals, and ogruks (fat, bearded cousins to the seal), whales, and bears; fish; the tundra stretching inland, flat and treeless and spotted with little lakes.

In summer the land was bright with grass and wild flowers and berries; in winter it was bleak and white, and dogs trekked across it pulling sleds. Around the horizon the sun swung in a slow circle, shining at midnight to produce continuous daylight in the summer, disappearing entirely for continuous darkness in the winter. Winter moonlight was brilliant over the gleaming snow, and at times the northern lights flicked over the sky in flaming tongues of color.

Once a year the U. S. revenue cutter *Bear* arrived with mail and supplies, carrying away furs, skins, and the ivory of walrus teeth. Once in a while whalers and seamen were wrecked on the Point, and had to be brought in to the mission doctor. Those were the things that Roy remembered as a natural part of his life.

At a government school with mission teachers, he learned a little English, studied numbers, geography, and history. At Sunday school he learned strange stories from the Bible. He never missed going to church with his father and mother, who had been among the first Christian converts in this northernmost mission in America.

His schooling was spasmodic because it was frequently interrupted by hunting and fishing trips. Sometimes Roy went with his father far into the interior with the dogs and the sleds, trapping mink and marten along the streams, coming back tired, but satisfied, with piles of valuable furs.

The school at Barrow afforded only an elementary education. Roy, finishing the eighth grade, began to act as assistant to the schoolteacher. From 1913 until 1925 he taught in the school. He married one of the teachers, who died shortly after their marriage. In 1920 he married Isabel Manuluk, his present wife, who was a Barrow girl.

In 1921 Dr. Henry W. Greist arrived to take charge of the mission hospital at Barrow. He had the usual struggle with the Inupiat language, and Roy made himself useful as interpreter. Roy was excellent in that capacity, for his mind was quick and his understanding of the Bible clear. He brought to his interpreting a poetic spirit.

"You, Roy," the doctor used to say to him, "could be a minister to your people in your own right. You could give them the gospel in their own tongue. Why not take the time to study for it? You are needed, you know."

But Roy said no. He hadn't the education, and in other ways he was not fitted for that sort of work. Besides, he had his family, and it was growing fast. Already by 1927, there were four children. How would he feed them, if he gave up business for study? He wanted to be just what other Eskimo men were, a hunter and a fisherman. That and no more.

So he packed himself and his family out into the wilderness eastward. He went deliberately, turning his back on books and studies. At the same time, "You are running away," a voice in his heart kept saying. And he refused to listen.

Hunting was good, and so was trapping. Roy Ahmaogak amassed piles and piles of furs, now and then making a run from his camp to the village to trade them for provender. He fed his children well, and they were content; content, and a little wild, too; ignorant, except for what he and their mother could teach them.

For four years they stayed out in the wilds. Two more children were born there. By the end of that time the older children were in real need of schooling. For their sakes, he would have to go back to Barrow.

Dr. Greist was glad to see him, and before he knew it he was interpreter again, and active in the church. But when the doctor urged him to do extra studying, he studied only a little. When the Reverend and Mrs. Frederick Klerekoper arrived in Barrow in 1936, they, too, commandeered his services.

Roy felt really sorry for Mr. Klerekoper. He was so in earnest about learning the language and so discouraged because he could not see it in written form. There was no grammar, no primer, no dictionary. The two of them began to work on a dictionary, slowly, for neither of them knew how to set the Inupiat sounds to letters. As best they could, they made a list of about two thousand words. Though not completely satisfying, it was a help.

When the time came for the Klerekopers' furlough in 1939-40, Mr. Klerekoper asked Mr. Ahmaogak to take charge of the church while he was away. As an elder, he could be licensed to preach, if he would.

If once he consented to preach the gospel for a whole year, would he be able to escape from it afterwards?

Knowing the danger, he tried one last time to avoid it, setting off on a hunting trip alone, except for his dogs, to fight out the matter with his conscience. He was a dot in the wide Arctic—small, very small. Yet the struggle within him was immense.

What voice came to him out in the wide spaces who knows except the man himself? He cannot tell it clearly, but he has acted his answer. He has not been disobedient to his vision. Right-about-face for the dog team. Right-about-face for the man.

He spent the year preaching for Fred Klerekoper. Then he took a church at Wainwright, ninety miles down the coast, where the natives spoke his own Inupiat dialect.

In 1946 opportunity came for Ahmaogak to spend a year in the States in special study. He decided to accept the offer, even though he was reluctant to leave his family for so long a time. His children now numbered eleven and most of them were still at home.

With the help of the American Bible Society, special courses at Bloomfield Seminary, New Jersey, and friends at the Board of National Missions, he was able, while preparing for ordination, to complete an Inupiat alphabet, produce an illustrated primer, and translate the Books of Mark, Romans, and parts of John's Gospel.

It was a hard task. In order to express ideas foreign to the Arctic, new words had to be invented. A camel had to be called a "big hump animal," honey was "that which bees eat," and grasshoppers were "insects that jump." Part of Mr. Ahmaogak's education was a trip to the zoo to inspect actual sheep, lions, and camels.

The man who could keep an unwavering course over hundred-mile stretches of tundra even in a blizzard found city life fearfully confusing. Paved streets, "hard trails," were good for cars, but he wished the cars would not go so wildly in so many directions. Traffic noises, surging crowds, trains, buses, elevators—all were parts of a strange new civilization. He yearned for the peace of the Arctic.

Back in the North again, however, at the end of the year, he saw some value in the gadgets of civilization. He found travel by dog sled extremely slow. He regretted having to spend so much time cutting ice by hand for his water supply. He longed for city electricity instead of the small home plant that required so much tinkering to keep in order.

However, these were minor matters. The great matter was that he was with his family again, and that he was a real minister. He was ordained at Barrow in June, 1947. A minister at last, at forty-nine, he took full charge of the church at Wainwright. He began teaching his alphabet and primer up and down the coast, and continued his translation of the Bible.

As he returned to the Arctic Coast he felt his life was just beginning because he had in his possession the word of God in the language of his people and the authority of his church for a full ministry to his people. From week to week and year to year he hunts now for the souls of his people to bring them to Christ, their Lord and Saviour.*

In the years since "Eskimo Preacher" was written, Alaska has finally achieved her statehood. United States defense activities, growing commercial developments, and increased use of the Alaska Highway have introduced many material aspects of Western civilization.

Roy Ahmaogak continues to serve the land he knows best. Recently he drove a station wagon from Wainwright to Barrow and back, beating his own

* Abridged from *Presbyterian Life* (December 9, 1950). Used by permission of the publisher.

THE CHURCH AND THE FINE ARTS

road over tundra and Arctic ice—the first time a vehicle not especially equipped for Arctic travel had made the trip. At home in Wainwright, his church— Ulgunik Presbyterian Church—his old manse, now used for group activities, and his new manse form a considerable nucleus for Christian work.

✝

O NORTH, WITH ALL THY VALES

"WHAT are you?" the Canadian asks his country. And his country replies, "I am the wind that wants a flag . . . America's attic, an empty room, a something possible, a chance . . ."

The western hemisphere, throughout all of its long length and wide expanse, is "something possible, a chance." It is still young; it is still growing. The adventuresome persistence by which our people continue to master the elements at the poles, whether by dog train, ship, airplane, or now atomic submarine, gives some sense of the restless determination of those who keep pushing civilization out into the farthest reaches of Canada and Alaska. Almost a century ago William Cullen Bryant dreamed of the triumphant and fruitful union of all the points of the compass into a new and glorious people:

> O North, with all thy vales of green!
> O South, with all thy palms!

With North and South, East and West, joined in antiphonal psalms of praise he sees God bringing "a train of brighter years; His kingdom is begun." Bryant sees this union of men as intimating that God's "Promised hour" is at hand when

> . . . at his feet shall lie
> All rule, authority, and power
> Beneath the ample sky;
> When he shall reign from pole to pole,
> The Lord of every human soul.

It is ours to work and pray that in us men who conquer space, God may win "The mightier conquest over sin."

William Cullen Bryant was born in Massachusetts in 1794, and died on Long Island, New York, in 1878. A lawyer for ten years, he turned to journalism, founding *The New York Review* and editing *The New York Post* for many years. He began early to write poetry. The well-known *Thanatopsis,* an uncommonly serious poem for a young man, was written when he was only eighteen years old. His church interests were somewhat eclectic as he affiliated variously with Congregational, Episcopal, and Presbyterian Churches, and at the age of sixty-four was immersed by a Baptist minister.

An admirer of Watts' hymns, Bryant wrote some hymns in stately meter,

O North, with all thy vales *

MACH'S MIT MIR, GOTT   8.6.8.6.8.8.

William Cullen Bryant, 1869   *Johann Hermann Schein, 1628*

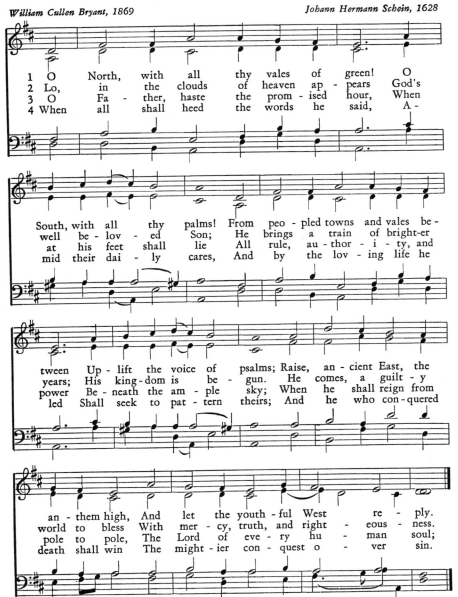

1. O North, with all thy vales of green! O God's
2. Lo, in the clouds of heaven ap - pears When
3. O Fa - ther, haste the prom - ised hour, A -
4. When all shall heed the words he said,

South, with all thy palms! From peo - pled towns and vales be -
well be - lov - ed Son; He brings a train of bright - er
at his feet shall lie All rule, au - thor - i - ty, and
mid their dai - ly cares, And by the lov - ing life he

tween Up - lift the voice of psalms; Raise, an - cient East, the
years; His king - dom is be - gun. He comes, a guilt - y
power Be - neath the am - ple sky; When he shall reign from
led Shall seek to pat - tern theirs; And he who con - quered

an - them high, And let the youth - ful West re - ply.
world to bless With mer - cy, truth, and right - eous - ness.
pole to pole, The Lord of eve - ry hu - man soul;
death shall win The might - ier con - quest o - ver sin.

*From Geer's *Hymnal for Colleges and Schools.* Used by permission of Yale University Press.

of which the most frequently printed is "Thou, Whose Unmeasured Temple Stands," a hymn written for the dedication of a chapel in Prince Street, New York, in 1835, and widely used in church dedications.

The composer of the music for "O North, With All Thy Vales," Johann Hermann Schein, was born in Germany in 1586. The son of a Lutheran pastor, he became a singer in the Court Chapel of Dresden at the age of thirteen. After study in the University of Leipzig he became Court Kapell-meister at Weimar in 1613. From 1615 until his death in 1630 he was cantor of St. Thomas' School in Leipzig. Schein was one of the most distinguished musicians of his time. He added largely to the literature of the chorale, composing many hymn tunes. He is best known by the great hymnbook he edited for the Lutheran Church in 1627.

✢

MY FAITH IT IS AN OAKEN STAFF

PIONEERS are pilgrims; they are people on a journey, moving out into new and unexplored areas of life as well as of space. Thomas Toke Lynch's sturdy hymn, "My Faith It Is an Oaken Staff," with fine expressiveness sets out the hardy faith of the soldier-pilgrim. Here faith is an oaken staff, a weapon stout, a trusted blade. And here is the man of faith, who travels on, by perils undeterred, unmoved by pain, unstayed by pleasure, always onward. This is the man who discovers new continents and inhabits them.

Lynch, himself, needed faith like "an oaken staff" for his own life. He was a frail man with unattractive appearance and no popular gifts. Because of ill health he was in and out of the ministry of the Independent Church. Nevertheless the freshness and spirituality of his preaching brought him select, if small, congregations.

In 1855, he published *The Rivulet, Hymns for Heart and Voice,* and in a later edition (1868) added sixty-seven more hymns. His hymns are marked for gracefulness and felicity of diction, picturesqueness, spiritual freshness, and the sadness of a profound soul struggling with a weak body. He published *The Rivulet* for his own congregation as a supplement to Watts. Actually the book stirred up a great controversy in the English Congregational Church, a controversy which hastened Lynch's death.

He was born in Dunmow, Essex, in 1818, and died in London in 1871.

The tune is a folk melody of unknown origin and is wholly suited to the text. The music score and words appear on pages 659 and 660.

My Faith it is an Oaken Staff *

English Traditional Melody
Arranged by Stanley L. Osborne, 1939

MUSWELL HILL 8 6 8 6 8 8 8 6

A - men.

*From *The Canadian Youth Hymnal*. Used by permission of Stanley L. Osborne and Ryerson Press.

My faith it is an oaken staff,
　　The traveller's well-loved aid;
My faith it is a weapon stout,
　　The soldier's trusted blade.
I'll travel on and still be stirred
By silent thought or social word,
By all my perils undeterred,
　　A soldier-pilgrim staid.

I have a Guide, and in His steps
　　When travellers lone have trod,
Whether beneath was flinty rock
　　Or yielding grassy sod,
They cared not, but with force unspent,
Unmoved by pain they onward went,
Unstayed by pleasures till they bent
　　Their zealous course to God.

My faith it is an oaken staff,
　　O let me on it lean;
My faith it is a trusty sword,
　　May falsehood find it keen;
Thy spirit, Lord, to me impart,
O make me what Thou ever art,
Of patient and courageous heart,
　　As all true saints have been.*

* From *The Canadian Youth Hymnal*. Used by permission of Stanley L. Osborne and Ryerson Press.

CONTENTS

PART V   SECTION 6

THE CHURCH IN THE MODERN ERA

---✠---

And he that sat upon the throne said, Behold, I make all things new.—REVELATION 21 :5

---✠---

PICTURES: PAGE
  Interpretation: Cathedral Church of St. John the Divine, New York
    City—*Cram* 662
  Picture: Cathedral Church of St. John the Divine, New York City—*Cram* .. 663
  Interpretation: First Christian Church, Columbus, Indiana—*Saarinen* 664
  Picture: First Christian Church, Columbus, Indiana—*Saarinen* 665
  Interpretation: St. Clement's Church, Alexandria, Virginia 666
  Picture: St. Clement's Church, Alexandria, Virginia 667

POETRY:
  Exit God—*Bradford* 669
  Witnesses—*Clark* 669
  Serve Where There Is Need—*Pugh* 670
  Countryman's God—*Stuart* 670
  A Worthy Church—*Seeley* 671
  An Airman's Prayer—*USAF Pilot* 672
  Churches—*Author Unknown* 672
  Dusk at the Airport—*Clark* 672

STORIES:
  A Message from the Second Assembly of the World Council of Churches
    —*Newbigin* 673
  Early Winter in a Rural Parish—*Gebhard* 675
  Bridgehead in East Harlem—*Presbyterian Life* 679

MUSIC:
  Interpretation: O Holy City, Seen of John—*Bowie* 681
  Music: O Holy City, Seen of John—*Maker* 682
  Interpretation: The Voice of God Is Calling—*Holmes* 683
  Music: The Voice of God Is Calling—*Lloyd* 684

661

CATHEDRAL CHURCH OF ST. JOHN THE DIVINE, NEW YORK CITY

ONE of the most massive sanctuaries in the world is the Cathedral Church of St. John the Divine in New York City (see photograph on p. 663). In a metropolis where many buildings demand superlatives, St. John's gathers the honors for magnificent dimension, inspiring impression, and glorious beauty.

The longest unbroken cathedral vista in Christendom may be viewed from the rear of its nave, a distance of six hundred one feet. Below, foundation stones pierce more than seventy feet to the solid rock, and above, the nave itself, apart from the towers, is seventeen stories in height. Morningside Heights is already a region of impressive monuments to the educational, religious, and philanthropic genius of modern man, but even here St. John's overshadows the neighboring edifices as it moves into the final third of its construction.

Dr. Ralph Adams Cram's design for the completion of the cathedral is basically French Gothic, but developed with such boldness of invention as to form a new and distinctly American chapter in this style. To mention only a single example, there are, on the west facade, not the shallow porches of Bourges, but deep ones like those at Rheims and Amiens, with their strong shadows, while the great verticals of Bourges and Wells are combined with the powerful horizontals of Paris and Amiens.

The cathedral is built entirely of stone, as in ancient times. The only steel in its mighty frame is in the ridge of the nave roof, where, in the old cathedrals, wooden beams were used. Its seating capacity is about ten thousand, with standing room for thousands more.

Between the ornate and massive bronze doors of the central portal is the imposing statue of St. John the Divine, for whom the cathedral is named. A favorite entrance is the Martyrs' Portal, in the north tower, richly and reverently carved with symbolic figures. Immediately inside and high above the central doors is the great rose window. Beneath this flare the state trumpets, sounded when the Bishop of New York enters ceremonially. These are decked with the banners of the original peoples of the Anglican Communion —represented by St. George of England, St. David of Wales, St. Patrick of Ireland, and St. Andrew of Scotland.

No brief sketch can describe the cathedral adequately, but the mention of a few rich appointments suggests the wealth of devotion here assembled: the eight great granite columns which rise majestically behind the altar, the ninety Burmese teakwood doors of the nave. American granite, marble, and limestone are the principal materials, but the snow-white marble of Carrara and its red counterpart from Sienna decorate the Chapel of St. Saviour. The baptistry is considered by experts to be one of the finest in the New World.

Courtesy The Cathedral Church of St. John the Divine, New York

CATHEDRAL CHURCH OF ST. JOHN THE DIVINE, NEW YORK CITY
—*CRAM*

Reverent devotion is found in small things. The Magna Carta pedestal, at the right of the high altar, is supported by a shaft of three stones from the high altar of the Abbey of Bury St. Edmunds in England. Within the corner-stone is a portion of a brick from the first Christian Church in the New World, erected by Christopher Columbus in Haiti in 1493. The richly ornate Barberini tapestries, seventeenth-century treasures designed for the Barberini Palace in Rome, and the Mortlake tapestries, woven from Raphael's cartoons and dating from the same century, are hung in the various bays.

Begun in 1892, the Cathedral of St. John the Divine is moving steadily toward completion. With sober grandeur it symbolizes the abiding deposit of religious faith deep in the heart of modern man.

✠

FIRST CHRISTIAN CHURCH, COLUMBUS, INDIANA

THE fountainhead of functionalism, or "modern," in church architecture is to be seen in a homey, typically American county-seat town, at Columbus, Indiana. It is the work of a great architect, who had formerly avoided ecclesiastical commissions; he was persuaded to begin his revolutionary career in this field because of an appeal from the building committee of this modest church amid the flat farmlands of the Middle West.

Eliel Saarinen, born in Finland, was the head of the Cranbrook Academy of Art in Michigan, assisted by his son Eero. His strictures on church design were severe, and well known. Most patterns, he said, were "an imitation of Gothic or some other historical style. Our forefathers, fathers, and we ourselves have been using the dead styles of alien cultures. We have remodeled them to serve any purpose, no matter whether they were appropriate to that purpose or not."

A committee of well-informed church members, who were successful business men from the Irwin, Miller, Reeves, and other families, appealed to the Saarinens to make a fresh approach to Christian symbolism in architecture. Speaking for their communion as a whole, they said, "We attach much importance to our effort to preach and to practice primitive Christianity and nothing else, for we believe that in it lies the hope of the world. . . . We are confronted with this ideal in our communion service and in our sermons, but every other part of worship and work should be planned to remind us continually and impressively of the obligation and privilege of a Christian life in this world." After many other words of perceptive insight about the nature of Christianity in its pristine days they concluded, "We are asking you to build a church which will interpret the spirit of Christ and of the gospel and which will also promote these ideals and assure their perpetuation among us."

Only a part of the result of this encounter of religious ideals with a craftsman skilled in the expression of them is to be seen in the picture on page 665.

FIRST CHRISTIAN CHURCH, COLUMBUS, INDIANA—*SAARINEN*

The lines are as direct and plain as the simple teachings of the Master. Without the pretense of flying buttresses where steel and brick do not require them, devoid of the romance of carved stone and stained glass, basic ideas are embodied in simplest forms. The prismatic tower rises one hundred sixty feet to suggest a heavenward look and oversight, housing musical chimes and an old bell from the house of the original congregation, organized in 1829. A large reflecting pool is crossed by a bridge with two stories of offices and other rooms, and wide halls of access to the further educational and fellowship areas. The grounds, from which the first railroad line in Indiana was relocated to clear the entire block for the church, are harmoniously dressed.

Windows occupy only one side of the sanctuary, throwing their light forward to the great cross which commands the altar wall. A huge tapestry above the choir, designed by Mrs. Saarinen, depicts the Sermon on the Blessed Life. An organ ranked as one of the ten best in the nation and adequate in range and power to serve the largest cathedral in the world, meets every need. A special hymnbook was prepared for the worship here and its use has spread to almost every state. Starlike recessed ceiling lights eliminate any need for extra fixtures. The communion table below the cross is centered in the altar area.

The reverent and effective simplicity of design in this church was immediately appreciated and recognized. From this work its architect went on in this new department of his significant career.

✛

ST. CLEMENT'S CHURCH, ALEXANDRIA, VIRGINIA

A LARGER proportion of the people in North America attend church worship than in any other country of Christendom. The voluntary principle in religion has won a victory in the hearts of men never gained by state enforcement of faith.

One reason for this profound accomplishment is the recapturing of the family concept in worship. A translation of this ideal into architecture and liturgy is the achievement of the Protestant Episcopal parish church of St. Clement in Alexandria, Virginia.

It is appropriate that this church should honor Titus Flavius Clemens, pioneering teacher in ancient Alexandria, Egypt, in the second and third centuries. St. Jerome, translator of the Vulgate, pronounces him the most learned of the ancients, while Eusebius, the church historian, applauds him as an "incomparable master of Christian philosophy." The church building in this new Alexandria, erected in 1948, is an architectural enterprise in the Clementine tradition—an effort to relate the eternal in Christian art and liturgy to the changes and concerns of contemporary life.

It is entirely possible that there may be found here a means of union between two contrary strains of thought in historic Christian worship. The

ST. CLEMENT'S CHURCH, ALEXANDRIA, VIRGINIA

Photo by Charles Baptie, Annandale, Va.

Dark Ages left a deposit of despair which separated the altar area completely from common life; no ordinary layman could set foot in it. Modern evolutionary optimism beckoned man to trust only in nature, where cross and crown are intruders. The mediating truth perceived in the fresh, clear air of the new land of democracy remains aware of God's holiness and supranatural character, worthy of all worship, but whose life and love is knowable fully only in human relations. These relations are experienced best in the family.

This sanctuary says that the Church is a family called into being by its Father which is God. In the very center is His symbol, the altar, with the family members gathered all around. Over the altar hangs the empty, oak cross, in an illusion of hovering (it is suspended by a chain from the ceiling), symbol of the sacrifice through which the committed life is saved.

The pulpit-lectern, the place of the Word, or Bible read and preached, is at one face of the altar. The font, the place of birth into the Christian family, is at the other face of the altar by the main entrance. The building in its entirety represents the first installment of life in heaven which is the realization of God's fully achieved presence. The worshiper looks up into a darkness which speaks of the vastness of the mystery of the over-brooding presence of God as does a night sky.

The dominant colors, especially in vestments and altar hangings, are blue, white and red, respectively for the Father, the Son, and the Holy Spirit. There is a fascinating continuity in their liturgical use by the ancient Jewish Temple, the early Christian Church, and in the heraldic colors of the British and American nations. Outside, however, another color, gold, is given striking play.

Unique among American churches is the force given to a mural message. In two panels, each twelve by twenty feet, heroic figures of Moses and Elijah (see page 667) depict the Law and the Prophets. On the left, approaching the church, is shown Moses, the Giver of the Law; the destruction of the Egyptians in the Red Sea; the beseeching hands of the Israelites in captivity; the Holy Tree coming into leaf, symbolizing their deliverance; and the fiery Hand of God over all. On the right, Elijah, representing the Prophets who declare man's breaking of the Law, is shown surrounded by symbols such as the stoning of Naboth; the false idol, with Jezebel, its importer, seated on its back; the fiery chariots coming in the whirlwind to receive Elijah; and, over all, the Hand of God bringing rain at Elijah's request.

Passing under the cross, which stands flush with the two large murals, one comes to the front doors. Above them is a true fresco (the large murals are painted on dry cement with a new ethyl silicate medium) done in the fresh, wet material. It shows Christ in judgment. By this arrangement the Judgment Mural cannot be seen except under the arms of the cross, a symbol of God's agape or free-flowing love. The cross itself is made of white marble chips. The free use of gold, which a color reproduction would show, is in mosaic blocks.

The Church speaks to men in buildings as well as in sermons. Throughout her long history she has been at her best when she used the language of the day in both. Not for two centuries had the Church expressed herself in contemporary architecture. The congregation of St. Clement's has taken its place in the vanguard of a movement to awaken the Church to the effectiveness of building in the pattern of this age.

✤

EXIT GOD

Of old our fathers' God was real,
　Something they almost saw,
Which kept them to a stern ideal
　And scourged them into awe.

They walked the narrow path of right,
　Most vigilantly well,
Because they feared eternal night
　And boiling depths of Hell.

Now Hell has wholly boiled away
　And God become a shade.
There is no place for him to stay
　In all the world he made.

The followers of William James
　Still let the Lord exist,
And call him by imposing names,
　A venerable list.

But nerve and muscle only count,
　Gray matter of the brain,
And an astonishing amount
　Of inconvenient pain.

I sometimes wish that God were back
　In this dark world and wide;
For though some virtues he might lack,
　He had his pleasant side.*

　　　　　　　　　　—Gamaliel Bradford

WITNESSES

The spires of country churches
Are simple, tall and true,
Built by village carpenters,
A craft the Master knew.

The bells of country churches
Are solemn, sweet, and clear,

* From *Masterpieces of Religious Verse*, edited by James Dalton Morrison, p. 41. Published in 1948 by Harper & Brothers.

Singing across the sunny fields,
Calling that He is near.

The folk of country churches
Follow where He trod,
Loyal as were His fishermen—
Witnesses of God.*

—*Leslie Savage Clark*

SERVE WHERE THERE IS NEED

The paths of service lead afar;
The start is near at hand;
Wherever we and others are,
In this and every land.

So look thee down the trail of life
To find a goal or creed—
And set thee out where sin is rife
And serve where there is need.

Oh—need is where the eye will see
And where the ear will hear
And where the heart will feel the plea
Of every human tear.**

—*Samuel F. Pugh*

COUNTRYMAN'S GOD

Who reaps the grain and plows the sod
Must feel a kinship with his God.

For there's so much on earth to see
That marks the hand of Deity.

When blossom springs from tiny shoot;
When orchard yields its luscious fruit;

When sap is running from great trees—
On all occasions such as these

The man who breathes fresh country air
Must know full well that God is there.***

—*Roger Winship Stuart*

* From *The Christian Century*. Used by permission of the author and Christian Century Foundation.
** From *Between-Time Meditations* by Samuel F. Pugh, p. 38. Copyright 1954 by Bethany Press. Used by permission of the author and the publisher.
*** From *Masterpieces of Religious Verse*, edited by James Dalton Morrison, p. 69. Published in 1948 by Harper & Brothers. Used by permission of the publisher.

A WORTHY CHURCH

Foundation . . . walls,
Ceiling . . . floors,
Rooms . . . halls
Windows . . . doors.
All these it takes to make a Church . . .
But, most of all, people.

Wood . . . steel,
Bricks . . . mortar
Plaster seal,
Stones in order,
All these it takes to make a Church . . .
But, most of all, people.

Pulpit . . . lectern
Organ . . . pews
Baptistry,
Lord's Table, too—
All these it takes to make a Church . . .
But, most of all, people.

Pictures . . . Bible,
Tables . . . chairs,
Books for teachers,
Some to share
All these it takes to make a Church . . .
But, most of all, people.

Without a Godly people
Seeking after Truth,
Barren be the building . . .
Needless, then, the roof,
Yes, it takes much to make a Church
But, most of all, the people.

May this day find us eager
To follow in His way,
To dedicate anew our lives
For service day by day . . .
That this may be a worthy Church,
And we, for aye, His people.*
—*Ann McDevitt Seeley*

* Used by permission of the author, Mrs. Kenneth B. Seeley.

AN AIRMAN'S PRAYER

Hear, O God, these words from men who fly.
May we, who are lifted from this world's surface, rise out toward Thee
Free of worldly weights of selfishness, of covetousness and of hate.
Thus unburdened, in the vast reaches of the sky,
May we come ever closer to the heights that Thou hast set for man to reach.
Upon returning from these flights above the lands and seas,
Help us to bring back some remnants of the beauty;
Better knowledge of the awe, and more abundance of the vision,
That Thou didst grant us there.
Teach us, by these gifts and by the closeness of Thy presence gained,
To strive to live our lives as men of Purpose,
Of Integrity, of Courage, and of Love for Thee.*

—*USAF Pilot*

CHURCHES

Beautiful is the large church,
With stately arch and steeple;
Neighborly is the small church,
With groups of friendly people;
Reverent is the old church,
With centuries of grace;
And a wooden church or a stone church
Can hold an altar place.
And whether it be a rich church
Or a poor church anywhere,
Truly it is a great church
If God is worshiped there.

—*Author Unknown*

DUSK AT THE AIRPORT

"Is not God in the height of heaven?"—Job 22:12

The flocks of silver birds come home
Across a darkening sky,
With stars above, and stars below
Where lighted cities lie.

* From *Chaplain Newsletter*, Vol. 3, No. 1 (September 1956). Used by permission of Air Force Chaplain (Maj. Gen.) Charles I. Carpenter, Chief. Chaplain (Lt. Col.) Joseph D. Andrew, Staff Chaplain, Hq. EADF, forwarded a copy of a poem written by a Command Pilot in his Command, who wishes to remain anonymous. As Chaplain Andrew notes, "This prayer is of a kind to make one marvel—it is so clear, so simple, so surprising in beauty. It reflects a pilot who has fine perception, devout thoughts, and a virile faith."

And some will climb the dark again
Toward far dim pathways drawn
By Vega, Mars and cresent moon,
And some will greet the dawn.

So small is man—so vast the night,
O Lord of earth and air
For every starward mounting bird
Hear our winged prayer.

Be present, O Merciful God, and protect us through the silent hours of this night, so that we, who are fatigued by the changes and chances of this fleeting world, may repose upon Thy eternal changelessness; through the everlasting Christ, our Lord. Amen.*

—*Leslie Savage Clark*

✠

A MESSAGE FROM THE SECOND ASSEMBLY OF THE WORLD COUNCIL OF CHURCHES
Bishop Lesslie Newbigin

To all our fellow Christians, and to our fellow men everywhere, we send greetings in the name of Jesus Christ. We affirm our faith in Jesus Christ as the hope of the world, and desire to share that faith with all men. May God forgive us that by our sin we have often hidden this hope from the world.

In the ferment of our time there are both hopes and fears. It is indeed good to hope for freedom, justice, and peace, and it is God's will that we should have these things. But He has made us for a higher end. He has made us for Himself, that we might know and love Him, worship and serve Him. Nothing other than God can ever satisfy the heart of man. Forgetting this, man becomes his own enemy. He seeks justice but creates oppression. He wants peace, but drifts towards war. His very mastery of nature threatens him with ruin. Whether he acknowledges it or not, he stands under the judgment of God and in the shadow of death.

Here where we stand, Jesus Christ stood with us. He came to us, true God and true Man, to seek and to save. Though we were the enemies of God, Christ died for us. We crucified Him, but God raised Him from the dead. He is risen. He has overcome the powers of sin and death. A new life has begun. And in His risen and ascended power, He has sent forth into the world a new community, bound together by His Spirit, sharing His divine life, and commissioned to make Him known throughout the world. He will come again as Judge and King to bring all things to their consummation. Then we shall see Him as He is and know as we are known. Together with the

* From *With All Thy Heart*, by Leslie Savage Clark, p. 13. Copyright 1957 by The Broadman Press. Used by permission of the author and the publisher.

whole creation we wait for this with eager hope, knowing that God is faithful and that even now He holds all things in His hand.

This is the hope of God's people in every age, and we commend it afresh today to all who will listen. To accept it is to turn from our ways to God's way. It is to live as forgiven sinners, as children growing in His love. It is to have our citizenship in that kingdom which all man's sin is impotent to destroy, that realm of love and joy and peace which lies about all men though unseen. It is to enter with Christ into the suffering and despair of men, sharing with them the great secret of that kingdom which they do not expect. It is to know that whatever men may do, Jesus reigns and shall reign.

With this assurance we can face the powers of evil and the threat of death with good courage. Delivered from fear, we are made free to love. Far beyond the judgment of men and the judgment of history lies the judgment of the King who died for all men, and who will judge us according to what we have done to the least of His brethren. Thus our Christian hope directs us towards our neighbor. It constrains us to pray daily, "Thy will be done on earth as it is in heaven," and to act as we pray in every area of life. It begets a life of believing prayer and expectant action, looking to Jesus and pressing forward to the day of His return in glory.

Now we would speak through our member churches directly to each congregation. Six years ago our churches entered into a covenant to form this Council, and affirmed their intention to fellowship during these six years. We enter now upon a second stage. To stay together is not enough. We must go forward. As we learn more of our unity in Christ, it becomes the more intolerable that we should be divided. We therefore ask you: Is your church seriously considering its relation to other churches in the light of our Lord's prayer, that we may be sanctified in the truth and that we may all be one? Is your congregation, in fellowship with sister congregations around you, doing all it can do to ensure that your neighbors shall hear the voice of the one Shepherd calling all men into the one flock?

The forces that separate men from one another are strong. At our meeting here we have missed the presence of Chinese churches which were with us at Amsterdam. There are other lands and churches unrepresented in our Council, and we long ardently for their fellowship. But we are thankful that, separated as we are by the deepest political divisions of our time, here at Evanston we are united in Christ. And we rejoice also that, in the bond of prayer and a common hope, we maintain communion with our Christian brethren everywhere.

It is from within this communion that we have to speak about the fear and distrust which at present divide our world. Only at the cross of Christ, where men know themselves as forgiven sinners, can they be made one. It is there that Christians must pray daily for their enemies. It is there that we must seek deliverance from self-righteousness, impatience and fear. And those who know that Christ is risen should have the courage to expect new power to break through every human barrier.

It is not enough that Christians should seek peace for themselves. They must seek justice for others. Great masses of people in many parts of the world are hungry for bread, and are compelled to live in conditions which mock their human worth. Does your church speak and act against such injustice? Millions of men and women are suffering segregation and discrimination on the grounds of race. Is your church willing to declare, as this Assembly has declared, that this is contrary to the will of God and to act on that declaration? Do you pray regularly for those who suffer unjust discrimination on grounds of race, religion or political conviction?

The Church of Christ is today a world-wide fellowship, yet there are countless people to whom He is unknown. How much do you care about this? Does your congregation live for itself, or for the world around it and beyond it? Does its common life, and does the daily work of its members in the world, affirm the Lordship of Christ or deny it?

God does not leave any of us to stand alone. In every place He has gathered us together to be His family, in which His gifts and His forgiveness are received. Do you forgive one another as Christ forgave you? Is your congregation a true family of God, where every man can find a home and know that God loves him without limit?

We are not sufficient for these things. But Christ is sufficient. We do not know what is coming to us. But we know Who is coming. It is He who meets us every day and who will meet us at the end—Jesus Christ our Lord.

Therefore we say to you: Rejoice in hope.*

✤

EARLY WINTER IN A RURAL PARISH
Anna Laura Gebhard

FRIDAY, OCTOBER 15

"And here, Laurie, is our church."

Our car came to a stop. With eager anticipation I looked out at the one-room building before us. I could think only of a little stray white dog at a deserted intersection.

"I warned you not to expect too much," Ed said. "After all, it's the people we're here to serve."

"I know, Ed. And we asked for a rural parish, didn't we?"

We crossed the dirt path to the chipped concrete steps. We opened the ill-fitting door and stepped into the empty room. In the rear stood an old wood stove, an immense jacket around it. My eyes followed the straight black stove-pipe the full length of the room to the front of the church. There underneath the chimney hole was a simple altar, adorned by a white wood cross and two

* Abridged from *The Evanston Report; The Second Assembly of the World Council of Churches 1954*, p. 1. Published in 1955 by Harper & Brothers. Used by permission of the publisher.

candlesticks, with a backdrop of purple velvet. It was the one touch of beauty in the entire barren room.

"It's remarkable what it becomes when the pews are full of people," Ed assured me. "Anyway, Laurie, take heart. Gorman is just one of our churches. We've a couple of others, you know. You'll like the neat white building at the Fairhaven crossroads."

"And Gold Valley?"

"Well, it's like the town—sorta run down and discouraged."

"It's going to seem strange, living here at Gorham but belonging to three communities."

"Just wait till you ride the circuit for a while," Ed told me. "It's like a merry-go-round—Wednesday, Gorman; Thursday, Fairhaven; and Friday, Gold Valley."

"And Sundays, all three. Well, at least we won't carry all our eggs in one basket!"

THURSDAY, OCTOBER 21

"Now you folks come on out and see us," Farmer Stanton admonished after the Fairhaven service last Sunday. Today we drove north to the rolling hills around Fairhaven crossroads that shelter a hundred sky-filled lakes and hold rolling fields with fringes of wilderness upon their backs. The haze of late autumn was upon the hills today.

Ed found Farmer Stanton plowing the west forty, and I found Mrs. Stanton in the neat farm kitchen, lifting hot loaves of bread from the oven.

We stayed for supper, for the warmth and charm of the farm home made us feel as though we belonged. In the kitchen Mrs. Stanton and I visited as we washed the dishes and separated the milk.

"Your job's a lot like a farmer's wife's, ain't it? Your husband's work wouldn't amount to much without your help," she said to me when I told her how I plan to ride the circuit with Ed.

When we finally prepared to go, they followed us to the car. "Ye'll come agin soon, won't ye?" Farmer Stanton asked. "You young folks fill an awful empty spot in this house. Marian lives in the city and don't git home often."

We drove home through the frosty, still night thankful for the gracious, kindly friends who fill our life.

TUESDAY, OCTOBER 26

I think I'm going to like Ladies' Aids. At least I enjoyed my initiation at Gorman today. The meeting turned into a bride's shower for me, and I came home laden with a handsome chair and a handful of household hints and favorite recipes. I'm sure I'll need them all.

But I think I appreciated even more the warmth of the welcome I received. Ed's remark of the other day kept singing through my mind: "It's the people who make the church; it's the people we're here to serve."

Thursday, October 28

Today has belonged to Fairhaven. We left at noon in our little car and returned tonight with the great, star-filled sky overhead. This afternoon we drove past the neat church to the farmhouse on the broad fields beyond.

The large front rooms were already filled when we got there. I found an empty chair and listened to members of the Sunshine Committees give their reports.

"Did you ever notice," asked the president, "how much the Bible says about the fatherless and widows? Now, we don't have many widows around Fairhaven, but we've got several widowers. Don't you suppose they'd enjoy a pan of hot rolls next baking day? I've just sorta been going on the assumption that Jesus was right when He said, 'Seek ye first the kingdom of God, and his righteousness; and all these things shall be added unto you.' "

Friday, October 29

Ed's leaning over the table in the dining room putting bright-colored thumbtacks into our improvised map of Gold Valley. We spent the afternoon there visiting, asking questions and collecting information. Finally we stopped at the general store and spent an hour with Ma Thompson, checking on the notes we had made.

Our survey seems to be confirming our impressions. Seventy per cent of the families in the village are unchurched—have even no religious preference. In the countryside surrounding the village the percentage is much higher. Thirty-five of the forty-two families in the community are on either government relief or state old-age pension rolls. And ours is not only the only church but, except for the little two-room school, the only constructive agency in the bewildered little town. Our hands seem weak in the face of such responsibility.

Sunday, November 28

Ed rode the circuit alone this Sunday. At the Gorman Sunday-school board meeting last week I promised to visit the Gorman Sunday school. Each Sunday morning during the closing hymn I have seen the children collect outside the church for their Sunday-school session. Very often the noisy gang of boys playing tag around the church has detracted somewhat from the closing prayer.

After the adults filed out of the church, the children spilled in. I counted eight classes crowded into the small room, and the confusion of sounds rivaled the tower of Babel.

Mrs. Larson asked me to teach the kindergarten class; the children and I could scarcely hear each other above the noise of the classes around us, and holding the attention of a few was like trying to teach a flock of twittering sparrows.

"Now, Laurie," Ed said at dinner, "you've been introduced to the dilemma of the one-room church."

I looked around the dining room. "Say, Ed, how'd it be to turn the parsonage into Sunday-school rooms? The primary class could hold forth in the living room, and the little tots in here."

Mrs. Larson came past this afternoon, and I ventured our suggestion. She hesitated, fearing the imposition.

"You'll never be in our way," Ed reminded her. "We're at Fairhaven while you're at Sunday school."

So the parsonage is the new church addition.

WEDNESDAY, DECEMBER 8

It's eerily bright out tonight. The moonlight on the billowy snow makes day out of the night, a cold sort of northern day that doesn't invite one into the open. We're glad for the warmth of our cozy rooms, for popcorn from the Gunter garden, and for books from the study shelves.

Despite the frosty air a dozen Junior Leaguers piled into the parsonage after school today to finish the little white church model they have been making. It is standing up in front of the church altar table now, with its tall spire, stained-glass windows, and open door through which one can see the little pews and altar inside.

We were talking several weeks ago about what makes a church, and I showed the children several pictures of great cathedrals.

"But those are all big churches," Betty Berg remarked. "I like little churches best because they are more friendly."

"Why can't we make a church—the kind we wish we had?" Jack Adams asked.

I showed the children how to make simulated stained-glass windows by using water colors on heavy wrapping paper, then oiling the back of the paper to make it translucent.

When we had our little model completed this afternoon, we took it over to the church and put it in place.

"Can we leave it up in front of the altar table so everybody can see the kind of a church we'd like?" Betty asked wistfully.

"A little child shall lead them."

FRIDAY, DECEMBER 24, CHRISTMAS EVE

Christmas Eve! We've just returned from our Christmas calls. Out in the Fairhaven hills we took old Mr. Miller a basket of bright fruit. In Gold Valley we left the Meads a box piled high with Christmas goodies, and at Grandma and Grandpa Morris' we left a little gift from the Sunday-school children and had prayer with them. On the way back we stopped at the Byrons' and left a small tree, full of lights and cookies, and a box of Christmas extras for the whole family. Then a few moments ago we paused outside the Gunters' living-room window, where a single candle made a pool of light on the snow outside, to sing a carol or two. Mr. Gunter threw open the door and asked us in. Their kind old faces shone as we told them of our Christmas errands.

"And ye'll read the Christmas story and have prayer with us afore ye go?" Mr. Gunter asked when we were ready to leave. Ed read from the Gospel of Luke, and then in the serenity of their fellowship we prayed together.

O God, be born anew in our hearts this Christmastide. Help us remember Him for whom "there was no room." May there be none in our town who cannot see the Christmas star or hear the angels sing because their hearts are left dark through our neglect.*

✛

BRIDGEHEAD IN EAST HARLEM

ONE Sunday morning in October, 1948, two young clergymen, Donald L. Benedict and Archie Hargraves, stood by the open door of a bare storefront on 102nd Street beneath the shadow of New York's Third Avenue Elevated. It was the first worship service of the East Harlem Protestant Parish, and the two ministers, just out of seminary, waited patiently for some of the local residents they had called on during the previous weeks to appear.

Finally one elderly Puerto Rican woman who lived next door walked in. For several weeks she and a group of children who came for church school were the only inhabitants of the crowded blocks to worship in the storefront. It was a long time before East Harlem Protestant Parish was to allay the community's suspicions and apathy.

The founders of the Parish, as students at Union Theological Seminary, had become appalled by the fact that the major Protestant denominations had largely abandoned East Harlem, one of the most congested areas in the world. Built up sixty years before to house the immigrants pouring into Manhattan, the area, in 1948, was peopled by Italians, Puerto Ricans, American Negroes, and remnants of the older immigrant groups. Here poverty had accentuated the whole range of social and economic dislocations modern urban life is heir to. Here men and women found little meaning in their treadmill jobs and lacked a sense of purpose in life.

As an interdenominational venture, supported by several denominational mission boards, the new Parish set out to present the gospel of Jesus Christ in new and vigorous ways.

Nearly eleven years later the Parish is world-famous. It has been described as "a place where Protestantism is meeting with power the challenges of modern economic life." Yet its staff is quick to state that the Parish has made no monumental impact on East Harlem. In terms of statistics, its witness has not been especially impressive; the section of East Harlem it serves,

* Abridged from *Rural Parish!* by Anna Laura Gebhard, pp. 9-40. Copyright 1947 by Stone & Pierce. Used by permission of Abingdon Press.

from 96th Street to 106th, from Lexington to First Avenues, houses some thirty thousand persons, but only four hundred have actually become members of the Parish with its four churches and one other affiliated congregation. The Parish, nevertheless, has met head-on the inner-city's resistance to the gospel. It has become a laboratory for the whole of Protestantism in facing twentieth-century issues.

Today the life and work of the Parish radiate out from storefronts, a Presbyterian and a Reformed Church building, rented offices and apartments, a retreat center in Putnam County, New York. In these scattered quarters, the Parish has set up a service network. The conviction that Christ is Lord of all of life is expressed not only in worship but through a medical clinic, a legal aid program, a federal credit union, two social clubs for teen-agers, and a clinic for narcotic addicts.

During the past ten years the Parish had developed an unusual group ministry. To identify themselves with the life of East Harlem, "to be native in all things save faith and morals," the staff members, most of whom have young families, live in the district's tenements and housing projects, and participate in its social, economic, and political activities. At present, the staff includes eight ministers, two internes, and six lay workers in addition to office assistants.

Recently lay members of the Parish churches have assumed responsibility and authority that in the early years had to be exercised by the staff. More and more of the major decisions and policies are determined by the Parish Council with its lay and staff delegates.

Convinced that God uses the whole Christian community for the doing of His will in the world, East Harlem Protestant Parish laymen are active in the narcotics committee, in teaching, in running the clubs for teen-agers, and in evangelistic calling.

When East Harlem teen-agers join the Parish-sponsored Conservatives' Social Club, they signify their exit from a fighting gang by pressing their silver-painted hands on the clubhouse walls. Nucleus of the Conservatives was a group of members of the Enchanters, an active fighting gang. When the gang veterans wanted "to go social," they enlisted the aid of Ramon Diaz, a member of the Parish's 100th Street Church. In turn, he convinced the Parish to provide a clubhouse where the youths and girls would have a place to go. Mr. Diaz, now director of the Social Club, spends from three in the afternoon until at least one in the morning, 365 days a year, with his young people.

The message ("In Unity—For Mission") of the uniting assembly of The United Presbyterian Church in the U.S.A. affirmed that "God summons us to journey not only along desert paths and jungle trails, but in the teeming alleys of our cities. . . . For the Church in the discharge of its God-given mission, the frontier is more than a location. It is wherever any sector of thought or life has to be occupied in the name of Jesus Christ."

Because the East Harlem Protestant Parish is a tangible demonstration of these principles, the eyes of the entire Christian community are noting this gallant mission in New York.*

✛

O HOLY CITY, SEEN OF JOHN

THE most vigorous and influential movement in American Christianity in the early decades of the twentieth century had to do with the concern to relate the Christian faith and gospel to the economic, political, and social life of the times. Men were now not so much troubled by the old threats to existence as by new anxieties and insecurities issuing from twentieth-century patterns of life.

We found ourselves at the end of the agricultural economy in its older form and in the full flush of the new machine civilization. Great masses of people were being uprooted and swept into the industries. Our cities were growing by leaps and bounds. Yet, with all its feverish successes, the world seemed only to be moving with relentless struggle for power, whether to amass quick wealth within nations, or to achieve, by military and political warfare, control of the international scene in order to maintain control, as it was believed, of the conditions of prosperity. The most characteristic American hymns of the period are therefore hymns of the "social gospel." Among these is Walter Russell Bowie's "O Holy City, Seen of John."

The vision of the city splendid, as projected in Chapter 22 of the Book of Revelation, is set out in the first stanza. The city of God, "where Christ, the Lamb, doth reign" is the city which knows neither "night, nor need, nor pain." The summons of the hymn is to men here and now to turn away their gaze from the far-distant city of ultimate hope and "seize the whole of life and build its glory" here. The world's oppressed cry out from their impoverishment and debasement to those who

> . . . rest content
> While lust and greed for gain
> In street and shop and tenement,
> Wring gold from human pain.

Importunate in prayer, man beseeches God for strength to build

> The city that hath stood
> Too long a dream.

And since the city already "riseth fair" in the mind of God, man dares to hope and to build.

Dr. Bowie (1882-   ) is a minister of the Protestant Episcopal Church. After his extended pastorate at Grace Church, New York City, from 1923 to 1939, he became professor of practical theology at Union Theological

---

* Abridged from *Presbyterian Life* (May 15, 1959). Used by permission of the publisher.

O Holy City, Seen of John

FORD COTTAGE. 8. 6. 8. 6. 8. 6.

WALTER RUSSELL BOWIE, 1882–

F. C. MAKER, 1844–1927

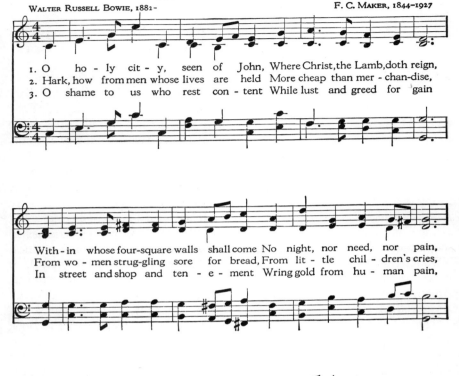

1. O ho - ly cit - y, seen of John, Where Christ, the Lamb, doth reign,
2. Hark, how from men whose lives are held More cheap than mer - chan-dise,
3. O shame to us who rest con - tent While lust and greed for gain

With - in whose four-square walls shall come No night, nor need, nor pain,
From wo - men strug-gling sore for bread, From lit - tle chil - dren's cries,
In street and shop and ten - e - ment Wring gold from hu - man pain,

And where the tears are wiped from eyes That shall not weep a - gain!
There swells the sob-bing hu - man plaint That bids Thy walls a - rise!
And bit - ter lips in blind de-spair Cry, "Christ hath died in vain!" A - MEN.

4 Give us, O God, the strength to build
   The city that hath stood
Too long a dream, whose laws are love,
   Whose ways are brotherhood,
And where the sun that shineth is
   God's grace for human good.

5 Already in the mind of God
   That city riseth fair:
Lo, how its splendor challenges
   The souls that greatly dare —
Yea, bids us seize the whole of life
   And build its glory there.

Seminary in New York, and somewhat later, dean of students. He wrote our hymn in 1909, at the request of Henry Sloane Coffin, who was looking for hymns which would show that the exalted Christian hopes might be brought out of the end-time into the here and now. Appropriately, the hymn was first published in 1910 in Dr. Coffin's *Hymns of the Kingdom*.

The tune, "Ford Cottage," by Frederick Charles Maker (1844-1927), seems to have first appeared in 1909 as the setting for Dr. Bowie's hymn in *The Fellowship Hymn Book*. Mr. Maker was an English organist-composer.

✣

THE VOICE OF GOD IS CALLING

JOHN HAYNES HOLMES (1879-   ) was one of the most challenging American voices of the first half of the twentieth century. For forty-two years pastor of the Church of the Messiah (Unitarian), now the Community Church, Dr. Holmes thundered from his pulpit like a new Moses on a New York Sinai. Not only was he heard from his pulpit, but in continuous lecturing and writing he was heard and read by people across the continent.

Although affiliated with the Unitarian Church as a minister from 1904-1919, and chairman of its General Conference from 1915-1917, in 1919 he left Unitarianism to become an Independent. Through these long years, Dr. Holmes, an independent indeed, has spoken as forcefully as he has spoken courageously on the many controversial subjects of our century as they have concerned faith and practice.

"The Voice of God Is Calling" reveals very clearly the point of impact at which its author struck the American community as with the stroke of a great bell. Once again the Lord roars from Zion. As He hears His people crying "In cot and mine and slum," as He sees His people falling "In darkness and despair," He sends out the summons "Whom shall I send, and who will go for us?" And as Isaiah replied, "Here am I, send me," so the Church now answers: "Here are we! Send us upon thine errand, Let us thy servants be!"

And then follows the tremendous fourth stanza:

> From ease and plenty save us;
> From pride of place absolve;
> Purge us of low desire;
> Lift us to high resolve;
> Take us, and make us holy;
> Teach us thy will and way.
> Speak, and, behold! we answer;
> Command, and we obey.

The hymn was written in 1913, while Dr. Holmes was on board ship returning from Europe. He had previously been requested to provide a

The voice of God is calling *

MEIRIONYDD   7.6.7.6.D.

John Haynes Holmes, 1913

Wales

Arranged by William Lloyd, 1840

1 The voice of God is call-ing Its sum-mons un-to
2 I hear my peo-ple cry-ing In cot and mine and
3 We heed, O Lord, thy sum-mons, And an-swer: Here are
4 From ease and plen-ty save us; From pride of place ab-

men; As once he spake in Zi-on, So now he speaks a-
slum; No field or mart is si-lent, No cit-y street is
we! Send us up-on thine er-rand, Let us thy serv-ants
solve; Purge us of low de-sire; Lift us to high re-

gain: Whom shall I send to suc-cor My peo-ple in their
dumb. I see my peo-ple fall-ing In dark-ness and de-
be. Our strength is dust and ash-es, Our years a pass-ing
solve; Take us, and make us ho-ly; Teach us thy will and

need? Whom shall I send to loos-en The bonds of shame and greed?
spair. Whom shall I send to shat-ter The fet-ters which they bear?
hour; But thou canst use our weak-ness To mag-ni-fy thy power.
way. Speak, and, be-hold! we an-swer; Com-mand, and we o-bey.

*From *Geer's Hymnal for Colleges and Schools.* Words used by permission of John Haynes Holmes. Music used by permission of Yale University Press.

hymn for the annual fall assembly of the Young People's Religious Union (Unitarian). Done at a single sitting, the hymn has happily proved to be one of our most challenging hymns for youth.

The tune, "Meirionydd" (pronounced Mer-i-on-eth') was arranged by the Welsh farmer-musician, William Lloyd (1786-1852), from a tune perhaps given him in manuscript; it was published in 1840. The tune is a typical Welsh tune. Meirionydd is the name of the remote western county adjoining the county of Carnarvon, Lloyd's home county.

CONTENTS

PART V   SECTION 7

CHRISTIANITY AND EDUCATION

✢

Who is a wise man and endued with knowledge among you? let him shew out of a good conversation his works with meekness of wisdom.—JAMES 3:13

✢

PICTURES: PAGE

Interpretation: Bethany College, in the Hills of West Virginia 687

Picture: Bethany College, in the Hills of West Virginia 689

Interpretation: Window of the Great Commission, Pacific School of
    Religion—*Wallis–Wiley Studio* 688

Picture: Window of the Great Commission, Pacific School of Religion
    —*Wallis–Wiley Studio* 691

Interpretation: Modern Altar, Massachusetts Institute of Technology
    —*Saarinen* 692

Picture: Modern Altar, Massachusetts Institute of Technology—
    Saarinen 693

POETRY:

Let There Be Light—*Marlatt* 694

Evolution—*Bryson* 694

A Spirit Muses—*Williams* 695

The Silent Wooded Place—*Graves* 696

The First Autumn—*Schacht* 696

Portrait of a Pastor—*Clark* 697

To a Fossil Fern—*Foote* 697

STORIES:

Early Days at Yale—*Beecher* 698

Proposals for the Union of Christians—*Campbell* 699

Church, School, and State—*Brown* 701

MUSIC:

Interpretation: Life of Ages, Richly Poured—*Johnson* 704

Music: Life of Ages, Richly Poured—*Medieval French Melody*
    harmonized by *Richard Redhead* 705

Interpretation: Let There Be Light, Lord God—*Vories* 704

Music: Let There Be Light, Lord God—*Mason* 706

BETHANY COLLEGE, IN THE HILLS OF WEST VIRGINIA

THE taming of the American frontier wilderness was an achievement for more than ax and plow. Settlers in the New World came to procure freedom in religion and in government, but they cherished another fond hope—that their children might stand straight and tall, as only masters may. Their masters in the Old World held their places in large part because they *knew* more than the common man. Education, the freeing of the mind, was the key to power over nature and over the encrusted forms of social cleavage. Full education of every able man, and later of women, became the glittering goal of the new democracy, where men must be their own masters.

The first brave steps toward widespread education at the high, collegiate levels were taken by churches and dedicated individuals. Utopian hopes and dreams often ran aground on the hard fact of the great cost of good learning, and more colleges expired than survived. One that battled persistently on the rugged frontier and lived to tell the tale was Bethany College.

Its very name speaks of religious faith. The principal founder, Alexander Campbell, embodied a typical American success story. Starting as a Scotch-Irish immigrant who toiled on a farm in Pennsylvania but never neglected his studies, he rose to political prominence, personal wealth, and a unique religious achievement—for he called together the largest church body originating in America, the Christian Church (Disciples of Christ).

Unlike most colleges in the South and West, Bethany sprang into being full-fledged in 1840, without transition from a forerunning academy. The founder gave the ground and raised money, much of it his own, for the buildings. In the secret places of his mind was a grand ideal. It was to plant upon the almost mountainous hills of his adopted West Virginia a college whose buildings would be no less imposing in substance, and its faculty no less solid in learning, than that of the University of Glasgow where strange fortune had once permitted him to spend a winter term!

At long last the permanent main structure was began. It projected along the brow of a commanding hill four hundred twenty feet of collegiate Gothic architecture, with a tower ninety-six feet high surmounted by a spire whose tip was one hundred twenty-two feet above the ground. A wide corridor along the back opened through great arches upon the steep decline and gave a long, cloistered walk appropriate to the long thoughts of youth and the solitude productive of scholarly contemplation.

The cost was great for that day. But the founder traveled widely raising funds, with one audience in Washington including the friendly President Buchanan. General James Garfield, destined to be another President, served on the Board of Trustees.

This was the first college in America to make the Bible a textbook for study, upon the same terms as any other classic.

Costs to students were amazingly low. One hundred and fifty dollars paid

for board, lodging, tuition, and laundry for the entire college year. Econo-
mies were expected, of course. One regulation read: "Agreeable to the
original plan and terms of this institution all studying rooms shall be furnished with lights in proportion of one candle to every two students till bed
hour and also with the necessary fuel, but that in all rooms which are occupied
as bed rooms all lights and fuel shall be furnished by those who occupy
said rooms."

The impressive old line of halls still serves as the main building of this
pioneering college (see page 689). The purely ornamental embellishments in
brick, stone, and wrought iron, and the arched walkways, continue their
pronouncement that life without beauty is mere existence, and that work
without wisdom is wasted toil.

✣

WINDOW OF THE GREAT COMMISSION, PACIFIC SCHOOL OF RELIGION

Few movements have impelled so many young men and women to committed lives in Christian service as did the Student Volunteer Movement,
organized in 1886. Its slogan, "The evangelization of the world in this generation," caused thousands to turn to missionary tasks under the zeal of a
great affection.

Back of the SVM, exactly eighty years before, was one of those provi-
dential episodes on which history turns. Samuel J. Mills and four other
students at Williams College, in Massachusetts, were on a hike when rain
drove them to seek shelter in a haystack. A serious discussion of their duty as
young Christians developed, and in solemn prayer they promised their lives
to assault barricaded heathenism.

This "haystack prayer meeting" of 1806 spread to other colleges, creating
missionary power. A whole series of movements and societies came into being
to serve the new stream of zeal. Dwight L. Moody aided the impulse through
the Student Missionary Movement, in 1879. A new fire was kindled by him
in a YMCA student conference at Mount Hermon, Massachusetts, in 1886.
One hundred of the two hundred fifty-one present volunteered. John R.
Mott was among them and became the chief promoter of the Student Volunteer Movement for a lifetime.

The "Y" touched Galen Merriam Fisher at the University of California and
he gave much of his rich talent to it. A sudden critical need for a Y leader
in Japan arose in 1897, and Mott asked Fisher to accept the call. Interrupt-
ing his plans to become a minister, he gave more than a score of years of
service through the YMCA as a layman. Next he served the Rockefeller Institute of Social and Religious Research, directing studies in India, China,
and Japan, resulting in the notable Laymen's Foreign Missions Inquiry in
1931. Later, in "alleged retirement," he headed civic and community move-

Courtesy Bethany College, Bethany, W. Va.

BETHANY COLLEGE, IN THE HILLS OF WEST VIRGINIA

ments in Berkeley, and was Chairman of the Board of Trustees of the Pacific School of Religion, in the same city. During World War II he courageously championed the rights of Orientals on the West Coast, organizing the Fair Play Committee. In 1950, while he was on a trip to the Orient, the Emperor of Japan conferred upon him the Third Order of Merit of the Order of the Sacred Treasure.

A chapel was constructed for the Pacific School of Religion, dedicated in 1956. Its design presented an ideal space for a large window, and a memorial to Dr. Fisher (who died in 1955) was a natural thought. The character of his life determined its theme—a "Window of the Great Commission."

A powerful figure of Jesus dominates the window (see page 691), voicing His command, not only for His contemporaries, but for all who would follow in His footsteps. Going forth from Him in all directions are smaller-scale figures of the disciples. Some are shown preaching, some teaching, some baptizing, and some offering Communion. The torch, open Bible and Lamp of Knowledge are shown to represent the Christian enlightenment being carried to all parts of the world. To emphasize the feeling of distant parts of the earth, there are worked into the window small areas of varying types of landscapes: the frozen north, the burning desert, mountains, seas, Oriental architecture, and great cities.

Across the entire window are lettered the actual words from Matthew 28:19, "Go therefore and make disciples of all nations." At one side of the lettering is the seal of the World Council of Churches, and at the other are the Cross and Orb, ancient symbol of the triumph of the gospel.

As chroniclers of the Good News, which Christ's apostles may carry to all peoples, the four Evangelists occupy an important place in the window and are represented by their traditional symbols: St. Matthew, the angel; St. Mark, the winged lion; St. Luke, the winged ox; and St. John, the eagle.

The over-all coloring of the windows is warm and golden. The figures and features are made in strong, rich colors and are silhouetted against a background of lighter, subtly blended colors. The glass used in this window came from many countries—Germany, France, England, Belgium, and the United States. Each of the hundreds of pieces was selected with great care by the Wallis-Wiley Studio, who also gave particular attention not only to color but also to texture.

Galen Fisher's favorite sport was mountain-climbing, and his world travels gave him opportunity to reach the top of many famous peaks—Shasta, Half Dome, Lyell, Whitney, Fujiyama and the Matterhorn. His favorite poem was Coleridge's "Hymn Before Sunrise," written on Mount Blanc. Its lines depict his faith and life:

> Thou kingly Spirit throned among the hills,
> Thou dread Ambassador from Earth to Heaven,
> Great Hierarch! tell thou the silent sky,
> And tell the Stars, and tell yon rising Sun,
> Earth, with her thousand voices, praises God.

WINDOW OF THE GREAT COMMISSION, PACIFIC SCHOOL OF
RELIGION—*WALLIS-WILEY STUDIO*

MODERN ALTAR,
MASSACHUSETTS INSTITUTE OF TECHNOLOGY

"AT the top of the ladder," goes the old saying, "there is plenty of room." In this day when science is king, only a few names vie for leadership among the institutions in the United States dedicated to pure and applied science. One in this company is known affectionately as "M.I.T."—the Massachusetts Institute of Technology.

A monument to faith in a citadel of science is the windowless, cylindrical chapel at M.I.T. First used as a place of worship in 1955, it is easily one of the most extraordinary religious buildings of this age. Its facilities, with only the most moderate changes, can be adapted to the forms of worship used by Protestants, Catholics, or Jews.

The soaring artistry of Eero Saarinen has created here a chapel in the form of a brick cylinder, standing in a water-filled moat. The result is a complete separation of interior from exterior. The building amounts to a platform for the congregation and altar which seems to be out in space, away from worldly things, for this platform is surrounded by the water of the interior and exterior moat, and the encompassing walls rise from irregularly spaced arches cut into the bottom of the chapel cylinder. Natural light enters by reflection from the water of the moat to the dark interior through these arches. Additional soft light may be provided by pinhole ceiling ports.

Within the chapel is a solid marble pedestal, rectangular and about three feet high. The special religious objects required by the different faiths may be placed on this pedestal as they are needed.

Separate vestment and storage rooms are provided in the basement of the chapel below the pedestal and changes in the furnishings of the altar are facilitated by elevator service between the basement and the main chapel floor. The pedestal receives its own special light from a circular glass ceiling port called a lantern. The lantern also provides artificial illumination for nighttime use. Both the daylight and artificial light from the lantern enter the chapel from behind a honeycomb grill.

The altar light presents a striking contrast to the dimmer illumination reflected from the moat. This contrast is further accentuated by a metal screen that hangs from ceiling to floor behind the altar. There is an illusion here of the stars in unlimited space, providing the backdrop and the frame of reference for the worship which man offers out of his life and work. Designed by the noted sculptor Harry Bertoia, the screen is not a solid partition but an open fret of slim metal rods and cross plates. It is an ornamental separator which serves to heighten the effect of the lantern light above the altar.

The walls of the chapel are brick inside and out. Each individual brick had to be cut to shape and no two bricks are the same.

For acoustical reasons, the inside brick walls were made wavy or serpentine in shape. The chapel floor is travertine marble set in an unusual diamond

MODERN ALTAR, MASSACHUSETTS INSTITUTE OF TECHNOLOGY—
SAARINEN

pattern, and the inner brick is softened with wood wainscoting.

The chapel seats are individual ladder-back chairs instead of conventional pews. They were especially designed by Saarinen for the chapel and heighten the element of individual responsibility as one joins the group apparently floating in space under the overarching Providence.

Leading into the chapel, the long narthex or passageway is walled in glass stained in antique gray. Directly above the entrance of the narthex is the organ built by Walter Holtkamp, renowned organ maker.

The outer brick cylinder of the chapel is about fifty feet in diameter and thirty feet high. It is topped by an aluminum spire taller than the cylinder itself. The spire is the creation of Theodore Roszak, the sculptor, who also designed the bell which hangs at its base.

The M.I.T. chapel was planned as a quiet retreat. Its isolation is achieved in part by the device of the moat and by the solid windowless cylinder wall.

The approach from the main campus is through a grove of trees beside a screening wall of brick. The light dims in the stained-glass entryway of the narthex and, except for the altar light, becomes even softer within the chapel itself. The separation from the outer campus is complete.

✛

LET THERE BE LIGHT

Through the dark the dreamers came,
Melchior, Balthasar,
Casper, following the flame
Of a star:
    Via, Via!
    De profundis via!

But the way did not seem
Shadowy or long;
It was brightened by a dream
And a song:
    Gloria! Gloria!
    In excelsis gloria!

It was worth the journeying
To the weary end;
For they found their dream, a King
And a friend.
    Maxima, maxima,
    *Gloria Dei maxima!**

—*Earl Marlatt*

EVOLUTION

I like to think that it is true
Birds once were creeping creatures, too.
That somehow in the maze of things
Their struggles upward gave them wings;

* From *Cathedral: A Volume of Poems*, by Earl Marlatt, p. 78. Copyright 1956 by Earl Marlatt. Published by Parthenon Press. Used by permission of the author and the publisher.

That even as a bird can fly,
So, spiritually indeed, may I;
That every soul that longs for God
Will surely find Him as the clod
Which housing seed through wind and shower
Reveals its soul in leaf and flower.*

—Artemisia B. Bryson

A SPIRIT MUSES

Three thousand dollars to repair the church!
I reckon in my day that would have bought
The souls of half the austere congregation.
Times change. We scarcely dreamed, the frosty day
We raised her frame of honest hand-hewn beams,
That she would ever fetch a tithe of that.
It was a raising bee to be remembered—
The men with all their families and their workers,
A brace of hymns, a prayer, a dram of rum,
(I vow the latter did the trick) and up
She went, as neat a frame as you could find
This side of Goshen. Yes, and there she stands,
For in those days we builded for the ages.

Three thousand to repair the meeting house,
The church we fashioned in the latest style.
Three thousand to preserve it as a relic!

Somehow, it seems the settler's steadfast faith
Should have a monument. Religion was
Not merely Sunday fare for pioneers.
A mile of woods between you and your neighbor,
With wolves, and maybe a stray Indian,
Stir up your thoughts of powder and of God—
You wonder that we joined to build a church?

Three thousand dollars to repair the church . . .
Three thousand will restore that antique spire
That points its slender finger heavenward,
The perfect tribute to his steadfast faith;
His living faith—I do not think it dead,
Although the pews stand empty in the dusk.
Along the roads, in town and city streets,
New churches stretch their towers skyward now.
I never was so finicky for creeds;
I left that safely to the minister,
And maybe I was right, and maybe he.

* From *Poetry Out Where the West Begins*, p. 86. Copyright 1949 by Grace Ross and Mabel M. Kuykendall. Used by permission of the author.

Three thousand dollars to repair the church . . .
I guess, about a dollar for each soul.*
                    —*Franklin B. Williams (Syracuse Chapbook)*

THE SILENT WOODED PLACE

Have you ever felt the beating of the rain
    upon your face?
Have you ever tramped the dampness of a silent
    wooded place?
Have you felt the moist winds around you bathing you
    in heaven's dew,
So you scarcely could imagine that this new-world
    thing was you?
Ah, then you've lived as I have lived, in wooded
    prairie land,
Where wind-swept trees make reverent bow to strength of
    God's command;
Where man can see his heaven and earth, his field, his grass,
    his tree,
Where God is near, and stretches down His hand to you
    and me.
With rain-soaked leaves upon your feet, the mist upon
    your face,
You may walk unseen, but seeing, through your silent
    wooded place!**
                    —*Rachel E. Miller Graves (Rockford College)*

THE FIRST AUTUMN

Where God had walked
The goldenrod
Sprang like fire
From burning sod.

The purple asters,
When He spoke,
Rose up beautifully
Like smoke,

And shouting glory
To the sky,
The maple trees
Where He passed by.

But when God blessed
The last bright hill
The holy world
Grew white and still.***
                    —*Marshall W. Schacht (Dartmouth Verse)*

* From *Cap and Gown: Some College Verse*, 4th series, edited by R. L. Paget, p. 82. Published 1931
by L. C. Page & Company. Used by permission of the Syracuse University Press.
   ** *Ibid.*, p. 349. Used by permission of the author and the publisher.
   *** *Ibid.*, p. 203. Used by permission of Dartmouth Publications.

PORTRAIT OF A PASTOR

He gave . . . pastors . . . for the perfecting of the saints, for the work of the ministry, for the edifying of the body of Christ.—EPHESIANS 4:11-12

As strong he towers as mountain peak
That, radiant, holds the sun
Long after shadows darken field
And lane and over-run
The minds of men. And we, earth-bound,
Look up with faith renewed
To brave the gathering dusk who see
His spirit's altitude.*

—*Leslie Savage Clark*

TO A FOSSIL FERN

When I behold the lacelike tracery
　With which the ponderous force of nature tells
In delicate and graceful charact'ry
　Etched during aeons in earth's remotest cells,

How first in epoch eld you humbly grew,
　And strove to drape your mother's rugged breast
With all the splendor of your verdant hue,
　'Til in her deepest bosom you were prest;

Then do I marvel at the mighty Will
　Whose power, sustaining planets in the sky,
Would all the praise of heav'nly glory still
　To hearken to a wounded sparrow's cry.

Lo! all our deeds are ferns, would we might know
How, in the test of years, their fronds will show.**

—*John A. Foote*

* From *With All Thy Heart,* by Leslie Savage Clark, p. 40. Copyright 1957 by The Broadman Press. Used by permission of the author and the publisher.
** From *The Georgetown Anthology,* edited by James S. Ruby and Aloysius P. Kane. Published by Dorrance & Company. Used by permission of James S. Ruby, President of the Georgetown Alumni Association.

EARLY DAYS AT YALE

Lyman Beecher

BEFORE [Dr. Timothy Dwight] came [in 1796] college was in a most ungodly state. The college church was almost extinct. Most of the students were skeptical, and rowdies were plenty. Intemperance, profanity, gambling, and licentiousness were common. I hardly know how I escaped. Most of the class before me were infidels, and called each other Voltaire, Rousseau, D'Alembert, etc., etc.

They thought the Faculty were afraid of free discussion. But when they handed Dr. Dwight a list of subjects for class disputation, to their surprise he selected this: "Is the Bible the word of God?" and told them to do their best.

He heard all they had to say, answered them, and there was an end. He preached incessantly for six months on the subject, and all infidelity skulked and hid its head.

He elaborated his theological system in a series of forenoon sermons in the chapel; the afternoon discourses were practical. The original design of Yale College was to found a divinity school. To a mind appreciative like mine, his preaching was a continual course of education and a continual feast. He was copious and polished in style, though disciplined and logical.

There was a pith and power of doctrine there that has not been since surpassed, if equaled. I took notes of all his discourses, condensing and forming skeletons. He was of noble form, with a noble head and body, and had one of the sweetest smiles that ever you saw. He always met me with a smile. Oh, how I loved him! I loved him as my own soul, and he loved me as a son. And once I told him that all I had I owed to him. "Then," said he, "I have done a great and soul-satisfying work. I consider myself amply rewarded."

Intellectually, the Senior year was the best to me. We all looked forward to Dr. Dwight's instructions with interest. We began with Blair's Rhetoric, half an hour's recitation, and an hour or hour and a half of extempore lecture. He was full of anecdote and illustration, and delighted to talk as much as we did to listen, and often he was very eloquent in these class lectures. It was not all ornament, however, but he showed a thoroughgoing mastery of the subject. Then we took up logic and metaphysics—Duncan and Locke were our authors. In ethics we studied Paley, our recitations all conducted as before. This took up three days of each week. On two other days we had written or extempore debates before Dr. Dwight, he summing up at the close. On Saturday we had the Catechism, Vincent's Exposition, followed by a theological lecture. You see it was more than a college—it was partly a divinity school. That was the idea of its original founders.*

* Abridged from *Autobiography, Correspondence, Etc., of Lyman Beecher, D.D.*, edited by Charles Beecher.

PROPOSALS FOR THE UNION OF CHRISTIANS
Thomas Campbell

Pushing his spectacles up to his forehead with a habitual gesture, the gentleman of kindly face rustled and evened the edges of several sheets of foolscap before him. At middle age Thomas Campbell had prematurely gray hair. His stay in and around the little town of Washington, Pennsylvania, for the two years prior to 1809 had been eventful as he awaited the arrival of his wife, Jane, his eldest son, Alexander, and the younger children. Neighbors had sought the liberties of the new nation, but chafed under the ancient religious restrictions brought by their clergymen, still shackled by Old World training and ties. These men had commissioned Mr. Campbell to express their "religious declaration of independence" in the new land, with loyalty retained not for human custom and creed but for the source book of revelation, the Bible. This document was essentially a reasonable and educational approach to the problem of church union amid the unprecedented religious freedom enjoyed in the burgeoning new nation.

Utterly unaware that his pages, entitled simply "A Declaration and Address," would generate the largest religious communion originating in America, he read:

BEING well aware, from sad experience, of the heinous nature and pernicious tendency of religious controversy among Christians, tired and sick of the bitter jarrings and janglings of a party spirit, we would desire to be at rest; and, were it possible, we would also desire to adopt and recommend such measures as would give rest to our brethren throughout all the churches: as would restore unity, peace and purity to the whole church of God.

Let all the churches of Christ unite in the bonds of an entire Christian unity—Christ alone being the *head,* the center, His word the rule; and explicit belief of, and manifest conformity to it in all things—the *terms.*

. . . Truths demonstrably evident in the light of Scripture and right reason are stated in these propositions.

1. That the Church of Christ upon earth is essentially, intentionally, and constitutionally one; consisting of all those in every place that profess their faith in Christ and obedience to Him in all things according to the Scriptures, and that manifest the same by their tempers and conduct, and of none else; as none else can be truly and properly called Christians.

2. That although the Church of Christ upon earth must necessarily exist in particular and distinct societies, locally separate one from another, yet there ought to be no schisms, no uncharitable divisions among them. They ought to receive each other as Christ Jesus hath also received them, to the glory of God. And for this purpose they ought all to walk by the same rule, to mind and speak the same thing; and to be perfectly joined together in the same mind, and in the same judgment.

3. That in order to do this, nothing ought to be inculcated upon Christians as articles of faith; nor required of them as terms of communion, but what is expressly taught and enjoined upon them in the word of God.

4. That although the Scriptures of the Old and New Testaments are inseparably connected, making together but one perfect and entire revelation of the Divine will, for the edification and salvation of the Church, and therefore in that respect cannot be separated; yet as to what directly and properly belongs to their immediate object, the New Testament is as perfect a constitution for the worship, discipline, and government of the Church, and as perfect a rule for the particular duties of its members, as the Old Testament was for the worship, discipline, and government of the Old Testament Church, and the particular duties of its members.

5. That with respect to the commands and ordinances of our Lord Jesus Christ, where the Scriptures are silent as to the express time or manner of performance, if any such there be, no human authority has power to interfere, in order to supply the supposed deficiency by making laws for the Church; . . . Nothing ought to be received into the faith or worship of the Church, or be made a term of communion among Christians, that is not as old as the New Testament.

6. That although inferences and deductions from Scripture premises, when fairly inferred, may be truly called the doctrine of God's holy word, yet are they not formally binding upon the consciences of Christians farther than they perceive the connection, and evidently see that they are so; for their faith must not stand in the wisdom of men, but in the power and veracity of God.

7. That although doctrinal exhibitions of the great system of Divine truths, and defensive testimonies in opposition to prevailing errors, be highly expedient, and the more full and explicit for those purposes they be, the better; yet, as these must be in a great measure the effect of human reasoning, and of course must contain many inferential truths, they ought not to be made terms of communion; . . .

8. That as it is not necessary that persons should have a particular knowledge or distinct apprehension of all Divinely revealed truths in order to entitle them to a place in the Church; neither should they, for this purpose, be required to make a profession more extensive than their knowledge; . . .

9. That all are enabled through grace to make such a profession, and to manifest the reality of it in their tempers and conduct, should consider each other as the precious saints of God, should love each other as brethren, children of the same family and father, temples of the same Spirit, members of the same body, subjects of the same grace, objects of the same love, bought with the same price, and joint heirs of the same inheritance. Whom God hath thus joined together no man should dare to put asunder.

10. That division among the Christians is a horrible evil, fraught with many evils. It is anti-Christian, as it destroys the visible unity of the body of Christ; as if He were divided against Himself, excluding and excommunicating a part of Himself.

11. That (in some instances) a partial neglect of the expressly revealed will of God, and (in others) an assumed authority for making the approba-

tion of human opinions and human inventions a term of communion, by introducing them into the constitution, faith, or worship of the Church, are, and have been, the immediate, obvious, and universally acknowledged causes, of all the corruptions and divisions that ever have taken place in the Church of God.

12. That all that is necessary to the highest state of perfection and purity of the Church upon earth is, first, that none be received as members but such as having that due measure of self-knowledge described above, do profess their faith in Christ and obedience to Him in all things according to the Scriptures; nor, secondly, that any be retained in her communion longer than they continue to manifest the reality of their profession by their temper and conduct.

13. Lastly. That if any circumstantials indispensably necessary to the observance of Divine ordinances be not found upon the page of express revelation, such, and such only, as are absolutely necessary for this purpose should be adopted under the title of human expedients, without any pretence to a more sacred origin, so that any subsequent alteration or difference in the observance of these things might produce no contention nor division of the Church.*

✛

CHURCH, SCHOOL, AND STATE
Samuel Windsor Brown

FOR somewhat over a century there has been going on in the United States a gradual but widespread elimination of religious and church influences from public education. During the early years of our history, especially during the colonial period, education and religion, the school and the Church, were close allies. One of the aims of elementary education was to inculcate religious beliefs; of higher education, to prepare religious teachers. The subject matter of instruction was largely religious in nature. Church authorities exercised considerable control over education affairs. The warmest advocates of education were those who had in view the needs of the Church. Today we find in every state a system of public education in which civic and industrial aims are dominant, in which religious instruction is either entirely eliminated or else reduced to the barest and most formal elements, and the control of which is vested well nigh exclusively in the state or some subdivision thereof.

So long as suffrage depended upon property, or some other qualification than mere manhood, the state needed to concern itself little about education. To private enterprise and religious zeal, assisted and encouraged at times by the State, could usually be intrusted the care of instructing the children and youth. But immediately manhood suffrage became universal, education began

* Abridged by A. T. DeGroot from *Declaration and Address*, pp. 48-58, as found in *The Disciples of Christ* by Errett Gates. Published 1905 by The Baker and Taylor Company.

to assume too great an importance from the standpoint of civic and national welfare for the state any longer to neglect it or entrust it to any other than its own agents whom it could hold responsible for standards and results.

So long as population regions were relatively homogeneous in matters of religious faith, nothing could be more natural than that the public school should be used to transmit unto the children the faith of the fathers. For centuries, under an alliance of Church and State, more or less close, the schools had been so used. But with the influx of immigration which set in about the third decade of the last century and continued to grow with ever-increasing volume during the succeeding decades, composed of the oppressed of all nations, our population regions, from being relatively homogeneous in religious matters, rapidly became most heterogeneous. The territories upon our western borders rapidly filled with streams of settlers drawn from the original seacoast states as well as from various European countries. Nor were the original states unaffected by this influx of European immigration. All this resulted in a thorough mingling of diverse religious and sectarian elements.

Education immediately began to assume great importance as a means of Americanizing the diverse racial and cultural elements composing our population, and the State began more and more to foster schools and the means of instruction. The great variety of religious opinion and belief existing in every state or territory made the question of religious instruction in the schools a crucial one. On the one hand there was a widespread belief that the chief purpose of all education was the formation of character and that religion was a necessary element therein. On the other hand, there was a tenacious adherence by the representatives of every shade of religious belief, to the particular tenets of their creed. To allow their children to be taught less than they believed, or other than they believed, was to them unthinkable. So long as the determination of the instruction to be given and the books to be used could be left to each individual community a certain amount of adaptation was possible. The majority at least in each community could have its preferences therein carried out.

But with state support and state control of education came, too, centralization and uniformity, which were demanded by considerations of efficiency and economy. So it has come to pass that necessity has led the State to provide for education; and sectarian differences have made it necessary that this education should be non-sectarian or non-religious.

That the aim of education in America as conceived at various times in our early history by our highest legislative authorities was largely religious, can be abundantly shown by citations from the enactments of the said authorities. This dominant religious aim is evident in the favorable attitude of the colony of Connecticut toward Yale College. The original act of incorporation of Yale is prefaced by the following: "Whereas several well disposed and public spirited persons, of their sincere regard to and zeal for the upholding and propagating of the Christian protestant religion by a succession of learned and orthodox men, have expressed by petition their earnest desire that full liberty and privilege be granted unto certain undertakers, for the founding and suitably endowing and ordering a collegiate school, within His Majesty's Colony of Connecticut, wherein youth may be instructed in the arts and sciences who, through the blessings of Almighty God, may be fitted for public employment both in church and civil state. To the intent therefore that all due encouragement be given to such pious resolutions and that so necessary and religious an undertaking may be set forward, supported, and well managed: Be it enacted by the Governor and Company of the said colony of Connecticut in general court assembled," etc.

The charter of King's College, now Columbia University, contained a provision for the establishment of a professor of Divinity for the Reformed Protestant Dutch Church, even though by the time of its founding, 1755, one might have expected the college to emphasize the English Church. The provision shows how the colonial government tried to provide for religious differences and still keep religion central in the college.

The charter of William and Mary, 1692, provided for the establishment of a "place of universal study, or perpetual College of Divinity, Philosophy, Languages, and other good arts and sciences."

The State provided for certain control by the Church or by religion over general education even past the middle of the nineteenth century. Georgia required all members of the trustees and faculty of the University to be of the Christian religion as late as 1861. Minnesota in 1867 provided that two-thirds of the board of trustees of Minnesota Central University be of the Baptist denomination. New York provided for the appointment of a member of the regents of the University of New York to be appointed by the religious denominations of the state.

Some states provided for the support of schools more or less under the control of denominations. As late as 1874 in Texas, a provision was made whereby a school district could contract with a private school for the instruction of the children of the district and share in the distribution of public funds.

Many of the regulations, however, of which the above are only a few examples, were changed in the latter part of the nineteenth century and early twentieth century to complete the picture of separation of religion and denominational instruction from the state-supported educational system. The Political Code of South Dakota in 1903 states with regard to the state university: "No instruction either sectarian in religion or partisan in politics shall ever be allowed in any department of the University." Utah, in 1892, shows how a state tried to avoid sectarianism and yet maintain the moral or religious undergirding of instruction. "No atheistic, infidel, sectarian, or denominational doctrine shall be taught in any of the district schools of the state. Moral instruction, tending to impress upon the minds of pupils the importance of good manners, truthfulness, temperance, purity, patriotism, and industry shall be given in every district school."

Religion as an aim of education is mentioned in relatively few of the state constitutions now in force, although almost all of them emphasize civic, professional, or industrial aims. Knowledge, morality, virtue are recognized as essentials of good citizenship, and it is assumed to be the function of the school to impart the same, but little is heard of religion or the service of the Church in this connection.*

✛

LIFE OF AGES, RICHLY POURED

FOR most of us the campuses of the universities of the world exude an almost holy air. For here through the centuries men have devoted themselves to the accumulation, preservation, and dissemination of learning. The centuries seem quietly gathered here and in patience wait to bless all coming generations of men. Unhurried, yet eager and alert, this quintessence of man's striving, this precious deposit of the ages, offers its free and generous wealth to all who come.

Samuel Johnson's hymn, "Life of Ages, Richly Poured," breathes this same immensity, as it describes the "life of ages," God's love, richly poured, yet unspent, flowing in prophetic insight and speech, issuing in the freedom of man's spirit. In all the vast and teeming life of the world, God's life is visible. For His is every time and place. Every time He freshens with His "truth and good," for He is the "fountain sweet of heart and mind." And if God's love breathes in "the thinker's creed," it also pulses in "the hero's blood." It consecrates "art and song, holy book and pilgrim track." It stands as a great bulwark against the "floods of tyrant wrong." And so it is Church and school together which maintain freedom for the prophet's word and which guard the people's liberty.

The hymn was first published in 1864 in *Hymns of the Spirit,* edited by Samuel Johnson and Samuel Longfellow.

The tune, "Orientis Partibus," had its origins in a medieval sacred folk song. It is commonly ascribed to Pierre de Corbeil, Archbishop of Sens in the thirteenth century. The Latin name of the tune comes from the first two words of the play, the *Feast of the Ass,* commemorating the Flight into Egypt. At the proper place in the play, the priests and people chanted, to a curious mixture of French and Latin, this tune. Older variants of the tune are in triple time. Richard Redhead (1820-1901), an English church organist, made this duple-meter adaptation for his *Church Hymn Tunes* (1853).

✛

LET THERE BE LIGHT, LORD GOD

How can man become wise? Where shall wisdom be found, and where is the place of understanding? These are old questions. But the Church has an answer,

* Abridged by Karl E. Snyder from *The Secularization of American Education,* by Samuel Windsor Brown. Published 1912 by Teachers' College, Columbia University. Used by permission of the publisher.

Life of ages, richly poured *

ORIENTIS PARTIBUS 7.7.7.7.

Samuel Johnson, 1864

Medieval French Melody
Adapted and harmonized by Richard Redhead, 1853

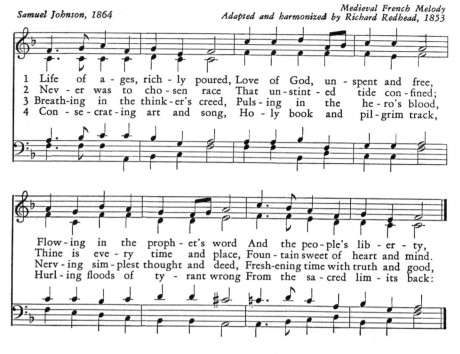

1 Life of a - ges, rich - ly poured, Love of God, un - spent and free,
2 Nev - er was to cho - sen race That un - stint - ed tide con - fined;
3 Breath-ing in the think - er's creed, Puls - ing in the he - ro's blood,
4 Con - se - crat - ing art and song, Ho - ly book and pil - grim track,

Flow - ing in the proph - et's word And the peo - ple's lib - er - ty,
Thine is eve - ry time and place, Foun - tain sweet of heart and mind.
Nerv - ing sim - plest thought and deed, Fresh-ening time with truth and good,
Hurl - ing floods of ty - rant wrong From the sa - cred lim - its back:

5 Life of ages, richly poured,
   Love of God, unspent and free,
   Flow still in the prophet's word
   And the people's liberty!

*From Geer's *Hymnal for Colleges and Schools.* Used by permission of Yale University Press.

and it is an old answer which yet is always new: "If any of you lack wisdom, let him ask of God, that giveth to all men liberally, and upbraideth not; and it shall be given him." Hence man *prays* for wisdom, and only as he prays with deep sighing and tears can the mysterious and relentless powers of ignorance be driven back and overcome.

What the world now needs is that wisdom which is from above that is "first pure, then peaceable, gentle, open to reason, full of mercy and good fruits, without uncertainty or insincerity." It is a wisdom which brings to birth "broad humanity," which issues in deeds, not boasts. It is a wisdom which quiets passion, brings strain and strife to an end, purges "from lusts that curse and kill." It opens men's eyes that they may see in their brothers' good their own, and find in the common joys and the common sufferings that perfect love which casts out fear. Then the "woe and waste" of war will come to an end, and man's labor will build fruitful homes filled with joy and laughter.

In many ways the hymn is an epitome of the long and creatively fruitful life of its author. Born in 1880 in Kansas, Mr. Vories quickly became interested in missions abroad. In accord with his pioneering spirit, he determined to serve as a layman, to work in a hitherto neglected area, to be independent of any church body, and to earn his own living while on the field, without salary from home.

In 1905 a teaching position was obtained for him in Omi-Hachiman, Japan. As the result of a long life devoted to Omi-Hachiman, sometimes in the midst

Let there be light, Lord God*
ELTON L.M.

William Merrill Vories, 1908   *Lowell Mason, 1854*

1 Let there be light, Lord God of hosts, Let there be
2 With - in our pas - sioned hearts in - still The calm that
3 Give us the peace of vi - sion clear To see our
4 Let woe and waste of war - fare cease, That use - ful

wis - dom on the earth! Let broad hu - man - i - ty have
end - eth strain and strife; Make us thy min - is - ters of
broth - ers' good our own, To joy and suf - fer not a -
la - bor yet may build Its homes with love and laugh - ter

birth! Let there be deeds in - stead of boasts!
life; Purge us from lusts that curse and kill!
lone— The love that cast - eth out all fear!
filled! God, give thy way - ward chil - dren peace!

*From Geer's *Hymnal for Colleges and Schools.* Used by permission of The American Peace Society and Yale University Press.

of violent opposition and personal persecution, there has come into existence the Omi Mission, and within the Mission, the Omi Brotherhood, a closely-knit, self-sacrificing community, living to build the larger community, the empire, and the world on Christian principles of love.

During the long years in which Dr. Vories has been the soul and center of the Mission, the town of Omi-Hachiman has almost been made new. The Mission specializes in women's work, kindergartens, playgrounds, newspaper evangelism, publications, and all activities which have to do with making life both rich and Christian. The architectural department has built important buildings throughout Japan. The tuberculosis hospital is the most complete and modern in all Japan. The Mission operates the *Galilee Maru*, a steamship on Lake Biwa, used for preaching purposes. And although the Omi Sales Company, Ltd., has sold dozens of American products in Japan and China, no personal profit has ever been derived from these enterprises. The profits from the vast business go to support the work of the Mission. Given the complete identification of himself with the people of his choice, it is not surprising that Dr. Vories married a Japanese wife and later became a Japanese subject.

Our hymn was written as early as 1908, but it gives classical statement to the Christian concerns which have possessed Dr. Vories in the changing and difficult times which Japan and the world have seen in this century.

The tune, "Elton," was composed by Lowell Mason (1792-1872), one of the most important of our nineteenth-century composers. He was editor or co-editor of almost forty hymnals, and himself composed, arranged, or adapted nearly seventeen hundred tunes.

PART VI

CHRISTIANITY, A WORLD-WIDE RELIGION

by

CYNTHIA PEARL MAUS

1. THE CHURCH OF CHRIST IN JAPAN ...... *page* 710

2. THE CHRISTIAN WITNESS IN CHINA, FREE CHINA, AND FORMOSA .... *page* 733

3. THE CHRISTIAN WITNESS IN KOREA ...... *page* 758

4. CHRISTIANITY IN THE PHILIPPINES ..... *page* 782

5. THE CHURCH OF CHRIST IN INDIA .... *page* 803

6. THE CHURCH OF CHRIST IN AFRICA ...... *page* 828

7. THE CHRISTIAN WITNESS IN LATIN AMERICA *page* 857

CONTENTS

PART VI SECTION 1

THE CHURCH OF CHRIST IN JAPAN

✠

In the mouth of two or three witnesses shall every word be established.—II CORINTHIANS 13:1

✠

PICTURES: PAGE
    Interpretation: The Three Saints—*Sadakata* 711
    Picture: The Three Saints—*Sadakata* 712
    Interpretation: Anglican Episcopal Church, Nara, and Matsuzawa Church,
       Tokyo 711
    Pictures: Anglican Episcopal Church, Nara, and Matsuzawa Church, Tokyo 714
    Interpretation: Woman's Christian College, Tokyo—*Raymond* 715
    Picture: Woman's Christian College, Tokyo—*Raymond* 716

POETRY:
    Prelude—*Erickson* 715
    Christmas—*Yamamoto* 717
    Holding the Cross—*Hayashi* 717
    Entrusting All—*Kanda* 718
    Christ Liveth in Me—*Kagawa* 718
    The Carpenter—*Yamamuro* 719
    A Holy Temple—*Handa* 720
    Glory to God—*Handa* 720
    The Living Christ—*Kagawa* 721
    Love's Gife—*Author Unknown* 721
    In All Things, Victory!—*Nagata* 722
    Discovery—*Kagawa* 722

STORIES:
    Kagawa, God's Hand in Japan—*Kagawa* 722
    Keizo Finds a New Way of Life—*Nagata* 725
    The Hiroshima Maidens—based on *Saturday Review* 727

MUSIC:
    Interpretation: More Love to Thee, O Christ—*Prentiss* 730
    Music: More Love to Thee, O Christ—*Doane* 730
    Interpretation: O For a Closer Walk with God—*Cowper* 731
    Music: O For a Closer Walk with God—*Cottman* 732

THE THREE SAINTS

Kwaiseki Sadakata

IN THIS painting by the Japanese artist Kwaiseki Sadakata (p. 712), we see an attempt to unite in one picture three religious leaders widely known throughout Japan and the Orient: Confucius on the left, Buddha on the right, Christ in the center. Confucius and Buddha are dressed in their traditional garb; the figure of Christ is gowned in the Oriental robe of His times. The right hands of the three saints are clasped together as if to indicate a partnership in their efforts to lift people to higher mental, moral, and spiritual levels.

"When Christianity leaves Palestine and enters another culture, a decision has to be made by artists as to whether one should aim at historical, ethnological, and archeological accuracy when painting Biblical scenes, or whether local models and backgrounds may be used with the main interest liturgical or spiritual."* Sadakata shows in the faces and figures of the three saints the characteristics of their national and racial backgrounds: there is the suggestion of a Japanese face for Confucius and for Buddha, while Christ's face resembles many modern concepts of the Christ of the Western world.

Sadakata is a devout Methodist and an outstanding contemporary Japanese artist, who feels that painting in the Christian tradition is a form of worship. His present-day use of old techniques and stylistic forms to portray new values and insights under the inspiration of Christianity can play a very real part in helping all of us toward a world Christian community. Just as in past centuries an entire community flowered in the building of great cathedrals, so today the efforts of artists of all races and among all nations help us to see the hand of God at work, enriching and developing appreciation for universal Christian concepts and patterns of thought and action throughout the wide, wide world. This spiritual task will not be completed in one generation, and in its consummation each nation, race, and culture must be encouraged to bring its distinctive gifts.**

✠

ANGLICAN EPISCOPAL CHURCH, NARA
AND MATSUZAWA CHURCH, TOKYO

THE upper view on p. 714 shows the Anglican Episcopal Church at Nara, Japan, sometimes called "Christ's Church." During the eighth century Nara was the capital of Japan, the center of administration and of the cultural communications between China, then under the T'ang dynasty, and Japan. It was then that the great Buddha's Temple was constructed in Nara and dedicated

* From *Each with His Own Brush* by Daniel J. Fleming, p. 7. Published 1952 by Friendship Press. Used by permission of the author and the publisher.
** From the Abbott Book Library of Art. Arranged by special permission.

711

THE THREE SAINTS—*SADAKATA*

by order of the Emperor. Many other temples of grandeur and importance were built there before the capital was transferred to another city.

A poem from the Mannyoshu, a ten-thousand leaf anthology of the period, describes the beauty of the old capital. Here is the poem in Japanese and in English:

Aoni yoshi	Nara, the Capital,
Nara no miyako wa,	In milliard colors gay,
Saku hana no,	Is in her prime today
Nio ga gotoku,	Like flowers blooming full,
Ima sakari nari.	Fragrant and beautiful.

Nara is also famous for a kind of cherryblossom known as the *Yaezakura,* which means "the eightfold cherryblossom of Nara." This cherryblossom is outstanding for its beauty, although it is hard to grow and still more difficult to transplant.

Those who have traveled to Nara will not soon forget its beauty and elegance, although much of the glory of this ancient city is now a matter of history.

The lower photograph on p. 714 shows the chancel end of the new chapel of Matsuzawa Church, built in 1940. This is in the village of Setagaya, a suburb of Toyko. Its pastor is the Rev. Kanzo Ogawa, and Dr. Toyohiko Kagawa is the associate pastor. (See "Kagawa, God's Hand in Japan," p. 722.)

Dr. Kagawa often used to come to this calm village to rest while conducting some special campaign in Tokyo, and he spent considerable time here after the great earthquake in 1923, when the entire city of Tokyo was damaged. He and a group of followers founded the Matsuzawa Christian Church in 1931.

Dr. Kagawa feels that church buildings should be used every day in the week, and in connection with this church a daily kindergarten was opened which serves more than two hundred children. This is in addition to the Sunday school, whose average weekly attendance is one hundred fifty children. Exactly how many churches Dr. Kagawa has had a hand in helping to build throughout Japan is not known, but at least fifty kindergartens or child-care stations around the country owe their beginnings to him.

One of the distinctive features of the Matsuzawa Church is the custom of gathering together in the chapel every morning at six to pray for world peace. Another unique custom is that of having a luncheon each Sunday after the morning service to promote Christian fellowship among the members. A system of mutual financial help also exists among the members, who contribute monthly to a fund from which interest-free loans are available to any needy person.

The Matsuzawa Church carries out the Master's example: "I am among you as one that serveth."

ANGLICAN EPISCOPAL CHURCH, NARA

MATSUZAWA CHURCH, TOKYO

WOMAN'S CHRISTIAN COLLEGE, TOKYO

SPEAKING of Japanese art, Daniel J. Fleming says: "The question as to whether Japanese symbolism should be used in the decoration of the Church and Christian institutions awakens very little interest among Japanese Christians. . . . When the process of absorption of Western culture began in Japan, nearly a hundred years ago, Christianity was scarcely differentiated from Western civilization; the Western religion and its Western cultural expression were taken quite naturally together."*

The Woman's Christian College in Tokyo is one of the most beautiful modern structures in the Orient. Built in 1938, it miraculously escaped destruction during the war. It is not an example of Japanese art, but is of a style frequently described as California Gothic. It was designed by a Czech architect, Mr. Antonio Raymond, an admirer and follower of Frank Lloyd Wright.

The chapel-auditorium, shown on p. 716, is described by Miss Constance Chappell: "The larger side to the left is an auditorium seating about a thousand people. The other side, with the decorative windows, is the chapel, which seats about three hundred. The chapel is used every day for the worship services of students and faculty. The auditorium is used for the weekly general assembly and for all special occasions such as graduation, Christmas, baccalaureate services, etc. One unique feature of this building is that just below the tower there is an organ, so arranged with sliding doors that it can be played for either the auditorium or the chapel."

One of the most beautiful parts of the chapel is the series of windows in a continuous lattice of crosses, diamonds, circles, and squares, framing colored glass of rainbow shades. Inside, the huge cross at the altar stands out in white, and on the altar are a broken Japanese reed, a lily, and an oak leaf, symbolizing man's weakness transformed through the Resurrection into strength.

The Woman's Christian College was founded and is supported by a number of mission boards of different denominations. It is one of Tokyo's most beautiful and significant buildings dedicated to Christian learning and culture.

✠

PRELUDE

I have seen beauty—
Flaming clouds at sunset;
Seas dyed to scarlet as
   the night comes on;
Bowers of flowers mirrored
   in the lakelets;
Grandeurs of gorges,
   Fuji in the dawn!

* From *Christian Symbols in a World Community* by Daniel J. Fleming, p. 103. Copyright 1940 by Friendship Press. Used by permission of the author and the publisher.

WOMAN'S CHRISTIAN COLLEGE, TOKYO—*RAYMOND*

Lacy green trees outlined
　　in misty vistas
Suddenly lighted by a flare
　　of maple leaves;
Far below the mountaintop
　　the ripening rice fields waving
'Round little brown mud hovels
　　with a straw-thatched eaves.

Now War and Death
　　have come to you
O Lovely Land of Morning,
Dull despair of sorrow
　　and bitterness of pain;
God grant us both forgiveness
　　for the wrongs we did each other—
Out of deep hatred
　　bring us Love again!*

　　　　　　　　　　　　　　—Lois J. Erickson

CHRISTMAS

Two thousand years ago the Star appeared
　　To wondering men;
　　Tonight it shines above our isle
　　As bright as then;
　　Lo, let us, let us go
　　To Bethlehem!

All quietly the maples glow red
　　That once were green;
　　Without the Camp
　　All silently,
　　Tonight the Christ is seen,
New-born and helpless, now as then,
　　Lo, let us, let us go
　　To Bethlehem!**

　　　　　　　　　　　　　　—Yamamoto

HOLDING THE CROSS

Bearing reproach and shame,
Suffering pain and loss,
My Soul undaunted still shall march
Holding aloft the Cross!***

　　　　　　　　　　　　　　—Hayashi

* From *Songs from the Land of Dawn* by Toyohiko Kagawa and other Japanese poets, translated by Lois J. Erickson, p. xvi. Copyright 1949 by Friendship Press. Used by permission of the publisher.
** From *Hearts Aglow* by Honami Nagata and Lois J. Erickson. Published by American Mission to Lepers. Used by permission of the publisher.
*** From *Souls Undaunted*, translated by Lois J. Erickson. Published by American Mission to Lepers. Used by permission of the publisher.

ENTRUSTING ALL

I would not change one little jot
    Of His dear will for me;
But in my weakness I would go,
Entrusting all my load of woe
    To Him Who walks with me.*

—*Keizo Kanda*

CHRIST LIVETH IN ME

"That Christ may dwell
Within your hearts
By faith,"
Thus did Paul write
To friends in Ephesus.

For Christ to Paul
Was not a Being
To be worshiped from afar,
But One Who dwelt within.

When Thought Police
Threw me in jail,
(For Jesus' sake)
I sat two days and nights
Upon the prison floor,
My head upon my knees,
Discouraged, miserable, and prayed.

And then the vision came—
I had been seeking for the Christ
Too far away;
But now I saw
That He could live in me!

Live with me always—
In the night
Came comfort,
For I tried to feel
That He was there,
And in the morning
That His love awaited me.

Then as I paced the prison grounds
He walked with me;

* From *Hearts Aglow* by Honami Nagata and Lois J. Erickson. Published by American Mission to Lepers. Used by permission of the publisher.

And as I read the books allowed
(The books on science),
Then He talked with me,
And made me know
That real truth is of God;
Shimbashi Prison thus became
    God's temple!

For from the very moment
When my vision came,
My tears were gone
And all my fears swept away.

Christ was with me
As I faced examination
By the fierce police;
And He was there
When I was brought
Before the judge,
Expecting death,
And praying that I might not shame
The Christ within my heart.

Christ, Who didst walk on Galilee,
Lead me to peace in this sad world;
Thou Who didst fall asleep in that frail boat
    On a storm-tossed sea,
Oh, lead me to that world where all is understood—
    Live Thou, O Christ, in me!*

—*Toyohiko Kagawa*

THE CARPENTER

Long, long ago
Beside a little grass-grown street
Of Nazareth,
Within a quiet shop,
He bent to plane tough boards
And saw hard wood,
While sweat dropped from His brow—
Our Lord and Master
In the form of man,
Who showed us thus
The worth of labor.

His salvation comes
Not from man's wisdom

* From *Songs from the Land of Dawn* by Toyohiko Kagawa and other Japanese poets, translated by Lois J. Erickson, pp. 24-26. Copyright 1949 by Friendship Press. Used by permission of the publisher.

Nor the lore of books,
But to those born again,
Whose hearts are made anew,
Be they but toilers, traders,
Peasants, poorest of the poor.

The grace of God
Is never limited
To men in gorgeous robes,
Who dwell in jeweled towers;
But He abides
Beside the hearths of hovels,
Where at morn and night
His children kneel
To lift their hearts to Him.

In faith then,
Let us pull the heavy wheels;
And in the Spirit
Draw the water
For our paddy fields,
Remembering that long ago
Jesus of Nazareth
Daily carved His wood,
And planed His long, hard boards.
So let us hold
His will for us
Deep in our hearts
And labor on and on.*

—*Gumpei Yamamuro*

A HOLY TEMPLE

Men hate me for the curse I bear,
    (I know it well)
  But shall I heed them
  Since my heart can be
   A holy temple
Where my God can dwell?**

—*Handa*

GLORY TO GOD

Glory to God Who sent His Son
To save the sad, dark earth;
And as we praise Him on this day

---

* *Ibid.*, pp. 48-49.
** From *Souls Undaunted*, translated by Lois J. Erickson. Published by American Mission to Lepers. Used by permission of the publisher.

That gave Him birth,
The hymns that herald how each heart rejoices
Mingle with angel voices!*

—Handa

THE LIVING CHRIST

Paul was the only man
Who ever saw our Lord
After His entrance
Into Heaven
To dwell with God.

Paul met Him
On the rough Damascus Road.
And from that time
Christ dwelt in Paul,
Giving him help,
Comfort in sickness,
And in persecution, strength—
Christ was his whole existence.

So to us
Today
Christ gives eternal life,—
He Who was crucified,
And triumphed,
Through the Power of Love.
Our Lord is in our hearts
And flesh and blood,
Helping us always.

Why should we speak
Of "Christianity"
As though it were
Dead doctrine?
Jesus is not dead;
Still as of old,
He seeks His sheep.

The Christ is everywhere—
The lepers find Him
In their dark despair;
He shines in the grey dawn
Beyond the dungeon bars;
And by our death beds
He is there!

Children of Japan,
Dumb in defeat,
Struggling to live,
Wipe, wipe away your tears,
Look at the living Christ;
He stands
*Here at your side.***
—Toyohiko Kagawa

LOVE'S GIFT

Love gave a gift to God—
    A little thing—
He used that gift to make
    Nagata sing.

Some widow brought her mite,
    And through God's grace
That glorious light was born
    On Keizo's face.

Christ walks no roads today,
    But 'tis His will
That those who love Him shall
    Touch lepers still!*

—Author Unknown

* From *Hearts Aglow* by Honami Nagata and Lois J. Erickson. Published by American Mission to Lepers. Used by permission of the publisher.
** From *Songs from the Land of Dawn* by Toyohiko Kagawa and other Japanese poets, translated by Lois J. Erickson, pp. 10-11. Copyright 1949 by Friendship Press. Used by permission of the publisher.

IN ALL THINGS, VICTORY

He hears me pray to Him upon the deep,
When masts are gone, and tattered sails are blown
By storms that drive my frail boat out to sea;
He hears, and sends the wind that wafts me home.

Naught that can come shall bring despair to me,
Gaining in all things more than victory!

He hears me pray to Him when I am lost
Amid wild mountains, and no path can see;
He saves me from the beasts and from the night,
And gives the comfort of His strength to me.

He hears me pray to Him when my tired feet
Struggle across the desert's burning sand;
With His own blood restores my fainting soul,
And to green pastures leads me by the hand.

The limits of the earth are wide and vast,
And vaster still its smiling dome of blue,
Yet through this space I always hear His voice,
"O little one," He says, "I died for you!"

My Lord in me has found a dwelling place,
And I in Him. Oh, glorious boon to gain
To be His temple! Gladly will I face,
In His great strength, all bitterness and pain!*

—*Honami Nagata*

KAGAWA, GOD'S HAND IN JAPAN

DISCOVERY

I cannot invent
New things,
Like the airships
Which sail
On silver wings;
But today
A wonderful thought
In the dawn was given,

And the thought
Was this:
That a secret plan
Is hid in my hand;
That my hand is big,
BIG,
Because of this plan.

* From *Hearts Aglow* by Honami Nagata and Lois J. Erickson. Published by American Mission to Lepers. Used by permission of the publisher.

And the stripes on my robe,
Shining from wear,
Were suddenly fair
Bright with a light
Falling from Heaven—
Gold, and silver, and bronze
Lights from the windows of Heaven.

That God,
Who dwells in my hand,
Knows this secret plan
Of the things He will do for the world
Using my hand!*

—Toyohiko Kagawa

TOYOHIKO KAGAWA was born in Kobe, Japan, July 10, 1888. His father was first head of some nineteen villages in his native province of Awa, and later was elevated to secretaryship of the Privy Council which, because of its function of advising the Emperor, was the most influential body in the Empire. Kagawa's childhood was a sad one, for he was the son of one of his father's concubines, and both parents died when he was four years old. He went to live in the ancestral village of Awa, in the care of his father's neglected wife and a foster grandmother. Here, in a great thatch-roofed farmhouse, he lived a lonely life, abused and humiliated because of his birth.

He knew little real affection until he entered school in the city of Tokushima. Love came into his life in the person of two missionaries, Dr. H. W. Myers and Dr. C. A. Logan. Both were friends and counselors to the lonely lad, and it was through them that he came to know the personality of Christ, and to find purpose and meaning in life. With the heartfelt prayer, "O God, make me like Christ," he entered upon that fellowship with God to the reality of which his whole subsequent life has been a testimony.

Reading of the work of Canon Barnett in the slums of London, he dedicated his life to service of the poor. The choice brought down upon him the wrath of his uncle, the head of the family, and resulted in his being disinherited. In 1905 he entered the Presbyterian College in Tokyo, in preparation for the ministry. There he distinguished himself as an omnivorous reader and as a lover and defender of the weak and needy.

At the time of the Russo-Japanese War, Kagawa, who had been deeply influenced by Tolstoi, declared himself a pacifist, and as a result one night was taken out by his fellow students and beaten. Years later, one of those again laid hands upon him, this time to offer his ordination prayer!

In the second year of college he was stricken with tuberculosis, and had to seek health on the seashore, where he spent himself in the service of the fishing folk about him. It was there that he drafted his first novel which was one day to give him a foremost place among the writers of Japan. He wrote in such poverty that his story had to be inscribed on the pages of castaway magazines.

When only partially recovered he went to Kobe to enter the theological seminary, and felt the call of the slums of that city, the worst, perhaps, in all the world. At that time there were in this section, known as the Shinkawa,

* From *Songs from the Slums* by Toyohiko Kagawa, p. 66. Copyright 1935 by Whitmore & Sons. Used by permission of Abingdon Press.

some twenty thousand outcasts, paupers, criminals, beggars, prostitutes, and defectives, who lived in human kennels of filth and vermin and disease.

Kagawa's one room was about six feet square, without bed, stove, table, or chair. Here [he] cared for the sick, washing their infected clothes with his own hands, and holding classes in reading and writing at an early hour before his students went out to work. Here he became the champion of babies and children who had been rented out to old women by parents who did not want them, and who were slowly allowed to starve. Kagawa adopted one such child and while still carrying on work in the seminary, nursed it back to life. He continued to live in his six-by-six room, but as his duties increased he added another room which served as dispensary and hospital.

After his first novel had been discovered one day by a publisher who called at his home in search of material for a magazine, it was published, and in a short time Kagawa's name was a household word over the Empire. Other books rapidly appeared, all of them eagerly devoured by the public.

While Kagawa was attending the seminary he came to know a "Miss Spring," a young woman who was a worker in a factory where he had preached. Under his influence she accepted Christ's way of life, and longed to give herself in the same hard, high service. It resulted in a long and happy marriage.

In 1914 the way opened for Kagawa to study for two years in America. Lucrative positions were offered him on his return to Japan, but he refused them all and returned to his little room in the slums.

In the course of time he found himself involved in social issues which affected the well-being of millions throughout Japan. In 1921 he led striking workers demanding the recognition of their union and voicing their radical demand: "Laborers are personalities. They are not commodities to be bought and sold according to the scale of wages based on the market price." More than once Kagawa was arrested.

It was not the army of industrial workers alone, however, that called forth the creative sympathy of Kagawa. The majority of Japan's workers are farmers, and the life of the rural population is particularly hard. Forty-six per cent of them were tenant farmers, and Kagawa found that the struggle for existence was constantly driving many of these to the cities, to swell the population of the slums. In 1931, in Kagawa's hut in the Shinkawa, the first true peasant union in Japan was organized.

He has stood uncompromisingly against extreme tactics of violence and hatred. As a pacifist, committed to the elimination of the economic causes of war, Kagawa organized the National Anti-War League of Japan in 1928.*

Between 1930 and 1940 Kagawa went on a speaking tour from Australia to America, where he spoke in two hundred cities in the United States and Canada, asking Christian peoples to put Christian beliefs into practice. When, in 1941, it became apparent that war between Japan and the United States

* Abridged from *Songs from the Slums*, by Toyohiko Kagawa, pp. 91-96. Copyright 1935 by Whitmore & Sons. Used by permission of Abingdon Press.

was imminent, he came to the United States again with a deputation representing Japanese Christians. They conferred with leaders of American Protestantism in search of peace, but to no avail. Finally Kagawa had to go back to Japan, and caught the last steamer that sailed from the United States before the attack on Pearl Harbor.

During the war Kagawa's writings were banned in his own country, and he was asked to keep silent. Even so, he was arrested three times and charged with being anti-war. Toward the end of the war he was forced to flee into the forests about a hundred miles north of Tokyo, where he lived for four or five months.

After the defeat of Japan, Kagawa was asked by the Japanese Cabinet to request food and supplies from General MacArthur for war refugees. The supplies were made available, and the "most peaceful occupation in history" was begun. Kagawa helped establish many settlements for war refugees all over Japan.

Japan has changed greatly since World War II. Women have received the vote; the budget once spent on armaments now goes for education; over four million acres of land have been purchased by the government and turned over to former tenant farmers. The Kagawa National Committee in the United States reports that Kagawa has over forty workers employed in thirty-nine projects—slum centers, day nurseries, orphanages, evangelistic centers, etc. In spite of his continuing poor health, Kagawa's great work goes on.*

✠

KEIZO FINDS A NEW WAY OF LIFE
Honami Nagata

IT WAS the year of the rice riots in Japan. War had poured a stream of money into the laps of many humble Japanese, and they were spending it in reckless ostentation. News of [his wife's] departure and their boy's death sent Keizo [a leper] into the fight against profiteers. Desire for revenge made all the world an enemy, and he took delight in helping to burn the great warehouses and threatening death to those the crowd held responsible for its troubles.

One day in July, Keizo and three of his companions left their battered cart and bony cur by the roadside, and hid themselves at the edge of a cemetery. The tall, closely packed gravestones, almost touching each other, and black with the weathering of five hundred years, made a hiding place visible only from the steep bluff just above. A smooth expanse of granite at the base of a headless Buddha made a good spot for throwing dice. A gourd of *sake* leaned against a cracked vase of wilted flowers. One of the four at play was a woman. A woman whom the disease had robbed of all beauty and attractiveness, and yet when *sake* and gambling had done their work, the men fell to quarrel-

* Based on information in *Unconquerable Kagawa* by Emerson O. Bradshaw, published in 1952 by Macalester Park Publishing Co., and in *The Christian Century* (December 7, 1955).

ing about her. Someone on the bluff heard the noise, saw knives drawn, and hurried to the telephone. A motorcycle policeman rushed around the curve just in time to prevent tragedy. Shortly after, pilgrims, dogs, and wabbling cart were taken to a house of detention. Next day the four were ordered to the Government Hospital at Oshima.

They huddled together half apprehensively as the doctor's launch towed their *sampan* through the morning mist. Sea and island and sky, subdued by the soft light, made a picture in apple green, slate gray and silver. Presently details stood out clearly. Beyond a crescent beach two hills were connected by a low-lying plain, and here there were wide buildings: the hospital, administration department, laboratories, electric lighting plant, and assembly hall. Farther back were tennis courts, and the tall chimney of the crematory. Through the trees were glimpses of the patients' cottages hugging the hillside, with tiny paddy fields or patches of vegetables beside them. And winding its length between the big, low buildings and the cottages, a barrier of barbed wire, beyond which no leper is allowed to go alone.

Keizo loitered about in the hot July evening, grateful to the strong breeze for its cooling. Down on the beach the massive roots of the pine trees lay black upon the sand. Groups of patients sat among them in the moonlight. At hand was the music of the tide, and beyond, silver waves and far-flung islands.

As he tried to go to sleep in his breathless little room, recent events circled before his eyes. He saw the dusty roads and the hiding place behind the graveyard, and heard the foolish giggle of the leper woman who had been with them. He cringed at the glare of hate on the men's faces as they drew their knives. Then came the blast of the policeman's horn; the tangled traffic of the city streets; the confusion at the house of detention; the freshness of the morning boat ride; the bewildering business of examination, disinfection, and finding quarters.

Maples flared upon the heights above the jade-green water. Wild flowers made the island a purple paradise. Summer came again. Through such seasons Keizo sang and laughed and told his jokes.

The more intelligent patients still afoot at Oshima are asked to help with the bedridden cases. Keizo, in a long white cotton coat, stood about the ward one day assisting with dressings, cleaning up after operations, doing orderly's work. Some score or more lay in their beds, usually suffering most and dying from some disease not leprosy. Poor creatures with paralyzed throats whistled through breathing tubes. Heavy over the room hung the sickening smell of iodoform.

A little band of men and women paused to leave their footwear at the door before entering the ward. Nagata left his made leg also, and crawled across the room to the bedside of Shimamoto. Books bound in black and gilt were taken from bandannas. Quavering hymns were sung. Keizo edged nearer to listen. By and by arms were folded; eyes closed; heads upraised, and Miyauchi's voice spoke confidently. Keizo, hearing, knew that he talked to God.

"Our Father, we thank Thee that we know that Thou art very near. Our brother suffered much in journeying to find Thee, and through his pain he came to fear and hate Thy name. We thank Thee that the body's agony is not needful, but that Thou dost hear the cry of every contrite heart. That Thou dost give cleansing from all evil, peace and joy. That Thy Holy Spirit doth find a temple in every child of Thine. That death brings not to such rebirth, nor retribution, but that Thy loved ones go on to be forever with their Lord."

That evening, as Keizo strolled toward the beach, he stopped to listen at the Christians' tent. The curtains were tied back, and he could see the rough pulpit, folding organ, song-sheet, and the little company of believers sitting on camp stools around a table covered with a faded cloth. Hoarsely, unmusically, but joyfully, they were singing,

> Though I do climb the mountain path alone,
> Where tempests rage, and mighty torrents flood,
> I hear above their roaring heavenly songs,
> And I am safe while I can cling to God.

I saw Keizo when I was at the hospital the other day. He is quite blind now. But for years the marks of dishonesty, sensuality, hate and despair have gone from his face. Behind all the distortion shines a happiness which startles. Nagata, fellow sufferer, ends his story thus quaintly: "The knowledge of this good doctrine caused the wish to hear to boil up within him. From baptism Keizo is a man living a resurrected life. In joy or pain, grief or gladness, he gives thanks. We can prophesy the future with confidence, for Christ liveth in him."

> "The old self
> And the sin,
> All cleansed and purified before the Cross,
> *The new man stands forth shining!*
> O Keizo, blind,
> But praying always with deep love and tears,
> Salt of the earth, light of the world,
> May all the journey left you be
> Of Heaven truly more than blessed.
>   Amen."*

✠

THE HIROSHIMA MAIDENS

ON the morning of August 6, 1945, several small girls, ranging in age from nine to fourteen, who had arrived at their public school in Hiroshima, were in the school basement, helping to start the school day by getting chalk or erasers or other classroom supplies. That was the morning the atomic bomb was dropped on the Japanese city.

---

* Abridged from *Hearts Aglow* by Honami Nagata and Lois J. Erickson, pp. 19-28. Published by American Mission to Lepers. Used by permission of the publisher.

When the bomb burst, the little girls raced upstairs to see what had happened, and found that the school had been totally demolished and that most of the students and teachers had been killed. In trying to make their way from the remains of the building the girls were severely burned or irradiated or both.

Those who survived, like many thousands of others in Hiroshima, received little or no medical or hospital treatment. Never before had so many people living in a crowded area been so seriously injured at one time, and the emergency medical crews could hardly begin to take care of more than a hundred thousand survivors. Most people had to look after themselves as best they could.

Among the most poignantly suffering cases were those who came to be known as the "Hiroshima Maidens," a group of about twenty-four girls, including those who had been trapped in the Hiroshima school and others of the same age whose injuries had also been severe. By 1953, when this story begins, the girls had reached marrying age, but were so badly scarred or disfigured that they shrank from appearing in public. Some of them had obtained jobs as seamstresses or in factories but were forced to give up their work because their burns, never properly treated, caused skin and muscles to contract so that they could not move their hands and arms normally.

The group of girls had come together in the church of the Reverend Kiyoshi Tanimoto, the Methodist minister who was one of the key figures in John Hersey's book *Hiroshima.* They had withdrawn almost entirely from any community life, seeking each other's company only and living on whatever meager subsistence they could obtain from their families or friends.

Mr. Tanimoto tried to find work for his new charges that they could do and that did not require them to be seen; he provided recreation for them; and he gave them psychological and spiritual help. He also started a public campaign to send some of the girls to Osaka or Tokyo for plastic surgery.

The plight of this group of young women came to the attention of Norman Cousins, editor of *The Saturday Review,* who was traveling in Japan in 1953. Few hospitals there could undertake the complicated and expensive surgery that would be needed, and it had been Mr. Tanimoto's dream that the girls might be brought to the United States for treatment. Quite aside from helping the girls themselves, he felt that such a project could become a powerful symbol of good will, at a time when there was much ill feeling in Japan against America.

For many months after his return to the United States, Mr. Cousins sought the means for making the project possible, and at last arrangements were completed. Mount Sinai Hospital in New York volunteered to supply operating facilities and hospital bed-care free of charge; the U. S. Air Force agreed to fly the girls from Tokyo to New York; private homes were located where the girls could stay between trips to the hospital.

By this time, however, news of the project had spread in Japan, and forty-three girls had asked to be included. As it was not possible to double the accommodations on short notice, the committee responsible for the project [which included Mr. Cousins, two American doctors, and an interpreter] faced the difficult and painful problem of choosing among them.

On the evening before the final selections were to be made, the Maidens went to Mr. Tanimoto's church for special services. Each of the girls had a prayer to offer. Most of the prayers were in two parts. The first part was for the American doctors, that they might know no anguish for not having been able to take all the girls, and that they might realize that the girls themselves understood. The second part was for the selection of the next girl.

Some additional decisions were made by the committee the next day. One was that the project would not end with the group selected to go to America, but that American doctors would be sent to Hiroshima to help provide treatment there and that two or three Japanese doctors would be brought to New York for further training. Another was that another group be chosen from similar victims in Nagasaki, which had also been bombed, though less severely than Hiroshima. The final decision was that twenty-five of the forty-three Hiroshima Maidens be taken, rather than trying to cut the list to the twenty originally planned for.

As a result of the Reverend Tanimoto's work with and concern for the girls, they had learned how to appear in public without feeling self-conscious, and their poise and charm made a deep impression not only on the committee and the doctors who first met them in Japan, but on everyone who met them in the United States.

The families who took the Japanese girls into their homes found them gay and spirited guests, and their courage and cheerfulness during the course of the many operations won the respect and admiration of the doctors and nurses at the hospital.

As time went by and the operations gave the girls back the use of their arms and hands, they began learning new skills. Some of them became expert hairdressers; one of the girls learned to make ceramic jewelry; others studied dressmaking.

After the Maidens had been in the United States about a year, one of them, who had already undergone several operations, suddenly died under anesthesia. It was feared that the others might lose heart and not wish to go on with the treatment and additional operations that were necessary, but the very next day another of the girls arrived at the hospital for her scheduled operation, with no hint of apprehension or misgivings. No other such tragedy occurred during the Maidens' stay; they mourned for their friend, but they went on cheerfully with their treatment and their various studies.

At the end of 1956, the Hiroshima Maidens returned to Japan, all except one who stayed behind to continue her very promising career as a fashion designer. Greatly changed in physical appearance, with many new friends in America, and with a new and hopeful future ahead, they went back home to begin their lives again.

The New York Friends Center, which keeps in touch with the girls, reports that most of them are still pursuing their studies or continuing at their jobs.

One girl, always frail, has died of cancer. Of the rest, several are happily married. The girl who stayed behind in America hopes some day to have a dressmaking house in Tokyo in which the Maidens who are dressmakers—there are several—can make their living and help support their parents.

In the meantime, the Japanese government is financing a program of plastic and reconstructive surgery in Hiroshima, performed by the Japanese doctors who accompanied the girls to America. The young women who had wanted to come to the United States but were unable to do so have been "adopted" by Friends who correspond with them, exchange Christmas and birthday gifts, and maintain an interest and friendship which makes that group of Hiroshimans feel they are not forgotten in America.*

More Love to Thee, O Christ *

Elizabeth P. Prentiss, 1869

William H. Doane, 1832-1915

*From *Japanese Christian Hymnal*. Used by permission of the publisher.

MORE LOVE TO THEE, O CHRIST

THE words to this memorable hymn were written by Elizabeth Prentiss (1818-1878), and have been translated into the language of nearly every country into which the message of Christ has gone. It is one of the great fellowship and communion hymns of the Church.

The tune to which it is usually sung was composed by William Howard

* Based on editorials by Norman Cousins in *The Saturday Review* (April 19, 1955; May 14, 1955; October 15, 1955; June 9, 1956; June 14, 1958). Used by permission of the publisher.

Doane (1832-1915). It should be sung at a moderate tempo and in the spirit of prayer, for it is in reality the prayer of every devout Christian in search of companionship with Christ, whose servant he is.

The music score on p. 730 shows the words of the first verse as they would appear in a Japanese hymnal. The English version of the entire hymn appears below.

More love to Thee, O Christ,
　More love to Thee!
Hear Thou the prayer I make
　On bended knee;
This is my earnest plea,
　More love, O Christ, to Thee.
More love to Thee,
　More love to Thee!

Once earthly joy I craved,
　Sought peace and rest;
Now Thee alone I seek;
　Give what is best:
This all my prayer shall be,
　More love, O Christ, to Thee,
More love to Thee,
　More love to Thee!

Then shall my latest breath,
　Whisper Thy praise;
This be the parting cry
　My heart shall raise;
This still its prayer shall be,
　More love, O Christ, to Thee,
More love to Thee,
　More love to Thee!

Amen.

—*Elizabeth Prentiss*

✠

O FOR A CLOSER WALK WITH GOD

"O FOR a Closer Walk with God" is another of those great devotional hymns that have stood the test of centuries. This hymn has been translated into nearly every tongue, the world around, into which the message of Christianity has gone. You will find it in the hymnbooks of all the Oriental countries. It is sung with deep devotion in the heart of Africa. Our Spanish-speaking neighbors in Mexico and Central and South America include this great song in their hymnals.

The words were written by the poet William Cowper in 1772. The melody to which it is usually sung was composed by Arthur Cottman in 1872. It should be sung in moderate tempo because of its deeply devotional character.

The verses below express the sentiment of this hymn in English. The music score on p. 732 shows the first verse as it would appear in a Japanese hymnal.

O For a Closer Walk with God*

8 6 8 6

William Cowper, 1772 — Arthur Cottman, 1872

O for a closer walk with God

*From *Japanese Christian Hymnal*. Used by permission of the publisher.

O for a closer walk with God,
A calm and heavenly frame,
A light to shine upon the road
That leads me to the Lamb!

Return, O holy Dove, return,
Sweet messenger of rest!
I hate the sins that made Thee mourn
And drove Thee from my breast.

The dearest idol I have known,
Whate'er that idol be,
Help me to tear it from Thy throne,
And worship only Thee.

So shall my walk be close with God,
Calm and serene my frame;
So purer light shall mark the road
That leads me to the Lamb.

Amen.
—*William Cowper*

CONTENTS

PART VI SECTION 2

THE CHRISTIAN WITNESS IN CHINA, FREE CHINA, AND FORMOSA

He that believeth on the Son of God hath the witness in himself.—I JOHN 5:10

PICTURES: PAGE
Interpretation: "Go Teach All Nations"—*Hung-nien* 734
Picture: "Go Teach All Nations"—*Hung-nien* 735
Interpretation: Moore Memorial Church, Shanghai 734
Picture: Moore Memorial Church, Shanghai 737
Interpretation: Lok-seng-i Presbyterian Church for Lepers, Taiwan 736
Picture: Lok-seng-i Presbyterian Church for Lepers, Taiwan 739

POETRY:
Flowers for the Altar—*Ely* 740
Oh, Holy Spirit—*Chao* 741
Fulfillment—*Ely* 741
Magnanimity and Restraint—*Anonymous Chinese Prayer* 742
Acceptable—*Ely* 742
For Broken Families—*Anonymous Chinese Prayer* 743
Infiltration—*Ely* 743

STORIES:
Preacher Yu—*Lewis* 744
Stranger Than Fiction—*Dickson* 747
Hong Kong—Taiwan—China—*Presbyterian Commission on Ecumenical
Mission and Relations* 750

MUSIC:
Interpretation: A Hymn of Praise—*Conder* 754
Music: A Hymn of Praise—*Ancient Chinese Lute Tune* 755
Interpretation: O Christ Our Great Foundation—*Lew* 754
Music: O Christ Our Great Foundation—Transcribed by *Lum* 756

"GO TEACH ALL NATIONS"
Lu Hung-nien

UNTIL the Communist People's Republic took control of China, beginning in 1949, great interest in portraying Christian themes had been displayed among Chinese artists—probably more than anywhere else in Asia. During the late 1930's a number of exhibitions of paintings in the Christian spirit were held in Peking and Nanking, and loan exhibits were sent to Budapest, Vienna, and the Vatican in Rome.

Lu Hung-nien is regarded by many as one of the greatest of the Chinese Christian artists. His collection includes more than a dozen paintings on New Testament themes, including the one shown on p. 735.

In the foreground the Master of men stands pointing to the distant fields "white unto the harvest." Three groups of disciples are near Him: five are standing at His right hand, two are seated by a nearby tree, and four others are facing Him as He gestures toward the distance. All are listening intently to His command.

Near at hand is a haystack that has been gathered against the oncoming winter. In the background one can see a rugged mountain peak with the homes of a small Chinese community nestling at its base.

Nowhere else can one find a more delicate and beautiful portrayal of trees and flowers than in Chinese landscapes. The Asiatic artist is a master at suggesting in a few strokes mountains, rivers, and seas, with flowering trees and slender bamboos trembling in the wind.*

✦

MOORE MEMORIAL CHURCH, SHANGHAI

IN days gone by, the Moore Memorial Church (Methodist) in Shanghai was one of the great institutional churches in the Orient. A gift in memory of Rosa Lee Moore, child of Mr. and Mrs. L. R. Moore of Kansas City, Missouri, it maintained a seven-day-a-week program of teaching, worship, and service in one of China's great cities. It also provided a boarding home for Chinese girls, many of them away from home for the first time.

Before the present period of Communist domination of China, the Sunday school of the Moore Memorial Church was one of the largest in China, and its auditorium served not only as a place of worship but also for such happy occasions as weddings, both among Chinese Christians and other nationalities that found in China a second home. The view on p. 737 shows the church decorated for a wedding.

The building is Gothic in style, and each of its unique windows bears in

* Based on information from the Abbott Book Library of Art.

734

"GO TEACH ALL NATIONS"—*HUNG-NIEN*

the center a Chinese ideograph representing the "fruit of the spirit." The beautifully carved pulpit and the three great chandeliers (only two of which appear in this picture) lend grace and dignity to this magnificent church.

In the course of the war with Japan, long before the present Communist regime, the church was badly damaged by Japanese soldiers. The pews were burned, and had to be replaced before the auditorium could be used again. During the war with Japan and the Pacific wars the church was used as a refugee center with an extensive program of relief.*

One cannot help but feel that China will one day again be free to worship God in the beauty of holiness, and that Moore Memorial Church will ring again with the praises of a grateful people.

✢

THE PRESBYTERIAN CHURCH OF TAIWAN
(LOK-SENG-I CHURCH FOR LEPERS)

TAIWAN (Formosa) has been known as the Presbyterian Island. This is because the Presbyterian Church in the island not only has been an over-whelming Christian religion, but also has had the early and long history of the reformed heritage. The Reformation began and its influence soon reached this remote island in the first half of the seventeenth century. During the period 1624-1661, the Dutch East India Company possessed this island and its missionaries worked among the people. Then during the years of the nine-teenth century both the Presbyterian Church of England and that of Canada came side by side to the island.

Like the Nestorian Church on the China mainland, the Early Dutch Re-formed Mission in Taiwan is one of the lost missions in the Orient. However, the relics of its missionaries preserved in Holland tell the story. The first missionary was Georgius Candidius, who arrived in the island in 1627. Follow-ing this pioneer, thirty-six other missionaries labored during the period. They erected chapels and schoolhouses in every important village, and their work soon spread from Longkiau in the south to the villages of the Kabalan Plain on the northeastern coast, winning many thousands of the inhabitants for Christ.

After thirty-seven years, in 1661, the missionary works were rudely stopped by an armed group of refugees from the China mainland under their chieftain Koxinga. He drove the Hollanders from the island and stopped their propa-gating Christianity among the islanders. After that the Christians in Taiwan were cut off from the people of Christendom for more than two hundred years, or until the nineteenth century.

In 1865 the Presbyterian Church of England broke ground in the south; and in 1872 the Presbyterian Church of Canada commenced a Protestant Mission

* Information supplied by the Board of Missions of the Methodist Church.

MOORE MEMORIAL CHURCH, SHANGHAI

at Tamsui in North Taiwan. The pioneer days of the South Church ended by the formation of her presbytery in 1896; the formation of the Northern Presbytery was delayed until the year 1904. Ultimately in 1912 these two presbyteries united under one Presbyterian Synod of Taiwan.

During this period both the Presbyterian churches lived under unsettled conditions of persecutions and untimely warfare. This was the period of transition from the last regime of the Chinese Empire to the Japanese occupation of Taiwan. However, God favored His workers. Having been driven out in 1865 from Tainan, then the capital, Dr. James L. Maxwell and his assistants began the missionary work at Takow. Dr. Maxwell was the pioneer medical missionary, but after that many medical doctors came to the island. Of the four original treatment centers there now remain but Chang Hua Hospital and Tainan Clinic, because there are so many government hospitals and practitioners on the island. However, the mission hospitals have made many valuable contributions to the Church.

The recent twenty-five years of our history, covering the whole period of World War II and its post-war years, brought about great changes to the Taiwan churches. Since 1931, when the Japanese inaugurated their aggressive warfare in Manchuria, the churches in Taiwan as well as those in Japan suffered a great deal from the rise of nationalism and totalitarianism, by which aggressors were supported in order to invade China. As a result in 1934 the Presbyterian Middle School at Tainan (first built in 1885, then rebuilt in 1916) was reformed under Japanese leadership; while Tamsui Middle School in the north (built in 1914) had to be given up to a non-Christian community in 1936. Fortunately, by that time, an effective evangelism was begun. Subsequently the North Church was divided into three presbyteries, and in 1940, the Synod of North Taiwan was formed.

With the outbreak of the Pacific War, the oppression of the Japanese against our Church became more severe day by day. Not only were our remaining institutions—such as the hospital and theological college—taken, but our church also was annexed to the *Kyodan* or "Christian Community," which was under the control of the Japanese. During this period, the evangelistic work among the hill tribes disappeared owing to cruel persecutions. It turned into an underground movement till the very end, 1945, when the Japanese surrendered to Allied forces.*

The Lok-seng-i Presbyterian Church, shown on p. 739, is a church for lepers, located near the government leprosarium where there are about a thousand patients. It is comparatively new, having been built since 1950. Already there are 372 baptized Christians.

* Arranged from an article by Hsu Chien-hsn and S. Y. Yang in *Island Beautiful*, edited by Claire Randell. Published in 1956 by the Commission on Ecumenical Mission and Relations, United Presbyterian Church in the USA. Used by permission of the publisher. The authors are professors at Taiwan Presbyterian College, Taipei, and Presbyterian Theological College, Tainan.

LOK-SENG-I PRESBYTERIAN CHURCH FOR LEPERS, TAIWAN

FLOWERS FOR THE ALTAR

Dapper in new fall tweeds young Doctor Wang
Walked briskly down the narrow cobbled street
Enjoying the crisp freshness of the air.
Proud in his own first tailored suit, his son,
Hwei-lo, beside him bounded happily,
Trying to match his father's longer stride.

Friends hailed the doctor as he passed. Some asked,
"Where are you bound so early this fine morn?"
"To church and Lord's Day school," came the reply.
"Come worship with us. You'll be greatly blessed.
This is our harvest festival, a day
Of joyous praise and thankfulness to God."

The doctor and his son a secret shared:
As they approached the church the little boy
Asked anxiously, "Where is Lao Lee? He should
Be here." "Don't worry. Here he comes! A crowd
Is following to admire our splendid blooms."
"And father! Watch Lao Lee! He's very pleased!"

"He well may be. Such a chrysanthemum
Display our town has never seen! Just hear
The folks exclaim!" Two plants that spanned the street
Swung from the ends of Lao Lee's carrying pole.
Like rounded trees they were! Their size, their form,
Their glory, their perfection, surpassed a grower's dreams.

Arrived at church the doctor and Lao Lee
Arranged the plants beside the entry doors—
Twin plants with lush green leaves and each ablaze
With four-score garnet balls, their petals lined
With gold! "A timing miracle," the pastor said,
"To have them open for this very day!"

The doctor laughed. "I raised these blossoms for
The altar, but they grew too large and hence
We placed them here to welcome worshipers."
"A fine idea! But how," the pastor asked
"Have you produced so much magnificence,
So many perfect blooms, so exquisite?"

"We chose good stock. Our growing season was
Most favorable. Lao Lee knows 'mums and tends
Them faithfully. He gave, withheld, with just
One end in view—their perfect growth. When there

Was need for pampering, all of us helped.
Even my busy nurses lent a hand!"

"Our people will be grateful that you chose
Thus to adorn the church," the pastor said.
"The Heavenly Father, too!" Hwei-lo remarked
As they went through the sanctuary door:
"He's glad we worked with Him to raise our flowers.
I know he's glad we brought them to His church."*

—*Lois Anna Ely*

OH, HOLY SPIRIT

Oh, Holy Spirit, pierce through my heart-depths,
Pierce through me deeply as with a sharp sword.
Make me surrender my whole heart to Jesus,
Cast from it all the sin that resists.
Give me thy comfort. I must yield my heart to Him.

Oh, Holy Spirit, pray for me deeply,
Help me, and pity my weariness and labor.
Drive away all my soul's deep sorrow,
Help me to know that Christ is my Saviour,
Help me to love Him—more precious than jade.

Oh, Holy Spirit, stay ever with me,
Shine through my heart like the radiant sun.
Teach me to worship with deep adoration,
God's Love far broader than bright clouds and seas.**

—*The Reverend Tsu-chen Chao*

FULFILLMENT

"O happy day."
I'll always love that hymn.
They sang it on the day I was baptized.
That *was* a happy day!
I turned from Buddha to the living Christ
My Lord and King.

Yet happier days
Were those when my two sons
Began to serve my dear Lord, Jesus Christ.
My wife was tardier.

* Written especially for this anthology by the author, a retired missionary who gave many year of service in China for the Disciples of Christ.
** From *The World at One in Prayer*, edited by Daniel J. Fleming, p. 48. Copyright 1942 by Harper & Brothers. Used by permission of the editor and the publisher.

She clung to Kwan Yin and the other gods
Her tiny room enshrined.

Her rosary
She treasured most of all,
Reciting tirelessly her endless prayers.
We taught her and we prayed
That she might seek and find our loving Lord.
One day the Lord found her!

Her radiant face
When I returned from work,
Proclaimed a soul's rebirth. No need for words!
Her gods were gone! Gone was her rosary!
She'd swept her home and heart of all distrust
And Jesus entered in.

Togetherness
Has blest our home since then.
Today our cup o'erflowed. Our church chose us
To pass the sacraments.
My wife and I were honored to accept
That very sacred trust.

Our happiest day
Shall be next Lord's day when
We first shall serve the Christian family.
We shall stand tall as we
Receive the bread and wine, but bow our hearts
In deep humility.*

—*Lois Anna Ely*

MAGNANIMITY AND RESTRAINT

Help each one of us, gracious Father, to live
in such magnanimity and restraint that the Head
of the church may never have cause to say to any
one of us, This is my body, broken by you.**

—*Anonymous Chinese Prayer*

ACCEPTABLE

His name eludes me but his gentle mien
  Is etched in my memory.
Always I saw him in a silken gown,
  Its color neutral from long years of wear.

* Written especially for this anthology.
** From *The World at One in Prayer* edited by Daniel J. Fleming, p. 46. Copyright 1942 by Harper & Brothers. Used by permission of the editor and publisher.

His steps, though slowed by age, as were his thoughts,
  Had rhythm in them still.
A man of dignity and quiet soul,
He daily tried to do his Christian best.

One Lord's day at the sanctuary door
  He paused inquiringly,
His hands extending harbingers of spring—
Three Shantung peonies, the king of flowers.

A precious gift, nurtured most tenderly
  Through winter's bitter cold,
He'd brought to grace the altar. On that day
The *Gloria Patri* rang exultantly!

The thoughtful sharing of those perfect blooms
  Made memorable a day,
And blessed the hearts of all the worshipers.
For me the blessing lasts across the years!*

—*Lois Anna Ely*

FOR BROKEN FAMILIES

  Look with pity, O Lord, upon the broken families
of the earth, driven from their homes to wander as
refugees in strange places, or divided by the exi-
gencies of war.

  Look with pity upon this whole generation of thy
children, so far strayed from thy ways, so full of
misery of their own contriving, so anxious for the
fulfillment of life and so frustrated by their own
passions. Lord, have mercy upon us, through Jesus
Christ, Our Lord. Amen.**

—*Anonymous Chinese Prayer*

INFILTRATION

Christians? Not one!
Not in the whole commercial school!
Then why the *cross?*
Their English teacher at year's end
Was going home.
Their parting gift to honor her
A satin scroll.

* Written especially for this anthology.
** From *The World at One in Prayer*, edited by Daniel J. Fleming, p. 51. Copyright 1942 by Harper &
Brother. Used by permission of the editor and publisher.

On it a cross!
Who chose to paint that symbol rare
To Chinese art?
And why no signature, no seal?
Embarrassment
At questions in a comrade's eyes?
Timidity?

Or was it fear
Of erring use of sacred things?
It matters not. It stands—a rugged, wooden cross,
Reminder of
The King
Their teacher claimed had died
For all mankind.

About the cross,
Embracing it, three royal flowers
Twine gracefully—
China's beloved tree peonies.
A fitting gift,
That scroll, for a recipient who served
The King of Kings.*

—*Lois Anna Ely*

✠

PREACHER YU

Alice Hudson Lewis

THE village congregation sat drinking in the words of the young visiting
preacher-evangelist—words of comfort, words of courage, words of faith, all
drawn from the little black-covered Testament he held in his hand. Suddenly
their peace was shattered by a wild-eyed man who ran through the chapel.

"Run! Run!" he shouted. "The soldiers are here. Run for your lives!"

In less time than it takes to tell it, the room was deserted by all but the
young preacher. It was indeed dangerous to be found in a meeting in those
days—any meeting. They ran for their homes or took refuge with neighbors.

But Yu had no home to run to. He knelt in prayer. And so the soldiers
found him when they burst into the chapel. They seized him, jerked him to
his feet, and bound him. But not before he had thrust his Bible inside his shirt.
Dragging him outside, they pushed him into a truck where he found twenty
of the villagers bound as he was, huddled on the floor of the truck, weeping
and wailing over the fate they knew was before them, for the families they
would never see again.

* Written especially for this anthology.

A strange peace filled his heart. The small ropes cutting into his flesh did not seem to matter. Here were men who needed him. Somehow he got to his feet, braced himself, and began to sing:

> "I can hear my Saviour calling,
> I can hear my Saviour calling,
> I can hear my Saviour calling,
> 'Take your cross and follow, follow me.'
>
> "God will take care of you,
> Through every day,
> O'er all the way.
> He will take care of you,
> God will take care of you."

The truck lurched and jolted over the rutted road. But there Yu stood, face to the sky, eyes alight, voice ringing loud and clear and true:

> "For I know whom I have believed,
> And am persuaded that He is able,
> To keep that which I've committed
> Unto Him against that day."

And so he sang until they reached the military headquarters, and he, with the other prisoners, was thrown into a filthy cell, where, without food and water and in agony from their bonds, they spent the long hours of the night.

Yu did not sleep; he did not rest. Bound like the others, he could not help them physically, but he did not cease his efforts to relieve, in such measure as words of faith and promise can, the human suffering of his fellows.

When dawn came, the twenty-one men were driven into the courtyard for examination. The terror of the villagers worked against them. "It is plain that these cowards are guilty. They are guerrillas and no mistake." That was the verdict. And one by one, Yu, in helpless agony, saw his comrades questioned, condemned, and killed. Then his turn came. Forced to his knees before the officer, he made no outcry.

"Who are you? What is your name, fellow?"

"My name is Yu. I am a Christian preacher. I came to the village to conduct a worship service."

"Ha! A preacher, no less. And what proof have you to offer?"

"If you will open my shirt, you will find there my Bible."

His shirt was torn open. Sure enough, there was the Book.

"Anyone can carry a book in his shirt," said the officer roughly. "Give it to me. I'll soon see if the book is his or not. Hmm! All this red ink. Well— 'For God so loved the world—' Finish it, Preacher Yu."

" '—that he gave his only begotten Son, that whosoever believeth in him should not perish, but have everlasting life.' "

One after another, certain passages were selected, but Pastor Yu knew his Bible, and he passed the test.

"Well, he's a Christian, all right, but—is he the preacher he pretends to be? Preach us a sermon, Preacher Yu."

Bound and still on his knees, Yu raised his head and looked his captors in the eye. Quoting his text, "Love thine enemy; and pray for them that persecute you," he launched into a sermon.

"Enough," said the commanding officer. "This man has spoken the truth. Loose him; bring him to my quarters. Order food."

What happened next was pure miracle. The bonds were cut from his wrists, and Pastor Yu was pulled to his feet. He was taken to the officer's headquarters and given the comfort of hot water and tea. Then to his astonishment he was told to sit at the officers' table. The sight and fragrance of hot food was almost too much for him. The room whirled about him. He was half led, half pushed to a chair, and there he sat across the table from the man who only an hour before had ruthlessly ordered twenty villagers to die and might have done the same for him. What did it mean? Was it a trick?

But no—the officer's voice was gentle and full of a friendliness that cannot be counterfeited. Yu picked up his chopsticks. His stomach said, "Eat." His mind said, "What does it all mean?" His heart said, "This is God's doing." His lips said, "Let us give thanks."

The food warmed him, but no more than the thought of God's care. His mind was still seeking for a meaning when the officer took up the Bible, his own Bible that they had snatched from its hiding place inside his shirt. "I would like to know more about this book," the officer said simply.

Hours later, the scars of his bonds still deep upon him, Yu was on his way back to his own home village, riding a bicycle the Japanese officer had given to him to help him in his work. They had been praying for more than twenty-four hours, praying for his safe return.

Great was their rejoicing when Yu appeared, but greater was their amazement when, the next day, he announced that he was returning to the Japanese headquarters.

"Get me a hundred eggs," he said, "I want to buy a hundred eggs to take to that officer."

"What? You would make a gift to that enemy of our country?" His people were horrified.

"No," said Yu quietly, tying his basket of eggs firmly to his bicycle. "I would make another occasion to preach the gospel of repentance and salvation to a man who needs it." *

* From *Tales from China* by Alice Hudson Lewis, pp. 68-71. Published by Friendship Press; now out of print. Used by permission of the publisher.

STRANGER THAN FICTION

James Dickson

FAR back in the deep gorges and high mountains of Formosa live an interesting group of people known as the aborigines. The origin of these people is shrouded in mystery, but they resemble some of the tribes in the Philippine Islands and the South Seas. It is therefore taken for granted that they migrated from the south in the far distant past. They have sometimes been known to people in other lands as "The Formosan Head-Hunters."

In 1895, after the Sino-Japanese War, China was compelled to cede Formosa to Japan. The people of Formosa, however, refused to recognize this treaty and declared Formosa to be a republic. The Japanese Navy promptly made a landing in Formosa, and the local government soon disappeared before their superior arms. Only the aborigines up in the mountains continued to fight on. The Tyals entrenched themselves in the mountains and in this place of natural advantage, the Japanese soldiers were unable to overcome them. These courageous, liberty-loving people were the only group in the island who were not conquered by Japanese arms. Later on it was decided to negotiate peace with the Japanese, and this peace was negotiated by a remarkable Tyal woman by the name of Chi-oang, a name which is now famous in the history of the Christian Church in the island.

In 1929 when I visited the East Coast of Formosa for the first time, a missionary colleague said, "There is an aboriginal woman on the East Coast by the name of Chi-oang who is a believer. Try and get her to come over and attend the Woman's Bible School."

On the East Coast I found a frail old woman past middle age, with the distinct marks of the Tyal tribe upon her face. She was the first aboriginal person I had met who could talk the Formosan (Chinese) dialect. I urged her to come to the Bible School, but she hesitated. She would like to come, but was she not too old? However, she finally decided to come and accompanied a Formosan minister and myself back to Tamsui, where the school was situated. There she enrolled and took a two-year course.

One might have questioned the wisdom of having a woman like Chi-oang take such a course. She was already past middle age and not in good health. Also she had little educational background. Yet none in Formosa and few anywhere have been used of the Lord to accomplish more in so short a period of time than she. Two years later she went back to the East Coast and quietly began to work. She taught little groups in the Tyal villages, as well as individuals, and started a movement which continued to grow in momentum. The Japanese police learned of her activities and demanded that a stop be put to them. She continued to attend secret night meetings in nearby villages where she taught the people.

Dowai, a Tyal young man, in the meantime had also gone to Tamsui for a two-year course, and came back to work among his own people. He also was told by the police that he was to hold no meetings. The Japanese police told him that they were giving the mountain tribes a religion, and that Christianity was not needed. His work also had to be done largely at night. There was one thing for which to be grateful: all the young people had learned Japanese, and Bibles in that language were made available to those who were interested. The police found some of these Bibles and collected and burned them, for the Bible was a banned book.

When they continued to discover Bibles in various villages, they became angry and arrested Dowai, and put him in prison. Why they did not arrest Chi-oang, we never knew. Perhaps it was because she was the woman who had negotiated peace between the Japanese Army and the Tyal tribe, and was, therefore, held in considerable respect by the Japanese authorities.

Rumors came through from the East Coast that there were groups of believers in various places, but no one knew much about them. Then the curtain of war came down over the scene, missionaries were withdrawn, and nothing more was heard of this movement for nearly five years.

In 1945, when the first missionary returned after the war, a great surprise awaited him. It was reported that there were about four thousand believers among the aborigines. They had erected twelve churches and others were being built.

The story of the growth of this Christian community and of how the Gospel message spread from place to place was gradually pieced together. It is one of the most amazing stories of modern missionary history. In most places the story is somewhat the same. Chi-oang with her Bible taught a small group in one of the homes, and some of them became believers. Then the police learned of the meetings and ordered them stopped, Chi-oang could no longer visit the village, and the believers would have to carry on their meetings secretly, at night, or up in the hills with someone on guard, so no one could approach them without warning. Chi-oang's movements later became so restricted that she spent most of her time at a little house at Ka-le-oan, where church leaders and others came to her for instruction.

Near Hoeliankang in the foothills is the village of Sakura. The outstanding man in this village is Wiran Takko. He heard the gospel from Chi-oang in 1938, and was the first believer in his village. He then started making trips to Ka-le-oan, about fifteen miles away, to learn from Chi-oang. He then won over his relatives and several others, and started holding group meetings every night. He did not have much education, and continually prayed for someone to teach them in the village. Several from the village started going to Chi-oang for instruction. She taught them about God, and how to pray, and read the Bible to them.

From this time on things became difficult for the Christians. They did not again dare to meet during the day, but met after midnight. They had to avoid being seen by unbelievers who would report them. In 1943 one of their meetings was reported by nonbelievers and they were called up by the police and ordered to hand in their Bibles. They brought a few old ones, but the others were hid out of doors. About twenty believers were called up this time. A search was made, and more Bibles were found in the trunk of a tree in the woods. Also a search was made in their homes, and any who had hid their Bibles in their bedding or elsewhere lost them.

From this time on they divided into three groups for meetings, in order that they would not be detected. On Sundays they went in their working clothes to the fields, and there gathered for service.

One night two young men came to Wiran's house for instruction. The police were watching, and found them there. They declared that Wiran was still teaching. That night two policemen beat Wiran until he was almost dead. The chief policeman asked Wiran if he would say clearly whether he would stop believing or not. Wiran said he could not forget the gospel. He was hit on the head and lost consciousness. Later he was carried home by a Christian who had believed less than a month. He was unconscious for two days. His family thought he was near death, and prayed earnestly for him. The third day he recovered.

Wiran continued to hold secret meetings in the hills. When the surrender of Japan took place, the Christians began to hold open meetings, and made plans to build a church. This new freedom brought great joy to the Christians. In a short time they had built their church.

In 1945, when the writer returned to Formosa, he learned that the work had spread down the East Coast wherever the Tyals lived. While on the train going along the coastal plain, a young woman of the Tyal tribe greeted me. I took for granted that she must be a Christian, and was informed by her that she was. I asked her where she was from, and she replied, "From Mikasa Yama." This was a new place to me, some forty miles south of Hoeliankang.

"Are there Christians there?" I asked.

"All the people are Christians," was her reply. "We have a church." She said they had heard that a missionary had returned, and they were waiting for him to visit their village. "Chi-oang told us," she said, "that when the war was over the missionaries would return. We have waited a long time for you."

The sufferings which the Christians endured at the hands of the police will never be fully known. They were treated as the worst of criminals, and their crime was that they believed in God, and were determined to obey Him. The surprising thing is that they have harbored so little resentment toward their persecutors. Their attitude is summed up in the words of one of the Christians who was severely beaten by a Formosan Chinese official after the end of the war. In the courtroom the aboriginal Christian said: "I have no charge to make against him. He is not a Christian, and therefore did not know better. I am ready to forgive him."

When the war came to an end, and Japan had lost, the Christians took great courage. Christianity, which had, of necessity, been a secret movement, now came out into the open. Within a short time, churches were going up in a dozen communities. Some Christian Tyals came down from the high mountains and inquired of a young minister at Hoeliankang, "How do you build a church?" He took a piece of paper and drew a rough sketch, while he told them something of what it should be like, saying, "I am coming up there in a few weeks, and will discuss the matter with you more in detail." That was too long to wait for them, and when he arrived, the church was completed.

At Siong-Tai-ho a small church was erected by a few earnest Christians shortly after the close of the war. This building was outgrown within a few months, and a larger one was erected. The second one was likewise soon outgrown, and now a third one has been built. These three churches were built within a period of two years.

The aboriginal church has from the beginning been a witnessing church. Those who believe the gospel have immediately sought to win others. The work has been carried on by laymen, who have given their time and endangered their safety, in order to tell others. Some converted their friends as they worked in the fields.

Gospel fires have been lighted in a dozen places on the West Coast, far back in the mountain gorges. The minister at Sintek, with his son, began work two years ago at a place called Chiam-chioh. He went there to preach as often as he could spare time from his own large and busy parish. There was at that time a hopeful group of about thirty believers. Again a year later I made another visit to this community, and was amazed to find that there are now over six hundred believers. They also have built a church—the first aboriginal church on the West Coast. The total number of people in this district is a little over three thousand.

The Paiwan Tribe, numbering forty thousand, has hardly been touched. I preached in several villages of this tribe and the message received a great welcome. An influential chief arose in one village and said, "I have never heard anything like this. If what we have heard today is the Christian religion, I am ready to accept it, and I would like to see all of my people accept it."

May it be that we may so dedicate ourselves and our substance to the work of the Master, that before long no one will be able to say, "I have never heard."*

☩

HONG KONG—TAIWAN—CHINA

PACKED within the narrow confines of less than four hundred square miles of mountainous terrain, Hong Kong's three million people maintain a small foothold of the free world upon the threshold of Communist China. The economy of the colony is vulnerable; its resources are severely limited. Nevertheless, under wise and progressive administration, Hong Kong continues to face its problems courageously and strives to make a home and provide

* Abridged from *Stranger Than Fiction* by James Dickson, pp. 5-41. Published by Evangelical Publishers, Toronto. Used by permission of the publisher.

a livelihood for its abnormally increased population composed mostly of refugees from the mainland.

The phenomenal building activity continues and old landmarks are rapidly vanishing. Multistory banks, hotels, business houses, apartments, and public buildings replace the low outmoded structures of an earlier era. Kowloon and Victoria City are both developing a conspicuous skyline. Reclamations are changing the contours of the harbor. The new Kai Tak Airport runway has been built out into the sea. Satellite cities are coming into existence in the New Territories. Industrial development is intensifying, and industrialization is the one hope of meeting the problem of the swollen population of Hong Kong. Population is increasing at the rate of more than 120,000 per year. The supply of jobs, water for consumption, housing, hospitals, and schools is not keeping up with the demand.

Communist China is unloading food and manufactured products on this free market with the design of disrupting business and worsening its position. It is also hindering the fishing industry of the colony by establishing a twelve-mile territorial limit. Meanwhile, markets for local manufactured goods are becoming less accessible and there is discrimination against Hong Kong products. Other unsolved problems are the drug traffic, the chief cause of crime, and tuberculosis, number one killer with from fifty to seventy deaths per week. However, Hong Kong's natural beauty is unimpaired. The shops are filled with beautiful merchandise and the casual visitor is not concerned with existing conditions.

Within the Church in Hong Kong much progress is being made. New churches can accommodate growing congregations and new schools provide for increasing numbers of children. Among the undertakings in the New Territories are a church and school in industrial Tsuen Wan; a church and school in agricultural Yuen Long; a school for fishermen's children on Cheung Chau Island; a church for the fishermen population on the eastern part of Hong Kong island; and the Morrison Memorial Church Center in Kowloon. A Mandarin-speaking congregation is still seeking a church home.

The relief, family welfare, and children's centers are serving to the utmost of their capacity. Nearly every refugee family and child with which these agencies deal epitomizes the grimness of the struggle for survival. For many, Hong Kong offers little more than freedom to starve.

An historic ecumenical Church event occurred in November, 1958, when the first Asian Church Women's Conference was held in Hong Kong. More than fifty delegates from churches in nine Asian countries met together for two weeks to study and counsel together on ways and means to further women's work within their respective churches and foster an ecumenical Church fellowship.

In retrospect, there are grounds for thankfulness for local churches alive to the spiritual needs of men, for Christian schools that give promising youth a chance to grow in mind and spirit, and for agencies that relieve bodily needs and suffering. The patience and endurance, the cheerfulness, the courage, and the amazing stamina of people without a country living in Hong Kong shame the more fortunately situated dwellers in this crowded community.

The island of Taiwan, commonly called Formosa, a hundred miles off the coast of South China with an area of fourteen thousand square miles, now has a population of ten million. When the Nationalist government of China established itself on Taiwan, the island was the permanent home of six and a half million people. Two million refugees and the natural increase since 1949 have brought the population to a size that is beginning to create pressure on the resources of the island. Fortunately, the production of food is ample. The surplus manpower is not fully utilized, since a relatively small number of the newer elements of the population can be placed on the land, and industrial production still is not sufficiently large to absorb the number needing jobs. There is evidence of made work in some places so as to give more mouths access to the rice bowls.

Taiwan has been the center of world-wide attention in connection with the threat of Communist China against the Quemoy-Matsu group of islands near the coast of the mainland. Despite this, the life of the people in general has gone on normally. Many Christian churches suffered damage and thousands of homes were destroyed in the Hwalien area during a severe typhoon which struck the eastern coast.

The oldest Protestant churches on the island, which are the fruitage of the work of the English Presbyterian Mission in the South and the Canadian Presbyterian Mission in the North, have become more closely unified under the name of the Presbyterian Church of Formosa. Among the issues brought before the recent General Assembly was the action of government agencies banning the use of the Bible printed in the romanized Amoy Chinese—"a book precious to the Church through a century of history." The use of the Bible in Japanese, previously banned, had deprived the people of the mountain tribes of the only written language they knew. According to the government's view, the use of the banned languages interferes with the attainment of literacy in the Mandarin language. The request of the General Assembly for the withdrawal of the police order banning these editions of the Bible was based on the constitutional provision guaranteeing freedom of religion.

The increase of Christian congregations among the mountain tribes to three hundred within a decade is indeed impressive. Lowland churches also report a steady growth. The opportunity for evangelism still attracts new religious groups to the island.

Foreign travelers into the Peoples' Republic of China bring back such sharply divergent accounts that it often seems they have visited entirely different countries. Their reports are quickly out of date since the revolution in China goes on rapidly from stage to stage, with programs and campaigns succeeding one another with great rapidity.

Nothing has occurred since the establishment of the Communist regime that is comparable to the launching of the Peoples' Communes in its implications for the culture and civilization of China. This new attack upon the inner life of the people is so far-reaching that if it succeeds the family will be practically broken up and a kind of mass slavery will have come into being on a country-wide basis. This socio-economic organization will absorb the newly-established agricultural co-operatives, promote industry, and foster military training. Traditional village, town, and city life will disappear, and communal existence for the people will take its place.

Reports are trickling in to show how the individual family will fare under the new system. A refugee here has learned that his wife was sent into one commune, his fourteen-year-old daughter into another, and a sixteen-year-old daughter into a third. They have completely lost touch with one another and he is doubtful of eventual reunion. Soon the only food available will be served in the common mess halls. Private homes are now being torn down to provide materials for the central mess halls, nurseries, and "happiness homes" for the aged. The average commune will include ten thousand to thirty thousand families. The entire program of life will be under the management of a party organization within the individual commune.

A new mass labor program is also under way. Everyone must participate. Those who are not sent away from home for such work must participate where they live. Even professional people are being sent out to sweep the streets daily in their neighborhoods.

Another period of persecution has begun and many people are being sent to prison. Not a few are Christian leaders. It is not clear what the charges are, except that the victims are accused of being rightists, deviationists, and anti-Communists. Church gatherings, other than worship meetings, were under attack as "interfering with production efforts." Some Christians have been re-arrested and put in prison. One well-known educator has died in prison.

Reports have come that church congregations have been *persuaded* to unite so as to free property for other uses. After people have been herded into the communes, it is reported that no religious practices will be permitted within the communal buildings. Whether Christians will still be free to worship in their remaining churches is not yet known.

As the year 1958 closes, there are signs that the Communist rulers of China may have overreached themselves in forcing the commune system so rapidly upon the long-suffering people. Sufficient resistance has accumulated to warn the authorities that a slowdown, at least, has become advisable and the establishment of communes in the larger cities is to be postponed. The true interpretations of recent events cannot be made as yet. Colossal changes are taking place in China as its leaders ruthlessly pursue their drive for power.*

* Abridged from *The First Annual Report of the Commission on Ecumenical Mission and Relations of the United Presbyterian Church in the USA.* Used by permission of the Commission.

A HYMN OF PRAISE

MUSIC is said to be the language of the heart. It is, therefore, one of the best mediums for appreciating the spirit of a people.

It is true that Chinese music is written in a notation that is almost incomprehensible to people of the Western world. Some of the best-loved music in China, however, is not written down at all. As a result no two persons will sing the same song in the same way. Then, too, most of the songs in China are sung all in unison, and to be used in the Western world they have to·be harmonized.

Many Christian hymns have been harmonized to Buddhist tunes. This hymn (see p. 755 for the music score) is sung to a harmonized ancient Chinese Lute tune. The English words were written by George W. Conder. It was later published in America by the Church Committee for China Relief, 105 East 22nd Street, New York, N. Y.

Many Chinese songs sing of mountains, running brooks, moonlight gardens, birds, and flowers. This hymn of praise reveals this tendency to praise God by relating His majesty and power to the human and nature elements to be seen at every hand.

The first verse praises the Lord of heaven and earth, for sea and air. The second sings praise for the silent night, the power of the sun's rays—all things praising the Lord. The third verse sings of rain and dew, "crimson sunset, fleecy cloud, rippling stream and tempest loud"—all singing praise to the Lord of life. The fourth verse sings of the Great Creator, whose powerful Word and omnipresent Spirit make men and women everywhere lift their hearts in praise.*

✣

O CHRIST OUR GREAT FOUNDATION

THIS hymn, "O Christ Our Great Foundation," is from a collection of twenty-three hymns translated by Frank W. Price. This collection was chosen from the Chinese *Hymns of Universal Praise,* a hymnal which was published jointly in 1936 by six major church bodies in China, and which has sold nearly a half million copies since that time. A "younger church" which has produced such a hymnbook, including its own poetry and music, will not die.

Melodies which spring from the heart of a nation have a universal appeal. Confucian chants and old Chinese folk melodies have been captured for Christ and His Church, as was the music of Bach, Beethoven, and Handel in the Western world. It is especially appropriate that the Christians in China,

* Abridged from *Songs of Cathay* by T. Z. Koo. Published by Association Press, Shanghai. Used by permission of the publisher.

A Hymn of Praise*

Original Chinese Hymn Tune

極樂吟 CHI LO YIN
(Song of Greatest Joy)
7. 7. 7. 7. 7. 7.

English words
By George W. Conder

Ancient Chinese Lute Tune

1. All things praise Thee, Lord Most High; Heav'n and earth and — sea and sky,
2. All things praise Thee: night to night Sings in si - lent — hymns of light;
3. All things praise Thee: high and low, Rain and dew and — sev'n-hued bow,
4. All things praise Thee: gra - cious Lord, Great Cre - a - tor, — pow'r-ful Word,

1. All were for Thy Glo-ry made, That— Thy great -ness thus —— dis- played,
2. All things praise Thee: day to day Chants— Thy pow'r in burn - ing ray;
3. Crim-son sun - set, fleec-y cloud, Rip-— pling stream and temp - est loud,
4. Om ni - pres - ent Spir-it now At-— Thy feet we hum - bly bow;

1. Should all wor-ship bring to Thee; All things praise Thee: Lord, may we. A - men.
2. Time and space are prais-ing Thee; All things praise Thee: Lord, may we. A - men.
3. Sum-mer, win-ter—all to Thee Glo - ry ren - der: Lord, may we. A - men.
4. Lift our hearts in praise to Thee; All things praise Thee: Lord, may we. A - men.

*From *Songs of Cathay* by T. Z. Koo. Published by Association Press, Shanghai. Used by permission of the publisher.

O Christ Our Great Foundation*

Timothy T'ingfang Lew
Tr. by Frank W. Price

"T'ung Fu"
7.6.7.6.D

Maryette H. Lum

1. O Christ, our great foun-da-tion On which the Church does stand,
2. Bap-tized in one con-fes-sion Chris-tians o'er all the earth
3. Where ty-rants' hold is tight-ened, Where strong de-vour the weak,
4. Chris-tians in ev-ery na-tion, Join hands and prove your worth;

To preach Thy true sal- va- tion In ev- ery age and land:
Bear, Sav-iour, Thy im-pres- sion, Sign of their sec- ond birth.
Where in-no-cents are fright-ened, Where bad men ven-geance wreak;
Seek now the con-sum-ma- tion, Christ's ho-ly Church on earth,

Thy life and cross in- spire men To make the Church more pure,
One fel- low-ship u- nit- ed In love be- yond their own,
There may Thy Church a- wak- ing At-tack the hosts of sin,
A new di- vine cre- a- tion Of good-ness, truth and love;

And keep her faith un-bro-ken As long as worlds en-dure.
One Church whose lamps are light-ed Wher-ev-er Thou art known.
And all their ram-parts break-ing For Thee the vic-to-ry win.
The per-fect Ref-or-ma-tion, God's King-dom from a- bove. A-men.

now sorely tried, can share songs of faith with fellow Christians throughout the world.

As we read the verses of this great hymn, we feel the heart throb of the Christians of China, now isolated in a peculiar and tragic way from the rest of the Christian world, and our own faith in Christ as the foundation of all righteous living which looks forward to a world of "peace upon earth among men of good will," is strengthened.*

* Abridged from *Chinese Christian Hymns.* Copyright 1953 by Frank W. Price. Used by his permission.

CONTENTS

PART VI SECTION 3

THE CHRISTIAN WITNESS IN KOREA

✠

And it is the Spirit that beareth witness, because the Spirit is truth.—I JOHN 5:6

✠

PICTURES: PAGE
   Interpretation: "Long Hast Thou Stood"—*Rupp* 759
   Pictures: "Long Hast Thou Stood" (Church in Wonju, Korea)—*Rupp* ... 761
   Interpretation: Grandmother's Prayer 759
   Picture: Grandmother's Prayer—*McInnes* 763
   Interpretation: Kite-Flying in Korea—*Keith* 762
   Picture: Kite-Flying in Korea—*Keith* 765

POETRY:
   O God—*Pyun* 764
   Korean Youth—*Baker* 766
   Old Korean Song—*Author Unknown* 766
   The Hills in Autumn—*Chasin* 767
   Triangle Mountain—*Sanghun* 767
   The Church Gives Strength—*Baker* 767
   Charity—*Pyun* 768
   Yosu Village—*Baker* 768
   Korean Flag—*Baker* 769

STORIES:
   A Christian World Statesman and Patriot—*Oliver* 769
   Take to the Air—*Presbyterian Commission on Ecumenical Mission and
      Relations* 773
   Bricks and a Dream—*Kelsey* 774

MUSIC:
   Interpretation: Peace Through His Cross—*Baker* 777
   Music: Peace Through His Cross—*Wesley* 779
   Interpretation: To Work, to Work—*Old Korean Song* 778
   Music: To Work, to Work—*Old Korean Melody* 781

"LONG HAST THOU STOOD"

THE recent war in Korea brought disaster to many public buildings. The Church, too, often suffered immeasurable loss. The pictures on p. 761 show how great these losses often were. At the top is the church in Wonju, Korea, before the war; below is all that remained after the town was practically wiped out in 1950.

Twice the armies fought through the streets. Bombs, mortars, rockets, machine guns, and artillery destroyed nearly everything.

This brick and stone church had parts of its four walls still standing when I visited Wonju for the first time in August of 1951. Shell and rocket holes made crazy patterns in the walls, and weeds grew where the floor had been.

The winter of 1951 was cold. The people wore cardboard under their rags to break the cold wind. They also wore crudely fashioned rubber shoes and no socks in ten-below-zero weather.

There was only a little food, maybe a few dried fish and vegetables for the lucky. The homeless built shacks with discarded GI ration cartons and hung burlap sacking for a door. Heartache, sacrifice, and suffering were coupled with a heroic effort to survive.

In the midst of all this devastation, suffering, and want, the people of Wonju began rebuilding their church. First, brick by brick, the old structure was taken down. All winter the piles of reclaimed material grew. In the spring the new walls went up, built with bricks from the old building.

The new building, completed in 1952, lacks the majesty of the old one. It looks like a new church now. Only the people know how old it really is.*

✛

GRANDMOTHER'S PRAYER

When families returned to their little farms on the island of San Ai near Seoul, Korea, after months of fleeing from the bombings and gunfire of war, they found their church and their homes in ruins. The United States Army Corps gave the small congregation a quonset hut for a church. The Bible Club, with its daily program of school subjects, devotions, and sports, was held there. Ma-si's grandmother would not go to church. Ma-si prayed for Grandmother's return.

EVERYONE has someone but me, Ma-si thought as she looked at the families around her in church. Kim-si, her best friend, sat with her mother and father.

Ma-si listened as Mrs. Boyd, the missionary from Seoul, said, "I will visit those who cannot come to church."

* Adapted from "Long Hast Thou Stood" by Virgil Rupp. From *Korean Survey* (February 1957). Published by The Korean Pacific Press. Used by permission of the publisher.

After church, Ma-si met Kim-si outside. "Will Mrs. Boyd visit your grandmother?" Kim-si asked as they walked along.

"I don't know," Ma-si said. "I cannot tell Pastor Chu that she will not come to church."

Ma-si knew one reason why Grandmother Pak did not go to church. Bombs had killed Ma-si's father and mother during the war. Church made Grandmother miss them more.

"I remember when we came back," Ma-si said. "We looked for our church. Tears ran down Grandmother Pak's cheeks when she saw the scattered piles of rubble. 'The church is gone,' she said. 'My son is gone.' "

Kim-si nodded. "We looked for the church, too."

"When we reached our farm, the house my father built was gone. There was no rice paddy. 'What shall we do now?' I asked Grandmother Pak. I cried.

" 'Do?' She looked at me," Ma-si went on. " 'We'll build a new house.' She wiped away my tears with a corner of her skirt. 'Go down to the river,' she said. 'Look for scraps of lumber washed ashore.' "

"One wall of our house still stood," Kim-si said. "Doesn't your grandmother like our quonset-hut church?"

"I don't know," Ma-si said.

"She could come to church now. Your house is finished."

"I know," Ma-si answered. She thought of the floods that had washed away most of the rice and all of the cabbages. That was another reason Grandmother Pak did not go to church. She did not have even a handful of rice to give.

"I should quit school," Ma-si said, "and work on other farms to get rice for the long winter ahead. Sometimes I think I shall never go to church again until Grandmother Pak goes, too."

When Grandmother Pak saw the girls coming, she took the kettle from the cooking fire outdoors and went inside. Ma-si said goodby to Kim-si and followed her grandmother into the house. She watched her spoon out thin rice gruel into two bowls. What would Grandmother Pak say if the missionary came? Something had to be done.

"Grandmother Pak," Ma-si asked, "why should I go to Bible Club school? Why should I go to church?"

"How foolish! There is no other school for poor children," Grandmother Pak said. "The church—"

"You do not go to church," Ma-si interrupted.

"I cannot go. I have nothing to give," Grandmother Pak said.

"I shall not go alone again," Ma-si said. "Families go together."

Tears brimmed out of Grandmother Pak's tired old eyes and ran down the furrows in her wrinkled cheeks. "There is nothing in church for me."

Ma-si could not watch her cry. "I'm not hungry," she said. She pushed open the door and ran down the hill to the Han River.

Church at Wonju, Korea

Wonju Church after Bombing

"LONG HAST THOU STOOD"

Grandmother Pak heard Pastor Chu call, "Anyone home?"

Mrs. Boyd was with him. "I'm sorry you couldn't come to church."

"Ma-si was at church," Grandmother Pak said. "I do not go to church. I have nothing to give."

"You have lost much," Mrs. Boyd said. "Pastor Chu told me. But you have Ma-si. Everyone can give something. God needs everyone."

Suddenly Grandmother Pak admitted what she knew in her heart. "I need the church," she said aloud. And if God needed her too— "I will come to church again."

Mrs. Boyd left a package. "From friends who want to share," she said. Inside were rice, cabbage, a can of dried milk, and a candle.

Ma-si walked alone along the river bank. Pastor Chu said that someday a prayer would bring everyone on the island into the fellowship of those who trusted God. That meant Grandmother Pak, too, she thought. Maybe God had heard her prayers.

When Ma-si got home, Grandmother Pak had heaping bowlfuls of rice and cabbage ready. The new candle was lighted. Before they ate, Grandmother Pak bowed her head.

"Thank you, God," she said, "for this food and candlelight. Bless those who sent these gifts to us in love."

Ma-si thanked God, too. She knew now they would go to church together again.*

The beautiful photograph by John McInnes on p. 763 shows better than words the spirit of quiet devotion characterized in Grandmother Pak and many other courageous women of Korea whose faith withstood the test of tragedy and loss.

✢

KITE-FLYING IN KOREA
Elizabeth Keith

FAMILY legends in Korea give some basis for the belief that kite-flying was popular in that peninsula two thousand years ago. The first authenticated written record of kite-flying comes from the Silla Dynasty and was dated approximately thirteen hundred years ago. This record relates that General Kim Yu-shin employed a kite as a psychological-warfare weapon during the suppression of a religious rebellion in the year A.D. 647. Other written records confirm that in the fourteenth century kite-flying was still a part of the military arts.

In later years kite-flying has had no serious purpose other than as a game or sport. Just when it became popular nationally is not known, but family legends

* Abridged from *World Family* (February 1959). Published by Board of National Missions and Commission on Ecumenical Mission and Relations, The United Presbyterian Church in the U.S.A. Used by permission of the publisher.

Courtesy John McInnes—RNS Korea

GRANDMOTHER'S PRAYER

confirm that annually, usually during the first days of spring, the staid citizens put aside their dignity and competed in flying kites.

Not long after the turn of the current century, Koreans learned that not all rulers are interested in letting them enjoy themselves. The Japanese, who annexed the peninsula in 1910, saw Korea only as a source of rice and a corridor through which they could travel to conquer China. They did not actually ban kite-flying, however, until the mid-1930's.

Following liberation after Japan's defeat in World War II, the problems created by the artificial division of the country, and the activities of Communists who devastated Korea and took many lives in bloody war, allowed little opportunity for such peacetime pleasures as kite-flying. But Koreans continued to remember longingly the old sport.

President Syngman Rhee took cognizance of this feeling in January, 1956, and the Republic's first national kite-flying contest attracted a tremendous crowd.*

The typical group of children (p. 765) playing against the background of the old city wall of Seoul which winds up and down the hillside—today, alas, with many breaks and gaps—portrays the kite-flying one can still see in Korea. Since the hills around Seoul are not too steep for boys and girls to climb, the city is an ideal spot for this fascinating game, and nowhere are there more daring and skillful fliers.

At the New Year, grownups have contests in kite-flying. The object is to cut the rival's strings. This is done by rubbing the strings with ground glass and porcelain mixed with glue. Some American observers have said that they consider these kite-flying contests as exciting as anything to be seen on an American baseball field.

✠

O GOD

O God!
Thy fire is spent;
Thy tent is rent;
My back is bent;
My shattered elements remold;
Thrill this cold clay with interest bold;
Fix a new soul of kingly hold!

O God!
Thy work is done;
'Tis all or none—
This smallest son.
Nay, I am spent but Thou ne'er art!
Rather play Thine creative part,
And million other ventures start!

* Arranged from *Korean Survey* (June-July, 1956). Published by the Korean Research and Information Office. Used by permission of the publisher.

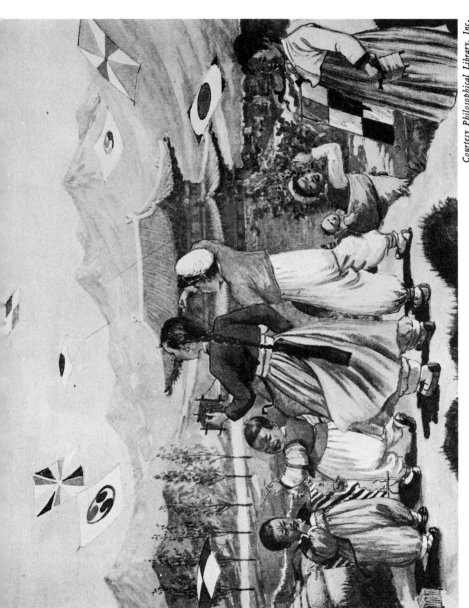

KITE-FLYING IN KOREA—KEITH

O God!
Yet leave me not
A broken pot
No longer sought!
O lash me, lash my duty-sense,
That in the end, through fight intense,
I reach Thy good pure and immense!*

—*Y. T. Pyun*

KOREAN YOUTH

The dawn is freighted with deep quietness,
Then suddenly fills resonant with sound
    Of voices raised in prayer.
Young women and young men have heard the call,
Christ's call, to follow Him. They pledge to live
    For Him, to greatly dare.

These Christian armies plan their march against
Idolatry and ignorance. Each finds
    His own appropriate tool
For teaching, medicine, for husbandry,
For trade—their loftiest aim, the Christian Church
    The Christian home and school.

So youth by thousands bow in reverence
Preparing for the day. Behind them, fires
    Of suffering and blight;
Before them, rising from the ashes, hope,
Their native land like stronghold on high hill,
    Each dwelling place, a Light.**

—*Catherine Baker*

OLD KOREAN SONG

Mount Tai-sen is a lofty one
But still it is beneath the sky,
However high. If one climb on
And on, he'll top it certainly.
Who must their idleness confess
Prefer to blame its loftiness.***

—*Author Unknown; translated by Y. T. Pyun*

* From *Songs from Korea*. Published by The International Cultural Association, Seoul. Used by permission of the publisher.

** Written especially for this anthology.

*** From *Korean Survey* (February 1955). Published by The Korean Research and Information Office. Used by permission of the publisher.

THE HILLS IN AUTUMN

The hills in autumn receive the setting sun
And are reflected on the surface of the river.
With a fishing pole on my shoulder,
I sit in my small boat.
God, perceiving my loneliness,
Sends me the moon.*

—Yu Chasin

TRIANGLE MOUNTAIN

Triangle Mountain, I leave you.
Han River, stay in good health.
I do not wish to depart from you,
O hills and streams of my native land!
Yet leave I must, and in these troubled times
I may never see you again.*

—Kim Sanghun

THE CHURCH GIVES STRENGTH

This small peninsula, her history
Was dark for centuries. She lived a slave
To foreign powers, but through the years she grew
Strength to withstand oppressing tyrant, knave . . .

Have we forgotten persecution, death,
Hunger, the "fate unknown," of recent days?
The tortured, broken bodies, children lost,
Family severed; churches, homes ablaze—
We cannot name the villages destroyed,
The foe spared nothing—house or dugout, hut;
Old men and youth, women, endured assault
Unspeakable to human dignity—but

That strength? Whence came it? From the ONE who taught
Forgiveness. Faith—faithfulness, dual rock
On which they build. In prison and in camp
They hear the accents, "Fear not, little flock."
In every distant outpost they erect
A house of prayer, in toil they pay the price,
Using discarded boxes, metal, brick—
Slaves only to their Lord, the ageless Christ.

* *Ibid*. Used by permission of the publisher.

On dusty road, up hill and down,
In rain or shine, heat, cold, they walk
To meetinghouse, in search
Of truth—eager, determined file,
Women with babies on their backs—
Old, young—their goal the Church.*

—*Catherine Baker*

CHARITY

Smile a genuine smile,
You'll save many a mile.

Try the feeling hand,
You'll find the heavenly land.

Tend a true need found,
You'll see the world come round.

Have one kind mite thrown,
It will buy you a crown.**

—*Y. T. Pyun*

YOSU VILLAGE

After the pastor's village was destroyed,
Among the enemy, a boy
Shot down the father's dearly cherished sons—
Gone from the home the laughter, joy.
Later the murderer was brought to trial,
Misguided lad, condemned to die—
"No," said the father, "punishment cannot
Bring back my sons. Please let me try
To teach the youth of Christian ways, may he
Become as one of ours, endeared,
And do the work my sons have left undone."
The father's faith had rich reward.***

—*Catherine Baker*

---

* Written especially for this anthology.
** From *Songs from Korea*. Published by The International Cultural Association, Seoul. Used by permission of the publisher.
*** Written especially for this anthology, and based on a true happening during the Korean War.

KOREAN FLAG

Historic emblem eloquently telling
Of years you hid concealed from hostile eyes,
Today you represent endurance, Freedom
To think and act, man's worth-the-striving prize.

Flag, symbol dear to patriot Korean—
White field; in corners cryptic bar design:
Circle enclosing blue and red—union;
Good-ill, day-night, life-death, all intertwine.

You represent your country's beauty; emblem
Of era, you, when feud and warfare cease;
You hold the prophecy, a bond-free future.
God bring the land you symbolize His peace.*

—*Catherine Baker*

✜

A CHRISTIAN WORLD STATESMAN AND PATRIOT
Robert T. Oliver

SYNGMAN RHEE's long life has been distinguished by a remarkable consistency of principles and by an unusual record of success in foreseeing and foretelling the course of events. He has won and held the devotion of his people as no other man has ever done in Korea and as few have done in any country. He has suffered physical tortures and the long maddening misery of condemnation and rejection of his views by the major statesmen of the world. When the sharpest crisis in the struggle between Communism and the free world was precipitated, he was on the spot and was equipped with the courage to confront it and to make the only decision which could serve the fundamental welfare of free people everywhere. He has been often condemned—usually for upholding policies which events have lost little time in justifying. He is near the end of his life, but he fights on with the strength of enduring convictions.

Although his name is widely known, the nature of the man himself remains obscure. It is easy to say that Rhee is often misunderstood. But why should he suffer more than other public men from prejudiced, or misinformed, or ill-natured reporting? The question is a fair one and the answer is not hard to find. Rhee has been associated with a cause, the establishment and defense of Korean independence, which has long been and still remains unpopular. He advocated freedom for Korea while it was under Japanese rule and the United States was at peace with Japan. He denounced Communism

* Written especially for this anthology.

and warned against Russian treachery while the free world was allied with the Soviet Union. He opposed methods and policies of the American Military Government in Korea. He was against the policy of "waiting for the dust to settle in the Far East." He has warned against errors and has forecast disaster. When his judgment was vindicated by the Communist attack on Korea, the United States and the United Nations were drawn into the Korean war and nobody liked either the war itself or the limitations under which it was fought. The general public distaste with involvement in the Korean war came into focus against Syngman Rhee—the highly vocal leader who stood out boldly calling for stronger measures and more determination.

Among the newspaper readers in this turbulent period President Rhee is most widely known for his adroit capacity to set the world by its ears. He is also known, in some quarters with admiration, in others with dismay, as one of the most influential men of our time.

Rhee had reached the age of customary retirement before the start of World War II, yet his period of most influential leadership came a full decade later. He was editor of Korea's first daily newspaper in 1895 and a member of the Emperor's Privy Council in 1897. Yet almost sixty years later he was the pivotal figure around whom revolved the questions of war or peace in the crucial struggle between the Communist and democratic worlds. Few men have played so significant a role in the twentieth century as has Syngman Rhee. Yet among all the important figures of our era, he is perhaps the least known.

It is the destiny of Syngman Rhee that he stood at the crossroads of Korean history in a period when Korea has been a focal center of the global power struggle. He has had the clarifying gift of being able to see the essential simplicity of issues which have confused other national leaders because of their seeming complexity. In the history of Korea his name will stand out as by far the greatest statesman yet produced by that prolific land. But in this era of the interrelationship of peoples, Syngman Rhee belongs to America and to the entire free world, as well.

It is not because of Dr. Rhee's education and forty-year residence in the United States that he has become a part of American history. Nor is it because his political and social thinking became Americanized—though in the long perspective his success in planting the roots of genuine democracy on the continent of Asia may prove the most significant turning point in the relationship of the two hemispheres. His significance for us arises only in part from the fact that he identified himself so closely with the United States that he has not been able to avoid looking at problems largely from the American point of view, nor has he at any time since 1904 thought of world or of Korean problems except in relation to official policies and public opinion in our country.

His basic connection with America's destiny in the Pacific is that he offered guidance for our Far Eastern policies which, to our cost, we ignored, and through his unswerving resistance to the communization of Asia he provided the United States and the United Nations with an opportunity for bringing to a halt the long forward sweep of Soviet aggression. If the Pacific basin continues to grow in world significance, as it seems certain to do, historians of the future will devote increasing attention to the role played by Syngman Rhee in the westernization, the modernization, and the democratization of that half of the world.

The story of the life of Syngman Rhee is one of the most dramatic and sensational chronicles of this century. It is also one of the most enlightening and suggestive life stories of our time; for he has lived in and through successive crises which for seventy-five years have jarred and shaken the tenuous relationship between the West and the East.

It is a curious anomaly that Rhee has been commonly rated even higher by his critics than by his friends. He has been the recipient of some of the sharpest notes ever dispatched to the head of a friendly state by two presidents of the United States, two prime ministers of Great Britain, the officials of Australia, India, and Canada, and by two secretaries-general of the United Nations. He has long been a favorite whipping boy of the press in the Western nations and has concurrently been a chief target for vituperation in the Communist press. Like Washington, Jefferson, and Lincoln in their times, he has had the capacity of arousing virulent denunciations and astonishingly zealous devotion and loyalty. He has become one of the epicenters of his age—a symbol, a magnet, a target; and also a prophet and a statesman as well.

The truly amazing vitality of Rhee after he became president of the new Republic of Korea in his mid-seventies had led to an unnatural concentration of attention on his age. Every successive year, as his birthday rolls around and another year is tallied, perplexed observers ask doubtfully, "Can it be true that he is *only* seventy-eight?" (or whatever his current age might then be).

By his critics even more than by his friends, "this old man" is credited with abilities and energy truly beyond human endurance. *Time* credits him with an appointment schedule of thirty visitors a day—an exaggeration, but wholly in line with the widely-held theory of his omniscient grasp of every phase of Korean life. Aside from these exaggerations, it is true that most of the great number of people he does see go out from their conferences with him amazed by his detailed knowledge of the special project they have come to discuss.

Those who hate Rhee (without knowing him) spare no lengths in their vilification. If it were not for the unparalleled loyalty and affection of the people of Korea for him and the high praise from notable men who know him well, it might be thought that Rhee has a talent for inspiring dislike. But to General James A. Van Fleet, who worked closely with him in the Korean War for two years, he is "worth his weight in diamonds," and "one of the greatest statesmen who ever lived." To his long-time Methodist pastor and chaplain of the United States Senate, Reverend Frederick Brown

Harris, Rhee is "one of the gentlest and truest Christian gentlemen I have ever known." [The late] U. S. Secretary of State John Foster Dulles [was] proud to refer to him frequently as "my friend" and as a "genuine statesman." He has been highly admired and indeed loved by men as diverse as Woodrow Wilson and Douglas MacArthur. His worst critics have paid tribute to his selfless patriotism and to the tenacity with which he stands by his principles.

The truth about Syngman Rhee is that he is that rare being, an *original,* who follows his own convictions even though they lead him into the teeth of direct opposition by world opinion and by the policies of the strongest states. If the events of the past three-quarters of a century had proved him to be wrong, he would be relegated to oblivion among the countless mistaken doctrinaire thinkers. But since the course of twentieth-century history can be pretty well traced in terms of the causes for which he has fought, he has become a major influence in our time, and must be numbered among the great political prophets of history.

For all his achievements as a prophet whose vision has not been distorted by his struggles with power politics, Syngman Rhee is a humble and simple man. He neither drinks nor smokes, yet is not at all an ascetic. He enjoys good food, good books, good talk, and such pleasant diversions as fishing, tennis, working in his garden, playing with his dogs, and writing Chinese calligraphy. He chuckles with solid enjoyment over good stories and mercifully forgets them so quickly that his appreciation extends through several re-tellings. He has a great capacity for enjoying the companionship of friends and is fortunate in possessing the essential quality of being able to relax and forget the care and responsibilities of office when his day's work is done. More basically, despite his alleged involvement in every minutia of his government, in actuality he holds himself aloof from the detailed operations of his administration and is thus enabled to keep his attention concentrated on the underlying principles and over-all policies.

Rhee is not a man who gains dignity from his executive position, but rather he is one who imparts meaning and significance to whatever he may do or whatever he may be. This quality is not alone apparent to his intimates but is instantly transmitted to great crowds when he speaks to them or officiates in public ceremonies. His very presence radiates the calm conviction of command, the assurance of knowing what he is about, the consciousness of being a leader—and this he does with no strutting, no pomposity, no pretense. He is inwardly serene, both because he feels himself to be in the right and because he never doubts that both his own people and history are with him.

Syngman Rhee's basic humility derives from his deep spirituality. From his earliest manhood he has been convinced of the eternal justice and compassion of God, and has found his greatest source of strength in prayer. For many years he has accompanied his breakfasts with his wife by reading aloud one or more chapters from the Bible. Frequent solitary prayer has been for him not so much a solace as an unfailing stimulus to hopeful reaffirmation of his faith. Among all the national leaders of our time, there are few others who rest as solidly as does Rhee upon a bedrock of religious faith.

Finally, in assessing his unique position of world-wide influence, there must be noted his native intellectual capacity and excellent education. In his youth he attained the highest levels of achievement in mastery of the old Chinese classics. He earned three degrees from three of America's best universities after he had undergone a period of leadership and trial which provided for him an unusual maturity of judgment to guide his studies. In his college work he majored in international relations, specializing in United States policies of neutrality in dealing with the Far East. He is one of the very few men who ever rose to the presidency of a nation after earning the Ph.D. degree. He combined in his own person the best education of the East and the West; he devoted himself unselfishly to the determined pursuit of a great ideal; and when the time came he was ready not only to lead his own people but also serve the needs, in a time and place of great crisis, of all the free peoples of the world.*

✛

TAKE TO THE AIR

FORTY miles from the tightly closed "bamboo curtain" a radio tower stands incongruously surrounded by rice paddies. A few buildings at the foot of the tower hold the studios for the Christian broadcasting station HLKY, "Radio Voice of the Church in Korea," which celebrated its fifth birthday December 15, 1959. A project of the Korean National Christian Council, HLKY is the first privately-operated radio station to be granted a permit by the Republic of Korea. Since its beginning it has been a lighthouse of hope in a nation still recovering after the tragedy of the Korean War.

On the air sixty-two hours a week now, HLKY is reaching out into the villages of Korea where ninety battery radios, "portable missionaries," have been distributed to as many country churches. Using the village church as a listening center, groups of thirty or more persons gather daily around each radio to hear a variety of gospel programs, dramas, fine music, and English lessons. Although listening to Christian programs is strictly forbidden north of the thirty-eighth parallel, once in a while the station learns that it is being heard as far away as the Yalu River, which divides Korea from China. At the edge of the demilitarized zone ROK soldiers often hook a receiver to amplifiers and broadcast the Christian message across the valley to Communist troops on the opposite hill. With Communist-dominated North Korea in mind, HLKY has added special programs that last until midnight every Saturday.

The evangelistic potential of consistent programming was illustrated at

Chinha Naval Base on the southern tip of Korea where three Christian seamen invited their buddies to listen to HLKY. By the end of six months twenty seamen had become Christian and, with a chaplain's help, the group started a regular weekly worship service.

Under the direction of Presbyterian missionary Otto DeCamp, HLKY has presented such fine programs that the standards of broadcasting in the whole country have been raised. By popular demand even Roman Catholic newspapers carry HLKY program listings, and a survey indicates that the people of Seoul devote an average of one-third of their listening time to the Protestant station.

The pastor, Dr. K. C. Han, and the session of the Yung Nak Presbyterian Church in Seoul have decided to put special emphasis on radio evangelism. This church of forty-five hundred members is supplying a wide range of fine music, and Dr. Han, an effective radio and pulpit preacher, is giving a weekly message in a new program called "The Hour of Hope."

Plans are well under way to open the first Christian relay station in Taegu. Programs taped in Seoul will be broadcast daily from the new transmitter of Station HLKT in Taegu. The Christian network expects to include other cities of South Korea as the way opens.

The "bamboo curtain" in Korea cannot keep out the "old, old story" when it is beamed by radio.*

✠

BRICKS AND A DREAM
Alice Geer Kelsey

It was the gayest time of the year—the fifteen days of the New Year's Festival in January. Like children all over Korea, the boys and girls of a farming village on Tourodo Island in the Taedong River were celebrating.

The air was full of the boys' New Year's kites. They were small square kites, so cleverly built that they needed neither wings nor tails to keep them afloat, so cleverly flown that they soared and dived and fought air battles with one another. Their colors were as bright as the New Year's costumes of the boys who flew them. Only for the big festivals of the year did the boys take off their cotton clothes and put on their silk outfits of green blouses, blue vests, and baggy yellow pants.

The girls also were dressed in their silken New Year's costumes of long full rosy-red skirts and short green jackets with flowing sleeves of many colored stripes. Their special New Year's game was the teeter-totter. One girl sat in the center of a long plank to balance it on its pile of blankets or rags. Two other girls stood on the plank, one at either end. As each one in turn

* Condensed from *Current News* (Korea: Autumn 1958; and Korea, Hong Kong, Taiwan: Spring 1959). Used by permission of the Commission on Ecumenical Mission and Relations of the United Presbyterian Church in the USA.

jumped down on her end of the board, the other one bounced high into the air, then landed again on her end to send her companion bouncing up. Sookney Lee, who was slim and lithe for her twelve years, would bounce especially high, but always landed in exactly the right spot.

There was top-spinning, too, and the eating of quantities of sweets made from barley and rice water.

Best of all, was the singing. Boys and girls dressed in their New Year's silks went in a group through the market place or to the houses of farmers who worked the fields surrounding the village. Men who liked their singing would drop coins into the girls' embroidered silk purses or into the purses that formed the end of each boy's bright sash. The children were sure of gifts when they sang in their most plaintive voices the beautiful and tragic "Song of Arirang," the favorite folk song of Koreans for three centuries.

> Arirang, Arirang, Arari-o!
> Crossing the hills of Arirang,
> There are twelve hills of Arirang
> And now I am crossing the last hill.

Then the children would shift to a lighthearted tune. Sometimes Sookney Lee and her friends would sing their church songs, "This Is My Father's World" or "For the Beauty of the Earth." The Christians—and these were many—were happy to hear the glad songs of their own faith.

Other boys and girls were collecting coins to buy sweets or toys or something needed at home, but the Christian children had a special reason for singing. Their coins would go into the slowly growing fund for building a church. They worshiped now in the same three-room schoolhouse where they went on weekdays to study. They had seen the brick church at Pyongyang on the mainland and dreamed of one of their own like it.

This new church meant more to Sookney Lee than it did to some of the other children. It was a part of the dream she carried in her heart—of giving all of her life to the teaching of Christianity.

Soon the fifteen days of the New Year's Festival were over. The last kite had been released to fly off into the sky. Every teeter-totter had become an ordinary plank. The New Year's outfits had been packed away to await the next festival. The children went back to school.

The work of the Korean year began. The men and big boys fertilized and planted the dry fields. The women and big girls worked at their sewing, their weaving, their baby-tending, and the never-ending washing and smoothing of the white cotton clothes that were the everyday dress of the men and women of Korea. And the children learned their lessons in the three-room school-house. In the spring the rice seedlings were started for transplanting later to the flooded fields. As they worked, the Christians of Tourodo Island continued to save and to sacrifice for the new church. Coin by coin, the fund grew.

At last there was enough money to order bricks from the mainland. During the sixth and the seventh months, the Christians of Tourodo watched for the flat boats, lying low in the water because of their weight of red-burnt bricks, to come rowing toward them on the Taedong River.

By the eighth month, men and women were weeding knee-deep in the wet rice fields from daybreak till sunset. After school the children helped, too. Weeds must not choke the fast-growing rice.

One day at recess, Pokdong stared toward the river.

"Boats are coming!" he shouted.

"Their load is heavy," said Soonam. "Like bricks!"

The children watched the first flat boat pull up to the landing. Sure enough, it was full of bricks. No strong men rushed out to meet it. They were all in the rice fields. The children saw the oarsmen moor their boat and look for men to help with the unloading. But the men were knee-deep in their wet rice paddies, pulling weeds.

"Who will unload the bricks?" Soopok asked the other children. They all stood there wondering the same thing.

"Bricks are not too heavy for us to carry—a few at a time," said Soonam.

"And it's our church," said Sookney.

In the schoolroom the three teachers looked into one another's eyes. They were all having the same idea at the same time, as often happens when Christians are working together.

"It would be worth more than a day with slates and books," the first-and-second-grade teacher said.

"We have two hundred children," reckoned the fifth-and-sixth-grade teacher. "They could form a line from the boat to the church site and pass the bricks from child to child."

At last the orders came, and the children raced to their places. Two hundred boys and girls and three teachers stretched in a thin line from boat to church lot. The little children stood close together so that they could pass the bricks easily. The middle-sized boys and girls stood farther apart. Each had to stretch and take a few steps as he handed the bricks to the one next in line. The fifth and sixth graders were spread out so that each must run to keep the stream of bricks flowing.

The August sun beat hotly on the working children. The edges of the bricks were rough enough to bruise small hands. There was an occasional squeal of pain as a brick dropped on toes that were bare or covered only by thin sandals of rice straw.

Someone started singing a song they had learned in the church service on Sundays in their schoolhouse, "Work, for the Night Is Coming." The bricks seemed lighter as they passed along in rhythm with the song. Finally one boat was emptied. By late afternoon the second boat's last bricks were being carried away. Grownups were coming home from their weeding. Mothers were calling their families in for evening rice and barley with good cabbage pickle. There was praise of the children and their pile of bricks.

"May we work again tomorrow?" asked Sookney Lee, the girl with the dream to work always for her church.

"If more bricks come," answered her teacher.

More bricks did come—the next day and for two days after that. Except for the rest-time at noon when the August sun was very hot, the two hundred children formed their living chain to pass bricks from early morning till it was too dark to see. Hands were scratched and blistered. Muscles were sore. Faces were sunburned. Backs were lame. Whenever it seemed that the next brick would be one too many, someone started a song that put life into them again. Even children who were not Christians enjoyed singing the songs with the strange but stirring Western tunes. There was a special song in the heart of Sookney Lee.

"May we help some more?" the children asked when the pile of bricks stood red and solid, a promise of the church that would soon rise in that spot.

At first the men of the church answered, "No. You are too young." Then they remembered that the ninth month would soon be there when the rice must be cut, carried home, and threshed. There might still be work for the boys and girls.

"Let's ask the bricklayers," said the men.

"The small children can wash the bricks," said the bricklayers. "The middle-sized boys and girls can bring us clean bricks in baskets. As the walls grow, the largest boys can carry the bricks up the ladders."

And so, through long hot days, the boys and girls kept building. Not so many were needed as had worked in the chain of children from boat to church lot. The lazy ones slipped away. The rest took turns.

So much work was done by the children that the grownups agreed on one thing when the church was finished. "The children must have a big part when we dedicate our beautiful new building," they said.

"Let's have a choir of children," someone suggested. The idea was received with favor.

Later all agreed that the best part of the dedication service was the children's choir, singing with gladness in their voices and joy on their faces "I love thy church, O God."

There was a special shine on the face of Sookney Lee. The music of children's voices raised in joyous praise—this, too, was part of the dream she carried in her heart.*

✣

PEACE THROUGH HIS CROSS

IT is well-nigh impossible for most of us to comprehend the poverty and misery caused by the recent war in Korea. Hundreds of families joined the hordes of refugees fleeing south toward Pusan. The suffering and privations of these families, who had to make that long trek carrying whatever they could

---

* Abridged from *Many Hands in Many Lands* by Alice Geer Kelsey. Reprinted in *Missionary Stories to Play and Tell*, edited by Nina Millen. Copyright 1958 by Friendship Press. Used by permission of the publisher.

of their personal belongings, can never be fully told.

Hungry, worn out, and desperate, they finally reached their goal, only to find that Pusan was in confusion and that starvation and sickness were on every hand. Some four or five million refugees were crowded into that small corner. Many wandered the streets for days unable to find shelter. Churches had been devastated, homes wrecked, and the organized charities of the city taxed beyond their power to help any but the most desperate cases.

It was out of the knowledge of such suffering and despair that the hymn "Peace Through His Cross" was born. Miss Catherine Baker, the author of the words, served as a missionary and teacher for the Methodist Church at Ewha College (now Ewha University) in Seoul for thirteen years. She knows from personal experience some of the tragedy and heartache the Korean people have suffered, and in this beautiful hymn, sung to the tune "Aurelia," she shows us their suffering as she lifts our eyes to a permanent and enduring peace through His cross.

✛

TO WORK, TO WORK

THE hymn "To Work, to Work" is especially dear to the Korean people. On p. 781 you will find the music score, with the words written in the Korean language. The words appear in English below, as translated by Miss Catherine Baker, who also wrote the words to the preceding hymn, "Peace through His Cross."

The Korean people love to sing; they sing at their work and at their play. They also love their land, with its towering mountains, its rivers and green valleys.

This Christian hymn recognizes God's ownership of all nature and His partnership with men as they work to make their country strong and beautiful.

<blockquote>
God gave us mountains, valleys, and rivers,
    Three thousand li[1] of country.
God gave us mountains, valleys, and rivers,
    Three thousand li of country.

People, there is much work to do—
From mountain, river, town, and valley.
God calls for helpers, don't delay,
Who goes in answer to that call?
</blockquote>

Refrain

[1] One-third of a mile.

Peace Through His Cross*

Aurelia 7.6.7.6.D

CATHERINE BAKER   SAMUEL WESLEY, 1810–1876

1. War's mad - ness and con - fu - sion On land and o - cean cease,
2. His cross— the sym - bol calls us To con - tem- plate its prayer,
3. Comes peace, world un - der - stand - ing, Su - prem - a - cy of good—

For at this ve - ry mo - ment Christ works en - dur - ing peace.
To speak with cheer and wis - dom, To give the need - y care;
All peo - ples, class - es, ra - ces, Be - liefs, a bro - ther - hood.

In spite of black - ened land - scape, The waste, the grief, the loss,
To bring the means of heal - ing Where sick in an - guish toss,
Greed, sel - fish - ness and hat - red Melt as un - want - ed dross—

The count-less homes made lone - ly— Love sig - nals from the cross.
To help eyes tor - ture - blind - ed Be - hold the light - ed cross.
Through rec - on - cil - ing pow - er Peace comes, peace thru His cross. A - MEN.

*From *The Methodist Woman* (November 1945). Used by permission of the author and publisher.

Three thousand li of waiting country
Must hear about the Saviour.
Christians, go work in every village,
Go preach the gospel, God commands you.

God gave us mountains, valleys, and rivers,
    Three thousand li of country.
God gave us mountains, valleys, and rivers,
    Three thousand li of country.

When springtime comes, we plough our fields,
God calls for workers where bare regions
Wait for life-giving seed, His word;
Who goes in answer to that call?

Refrain

God gave us mountains, valleys, and rivers,
    Three thousand li of country.
God gave us mountains, valleys, and rivers,
    Three thousand li of country.

Yes, plant the precious seed today
And it will bear immortal harvest.
God calls for workers, who will hear?
Who goes in answer to that call?*

Refrain

* From *Land of Morning Splendor* by Catherine Baker, pp. 22-23. Published by Dierkes Press. Used by permission of the author and the publisher.

일흐러가세
To Work, To Work*

NAM KUNG OK

삼천리반도 금슈강산 하느님주신 동산 삼천리반도 금슈강산

하 느 님주신 동산 이동산에 홀일만하 스방에일군을 부르네 곳

금일에 일 가랴고 누구가더답을 홀가 일흐러가세 일흐러가 삼

후렴

천리강산 위히 하느님명령 밧앗스니반도 강산에일흐러 가세

*Courtesy Korean Hymns.

CONTENTS

PART VI SECTION 4

CHRISTIANITY IN THE PHILIPPINES

--✝--

For whom the Lord loveth he chasteneth, and scourgeth every son whom he receiveth.—HEBREWS 12:6

--✝--

PICTURES: PAGE
    Interpretation: The Symbolism of Central Christian Church, Manila—
        Arellano 783
    Picture: The Symbolism of Central Christian Church, Manila—*Arellano* .. 784
    Interpretation: United Protestant Youth Center, University of the Philippines 785
    Picture: United Protestant Youth Center, University of the Philippines 786
    Interpretation: Silliman University Church, Dumaguete 787
    Picture: Silliman University Church, Dumaguete 788

POETRY:
    Judas Iscariot—*Nabong* 787
    Philippine Hymn—*Author Unknown* 789
    Longinus—*Demetillo* 790
    Prayer for Our Country—*Reyes* 790
    This Is to Live—*Ordinario* 790
    Those Between—*Reyes* 791
    Increase My Love, O God—*Pugh* 792

STORIES:
    Librada Javalera of the Philippines—*Lee* 792
    Healing for Body and Spirit—*Presbyterian Commission on Ecumenical
        Mission and Relations* 795
    Pablo Helps with the Writing—*Niedermeyer* 797

MUSIC:
    Interpretation: O Zion, Haste, Thy Mission High Fulfilling—*Thomson* 799
    Music: O Zion, Haste, Thy Mission High Fulfilling—*Walch* 800
    Interpretation: In Christ There Is No East or West—*Oxenham* 801
    Music: In Christ There Is No East or West—*Reinagle* 801

THE SYMBOLISM OF
CENTRAL CHRISTIAN CHURCH, MANILA

"Strength and beauty are in His sanctuary."—THE PSALMIST.

THERE is justification for the use of symbols in the construction of a church. The temple built by Solomon was rich with symbols, which are described in the third and fourth chapters of II Chronicles. Among such symbols were a molten sea, the cherubim, pomegranates, lilies, candlesticks, and lamps. What are many of the Lord's parables but symbols? Think of the sower and the seed, the wheat and the tares, the mustard seed, the leaven, the treasure hid in the field, the pearl of great price, and the net (Matt. 13).

Central Church, as a whole, is cruciform or cross-shaped: the nave and the chancel form a cross with the transept. Above the facade is another cross. Rising high above the church is a spire, which represents the heavenward longing of the Christian soul. Superimposed upon the spire is a cross, signifying that the Christian life should be ruled by the sacrifice of Christ on Calvary.

The architectural style of Central Church, designed by a leading Filipino architect, Mr. Juan Arellano, is modern or Gothic simplified. One of the chief characteristics of the Gothic style is the pointed form of the arches and vaulting, a form which points toward our Father who is in heaven. Standing between the Romanesque (eighth to eleventh centuries) and the Renaissance (fifteenth to seventeenth centuries), Gothic architecture may be said to be distinctly Christian. It symbolizes the best and the highest of Christianity in the Middle Ages.

In the chancel, the central symbol is Da Vinci's "The Last Supper" carved in relief by Graciano Nepomuceno, an outstanding Filipino sculptor. It is highly fitting that the principal symbol should be the picture of that sacred moment of loving farewell of the Master to His disciples. Just above "The Last Supper" is a vine, to depict the words of Jesus when He said: "I am the vine, ye are the branches" (John 15:5).

Below "The Last Supper" is the communion table. Underneath this table, facing the congregation, are the Greek letters Alpha and Omega, from Revelation 21:6: "And he said unto me, It is done. I am Alpha and Omega, the beginning and the end." Between these two letters are letters used by the early Christians meaning the Lord Jesus.

On the upper part of the panels on the three sides of the chancel are rows of carved symbols: a nipa house, a torch, a lily, a rose, and a sheaf of rice. The nipa house signifies the Christian home. The torch stands for the light of education. The lily means purity of life. The rose represents truth, which blossoms in the life of every Christian. And the sheaf of rice symbolizes God's bounty.

Inscribed on each of three sides of the pulpit is a rose, in the center of which are a heart and a cross. This was Luther's shield meaning truth,

THE SYMBOLISM OF CENTRAL CHRISTIAN CHURCH, MANILA—
ARELLANO

courage, and salvation. And on each of three sides of the lectern, from which God's Word is read, is carved the open Bible that all persons may freely read the Holy Writ. Thus everyone should be guided by his own conscience in understanding the way of salvation through Jesus Christ.*

Pictures of the interior and exterior of this beautiful church may be seen on p. 784. It is indeed a fitting place in which to meet God in the beauty of holiness.

✛

UNITED PROTESTANT YOUTH CENTER, UNIVERSITY OF THE PHILIPPINES

THE proverb "Great oaks from tiny acorns grow" is seldom better illustrated than in the United Protestant Christian Youth Movement of the Philippines, which was formed in 1947, when a group of evangelical students met at Union Theological Seminary Chapel in Manila. With the transfer of the University of the Philippines to Dillman, near Manila, in 1949, an enlarged program of weekly meetings, symposia, lectures, and musicales was initiated. The group made a spiritual retreat during 1950, an experiment which met with such success that it has been repeated from year to year.

The building of a church on the campus of the University of the Philippines had long been in the minds of the Protestant leaders. As early as 1947 an appeal was made to friends in the United States for funds to help realize this dream. Since the majority of the leaders in all phases of work in the Philippines come from among the University's graduates, such a center was envisioned as a lasting spiritual influence throughout the islands. The young people themselves felt the need of a fourfold program that would include worship, religious education, fellowship, and friendship.

Over the years, the sum of nearly one hundred thousand dollars has come from the Boards of Foreign Missions of several denominations, along with ten thousand dollars contributed locally. This has gone to build the chapel (see p. 786), completed in 1954, the Fellowship Center, and the parsonage.

Through the Youth Center, evangelical young people come to know one another better, make new friends, and receive guidance and counseling. Sunday-school classes for children and adults make possible the study of the Bible and the Christian way of life. The Fellowship Center provides a sanctuary where students can undergo a reverent, dynamic worship experience which has been the heart of their movement from its beginning. The United Protestant Youth Center is meeting in a full-rounded way the needs of Filipino young people as they grow into Christian manhood and womanhood.

* Arranged from an article by Dr. Jorge Bocobo in *The Central Spire* (February 19, 1950). Used by permission of the author and Central Methodist Church.

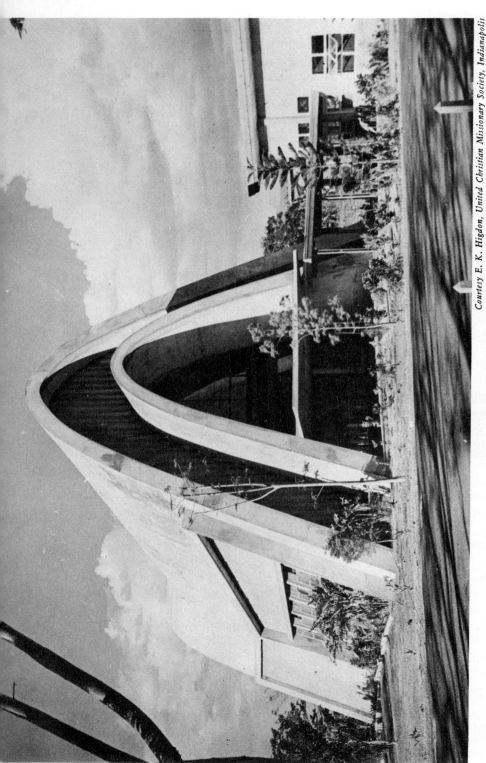

UNITED PROTESTANT YOUTH CENTER, UNIVERSITY OF THE
PHILIPPINES

SILLIMAN UNIVERSITY CHURCH, DUMAGUETE

THE United Church of Christ in the Philippines was organized in 1903 as the First Presbyterian Church, but it has always been known as Silliman University Church.

In 1899, the Reverend David S. Hibbard, a Presbyterian missionary, made a survey of several towns in the Philippines with the object of finding a suitable location for a school. He finally chose Dumaguete because the people there were responsive and interested in his plan. In 1901 he and his wife organized the first classes of the school that has since come to be known as Silliman University.

The work of the church in those early years was very closely tied up with the University. The faculty members taught classes in the church's school, and senior college students helped conduct Sunday-school classes. The great event of the year was at Christmas time, when the Silliman Church Choir and the Children's Choir joined in a musical festival. In addition to these choirs there was also a speech choir, which attracted wide publicity.

Many members of Silliman Church went out regularly to neighboring towns and *barrios* (villages) to teach Sunday-school classes of children and adults. They frequently brought back testimony of the power of God's word in the lives of these neglected and often underprivileged communities. Smaller churches in surrounding towns looked to Silliman Church for inspiration and guidance.

In August of 1941 the cornerstone of the new church building was laid, and construction was begun even though rumors of war were increasing. Only the outer shell of the building had been completed when the Japanese invasion came. Japanese forces occupied the campus of the University and used the church as a warehouse.

When the University reopened after the war, efforts were renewed to finish the building and its furnishings. People of many different nationalities and religious faiths contributed generously to the church, and slowly it was completed.

On Palm Sunday, April 2, 1950, Silliman University Church was dedicated, an inspiring expression of the great ecumenical fellowship which is the Christian Church. The picture on p. 788 shows the church as it stands today.*

✠

JUDAS ISCARIOT

I was there, standing near and below
The place called the "skull."
I watched: They cursed and scourged
And goaded a King.

* Based on information provided by Mrs. Portia Mapanao of Dumaguete, P. I.

SILLIMAN UNIVERSITY CHURCH, DUMAGUETE

In the torturous hours
Of gall and suffering . . . strange!
What power and love and humility
From His heart poured forth.

I felt the wormwood and the gall:
Oh, my Lord, and Master—
For a kiss and thirty pieces of silver
I betrayed Thee.

Soon the earth trembled and quaked—
The heavens tossed and rolled to proclaim
Him, the Saviour—Victor over sin and death!
Victor over man's inhumanity!

Yet I, Judas, called Iscariot,
Had already betrayed innocent blood!
I sold Him into bondage and suffering.
I am condemned. I am accursed!

Nothing is left now for me to do:
A piece of rope, a sycamore tree awaits—
And darkness for my furious
Lamentations eternally to come.*

—*Juan C. Nabong, Jr.*

PHILIPPINE HYMN

Land of the morning,
Child of the sun returning,
With fervor burning,
Thee do our souls adore;
Land dear and holy,
Cradle of noble heroes,
Ne'er shall invaders
Trample thy sacred shore.

Ever within thy skies
And through thy clouds
And o'er thy hills and sea
Do we behold the radiance,
Feel the throb
Of glorious liberty.
Thy banner, dear to all our hearts,
Its sun and stars alight.

O, never shall its shining field
Be dimmed by tyrant's might
Beautiful land of love,
O land of light,
In thine embrace 'tis rapture to lie,
But it is glory ever,
When thou art wronged,
For us, thy sons, to suffer and die.**

—*Author Unknown; translated by*
M. A. L. Lane and Camilo Osias

* Used by permission of the author, a senior in the College of Law, University of the Philippines.
** Music score for this hymn may be procured from Silver Burdett Company.

LONGINUS

I felt that I had seen a god
Gripped by the bloody nails,
Who writhed beneath the rod.
I laughed to see him die.

But as I trudged home from the hill
Where the cross loomed,
A lonely shadow hemmed me in,
Like shuttered doom.

Now haunted by the thorny brow
That I helped pierce,
I run, feeling accurst,
Pursuit behind.

But every step the shadow gains.
I faint in dread.
The dark, shot through with light,
Reveals the young God's head.*

—*Ricardo Demetillo*

PRAYER FOR OUR COUNTRY

Our land and people bless, O God,
Thou Saviour through our darkest years—
Make Thou us solid—strong and one,
Keep Thou us free from harm and fears.

We pray Thee, now, unite us all!
Let strength upon our union be!
And keep us safe from hunger, God,
Enrich, help grow a nation free!

Together hold our people, Thou
Who saw how martyrs sought our peace,
Who saw our braves fall in the night,
Their wish: that we their sons might live.

Now help us build more happy homes!
The harvests of our fields increase!
Unite us! Bind us in Thy fold!
Bless Thou, O God, our Philippines.**

—*James Servel Reyes*

THIS IS TO LIVE

To love without pretentious adoration,
    To keep the heart from wanton hate and pride;
To graciously acclaim His love's creation,
    Nor think each seemingly dark day too bright;
To greet each morn with gladness at its coming,
    To make each moment live as 'twere the last—
To be alive within the living present
    To bid goodbye to every gloom of past.

* From *No Certain Weather* by Ricardo Demetillo. Published by Guinhalinan Press. Used by permission of the author and the publisher.
** From *The Manila Times* (July 4, 1957). Used by permission of the author and the publisher.

To meet each sorrow with a heart of lightness,
    To taste life's pleasures but never take too much.
To hate sin's pride, and cleave to all that's goodness;
    To turn from that which comes from sin's strong clutch.
To have a will that sways with no temptation,
    And changes not unless it does for right.
To gain control o'er every power and action,
    Nor be a slave of willful force and might.

To seek His presence in the still, small hours,
    To bear His image while the tasks are done;
To dwell harmonious with each fellow being,
    Regard the poor and rich as though they're one.
To be a friend in joy, in mirth and pleasure,
    To be a comrade with the ones in need.
To know joy's pains and sorrows' living treasure,
    To laugh, to lift, to love . . . this is to live.*

—*Ruby Leah Ordinario*

THOSE BETWEEN

Between the act and a desire
Compel me, Lord, to fear the mire
So I may tread a safer path
Preferring well Your smile to wrath.

Between this day and after-years
Lord, make me offer more than tears
For causes worthier than my own,
Such deed a gift and not a loan.

Between forgiving and revenge
Remind me, Lord, to build a fence
Confining me in peace from war
So I may have no other scar.

Between the sunshine and the rain
Lord, make me stock my needed grain
So when my winter starts to fall
I shall not beg from You at all.

Between my woman, God, and me,
Lord, make me ponder deep in Thee
That I may know when we may cease
From feeling heaven in a kiss.

* Written especially for this anthology.

Between the Virtue and the Vice,
Between the Self and Sacrifice,
Between Preparedness and the Rod:
Afflict my heart with Thee, my God!*
                    —*James Servel Reyes*

INCREASE MY LOVE, O GOD

Increase my love, O God,
    To take in every man
Of every clime, and every race,
    As well as my own little clan.

Increase my sight, O God,
    That I may come to see
In every bit of beauty here
    A touch of thy divinity.

Increase my will, O God,
    That I may have the power
To live the way I want to live—
    Through every week, and day and hour.

Increase my strength, O God,
    That I may come to do
This fascinating work of thine—
    Till every task is through.**
                    —*Samuel F. Pugh*

✛

LIBRADA JAVALERA OF THE PHILIPPINES
Elizabeth Meredith Lee

A MAN and a girl jogged along in a horse-drawn carriage toward Manila, city of wonders. As they crossed the plaza of the provincial town of Imus, the girl glanced back with awe at the statue of her maternal grandfather, erected in the square by admiring fellow townsmen. In his day the old gentleman had been a revolutionary. His nineteen-year-old granddaughter hardly yet recognized that she belonged to this same independent breed. She had just won her first victory by stubborn resistance to tradition. Now she was on her way to a new life, which none of her friends could understand. She herself, that day, had no notion how far this journey would lead her.

* From *Evening News Saturday Magazine* (January 1951). Used by permission of the author and *The Manila Times*.
**From *Between-Time Meditations* by Samuel F. Pugh, p. 26. Copyright 1954 by Bethany Press. Used by permission of the author and the publisher.

A few weeks earlier, Librada Javalera, following Philippine custom, had called on her kinsfolk to inform them that she was leaving home to study nursing. Stanchly she stood up against the opposition that blasted forth. Aunts, uncles, and cousins scornfully exclaimed, "Nurse! That work is left to servants. Why should you leave home and go to Manila to do the work of a maid?" And the school principal reminded the nineteen-year-old teacher that she was soon due a promotion. "You are crazy to choose nursing. I have just been in a hospital and I know the menial work nurses do."

The girl calmly replied, "When I am in Rome I can do as the Romans do!" So, she and her father, who with her mother had upheld her choice, drove on toward Manila and the Mary Johnston Hospital.

In the veins of this young Filipina the grandfather's blood flowed strongly. As a child she had been entranced by his tales of revolutionary days. He was a leader against Spanish aggression and he even chose to burn his big home rather than to have it used as enemy headquarters.

Grandfather was a man of revolt in religion as well as in politics. He brought up his family as Independent Catholics, a church that was a dissenter from Spanish Catholicism. The Javaleras had ten children, one of whom died in infancy. The family was not rich, and the children could hardly believe their mother's tales of the grandeur in which she was brought up on her father's estate. The children remembered vacations when they roamed the woods, rode *carabaos* [water buffaloes], drank cane juice, and reveled in outdoor meals with friendly farmhands.

Librada, the oldest child, went through elementary school, which, in those days, fitted her to teach primary grades. Her first salary was ten dollars a month, which helped to educate the younger children. But revolution was in her blood. She wanted to do something else, but couldn't tell what. During this period her mother gave birth to her tenth child, in difficult labor. The only help came from a friendly neighbor who was a nurse. In that hour Librada decided her destiny. She would be a nurse, too.

A family friend, dietitian at Mary Johnston Hospital, a Methodist institution in Manila, helped the girl obtain an application blank. The letter of admission finally came, and the girl headed toward Manila. It was the year of 1919.

Time passed, and it was 1945. War had ravaged the Philippines for three years. Missionary doctors and nurses of the Mary Johnston Hospital were interned by the Japanese. Librada Javalera, graduate of the class of 1922, was ready to take responsibility. She had run the gamut of nursing services, from humble dietary assistant to Superintendent of Nurses. At an Epworth League meeting in her student days she had found the living Christ and had witnessed so well that not only most of her students but also every member of her family had accepted the Protestant faith.

Always a revolutionary, Miss Javalera had forged ahead in the nursing field. After obtaining her high-school diploma in evening classes, she took a degree at the University of the Philippines. In 1932, helped by admiring

relatives, she studied in the United States. Following that American training, Miss Javalera returned to the Mary Johnston Hospital as head nurse.
Soon she was active in the Philippine Nurses' Association, setting standards
for the entire country.

After the missionaries were interned on July 7, 1944, Miss Javalera continued to keep the hospital open, though it was under strict Japanese
surveillance. This institution had served only women and children, but
tradition had been thrown to the winds. Wounded soldiers (some Japanese)
and civilians were cared for, and even a few Filipino guerrillas were
smuggled in.

Inflation made it difficult to obtain food in Manila, so Miss Javalera frequently made dangerous boat trips across Manila Bay to her old home, to
obtain rice, meat, and vegetables for the hospital. At the risk of her life she
sent food to missionaries in internment camps. Mary Johnston Hospital was a
haven of refuge and healing and Christian spirit, led by this brave nurse, now
in her middle forties.

February 5, 1945, brought to Tondo District blood, fire, and death. Bombs
fell, and in the early evening fire broke out within the hospital block. People
stampeded the hospital for shelter. Miss Javalera took charge, guiding the
frantic to safety, carrying out what could be saved, directing doctors and
nurses. The fire died down in one spot; flared up in another. Now it was a
square of fire on three sides, with the bay at the back. A lurking Japanese
sentry shot down a church member looking out a window of the hospital.
The public school building had just caught fire, then the church and the
dormitory opposite Mary Johnston. Explosions added to the uproar. It was
dangerous to move about for fear of being shot down by the invading
soldiers. The night was filled with terror.

As dawn broke over the city, the little crowd from the hospital sat on
the sidewalk, waiting for the worst. In the midst of destruction the beloved
house of healing stood like a lone sentinel over the holocaust. At six-thirty
in the morning it caught fire. "With bowed heads and with our backs to
the hospital," wrote Miss Javalera later, she led her group out into the bay,
the only way of escape. In two hours it was gone, all except the concrete
porch with the name on the wooden sign. The bedraggled group came out of
the water and sought the only shelter available—the remaining balcony of
the ruined Methodist Church across the street. For three weeks they lived
there, as the battle raged across the Pasig River.

Even before the Americans had liberated Manila, these Christian doctors
and nurses were making plans for the future. Soon missionaries were permitted to return to assume part of the burden of rebuilding. A Crusade
Scholarship of the Methodist Church was made available to Librada, which
made possible two years of study at Vanderbilt University and the obtaining
of a B.S. degree in nursing education. Upon her return this time, Miss
Javalera became the first Filipina director of Mary Johnston School of
Nursing.

The Board of Missions in New York also had its eye on the situation in Manila, and began work on reconstruction plans for a general hospital for men and women, to be maintained by both the Division of World Missions and the Woman's Division of Christian Service. As a member of the building committee, Librada kept her own eyes on the blueprints for the School of Nursing, determined to make it the best of its kind in the Orient. In August, 1952, the new Mary Johnston Hospital was dedicated.

Wherever MJH graduates work, they carry with them the high professional standards set by their teacher and also an appreciation, caught from their leader, of the arduous years of devoted labor given by missionary women doctors and nurses who established the hospital and bore its burdens for so many years. Miss Javalera never forgets her gratitude for these colleagues who took her in as a girl, nurtured her in her profession and in her Christian faith, were tolerant of her revolutionary ideas, and let her move forward. In the difficult years of the war, when she had to assume the heavy responsibilities, she said, "Our happiness was in the justification of the labor of our beloved missionaries."

Today the "Life-Saving Station of Tondo" is the most modern hospital in the Philippines. It ministers to men, women, and children, regardless of race, color, or creed. Its revolutionary angel has made its School of Nursing known throughout the land. She used to say shyly that she had worked herself out of a job, since one of the standards she set was that every director of a school of nursing in the Philippines must have an M.A. in nursing education. "And I have only a B.S.!"

She had no M.A. then, but in September, 1955, Miss Javalera came to the States and entered the University of California. Here she obtained her master's degree in School Administration. Returning to Manila in May, 1957, she has continued her crusading for the highest and the best for her students, emphasizing always the need for the spiritual qualities along with the intellectual.

Today Miss Librada Javalera stands at the top in the field of nursing education in her own country, and her revolutionary spirit lives on in the lives of those who have been her students.*

✤

HEALING FOR BODY AND SPIRIT

BETWEEN one and three o'clock all good Filipinos take a long lunch hour and a short nap to escape the tropical heat. But for the staff of the Masbate Mobile Clinic, siesta time is a restless two hours. Children are constantly knocking at the door to ask Gorgonia to tell another Bible story or Fe to teach another gospel chorus.

* Abridged from *Thirteen Biographies* by Elizabeth Meredith Lee, pp. 11-15. Published in 1958 by the Woman's Division of Christian Service of the Methodist Church. Used by permission of the author and the publisher.

The Christian clinic spends months at a time ministering to *barrios* (villages) on the island of Masbate, and the clinic's staff is a team well trained to meet the physical and spiritual needs of these isolated villagers. Gorgonia is the team's Bible woman. She spends her day teaching and visiting *barrio* families. Fe is the cook. She prepares three meals a day for the team on a one-burner stove, without running water, in someone else's kitchen. She can often be found on a neighbor's veranda playing gospel recordings for a crowd of children who beg for "just one more."

Other members of the staff are Marietta, the curly-headed dentist who, like the other girls, often doubles as nurse; Juan the jack-of-all-trades; and Dr. William McAnlis, a Presbyterian fraternal worker who is the doctor and director of the team.

It is a hectic schedule the group keeps during itineration in rural sections of the island; clinic, teaching, pastoral calling, and distributing literature during the day, films and worship in the evening. After a week in one village, the team moves on, carrying its equipment, food, and medicine by trailer or, where there are no roads, by boat.

The evening meetings are the clinic's first evangelistic approach to people. Often meetings are held in the open, but when it rains, the team must find a sheltered spot like a cockpit or the town market stalls. In one village the team has the use of a large empty storehouse open on two sides. The evening that the team arrives, the villagers have already gathered, and in five minutes Juan has the generator going and the projector hooked up for a film on malaria or yaws. After the movie the congregation sings gospel hymns and one of the team tells the message of Christ. If there is time, the program ends with filmed portions of *The King of Kings*.

The clinic program has brought fine results. Besides providing medical care for dozens of isolated *barrios,* it has brought a number of people to Christianity.

Then there are the children in the cities. Like every large city, Manila has its slums. In one area near the Ellinwood Bible School there is a huge, war-damaged, concrete tenement. Families have made small apartments in it by building partitions of galvanized iron, old boards, and heavy cardboard. There is no light, no sanitation, no running water. The place is dark and evil-smelling.

In the spring of 1958 fourteen children from this tenement made up the kindergarten at Ellinwood Bible School. On the opening day they nearly went wild. They had never possessed toys of their own, so they ran from one plaything to another, fighting over them but never playing long with one toy before another caught their attention. After that first day a student teacher said, "To be a kindergarten teacher you have to be like the wheels in Ezekiel's prophecy, with eyes on all sides."

Not many days passed, though, before the youngsters learned to play together, to sit fairly still during conversation periods, to enjoy the rest period and noonday lunch.

The slum children presented special problems. The five-year-olds sometimes startled teachers by discussing whether or not they wanted to be drunkards when they grew up or by relating the latest episodes at a nearby cabaret (named the Sputnik Club!) where vice flourished in all its forms.

The results of good teaching began to show by the end of the school. Parents came with reports of better discipline at home, and some were amazed when their children insisted on prayer before meals or on wearing clean clothes. One tiny girl always insisted on dressing and acting like a boy. It was a real triumph when she came to school one morning in a starched dress and headed for the dolls. "At last we have a girl," said her grateful father.

The kindergarten is designed as a three-month laboratory course where seniors gain experience in teaching, curriculum writing, and developing equipment, and is part of the field work required during the three-year course at Ellinwood. It goes hand in hand with the curriculum of Bible, administration, home nursing, Church history, and teaching methods, which prepares young Filipinas to become deaconesses (Directors of Christian Education) in the United Church of Christ. Deaconesses perform valuable tasks in the churches they serve, and many small congregations are kept alive by these faithful, well-trained women.*

✤

PABLO HELPS WITH THE WRITING
Mabel Niedermeyer

PABLO sat in the shade beneath his house-on-stilts in the Philippines. How he wished he could help with the writing of the Book! But he was only a boy, and the Señor Missionary had asked for men to do the writing.

Pablo could remember clearly the words that the missionary had spoken in chapel the evening before. "This Book, the Bible, is written in many languages. It can be written in the words you speak, too, if some of you will help me with the writing. I shall need men who can teach me your words. With their help I shall change the English words into your words. Thus we shall do the writing together."

Pablo thought of his older brother, José, who was already grown.

"If I were a man like José, then I could help," he said to himself.

A man like José! That thought gave Pablo an idea. Quickly he jumped and ran off in search of his brother.

He found him cutting bamboo to build a new ladder to their home. "José," he said, "if you want to help with the writing, I could do your work for you."

"What writing?" José asked.

"The writing that the Señor Missionary told us about last night," Pablo explained. "He wants men to help him. I am not a man. I am only a boy.

* From *Current News* (The Philippines: Autumn 1958 and Winter 1958). Used by permission of the Commission on Ecumenical Mission and Relations of the United Presbyterian Church in the USA.

Could not a boy help to do the work of a man, so the man could do the writing?"

"That is well said," José said kindly. "But the work I do is a man's work and not for a boy like you, Pablo. Soon there will be the planting of the rice—"

"Ho, the planting of the rice," Pablo interrupted, standing as straight and tall as he could. "That is nothing more than sticking the small plants in the mud. I have watched the workers and I know how that is done. The planting of the rice, that I can do."

José said more, but Pablo would not let his idea go. Finally José agreed. "But when my work becomes too heavy for you, then my help with the writing must come to an end," he added.

The next day Pablo began doing the tasks of his older brother so José could help the Señor Missionary. He polished the bamboo floor of their home-on-stilts. But Pablo did not think that was work. It was fun to stand on the banana leaves and skate back and forth across the floor. Pablo did not stop until he was sure the bamboo boards shone as they did when José did the polishing.

"I can do this always," he said, as he skated back and forth. "Even when José is not busy with the writing."

Soon after, Pablo went with his mother to the market, helping her carry her load. There under the hot iron roof of the market place, he waited while she sold the woven pieces of cloth and scarves that she had made. No other pieces seemed quite as fine to Pablo as those that had been made by his own mother.

Then came the time for the planting of rice. Early one morning Pablo went with the other workers to the field. Each time he bent down, he stuck a rice plant in the mud. Each time he stood up, he took a plant from the bunch in his left hand and held it ready for planting.

Pablo joined in the singing of the other workers as he planted to the rhythm of their song.

> Planting rice is never fun;
> Bent from morn till set of sun.
> Cannot stand, cannot sit,
> Cannot rest for a little bit.*

Pablo thought planting rice was fun when he started. But as the sun climbed higher in the sky, he began to get tired. His broad straw hat protected him from the heat of the sun, but his back ached from constant stooping. Down, up. Down, up. Down, up. Perhaps he had been wrong when he had boasted to José that he could do the planting of the rice. Down, up. Down, up. Down, up. Should he tell his brother that the work was too heavy for him? No, he decided. He would work on until the writing was finished.

One evening toward the end of the rice planting time José said, "A few

* The music for this song may be found in *The Whole World Singing*. New York, Friendship Press, 1950.

more days and our work on one small part of the Book will be finished. Then will come a meeting at the chapel when the writing will be made known."

In the days that followed, Pablo thought much about that meeting. How proud he would be when the people knew that José had helped the Señor Missionary!

At last the day came when the writing was finished. The people in the village met together in the chapel as José had said. It seemed to Pablo that the singing had never been quite so beautiful before. "It is a song of gladness," he thought, "because part of the Book is written in our language."

After the singing, the Señor Missionary showed the part of the Book that had been written. Slowly and clearly he read from it so that all could understand. Then he spoke.

"We have come tonight because a part of a great work is finished. A part of the Bible has been written in your language. The words that I have read tonight are from this new writing. It has been done with the help of men among us. Fidel Miguel, Juan Rodríguez, and José Martínez have met with me day after day to give help in this work."

The Señor Missionary paused a moment and looked at the people before he went on.

"There has been another who helped," he said. "He is Pablo, the younger brother of José. Each day since the work began, Pablo has done many of the tasks of his older brother. Thus José was free to work with us. To Pablo, too, go our thanks that this work has been done."

Another hymn was begun, and Pablo sang as he never had before. He forgot the long days of bending over the rice plants. In his heart was a great happiness. He, too, had helped with the writing.*

✠

O ZION, HASTE, THY MISSION HIGH FULFILLING

THIS missionary hymn is a real favorite among Christians in the Philippines. The words were written by Mary Ann (Faulkner) Thomson (1834-1923), whose father was an Anglican priest. When she came to America as the bride of John Thomson, librarian of the Philadelphia Free Library, she became a member of the Episcopal Church of the Annunciation. She was the author of more than forty hymns, but only this one has survived in most modern hymnals.

The message of this hymn is addressed to the Church under the fanciful name of Zion, the name applied to Jerusalem in II Samuel 5:7. By a Christian metaphor the term came to represent the church on earth (Heb. 12:22), eventuating in the New Jerusalem in heaven (Rev. 21:2). Every verse of the hymn proclaims that God is Light and Love and that every

* From *My Story Book about the Bible* by Mabel Niedermeyer. Reprinted in *Missionary Stories to Play and Tell*, edited by Nina Millen. Copyright 1958 by Friendship Press. Used by permission of the publisher.

O Zion, Haste, Thy Mission High Fulfilling

TIDINGS. 11. 10. 11. 10. with Refrain

MARY A. THOMSON, 1834–1923
With spirit and dignity

JAMES WALCH, 1837–1901

1. O Zi - on, haste, thy mis- sion high ful - fill - ing, To tell to all the
2. Pro - claim to ev - ery peo-ple, tongue, and na- tion That God, in whom they
3. Give of thy sons to bear the mes-sage glo - rious; Give of thy wealth to

world that God is Light, That He who made all na - tions is not will - ing
live and move, is Love; Tell how He stooped to save His lost cre - a - tion,
speed them on their way; Pour out thy soul for them in prayer vic - to -rious;

REFRAIN

One soul should per - ish, lost in shades of night.
And died on earth that man might live a - bove. Pub - lish glad tid - ings;
O Zi - on, haste to bring the bright-er day.

Tid -ings of peace; Tid-ings of Je - sus, Re-demption and re-lease. A-MEN.

Christian should strive to carry His Word to the whole world.

The tune to which this hymn is usually sung is "Tidings," composed by James Walch (1837-1901) an English organist and composer.

Two of the original verses have been omitted from the music score that appears on p. 800. These, the second and fifth, are:

> Behold how many thousand still are lying
> Bound in the darksome prison house of sin,
> With none to tell them of the Saviour's dying,
> Or of the life He died for them to win.

> He comes again: O Zion, ere thou meet Him,
> Make known to every heart His saving grace;
> Let none whom He has ransomed fail to greet Him,
> Through thy neglect, unfit to see His face.

In Christ There Is No East or West

ST. PETER. C. M.

JOHN OXENHAM, d. 1941
In moderate time

ALEXANDER R. REINAGLE, 1799-1877

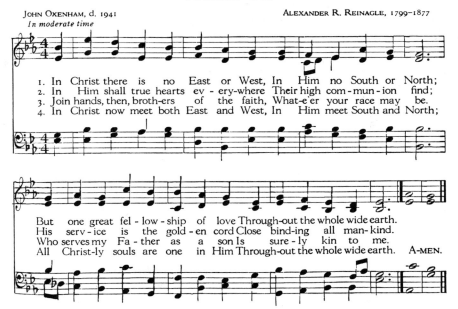

1. In Christ there is no East or West, In Him no South or North;
2. In Him shall true hearts ev - ery-where Their high com - mun - ion find;
3. Join hands, then, broth-ers of the faith, What-e'er your race may be.
4. In Christ now meet both East and West, In Him meet South and North;

But one great fel - low-ship of love Through-out the whole wide earth.
His serv - ice is the gold - en cord Close bind-ing all man-kind.
Who serves my Fa - ther as a son Is sure - ly kin to me.
All Christ-ly souls are one in Him Through-out the whole wide earth. A-MEN.

IN CHRIST THERE IS NO EAST OR WEST

RUDYARD KIPLING wrote:

Oh, East is East and West is West, and never the twain shall meet, Till Earth and Sky stand presently at God's great Judgment Seat.

Another British poet wrote: "In Christ there is no East or West." As inventions of various sorts succeed in lessening physical distances, there must also come a corresponding lessening of spiritual distances if "peace on earth, and good will toward men" is ever to be fully realized.

John Oxenham, who passed away during World War II, is the author of this sublime and prophetic hymn of the new day yet to come. Mr. Oxenham, whose real name was William Arthur Dunkerley, received his education at Victoria University in Manchester, England, and then entered business, traveling extensively, and living at various times in France, the United States, and Canada. The British *Who's Who* indicates that he took up writing as "an alleviation and alternative from business and found it much more enjoyable, so he dropped business and stuck to writing."

One of his best-known poems is titled "In Christ There Is No East or West." It comes from *Pageant of Darkness and Light,* which was widely produced throughout England and the United States during the years from 1908 to 1914. John Oxenham wrote the entire text, which includes many exquisite lines.

The melody "St. Peter" to which Oxenham's words are ordinarily sung was composed by Alexander A. Reinagle (1799-1877) for Psalm 118. It was named for the church in Oxford where the composer was the organist for thirty-one years.*

* Arranged from *Lyric Religion* by H. Augustine Smith, pp. 170-74. Copyright 1931 by H. Augustine Smith. Published by Fleming H. Revell Company. Used by permission of the publisher.

CONTENTS

PART VI SECTION 5

THE CHURCH OF CHRIST IN INDIA

✝

John to the seven churches which are in Asia: Grace be unto you, and peace, from him which is, and which was, and which is to come; and from the seven Spirits which are before his throne.—REVELATION 1:4

✝

PICTURES: PAGE
Interpretation: "I Will Come Again"—*Thomas* 804
Picture: "I Will Come Again"—*Thomas* 805
Interpretation: Anglican Cathedral, Dornakal 806
Picture: Anglican Cathedral, Dornakal 807
Interpretation: Chapel of Women's Christian College, Madras—*Dunn* 806
Picture: Chapel of Women's Christian College, Madras—*Dunn* 809

POETRY:
The Cross Is Lifted—*Devanesen* 808
From This Day On—*Tilak* 810
Christ of the Indian Road—*Devanesen* 811
The Guardian—*Goreh* 812
Hedges—*Devanesen* 813
India—*Oxenham* 813
Thy Yoke—*Devanesen* 814
Prayer—*Tilak* 814
Discovery—*Devanesen* 815
Adoration—*Pillai* 815

STORIES:
Village Life in Rural India—*Bryce* 815
Lines to a Rickshaw Puller (A Poetic Story)—*Devanesen* 819
The Ministry of Health and Healing—*Bryce* 821

MUSIC:
Interpretation: Light Thou the Lamp *(Jiwan Deep Jalao)*—*Masih* 823
Music: Light Thou the Lamp *(Jiwan Deep Jalao)*—*Masih* 824
Interpretation: Listen to Our Prayer *(Binti Hamari)*—*Indian Folk Song* .. 825
Music: Listen to Our Prayer *(Binti Hamari)*—*Indian Folk Song* 826

"I WILL COME AGAIN"

Alfred David Thomas

THIS beautiful water color (p. 805) is by the contemporary Indian artist, Alfred David Thomas, and comes to us from Madras.

Jesus had promised His disciples that He would come again. "It is expedient for you that I go away: for if I go not away, the Comforter will not come unto you; but if I depart, I will send him unto you" (John 16:7).

Occasionally you hear people bemoaning the fact that Jesus is no longer visible to the human eye. Yet we know that when He was present in the flesh, He was bound as we are bound. When He was in Nazareth, He could not be in Bethany at the same time; and when He was in Galilee, He could not be in Jerusalem. Even after His Resurrection He was limited, although not to so great a degree.

We may never know all that transpired during the forty days after His Resurrection, during which He frequently reappeared to men; but we do know that what He said and did opened the eyes of His followers to receive His truth in a larger and fuller way than ever before. He became, not only a Risen Saviour, but the Almighty, the all-powerful Son of God, to whom the lives of His followers were dedicated in service throughout all time.

Mr. Thomas' painting shows Jesus standing on the rim of a sphere, His right hand raised in blessing and in His left a shepherd's crook. Around Him is the host of ministering angels to which He had often referred during His earthly ministry, and who had come to escort Him in glory to His heavenly home.

He looks down toward the group of His followers who are watching Him depart. His disciples asked the question recorded in Acts 1:6: "Lord, wilt thou at this time restore the kingdom of Israel?" Jesus replied: "It is not for you to know the times or the seasons, which the Father hath put in his own power. But ye shall receive power, after that the Holy Spirit is come upon you: and ye shall be witnesses unto me both in Jerusalem, and in all Judea, and in Samaria, and unto the uttermost part of the earth." They were not to expect His reappearance, but to await the coming of the Holy Spirit, which was to guide them into all the fullness of truth.

We need to be reminded that it is by the power of an ascended Christ that the Holy Spirit receives the word that is spoken and the song that is sung and causes the plans for the kingdom made by His followers to come to pass. The frail human effort that we, His followers make, and its effect on the hearts and consciences of people everywhere—these are the evidences of His Holy Spirit motivating the hearts and lives of men and women in all lands.*

* Used by special permission of the Abbott Book Library of Art.

"I WILL COME AGAIN"—*THOMAS*

ANGLICAN CATHEDRAL, DORNAKAL

"BISHOP AZARIAH of Dornakal, the first Indian bishop, believes the Church of India, Burma, and Ceylon should aspire to give a characteristically Indian flavor to the common faith. He desires that the permanently valuable elements in Indian culture should 'be consecrated to the service and worship of the Padma-feet of our Saviour Christ.'

"Ceremonial bathing before worship is common in India and facilities for this are generally provided outside mosques and temples. In India, therefore, washing as a symbol of purification is traditional and understood. Hence this symbolism has been adopted by at least a few churches, which have provided pools near their entrances.

"Moslems and Hindus take off their sandals before entering their mosques and temples as a symbol of reverence. This practice is continued by Christians in many country churches."*

It was the late Bishop Azariah who was sent from Tirunelveli to start work in the Dornakal area, and the Anglican Cathedral at Dornakal (p. 807) stands as a memorial to his great efforts. The structure is different from most church buildings, since it incorporates many distinctly Indian features. The twin domes and minarets suggest the Moslem type of architecture. The supporting pillars are Dravidian; many of the Christians who worship at this church come from the Dravidian peoples. The walls are also typically Indian, although the rounded chancel and the cross indicate that the cathedral is a Christian one.

Inside the church are more Dravidian pillars, on which are repeated the design of the cross and the lotus, symbolizing to the Hindu the foot of God touching the earth and to the Christian the incarnation. In this way is represented the divine Saviour who brought life out of death and ever lives to communicate that life to others.

✣

CHAPEL OF WOMEN'S CHRISTIAN COLLEGE, MADRAS

THE Women's Christian College in Madras, India, owes its origin and development to the united efforts of twelve missionary societies in Great Britain, Canada, and the United States, and of its sister college in America, Mount Holyoke (Massachusetts). It was founded in 1915, with the object of providing for Indian women the opportunity to obtain on moderate terms a sound Christian education, and has for its motto, "Lighted to lighten." This phrase was chosen by forty-one students of that first year, during their first week at college. Since then more than two thousand women have passed

* Abridged from *Christian Symbols in a World Community* by Daniel J. Fleming, p. 45. Copyright 1940 by Friendship Press. Used by permission of the author and the publisher.

ANGLICAN CATHEDRAL, DORNAKAL

Photo by Korteling, Courtesy National Christian Council of India, Punganur, South India

through its portals, and today there are more than three hundred students annually—Christians, Hindus, Muslims, Sikhs, Jains, Parsees and others from all parts of India, Burma, Ceylon, Malaya, East Africa, and Ethiopia.

For its first thirty-five years, the college was governed by boards in Britain and America, with a local Council in Madras acting under their direction. On March 3, 1952, a very important step was taken when the governing boards transferred to the College Council in India the final authority and control over the Women's Christian College.

This transfer of power brought with it new responsibilities. It is the desire of the Council to maintain the college as a small one and to preserve its traditions. The supporting missions continue to foster interest in the work of the college, but there is still need for continued and increased local and world-wide support.

Slightly more than 60 per cent of the students live in the hostels attached to the college. The staff, composed of women of many nationalities, lives with the students, sharing and enriching all aspects of their college life. This daily contact with mature minds, as well as the system of student government, helps to provide a sense of public responsibility and good citizenship.

The students have always taken a keen interest in the social work which they do in the slum villages nearby. The flourishing little nursery school in one of these villages was founded by college alumnae in memory of Miss McDougall, the first principal. The school now receives an annual grant from the government, but is still chiefly supported by the alumnae.

Religion has been central in the life of the college since its founding. In the beautiful chapel (p. 809) the staff and students gather every day for worship. The architect, Mr. Dunn, has tried to express in the building the Christian as well as the Indian spirit. The chapel's seventeen doors are always open during the day, and seem almost to bring the surrounding gardens inside. Everything in the chapel except the organ is of local material. The walls are of "country brick" (Cuddapah slabs); the great standing cross is of Indian rosewood, and the apse is lighted by a pierced brass hanging lamp. For the regular services woven mats are used instead of chairs.

The chapel was the gift in 1923 of "an unknown American friend," and is always open for meditation. It is a great source of strength and inspiration to the entire college community.*

✧

THE CROSS IS LIFTED

Two thousand years have slipped by
like freshets in the Ganges
since St. Thomas came to our land.
Here, though the cross is lifted

---

* Arranged from *1955 Bulletin of Women's Christian College.* Used by permission of the College.

CHAPEL OF WOMEN'S CHRISTIAN COLLEGE, MADRAS—*DUNN*

amidst the paddy fields and coconut palms
and white-clad Christians flock to the churches
when the bells call them to worship;
our wise men have not yet seen the star
and the manger of Bethlehem
is not yet the cradle of our land.
But Christian hope never dies
and the ends of the strands of destiny
are held safe in the hands of God.

Pass it on to the ends of earth!
Christ is the answer—Ours! Yours!*

—*Chandran Devanesen*

FROM THIS DAY ON

From this day onward Thou art mine,
Brother beloved and King divine,
    From this day on.

My food I'll get in serving Thee;
Thy thoughts shall be as eyes to me.
I'll live and breathe to sing Thy praise
From this time onward all my days.
Thy feet I choose, the world resign,
For Thou, from this day on, art mine,
Brother beloved and King divine!

To Thee I offer child and wife,
My home and all my worldly life;
To Thee this body, too, I bring,
To Thee surrender everything.
My very self henceforth is Thine.
O take it, Lord, for Thou art mine,
Brother beloved and King divine!

My thoughts and words are all of Thee,
Thou—Wisdom, Joy and Liberty.
Now Thee and me no rift can part,
One not in semblance but in heart.
Set free am I, and for me shine
The joys of heaven, since Thou art mine,
Brother beloved and King divine!

From this day onward Thou art mine,
Brother beloved and King divine,
*From this day on.**

—*Narayan Vaman Tilak*

CHRIST OF THE INDIAN ROAD

Have you heard about Him,
O my brothers?
Do you not know about Him,
O my sisters?

He was a carpenter,
the wood yielded to His hands.
His yokes were easy upon the ox's neck,
and sweat was upon His brow.
He called Himself the Son of Man.
He did not despise the *devadasi*.[1]
He cared for the beggar and the dog
that licked the beggar's sores.
He brought sight to the blind
and healed the leper.
He cured the diseased in mind
and gave them new life. . . .

He gives a dream that will not
let a young man sleep.
He gives an adventure that will not
let a young man rest. . . .

He can give you life that is as bread
to your hungry bellies.
Listen to Him, O *babu*,[2] toiling in your office.
He can give you life that is as hours
spent away from your desk. . . .

Listen to Him, O men and women of India,
you and your children.
The hands that are His
will speed the plow through our fields of poverty.
The minds that are His
will create the plan which hums
in the roar of the city,

* From *Narayan Vaman Tilak* by J. C. Winslow, p. 109. Published in 1923 by Association Press, Calcutta. Used by permission of the publisher.
  1 A harlot; literally, a girl dedicated to the god of the temple.
  2 Gentleman.

which throbs in the rhythm of the *tabla*[3]
beaten in the village.
The hearts that are His
will clear the way and build the
road that is gentle even to crippled feet.
Let Him lead us in the march of Humanity,
to the wonder that awaits,
to the eye-unseen, the ear-unheard Future
that leads over star-track and Beyond!*

—*Chandran Devanesen*

THE GUARDIAN

I lay me down in peace
    Beneath Thy wing,
    And safely sleep.
Thy watch can never cease;
    For Thou, O King,
    My soul dost keep.

For all the tenderness
    Which Thou hast shown
    To me this day:
For strength in feebleness
    To Thee alone
    My thanks I pay.

And if before the morn
    Thou bidst me rise
    And come to Thee,
Then homeward swiftly borne
    Beyond the skies
    My soul shall be.

Or if it be Thy will
    That I should see
    Another day,
Oh, let Thy presence still
    Remain with me
    And be my stay.**

—*Ellen Lakshmi Goreh*

3 A kind of drum.
  * From *The Cross Is Lifted* by Chandran Devanesen, pp. 51-52. Copyright 1954 by Friendship Press. Used by permission of the author and the publisher.
  ** From *Devotees of Christ* by D. S. Batley and A. M. Robinson, pp. 63-64. Published in 1938 by Zenith Press, London. Used by permission of Miss Goreh and the publisher.

HEDGES

When I see a single flower
blooming in lonely splendor
in the midst of a thorny hedge
I stop and gaze at it
in silent admiration.
When I glimpse a truth of God,
a single bloom of wisdom
in a hedgerow of life's perplexities,
I stop and bow my head in silent adoration.

And so I pass
from flower and grass
to the very essence
of His holy Presence.
The hedgerows of earth
are the battlements of heaven.*

—*Chandran Devanesen*

INDIA

A land of lights and shadows intervolved,
A land of blazing sun and blackest night,
A fortress armed, and guarded jealously,
With every portal barred against the Light.

A land in thrall of ancient mystic faiths,
A land of iron creeds and gruesome deeds,
A land of superstition vast and grim,
And all the noisome growths that Darkness breeds.

Like sunny waves upon an iron-bound coast,
The Light beats up against the close-barred doors,
And seeks vain entrance, yet beats on and on,
In hopeful faith which all defeat ignores.

But—time shall come, when, like a swelling tide,
The Word shall leap the barriers, and The Light
Shall sweep the land; and Faith and Love and Hope
Shall win for Christ this stronghold of the Night.**

—*John Oxenham*

* From *The Cross Is Lifted*, p. 28. Copyright 1954 by Friendship Press. Used by permission of the author and publisher.
** From *Bees in Amber* by John Oxenham, p. 73. Used by permission of Miss Erica Oxenham and Methuen Co., Ltd.

THY YOKE

O Lord, Thy yoke is easy
and Thy burden light,
but my neck is obstinate
and my back unbending.
My eyes wander from the paths
in which Thou wouldst direct me
to green grasses of distraction
and tempting leaves of desire.
When Thou dost want me to run
I stumble and fall.
When Thou dost want me to walk
I lie down to chew the cud
of idleness.
O Lord, forgive my stubbornness
and my foolish ways.

Be patient with me
Till I have learned Thy discipline
in the gentle pull of Thy rope
which is my true comfort and freedom.*
                            —*Chandran Devanesen*

PRAYER

Prayer to a heart of lowly love
Opens the gate of heaven above.

Ah, prayer is God's high dwelling place
Wherein His children see His face.

From earth to heaven we build a stair—
The name by which we call it prayer.

Prayer is the gracious Father's knee;
On it the child climbs lovingly.

Love's rain, the Spirit's holy ray,
And tears of joy are theirs who pray.

To walk with God, to feel His kiss,
Yea, prayer, His servant owns, is this.*
                            —*Narayan Vaman Tilak*

* From *The Cross Is Lifted* by Chandran Devanesen, p. 17. Copyright 1954 by Friendship Press. Used by permission of the author and the publisher.
** From *Narayan Vaman Tilak* by J. C. Winslow, p. 105. Published in 1923 by Association Press, Calcutta. Used by permission of the publisher.

DISCOVERY

When a little child
laid its head upon my shoulder
I found Faith. . . .

When a blind man smiled
despite his sightless eyes
I found Hope. . . .

When a wooden cross
bore a broken body upon it
I found Love. . . .*

—*Chandran Devanesen*

ADORATION

O Truth, thou stainless One!
O thou who art wholly Purity!
Spirit in ecstasy
Glowing refulgent Trinity
Whereby shall I thy slave
Attain salvation, set free from sin?
O God, save only thee,
Who then my Comfort, my Guide and Friend?**

—*Krishna Pillai*

✠

VILLAGE LIFE IN RURAL INDIA

L. Winifred Bryce

MOST of the villages [in India] are small, mere hamlets. When a man walks home in the evening with his plow over his shoulder, he does not have a great way to go. There are about seven hundred thousand villages in India, and it is reckoned that if our Lord had begun to visit one every day when He was here in the flesh, He would hardly have made the rounds even yet. Over 85 per cent of the people in India live in villages.

In all the provinces and states of India more than two-thirds of the people are directly employed in agriculture. Among the civilized countries of the world India has the highest proportion of people dependent on agriculture

* From *The Cross Is Lifted* by Chandran Devanesen, p. 8. Copyright 1954 by Friendship Press. Used by permission of the author and the publisher.
** A Tamil hymn (1890) by a learned Hindu Pandit who became a Christian. From *The World at One in Prayer*, edited by Daniel J. Fleming, p. 79. Copyright 1942 by Harper & Brothers. Used by permission of the editor and the publisher.

and the lowest proportion of those employed in industries, trade, and transport.*

The density of the population is always to be taken into consideration when one discusses the pressure on the land. In the United States it is 41 persons to the square mile; in China 200; in Japan, rather more; in India it is 254.

Some of the Indian crops that are of importance in world economy are rice and tea, in which India is second only to China; wheat, in which India equals Canada's production; sugar cane, in which she stands second among the nations; and peanuts, of which she raises half the world's crop.

One of the most important problems in connection with Indian economy is the dependence of agriculture on the monsoons, the seasonal winds that cause the rainfall. The rain for most of India comes with the southwest monsoon winds, which blow from May to September. In every five-year cycle there is usually one year of good rains, one of scanty or no rain, and three that have been described as "middling." It is therefore necessary for science to devise ways of meeting the vagaries of the monsoons.

One of the greatest triumphs has been the creation of the largest system of irrigation in the world. Irrigation has, of course, been known in India from time immemorial. Most of the supply of water came from wells, which are still extremely important. There were also constructed what are known as tanks, i.e., reservoirs with high sides or embankments of earth or of masonry in which rain water is stored; they are most common in Madras. In South India, too, is found the Grand Anicut Dam, which for sixteen centuries has been holding back the waters of the Cauvery River. In recent years the skill of modern engineering has harnessed the larger rivers of India and turned water into canals, which have literally made the wilderness blossom.

Over fifty-five million acres in India, or about 26 per cent of the cultivated area of the country, are now watered by government works. The crops that result are valued at more than four million dollars a year. The system was inaugurated with British capital and engineering skill, but is now maintained and owned by India. There are moderate charges for the use of water, and the net profit of 5.71 per cent on the capital contributes forty-eight million dollars a year to the budget of the government of India. It is an example of successful public ownership.

Some very important schemes are under consideration to bring under cultivation an additional 170,000,000 acres, but whether it can be done economically has yet to be demonstrated. The need of making available more arable land may be seen from the fact that the number of cultivated acres per cultivator varies from 12.2 per cent in Bombay Presidency to 2.5 per cent in the United Provinces.

One cause of poverty is soil erosion. There are several causes for the erosion that is taking place. The first is common to many countries, viz., the destruction

* *Indian Economics, a Comprehensive and Critical Survey* by Jathar and Beri. Bombay, Oxford University Press, 7th ed., 1942. The statistics included here are based on findings of the census and on Indian authorities.

of forests in the hills and mountains. This the forestry service is trying to check. Another cause is excessive grazing by the large numbers of useless cattle, and a third, unwise methods of cultivation. Soil erosion is one remediable cause of large-scale poverty.

Like a chain about all progress in India is the prevalence of debt. The Debt Conciliation Boards are making a worth-while contribution in giving the creditor his just due, but no more. Credit societies have done much to extricate men from the burden of debt, and the habit of banking thus acquired is teaching men to use their money productively instead of spending it on useless social ceremonies, such as lavish wedding or funeral feasts. It also brings into circulation hoards that are lying unused.

Other forms of co-operation such as producers' and consumers' societies are being recognized as extremely valuable, and are sponsored by the Indian Federation of Labor and other influential groups.

It may perhaps not be realized that there is in India a complete organization for bringing the results of the application of science into the village. At one end of the scale are the agricultural colleges and research institutes—at the other thousands of village demonstration plots where the effect of improved seed, methods, implements, and manures is shown under the cultivator's own conditions. Intermediate links in this chain are the experimental farms, where scientific research is translated into field practice, demonstration and seed farms and seed stores. As in America, not all this knowledge is used, but it is available to be appropriated in India as in the United States and Canada.

While rejoicing over the contribution of science, we may well remember the words of Tagore: "Village life is a whole life. The development of scientific technique by itself will not build a new village India. The spirit must be lifted and formed." To which the Christian's comment is: "The spirit of man is the candle of the Lord."

Perhaps the most outstanding [characteristic of the Indian peasant] is his capacity to win the admiration and liking of all who come to know him, even foreigners. The peasant is no fool. He often has good ways of doing things, though he can seldom, if ever, give you the reason. That he has not succumbed long ago to all his adverse circumstances shows that he is possessed of remarkable stamina.

He has extraordinary dignity. His clothing may be threadbare or scanty, his house may seem little better than a hut, his fare may be meager, but when he offers you hospitality, be it simply a cup of milk, he has the dignity of a prince, and the chances are that he will have more *savoir faire* than you will!

He is deeply devout and quite natural and direct in his approach to the manifestations of God as he has seen them. The songs he sings at his plow, or his wife sings at her spinning, reflect the nearness of the divine in everyday life. Music is part of his nature and makes a strong appeal to him.

More and more the Indian peasant finds in the Church an understanding and consecration of his folk ways. Witness the blessing of fields and gardens as it takes place in a Methodist circuit: "At the first village they were about to plant rice. The village basket maker gave us a cross of split bamboo to place in the corner of the field which was dedicated as a contribution to the church. When the paddy was put in my hand by the owner of the field, I very naturally broadcast the seed in the manner of ancient usage. This was done before the cross was put in place. It is a ceremonial that comes of the villager's sense of the mysteriousness of things."

Illiteracy is, surely, one of the greatest handicaps of the Indian peasant. The bulletins issued by the agricultural department of the government, the accounts of the moneylender, the market quotations that are issued in centers of agricultural marketing, the general news of the day that shows how world conditions may influence cash crops, information on the care of cattle—all these helps are available in India; but they are beyond the reach of the illiterate farmer. Literacy campaigns are now making progress, and Christian farmers in particular like to learn to read. The farmer, however, even when illiterate is a man of common sense. He likes to be shown rather than to be told, and agricultural fairs and demonstrations usually meet with a ready response.

The Christian Church realizes that not only is there need of economic salvation but it offers a message of hope and practical work to show the wholeness and the fullness of life that God wants His children to have.

In South India, in the Vikarabad district of the Deccan, is an area that has achieved conspicuous success through village centers. Preaching, teaching, and healing are here combined by the Methodist leaders in one work unit, which is of course strategically situated to be the center for a wide ministry to neighboring villages. The buildings are in keeping with their surroundings, but when the pastor's house has windows that give sufficient light and air, and screens on doors and windows, the villagers study such a house with great interest. Add to it a smokeless kitchen and simple but adequate sanitary arrangements and you have a situation that commands both attention and respect.

In the school, which is part of the center, classes are held in the daytime for the children and at night for adults. It is the teacher who is the spearhead for personal and community cleanliness. Indian people have a high standard of personal cleanliness where they have the means to practice it; but it is not always easy for poor people to get water for bathing, and soap is a real luxury.

The dispenser of medicines and first aid, or the health nurse, is also an important part of the program of work. The women are taught how to care for their babies, and all the physical suffering that is so characteristic of village life is prevented as far as posisble, and cured in many other cases.

The heart of the life of the village center lies in its worship service. One end of the open courtyard has walls on three sides and is used as a chancel. On the back there is a cross made of iron spoons inserted into the wall. The women of the village appreciate the honor of providing the oil whereby these spoons are turned into lamps, and the lovely lighted cross makes a strong appeal. A visitor describes an evening service: "There was evening worship in a village twenty miles from a railway. One hundred and fifty people sat in straight rows (on the floor) facing a lighted cross. The singing was made more vivid by homemade cymbals and village drums. The sermon was listened to attentively throughout. These village people are a worshiping people."

There is another type of village that is found in a number of places in India. It is a settlement of Christians who have had the opportunity to acquire land and live together in a Christian colony. One such village in the far south is called Nazareth. One in the north, in the Punjab, is called Bethlehem. It is the latter that we shall briefly describe, partly because the presiding genius of the place is a remarkable woman, Miss Komolini Sircar.

When one of the great canals began to irrigate some of the hitherto unproductive land of the Punjab, new settlers were invited to colonize the area. In 1916 space was offered to Christians who wished to take up land and farm, and the district Montgomery was selected.

To establish a village of their own instead of being a small minority in a non-Christian village was a new and challenging adventure. The pioneers set to work to build their sturdy mud-walled homes, and then joined together to construct a humble church with their own money and their own hands. They chose their headman and their Committee of Five, and the village of Bethlehem was constituted.

An important event occurred in 1931 when the charming and gifted vice-principal of Kinnaird College, Lahore, Miss Komolini Sircar, resigned her position and became a missionary of the National Missionary Society. She went to live in Bethlehem, and within two years of her coming it was a transformed village. The secret of her success has been to awaken in others a sense of responsibility and power, so that Bethlehem has been spoken of as an example of what self-help can achieve. Bethlehem, like Miss Sircar, is radiantly happy.*

✠

LINES TO A RICKSHAW PULLER

(A Poetic Story)

Chandran Devanesen

I pass you every morning
on my way to the station.
The light is raw and the wind is keen.
All around you the city is stretching its limbs
and wiping the sleep from its eyes.
The raucous voice of the crow is everywhere.
But you hear nothing, you see nothing.
You lie curled up in your rickshaw
with sprawling limbs and inert body
like some tired animal.

* Abridged from *India at the Threshold* by L. Winifred Bryce, pp. 24-35. Copyright 1946 by Friendship Press. Used by permission of the publisher.

Some mother must have cradled you
pressing you against the soft comfort
of her warm breasts.
But now you shape your body
to fit the wooden embrace
of the hard sides of your rickshaw
for its walls are your home, your rented home.
Your intimacy with it is very great.
Your worldly possessions are in the box
under the seat with its torn fibre cushion
keeping company with your oil lamps,
the battered old *topee*[1]
you wear on rainy days,
and a few *beedis*.[2]
The shafts are worn smooth
by the contact of your forearms.
The rickshaw and you—
you belong together.
I have passed you by at other times—
when you were not asleep
and something of your life
has trailed after me.
I remember the laughter of your fellows
as you twitted the grain seller
who sits by the rickshaw stand
until the old hag exposed her gums
in a toothless grin. . . .
I have watched you fight with your creditors
with the ferocity of a trapped beast
over pitiful sums, the price of a packet of fags
I have heard you whine for a fare
when the day's earnings were poor.
I have seen you resentful and bitter
when you spat on the ground
and talked unconscious communism.
I pass you by like a hundred others
who also pass you by—
and the road may be the road
from Jerusalem to Jericho for all we know.
I would like to put my hand on your shoulder
and say to you, "Comrade,
There is One who died for us
and dying made of us blood brothers."
But I am filled with the cowardice of the well-dressed—
for clothes are by no means flimsy
when it comes to erecting barriers
between man and man.

1 Hat.
2 Cheap Indian cigars.

I am afraid you will wake with a start
and betray resentment in your eyes
as you see in me what I really am—
your well-dressed enemy.
And then you will acknowledge defeat
and put on your mask of patient stupidity.
You will jump up and dust the seat
and grin and point to it with a flourish of your hand.
You will want us to sell our brotherhood
for eight *annas*.[3]

Day after day I pass you by,
you the man by the roadside
and I the priest and the Levite rolled in one,
passing you by. [*]

✤

THE MINISTRY OF HEALTH AND HEALING
L. Winifred Bryce

IN 1918 a group of mission boards of Great Britain and North America united
to establish a Woman's Medical College at Vellore [in South India] with
Dr. Ida Scudder as principal. After twenty-five years of splendid service,
during which several hundred Christian women were prepared for medical
service, the college accepted the invitation of the Christian Medical Association
of India, Burma, and Ceylon to serve as the nucleus of an institution for the
training of both men and women, which should be the one Christian medical
college of full university grade in all India. The story of the achievements that
have been, and are still, taking place, is a moving one.

There has been nothing more inspiring in this effort than to see the way in
which Indian Christian medical men and women have rallied to its support.
Because they have set service in the forefront of their profession few of them
have what might be called lucrative practices, but they have come forward with
gifts of one to four months' salary. The rank and file membership of the
church has also participated in a most heartening way. For example, three
widows from the state of Manipur, which the Japanese invaded, sent two
rupees each as a thank offering for restored sight, which for women in their
circumstances was a very generous gift.

Dr. Hilda Lazarus, a Christian Indian doctor of high qualifications and ex-
perience in medical education, was asked to accept the principalship of this
Medical College. She was principal of the Government Medical College for
Women at Delhi (The Lady Hardinge College) and has since been serving as

---

[3] Coins worth about 1⅓ cents in American currency.

[*] From *The Cross Is Lifted* by Chandran Devanesen, pp. 46-48. Copyright 1954 by Friendship Press. Used
by permission of the author and publisher.

chief medical officer of the Women's Medical Service with the rank of lieu-
tenant-colonel. She could not be released until after the war, but expressed her
willingness then to serve the college at Vellore in any capacity.

Vellore is planning some important advances. One is a hospital for nervous
diseases. The Christian forces in India have hitherto been handicapped in
their desire to bring into service there the skills of psychology and psychiatry
on behalf of mental health. Anyone who has seen a psychiatrist without religious background and training attempting to deal with the phenomena of
religious experience will realize how great is the need. To hear such a one
trying to analyze the working of the grace of God is like seeing a color-blind
man trying to arrange traffic signals.

Another great venture that Vellore is making is in the establishment of a
Chair of Rural Medicine. Nearly all medical problems in India are connected
with rural life, but there has so far been no research on the proposed lines.
Medical authorities in India regard this as a great forward step.

Perhaps it is in the Christian medical work of India that one realizes most
vividly the continuity of the apostolic tradition. The Church in India is deeply
interested in Christian hospitals. Many hospitals now have chapels for prayer,
which are the loveliest that they can erect under the circumstances. The medical
workers have not been content to remain within hospital walls but have gone
out to the loneliest and most neglected areas. The backwaters of Travancore
with their floating dispensaries, the hospital van on rural roads, and the isolated doctor or nurse in a lonely and difficult post are all outreachings of the
love of God expressed by His Church in India.

"They went out and told the good news everywhere, and their Lord worked
with them and endorsed their message with His wonderful deeds."*

The work of America's Dr. Victor Rambo in traveling from village to village in India, establishing "eye camps" and performing scores of cataract operations daily—some days as many as one hundred—is another example of the
medical service of the dedicated work at Vellore. From the mountains of
Nepal to the jungles of Borneo these men and women of medicine are the
unofficial ambassadors of "Peace on earth and good will toward men."

The government of India has given a grant of $45,500 to Vellore for the
development of the radiology department for the treatment of cancer. This
is expected to aid in building a radium ward with twenty women's and eight
men's beds, a radium theater and three private rooms. Other grants from other
agencies, in varying amounts, have been received. One loyal supporter has
contributed five shares of gilt-edged bank stock. This brings her total to thirteen shares which are providing good revenue for Vellore.

An eminent New York doctor has contributed an X-ray machine and all
equipment. A New Jersey doctor offered his basal metabolism machine at
Vellore, which was gratefully received. A Methodist doctor in the West reg-

* Abridged from *India at the Threshold* by L. Winifred Bryce, pp. 117-19. Copyright 1946 by Friendship
Press. Used by permission of the publisher.

ularly assigns the rental of a property to the Vellore program of health and healing. A member of a medical group in the Midwest contributes $300 annually for a complete medical scholarship.

$525 maintains a free bed for a year
$500 trains a nurse with college degree
$ 52 buys a surgical bed
$ 25 provides a streptomycin course
$ 10 removes an eye cataract
$ 4 buys a pint of blood
30¢ provides a day's diet.

All gifts, large and small, are investments in the significant Christian witness and healing work at Vellore. At the present time Dr. John S. Carmen is the director of the Vellore Christian Medical College.

The Christian Medical College at Vellore, South India, is a great teaching and healing enterprise which is officially sponsored and supported by thirty-nine churches, societies, and mission boards in six countries—Australia, Canada, Denmark, India, the United Kingdom, and the United States. These denominations contribute by providing personnel for the staff, capital funds for buildings and equipment and grants for maintenance—all in greatly varying amounts.

In 1956 the institution received $495,952 on the maintenance account, of which 72.2 per cent came from Indian sources—patients' fees, government grants, students' fees, property and endowments, and the Orthodox Syrian Church; while 27.8 per cent came from overseas. The staff is composed of the following:

Doctors:	135 Indians,	26	Westerners
Nurses:	147 "	7	"
Administration:	10 "	4	"
Other employees:	66 "	12	"

There are 671 beds in the main and satellite hospitals—eye hospital, rural infirmary—of which 44 are for private patients. During 1956, 14,456 in-patients and 157,791 out-patients—a total of 172,247 individuals—were treated. These figures include 895 eye operations in village eye camps.*

✣

LIGHT THOU THE LAMP *(JIWAN DEEP JALAO)*

IN 1956 the people of the United States were honored by the visit of an all-India choir of eighteen musical ambassadors, both men and women. They toured the United States for six months, giving a series of thirty-three concerts

* From *Vellore News,* Vellore, South India (Spring-Summer 1957). Used by permission of the publisher.

Jiwan Deep Jalao
Light Thou the Lamp*

M. Masih

Jee - va-na dee-pa ja-la-o.
Light_Thou the lamp_ of my life;_

Jee - va-na dee-pa ja-la Pra-bhu jee
Light Thou the lamp of my life, O Sa-vior

me - re,
most _ ho - - - ly.

FINE

Jee - va na dee-pa ja la - o.
Light_Thou the lamp of my life._

Gho-ra an-dhe ra pa-tha na su -jhe,
Dark is the night and hid-den my path-way.

Sa-ta na-ga-ri -ko pa-un kai-say,
How_ can I find the cit -y of truth?_

Ha-tha pa-kar kar tum hi swa-mi
Hold Thou my hand, O Sa-vior, show me

Pre-ma ki ra-ha dee-ha-o Pra-bhu jee.
Which is the way_ of love, _O_Sa-vior.

*From *Joyful Songs of India*. Copyright 1954 by Cooperative Recreation Service, Inc. Used by permission of the publisher.

THE CHURCH OF CHRIST IN INDIA

in the spring and another series in the fall, singing in three different Indian dialects, Hindustani, Bengali, and Telegu. Their repertoire included folk songs from several different Indian provinces, as well as authentic Christian music of India—the *bhajans* or hymns taken from Indian villages and developed in Christian schools.

This group of Indian young people was known as the Centenary Choir, honoring the close of one hundred years of missionary work in India on the part of the Methodist Church. Many of the young people in this choir doubled as instrumentalists, playing typically Indian instruments: the *sitar,* the *tabla,* the *dilruba* and the flute.

The members of the choir were dressed in their native Indian costumes. The women wore varicolored *saris,* the men fitted coats and tight jodhpur-like trousers. Their leader, the Reverend Victor Sherring, is a native of Mathura, India, who studied music and theology in this country and returned to India to teach and to organize the Centenary Choir.

These young people came from a different world, certainly from a different civilization from that of the United States. Dirt roads, no electricity, no plumbing; cooking usually with a metal brazier on the floor—these are the conditions which prevail in most Indian towns and villages, and 85 per cent of the people in India live in villages.*

On p. 824 you will find the music score and words in both Hindi and English for the hymn, "Light Thou the Lamp," a song of praise to Christ, the Saviour of the world.

✢

LISTEN TO OUR PRAYER *(BINTI HAMARI)*

ONE of the most beautiful things about the Christian religion is the ease with which peoples of many lands, races, and cultural backgrounds sing together the great hymns of the church. Start a song fest among Christian people anywhere in the world, and the first time you begin to sing one of the well-known hymns you will note the universality in everyone's response.

Yet, comparatively speaking, Christianity is one of the newer religions of the world. It is only a little more than nineteen hundred years old; and it has been less than two centuries since what is known as the modern missionary enterprise began. Yet today people of many lands are singing the same Christian hymns, each in his own language. It is only a little more than a hundred years since American Methodist missionaries first translated some of the great Christian hymns into Hindustani so that the people of India could sing the "good news" of Christ's message of love in their own tongue. In a comparatively short time they were singing these hymns with a typically Indian

* Abridged from "Musical Ambassadors from India," *Music Clubs Magazine* (May 1956). Used by permission of the publisher.

accent and rhythm, making them sound different to our ears even when singing the same words that you and I sing.

In Indian music, bars or measures of different length are used, producing some very strange and interesting rhythmic patterns. There are some eight dif-

Binti Hamari
Listen to Our Prayer*

India

Bi - nti ha - ma - ri
Lis - ten to our prayer, — Lord;

Sun le Pra-bhu, Bi - nti za-
Hear our hum-ble plea. Lis-ten to our

Second time to CODA

ra _____ sun bha - g - wan.
prayer, — Lord; Hear our hum-ble plea.

1 GIRLS

Kan la - ga tu ha - ma-ri
Thy gra-cious ear, Lord, turn to us to-

BOYS

or, Sha - nti tu de, ae
day; O— give us peace, O—

D.C.   **2 CODA**   **Fine**

bha - g - wan,   A - min.
give us peace.   A - men.

ferent "Tals" or rhythm patterns in Indian music, and the variation in the rendering of these different patterns constitutes part of the charm of India's music.

Then, too, the accent is different in Indian music than in that of the Western world. In all the different "Tals" the heavy beat or emphasis is always on the first note. It is called the Sum. In the Dadra Tal, which has six beats in two measures, the heavy emphasis is on the first beat and the light, or least, emphasis on the fourth beat; while in the Tintal (the rhythm to which "Listen to Our Prayer" is sung) there are eight beats in two measures, with the heavy accent on the first and the light accent on the fifth. Some hymns have no particular mode or Tal.

The music score of "Listen to Our Prayer," arranged as the Indians would sing it, appears on p. 826. It is written in common or 4/4 time or tempo. The accent falls on the first syllable of the first note in the first measure; since in the Tintal rhythm there is only one accented note for each two measures, this accent is repeated every two measures throughout the hymn. If you arrange to have a group of young people sing this hymn in the Indian manner, it will add a new and unusual feature to your devotional program.

CONTENTS

PART VI SECTION 6

THE CHURCH OF CHRIST IN AFRICA

———————————————————✛———————————————————

And God, which knoweth the hearts, bare them witness, giving them the Holy Ghost, even as he did unto us.—ACTS 15:8

———————————————————✛———————————————————

PICTURES: PAGE
  Interpretation: Christ Falls under the Weight of His Cross—*Norbert* 829
  Picture: Christ Falls under the Weight of His Cross—*Norbert* 831
  Interpretation: The Kimpese Christian Institute, Belgian Congo 829
  Picture: The Kimpese Christian Institute, Belgian Congo 833
  Interpretation: Dr. and Mrs. Royal J. Dye Memorial Church, Belgian Congo 832
  Picture: Dr. and Mrs. Royal J. Dye Memorial Church, Belgian Congo 835

POETRY:
  Africa—*Anonymous* 834
  Bring Us the Light—*Oxenham* 836
  His Presence—*Edwards* 836
  Congo Christmas—*Poole* 837
  Livingstone's Soliloquy—*Oxenham* 838
  A Prayer for the Sacraments—*Pierre* 839
  The Bread of the Sacrament—*Author Unknown* 840
  The Wine of the Sacrament—*Yoane* 840

STORIES:
  The Sacrament of Christian Baptism—*Barron* 841
  "And Ye Shall Be My Witnesses"—*A true story* 842
  A New World Comes to Africa Through the Church—*Yoane* 843
  Every Man in His Own Language—*Nida* 847

MUSIC:
  Interpretation: Our Home (*Bola Bokiso*)—*Ekofo* 849
  Music: Our Home (*Bola Bokiso*)—*Ekofo* 850
  Interpretation: Storm on the Lake (*Bompompo Nda Jibeke*)—*Ekofo* 851
  Music: Storm on the Lake (*Bompompo Nda Jibeke*)—*Ekofo* 853
  Interpretation: Lord, Bless Africa (*Nkosi Sikelel' i Afrika*)—*Sontonga and*
    Mqayi 852
  Music: Lord, Bless Africa (*Nkosi Sikelel' i Afrika*)—*Sontonga* 854

CHRIST FALLS UNDER THE WEIGHT OF HIS CROSS
Nsimba Norbert

IN this sculptured reproduction (p. 831) of Christ falling under the weight of His cross, as He struggled up Calvary's steep hill, we see a truly African concept of that tragic event. The half-closed eyes of the Christ, the inert muscles of His tired body, the spent expression on His face—all speak directly to the human heart.

Nsimba Norbert, an African art student from the St. Luc School of Fine Arts in Léopoldville, in the Belgian Congo, has portrayed for us a Christ whose vitality has been sapped by His midnight betrayal and arrest, the long trying hours before the court of the Sanhedrin in Jerusalem, and the lonely wait in the dungeon into which He was thrown until He could be brought before Pilate for trial on Friday, the day of His Crucifixion.

In this carving, Christ has already fallen under the weight of His humiliating burden. Matthew, Mark, and Luke all tell us that when He was led out to be crucified, the Jews compelled a man from the country, Simon of Cyrene, to carry the cross for Him. Countee Cullen, one of America's greatest Negro poets, in his poem, "Simon the Cyrenian Speaks," gives us in four brief verses his interpretation of this tragic moment in human history. (This poem may be found on p. 402 of the revised and enlarged edition of *Christ and the Fine Arts* by Cynthia Pearl Maus.)

Although this carving represents a beginning in the field of Christian art, anyone who has visited Africa knows of the remarkably beautiful carvings in wood and ivory that these forest people make. They work with painstaking care, portraying with amazing realism and beauty the stately trees with their waving fronds, the animals of the jungle, and the people and events with which they are familiar. They polish their carvings patiently with the dampened leaves of the umbrella tree until they glow like satin.

The African's innate love of beauty is often expressed, but seldom more poignantly than in Mr. Norbert's exquisite work.

✛

THE KIMPESE CHRISTIAN INSTITUTE, BELGIAN CONGO

JUST as Paul and the other apostles found it necessary to supplement the extensive task of preaching by an extensive teaching program, so modern missionaries have found teaching an indispensable and richly rewarding part of their service.

Throughout the years the teacher-evangelist has been the key figure in the growth of both the Church and school in Congoland. Most of the Congo villages are small—a few hundred people at most, with vast stretches of plains, of hills, of forest or swamp or empty grassland between one village and the next. A single mission station may be responsible for the Christian witness in several hundred such villages.

It is these teacher-evangelists who have made it possible for the Congo to approach, even in the first generation, the ideal of a literate church in which every member should be able to read and study the Scriptures for himself. It soon became evident, however, that in addition to the rudimentary teacher-training carried out in the mission stations, higher and better courses were needed for a select few who might be expected to rise to leadership as native pastors, teachers, and supervisors.

One of the earliest central training schools was the Congo-Evangelical Training Institute, now named *École de Pasteurs et d'Instituteurs,* at Kimpese. It was opened in 1903 under the joint sponsorship of the British and American Baptist Missions. The Swedish Mission Covenant became a partner in 1937.

Thomas Lewis and Seymour E. Moon and their wives formed the initial staff, and the school started with seven student families in residence. Even from the outset this school had two characteristic emphases: that the whole family should be trained as a unit, and that the course should include practical skills that would enable the graduates not only to preach and teach, but also to lead the village people in creating better living conditions as well. Mornings were devoted to classes, afternoons to gardening, building, carpentry, and practice-teaching in the children's school. Visitors at the school were sometimes surprised to see the students laying bricks or thatching roofs under the hot afternoon sun instead of sitting in the shade and studying.

In 1912 the staff was reinforced by the addition of Dr. Catherine L. Mabie (who first came to Congo in 1898). From then until her retirement in 1940 she made an extraordinary contribution in the teaching of health and hygiene in terms of village life, and particularly in teaching students' wives better child care, nutrition, and housekeeping. She also wrote and translated many books, and shared her own genius for teaching with generations of students.

A number of other central training schools followed the pattern of Kimpese with local modifications. The Congo Christian Institute at Bolenge was established by the Disciples of Christ in 1928 under the leadership of Herbert Smith. This school devotes much attention to a study of tribal practices prevalent in the area in the light of the Gospel. This school was established by one mission, but certain neighboring missions now send students and help to provide faculty, thus greatly strengthening the work.*

The Kimpese Christian Institute is shown on p. 833, as the student body goes to its morning prayer service. The school is attended predominantly by boys, for the opportunity for women to receive an education is still very limited in the Congo.

* Abridged from *Highways for God in Congo* by George Wayland Carpenter. Published by the Leco Press, Léopoldville. Used by permission of the publisher.

CHRIST FALLS UNDER THE WEIGHT OF HIS CROSS—*NORBERT*

DR. AND MRS. ROYAL J. DYE MEMORIAL CHURCH, BELGIAN CONGO

ON Easter Sunday, 1957, we worshiped for the first time in the beautiful new Dr. and Mrs. Royal J. Dye Memorial Church in Bolenge, Congo-Belge, Africa. This church is the tangible result of the efforts, sacrifices, and prayers of Disciples of Christ "at home"; and those who were there that day wished that it might have been possible to share some of the joy of the occasion with those who were so many miles away.

The first service was in Lingala, and lasted for more than two hours. This new church in Bolenge was designed to seat six hundred persons; actually it will seat nearly a thousand, for in the Congo a church is never too crowded to make room for more.

If you have ever heard a thousand Africans lift their voices in song, you will know that it sounds more like two thousand people singing. What these people lack in training and ability they gladly make up in fervor and volume. Never have I been more thrilled than I was on that Easter morning as their voices rang out in "Christ the Lord Is Risen Today." One could feel the power of their faith, and it was very moving.

I found myself realizing more vividly than ever, "These people really know that Christ the Lord is risen." What a challenge it is to help channel this faith into God's will, and so to help bring about His will throughout the great continent of Africa!

Cynthia Pearl Maus, a noted Disciples of Christ author, who visited the Congo in 1956, gave a huge ebony (ironwood) cross inlaid with ivory and two sevenfold ironwood candlestick holders made by native Congo artists to be placed on the altar of the church. The dedication of that cross was a part of the Easter service, and it was very meaningful, combining the native arts of Africa with the message of Christ's death upon the cross and His glorious Resurrection.

The message that morning was based upon a text from Mark 16, which relates the story of the three women who went early to the tomb seeking Jesus on that first Easter morn. Our African preacher said: "No one told these women to go to the tomb; they went because of the love in their hearts for Him. As they went, they asked themselves, 'How will we roll away the stone from the tomb?' They realized that it was too great for them to roll away. Nevertheless, they proceeded on their way, trusting God to help them, and of course He did. After the women found that the stone was rolled away, they discovered that Christ was risen! He was not there! Then they turned to obey the angel who commanded them, saying, 'Go and tell my disciples that He is not here! He is risen!'"

Our speaker then applied these points to our own lives. We should neither have to be asked or urged to seek Jesus that we might serve Him. If we love Him we will seek Him ourselves. We know that there are always stumbling

Photo by C. Lamote, Courtesy Congo-Evangelical Training Institute, Kimpese, Africa

THE KIMPESE CHRISTIAN INSTITUTE, BELGIAN CONGO

blocks in our way, but we should not hesitate. We should continue in faith as did these three women.

We must also accept the command to go and tell others. If these three women in the Bible story had failed to obey that command, we would not have the gospel in the Congo today. Our speaker went on to say that because some people in America had heard the message, "Christ the Lord is risen," they, too, sought to tell others this good news. He said, "I cannot even imagine the love which the people in America have for their Lord that they would give without counting the cost, thus making it possible for this great church, the symbol of the resurrected Christ, to stand here in Bolenge. It is a witness to all who pass that 'Christ the Lord is risen!' "

Our speaker made us ready and eager to begin with the first village we find without a church or chapel. We feel constrained to build the living symbol of the resurrected Christ into the lives of the people along the "village to village" paths of Congoland.*

The pictures on p. 835 show the Royal J. Dye Memorial Church. The interior view shows the altar, the communion table with its inscription "Lonjofw' Me" (In Remembrance of Me). At the right stands the Reverend Bongalembe, the pastor, and at the left Captain John Inkima, the honored elder of the steamship *Oregon* fame. Behind them stand the ebony cross and the sevenfold candlestick holders against a cardinal-red velvet curtain. It is small wonder that Congo Christians love to linger in and near the church after each service to admire the beauty of Christ's church and its silent witness to the redeeming power of love.

✠

AFRICA

I slept. I dreamed. I seemed to climb a hard,
        ascending track
And just behind me labored one whose face was black.
I pitied him, but hour by hour he gained upon my path.
He stood beside me, stood upright, and then I turned
        in wrath:
"Go back," I cried, "what right have you to stand beside
        me here?"
I paused, struck dumb with fear, for lo! the black man
        was not there—
But Christ stood in his place!
And oh! the pain, the pain, the pain that looked from
        that dear face!

—*Anonymous*

* Abridged from an article by Ruth Peterson, a missionary in the Belgian Congo, which appeared in *World Call* (July-August 1957). Used by permission of the author and the United Christian Missionary Society.

Photos by Charles C. Mills, Courtesy United Christian Missionary Society, Indianapolis

DR. AND MRS. ROYAL J. DYE MEMORIAL CHURCH,
BELGIAN CONGO

BRING US THE LIGHT

I hear a clear voice calling, calling,
Calling out of the night,
O, you who live in the Light of Life,
    Bring us the Light!

We are bound in the chains of darkness,
Our eyes receive no sight,
O, you who have never been bond or blind,
    Bring us the Light!

We live amid turmoil and horror,
Where might is the only right,
O, you to whom life is liberty,
    Bring us the Light!

We stand in the ashes of ruins,
We are ready to fight the fight,
O, you whose feet are firm on the Rock,
    Bring us the Light!

You cannot—you shall not forget us,
Out here in the darkest night,
We are drowning men, we are dying men,
    Bring, O, bring us the Light!*

—*John Oxenham*

HIS PRESENCE

In the swamp-stream or the jungle
    On the path or river fair,
We are conscious of Christ's presence
    For our God is everywhere.

In the blossoms by the wayside,
    In the stately redwood tree—
In the welcome song of brother
    Surely God is everywhere.

What a blessing to be busy
    In His great unbounded plan;
Of peace on earth and good will—
    The world brotherhood of man!

* From *Bees in Amber* by John Oxenham, p. 65. Used by permission of Miss Erica Oxenham and Methuen Co., Ltd.

May this message from the Congo
   Cheer us on as hand in hand
We plant His loving Kingdom
   In the souls of every land.

When in time we come to harvest
   With our friends of every race,
We will sing with glad rejoicing
   In the brightness of His face!*

                      —*Edna V. Edwards*

CONGO CHRISTMAS

The village sleeps, the friendly fires are slumbering,
The night is black, and jungle voices fill the air,
As shadows move, the slinking leopard leaves his lair.
The moon's pale light makes lazy patterns everywhere.
The night hours pass, while fireflies dance then disappear,
The heavy scent of lilies opening fills the air,
               They wait . . .

The dawn bird calls the signal of approaching morn,
In darkness still, the village stirs remembering—
This day is Christmas. In the deep darkness
The people pour from doorways darker still.
Soon carols ring from Chieftain's court and village path
As singers in converging groups draw near the church,
              And soon . . .

Before the dawn's mysterious deep night has gone
The Church's silence is broken by entering forms.
All songs are still, all hearts in silence wait . . .
The break of dawn! It breaks! With the first gleam of light,
As with one voice, the song the angels sang on that first morn
Peals forth again in Congoland on Christmas Day . . .
              Joy to the world!

Outside the Church swift rises Congo's sun
Turning night's silver patterns into shining gold.
Victorious sun, its penetrating light
Quickens the deepest jungle forest into life.
Those who had entered in the darkness, leave the church
In brightest day. The Light of Life is born . . .
             The Son of Righteousness!

---

* Written especially for this anthology by the author, a retired missionary who gave more than thirty years of service in the Congo.

The morning hours pass, then the drums sound again,
The call to come and worship, bringing gifts of love;
For Congo folks pay grateful homage to their King . . .
A woven mat, some fruit or eggs—such homely gifts
That hands have wrought with patient toil are dear to Him
Who came to earth to dwell with men in lowly huts . . .
                    The King of Love!

The day is done, and sunset colors fill the sky,
The evening smoke pours through thatched village roofs
And blazing fires spread cheer around the hearth
Where young and old gather as the night draws nigh.
What matter if the dreaded evil spirits prowl—
They sleep in peace within the Father's care,
                    *On Christmas night!**
                                        —Edna Poole

LIVINGSTONE'S SOLILOQUY

            My heart to-day
Is strangely full of home!
How is it
With the dear ones over there?
            Five years!
            Five long-drawn years!
            And one short moment is enough
            To alter life's complexion for eternity.
            Home! Home! Home!

            How is it with you all
            At home?

And you, my dearest one,
Are ever nearer to me than the rest!
            Your body lies
            Beneath the *baobab*
            In far Shapanga;
But your soul is ever nearest
            When I need you most.
Where a man's treasure is
            His heart is.
And half my heart is buried there with you,
And half works on for Africa.
            Home! Home! Home!

* From *World Call* (December 1951). Used by permission of the author and the United Christian Missionary Society.

Why should such thoughts of home
      Drag at my heart to-day?
      Why should I longer roam?
      Why should I not go home?
Five years of toilsome wanderings
      May claim a rest!

      Nay! God knows best!
      When He sees well
He'll take me home and give me well-earned rest.
      The work is not yet done.
      This land of Night
Is not yet fully opened to the Son
      And His fair Light.
      But—when the work is done—
Ah—then!—how gladly will I go—
      Home! Home! Home!
      To rest.*

                  —John Oxenham

A PRAYER FOR THE SACRAMENTS

Heavenly Father, God of righteousness, purity and beauty,
You have given us the clean garments of Thy Spirit.
On this Lord's Day we come to You with
Hearts and spirits that are clean:
Even so, Father, here in Thy presence, we feel
Sorrow and shame for we know that we call to You
From hearts that are still tinged with evil.

We know that the Blood of our Lord, Jesus Christ,
Cleanses us from bad thoughts and deeds;
And in His name we come to Thee.
Father, if we truly make our hearts pure
We will see Thy face this day and on the morrow;
But if we do not make our hearts pure
We shall not see Thy face at all.

Feel pity toward us, our Heavenly Father,
And cleanse our hearts with the blood of Thy Holy Son,
Who was nailed to the cross
That we might be clean through His sacrifice.
Help us to examine our hearts this day,
Before we drink this cup, and bless us
With Thy blessing in the name of Jesus Christ, our Lord.**
                  Amen.
                  —Mojebo Pierre

* From *Bees in Amber* by John Oxenham, pp. 77-78. Used by permission of Miss Erica Oxenham and Methuen Co., Ltd.
** Used by permission of the author and Congo Christian Institute, Disciples of Christ, Bolenge, Belgian Congo.

THE BREAD OF THE SACRAMENT

Be thoughtful when you touch the bread,
Let it not lie unwanted, uncared for.

So often bread is taken for granted,
Yet there is so much of beauty in bread—
Beauty of the sun and the soil,
Beauty of human toil.
Winds and rains have caressed it,
Christ, Himself, blessed it.

Be prayerful when you touch the bread.
It is a symbol of His body,
Broken for you.

—Author Unknown

THE WINE OF THE SACRAMENT

Be thoughtful when you drink the wine,
Let it not make of you a glutton and a wine-bibber.
Jesus made the fruit of the vine
A symbol of His blood, shed for many
        Unto the remission of sins.

In an upper room on the outskirts of Jerusalem,
On the night of His betrayal and arrest
Jesus sat with the Twelve in His Last Supper.
He took the wine and blessed it, and giving
It to His disciples, He said:
"This is My blood in the new covenant
Drink this in remembrance of Me."

Later, Paul the apostle, urged Christians
To examine their own inner lives, and so to
Partake of the bread and the wine as not to
Eat and drink condemnation to themselves.

Be thankful, and prayerful, therefore
When you drink of the fruit of the vine.
It, too, is a symbol of Christ's blood
Shed on Calvary for you.*

—Wanga Yoane

* Used by permission of the author and Congo Christian Institute, Bolenge.

THE SACRAMENT OF CHRISTIAN BAPTISM

(MATTHEW 3:13-17; LUKE 3:21-22; JOHN 1:29-34)

Jack Barron

IT was a beautiful Sunday morning in early January of 1956. Thirty-two lepers were to be baptized that day. The baptismal service was to be held at six o'clock in the morning in the waters of the Congo River near Bolenge, one of the longest and finest navigable waterways in the world. The sun, partly concealed by clouds, sent spotlight reflections on the surface of the water.

I was the only white man present. Together with three native African ministers we performed this beautiful baptismal sacrament of cleansing. One of the native ministers was, himself, a leper. The thirty-two candidates for Christian baptism stood in a straight line on the river's bank, and entered the water in groups of four at a time. Their friends stood a short distance apart singing some of the best-loved hymns of the native church.

The place of baptism was a spot along the river's shore where the people of the village often came to do their laundry work; and frequently there were small canoes anchored to the shore line when they were not in use, as there were that Sunday morning; for these river-village people make their living by fishing. To the left and close to the bank three women were washing clothes in the blue waters of the Congo. They paused for a few moments from their labor to watch this early sunrise service. In the distant background a canoe containing two fishermen and their grass fishing nets drifted silently down the stream.

When the sacrament of baptism had been completed, the thirty-two lepers lined up on the edge of the river's bank, and, as is the custom in Congoland, the four ministers and many of the laymen marched up the line shaking hands with each one of the candidates and wishing them joy in their Christian life. Some of the newly baptized lepers had no fingers at all, and one of the arms had only half a hand.

As if to add its benediction to the beauty and solemnity of that early morning sacrament, the sun came out of its hiding place behind the clouds, and sent a strong beam of light which fell directly on the thirty-two new Christians standing along the river's bank. You could almost hear the voice of Jesus saying, "Arise, and walk ye in the righteousness of the Son of God. For ye are not your own, ye have been bought with a price: therefore glorify God in your body, and in your spirit, which are God's" (I Cor. 6:19-20).*

* Used by permission of the author, a Christian evangelist for the Congo Christian Institute, Bolenge.

"AND YE SHALL BE MY WITNESSES"

PHILLIP MANGOBE had come back to school. He was taking the short training course given to the teacher-preachers who had not been able to finish their education. For the past two years he had been the teacher-preacher for a village on the banks of the Ubangi River—a village where little progress had been made toward building a Christian community.

One day at recess time, the following conversation was overheard. Said one student, "I had a hard time in my village because there was an old witch doctor that tried to keep the people from coming to hear the words of God."

"Yes," answered Mangobe, "there are many difficult things to do when one is a teacher-preacher in a village. I remember one time when I had to do something that was very, very difficult."

"What was that?" asked one of the others.

"Well, I was busy working in my garden one day, when a boy came running to me and said, 'Teacher-Preacher, they are calling for you to come to the other end of the village.' I asked him why, but he was already hurrying back down the path. So I followed as fast as I could, wondering what it was that they wanted of me.

"Soon I came to where a large crowd of people had gathered. They were talking excitely but in hushed, scared voices. As I approached, a group of the elders turned to me and said: 'We are waiting for you to open that house.' They pointed to a nearby hut and said that a man had died inside. The odor of death was very evident and the people were afraid to touch even the mats that were tied over the door for fear that the 'Death Spirit' might get them too. They had discussed setting fire to the hut, but that, too, was a very awesome and daring challenge to the 'Death Spirit,' and besides they could not forget that there might be some property to share, as the old man had no family.

"The spokesman continued: 'This man here said that he had heard you say that the God whom you worship was stronger than any of the spirits and gods of our village. So we called you to come and open this house for us. If your God is so strong and powerful you do not need to be afraid.'

"Afraid! I was indeed afraid! To break into a house where a dead man was, would be terribly hard. I had never done anything like that! But when I looked around me, I saw that everyone had stopped talking and that they were all looking at me, and waiting. What could I do? That man had heard me declare that the true and living God was the Creator of all, and of course more powerful than any of the witch doctors, or any of the gods of our fathers. In my heart I truly believed that, but still I wasn't sure that I wanted to open that house with the dead man in it.

"Then I remembered that I could pray to God for strength and help in time of need. He was the great Heavenly Father and would hear and help. So in my heart I prayed: 'O Father God of all life, be with me now, strengthen my faith and give me courage to open that door so that I may prove to these people that you are truly the all-powerful Creator of all life and that you would be the Saviour of all men who seek you. Oh, help me to be strong in your power. They are counting on me to act in your name. Help me, O Father-God, help me.'

"Thus while my heart was seeking strength through prayer, I went to the door of the house and tore off the grass mats that were tied over the door. The stench was terrible, but I went inside, found the body, rolled it up in one of the mats and carried it outside. Everyone was still and tensely waiting to see if I would not be struck dead or at least punished in some awful manner by the 'Death Spirit.' When I asked about the burial of the corpse, no one was willing to touch the body of one who had died in such a mysterious manner. So I dug the grave myself and buried him.

"The people relaxed and began talking again. No one made any comments to me, so I returned to my own house and garden. But that was not the end of the story. There were very few in that village who had been baptized as Christians, and there were very few who came to hear the teachings each morning when the drum beat out the call to the services. But the next morning I was astonished and very happy to see a large number of folk coming into our little mud-walled house of God. One said: 'We've decided that we want to worship a God who is stronger than our vengeful spirits.' And now at this village of Bobangi, there are a lot of Christians, and we have built a new brick church with a tin roof."

"That's right," exclaimed one of the listeners. One of our missionaries told us that one of the strongest village churches in the whole area is the Bobangi church, where Phillip Mangobe is the preacher-teacher. In many difficult situations he is one of Christ's "ye are my witnesses."*

✛

A NEW WORLD COMES TO AFRICA THROUGH THE CHURCH
Wanga Yoane

Wanga Yoane is a real person. At present he is the native pastor of the Royal J. Dye Memorial Church at Bolenge, five miles from Coquilhatville, Belgian Congo, Africa (see photographs, p. 835). He does not know how old he is, because he was born before his section of Africa had any written language at all, therefore no record of his birth is available.

He became a freshman in the Congo Christian Institute, Disciples of Christ Christian Mission, when the school opened on November 11, 1932. He was somewhat older than most of the class and had had a much wider experience in many things, but he was there as a student and he did not push himself forward. On his graduation in 1935 he was asked to become a teacher in the Institute.

Wanga is married to Bombundo Louisa, who also taught at the Institute. They have no children, but have taken several orphans into their home and reared them as they would have cared for their very own.

* A true story, translated by Miss Edna Poole, Bolenge, Belgian Congo.

MY childhood was dark with the taboos of my people, many of which had never seen a white man until the missionaries came to our land. They worshiped ghosts, evil spirits, and charms of every kind. The reason why they were not Christians was that during their whole lifetime no teacher of Jesus Christ had ever come to live in their village.

When I first became a teacher in the Congo Christian Institute many visitors came to see me and my wife. Visiting has always been one of the strong ties in our African life. At school, however, we could have visitors only for brief periods, as the opportunity on the school grounds was limited. So I built a brick house out in the village, and in that we could do as our fathers had done before us—visit to our hearts' content.

In our home, visitors always found things strange to them. My wife and I eat our meals together. This is not done in most of the African homes. We read all the books, and especially the Bible, together. I have notebooks and school papers and maps that go with my school work. These maps on the wall were always a source of many new conversations.

One day five men came to our home for a visit. It happened that on this day I was just finishing a map of Palestine in the time of Christ. It was made on white cloth; the provinces were made of different colors and the roads and rivers likewise. As soon as my guests were seated, the oldest one, Bokungu, asked: "Did you make that map?"

"I have just made it," I replied. "It took me nearly a week and I have now hung it up to dry."

"I could never do anything like that," said Bokungu. "It is too hard a work and I am not skillful enough for anything like that."

"Don't forget the proverb of our fathers," I replied. "I am not able never does any work."

Bokungu replied, "I have often said the same thing to my son. Several years ago I went to school. I learned to read and write a little and do some simple sums; but when they began to teach geography and other things, I left school because I was not able to do the work. I think my god does not give me wisdom and therefore does not like me. Your god must like you because you can do so many things."

I said: "Our fathers always thought just as you do now, that each person had his own god or helper. Those thoughts are not correct, however. There is only *one* God. He is the Creator and Father of all men. He loves all men and He gives to each person all the powers he should have.

"When you went to school, if you had put all your heart into your work you most certainly would have been able to do such work as you now see on that map of Palestine. In the Congo Christian Institute, we try first to teach the right truths and attitudes regarding God, and when students get these thoughts correct they find they can do many other things."

There was a buzz among the visitors. It was plain that all did not agree with Bokungu about each man having his own little god. Finally Lyombe gained a hearing and said: "We are amazed at what many of them can do. These boys surprise their own fathers and mothers when they come back to their own villages. We watch them play ball in a way we never dreamed was possible, and we see them cutting grass with long, sharp knives. Their bodies shine in the sunshine and they work and act like giants. They are different, too, in many other ways. They are like people who have a purpose in life. What is it that you teachers do to these students? Do you give them some kind of charm, or some new kind of medicine which brings about so great a change?"

That is what our charmers and witch-doctors want the people to believe. "No," I said, "we do not give our students any charms or medicines to change them. In the hospital you will not find any medicine that will change the heart or mind or disposition. The teachers do one certain thing. They teach them certain truths. We try to give each student new knowledge and new opportunity for a different way of life from what our fathers knew."

Then Efomi, who had been looking hard at the map, and who had hardly been inside even a village school, said: "Is all the world shown on that map?"

"No, it is only a small part of the world."

"Is that so?" Efomi said. "We have heard that in this school you have a picture-like map that shows the whole world. Do you really have anything like that?"

I took out from a drawer the map of the world, and I said: "Behold the map of the whole world!"

Efomi and his friends looked at the map in wonder. I do not think that the map meant much to them. Finally I said: "The large parts of the land are called by different names. We speak of the continents of Africa, Asia, Europe, America and Australia. Then there are, of course, very many parts known as islands."

"What is a continent?" they asked.

"A continent is a very large piece of land, almost or wholly surrounded by water."

"Is there any difference between *continent* and *colony?*" they wanted to know. "These young boys are giving us new words, and we do not know what they mean."

I answered that "A colony might be an island or a part of a continent. It has to do with a piece of land that is ruled by men of another nation. For example, we live in Africa, which is a continent; but we also live in a colony, Congo-Belge. That is, the white men of Belgium rule this part of Africa and call it a colony."

"Now that is beginning to clear up," they said. "We now begin to see the way things are worked out."

I was just getting ready for more explanations when Bokungu said: "Teacher, there have been many things we have not thought about until these boy teachers and those grown-up teachers began to tell us new things. We used to talk about the debts we had, the wives that had run off, the dowry we had paid for those women, and hunting and fishing. Now, we hear new things all the time. For instance that our little village is flat; and if we could see the end of the path that comes into our village at one end and the other end that is lost again in the forest, the land would be mostly flat. These teachers say that the whole world is not that way, but resembles an orange on a very large scale. What do you say about that?"

"That is what we now believe," I said. "Africa has many hills and mountains, but here we live in a flat part of the country which is covered with forest. Now the whole earth has no small end or tip, like the tip of an arrow. It has no end like the farthest end of a village street. Truly the earth is round like the fruit of an orange."

Lyombe took me up and said: "'How do people know that the earth is like the shape of an orange?"

"Long, long ago, most men thought as you did," I explained. "They said that it was not safe to go on long journeys to unknown places. They were afraid they might come to the end or the beginning of the earth and fall off. Look at this orange. You can begin anywhere on that orange, and if you continue to go in the same direction you will come back to the place from which you started. Long ago, after the time of Jesus, men wanted to make long journeys. Some of them never came back. But other people took up the unfinished work. These people proved that if you keep going in the same direction long enough, you will return to the place from which you started.

"In school we read about David Livingstone and Henry M. Stanley. They are two among many who explored large parts of Africa. Livingstone was in parts of Africa now known as Congo-Belge, but our fathers did not see him because he was in the eastern part of this country. Stanley, however, was well known to our fathers. He was the first white man to come down the Congo River. Bofeko, who lives in the village of Bolenge, remembers the first visit of Stanley and other times that he visited these parts of Africa. These men helped to add to the knowledge of the world.

"In our school we teach the subject of geography, and the students not only learn about the surface of the earth, but the different people who live upon it. They learn about the food that grows there and how some of that food is brought to Africa and is now grown in our gardens. We also send many things from Africa to other parts of the world.

"Now our visit is over. I would like both those who are Christian and those who are not to hear a line or two of the Scriptures before you leave our home." I then took my Bible and found the place where Jesus spoke these words to all people everywhere: "Truly, truly, I say unto you, he who believes in me will also do the works that I do; and greater works than these will he do, because I go to my Father." He also said: "I came that they might have life, and have it abundantly."*

---

* Abridged from *Wanga Yoane, the Autobiography of Wanga Himself*, translated by Herbert Smith. Published by the United Christian Missionary Society. Used by permission of the author and the publisher.

EVERY MAN IN HIS OWN LANGUAGE
Eugene A. Nida

"BUT how do you say 'God redeemed us' so that your own Bambara people can understand?" the missionary inquired earnestly, as he endeavored to find out from his West African translation helper how to express in the Bambara language the meaning of "redeem"—that key word of the Scriptures.

"Why—we say 'God took our heads out,' " was the strange reply.

"But how will the people understand that?"

"Oh, that is easy. Perhaps you forget, but tales of the Arab slave raids into the interior live vividly in the memories of our fathers." And then this Bambara man continued to explain about the long lines of lash-driven men and women wearily walking to the coast, each with a heavy iron collar around his neck and with a chain leading from one slave to another. It so happened that at times in the villages through which these lines of condemned slaves passed, a local chief or king might see some friend being led away to slavery, and he would want to redeem him. This he could do if he paid the Arabs enough gold, silver, brass, or ivory. To redeem a friend he would literally "take his head out of the iron collar."

And so today Bambara evangelists, as they tell the people of God's redeeming love in Christ Jesus, explain to the huddled bands around the evening village fire that God saw us in slavery to sin and self, being driven under the lash of Satan, and so He sent His Son to die that men might live. Thus He redeemed us, literally, "He took our heads out." "And furthermore," they explain, "just as in ancient times a redeemed slave felt an obligation to serve for a lifetime the one who had thus redeemed him, so we may be the voluntary slaves of Jesus Christ."

This expression "to redeem," literally, "to take the head out," was born of the bitter experience of slavery, but it has come to be the very vehicle of thought by which men may know the truth of God, who alone can set them free.

Already the Bible or some portions of it have been translated into and published in 1,034 languages. However, there are at least one thousand more languages and dialects in the world which have absolutely nothing of the Word of God. Of course, the speakers of these one thousand languages do not represent large tribes and nations, but their total population is fully equal to that of the United States.

To meet the needs of the one thousand groups without the Scriptures and to provide the Word of God more adequately for those who already have some of it, there are today more missionaries engaged in Bible translating and revision than at any other time in the history of the world.

These missionary pioneers have rarely found a dictionary or grammar of the language which they determined to learn. In fact, in many instances there is not so much as an alphabet. One must simply sit down with natives and

848 — THE CHURCH AND THE FINE ARTS

begin to ask for words—sometimes without so much as being able to say, "What do you call this?" It may take weeks to stumble across this key phrase. At first, one may be forced to sit and stick out one's lower lip and in this way point to objects, for there are several places in the world where pointing with the finger is a very crude, vulgar gesture.

Sounds may give no end of trouble. The natives seem to understand one another perfectly, but the queer things that come out as sounds to be symbolized by an alphabet seem like so many squeals, squeaks, grunts, pops, and hisses, with queer vowels added at the most difficult places.

Some languages have clicklike sounds, where the air pops into the mouth before the following vowel comes out. Almost anyone can say Tsk! Tsk! (in admonishing children) or suck in the air along the sides of the mouth as when driving horses, but in the Bushman and Hottentot languages of South Africa there are twenty different types of these clicks, and all of them become a regular part of the word-making genius of the language.

If sounds were the only trouble, then it would be relatively easy, but some languages have grammars which almost defy description, at least for the beginner.

Some missionaries who have been undaunted in the face of strange and complicated grammars of so-called primitive languages have thought they might have clearer sailing when they came to learning the vocabulary of such "culturally inferior" peoples. But imagine their surprise to find in a language such as Zulu one hundred twenty different words to describe distinct kinds of walking—walking pompously, with a swagger, crouched, in tight clothes—to cite only a few. Or consider the consternation of the missionaries in Madagascar who found that the Malagasy-speaking native distinguishes more than two hundred different kinds of noises and has special words and phrases to differentiate over one hundred different colors.

With all the welter of strange sounds, queer grammatical forms, and myriads of new words, is it any wonder that one poor missionary in Central Africa was so confused that he told the people, "Go sit on a stick," rather than "Enter the kingdom of heaven"? Another missionary in Congo was always talking about John the Baptist "crying" in the wilderness and the prophets of old "crying" out to the people. But his literal translation applied only to the crying of little babies before they were old enough to talk. How utterly incomprehensible his message must have been—for all of God's messengers seemed to be squalling children.

It is one thing to speak of "heaping coals of fire on one's head" if one is talking to an English-speaking congregation; but if one speaks that way in some parts of Africa, he can be badly misunderstood, for that is one method of torture and killing.

Perhaps the gravest errors have come because a well-intentioned translator has simply taken a native's word for the meaning. Only after some time was it discovered that in one language of Liberia the natives were reciting a portion of the Lord's Prayer as "Do not catch us when we sin" rather than "Lead us not into temptation." Because of very inadequate knowledge of the native idiom, early missionaries had not been able to explain the Lord's Prayer—certainly not this phrase—and so the natives simply inserted what would make sense to them. To so many peoples of earth—primitive and "civilized"—sin is not sin unless one is caught.

Even those usages hallowed by time must not go unchallenged. In one language of East Africa missionaries have been saying for more than fifty years, "The Lord be with thy spirit," but they never realized until recently that because of subtle grammatical distinctions this important benediction actually implied, "Yes, the Lord be with *your* spirit, for we don't want Him." When this fact was discovered, the missionaries protested to their native brethren and demanded why they would permit missionaries to go on making such a mistake for so many years. The only reply from the natives was that the missionaries were in the habit of saying a good many strange things, and since the missionaries all agreed in making the mistake, it must have been true, regardless of the strange implications.

The journey into the soul of a language is often confusing because our idioms, which are the signposts of our thoughts, seem to have no counterparts, or at least no ready equivalents. For example, those long, lanky Shilluk natives of the Anglo-Egyptian Sudan speak of a stingy man as "having a big heart" and a generous man as "having a small heart." This seems ridiculous to us, but not to Shilluk natives, who are every bit as well prepared to defend their idiom as we are ours. They argue that a stingy, selfish man is one who has grabbed everything he can and has stored it away in his heart. Therefore, his heart is large. However, the generous man is one who has given away practically all that he has, and therefore his heart is small. This makes perfectly good sense and is fully as adequate as our corresponding idioms. But in the strangeness of much idiomatic metaphors we often become confused, and instead of blaming ourselves we are likely to insist that the natives are the ignoramuses, rather than ourselves.*

✠

OUR HOME (*BOLA BOKISO*)

JOSEPH O. EKOFO composed both the words and music of this hymn in 1943. Young Ekofo had been first attracted to the services of the Church of Christ in the Congo by the singing of the hymns in his own Lonkundo language. Loving music, he soon learned to sing many of these hymns, and so was led to give his heart to the Lord while he was still a young lad.

When he had finished his studies in the mission's primary school, he was sent to the Congo Christian Institute at Bolenge to study and to become a teacher-preacher. During his school days he was active in the

* Abridged from *God's Word in Man's Language* by Eugene A. Nida, pp. 13-19. Copyright 1952 by Harper & Brothers. Used by permission of the publisher.

OUR HOME

(BOLA BOKISO)

J. O. EKOFO

J. O. EKOFO 1943

AS WE GO A-LONG OUR WAY IN THIS WORLD MAY WE NOT STOP AND
A-KEND'I-SO NDA BO-KI-JI BONE TO-KA-NE-LE TE

THINK THAT OUR REAL HOME IS THERE IN HEA-VEN WITH HIM, OUR LORD
BO-LA BO-KI-SO BO-LE NDA LOO-LA E-KA YA-WE,

THAT PEACE-FUL HOME THAT HOME OF GREAT JOY! IN THAT PLACE CROWDS OF
BO-LA WA KU-CI L'OSALO BUKE EKO BANTO BU-

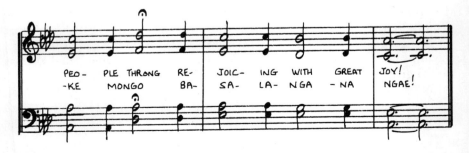

PEO- PLE THRONG RE- JOIC- ING WITH GREAT JOY!
-KE MONGO BA- SA- LA-NGA -NA NGAE!

church choir. After his graduation he was chosen as a teacher in the Institute. A missionary taught him to play the harmonium, and in his spare time he taught hymns to the students.

For several years he directed the choir of the Bolenge church. When he found new hymns in English that appealed to him, he would ask a missionary to tell him its thoughts in his own language. Then he would write the words in Lonkundo to fit the music, learn all the parts, and then teach it to others.

Eventually, sitting at the harmonium, Ekofo composed the melody, harmonized, and wrote the words of several hymns. This one, "Our Home," and the following, "Storm on the Lake," are his compositions. They show the influence of European music, but are nevertheless remarkable as early efforts of a first-generation Congolese Christian with little formal training in music.

The first verse of "Our Home," printed in both English and Lonkundo, appears in the music score on p. 850. The following three verses are printed below:

> How may we reach that lovely home above?
> Just by believing in Him, Jesus Christ,
> Who gave His life for us on the cross.
> He is our Chief for He reigns in heaven.
> He will take all His people there
> All who believe in Him.
>
> Jesus never refuses one who comes;
> He loves all those who truly believe Him
> Through persecutions in all the world,
> Never forsaking His name, no, never.
> He will abide with all His own
> When times of trouble come.
>
> On that day, when we finish our work here
> In this world, then we shall go to that home
> Where the Lord Jesus awaits us all.
> There He will give us the lovely mansions
> Which he did say when here on earth
> He'd go to prepare for us.*

STORM ON THE LAKE (*BOMPOMPO NDA JIBEKE*)
(Interpretation)

AFTER several years of teaching in the Congo Christian Institute at Bolenge, Africa, and one year at the mission school in Coquilhatville, a few miles

* Words and music used by permission of the author and the Congo Christian Institute, Bolenge.

distant, Joseph O. Ekofo, the composer of this hymn and the preceding one, moved to Léopoldville, the capital of the Belgian Congo, where he obtained a good position in a bank. He advanced in his work there, but his primary interest was in the church. He soon became the director of the choir, singing in Lingala, and translated a number of hymns into that language. Some of his choir numbers were recorded and quickly found favor among the Congolese. He became an elder of the church, and was for years its treasurer.

At the end of ten years in the bank's employ, Mr. Ekofo resigned his position and moved his wife and three children to Boende, a district capital, to become the pastor of the Church of Christ there. Although this change required considerable sacrifice for him, the work that he is doing in this growing center presents the kind of challenge that he, as a consecrated Christian, is eager to undertake.

The first verse of his hymn, "Storm on the Lake," is printed in both English and Lonkundo in the music score on p. 853. The following three verses appear below:

> Then the Lord took pity, to the sea He spoke,
> "Peace, be still, oh sea; ye waves and winds, be calm."
> So the storm did cease, the lake became so still.
> Then He said to them, "Oh why are you afraid?
> Is there not a little faith within your hearts,
> Know you not that I am He, the Lord of all?"
>
> But His followers were very sore afraid,
> And they asked each other, "Who can this One be?
> Even the storms and winds and sea obey His voice.
> Surely it is He, the One who was to come,
> Christ the Lord foretold to us in Holy Writ,
> It is He, the Son of God, Immanuel."
>
> And today when trouble comes to all of us
> When the storms and winds do blow around our heads,
> Many difficulties, great temptations, too.
> But if we just call Him, Jesus Christ will come,
> He will take away all trouble from our hearts
> Just as He did calm the waves upon the sea.*

✤

LORD, BLESS AFRICA (*NKOSI SIKELEL' I AFRIKA*)

WHEN the Bantu township of Nancefield or Klipspruit (eleven miles west of Johannesburg) was first settled as a suburb of the Rand Municipality, the late Enoch Sontonga (of the Mpinga clan among the Tembu tribes) was a teacher in one of the Methodist Mission schools. He had a gift for song, and

* Words and music used by permission of the author and the Congo Christian Institute, Bolenge.

STORM ON THE LAKE
(BOMPOMPO NDA JIBEKE.)

J.O. EKOFO   MARK 4:35-41   J.O. EKOFO 1943

ONE FINE DAY ON THE BLUE | LAKE OF GA-LI- LEE, | THERE, THE LORD TOOK HIS DIS-
NDA JI-BE-KE JIMO | JA NGALILAYA, | NKO-LO A-KE-NDA-KI

CI-PLES IN A BOAT. | THEN A VER- Y BIG STORM | CAME AND BLEW SO HARD
L'A-KI-MI BAKAE. | BO-MPOMP' OKUMBAKI | LA BOLO MONGO,

THAT HIS OWN DIS- CI- PLES | WERE SO FULL OF FEAR | THAT THEY CALLED THE CHRIST AND
BA-KI-MI BA-KI LA | BOFOJU BU-KE | BE-TA-KI MASIYA:

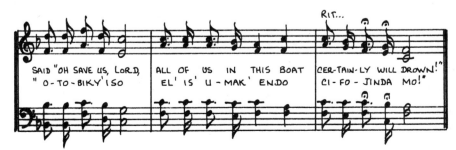

RIT...

SAID "OH SAVE US, LORD, | ALL OF US IN THIS BOAT | CER-TAIN-LY WILL DROWN!"
"O-TO-BIKY'ISO | EL'IS' U-MAK'ENDO | CI-FO-JINDA MO!"

constantly composed words and music for the use of his pupils at public entertainments. He wrote these down by hand in tonic sol-fa, including "Nkosi Sikelel' i Afrika," and eventually collected them into an exercise book, with a view to printing them. This was around the years of the Boer War (1899-1902). But he died before this ambition was realized.

"Nkosi Sikelel' i Afrika" was composed in 1897 and first publicly sung in 1899 at the ordination of the Reverend M. Boweni, a Shangean Methodist minister. The occasion was one of wide joy that a member of one of the more backward African tribes had attained to the honor of being a clergyman. The

Lord, Bless Africa*
Nkosi Sikelel' i Afrika.

ENOCH SONTONGA.

*From *Lovedale Sol-fa Leaflets*, No. 17. Used by permission of Lovedale Press.

composition was inspired by a depressed heart, and the refrain testifies to a somewhat melancholy strain. The black folk around Johannesburg were far from happy. The piece was commonly sung in native day schools and further popularized by the Ohlange Zulu Choir, a choir that visited the Rand giving concerts.

When the African National Congress flourished, its leaders adopted this piece as a closing anthem for their meetings, and this soon became a custom in the other provinces in connection with all types of Bantu organizations. The black races of the Union and the Protectorates by tacit assent adopted it as their recognized national anthem, sung before royalty and on the big public occasions.

Only the first stanza was originally composed by Mr. Sontonga, but S. E. Mqayi has made up seven additional stanzas, of which a free English translation is given here.*

> Lord, bless Africa;
> May her horn rise high up;
> Hear Thou our prayers
> And bless us.
>
> *Chorus*
>
> Descend, O Spirit
> Descend, O Holy Spirit.
>
> Bless our chiefs;
> May they remember their Creator,
> Fear Him and revere Him,
> That He may bless them.   *Chorus*
>
> Bless the public men,
> Bless also the youth
> That they may carry the land with patience
> And that Thou mayst bless them.   *Chorus*
>
> Bless the wives
> And also all young women
> Lift up all the young girls
> And bless them.   *Chorus*
>
> Bless the ministers
> Of all the churches in this land;
> Endue them with Thy spirit
> And bless them.   *Chorus*
>
> Bless agriculture and stock raising;
> Banish all famine and diseases;

* Abridged from *Lovedale Sol-fa Leaflets*, No. 17. Published by Lovedale Press. Used by permission.

Fill the land with good health
And bless it.   *Chorus*

Bless our efforts
Of union and self-uplift,
Of education and mutual understanding
And bless them.   *Chorus*

Lord, bless Africa;
Blot out all its wickedness
And its transgressions and sins,
And bless it.   *Chorus*

CONTENTS

PART VI SECTION 7

THE CHRISTIAN WITNESS IN LATIN AMERICA

---✠---

Ye are my witnesses, saith the Lord, and my servant whom I have chosen.—ISAIAH 43:10

---✠---

PICTURES: PAGE
  Interpretation: Jesus Christ Crucified—*Rebull* 858
  Picture: Jesus Christ Crucified—*Rebull* 859
  Interpretation: Union Evangelical Seminary, Río Piedras (San Juan)—*Díaz* 860
  Picture: Union Evangelical Seminary, Río Piedras (San Juan)—*Díaz* 861
  Interpretation: Christ of the Andes—*Alonso* 862
  Picture: Christ of the Andes—*Alonso* 863

POETRY:
  If You Love God—*Nervo* 864
  I Return—*Báez-Camargo* 865
  Peace Like a River—*Strange* 865
  Purification—*Báez-Camargo* 866
  Word Incarnate—*Strange* 866
  He Says—*Báez-Camargo* 867
  When I Have Food—*Pugh* 867

STORIES:
  A Young Christian Sees America—*Sosa* 868
  Lidia Vargas in Chile—*Lee* 870
  God's Gift to Paquito—*Allstrom* 873

MUSIC:
  Interpretation: O Jesus, I Have Promised (*Jesús, Yo He Prometido*)—*Bode* 876
  Music: O Jesus, I Have Promised (*Jesús, Yo He Prometido*)—*Mann* 877
  Interpretation: Jesus Is My Sovereign King (*Jesús Es Mi Rey Soberano*)—
    Mendoza 877
  Music: Jesus Is My Sovereign King (*Jesús Es Mi Rey Soberano*)—*Mendoza* 878

JESUS CHRIST CRUCIFIED
Santiago Rebull

"JESUS CHRIST CRUCIFIED" is from the brush of the Mexican artist, Santiago Rebull (1828-1902), and hangs in the *Académia de San Carlos* in Mexico City. It is strikingly beautiful in the simplicity of the artist's portrayal of the most dramatic event in the life of the Master Teacher of Galilee.

As we study the expression on the Master's face, we note that His eyes are lifted to the heavens, as though He might be saying to His Heavenly Father, "Into thy hands I commend my spirit" (Luke 23:46). It is a strong body in the prime of young manhood that Rebull has painted for the centuries to gaze upon, for the Master was a man of the out-of-doors, accustomed to hard work, long walks, and tireless days of preaching, teaching, and healing. He had crowded into three or four years more than the average man accomplishes in a lifetime.

His expression is not that of a dreamer only, but of one who has accomplished the task whereunto He was sent and who knows within Himself that He has fulfilled the prophecy: "And I, if I be lifted up from the earth, will draw all men unto me" (John 12:32).

I doubt that even His disciples understood the deep significance of those words at the time. But since then all the world has come to know their deep spiritual meaning. Christ seemed to know in advance that the shepherd must lay down his life for the sheep, that the only way the full-rounded love of God could be shown to man was by the way of the cross; and to that end, difficult and painful as it was, He steadfastly "set His face."

All of His disciples save John the beloved had run away, too scared or too shocked to understand this tragic end to the life of one who, they had supposed, was sent to "redeem Israel." Two or three women and one man only stood near the cross witnessing the end; they could not go away, even though the cause for which Christ had given His life seemed to have ended in disaster.

As yet there was no joy of the Resurrection morn, no coming of His Holy Spirit to comfort them and to bring to their remembrance all that Jesus had said and done.*

> With shudder of despair and loss
> The world's deep heart was wrung,
> As lifted high upon His cross,
> The Lord of Glory hung.
>
> When rocks were rent, and ghostly forms
> Stole forth in street and mart;
> For Calvary and Easter Day

* Arranged from the Abbott Book Library of Art.

JESUS CHRIST CRUCIFIED—*REBULL*

Earth's blackest day, and whitest day,
Were just three days apart.
                    —*Author Unknown*

✠

UNION EVANGELICAL SEMINARY, RÍO PIEDRAS (SAN JUAN)
Horacio Díaz

THE Union Evangelical Seminary in Río Piedras (San Juan), Puerto Rico, is an outgrowth of several earlier institutions. It was preceded by the Presbyterian Puerto Rican Theological Seminary at Mayagüez, the Baptist Grace Conway Institute in Río Piedras, the Methodist Robinson Institute in Hatillo, and the Disciples of Christ Institute in Bayamón. It is governed by a Board of Trustees representing the supporting Boards of Missions. The support comes from the American Baptist Home Missions Society, the Board of Missions of the Congregational-Christian Church, the United Christian Missionary Society (Disciples of Christ), the Board of National Missions of the United Presbyterian Church in the U.S.A., the Department of World Missions of the Evangelical United Brethren Church, and the Board of Missions of the Methodist Church.

The present seminary was founded in 1919 for the purpose of training ministers and directors of religious education for Puerto Rico's growing Protestant evangelical churches, and it has sent out graduates of various denominations to serve Puerto Rico, Cuba, and the Dominican Republic; Venezuela, Colombia, Costa Rica, and San Salvador; and churches in various parts of the United States.

Directly across the street from the seminary is the University of Puerto Rico, one of the largest universities in the western hemisphere. There is no direct relation between the two institutions, but their proximity permits the mutual use and enjoyment of library facilities, lectures, and concerts, to the advantage of both.

The new combined chapel and educational building (p. 861), dedicated on January 12, 1958, was designed by Sr. Horacio Díaz. The front and rear walls of the chapel, which seats ninety people, are of glass; directly behind the communion table is a curved wall paneled in bleached cypress. Also contained in the building are administrative offices, a library with space for over twenty thousand volumes, a dining-lecture hall, a recording room for the preparation of radio programs, and four classrooms.

With its new facilities, this growing institution continues to train Christian leaders not only for the Protestant churches in the beautiful island of Puerto Rico, sometimes called America's "Paradise of the Atlantic," but also for other countries near and far.*

---

* Compiled from information supplied by T. J. Liggett, president of Union Evangelical Seminary.

UNION EVANGELICAL SEMINARY, RÍO PIEDRAS (SAN JUAN)—DÍAZ

CHRIST OF THE ANDES

Mateo Alonso

ONE of the most significant art masterpieces in Latin America is the magnificent bronze statue of *Cristo Redentor* (Christ the Redeemer), which stands high in the majestic Andes on the long boundary line between Argentina and Chile. This world-famous statue is popularly known as "Christ of the Andes," and is surrounded by jagged, snow-covered mountains of great grandeur and beauty. It is a cherished symbol of peace and the brotherhood of man. Although the statue stands at an elevation of over thirteen thousand feet, overlooking the Pan-American Highway, it is overshadowed by Mount Aconcagua ("Rocky Sentinel"), which rises to more than twenty-three thousand feet above sea level.

The words most often evoked in connection with this famous statue are those spoken by the Chilean Bishop San Carlos de Ancud at its dedication: "Sooner shall these mountains crumble into dust than Argentines and Chileans break the peace sworn at the feet of Christ the Redeemer."

This statue (see p. 863) is a gigantic bronze figure of Christ, standing twenty-six feet high. The left hand supports a huge metal cross, while the right hand is raised in benediction over Argentina and Chile. The figure stands on a five-foot granite hemisphere on which the American continents are carved in bold relief in bronze.

The peoples of Chile and Argentina have always had many common bonds, but in 1902 their respective governments were preparing for war because of a boundary dispute. People of the two republics, recalling the encyclical of Pope Leo XIII of November 1, 1900, endeavored to persuade their governments to settle the dispute by arbitration. The encyclical called for the consecration of the entire world to Christ the Redeemer, ending with the words which the Master spoke: "And I, if I be lifted up from the earth, will draw all men unto me" (John 12:32).

The Bishop of San Juan, Argentina, Monsignor Marcolino del Carmel Benavente, inspired by this thought, proposed that a statue be erected in his diocese which would not only recall the consecration of the world to the Saviour, but also bring home to the minds of men that they, having been dedicated to the service of the Master, should adjust their differences and arrive at that mutual understanding which is the very essence of an enduring peace.

Much of the credit for carrying out Bishop Benavente's idea belongs to Sra. Angela de Oliveira Cézar de Costa of Buenos Aires. Through her efforts the money was obtained for casting the statue, patterned after a model by Mateo Alonso, an Argentine sculptor. The material for the statue was obtained by melting down old cannon captured from Spanish forces in the War of Independence.

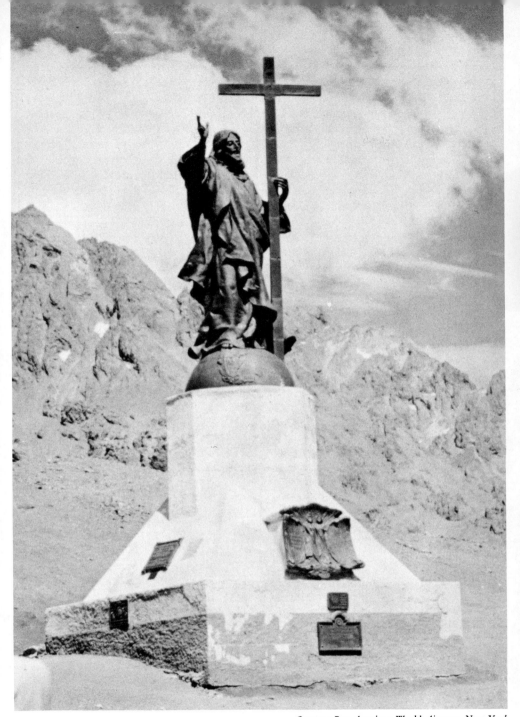

CHRIST OF THE ANDES—*ALONSO*

At this point an event occurred which gave to the erection of this statue special significance for both Argentina and Chile—the settlement by arbitration of the boundary dispute which had threatened to lead to war. In 1903 Argentina and Chile concluded a series of peace pacts and boundary treaties.

Sra. de Costa felt that the signing of these treaties should be signalized in some tangible form. To her mind the statue of Christ the Redeemer, set up at the highest accessible point on the boundary of the two countries, would be the most appropriate way to commemorate the pacific spirit behind these treaties. She presented her idea to President Julio A. Roca of Argentina and members of the Chilean Commission. They adopted her suggestion.

Uspallata Pass, between the giant peaks of Aconcagua and Tupungato, was the site chosen for the statue. It is here that the Andes reach their greatest elevation and are least habitable. Through this pass General José de San Martín and his army of the Andes marched in 1817, to free the Chilean people from Spanish rule. It is fitting that the statue of Christ the Redeemer, symbolizing the eternal peace between the two countries, marks the spot of their physical triumph over a tremendous barrier.

Several plaques have been affixed to the base of the statue of the Christ of the Andes. Across one is the inscription: "He is our peace who hath made us one."*

✠

IF YOU LOVE GOD

If you love God you will not feel
yourself a stranger anywhere,
because He will be everywhere;
in the sweetest essence of every scene,
in the undefined limits of all horizons.

If you love God, nowhere will you be sad,
for in spite of dire tragedy,
He fills the universe with joy.

If you love God, you will fear nothing
and nobody, for you can lose nothing,
and all the power of the cosmos would
be unable to take away your inheritance.

If you love God, you already have
a noble task for every moment,
for there will be no act performed
in His name, neither the humblest nor the noblest,
that does not testify of Him.

* Abridged from a pamphlet, *Christ of the Andes*. Published by the Pan American Union. Used by permission of the publisher.

If you love God, you will not desire
  to investigate the enigmas of life,
  for you will have Him who is the key
  to the solution of them all.

If you love God, you will no longer
  in anguish try to distinguish between
  life and death, for you are in Him
  and He remains safe and unharmed
  along all of life's pathway.*

—Amado Nervo

I RETURN

I will follow in Thy footsteps.
Lord, this is final.
I will drink only from Thy fountain;
I will love only the brightness of Thy stars.
And steadfastly journey toward Thy peace.

How terrible has been
My wandering adventure!
My flowers were thistles; my sweetness
The bitterness of the waters of Mara;
My light, shadow; and my warmth, coldness.

But now I return to Thee, Jesus, my brother,
And today my path again will have
The perfume of nard and the brilliance of stars;
For I will follow in Thy footsteps.
  Lord, this is final.*

—Gonzalo Báez-Camargo

PEACE LIKE A RIVER

A prophet who loved his people and longed for their release
From the burdens of care and the darkness of sin on earth
Promised them a great Light in the Coming Saviour's birth,
And a reign of justice and love with this Prince of Peace.
Peace, like every good and perfect gift from above,
Is from the Father of Lights, the wise omnipotent Giver;
It is the fruit of love, and can grow like a river
If we pay the price—heed His word and walk in love—
Like a river, gentle, quiet, content within its banks
To give the world a steady flow of power, service and life,

---

* From *Hartford Seminary Foundation Bulletin*. Translated by Jay C. Field. Used by permission of Hartford Seminary Foundation.

To mankind beauty and song, calmness and freedom from strife.
For this joyous life-giving water, oh Prince of Peace, our thanks.*
                                                —*Hallie Strange*

PURIFICATION

> This temple, my soul, Thy abode,
>   O Lord, my passions
>   Have turned into a den of thieves.
>
> Lord, see what is happening
>   Within my heart . . .
>   And yet Thou didst create it
>   To be called
> Thy house of Prayer.
>
>   Lord, Lord,
> My spirit cries out to Thee and longs
> For the glorious day
> Of Thy triumphal entry,
>   When, just as the raging wind
>   Drives the chaff before it,
> Thy holy wrath shall smite my passions
>   And drive out all the robbers
>   From the temple of my soul,
>   From Thy dwelling place,
> Thy House of Prayer!**
>   —*Gonzalo Báez-Camargo*

WORD INCARNATE

Word Incarnate, light of heaven and earth,
Only angels could sing those words sublime—
Truth divine revealed in Thy manger birth.
But shepherds heard, and mortals in their time
Have echoed this melody from above.
Let all who would pass on that glorious song
Of peace and good will, salvation through love,
See the secret in Thy life victorious.
Hear those lower supporting chords of work
Of Thy humble servant from above,
In perfect harmony. We would not shirk
Our part, but lift incense in praise to Thee—
Humble hearts, and clean hands in adoration—
Sowing Peace, perfect fruit of Creation. (PHILIPPIANS 2:5-11)*
                                                —*Hallie Strange*

* Used by permission of the author.
** From *Hartford Seminary Foundation Bulletin.* Translated by Jay C. Field. Used by permission of
Hartford Seminary Foundation.

HE SAYS

What is that poor, prostrate sinner trying to do,
Who with muffled moan lacerates his flesh?
  To find *the Way!*

And the ignorant sage as he explores
The mystery of obscure matter or stellar space?
  To find *Truth!*

And the deluded chemist who, with eager gaiety,
Mixes substances and dreams of an elixir?
  To find *Life!*

  And Christ?
They do not hear Him; they do not even see Him.
Yet there He stands at their side, with open arms
And outstretched hands, tenderly smiling, saying:
  I am the Way, the Truth, the Life.*
                              —*Gonzalo Báez-Camargo*

WHEN I HAVE FOOD

O God—When I have food,
Help me to remember the hungry;
When I have work,
Help me to remember the jobless;
When I have a warm home,
Help me to remember those who have no home at all;
When I am without pain,
Help me to remember those who suffer—
And remembering,
Help me to destroy my complacency,
And bestir my compassion—
And be concerned enough to help,
By word and deed,
Those who cry out
For what we take
For granted. Amen.**
                              —*Samuel F. Pugh*

  * From *Hartford Seminary Foundation Bulletin*. Translated by Jay C. Field. Used by permission of Hartford Seminary Foundation.
  ** From *Between-Time Meditations* by Samuel F. Pugh, p. 21. Copyright 1954 by Bethany Press. Used by permission of the author and the publisher.

A YOUNG CHRISTIAN SEES AMERICA

Pablo David Sosa

Pablo David Sosa, son of an Argentine Methodist pastor, studied on a Crusade Scholarship in the United States from September of 1954 to June 1957. He has now returned to Buenos Aires to occupy the professorship of Sacred Music in the Union Theological Seminary there. He gives here his impressions of the value of these exchange scholarships.

"To THE American University, please," I told the taxi driver. I was, of course, in Washington, D. C., to attend a two weeks' course of much needed "orientation" for the Methodist foreign students, commonly called "Crusade Scholars." That was the beginning of an adventure which lasted for three years and now seems but a distant dream.

It was late in the evening when I arrived at the American University, so I went straight to bed. When I awoke I realized that my roommate was a Korean. A minister. The first Korean I had seen in my life! The first of a great number of Christians from all over the world with whom I came in contact during my three years in the States. That was a real blessing for me. As I think of them now, scattered all around the globe, I have a much more real picture of the One Church of Christ, everywhere.

I had many occasions to meet many other foreign persons who were not actively engaged in the work of the Church. And while I saw what a tremendous benefit it was for the States to have represented in its population so many different nationalities and races which work and contribute from the wealth of their various backgrounds, I also realized that it was not easy to live together with people from other cultures and ways of life.

I spent one summer living in the lower east part of Manhattan, serving in the Puerto Rican work of the Methodist Church of All Nations. In a district where Puerto Ricans, Polish, Italians, Negroes, Irish, Jewish, and "native" Americans live side by side, but not together, I saw as much prejudice, hatred, and stupidity as there can be in a man's heart and mind. I had also occasion to visit the South and the Mexican border; and many of my friends came from the Far West. I believe this problem is one of the greatest challenges the Church of Christ has to face in the States. I also believe that the churches are doing much to answer it.

Something which impressed me deeply while in Washington, and which I confirmed later on, was the free and honest exchange of ideas and opinions, even between people of diametrically opposed convictions. Every morning during those two weeks, we had a lecture or a panel about some phase of American life. There we saw a Roman Catholic priest, a Protestant minister, and a Jewish rabbi discuss the religious problems of America; we also saw members of the two main political parties talk about the political situation in America; a Negro scholar presented the Negro problem for us, and so on. I can hardly think of many other countries in the world where that would be possible. It is something of which all North Americans have a right to be proud.

Being a foreign student in the United States is, no doubt, a position of privilege, for various reasons. First, because leaving one's own country to go anywhere else—but especially to the United States—gives a person a perspective, and above all an objective and impartial view of what he is leaving behind. And if the person is a student whose mind is not yet stiffly settled, many good things can happen for the benefit of all, the visitor and his country and the country he is visiting. I myself left my country after having lived since I was ten years old under the continuous pressure and propaganda of a dictatorship, my mind filled with prejudices and ignorance about fundamental principles. Fortunately I came back to a freer country, but many of my fellow countrymen are still trying to get rid of that terrible burden which I was able to throw away, not without difficulty, but definitely, as soon as I got away from home.

Secondly, the privilege of being introduced to a new country and at the same time of introducing one's own country is tremendously valuable. Hardly a month passed at school without our having an invitation to participate in some kind of church and school activities for foreign students. We were taken to visit homes, churches, schools, factories, etc. It was almost too much sometimes, for one felt that foreign students were something of a "curiosity" for North Americans, but after one had "officially" been introduced to every conceivable thing and the time came for real friendship we had a good chance to prove that it is not at all true—as some of us thought—that North Americans are not capable of having deep friendships as we have among us.

As to introducing my own country, I gladly, and must confess, proudly, spoke about it many times when asked, and many more when I was not, although many of the questions disappointed me as to the amount of information about us. I did not justify this ignorance, attributing it to a failure in the courses about Latin America offered in their schools, to the tremendous extension of the territory of the States with so much to know within its own limits, to a general lack of real interest in foreign countries due to the self-sufficiency of the States and the fear of having to interfere too much, economically or militarily, in a world which seems to do nothing but hate the U.S.A. When the Middle East crisis broke out during my last winter in the United States I had occasion to see some of my friends in college shut up with anger a television set which was informing them of the "mess" the world was in, thinking that they might have to pay even with their lives for what these "immature" countries were doing. I do not blame them, and yet . . .

As to my religious experiences in the States, I want to mention only one which I believe is the most important. I had two or three opportunities to attend large youth conferences intended primarily for the recruiting of missionaries. I had seen many missionaries when they arrived in my country. I

never worried too much about their place of origin, background, family, etc.
I always expected them to adjust themselves to our situation as soon as possible, and always blamed them if they were not able to do so. In the States
I had the opportunity of seeing the whole matter from the other side. I
heard missionaries on furlough present our country as if it were their own.
I saw young people dedicate their lives to serve God in the work of my
country, and start, with a devotion that touched my heart, to get ready for
that day when they would be able to come to us. And then, only a few months
ago, I saw a good friend of mine leave for the first time for a faraway
missionary field. I was there when he said good-by to his parents. I know
what it meant for him to leave his country, because I also had that experience
once. How could I ever feel toward missionaries in that same rather matter-
of-fact, impersonal way I did before?

I do thank God and also those in the Methodist Church in the United
States who provided for me and many other students from all over the world
this wonderful opportunity of widening our spiritual and mental horizons,
hoping that many others still will be able to do so too.*

✤

LIDIA VARGAS IN CHILE
Elizabeth Meredith Lee

IN AN upper, smoke-filled room in a business building of downtown Santiago,
Chile, thirty-one people sat around a table. Only one of them was a woman.
This was the quarterly meeting of the Association of Bookstore Managers of
Santiago, and the manager of the famous Protestant bookstore, El Sembrador,
was taking her rightful place. She was the only woman who had ever entered
their precincts, and the men hardly knew how to treat this wavy-haired, attractively groomed colleague. Sometimes they forgot her presence, in the stories
they told with raucous laughter. "At times," she remarked later, "I had to
remind them, to their faces, of their lack of good breeding."

This woman bookstore manager of Santiago has fought her way up until
she has won the respect and admiration of her men co-workers. Her firm
convictions, gently expressed, often have helped them understand the standards set by the Protestant Church. "She is so fair, so clear in her judgments,
so sure of what she believes. And she has good ideas about selling books,
too! We can all learn from her."

Lidia Vargas, now the head of El Sembrador, has loved books since she
was a child. Like most children of Chile, she was brought up in a Catholic
home. She remembers well her first visit to a Protestant church. She was
nine, and her father had just died. To add to the family despair, a little
brother of two years had suddenly been stricken with polio. Doctors could

* Abridged from Pampa Breezes (Oct.-Dec. 1957). Used by permission of the author and the Board
of Missions of the Methodist Church.

do nothing. The mother took the boy to the local Catholic church for the priest's blessing, but the indifference of the priest made the mother's faith waver. A friend suggested that Señora Vargas take the sick child to a Protestant church. She did, and her little daughter accompanied her. The warmth of the reception and the way the pastor brought them to the altar for prayer made a lasting impression on the little girl. "Their prayer that the will of God be done, that He bless my mother and the family was never forgotten. My brother died, but the church members did not abandon us. My mother was soon converted, and that very day I felt really called of God to accept Him."

The family was very poor and needed help, but the missionary pastor wisely led them to help themselves. Lidia was invited to come into the missionary home to help in the care of the children. That home seemed to the little Chilean girl, deprived of many of the niceties of life, a veritable paradise. She tells how much she admired everything surrounding her, and how when the missionary and his wife were absent and she was left alone with the children she used to open dressers and wardrobes and feast her eyes on "the wearing apparel, so elegant, so beautiful." She never wanted anything for herself, but she loved to look at the pretty garments. One day she opened the trunk where the missionary mother kept her wedding dress! Lidia stood there in ecstasy, but that turned to horror when she tried to close the trunk and found it was stuck. Petrified lest she be discovered in her "sin," she used all her might to force the cover down, but she always felt that the missionaries knew what had happened though they never said a word.

Between Lidia and her missionary friends there grew up a beautiful fellowship. The pastor, when she was twelve, arranged for her to go to Concepción College. With her tremendous interest in learning, Lidia was soon at the head of her class.

Her first real job was with the Methodist Mission, in the office of the treasurer. The longing to be a teacher never left Lidia. Soon she decided to take night classes in order to get her secondary-school diploma. After working all day, she attended classes till almost midnight. She completed the course successfully and received a prize for her "dedicated application."

No opportunity for growth was ever turned down. The teacher of her Spanish course recommended that the students read the works of famous Chilean writers in order to write their biographies. "If any of you should be able to have an interview with a famous writer, that would be all to the good."

The next day Lidia was downtown trying to get an interview with an author who wrote for a leading Santiago paper. After many attempts, she found herself in the presence of this well-known writer. She was tongue-tied. How did one begin to talk to such a great man? But the most amiable Daniel de la Vega must have sensed the girl's confusion. He began to ask her questions until she soon forgot her embarrassment and was eagerly telling Señor

de la Vega about herself and her aspirations. She came out of the office with
the gift of one of his books in her hands, positive proof that she had had
the interview! From that day the Spanish teacher took a special interest in
Lidia.

This thoughtful girl always stood up for her Protestant faith vigorously.
One of her professors, she recalls, presented religion so that anyone might
easily be convinced that a belief in God was the fruit of gross ignorance.
Lidia was not very good in argument or debate, but perhaps it was her manner
of expressing in class some of her own deep convictions that one day induced
a teacher to talk with her outside of class. "Señorita Lidia, how do you
explain your faith? I admire you but I do not understand you, because, for
myself, I cannot accept anything that I cannot explain rationally." "But for
me," the girl answered, "religion is something that one feels more than
something one can explain rationally." "But how do you *feel?*" the learned
professor then asked. Lidia had many such opportunities to hold conversations with her teachers who, while not accepting Christ, showed a sympathy
and respect for the Protestant faith.

Prepared to be a teacher, Lidia never taught. Among her church friends
she was known as a wide reader and lover of books. *El Sembrador* offered
her work in the bookstore for half a day, even while she was studying. Later
she was named assistant manager of this institution, which is sponsored
jointly by the Methodist and Presbyterian churches in Chile. She loved this
living with books day in and day out. But it was a surprise when, upon the
retirement of the missionary in charge, she was asked to take the responsibility of the store "till someone is found." Lidia accepted the challenge.

"It is difficult work, and sometimes not fully supported by the pastors and
church leaders themselves. But we will find ways of making our work efficient," the young manager said when she took over the job. Today the work
shows that her objective is gradually being reached. She looks upon the
distribution of Christian literature as a means of advancing the work of the
whole Church. Her dream is to reach by means of Christian literature all the
churches and every Protestant church member in Chile.

In the beginning Lidia found it very difficult to speak in public. But a part
of her strategy is to hold book exhibits in as many churches as possible. Of
course, the books have to be explained, so Lidia soon found herself with a
reputation as a public speaker who loves her subject and can make books
live.

When she is going out on a book trip into the wilder parts of Chile, up
in the Andes, or down in the beautiful lake region, Miss Vargas sends parcels
of books in advance. These she puts on display attractively. At each center
she speaks on the significance of reading matter for the Church and for the
individual church member. As a result she usually returns to Santiago empty-
handed. In one journey covering eighteen churches she made sales totaling
eighty thousand pesos.

Knowing that one person cannot do the job, Miss Vargas is training a
younger assistant who already goes about representing *El Sembrador* and

making further sales. Beyond this, however, Miss Vargas knows that real success lies in the enthusiasm of local people. To this end she is trying to recruit a church member in each area of Chile who will become an active local agent for the Protestant bookstore.

But Miss Vargas does not stop with the churches. She is finding ways to bring Christian literature to those who do not yet accept Christ, some in places where there is at present no established church. Thus her leadership in this commercial bookstore is developing her into an evangelist herself, eager to share the Christ she serves with all the people who need Him.*

✣

GOD'S GIFT TO PAQUITO

Elizabeth Allstrom

PAQUITO's village was perched on a hillside on the island of Puerto Rico. In his small house there was always work to do, but most of the time seven-year-old Paquito didn't like to help do it.

Usually when Mamá called, "Go to the store," or "Bring the water," Paquito grumbled. Then sometimes when Mamá didn't ask him at all, the full pail of water would be in the corner, the rice and beans on the table. Paquito liked to help when he thought of it himself.

One morning when Paquito had finished breakfast, he hurried out as usual to find his friends. He did not wash his face as Mamá asked nor put on a clean shirt nor go to the store. He thought only about playing.

On this morning as Paquito and his friends played a game called "The Stick" in a cleared space at the edge of the village, the rumbling sound of a truck came from the distance.

In another moment, the truck came into view and bumped its way across the play space to a noisy stop. Two men climbed out of the cab, went to the back, and began to unpack.

Paquito and his friends moved closer. Curious, Paquito spoke out, "¿ Que pasa?"

One of the men answered, pointing to the stacks of heavy brown cloth and to the long wooden poles now lying on the ground beside the truck. "I am a pastor, and this is a tent. When it is put up, there will be church meetings in it. Fathers and mothers will come at night. Children are invited for stories and songs. Come when you hear the gong this afternoon."

To Paquito the afternoon seemed a long way off, and he was more interested in the game. "It's my turn," he reminded the boys. "Let's play."

His friends paid no attention. They wanted to watch what the strangers were doing. They told the men, "We'll help you."

The men seemed pleased. "That will be fine," the pastor said. "You're

* Abridged from *Thirteen Biographies* by Elizabeth Meredith Lee, pp. 49-52. Published in 1958 by the Woman's Division of Christian Service of the Methodist Church. Used by permission of the author and the publisher.

hardly strong enough to pound the heavy stakes into the ground to hold the tent or tall enough to pull the ropes tight and tie the tent firmly in place. But I know a way you can help. You are just the right size to carry benches. You may bring some from your homes for us to use inside the tent."

"Yes, oh, yes!" the boys answered and hurried to their homes on their errand.

It was no fun to play alone. Paquito went home, too. Mamá was ironing. Paquito sat in the doorway. He sat there a long time, until the gong sounded clang, clang, clang.

"It's the pastor in the tent," Paquito told Mamá. "He came in a truck this morning. I must go to the tent now for stories."

Mamá stopped her ironing. "Paquito mío, you go first to the store to buy beans and rice for supper. The shelf is empty."

"But Mamá," Paquito grumbled, "the stories!"

Mamá took coins from a box and handed them to Paquito. Still grumbling, he took them and ran out through the gate to the store. When he came back, he dropped the bag on the table.

Mamá spoke again. "There is no water, Paquito mío. Go now and get it for me."

Mamá pointed to the pail. Paquito took it, dashed through the gate to the village well, and brought back the water as Mamá asked.

"Already I am late," he complained. "The others are in the tent." If only he had offered to help with the benches, he'd be there, too! But Mamá was talking again. "Paquito mío, you must have a clean face and a clean shirt when you go to listen to the stories."

Paquito, still complaining, dipped some of the water into a pan, splashed it on his face, then put on the fresh shirt Mamá handed to him.

At last, Mamá was satisfied, and Paquito hurried through the gate.

At the tent the story had begun. Paquito, late, tried to listen, but he could not keep his mind on the pastor's words. His starched shirt was scratchy. He wiggled and wiggled. Ladybugs came from their hiding places in the grassy tufts and crawled over his bare toes. Paquito reached down, picked up one, and put it into his pocket.

When he straightened up, the pastor was looking at him and speaking directly to him. "God has given a special gift to you. You must use your gift."

Paquito glanced around. He was sure there was a mistake. A gift from God to him? He had no gift from the good God. There was not even a gift from Mamá. Money at their house was spent for food, not gifts.

Now the pastor spoke the closing prayer. The meeting was over.

Paquito walked slowly up to the pastor. "I have no gift," he said.

The pastor's eyes twinkled as he answered. "I spoke the truth. You have a gift. Perhaps it is because you do not use your gift that you do not know about it. God has given it to you."

His glance was so friendly that Paquito smiled back. He would try to find the gift! All the way home, Paquito thought about it. When did God bring his gift? Where did God leave it?

At home Paquito searched in all the places he knew—on the shelf, behind the door, under the window. He found nothing.

Next morning Paquito told Mamá, "I'll bring the water!" The gift might be near the well. At the well Paquito saw only the usual things.

Back home again he told Mamá, "I'll go for rice and beans." The gift might be hidden along the path to the store. Paquito's eyes searched both sides of the path, but there were only many high weeds and a few small stones.

That afternoon Paquito remembered himself to wash his face and put on a clean shirt. He waited for the gong, and when it sounded, he darted through the gate and turned down the path that led to the tent. He would be on time today! He would find out more about the gift.

But there ahead, and in his way, Paquito saw a small donkey lying down in the path. Bent over the donkey was his old master, yelling angrily, pulling, tugging at the reins, trying to get the stubborn little creature to his feet.

In his hurry around the donkey and his master, Paquito stopped suddenly. "What a trouble!" he said. Scattered over the ground were vegetables— peppers, squash, beans—spilled out of the baskets on the donkey's back when the creature had decided to rest instead of walking on to the market.

"What a trouble! So much to pick up! No wonder the old man yells." Paquito passed by and went on his way. But not far!

In a moment he was back. "I'll help you," he called to the old man. Without waiting for an answer, Paquito scrambled around, picked up the vegetables, and put them into the baskets.

Suddenly the donkey, with a quick toss of his head and a shake of his body, got up on his feet. The old man was soon astride him and ready to continue his trip. He turned to Paquito.

"Gracias, gracias, thank you, thank you. In truth, your two hands are gifts from God Himself, and you have used them well to help me this day."

He snapped the reins, and the donkey moved off as though there had been no trouble.

Paquito stared down at his two hands. Were these a gift from God? Could the pastor in the tent have meant hands?

Paquito ran all the way to the tent and straight up to the front where the pastor stood, ready to begin the story. "I've found God's gift! I've had it all the time!"

The next day, and almost every day after that, Paquito remembered to use his gift.*

---

* Abridged from *The Singing Secret* by Elizabeth Allstrom. Reprinted in *Missionary Stories to Play and Tell*, edited by Nina Millen. Copyright 1958 by Friendship Press. Used by permission of the publisher.

O JESUS, I HAVE PROMISED *(JESÚS, YO HE PROMETIDO)*

CHRISTIAN hymns composed by natives of countries still regarded as mission fields are generally not yet available, and this is true of Mexico. Followers of the Christian way in such countries use translations of the great old hymns of the Church which have a common appeal to the human heart.

One such hymn is "O Jesus, I Have Promised." I suspect that one reason why its appeal to Christians everywhere is so great is that it expresses the common problems, temptations, and trials that beset the path of all who strive to live the Christian life.

There is a universal hunger in the hearts of all believing Christians to *feel* the indwelling of Christ's spirit in their daily lives. Young Christians especially know that if they are to follow in the Master's steps, they must always be conscious of His will. Above the storms of individual passions and desires, we need constantly to hear the voice of the Saviour of men, saying: "Be ye perfect, even as I am perfect." When the urge to follow the way of the flesh seems too insistent to bear, the courage to follow Christ can come only if we feel His presence with us as we walk, day by day, the Christian life.

What a pleasure it is to join our voices with Christians of other nations as we sing these great old hymns. We can feel the glow of oneness, even though we are expressing our Christian comradeship in a tongue unfamiliar to their ears.

The music score of "Jesús, Yo He Prometido" is found on p. 877. The English words appear below:

> O Jesus, I have promised to serve Thee to the end;
> Be Thou forever near me, my Master and my Friend:
> I shall not fear the battle if Thou art by my side,
> Nor wander from the pathway if Thou wilt be my guide.
>
> O let me feel Thee near me! The world is ever near;
> I see the sights that dazzle, the tempting sounds I hear;
> My foes are ever near me, around me and within;
> But Jesus, draw Thou nearer, and shield my soul from sin.
>
> O let me hear Thee speaking, in accents clear and still,
> Above the storms of passion, the murmurs of self-will;
> O speak to reassure me, to hasten or control;
> O speak, and make me listen, Thou guardian of my soul.
>
> O Jesus, Thou hast promised to all who follow Thee
> That where Thou art in glory there shall Thy servant be;
> And, Jesus, I have promised to serve Thee to the end;
> O give me grace to follow, my Master and my Friend.

O Jesus, I Have Promised*
Jesús, Yo He Prometido

Tr. J. B. Cabrera
John Ernest Bode

Arthur H. Mann

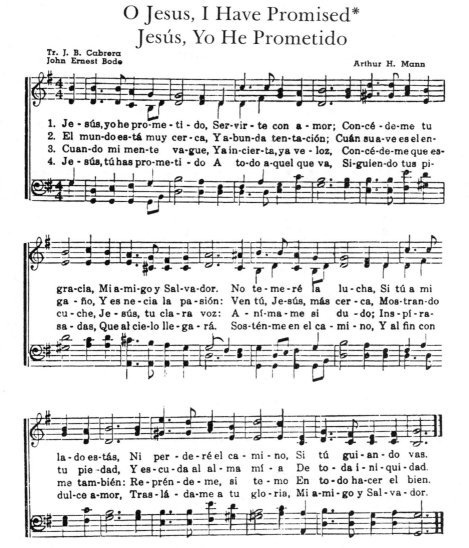

1. Je - sús, yo he pro-me-ti - do, Ser-vir-te con a - mor; Con-cé - de-me tu
2. El mun-do es-tá muy cer - ca, Y a-bun-da ten-ta-ción; Cuán sua-ve es el en-
3. Cuan-do mi men-te   va-gue, Y a in-cier-ta, ya ve - loz, Con-cé-de-me que es-
4. Je - sús, tú has pro-me-ti - do A   to-do a-quel que va, Si-guien-do tus pi-

gra-cia, Mi a-mi-go y Sal-va-dor.   No te-me-ré la   lu-cha, Si tú a mi
ga - ño, Y es ne-cia la pa-sión: Ven tú, Je-sús, más cer - ca, Mos-tran-do
cu-che, Je - sús, tu cla-ra voz: A - ní-ma-me si   du - do; Ins-pí-ra-
sa - das, Que al cie-lo lle-ga - rá.   Sos-tén-me en el ca - mi - no, Y al fin con

la-do es-tás, Ni per-de-ré el ca - mi-no, Si tú gui-an-do vas.
tu pie-dad, Y es-cu-da al al-ma   mí - a   De to - da i-ni-qui-dad.
me tam-bién: Re-prén-de-me, si   te - mo En to-do ha-cer el bien.
dul-ce a-mor, Tras-lá - da-me a tu   glo-ria, Mi a-mi-go y Sal-va-dor.

JESUS IS MY SOVEREIGN KING (*JESÚS ES MI REY SOBERANO*)

BOTH the words and music of this beautiful hymn-poem were composed by Vicente Mendoza, one of Latin America's favorite poets. It is a hymn of gratitude and praise to Jesus who, when enthroned in the human heart,

Jesus Is My Sovereign King
Jesús Es Mi Rey Soberano *

Vicente Mendoza   Vicente Mendoza

1. Je - sús es mi Rey so - be - ra - no, Mi go-zo es can-tar su lo-
2. Je - sús es mi A- mi - go an-he- la - do, Y en som-bras o en luz siem-pre
3. Se - ñor, ¿qué pu - die - ra yo dar - te Por tan-ta bon-dad pa - ra

or; Es Rey, y me ve cual her - ma - no, Es Rey y me im-par-
va Pa-cien-te y hu-mil-de a mi la - do, Y a-yu-da y con-sue-
mí; Me bas-ta ser-vir-te y a-mar-te? ¿Es to-do en-tre-gar-

te su a-mor. De - jan-do su tro-no de glor - ria, me vi-no a sa-car
lo me da. Por e-so cons-tan-te lo si - go, por-que él es mi Rey
me yo a ti? En-ton-ces a-cep-ta mi vi - da, que a ti so - lo que-

de la es - co - rria, Y yo soy fe - liz, Y yo soy fe - liz por él.
y mi A - mi - go, Y yo soy fe - liz, Y yo soy fe - liz por él.
da ren-di - da, Pues yo soy fe - liz, Pues yo soy fe - liz por ti.

becomes not only one's king, but also a friend, a brother, and a wise counselor, who patiently leads those who follow Him into paths of love, truth,
justice, and service.

It is not easy to translate poetry from one language to another. We are
indebted to Jay Carleton Field for his translation of this hymn. The music
score on p. 878 gives the words in Spanish; the English words are given
below, so that the English-speaking nations may join with their Latin
American neighbors in singing this truly great hymn of praise and thanksgiving.

> Enthroned in my heart I keep Jesus
> And joyfully I sing Him my praise.
> Though King, He me owns as a brother;
> Though King, freely He gives me His love.
> His throne in the sky He abandoned
> To save me from a life that is futile,
> So now I rejoice, for happy in Him I live.
>
> My friend most desired is Lord Jesus.
> In darkness or in light He's my Guide.
> He's humble and patient and leads me
> Forever with His counsel and aid.
> And so in His steps I will follow,
> For He is my King, and so friendly that I'm
> Happy! O so happy in Him I live.
>
> Lord, O that I might now repay Thee
> For Thy loving service to me!
> Enough that I serve and I love Thee?
> Enough that I surrender to Thee?
> Accept then my life; thus I pray Thee;
> And wholly for Thee it is given.
> For I'm O so happy! Happy in Thee I live.

INDICES AND ACKNOWLEDGMENTS

ACKNOWLEDGMENTS
page 883

INDEX OF ART AND ART INTERPRETATIONS BY ARTISTS
AND TITLES
page 895

INDEX OF POETRY BY AUTHORS AND TITLES
page 897

INDEX OF STORIES BY TITLES AND AUTHORS
page 899

INDEX OF MUSIC AND MUSIC INTERPRETATIONS BY TITLES
AND AUTHORS
page 901

ACKNOWLEDGMENTS

ACKNOWLEDGMENTS are here made for the gracious co-operation of friends, authors, publishers, libraries, and art agencies in the compilation of this anthology, *The Church and the Fine Arts.*

The author-compiler and her collaborators have made every effort to trace the ownership of all the poems, stories, pictures, and music contained in this volume through public libraries, art galleries and agencies, and publishers, and to the best of their knowledge have secured all necessary permissions from authors, artists, and composers, or their recognized agencies or both. Should there be any question regarding the use of a picture, poem, story, or musical composition without adequate permission having been obtained, regret is hereby expressed for such unconscious error. Upon notification of such oversight, the publishers will be pleased to make proper correction and acknowledgment in future editions of this anthology.

In addition to the acknowledgments that appear throughout this volume, the author-compiler wishes to express her sincere thanks to her four collaborators—Dr. John P. Cavarnos, Dr. Alfred T. DeGroot, Dr. Ronald E. Osborn, and Miss Jean Louise Smith—each of whom painstakingly compiled a major part of this anthology and contributed much original material to it. The addresses of the compilers are given below for the convenience of readers who may wish to correspond with them regarding the materials included in each part of this anthology.

Parts I and VI: Dr. Cynthia Pearl Maus, 2619 Wilshire Blvd., Apt. 810, Los Angeles 57, California.

Part II: Dr. John P. Cavarnos, Department of Classics, Austin College, Sherman, Texas (or 115 Gilbert Road, Belmont 78, Massachusetts).

Part III: Miss Jean Louise Smith, Box 113, Norwich, Vermont.

Part IV: Dr. Ronald E. Osborn, Christian Theological Seminary, Butler University, Indianapolis 7, Indiana.

Part V: Dr. Alfred T. DeGroot, Brite College of the Bible, Texas Christian University, Forth Worth, Texas.

For special help in finding materials for this anthology, deep appreciation is expressed to: the Los Angeles Public Library and the New York Public Library; the Libraries of the Board of Missions of the Methodist Church and of the National Council of the Episcopal Church, both in New York; the files of several departments of the United Presbyterian Church in the U.S.A.; the Metropolitan Museum of Art and the Frick Art Reference Library, both in New York; Mr. G. Fattorusso, Florence, Italy; and Mr. Abbott Book of the Abbott Book Library of Art, Piedmont, California.

The author-compiler also wishes to express her special appreciation for the generous contributions, some of them never before published, from a number of poets: Miss Catherine Baker, Mrs. Leslie Savage Clark, Chandran Devanesen and Friendship Press, Miss Lois Anna Ely, Miss Clarice White Luck, Mr. Earl Marlatt, Mr. Samuel F. Pugh, and the Reverend Henry C. Spear. Special thanks are also due to Miss Erica Oxenham for permission to publish a number of poems by John Oxenham.

Sincere thanks are also expressed to the following individuals, institutions, publishers, and art agencies for granting reprint permissions from their libraries and publications:

PICTURES

For providing the art reproductions and other photographs appearing in this anthology and for granting permission for their use:

Fratelli Alinari, 107 Via Nazionale, Florence, Italy, and their American representatives, Art Reference Bureau, P. O. Box 137, Ancram, N. Y., for "Judas Iscariot" by Andrea del Sarto, "St. Paul" and "St. Peter" by Fra Bartolommeo, "St. John, the Evangelist" by Carlo Dolci, "The Crucifixion of St. Peter" by Michelangelo, "The Emperor Justinian and His Court" by an unknown artist, "Christ Consigning the Keys to St. Peter" by Sanzio Raphael, "The Tribute Money" by Masaccio; and photographs of St. Paul's Cathedral in Rome and of the Upper and Lower Churches of St. Francis of Assisi.

The American Bible Society, 450 Park Ave., New York 22, N. Y., for "The Bible Goes to Press" from the motion picture, Our Bible—How It Came to Us, and its interpretation, reprinted from portions of the article, "500th Anniversary of the Gutenberg Bible" by Margaret T. Hills, which originally appeared in Bible Society Record for September 1956.

The American Waldensian Aid Society, 156 Fifth Ave., New York 10, N. Y., for the photograph of the Waldensian Fresco by Paolo A. Paschetto.

D. Anderson, 7-a Via Salaria, Rome, Italy, for "St. Matthew" by Guido Reni and photographs of St. Peter's Cathedral, Rome, and the Cathedral, Baptistry, and Campanile, Pisa.

Bethany College, Bethany, West Virginia, for the photograph of the college.

Mr. Abbott Book, 140 Arbor Dr., Piedmont 10, Calif., for "Christmas Night" and "The Ascension" by Fritz von Uhde, "The Holy Family" by Adelbert Franz Seligmann, "St. Paul Before the Altar of the Unknown God" by Luke Ch'en, "Christ or Diana?" by Edwin Long, "The Last Prayer" by Jean Léon Gérôme, "The Three Saints" by Kwaiseki Sadakata, "Go Teach All Nations" by Lu Hung-nien, "I Will Come Again" by Alfred David Thomas, and "Jesus Christ Crucified" by Santiago Rebull. He also supplied interpretative data about each painting.

Canterbury Cathedral, 6 Hawks Lane, Canterbury, England, for the photograph of the cathedral.

. Dr. Constantine Cavarnos, 115 Gilbert Road, Belmont, Mass., for "The Transfiguration of Christ" by Fotis Kontoglous.

Dr. John P. Cavarnos, 115 Gilbert Road, Belmont, Mass., for the photographs of Hagia Sophia at Constantinople and St. Panteleimon Monastery.

Mr. Samuel Chamberlain, 5 Tucker St., Marblehead, Mass., for the photograph of the Old Brick Church, Smithfield, Va.

Miss Constance Chappell for the photograph of Woman's Christian College, Tokyo.

Christian Education Press, 1505 Race St., Philadelphia 2, Pa., for "Head of Christ" by Jacques Barosin and for its interpretation by Miss Helen Groninger from Church Management of June, 1955.

Mr. Elmer T. Clark, Lake Junaluska, N. C., for "John Wesley, Ecclesiastical Statesman" by Frank O. Salisbury.

The Congo-Evangelical Training Institute, Kimpese, Africa, for the photograph by C. Lamote of the Kimpese Christian Institute.

Crusade Monthly, 30 Bedford Pl., London, W.C. 1, England, for the photograph of the statue by J. E. Boehm of William Tyndale.

Mr. Demetrios Dukas, 455 Essex St., Lynn, Mass., for a reproduction of his "Pantocrator" mosaic which appears at the dome of the Church of the Archangels at Stamford, Conn.

Earlham College, Richmond, Ind., for the painting by Marcus Mote of the Quaker Meetinghouse in Richmond.

L'Ecole Officialle d'Art, Léopoldville, Africa, for the photograph of the wood carving, "Christ Falls Under the Weight of His Cross," by Nsímba Norbert.

The First Baptist Church, 51 W. Olive Ave., Redlands, Calif., Frank B. Fagerburg, Minister, for the photograph by Daniel W. Brock, 2301 Echo Park Ave., Los Angeles 26, Calif., of "Christ and the Children of the World," a stained-glass window designed by Judson Studios, 200 S. Ave. Sixty-six, Los Angeles 42, Calif.

The First Christian Church, Fifth St. at Lafayette, Columbus, Ind., for the photograph of their church, designed by Eliel Saarinen.

The First Church of Oberlin, Oberlin, Ohio, Joseph F. King, Minister, for the photograph of the Congregational Meetinghouse, Oberlin.

The Fogg Art Museum, Harvard University, Cambridge, Mass., for the photograph of the Church of the Holy Sepulcher.

Forest Lawn Memorial-Park Association, Inc., Glendale, Calif., for the photograph of "The Last Supper" Window by Rosa Caselli-Moretti and for their interpretation of it.

The Franciscan Fathers, Old Mission, Santa Barbara, Calif., for the photograph of Santa Barbara Mission.

The Frick Collection, 1 E. 70th St., New York 21, N. Y., for "St. Jerome" by El Greco (reproduction copyrighted 1937) and "The Education of the Virgin" by Georges de la Tour (reproduction copyrighted 1948).

Frost & Reed, Ltd., Bristol, England, and their American representatives, Rudolf Lesch Fine Arts, Inc., 225 Fifth Ave., New York, N. Y., for "The Lord Turned and Looked at Peter" by Herbert Beecroft.

E. Houvet, 20 Rue de Rechevres, Chartres, France, for his photograph of the statue, "Christ Teaching," at the Cathedral of Notre Dame, Chartres.

The Iona Community, Glasgow, Scotland, for the photograph of St. Martin's Cross.

Jordan Tourist Office, 411 East 53rd St., New York, N. Y., for photographs of "The Church of the Holy Sepulcher" and "The Mount of Olives and Gethsemane."

Prof. Ernst Kitzinger and the Dumbarton Oaks Research Library and Collection, 1703 32nd St., Washington 7, D. C., for the reproduction of the "Gregory of Nyssa" mosaic from the Palatine Chapel at Palermo, Sicily.

The Korean Research and Information Office, 1828 Jefferson Pl., Washington 6, D. C., and Virgil Rupp for his photograph of the church in Wonju, Korea.

Kriebel & Bates, 4125 N. Keystone Ave., Indianapolis, Ind., for "Head of Christ" by Warner E. Sallman and its interpretation from the pamphlet, *The Story of Sallman's Head of Christ*, by Howard W. Ellis.

Lakeview United Church, Regina, Saskatchewan, for the photograph by R. F. Howard, 2731 S. Railway, Regina, of their Communion table.

Lutheran Church Productions, Inc., 11 W. 42nd St., New York 36, N. Y., for "Here I Stand" from the motion picture, *Martin Luther*.

Massachusetts Institute of Technology, Cambridge, Mass., for the photograph of the modern altar designed by Eero Saarinen in association with Anderson, Beckwith & Haible.

John McInnes of Tucson, Ariz., for his photograph of a Korean woman at prayer, here titled "Grandmother's Prayer."

The Board of Missions and Church Extension of the Methodist Church, Interchurch Center, 475 Riverside Dr., New York 27, N. Y., for the photograph of Moore Memorial Church in Shanghai.

The Metropolitan Museum of Art, Fifth Ave. at 82nd St., New York 24, N. Y., for the photograph of The Cuxa Cloister.

Mount Calvary Lutheran Church, 1444 Union Blvd., St. Louis, Mo., for the photograph of the wood carving, "The Last Supper," by Alois Lang.

The Museum of Art, Rhode Island School of Design, 14 College St., Providence, R. I., for "St. Andrew" by El Greco.

The Museum of Fine Arts, 479 Huntingdon Ave., Boston 15, Mass., for "Knight, Death, and the Devil" by Albrecht Dürer.

The National Christian Council of India, Punganur, Chittoor District, South India, Rev. Ralph G. Korteling, Field Director, for his photograph of the Anglican Cathedral at Dornakal.

The National Christian Council of Japan, 2-Chrome, Ginza, Chou-ku, Tokyo, Norimichi Ebizawa, Executive Director, for photographs of Anglican Episcopal Church, Nara, and Matsuzawa Church, Tokyo, and for information about both churches.

The National Gallery of Art, Washington 25, D. C., for "A Dominican Preaching" by Domenico Morone (Gift of Mrs. Felix M. Warburg) and "The Sacrament of the Last Supper" by Salvador Dali (Chester Dale Collection).

The National Gallery of South Australia, Adelaide, Australia, and Colin Ballantyne for "The Church on the Hill" by John Eldershaw.

The National Museum of Ireland, Kildare St., Dublin C. 17, Ireland, for a photograph of the Ardagh Chalice.

The Nebraska State Historical Society, 1500 R St., Lincoln 8, Neb., for a photograph of the First Presbyterian Church in Bellevue.

The Neighborhood Church of Pasadena, 215 W. California St., Pasadena, Calif., for a photograph by Julius Shulman, P. O. Box 46206, Los Angeles 46, Calif., of the Children's Chapel in Pasadena, designed by Smith & Williams.

Dr. Ronald E. Osborn, Butler University, Indianapolis, Ind., for his photograph of the Arnoldshain Altar, designed by Siegfried Moroder.

Pan American World Airways, New York, N. Y., for "Christ of the Andes," by Mateo Alonso.

Mr. Pericles Papahadjidakis, 14 Apollo St., Athens, Greece, for his photographs of "Anastasis" or "Resurrection," "St. Constantine and St. Helen," both by unknown artists, "Basil the Great" by Fotis Kontoglous, "Athanasius of Alexandria" by Theophanes of Crete, "St. John and St. Prochorus" by Manuel Panselenos, and "Iconostasis of the Protaton."

Philosophical Library, Inc., 15 E. 40th St., New York 16, N. Y., for reproduction of "Kite-Flying in Korea" by Elizabeth Keith.

Rijksmuseum, Hobbemastraat 21, Amsterdam, Neth., for "Old Woman at Prayer" by Nicolas Maes.

Rijksmuseum Kröller-Müller, Otterlo, Neth., for "The Good Samaritan" by Vincent Van Gogh.

St. Clement's Church, Alexandria, Va., for the photograph by Charles Baptie, Route 3, Annandale, Va., of the church.

The Cathedral Church of St. John the Divine, Cathedral Heights, New York 25, N. Y., for the photograph of the church, designed by Ralph Adams Cram.

St. Martin's Evangelical Lutheran Church, 100 E. 14th St., Austin, Tex., Edward V. Long, Pastor, for the photograph of the pulpit.

St. Paul's Church, Halifax, Nova Scotia, H. St. C. Hilchey, Rector, for the engraving by Fougeron of the church. The photograph was supplied by Royal Ontario Museum, 100 Queen's Park, Toronto 5, Ontario.

St. Philip's in the Hills, Rte. 5, Box 50, Tucson, Ariz., George W. Ferguson, Rector, for the photograph of the altar view.

The Trustees of St. Sophia Cathedral and the Reverend Leonidas Contos, 1324 S. Normandie Ave., Los Angeles, Calif., for the photograph of St. Sophia Cathedral.

St. Stephen's Episcopal Church, Fort Yukon, Alaska, The Ven. Norman H. V. Elliott, Archdeacon, for the photograph of their moosehide altar.

Mr. Walter Scott, Rock House, Thorncliffe Rd., Bradford, England, for the photograph of Glastonbury Abbey.

Le Secretariat de la Province de Quebec, Quebec, for the photograph of Cap-de-la-Madeleine.

Staatlichen Museen, Berlin, Germany, for "St. Thomas Visiting St. Bonaventura" by Francisco Zurbaran.

Stehli Brothers, Ltd., Stadelhoferstr. 12, Box 232, Zurich 24, Switz., for "Go Preach" by Eugene Burnand.

S.V.D. Catholic Universities, 316 N. Michigan Ave., Chicago 1, Ill., and Luke Ch'en and the Catholic University of Peking for "The Return of the Prodigal" by Luke Ch'en.

The Swiss National Tourist Office, 10 W. 49th St., New York 20, N. Y., for the photograph of the statue, "Pestalozzi and the Children," by Karl Alfred Lanz.

Mr. John Taylor, World Council of Churches, 17 Rue de Malagnou, Geneva, Switz., for his photographs of St. Peter's Cathedral and the Reformation Monument, both in Geneva.

The Parish of Trinity Church, 74 Trinity Pl., New York 6, N. Y., for the old engraving of Trinity Church.

Union Evangelical Seminary, Río Piedras, Puerto Rico, T. J. Liggett, Pres., for the photograph of the seminary and for information about it.

The Vestry of the Unitarian Church, Charleston, S. C., for the photograph of the fan tracery.

United Christian Missionary Society, 222 S. Downey Ave., Indianapolis 7, Ind., and Mr. E. K. Higdon for his photographs of Central Christian Church, Manila; United Protestant Youth Center, University of the Philippines; and Silliman University Church, Dumaguete. Also the Society and Mr. Charles C. Mills for his photograph of the Dr. and Mrs. Royal J. Dye Memorial Church, Bolenge, Belgian Congo.

The United Presbyterian Church in the U.S.A., Interchurch Center, 475 Riverside Dr., New York 27, N. Y., for the photograph of Lok-seng-i Presbyterian Church for Lepers, Taiwan, and for information about it from their publication, *Island Beautiful*, edited by Claire Rendell.

The Walker Art Gallery, William Brown St., Liverpool 3, England, for "And When Did You Last See Your Father?" by W. F. Yeames.

The Wallis-Wiley Studio, 2175 E. Foothill Blvd., Pasadena 8, Calif., for the photograph of the Window of the Great Commission, Pacific School of Religion.

The Wayfarers' Chapel, Portuguese Bend, Palos Verdes, Calif., Kenneth W. Knox, Minister, for the photograph of the chapel.

Mr. Zaphirios Zaphiriou, 6 G. Gennediou St., Athens, Greece, for his photograph of "John Damascene" by Fotis Kontoglous.

In addition to those already mentioned who have contributed interpretative material for the pictures, we are also indebted to the following:

Dr. Jorge Bocobo and *The Central Spire,* bulletin of Central Methodist Church, Manila, for the interpretation of "The Symbolism of Central Christian Church, Manila."

Mr. Joe Bragg, Jr., 407 Shore Crest Dr., Tampa, Fla., for the interpretations of "Pestalozzi and the Children" and "The Good Samaritan."

M. Daniel Buscarlet, Eglise Nationale Protestante, 24 Bourg-de-Four, Geneva, Switz., for the interpretation of "St. Peter's Cathedral, Geneva."

California Mission Trails Assn., Ltd., 4015 Wilshire Blvd., Los Angeles, Calif., for the interpretation of "Santa Barbara Mission," from *California's Missions,* edited by Ralph B. Wright.

Mr. George Wayland Carpenter and Leco Press, Léopoldville, Africa, for the interpretation of "The Kimpese Christian Institute," from his publication, *Highways for God in Congo.*

Dr. A. T. DeGroot and The Christian Board of Publication, Beaumont and Pine Blvd., St. Louis 3, Mo., for the interpretation of "Here I Stand," from "Scenes of the Protestant Reformation" by A. T. DeGroot, published in *The Christian Evangelist,* Vol. 92.

G. Fattorusso, Via Montebello 11 rosso, Florence, Italy, for the interpretation of "St. Peter's Cathedral, Rome," quoted from *Wonders of Italy.*

Friendship Press, Interchurch Center, 475 Riverside Dr., New York 27, N. Y., for the interpretations of "Go Teach All Nations" by Lu Hung-nine, from *Each with His Own Brush* and "Anglican Cathedral, Dornakal," from *Christian Symbols in a World Community,* both by Daniel J. Fleming, and for other short quotations from these two books.

Mr. Harold Johnson, Disciples of Christ, 222 S. Downey Ave., Indianapolis 7, Ind., for the interpretations of "Martin Luther" and "Old Woman at Prayer."

Mr. Donald C. Lacy, Minister, Webster Methodist Church, Rte. 1, Parker, Ind., for the interpretation of "John Wesley."

New York Graphic Society, 95 E. Putnam Ave., Greenwich, Conn., for a nine-line excerpt from *The Complete Letters of Vincent Van Gogh* which appeared in *This Week Magazine* on Nov. 16, 1958. The excerpt is quoted in the interpretation of "The Good Samaritan."

Miss Ruth Peterson, Nashua, Iowa, for the interpretation of "Dr. and Mrs. Royal J. Dye Memorial Church, Congo," from *World Call,* July-Aug. 1957.

Pilgrim Press, 14 Beacon St., Boston 8, Mass., for a portion of the interpretation of "The Crucifixion of St. Peter," from *The Gospel in Art* by Albert Edward Bailey.

Charles Scribner's Sons, 597 Fifth Ave., New York 17, N. Y., for the interpretations of "Christmas Night," "The Holy Family," "Go Preach," and "The Ascension," all from *Christ and His Gospel in Recent Art* by Albert Edward Bailey.

Prof. Walter W. Sikes, Christian Theological Seminary, Indianapolis 7, Ind., for the interpretation of "Knight, Death, and the Devil," selections from an unpublished sermon on justification by faith.

The United Presbyterian Church in the U.S.A., Interchurch Center, 475 Riverside Dr., New York 27, N. Y., for the story used as the interpretation of "Grandmother's Prayer." This story, originally entitled, "Grandmother's Return," appeared in *World Family* for February 1959.

Mrs. Evelyn R. Wagner, 5435 Carrollton Ave., Indianapolis 20, Ind., for the interpretation of "William Tyndale."

Women's Christian College, Madras, India, for the interpretation of "Chapel of Women's Christian College, Madras," quoted from the college's 1955 *Bulletin.*

POETRY

For granting permission to reprint poems already published or to publish those appearing in print for the first time:

Abingdon Press, 201 Eighth Ave., S., Nashville 2, Tenn., for "Discovery" from *Songs from the Slums* by Toyohiko Kagawa and "His Love Is Always Shining" by John Oxenham from *Meditations under the Sky* by Dorothy Wells Pease.

American Mission to Lepers, 156 Fifth Ave., New York 10, N. Y., for "Glory to God" by Handa, "Entrusting All" by Keizo Kanda, "In All Things, Victory" by Honami Nagata; and "Christmas" by Yamamoto from *Hearts Aglow* by Lois J. Erickson and Honami Nagata; and "A Holy Temple" by Handa and "Holding the Cross" by Hayashi from *Souls Undaunted,* translated by Lois J. Erickson.

Glenn H. Asquith and the American Baptist Convention, 152 Madison Ave., New York 16, N. Y., for his poem "The Church" from *Baptist Leader,* Dec. 1941.

Association Press, 5 Russell St., Calcutta, India, for "From This Day On" and "Prayer" by Narayan Vaman Tilak from *Narayan Vaman Tilak* by J. C. Winslow.

Miss Mary Austin and the University of New Mexico Press, Albuquerque, N. M., for

888   ACKNOWLEDGMENTS

"Litany for New Mexico" from *Signature of the Sun.*

Miss Catherine Baker, 275 Robincroft Dr., Pasadena 6, Calif., for "The Church Gives Strength," "Korean Flag," "Korean Youth," and "Yosu Village," from *Land of Morning Splendor,* written especially for this anthology.

The Baptist Home and Hospital, 316 Randolph St., Maywood, Ill., for "A Hymn Poem" by The Venerable Bede, translated by Elizabeth Charles and appearing in *The World's Great Religious Poetry,* edited by Caroline Miles Hill.

Bethany Press, 2640 Pine Blvd., St. Louis, Mo., for "Increase My Love, O God," "Lord, Must I Climb?" "O Lord, Forgive," "Petition," "The Quiet Hour," "Serve Where There Is Need," "When I Have Food," and "Why?" from *Between-Time Meditations* by Samuel F. Pugh; and "In Lincoln Cathedral" by Thomas Curtis Clark from *The Christian-Evangelist,* Nov. 12, 1936.

Mrs. James C. Blackie, 37 Greensbank Rd., Edinburgh 10, Scotland, for the English translation of "Its Only Joy, Saviour and Lord," Leo Jud's version of Psalm 25.

The Christian Century Foundation, 407 S. Dearborn St., Chicago 5, Ill., for "New England Spires" and "Witnesses" by Leslie Savage Clark and "Thoughts in a Cathedral" by Thomas Curtis Clark from issues of *Christian Century.*

The Christian Foundation, Inc., 301 Washington St., Columbus, Ind., and North River Press, 597 Fifth Ave., New York, N. Y., for "We Greet Thee, King of Mercy and of Grace" by John Calvin from *Christian Hymns.*

Christian Herald, 27 E. 39th St., New York 16, N. Y., and Margaret Chaplin (Mrs. J. S.) Anderson, 7807 Three Chopt Rd., Richmond 26, Va., for "And It Was Night" from the April 1958 issue; and Ralph T. Nordlund, Fostoria Baptist Church, 4th and Wood Sts., Fostoria, Ohio, for "A Prayer for Our New Church," also from *Christian Herald.*

Mrs. Leslie Savage Clark, 99 Monterey Rd., Rochester 18, N. Y., for "Architect," "Dusk at the Airport," "Man's Heritage," "Master Builder," "Memorial," "My Father's House," "Of Peter," "Portrait of a Pastor," "Prayer," "World Wide Communion," and "Worship," all from *With All Thy Heart,* published by Broadman Press, Nashville, Tenn.

Mrs. Thomas Curtis Clark, 242 Marshall Ave., Bellwood, Ill., and Miss Dorothy Wells Pease for "Trust the Great Artist" by Thomas Curtis Clark from *Meditations Under the Sky* by Miss Pease.

Dartmouth Publications, Dartmouth University, Hanover, N. H., and L. C. Page & Co., 101 Fifth Ave., New York 3, N. Y., for "The First Autumn" by Marshall W. Schacht from *Dartmouth Verse, 1925.*

Ricardo Demetillo and Guinhalinan Press, Quezon City, P. I., for "Longinus" from *No Certain Weather.*

The Devin-Adair Company, 23 E. 26th St., New York 10, N. Y., for "Be Thou My Vision," translated by Eleanor Hull, from *1000 Years of Irish Poetry,* edited by Kathleen Hoagland.

Miss Lois Anna Ely, 2429 Thirty-third St., Santa Monica, Calif., for "Acceptable," "Flowers for the Altar," "Fulfillment," and "Infiltration," written especially for this anthology.

Friendship Press, Interchurch Center, 475 Riverside Dr., New York 27, N. Y., and Chandran Devanesen for "Christ of the Indian Road," "The Cross Is Lifted," "Discovery," "Hedges," and "Thy Yoke" from *The Cross Is Lifted.* Also Friendship Press for "The Carpenter" by Gumpei Yamamuro, "Christ Liveth in Me" and "The Living Christ" by Toyohiko Kagawa, and "Prelude" by Lois J. Erickson from *Songs from the Land of Dawn.*

Dr. Michael G. H. Gelsinger, 524 Winspeare Ave., Buffalo, N. Y., for portions of his translation of "Good Friday Eve Encomia" from *Orthodox Hymns in English.*

Everett A. Gillis, 3202 32nd St., Lubbock, Tex., for "Circuit Rider" from *Southwester Anthology,* published by the American Poetry Assn., Dallas, Tex.

Miss Ellen Lakshmi Goreh, c/o Zenith Press, 19 Conway St., Fitzroy Sq., London W. 1, England, for "The Guardian" from *Devotees of Christ* by D. S. Batley and A. M. Robinson.

Rachel E. Miller (Mrs. H. D.) Graves, 1150 Western Way, Orlando, Fla., and L. C. Page & Co., 101 Fifth Ave., New York 3, N. Y., for "The Silent Wooded Place" from a Rockford College publication.

Harper & Brothers, 49 E. 33rd St., New York 16, N. Y., for "Exit God" by Gamaliel Bradford, "I Never Saw a Moor" by Emily Dickinson, and "Countryman's God" by Roger Winship Stuart from *Masterpieces of Religious Verse,* edited by James Dalton Morrison; "Anabaptist Martyr's Hymn" by Leonard Schiemer from *The Renaissance and the Reformation* by Henry S. Lucas; "Oh, Holy Spirit" by Tsu-chen Chao, "Adoration" by Krishna Pillai, and two Chinese prayers, "For Broken Families" and "Magnanimity and Restraint," from *The*

World at One in Prayer by Daniel J. Fleming; and "Indifference" from *The Sorrows of God* by G. A. Studdert-Kennedy.

Hartford Seminary Foundation, 55 Elizabeth Ave., Hartford 5, Conn., for "He Says," "I Return," and "Purification" by Gonzalo Báez-Camargo, translated by J. C. Field, and "If You Love God" by Amado Nervo.

Ann Louise (Mrs. Frank A.) Hayes, Carnegie Institute of Technology, Schenley Park, Pittsburgh 13, Pa., for "Sonnet for a Marriage" from *Poets of the Pacific,* published by Stanford University Press.

Houghton Mifflin Company, 2 Park St., Boston 7, Mass., for "Landing of the Pilgrim Fathers" by Felicia Hemans, "The Word of God to Leyden Came" by Jeremiah Eames Rankin, and "God Makes a Path" by Roger Williams from *Poems of American History,* edited by Burton Stevenson; and "An Epitaph on My Dear and Honoured Mother" by Anne Bradstreet and "The Problem" by Ralph Waldo Emerson from *American Poetry and Prose,* edited by Norman Foerster.

The International Cultural Assn., Seoul, Korea, for "Charity" and "O God" by Y. T. Pyun from *Songs from Korea.*

The Korean Research and Information Society, 1828 Jefferson Pl., Washington 6, D. C., for "The Hills in Autumn" by Yu Chasin and "Triangle Mountain" by Kim Sanghun from *Korean Survey,* Feb. 1955.

The Misses Grace Ross and Mabel M. Kuykendall, 4429 Foard St., Forth Worth 19, Tex., for "Evolution" by Artemisia B. Bryson from *Poetry Out Where the West Begins.*

Miss Clarice White Luck, P. O. Box 7, Columbiana, Ala., for her poem, "Intercessors," from *Alabama Christian Advocate,* Aug. 1952, and "The Star—The Cross—The Empty Tomb," written especially for this anthology.

Lutterworth Press, 4 Bouverie St., London, E.C. 4, England, for "In Convalescence" and "In the Midst of the Illness" by Huldreich Zwingli from *Zwingli the Reformer* by Oskar Farner.

The Macmillan Company, 60 Fifth Ave., New York 11, N. Y., for "The Nameless Saints" by Edward Everett Hale and "Doubt" by Helen Hunt Jackson from *The World's Great Religious Poetry* by Caroline Hill.

Miss Rosa Zagnoni Marinoni, Villa Rosa, Fayetteville, Ark., for "Christmas in the Ozarks" from *Signature of the Sun.*

Virgil Markham and Doubleday & Co., Inc., 575 Madison Ave., New York 22, N. Y., for "How the Great Guest Came" from *The Shoes of Happiness and Other Poems* by Edwin Markham.

Earl Marlatt, Perkins School of Theology, Dallas, Texas, for "Augustine," "Canticle to Il Poverello," "Far Music," "Francis," "John the Baptist," "Let There Be Light," "Mountain Communion," "Nameless, Not Unknown," "Paul," "People," and "Peter" from *Cathedral: A Volume of Poems,* published by Parthenon Press.

McClelland, Goodchild & Stewart, 25 Holinger Rd., Toronto 16, Ontario, for "Standing on Tiptoe" by George Frederick Cameron, "Harvest Hymn" by Charles Sangster, and "The Builder" by Duncan Campbell Scott from *Canadian Poets and Poetry,* edited by John W. Garvin.

New York University Press, Washington Sq., New York, N. Y., for "Song of Myself" (Section 48) from *Walt Whitman's Poems,* edited by Gay Wilson Allen and Charles T. Davis.

Miss Erica Oxenham, High Salvington, Worthing, Sussex, England, and Methuen & Co., Ltd., London, for "Bring Us the Light," "Credo," "India," "Liberty, Equality, Fraternity," "Livingstone's Soliloquy," "Quo Vadis?" and "Stephen—Paul" by John Oxenham from *Bees in Amber.*

The Provincial Elders Conference of the Moravian Church in America (Northern Province), 69 W. Church St., Bethlehem, Pa., for English translations of "Christian Unity" by Matthias Czerwenka, "Give to the Winds Thy Fears" by Paul Gerhardt, "An Evening Prayer" by Petrus Herbert, "The Word of God" attributed to John Huss, "The Moravian Emigrants' Hymn" by Henry Isaac, "Lord, Keep Us Steadfast in Thy Word" and "A Missionary Prayer" by Martin Luther, "Morning Prayer for the Day's Work" by John Matthesius, "The Church of Christ" by Augustus G. Spangenburg, and "Glory to God, Whose Witness Train" by Nicolaus L. von Zinzendorf from *Hymnal and Liturgies of the Moravian Church (Unitas Fratrum).*

Reilly & Lee Company, 325 Huron St., Chicago, Ill., and the late Edgar A. Guest for his poem, "God Builds No Churches," from *A Book of Collected Verse.*

James Servel Reyes and *The Manila Times,* 120 E. 56th St., New York 22, N. Y., for "Prayer for Our Country" and "Those Between" from *The Manila Times.*

Dr. James S. Ruby, Pres., Georgetown Alumni Assn., Georgetown University, Washington 7, D. C., for "To a Fossil Fern" by John A. Foote.

The Ryerson Press, 299 Queen St. W., Toronto, Ontario, for "The Builder" from *Selected Poems of Duncan Campbell Scott.*

Arthur M. Sampley, Box 5263, N. Texas Sta., Denton, Tex., for "R. I. P." from *Signature of the Sun.*

Charles Scribner's Sons, 597 Fifth Ave., New York 17, N. Y., for "A Ballad of Trees and the Master" from *Poems of Sidney Lanier,* edited by Mrs. Sidney Lanier.

Silver Burdett Company, Morristown, N. J., for "Philippine Hymn."

The Society of SS. Peter and Paul, 32 George St., Hanover Sq., London, for "In the Garden," "Jerusalem," and "The Road to Emmaus" from *Sonnets of the Cross* by Thomas S. Jones, Jr.

The Reverend Henry C. Spear, 128 Church St., Hartford, Wis., for "Apostle John," "Apostle Matthew," "Apostle Paul," "Apostle Peter," "John Mark," "Mary Magdalene," "Mary and Martha," "Mary, Mother of Jesus," and "Stephen," all written especially for this anthology.

Miss Hallie Strange, 4928 Homes St., Dallas 6, Tex., for "Peace Like a River" and "Word Incarnate."

Arthur Swallow, Publisher, 2679 S. York, Denver 10, Colo., for "The Mountain Cemetery" and "The Wise Men" from *The Form of Loss* by Edgar Bowers and "To My Father" from *No Moat No Castle* by Donald F. Drummond.

Syracuse University Press, University Sta., Syracuse 10, N. Y., for "A Spirit Muses" by Franklin B. Williams from *Syracuse Chapbook.*

Brig. Gen. Robert P. Taylor, Deputy Chief of Air Force Chaplains, Dept. of the Air Force, Hq USAF, Washington 25, D. C., for "An Airman's Prayer" by a USAF pilot from *Chaplain Newsletter.*

Miss Mary Agnes Thompson, 809 NW 22nd St., Oklahoma City 6, Okla., for "Prairie Woman's Prayer" from *Southwester Anthology,* published by the American Poetry Assn., Dallas, Tex.

University of Chicago Press, 5750 Ellis Ave., Chicago 37, Ill., for "Sea Lavender" by Louise Morey Bowman and "The Wayside Cross" by Frederick George Scott from *The Book of Canadian Poetry,* edited by A. J. M. Smith.

World's Student Christian Federation, 13 Rue Calvin, Geneva, Switz., for English translations of "Sitting Beside the Babylonian Waters" by Clement Marot and "The Cause for Which We Strive Is Thine" by Samuel Preiswerk and Graf F. Zaremba.

The following, each of whom contributed one poem to this anthology: A. L. Alexander, "The Church Within"; Ralph Spaulding Cushman, "My Petition"; Edna V. Edwards, "His Presence"; Paul Gilbert, "Your Own Version of the Gospel"; Beulah Hughes, "I am the Church"; Juan C. Nabong, Jr., "Judas Iscariot"; Ruby Leah Ordinario, "This Is to Live"; Ann McDevitt (Mrs. Kenneth) Seeley, "A Worthy Church"; and Mojebo Pierre, "A Prayer for the Sacraments," Edna Poole, "Congo Christmas," and Wanga Yoane, "The Wine of the Sacrament," the last three poems coming also through the courtesy of the Congo Christian Institute, Belgian Congo, Africa.

STORIES

For granting permission to reprint stories and other prose writings previously published:

Abingdon Press, 201 Eighth Ave. S., Nashville 2, Tenn., for "Move to Indiana," an abridgment from *Frontier Bishop* by Worth M. Tippy; "The Bell Founder's Window" and "Luca della Robbia's Singing Gallery" from *Great Art and Children's Worship* by Jean Louise Smith; "A Bible for Plowboys and Poets," an abridgment of the chapter on the English Bible from *How Came the Bible?* by Edgar J. Goodspeed; "Man with a Twa-Handed Sword," an abridgment of the chapter on John Knox from *Men Who Made the Churches* by Paul Hutchinson; "Early Winter in a Rural Parish," an abridgment from *Rural Parish!* by Anna Laura Gebhard; and "Kagawa, God's Hand in Japan," an abridgment from *Songs from the Slums* by Toyohiko Kagawa.

American Mission to Lepers, 156 Fifth Ave., New York 10, N. Y., for "Keizo Finds a New Way of Life" from *Hearts Aglow* by Honami Nagata and Lois J. Erickson.

Miss Ellen Baker and *Uplift Magazine,* Concord, N. C., R. Vance Robertson, Ed., for "Martin Luther and the Eisleben Choir."

The Baker & Taylor Co., Rte. 22 & Broad St., Hillside, N. J., for "Proposals for the Union of Christians" by Thomas Campbell, abridged from "Declaration and Address," as found in *The Disciples of Christ* by Errett Gates.

Bruce Barton, 383 Madison Ave., New York 17, N. Y., executor of the estate of William E. Barton, for "The Gospel According to Andrew" and "The Gospel According to Judas" from *Four Hitherto Unpublished Gospels* by William E. Barton, now out of print.

George Bell & Sons, London, for "St. Bernard of Clairvaux" and "St. Boniface" from *The Saints in Christian Art* by Mrs. Arthur Bell.

Cassell and Company, Ltd., 37-38 St. Andrew's Hill, London, E. C. 4, England, for "Handel's Messiah," an abridgment from *George Frederic Handel* by Newman Flower.

Catholic Foreign Mission Society of America, Maryknoll, N. Y., and McMullen Books, Inc., 839 Stewart Ave., Garden City, N. Y., for "The End Is a Beginning" from *The Meaning of Maryknoll* by Albert J. Nevins.

Caxton Printers, Ltd., Caldwell, Idaho, for "American Home Missionary Society and Oregon," an abridgment from *Home Missions on the American Frontier* by Colin Brummit Goodykoontz.

Christian Board of Publication, Beaumont and Pine Blvds., St. Louis 3, Mo., for an abridgment of the article "Our Protestant Heritage" by Walter W. Sikes from *The Christian-Evangelist,* Vol. 92.

Christian Herald, 27 E. 39th St., New York 16, N. Y., and Glenn H. Asquith, for "A House for God."

P. F. Collier & Son, 640 Fifth Ave., New York 19, N. Y., for "Quaker Individualism" from *More Fruits of Solitude* by William Penn, published in *The Harvard Classics,* Vol. I.

Columbia University (Teachers' College), New York, N. Y., for "Church, School and State" by Samuel Windsor Brown, abridged from *The Secularization of American Education.*

Commission on Ecumenical Mission and Relations of the United Presbyterian Church in the U.S.A., Interchurch Center, 475 Riverside Drive, New York 27, N. Y., for an abridgment of "Hong Kong—Taiwan—China" from the Commission's *First Annual Report;* "Take to the Air," an abridgment of news stories in *Current News:* "Korea": Autumn 1958; and "Korea, Hong Kong, Taiwan": Spring 1959; and "Healing for Body and Spirit," an abridgment of news stories in *Current News:* "The Philippines": Autumn 1958 and Winter 1958.

Congo Christian Institute, Bolenge, Belgian Congo, Africa, for "And Ye Shall Be My Witnesses," a true story translated by Edna Poole, and "The Sacrament of Christian Baptism" by Jack Barron; permission was also received from Miss Poole and Mr. Barron.

James Dickson and The Evangelical Publishers, 241 Younge St., Toronto, Ontario, for "Stranger Than Fiction" from the book of the same title.

Vernard M. Eller, c/o Pacific School of Religion, 1796 Scenic Ave., Berkeley 9, Calif., for "Sealed at the Lord's Table," a speech delivered in the Kneeland Speech Contest, May 1957, of the Pacific School of Religion.

Frederick J. Fawcett II, 129 South St., Boston 11, Mass., for "The Faith Healer" by William Vaughan Moody from the book of the same title.

Friendship Press, Interchurch Center, 475 Riverside Dr., New York 27, N. Y., for "Lines to a Rickshaw Puller" and "One of the Twelve Fell Away" from *The Cross Is Lifted* by Chandran Devanesen; "The Ministry of Health and Healing" and "Village Life in Rural India" from *India at the Threshold* by L. Winifred Bryce; "Junipero Serra: Father of the California Missions" from *Pioneers of Goodwill* by Harold B. Hunting; "Preacher Yu" from *Tales from China* by Alice Hudson Lewis; and "Bricks and a Dream" by Alice Geer Kelsey, "God's Gift to Paquito" by Elizabeth Allstrom, and "Pablo Helps with the Writing" by Mabel Niedermeyer from *Missionary Stories to Play and Tell,* edited by Nina Millen.

Kenneth F. Hall and Gospel Trumpet Co., Anderson, Ind., for an abridgment of "Through Peril and Fire" from *They Stand Tall: Life Stories of Fifteen Great Men and Women.*

Harcourt, Brace & Co., 383 Madison Ave., New York 17, N. Y., for "Music on the Muscatatuck" from *The Friendly Persuasion* by Jessamyn West.

Harper & Brothers, 49 E. 33rd St., New York 16, N. Y., for "The Pilgrimage to Bethlehem" and "Wise Men from the East," abridgments from *Ben Hur, a Tale of the Christ* by Lew Wallace; an abridgment of "Prisons—and the Golden Rule" from *Deeds Done for Christ* by Sir James Marchant; "A Spire on the Horizon," an abridgment from *Dig or Die, Brother Hyde* by William J. Hyde; "A Message from the Second Assembly of the World Council of Churches" by Bishop Lesslie Newbigin from *The Evanston Report;* "Every Man in His Own Language," an abridgment from *God's Word in Man's Language* by Eugene A. Nida; "St. Benedict" from *Great Men of the Christian Church* by Williston Walker; "Gregory Palamas:

Mystical Illumination," a condensation of pp. 274-79 of *The Holy Fire* by Robert Payne; "The Ministry of Friendship" from *The Spirit of American Christianity* by Ronald E. Osborn; "Peter, the Man of Impulse," an abridgment from *These Twelve* by Charles R. Brown; and "Father Tabart" from Chap. I of *The White Fathers* by Glenn D. Kittler (permission also of W. H. Allen & Co., Ltd., 43 Essex St., Strand, London, England, for British Empire rights).

Harvard University Press, Cambridge 38, Mass., and the Loeb Classical Library for "The Martyrdom of Polycarp," "The Vision of the Leviathan," and "Who the Christians Are" from *The Apostolic Fathers,* and for a condensation of *Barlaam and Ioasaph* by John Dama-scene.

Hodder & Stoughton, Ltd., St. Paul's House, Warwick Sq., London, E.C. 4, England, for an abridgment from Chap. V of *God in the Slums* by Hugh Redwood.

Houghton Mifflin Company, 2 Park St., Boston 7, Mass., for "Prayer and Creeds," an abridgment of *Self-Reliance* by Ralph Waldo Emerson from *American Poetry and Prose,* edited by Norman Foerster; and abridgments of "The Light of the World Is Come" and "This Is My Beloved Son" from *The Story of Jesus Christ* by Elizabeth Stuart Phelps.

Mrs. Paul Hutchinson and the Editors of *Life* Magazine, New York, N. Y., for permission to quote, in the Introduction to this anthology, a short passage by Paul Hutchinson from *The World's Great Religions.*

Institute of Social and Religious Research, 30 Rockefeller Plaza, New York 20, N. Y., for "The Tumult of Her Birth" by Claris Edwin Silcox from *Church Union in Canada.*

Alfred A. Knopf, Inc., 501 Madison Ave., New York 22, N. Y., for abridgments of "Jesus, As Seen by Joseph of Arimathea" and "Simon, Who Was Called Peter" from *Jesus, the Son of Man* by Kahlil Gibran.

Fotis Kontoglous, Athens, Greece, and *Kivotos* for "The Meek Icon," condensed and translated from the Greek by John P. Cavarnos, from *Kivotos,* Dec. 1952.

Elizabeth Meredith Lee and Woman's Division of Christian Service of the Methodist Church, 7820 Reading Rd., Cincinnati 37, Ohio, for abridgments of "Librada Javalera of the Philippines" and "Lidia Vargas in Chile" from *Thirteen Biographies.*

Lutterworth Press, 4 Bouverie St., London E.C. 4, England, for "Keeper of the City," an abridgment of a chapter on Theodore Beza from *Beza's "Icones"* by C. G. McCrie, and "Giving Worship Back to the People," an abridgment of the chapter, "The Consummation in Zurich," from *Zwingli the Reformer* by Oskar Farner.

The Macmillan Company, 60 Fifth Ave., New York 11, N. Y., for "The Winter of the Cross" from *Raymond and I* by Elizabeth Robins.

The Moody Press, 820 N. LaSalle St., Chicago 10, Ill., for "Stephen, the First Christian Martyr" from *Christian Martyrs of the World* by John Foxe and "Vignettes of the Apostles of the Early Church," arranged by Cynthia Pearl Maus from information in the same volume.

Robert T. Oliver and Dodd Mead & Company, 432 Fourth Ave., New York 16, N. Y., for "A Christian World Statesman and Patriot" from *Syngman Rhee, the Man Behind the Myth.*

Lovick Pierce, *Together* Magazine, 740 N. Rush St., Chicago, Ill., for "America's Fourth Faith" by T. Otto Nall from the July 15, 1958, issue.

Presbyterian Life, Witherspoon Bldg., Philadelphia 7, Pa., for abridgments of "Bridgehead in East Harlem" from the May 15, 1959, issue and "Eskimo Preacher" by Edith J. Agnew from the Dec. 9, 1950, issue.

Fleming H. Revell Company, Inc., Westwood, N. J., for "Attempt Great Things for God," an abridgment of the story of William Carey from *Epoch Makers of Modern Missions* by Archibald McLean and an abridgment of "By Invitation of Jesus" from *Mr. Jones, Meet the Master* by Peter Marshall.

St. Columbans' Foreign Mission Society, St. Columbans, Neb., for an abridgment of *White Martyrdom* by the Reverend John Henaghan.

The Saturday Review, 25 West 45th St., New York 36, N. Y., for "The Hiroshima Maid-ens," based on editorials by Norman Cousins appearing in issues of April 19, 1955; May 14, 1955; Oct. 15, 1955; June 9, 1956; and June 14, 1958.

Sheed and Ward, Inc., 840 Broadway, New York 3, N. Y., for "St. Joseph of Arimathea" from *New Six O'Clock Saints* by Joan Windham.

The Society for Promoting Christian Knowledge, Marylebone Rd., London, N. W. 1, England, and Harper & Brothers, New York, for a condensation of pp. 1-42 of *The Way of a Pilgrim,* translated by R. M. French.

Pablo David Sosa and The Board of World Missions of the Methodist Church, Interchurch Center, 475 Riverside Dr., New York 27, N. Y., for "A Young Christian Sees America" from *Pampa Breezes,* Oct.-Dec. 1957.

Vellore News, Vellore Christian Medical College Board, Inc., Vellore, South India, for statistics from the issue of Spring-Summer 1957, quoted at the end of "The Ministry of Health and Healing."

Wanga Yoane and the United Christian Missionary Society, Missions Bldg., Indianapolis 7, Ind., for "A New World Comes to Africa Through the Church" from *Wanga Yoane* (his autobiography), translated by Herbert Smith.

MUSIC

For granting permission to reproduce words and music of hymns previously published:

American Peace Society, 1307 New Hampshire Ave., Washington 6, D. C., for the words of "Let There Be Light, Lord God" by William Vories.

Association Press, 20 Museum Rd., Shanghai, China, for words and music of "A Hymn of Praise" from *Songs of Cathay,* compiled by T. Z. Koo.

Miss Catherine Baker, 275 Robincroft Dr., Pasadena 6, Calif., for the words of "Peace Through His Cross" and her translation of "To Work, to Work" from *Land of Morning Splendor,* published by Dierkes Press, Eureka Springs, Ark.

Baptist Publishing House, P. O. Box 4255, El Paso, Tex., for the Spanish versions of "Jesus Is My Sovereign King" and "O Jesus I Have Promised" from *El Nuevo Hymnario Popular.*

Bethany Press, 2640 Pine Blvd., St. Louis 3, Mo., for words and music of "Here at Thy Table, Lord" and music by Cleo Milligan for "To All the Nations, Lord" from *Christian Worship.*

Dean D. Bouzianis, 39 Newcomb St., Haverhill, Mass., for "Cherubic Hymn" and "Nativity Ode" and his transcriptions of all the Byzantine hymns.

The Christian Foundation, Inc., 301 Washington St., Columbus, Ind., for the words of "O Sacred Head, Now Wounded," "We Gather Together," and "Ye Servants of God, Your Master Proclaim."

The Church Pension Fund, 20 Exchange Pl., New York 5, N. Y., for permission to photograph "O Saviour, Bless Us Ere We Go," "O What Their Joy and Their Glory Must Be," and "The Royal Banners Forward Go" from *The Hymnal, 1940,* published by The Church Hymnal Corporation.

Cooperative Recreation Service, Inc., Radnor Rd., Delaware, Ohio, for words and music of "Light Thou the Lamp" and "Listen to Our Prayer" from *Joyful Songs of India.*

Purd E. Deitz, Board of National Missions, 1720 Chouteau Ave., St. Louis 3, Mo., for the words of "We Would Be Building" and for his explanation of how they came to be written.

Eden Publishing House, 1724 Chouteau Ave., St. Louis 3, Mo., for words and music of "All Glory, Laud, and Honor," and "Crown Him with Many Crowns," and music of "Father, We Praise Thee" from *The Hymnal.*

J. C. Ekofo and Congo Christian Institute, Bolenge, Congo-Belge, Africa, for words and music of "Our Home" and "Storm on the Lake."

Dr. Harry Emerson Fosdick, The Riverside Church, 490 Riverside Dr., New York 27, N. Y., for the words of "God of Grace and God of Glory."

Dr. John Haynes Holmes, The Community Church, 10 Park Ave., New York 16, N. Y., for the words of "The Voice of God Is Calling."

The Hymn Society of America, 297 Fourth Ave., New York 10, N. Y., for "I to the Hills Will Lift Mine Eyes" from *The Three Hundredth Anniversary of the Scottish Psalter, 1650–1950.*

Lovedale Press, Alice C.P., Africa, for words and music, as well as the interpretation, of "Lord, Bless Africa" by Enoch Sontonga from *Lovedale Sol-fa Leaflets,* No. 17.

Earl Marlatt, Perkins School of Theology, Dallas, Texas, for the words of "A Christmas Hymn for Peace" from his 1950 Christmas folder, *Journey's End.*

Stanley L. Osborne, Box 1330, Whitby, Ontario, and Ryerson Press for the music "Muswell Hill" for the hymn "My Faith It Is an Oaken Staff" from *Canadian Youth Hymnal.*

Miss Erica Oxenham, High Salvington, Worthing, Sussex, England, and Methuen & Co., Ltd., London, for the words of "In Christ There Is No East or West" from *Bees in Amber* by John Oxenham.

Oxford University Press, Warwick Sq., London, E. C. 4, England, for permission to photograph "Brief Life Is Here Our Portion," "Creator Spirit, by Whose Aid," "Disposer Supreme, and Judge of the Earth," "Hark! A Herald Voice Is Calling," "O Trinity of Blessed Light," and "Therefore We, Before Him Bending" from *Songs of Praise* and to include words and music of "My God, I Love Thee," reprinted from the same collection; for the words of "Father, We Praise Thee" and an adaptation of the interpretation of "Creator Spirit, By Whose Aid" from *Songs of Praise Discussed;* and for the music "Magda" by Ralph Vaughan Williams for the hymn "God of the Prairies" from *The English Hymnal.*

Presbyterian Board of Christian Education, Witherspoon Bldg., Philadelphia 7, Pa., for words and music of "O Love, How Deep" from *The Hymnal* and the special arrangement of "Finlandia" by Jean Sibelius used in "We Would Be Building" (permission also received from Breitkof & Härtel, Wiesbaden, Germany).

Frank W. Price, c/o Missionary Research Library, 3041 Broadway, New York 27, N. Y., for words and music of "O Christ Our Great Foundation" from *Chinese Christian Hymns.*

The Provincial Elders Conference of the Moravian Church in America (Northern Province), 69 W. Church St., Bethlehem, Pa., for words and music of "Through the Night of Doubt and Sorrow" from *Hymnal and Liturgies of the Moravian Church (Unitas Fratrum).*

Fleming H. Revell Company, Inc., Westwood, N. J., for the interpretation of "In Christ There Is No East or West" from *Lyric Religion* by H. Augustine Smith.

Cyril C. Richardson, 99 Claremont Ave., New York 27, N. Y., for the words of "God of the Prairies."

Thomas Tiplady, 22 Chester Way, London, S.W. 11, England, and the Hymn Society of America, New York, N. Y., for the words of "To All the Nations, Lord" from *Hymns for the Times.*

Westminster Press, Witherspoon Bldg., Philadelphia 7, Pa., for permission to photograph "City of God," "The Lord's My Shepherd," "O God, Beneath Thy Guiding Hand," "Saviour! Thy Dying Love," and " 'Thy Kingdom Come,' on Bended Knee" from *The Hymnbook.*

World's Student Christian Federation, 13 Rue Calvin, Geneva, Switz., for words and music of "Lord, Take Thou the Reins to Thee," "O Lord of All, Our Father," and "Thine Is the Glory" from *Cantate Domino.*

Yale University Press, New Haven, Conn., for words and music of "Life of Ages, Richly Poured" and "O North, with All Thy Vales" and for music of "Let There Be Light, Lord God" and "The Voice of God Is Calling" from Geer's *Hymnal for Colleges and Schools.*

INDEX OF ART AND ART INTERPRETATIONS BY ARTISTS AND TITLES

The *Italics* show the page on which the picture will be found; the Roman figures refer to the interpretation of the picture. Pictures of churches are listed by the name of the architect or by the name of the church.

Alonso, Mateo
Christ of the Andes, 863
Interpretation, 862
Anglican Cathedral
Anglican Cathedral, Dornakal, 807
Interpretation, 806
Anglican Church
Anglican Episcopal Church, Nara, 714
Interpretation, 711
Anthemios and Isadoros (architects)
Hagia Sophia at Constantinople, 167
Interpretation, 164
Artist Unknown
Anastasis or *The Resurrection, 148*
Interpretation, 145
Ardagh Chalice, The, 273
Interpretation, 272
Emperor Justinian and His Court, The, 255
Interpretation, 254
Gregory of Nyssa, 187
Interpretation, 186
St. Constantine and St. Helen, 165
Interpretation, 164
St. Martin's Cross, 271
Interpretation, 270
Barosin, Jacques
Head of Christ, 525
Interpretation, 524
Bartolommeo, Fra
St. Paul, 70
Interpretation, 69
St. Peter, 96
Interpretation, 95
Beecroft, Herbert
"The Lord Turned and Looked at Peter," 45
Interpretation, 42
Bethany College
Bethany College, in the Hills of West Virginia, 689
Interpretation, 687
Boehm, J. E.
William Tyndale, 467
Interpretation, 465
Burnand, Eugene
"Go Preach," 68
Interpretation, 67
Canterbury Cathedral
Canterbury Cathedral, 463
Interpretation, 462

Cap-de-la-Madeleine
Cap-de-la-Madeleine, 362
Interpretation, 361
Caselli-Moretti, Rosa
"The Last Supper" Window, Frontispiece
Interpretation, 38
Central Christian Church
The Symbolism of Central Christian Church, Manila, 784
Interpretation, 783
Ch'en, Luke
Return of the Prodigal, The, 384
Interpretation, 383
St. Paul Before the Altar of the Unknown God, 72
Interpretation, 71
Children's Chapel
Children's Chapel, Pasadena, California, 615
Interpretation, 613
Christ and the Children of the World
Christ and the Children of the World, Redlands, California, 617
Interpretation, 614
Church of the Holy Sepulcher
Church of the Holy Sepulcher, The, 147
Interpretation, 145
Cloisters, The
Cuxa Cloister, The, 295
Interpretation, 294
Congregational Meetinghouse
Congregational Meetinghouse, Oberlin, Ohio, 567
Interpretation, 565
Cram, Ralph Adams (architect)
Cathedral Church of St. John the Divine, The, New York City, 663
Interpretation, 662
Dali, Salvador
Sacrament of the Last Supper, The, 382
Interpretation, 381
del Sarto, Andrea
Judas Iscariot, 43
Interpretation, 41
Díaz, Horacio (architect)
Union Evangelical Seminary, Río Piedras (San Juan), 861
Interpretation, 860
Dolci, Carlo
St. John, the Evangelist, 100
Interpretation, 99

Dukas, Demetrios
Pantocrator, 230
Interpretation, 228
Dürer, Albrecht
Knight, Death, and the Devil, 409
Interpretation, 407
Dye Memorial Church
Dr. and Mrs. Royal J. Dye Memorial Church, 835
Interpretation, 832
El Greco
St. Andrew, 150
Interpretation, 146
St. Jerome, 253
Interpretation, 250
Eldershaw, John
Church on the Hill, The, 386
Interpretation, 385
First Presbyterian Church
First Presbyterian Church, Bellevue, Nebraska, 589
Interpretation, 588
Fort Yukon, Alaska
Moosehide Altar, Fort Yukon, Alaska, 641
Interpretation, 639
Fougeron, John (architect)
St. Paul's Church, Halifax, Nova Scotia, 635
Interpretation, 634
Gérôme, Jean Léon
Last Prayer, The, 126
Interpretation, 125
Glastonbury Abbey
Glastonbury Abbey, 275
Interpretation, 274
Grünewald, Matthias
Crucifixion, The, 339
Interpretation, 337
Hung-nien, Lu
"Go Teach All Nations", 735
Interpretation, 734
Keith, Elizabeth
Kite-flying in Korea, 765
Interpretation, 762
Kimpese Christian Institute
Kimpese Christian Institute, The, 833
Interpretation, 829
Kontoglous, Fotis
Basil the Great, 169
Interpretation, 168
John Damascene, 189
Interpretation, 186
Transfiguration of Christ, The, 208

Interpretation, 207
Korean Church
Church in Wonju, Korea, 761
Interpretation, 759
Lakeview United Church
Communion Table, Lakeview
United Church, Regina, Sas-
katchewan, 637
Interpretation, 636
Landowski, Paul, and Bouchard,
Henri
Reformation Monument, Geneva,
441
Interpretation, 438
Lang, Alois
Wood Carving of the Last Sup-
per, St. Louis, Missouri, 571
Interpretation, 570
Lanz, Karl Alfred
Pestalozzi and the Children, 499
Interpretation, 496
La Tour, Georges De
Education of the Virgin, The,
364
Interpretation, 363
Lok-Seng-I Presbyterian Church
Lok-Seng-I Presbyterian Church
for Lepers, Taiwan, 739
Interpretation, 736
Long, Edwin
Christ or Diana?, 122
Interpretation, 121
Maes, Nicolas
Old Woman at Prayer, 493
Interpretation, 491
Masaccio
Tribute Money, The, 336
Interpretation, 335
Matsuzawa Church
Matsuzawa Church, Tokyo, 714
Interpretation, 711
McInnes, John (photographer)
Grandmother's Prayer, 763
Interpretation, 759
Michelangelo
Crucifixion of St. Peter, The, 102
Interpretation, 99
Michelangelo and others (archi-
tects)
St. Peter's Cathedral, Rome, 251
Interpretation, 249
Moore Memorial Church
Moore Memorial Church, Shang-
hai, 737
Interpretation, 734
Moroder, Siegfried
Arnoldshain Altar, 523
Interpretation, 520
Morone, Domenico
Dominican Preaching, A, 293
Interpretation, 291
Mote, Marcus
Quaker Meetinghouse, Rich-
mond, Indiana, 569
Interpretation, 566
Motion Picture: Martin Luther
"Here I Stand", 415

Interpretation, 412
Motion Picture: Our Bible—How
It Came to Us
Bible Goes to Press, The, 413
Interpretation, 410
Mount of Olives
Mount of Olives and Gethsem-
ane, 8
Interpretation, 9
Norbert, Nsima
Christ Falls Under the Weight
of His Cross, 831
Interpretation, 829
Notre Dame, Cathedral of
Christ Teaching, Cathedral of
Notre Dame, Chartres, 317
Interpretation, 315
Old Brick Church
Old Brick Church, Smithfield,
Virginia, 547
Interpretation, 545
Panselenos, Manuel
St. John and St. Prochorus, 206
Interpretation, 204
Paschetto, Paolo A.
Waldensian Fresco, 443
Interpretation, 440
Pisa, Cathedral of
Cathedral, Baptistry, and Cam-
panile, Pisa, 316
Interpretation, 314
Poletti, L. (architect)
St. Paul's Cathedral in Rome,
124
Interpretation, 123
Protaton, Church of the
Iconostasis of the Protaton, 227
Interpretation, 225
Raphael, Sanzio
Christ Consigning the Keys to
St. Peter, 341
Interpretation, 340
Rebull, Santiago
Jesus Christ Crucified, 859
Interpretation, 858
Reni, Guido
St. Matthew, 98
Interpretation, 97
Saarinen, Eero (architect)
Modern Altar, Massachusetts In-
stitute of Technology, 693
Interpretation, 692
Saarinen, Eliel (architect)
First Christian Church, Colum-
bus, Indiana, 665
Interpretation, 664
Sadakata, Kwaiseki
Three Saints, The, 712
Interpretation, 711
St. Clement's Church
St. Clement's Church, Alexan-
dria, Virginia, 667
Interpretation, 666
St. Francis of Assisi, Church of
St. Francis of Assisi, Upper and
Lower Church of, 312, 313
Interpretation, 311

St. Martin's Church
Pulpit, St. Martin's Evangelical
Church, Austin, Texas, 591
Interpretation, 590
St. Panteleimon Monastery
St. Panteleimon Monastery, 205
Interpretation, 203
St. Peter's Cathedral
St. Peter's Cathedral, Geneva,
437
Interpretation, 435
St. Philip's
Altar View, St. Philip's in the
Hills, Tucson, Arizona, 593
Interpretation, 592
St. Sophia Cathedral
St. Sophia Cathedral of Los
Angeles, 229
Interpretation, 226
Salisbury, Frank O.
John Wesley, 495
Interpretation, 492
Sallman, Warner E.
Head of Christ, 18
Interpretation, 17
Santa Barbara Mission
Santa Barbara Mission, 359
Interpretation, 357
Seligmann, Adelbert Franz
Holy Family, The, 16
Interpretation, 15
Silliman University Church
Silliman University Church, Du-
maguete, 788
Interpretation, 787
Theophanes of Crete
Athanasios of Alexandria, 185
Interpretation, 184
Theotocopuli, Dominico—See
Greco, El
Thomas, Alfred David
"I Will Come Again", 805
Interpretation, 804
Trinity Church
Trinity Church, New York City,
549
Interpretation, 546
Uhde, Fritz von
The Ascension, 47
Interpretation, 44
Christmas Night, 14
Interpretation, 13
Unitarian Church
Fan Tracery, Unitarian Church,
Charleston, S. C., 551
Interpretation, 550
United Protestant Youth Center
United Protestant Youth Center,
University of the Philippines,
786
Interpretation, 785
Van Gogh, Vincent
Good Samaritan, The, 519
Interpretation, 518
Wallis-Wiley Studio (designers)
Window of the Great Commis-

sion, Pacific School of Religion, 691
Interpretation, 688
Woman's Christian College
Woman's Christian College, Tokyo, 716
Interpretation, 715
Women's Christian College

Women's Christian College, Chapel of, Madras, 809
Interpretation, 806
Wright, Lloyd
Wayfarers' Chapel, The, Palos Verdes, California, 619
Interpretation, 616
Yeames, W. F.

"And When Did You Last See Your Father?", 469
Interpretation, 468
Zurbaran, Francisco
St. Thomas Aquinas Visiting St. Bonaventura, 290
Interpretation, 289

✠

INDEX OF POETRY BY AUTHORS AND TITLES

Abélard, Pierre
To Gabriel of the Annunciation, 297
Albrecht of Brandenburg
Whate'er God Will, 344
Alexander, A. L.
Church Within, The, 103
Anatolios
Thy Kingdom, O Christ God, 152
What Shall We Bring to Thee, 172
Anderson, Margaret Chaplin
And It Was Night, 49
Andrew of Crete
Great Canon, The, 188
Anonymous
Africa, 834
Amergin, 299
Angel Unawares, An, 105
Basque Song, The, 321
Be Thou My Vision, 298
Behold the Bridegroom Cometh, 152
Bread of the Sacrament, The, 840
Charm for Bees, A, 297
Churches, 672
Communion Hymn-Poem of the Ancient Irish Church, 279
Crusaders' Song, 320
Ektenia *or* Great Collect, 231
For Broken Families, 743
Good Friday Eve Encomia, 233
Heavenly King, Comforter, 153
Lord My Creator, The, 210
Love's Gift, 721
Magnanimity and Restraint, 742
My Church, 573
Old Korean Song, 766
Philippine Hymn, 789
Rune of Hospitality, The, 278
With Shudder of Despair and Loss, 858
Arnold, Matthew
East London, 528
Arsenios
Order of Holy Unction, 192
Asquith, Glenn H.
Church, The, 103
Austin, Mary

Litany for New Mexico, 598
Báez-Camargo, Gonzalo
He Says, 867
I Return, 864
Purification, 866
Baker, Catherine
Church Gives Strength, The, 767
Korean Flag, 769
Korean Youth, 766
Yosu Village, 768
Balbulus, Blessed Notker
Alleluia!, 276
Baxter, Richard
Lord, It Belongs Not to My Care, 473
Bede, The Venerable
Hymn Poem, A, 296
Blake, William
Jerusalem, 527
Blunt, Wilfrid Scawen
How Shall I Build?, 389
Bobrov
Song of Cherubim, 211
Bowers, Edgar
Mountain Cemetery, The, 620
Wise Men, The, 621
Bowman, Louise Morey
Sea Lavender, 645
Bradford, Gamaliel
Exit God, 669
Bradstreet, Anne
Epitaph on My Dear and Ever Honoured Mother, An, 556
Browning, Robert
Religion, 103
Bryant, William Cullen
Forest Hymn, A, 575
Prayer to Make Your Own, A, 623
To a Waterfowl, 573
Bryson, Artemisia B.
Evolution, 694
Bunyan, John
Valiant Pilgrim, The, 474
Buonarroti, Michelangelo—See Michelangelo
Caedmon
Hymn of the World's Creator, 276
Calvin, John

We Greet Thee, King of Mercy and of Grace, 446
Cameron, George Frederick
Standing on Tiptoe, 643
Cassiani
On Mary Magdalene, 232
Chao, Tsu Chen
Oh, Holy Spirit, 741
Chasin, Yu
Hills in Autumn, The, 767
Clark, Leslie Savage
Architect, 103
Dusk at the Airport, 672
Man's Heritage, 20
Master Builder, 21
Memorial, 74
My Father's House, 20
New England Spires, 557
Of Peter, 101
Portrait of a Pastor, 697
Prayer, 130
Witnesses, 669
World Wide Communion, 130
Worship, 74
Clark, Thomas Curtis
In Lincoln Cathedral, 475
Thoughts in a Cathedral, 446
Trust the Great Artist, 19
Clement of Alexandria
Shepherd of Eager Youth, 153
Cosmas of Maiouma
Ode on the Nativity, 149
Tossed on the Sea of Life, 211
Transfiguration Canon, 151
Crashaw, Richard
Christ Crucified, 365
Crawford, Mary Ruth
Bless This Church, 106
Cushman, Ralph Spaulding
My Petition, 130
Czerwenka, Matthias
Christian Unity (Psalm 133), 420
Davenant, Sir William
Praise and Prayer, 365
Demetillo, Ricardo
Longinus, 790
Devanesen, Chandran
Christ of the Indian Road, 811
Cross Is Lifted, The, 808
Discovery, 815

Hedges, 813
Thy Yoke, 814
Dickinson, Emily
I Never Saw a Moor, 576
Doane, George Washington
Evening, 576
Donne, John
Hymn to God the Father, A, 471
Dracontius, Blossius Aemilius
Birds, The, 256
Drummond, Donald F.
To My Father, 621
Dryden, John
Veni Creator Spiritus, 256
Edwards, Edna V.
His Presence, 836
Eguren, José M.
Abbey, The, 390
Ely, Lois Anna
Acceptable, 742
Flowers for the Altar, 740
Fulfillment, 741
Infiltration, 743
Emerson, Ralph Waldo
Problem, The, 574
Ephraem the Syrian
For the Whole Church, 192
Two Natures of Jesus Christ, The, 192
Erickson, Lois J.
Prelude, 715
Foote, John A.
To a Fossil Fern, 697
Franck, Johann
Jesus, Priceless Treasure, 501
Gerhardt, Paul
Give to the Winds Thy Fears, 500
Gilbert, Paul
Your Own Version of the Gospel, 130
Gillis, Everett
Circuit Rider, 595
Goreh, Ellen Lakshmi
Guardian, The, 812
Graves, Rachel E. Miller
Silent Wooded Place, The, 696
Gregory the Great
Morning Hymn, 257
Gregory Nazianzen
Infinite Light, 171
Morning Prayer, A, 171
Guest, Edgar A.
God Builds No Churches, 4
Hale, Edward Everett
Nameless Saints, The, 556
Handa
Glory to God, 720
Hóly Temple, A, 720
Hayashi
Holding the Cross, 717
Hayes, Ann Louise
Sonnet for a Marriage, 622
Hemans, Felicia
Landing of the Pilgrim Fathers, 554
Herbert, George

Teach Me, My God and King, 472
Herbert, Petrus
Evening Prayer, An, 419
Hilary of Poitiers
Thou Splendid Giver of the Light, 258
Hughes, Beulah
I Am the Church!, viii
Hunt, Leigh
Abou Ben Adhem, 528
Huss, John (?)
Word of God, The, 417
Innocent III
Come, Thou Holy Spirit, 320
Isaac, Henry
Moravian Emigrants' Hymn, The, 419
Jackson, Helen Hunt
Doubt, 623
Jadovskaya, Julia
Prayer to the Virgin, 234
John Damascene
Last Kiss, The, 235
John the Monk
All Human Things Are Vanity, 211
Jones, Thomas S., Jr.
In the Garden, 50
Jerusalem, 48
Road to Emmaus, The, 52
Joseph of Studium
Thy Paternal Glory, 191
Jud, Leo
Its Only Joy, Saviour and Lord (Psalm 25), 445
Kagawa, Toyohiko
Christ Liveth in Me, 718
Discovery, 722
Living Christ, The, 721
Kanda, Keizo
Entrusting All, 718
Keble, John
New Every Morning Is the Love, 527
Kempis, Thomas à—See Thomas à Kempis
Ken, Thomas
Glory to Thee, My God, This Night, 474
Kennedy, Studdert, G. A.—See Studdert-Kennedy
Kipling, Rudyard
Recessional, 529
Lanier, Sidney
Ballad of Trees and the Master, A, 597
Leo VI, Emperor
Let Us Adore God in Holy Trinity, 209
Löwenstern, Matthäus Appelles von
Prayer for the Church, A, 500
Longfellow, Samuel
Church Universal, The, 595
Luck, Clarice White
Intercessors, 104

Star—the Cross—the Empty Tomb, The, 51
Luther, Martin
Lord, Keep Us Steadfast in Thy Word, 417
Missionary Prayer, A, 418
Marinoni, Rosa Zagnoni
Christmas in the Ozarks, 597
Markham, Edwin
How the Great Guest Came, 128
Marlatt, Earl
Augustine, 256
Canticle to Il Poverello, 319
Far Music, 644
Francis, 322
John the Baptist, 22
Let There Be Light, 694
Mountain Communion, 646
Nameless, Not Unknown, 51
Paul, 73
People, 127
Peter, 74
Marot, Clément
Sitting Beside the Babylonian Waters (Psalm 137), 445
Matthesius, John
Morning Prayer for the Day's Work, 418
Medici, Lorenzo de'
Orazione, 343
Methodios of Olympus
From on High, Virgins, Hark the Cry, 168
Metrophanes of Smyrna
Unity of Threefold Light, 191
Michelangelo Buonarroti
For Inspiration, 342
Milton, John
On His Blindness, 472
More, Sir Thomas
Consider Well, 342
Nabong, Juan C., Jr.
Judas Iscariot, 787
Nagata, Honami
In All Things, Victory!, 722
Neeman, Louis I.
Voice of God, The, 103
Nervo, Amado
If You Love God, 864
Nordlund, Ralph T.
Prayer for Our New Church, A, 105
Ordinario, Ruby Leah
This Is to Live, 790
Oxenham, John
Bring Us the Light, 836
Credo, 47
His Love Is Always Shining, 20
India, 813
Liberty, Equality, Fraternity, 127
Livingstone's Soliloquy, 838
Quo Vadis?, 77
Stephen—Paul!, 75
Pierre, Mojebo
Prayer for the Sacraments, A, 839
Pillai, Krishna

Adoration, 815
Ponce de León, Luis
Life of the Blessed, The, 343
Poole, Edna
Congo Christmas, 837
Proctor, Adelaide Anne
Give Me Thy Heart, 388
Prudentius
Before Meat, 258
Pugh, Samuel F.
Increase My Love, O God, 792
Lord, Must I Climb?, 622
O Lord, Forgive, 76
Petition, 553
Quiet Hour, The, 558
Serve Where There Is Need, 670
When I Have Food, 867
Why?, 572
Pyun, Y. T.
Charity, 768
O God, 764
Rankin, Jeremiah Eames
Word of God to Leyden Came,
The, 553
Rascas, Bernard
Love of God, The, 321
Reyes, James Servel
Prayer for Our Country, 790
Those Between, 791
Robert, King of France
Strength, Love, Light, 298
St. Bernard of Clairvaux
Thy Kingdom Come, 322
St. Columba
On His Exile to Iona, 278
St. Francis
Simple Prayer, A, 319
St. John of the Cross
O Flame of Living Love, 366
St. Patrick of Tara
Deer's Cry, The, 277
St. Teresa of Avila
If, Lord, Thy Love for Me Is
Strong, 366
Lines Written in Her Breviary,
367
Sampley, Arthur M.
R. I. P., 597

Sanghun, Kim
Triangle Mountain, 767
Sangster, Charles
Harvest Hymn, 642
Schacht, Marshall W.
First Autumn, The, 696
Schiemer, Leonard
Anabaptist Martyr's Hymn, 420
Scott, Duncan Campbell
Builder, The, 643
Scott, Frederick George
Wayside Cross, The, 645
Scottish Psalter
First Psalm, The, 473
Seeley, Ann McDevitt
Worthy Church, A, 671
Silesius, Angelus (John Scheffler)
Soul Wherein God Dwells, The,
367
Spangenburg, Augustus G.
Church of Christ, The, 503
Spear, Henry C.
Apostle John, 49
Apostle Matthew, 50
Apostle Paul, 75
Apostle Peter, 48
John Mark, 75
Mary Magdalene, 51
Mary and Martha, 21
Mary, Mother of Jesus, 21
Stephen, 73
Strange, Hallie
Peace Like a River, 865
Word Incarnate, 866
Stuart, Roger Winship
Countryman's God, 670
Studdert-Kennedy, G. A.
Indifference, 530
Synesios of Ptolemais
My Soul Uncrushed by Care, 171
Night Makes Me Sing to Thee,
170
Tappan, William B.
Robert Raikes, 503
Tennyson, Alfred
We Must Needs Love the High-
est, 128

Theoctistos of Studium
Supplant Canon to Jesus, 234
Theodore of Studium
Canon for Apokreos (Sexagesi-
ma), 209
Sunday of Orthodoxy Canon, 190
Thomas à Kempis
Trust, 345
Thompson, Francis
Hound of Heaven, The, 387
Thompson, Mary Agnes
Prairie Woman's Prayer, 594
Tilak, Narayan Vaman
From This Day On, 810
Prayer, 814
Unknown Authors See Anonymous
USAF Pilot
Airman's Prayer, An, 672
Vega, Lope de
Tomorrow, 344
Verlaine, Paul
Confession, A, 389
Watts, Isaac
Heavens Declare Thy Glory,
Lord, The, 502
Whitman, Walt
Song of Myself (Section 48), 596
Whittier, John Greenleaf
Vaudois Teacher, The, 447
Wilde, Oscar
E Tenebris, 390
Williams, Franklin B.
Spirit Muses, A, 695
Williams, Roger
God Makes a Path, 555
Yamamoto
Christmas, 717
Yamamuro, Gumpei
Carpenter, The, 719
Yoane, Wanga
Wine of the Sacrament, The, 840
Zinzendorf, Nicolaus L. von
Glory to God, Whose Witness
Train, 502
Zwingli, Huldreich
In Convalescence, 444
In the Midst of the Illness, 444

INDEX OF STORIES BY TITLES AND AUTHORS

Abbot and the Learned Woman,
The, 424
Desiderius Erasmus
Ambrose, the Reluctant Bishop, 263
Jean Louise Smith
American Home Missionary Society
and Oregon, 626
Colin B. Goodykoontz
America's Fourth Faith, 235
T. Otto Nall

"And Ye Shall Be My Witnesses,"
842
A true story
"Attempt Great Things for God,"
530
Archibald McLean
Barlaam and Ioasaph, 212
John Damascene
Bell Founder's Window, The, 350
Jean Louise Smith

Bible for Plowboys and Poets, A,
475
Edgar J. Goodspeed
Bricks and a Dream, 774
Alice Geer Kelsey
Bridgehead in East Harlem, 679
Presbyterian Life
By Invitation of Jesus, 134
Peter Marshall

Christian World Statesman and Patriot, A, 769
  Robert T. Oliver
Church, School and State, 701
  Samuel Windsor Brown
Conversion of Constantine the Great, The, 176
  Eusebios
Decree on the Veneration of the Icons, 193
  The Seventh Ecumenical Synod
Early Days at Yale, 698
  Lyman Beecher
Early Winter in a Rural Parish, 675
  Anna Laura Gebhard
End Is a Beginning, The, 394
  Albert J. Nevins
Eskimo Preacher, 652
  Edith Agnew
Every Man in His Own Language, 847
  Eugene A. Nida
Faith Healer, The, 624
  William Vaughan Moody
Father Tabart, 398
  Glenn D. Kittler
Giving Worship Back to the People, 448
  Oskar Farner
God in the Slums, 536
  Hugh Redwood
God's Gift to Paquito, 873
  Elizabeth Allstrom
Gorgonia, 178
  Gregory Nazianzen
Gospel According to Andrew, The, 80
  William E. Barton
Gospel According to Judas, The, 85
  William E. Barton
Gregory Palamas: Mystical Illumination, 218
  Robert Payne
Handel's Messiah, 504
  Newman Flower
Healing for Body and Spirit, 795
  Presbyterian Commission on Ecumenical Mission and Relations
Hilary of Poitiers, 260
  Samuel W. Duffield
Hiroshima Maidens, The, 727
  From The Saturday Review
His Mother's Sermon, 533
  John Watson (Ian Maclaren)
Hong Kong—Taiwan—China, 750
  Presbyterian Commission on Ecumenical Mission and Relations
House for God, A, 138
  Glenn H. Asquith
Innocent Veniaminov: The Greatest Missionary of American Orthodoxy, 216
  Bishop Nicholas
Jesus, As Seen by Joseph of Arimathea, 77
  Kahlil Gibran

Junipero Serra: Father of the California Missions, 370
  Harold B. Hunting
Kagawa, God's Hand in Japan, 722
  Toyohiko Kagawa
Keeper of the City, 454
  C. C. McCrie
Keizo Finds a New Way of Life, 725
  Honami Nagata
Librada Javalera of the Philippines, 792
  Elizabeth Meredith Lee
Lidia Vargas in Chile, 870
  Elizabeth Meredith Lee
Life of St. Anthony, The, 173
  St. Athanasios
Light of the World Is Come, The, 26
  Elizabeth Stuart Phelps
Lines to a Rickshaw Puller (A Poetic Story), 819
  Chandran Devanesen
Luca della Robbia's Singing Gallery, 348
  Jean Louise Smith
Man with a Twa-Handed Sword, 478
  Paul Hutchinson
Martin Luther and the Eisleben Choir, 428
  Ellen Baker
Martyrdom of Polycarp, The, 155
  Author Unknown
Meek Icon, The, 194
  Fotis Kontoglous
Message from the Second Assembly of the World Council of Churches, A, 673
  Bishop Lesslie Newbigin
Michelangelo Buonarroti, 345
  Clara Erskine Clement
Ministry of Friendship, The, 603
  Ronald E. Osborn
Ministry of Health and Healing, The, 821
  L. Winifred Bryce
Miracle of Kaisariani, The, 238
  Alexander Papadiamantis
Move to Indiana, 579
  Worth M. Tippy
Music on the Muscatatuck, 599
  Jessamyn West
New World Comes to Africa Through the Church, A, 843
  Wanga Yoane
One of the Twelve Fell Away (A Poetic Story), 59
  Chandran Devanesen
Our Protestant Heritage, 451
  Walter W. Sikes
Pablo Helps with the Writing, 797
  Mabel Niedermeyer
Patrick of Ireland, 283
  H. Leo
Pére Marquette, 373
  Father Quill
Peter the Hermit, 326

John H. Haaren and A. B. Poland
Peter, the Man of Impulse, 55
  Charles Reynolds Brown
Pilgrimage to Bethlehem, The, 22
  Lew Wallace
Pilgrim's Journey, 481
  John Bunyan
Prayer and Creeds, 578
  Ralph Waldo Emerson
Preacher Yu, 744
  Alice Hudson Lewis
Prisons—and the Golden Rule, 509
  Sir James Marchant
Proposals for the Union of Christians, 699
  Thomas Campbell
Quaker Individualism, 559
  William Penn
Robert Raikes and His Ragged Schools, 507
  J. Henry Harris
Sacrament of Christian Baptism, The, 841
  Jack Barron
St. Augustine of Canterbury, 259
  William Caxton
St. Benedict, 303
  Williston Walker
St. Bernard of Clairvaux, 328
  Mrs. Arthur Bell
St. Boniface, 280
  Mrs. Arthur Bell
St. Francis of Assisi, 323
  Abbie Farwell Brown
St. Francis Xavier: Apostle of the Indies, 368
  John O'Kane Murray
St. Hilda: Princess, Abbess, 279
  Sabine Baring-Gould
St. Joseph of Arimathea, 300
  Joan Windham
Sealed at the Lord's Table, 131
  Vernard M. Eller
Search for a Personal God, The, 560
  Roger Williams
Simon, Who Was Called Peter, 106
  Kahlil Gibran
Spire on the Horizon, A, 606
  William J. Hyde
Stephen, the First Christian Martyr, 113
  John Foxe
Story of the Mayflower Compact, The, 558
  Arr. Karl E. Snyder
Stranger than Fiction, 747
  James Dickson
Symeon the Stylite, 196
  Sabine Baring-Gould
Take to the Air, 773
  Presbyterian Commission on Ecumenical Mission and Relations
Temperance Pledge, The, 625
  Thomas Francis Marshall
"This Is My Beloved Son," 52
  Elizabeth Stuart Phelps

Through Peril and Fire, 421
 Kenneth Hall
Tumult of Her Birth, The, 646
 Claris Edwin Silcox
Venerable Bede, The, 299
 William Caxton
Vignettes of the Apostles of the
 Early Church, 108
 Arr. *Cynthia Pearl Maus*
Village Life in Rural India, 815

L. Winifred Bryce
Vision of the Leviathan, The, 153
 Author Unknown
Way of a Pilgrim, The, 242
 Anonymous
White Martyrdom: The Story of
 Father Damien, 391
 John Henaghan
Who the Christians Are, 158
 Author Unknown

Winter of the Cross, The, 649
 Elizabeth Robins
Winter, Stoves, and the Meeting-
 house, 576
 Samuel Griswold Goodrich
Wise Men from the East, 29
 Lew Wallace
Young Christian Sees America, A,
 868
 Pablo David Sosa

---✠---

INDEX OF MUSIC AND MUSIC INTERPRETATIONS BY TITLES AND AUTHORS

The *italics* indicate the page on which the music score will be found; the Roman figures refer to the interpretation of the music.

All Glory, Laud and Honor, 307
 Words: Theodulph of Orleans
 Music: Melchior Teschner
 Interpretation, 306
Brief Life Is Here Our Portion, 331
 Words: Bernard of Cluny
 Music: Henry John Gauntlett
 Interpretation, 330
Cherubic Hymn, 220
 Words: John Chrysostom (?)
 Music: Arr. Dean D. Bouzianis
 Interpretation, 219
Christ Is Risen, 245
 Words: Traditional Byzantine
 Music: Tr. Dean D. Bouzianis
 Interpretation, 245
Christmas Hymn for Peace, A, 116
 Words: Earl Marlett
 Music: Samuel S. Wesley
 Interpretation, 115
Church's One Foundation, The, 116
 Words: Samuel J. Stone
 Music: Samuel S. Wesley
 Interpretation, 115
City of God, 611
 Words: Samuel Johnson
 Music: Thomas Haweis
 Interpretation, 610
Creator Spirit, by Whose Aid, 308
 Words: John Dryden
 Music: Thomas Attwood
 Interpretation, 309
*Crown Him with Many Crowns,
 401*
 Words: Matthew Bridges
 Music: George J. Elvey
 Interpretation, 400
Day of Resurrection, 200
 Words: John Damascene
 Music: Tr. Dean D. Bouzianis
 Interpretation, 200
*Disposer Supreme, and Judge of
 the Earth, 378*
 Words: J. B. de Santeuil
 Music: Ravencroft's Psalter
 Interpretation, 376
Father, We Praise Thee, 286
 Words: Gregory the Great

Music: La Feillée's *Methode du
 Plain Chant*
 Interpretation, 286
Gladsome Light, 180
 Words: Athenogenes (?)
 Music: John Sakellarides; tr.
 Dean D. Bouzianis
 Interpretation, 180
*God of Grace and God of Glory,
 630*
 Words: Harry Emerson Fosdick
 Music: Henry Smart
 Interpretation, 631
God of the Prairies, 609
 Words: Cyril C. Richardson
 Music: Ralph Vaughan Williams
 Interpretation, 608
Great Doxology, The, 160
 Words: Traditional Byzantine
 Music: Hourmouzios Hartophy-
 lax; tr. Dean D. Bouzianis
 Interpretation, 159
*Hark! A Herald Voice Is Calling,
 285*
 Words: St. Ambrose (?)
 Music: William Henry Monk
 Interpretation, 284
Here at Thy Table, Lord, 64
 Words: May P. Hoyt
 Music: William F. Sherwin
 Interpretation, 65
*Here, O My Lord, I See Thee
 Face to Face, 118*
 Words: Horatius Bonar
 Music: Felix Mendelssohn
 Interpretation, 117
Hymn of Praise, A, 755
 Words: George W. Conder
 Music: Ancient Chinese Lute
 Tune
 Interpretation, 754
*I to the Hills Will Lift Mine Eyes,
 488*
 Words: Psalm 121
 Music: Scottish Psalter
 Interpretation, 487
*In Christ There Is No East or
 West, 801*

Words: John Oxenham
 Music: Alexander R. Reinagle
 Interpretation, 801
*Jesus Is My Sovereign King (Jesus
 Es Mi Rey Soberano), 878*
 Words: Vincente Mendoza
 Music: Vincente Mendoza
 Interpretation, 877
*King of Love my Shepherd Is, The,
 63*
 Words: Henry W. Baker
 Music: John B. Dykes
 Interpretation, 62
Let There Be Light, Lord God, 706
 Words: William Merrill Vories
 Music: Lowell Mason
 Interpretation, 704
Life of Ages, Richly Poured, 705
 Words: Samuel Johnson
 Music: Medieval French melody;
 har. Richard Redhead
 Interpretation, 704
*Light Thou the Lamp (Jiwan Deep
 Jalao), 824*
 Words: M. Masih
 Music: M. Masih
 Interpretation, 823
*Listen to Our Prayer (Binti Ha-
 mari), 826*
 Words: Indian Folk Song
 Music: Indian Folk Song
 Interpretation, 825
*Lord, Bless Africa (Nkosi Sikelel'
 i Afrika), 854*
 Words: Enoch Sontonga
 Music: Enoch Sontonga
 Interpretation, 852
*Lord, Take Thou the Reins to
 Thee, 457*
 Words: Huldreich Zwingli
 Music: Huldreich Zwingli
 Interpretation, 456
Lord's My Shepherd, The, 563
 Words: Scottish Psalter
 Music: William Henry Havergal
 Interpretation, 562
Megalynarion, 223
 Words: Traditional Byzantine

Music: Th. Phokaeus; tr. Dean
  D. Bouzianis
Interpretation, 222
More Love to Thee, O Christ, 730
Words: Elizabeth P. Prentiss
Music: William H. Doane
Interpretation, 730
My Faith It Is an Oaken Staff, 659
Words: Thomas Toke Lynch
Music: Folk Melody
Interpretation, 658
My Faith Looks up to Thee, 583
Words: Ray Palmer
Music: Lowell Mason
Interpretation, 582
My God, I Love Thee, 377
Words: St. Francis Xavier (?)
Music: Henry John Gauntlett
Interpretation, 376
Nativity Ode, 162
Words: Romanos the Melodist
Music: Har. Dean D. Bouzianis
Interpretation, 161
O Christ Our Great Foundation,
  756
Music: "Tung Fu"; tr. Mary-
  ette H. Lum
Interpretation, 754
O Come, O Come, Emmanuel, 33
Words: Old Latin
Music: Ancient Plain Song
Interpretation, 32
O For a Closer Walk with God,
  732
Words: William Cowper
Music: Arthur Cottman
Interpretation, 731
O God, Beneath Thy Guiding
  Hand, 562
Words: Leonard Bacon
Music: John Hutton
Interpretation, 561
O God of Love! O King of Peace!,
  92
Words: Henry W. Baker
Music: Henry K. Oliver
Interpretation, 92
O Holy City, Seen of John, 682
Words: Walter Russell Bowie
Music: Frederick C. Maker
Interpretation, 681
O Jesus, I Have Promised (Jesus
  Yo He Prometido), 877
Words: John Ernest Bode
Music: Arthur H. Mann
Interpretation, 876
O Lord of All, Our Father, 430
Words: Kliment Bosak
Music: Hussisches Graduale
Interpretation, 429
O Love, How Deep, 353
Words: Latin Hymn Poem
Music: "The Agincourt Song"
Interpretation, 352
O North, With All Thy Vales, 657
Words: William Cullen Bryant
Music: Johann Harmann Schein

Interpretation, 656
O Sacred Head, Now Wounded,
  513
Words: Author Unknown
Music: Hans Leo Hassler; har.
  Johann Sebastian Bach
Interpretation, 512
O Saviour, Bless Us Ere We Go,
  403
Words: Frederick William Faber
Music: William Henry Monk
Interpretation, 402
O Trinity of Blessed Light, 267
Words: St. Ambrose (?)
Music: Chartres Church Melody
Interpretation, 267
O What Their Joy and Their Glory
  Must Be, 332
Words: Pierre Abélard
Music: Adapt. from Methode du
  Plain Chant; har. John B.
  Dykes
Interpretation, 332
O Zion Haste, Thy Mission High
  Fulfilling, 800
Words: Mary Ann Thomson
Music: James Walch
Interpretation, 799
One Holy Church of God Appears,
  140
Words: Samuel Longfellow
Music: Raphael Courteville
Interpretation, 139
Our Home (Bola Bokiso), 850
Words: J. O. Ekofo
Music: J. O. Ekofo
Interpretation, 849
Peace Through His Cross, 779
Words: Catherine Baker
Music: Samuel S. Wesley
Interpretation, 777
Royal Banners Forward Go, The,
  266
Words: Fortunatus (?)
Music: Horatio Parker
Interpretation, 265
Saviour! Thy Dying Love, 585
Words: Sylvanus D. Phelps
Music: Robert Lowry
Interpretation, 584
Storm on the Lake (Bompompo
  Nda Jibeke), 853
Words: J. O. Ekofo
Music: J. O. Ekofo
Interpretation, 851
Therefore We, Before Him Bend-
  ing, 354
Words: St. Thomas Aquinas
Music: G. P. da Palestrina
Interpretation, 352
Thine Is the Glory, 541
Words: Edmond L. Budry
Music: George Frederick Handel
Interpretation, 540
This Day Salvation, 244
Words: Traditional Byzantine

Music: Manuel Protopsaltis; tr.
  Dean D. Bouzianis
Interpretation, 244
Thou Holy Spirit, We Pray to
  Thee, 432
Words: Martin Luther
Music: Gesangbuch
Interpretation, 431
Through the Night of Doubt and
  Sorrow, 539
Words: Bernard Severin Inge-
  mann
Music: William S. Bambridge
Interpretation, 538
"Thy Kingdom Come," On Bended
  Knee, 629
Words: Frederick Lucian Hosmer
Music: Day's Psalter
Interpretation, 628
To All the Nations, Lord, 91
Words: Thomas Tiplady
Music: Cleo C. Milligan
Interpretation, 90
To Work, to Work, 781
Words: Old Korean Song
Music: Old Korean Song
Interpretation, 778
Trisagion, 199
Words: Traditional Byzantine
Music: Iakovos Protopsaltis: tr.
  Dean D. Bouzianis
Interpretation, 198
Voice of God Is Calling, The, 684
Words: John Haynes Holmes
Music: William Lloyd
Interpretation, 683
Watchman, Tell Us of the Night,
  35
Words: Sir John Bowring
Music: Lowell Mason
Interpretation, 34
We Gather Together, 459
Words: Anonymous
Music: Netherlands Folk Song;
  arr. Edward Kremser
Interpretation, 458
We Hymn Thee, 181
Words: Traditional Byzantine
Music: Tr. Dean D. Bouzianis
Interpretation, 182
We Praise Thee, O God; We
  Acknowledge Thee (Te Deum
  Laudamus), 486
Words: Nicetas of Remesiana
Music: Henry Lawes and Robert
  Cooke
Interpretation, 484
We Would Be Building, 141
Words: Purd E. Deitz
Music: Jean Sibelius
Interpretation, 140
Ye Servants of God, Your Master
  Proclaim, 515
Words: Charles Wesley
Music: Johann Michael Haydn
Interpretation, 514